BF 1012 .555

A SKEPTIC'S HANDBOOK
OF PARAPSYCHOLOGY

A
SKEPTIC'S
HANDBOOK
OF
PARAPSYCHOLOGY

Edited by
Paul Kurtz

PROMETHEUS BOOKS
BUFFALO, NEW YORK

Library of Congress Card Catalog No. 85-43082
ISBN: 0-87975-302-1

Contents

Acknowledgments

My special gratitude in preparing this volume goes to Doris Doyle, senior editor of Prometheus Books, whose expert assistance has been invaluable. My appreciation also is due Beth Rosch, assistant editor, especially for her efforts in compiling the index, and to Judy Williams for her able editorial assistance. My thanks, too, to Bruce Carle, JoAnne Smyers, and Karen Neri, who as the typesetters are the unsung heroes of this book, and to Guy Burgstahler, the art director.

I am grateful to my colleagues Martin Gardner, Charles Akers, C. E. M. Hansel, James Alcock, Ray Hyman, and Gerd Hövelmann for their helpful advice on the selection of essays for this volume, and to Marcello Truzzi for his help in editing the posthumous paper of Piet Hein Hoebens. I am also indebted to Victor Gulotta, vice president, and Lyn Nisbet and Steven Mitchell, of Prometheus Books.

Introduction

More than a Century of Psychical Research

I

Many books and collections of essays on parapsychology have been published over the years, written and edited by and for those who support belief in psychic phenomena. There have been far fewer collections about the paranormal written by its critics. This volume is the first to bring together many of the leading skeptics to evaluate the entire history of the field of parapsychology and psychic research and to examine the results. The contributors were asked to focus on one or more aspects of the field: Does ESP exist? What is the evidence for it? How reliable is this evidence? Can two or more minds communicate outside normal sensory channels? Has precognition been demonstrated? What about psychokinesis and levitation? Can psychics assist the police in locating missing persons or in solving crimes? Does the mind survive the death of the body?

Although the contributors may be said to be predominantly skeptical of psychic claims, some parapsychologists have been included to defend the parapsychological point of view. Nineteen of the following chapters were written especially for this collection, and eleven previously published essays have been added to deal with particular issues. In some cases, these include important historical statements, such as the confessions of the spiritualist Margaret Fox and the alleged telepathist Douglas Blackburn. I have also included three important overviews of psychical research: one by Simon Newcomb, the first president of the American Society of Psychical Research, in which he evaluates the field in 1909 at the end of his career; the second is John Coover's survey of psychic research through 1927; and the third is by Eric Dingwall, who was intimately associated with the work of the British Society for Psychical Research for sixty years and summed up his appraisal in 1971.

II

Many people in modern society are convinced that paranormal realities exist. Often their belief is spawned by a body of "inexplicable" experiences in ordinary life. Someone has a strange dream that may later come true. Was this precognition? Just before the telephone rings one may think of the person who is about to call. Close friends and relatives sometimes claim to be able to read each other's minds and to anticipate what the other will think, feel, or say. Some persons may believe that they have been visited by the spirit of departed relatives or friends or that their houses are haunted. There have been numerous reports of rapping noises and of strange objects moving about. This they explain by reference to poltergeists or psychokinesis (PK). Reports of these phenomena have been common in human culture. The folklore tends to support the reality of paranormal events. Many people are convinced that, although causality operates in the everyday world, anomalous events occur that are exceptions to these regularities. Unexplained events mystify us. Can they be due to mere coincidence? Can we give naturalistic explanations? Or are there underlying causes that could account for puzzling phenomena? It is clear that, if people tend to believe in a mysterious or paranormal universe, they will more readily posit psychical explanations for otherwise inexplicable experiences.

Thus there is a fund of unexplained spontaneous events in everyday life, and old wives' tales and legends have grown up around us to interpret them. Most of this information is anecdotal and based upon hearsay. Some of it is grounded in personal experience. Is the willingness to give a psychical interpretation due only to ignorance and to a failure to understand the causes of how or what happens? The reports of such phenomena have been so widespread, from the earliest days of human history up to the present, that there have been demands that science account for them. Can we take such reports of psychic phenomena and test them by the methods of scientific verification?

There have been three critical phases in the development of scientific interest in parapsychology and psychic research and the effort to submit such claims to testing. The first was the dramatic growth of spiritualism, which holds the view that there are spiritual agencies and forces at work in the universe. The spiritualist movement may be said to have begun in 1848 in Hydesville, New York, when strange rappings were reported in a home occupied by a family with two young daughters, the Fox sisters. These rappings were believed to be caused by spirits of the dead communicating through these girls. Word of these eerie events spread rapidly and aroused the interest of the scientific community in confirming the veracity of the Fox sisters. Once on its way, spiritualism brought forth a series of other mediums, so-called gifted sensitives, who were allegedly able to elicit messages from discarnate spirits. These powers could be evinced, it was said, in a darkened séance room, where rappings, levitation of tables and chairs, automatic writing, and other physical evidences were manifested. D. D. Home, Henry Slade, William Eglinton, and other mediums displayed their talents. Home actually claimed to have levitated high above a street in London.

A number of notable scientists investigated these claims—Robert Hare, Michael Faraday, Sir William Crookes, Sir Oliver Lodge, and others—but their efforts were not systematic.

It was not until 1882, that the second phase of scientific interest in psychical research began, with the founding of the Society for Psychical Research (SPR) in Britain. The American Society for Psychical Research was organized three years later. The SPR took upon itself the task of systematically investigating paranormal claims. They examined thought transference (telepathy), automatic writing, and cross-correspondence. They also attempted to test leading mediums and psychics in controlled situations and to provide analyses of reports of apparitions and hauntings.

One of the chief motives of the members of the SPR was to give a new foundation to the traditional religious conception of reality, which had been undermined by the naturalistic, or physicalistic, interpretation of nature. Darwin's theory of evolution shocked many Victorians, for it seemed to invalidate orthodox biblical views of creation. Is there evidence of a spiritualistic realm? they asked. Is the mind separate from the body, and can it display properties that are independent of physical causality? Does the soul survive the death of the body, and can we in fact find rigorous scientific evidence to sustain this age-old article of faith? If this data could be establisned, it would provide scientific foundation for religious belief.

The SPR began testing a series of famous psychics and mediums to ascertain whether they indeed had the powers they claimed. Douglas Blackburn, G. A. Smith, and the Creery sisters were tested for thought transmission; Eusapia Palladino and Mrs. Leonora Piper, for trance mediumship. Those who conducted these tests became embroiled in heated controversy, because skeptics and critics believed that the controls placed upon the test subjects were not rigorous and that the possibility of fraud or sensory leakage was present. Indeed, so many cases of chicanery were uncovered that much of this research was discredited. This was all the more evident when Mrs. Mina Crandon ("Margery"), Eusapia Palladino, and other mediums were later found to be tricksters. The question was then asked, In spite of the evidence of fraud, isn't it possible that some of the phenomena are genuine?

The third phase of scientific investigation began in 1927, when Joseph B. Rhine established a parapsychological laboratory at Duke University in North Carolina. He deferred any attempt to confirm the survivalist hypothesis and, instead, focused on ESP (clairvoyance, precognition, telepathy) and PK. Rhine believed that only rigorous experimental and statistical methods should be used. His amazing results were hotly contested by members of the scientific community, who maintained that there were many flaws in his experimental procedures. Moreover, efforts by numerous researchers world-wide to replicate his experimental results generally failed. As conditions were tightened up, laboratory results were never again so high.

The great issue that emerged was the question of replication; for science requires that if a phenomenon has been discovered, then other independent and neutral researchers in other laboratories could go through the same steps and obtain similar results. Unfortunately, whether such conditions have been satisfied is open to dispute. Believers in ESP maintain that they have. Skeptics deny this, and hence do not accept the psi hypothesis.

One of the most interesting developments in this regard was the failure of repeated efforts in Great Britain to replicate Rhine's results. Parapsychologist G. S. Soal, in particular, claimed negative results. However, in the 1940s Soal went on to test Basil Shackleton and Gloria Stewart for precognition and telepathy, and he reported extraordinary results. Repeated trials seemed to demonstrate the existence of psi. The odds against these anomalies occurring by chance, Soal's supporters said, were billions to one. These experiments apparently convinced a great number of scientists and skeptics that ESP had been decisively demonstrated, though many others continued to harbor doubts. If such results were to be taken as veridical, then a major paradigmatic shift in our fundamental conceptions of physical reality had occurred. Some skeptics speculated that, rather than overthrow the "basic limiting principles" by which we interpret ordinary experience and the physical sciences, the hypothesis of possible fraud should not be dismissed. This was rejected as preposterous by the parapsychological community. Nevertheless, doubts continued to be expressed. But it was not until 1978, when Betty Markwick was able to clearly demonstrate that Soal had manipulated his data, that his findings were discarded.

The question thus remained, Has evidence of psi been replicated in the laboratory? Skeptics have perceived a pattern: The world of parapsychology becomes enamored with a new field of research; they proclaim a breakthrough eventually shown to be flawed; and many become disheartened or disenchanted with its findings until a new line of research appears and the cycle is repeated.

In recent decades a bevy of superpsychics has replaced the mediums of an earlier generation, but they too have had their credentials questioned: the American psychics Ingo Swann and Pat Price, the Russian Nina Kulagina, the Dutch clairvoyant Gerald Croiset, and especially Uri Geller from Israel. Geller, in particular, received considerable attention not only from the media but from the scientific community. His alleged ESP and psychokinetic feats have been easily duplicated by magicians, suggesting that he and others like him could simply be skilled at performing conjuring tricks. Similarly, a number of children have been tested for the "Geller Effect" but under controlled conditions were found to be metal-bending by sleight of hand.

For a time, a promising line of research was that being done by Walter J. Levy on precognition in animals. Levy was considered heir-apparent to J. B.

Rhine at Duke, and his work had been heralded as a new breakthrough in parapsychology. In 1974, however, Levy was caught in the act of tampering with his data and was forced to resign his post.

An area of recent intense interest is the ganzfeld experiments and dream research, in which subjects are isolated and deprived of sensory stimulation. It is claimed that under these conditions a subject can more easily receive messages or images by telepathy or clairvoyance. Some parapsychologists (such as Charles Honorton) claim that ganzfeld studies have produced replicable results. But skeptics have examined the reports of this research and have found serious flaws in the experimental procedures.

Two other areas of research that have been hailed of late are (a) experiments in psychokinesis using random-number generators, for which the probabilities can be easily calculated, and (b) remote-viewing experiments in which subjects are sent out into the field and transmit images of the target site to "receivers" in the laboratory. Again, results in both of these areas of research have been thrown into question.

Helmut Schmidt, Robert Jahn, and other researchers working with random-number generators claim that deviation from chance occurs over repeated trials, and this they attribute to psychokinetic activity. Moreover, it is maintained that other laboratories have replicated their results. But that this is the case has been disputed by skeptics. Have adequate safeguards been used in the experimental design? Even if there are deviations from chance, can these anomalies be attributed to psi—whether PK or precognition—or are there other explanations for the phenomena? It is one thing to demonstrate that above- or below-chance runs have occurred using a random-number generator; it is another to propose that the psi hypothesis is the most likely explanation. Similarly, Russell Targ and Harold Puthoff (at Stanford Research International) have repeatedly claimed that they have demonstrated the reality of remote viewing, but critics have pointed out serious flaws in the grading techniques and in evaluating what constitutes a "hit." Whether or not the matching procedure is reliable is questionable. Moreover, there have been PK and remote-viewing experiments in which the results are negative and may often go unreported. If *all* of these experiments were put in the hopper, it is possible that we would obtain only chance results.

Generally, the study of psychic phenomena has focused on the following three areas of research: First, there are the spontaneous experiences in everyday life, which are based upon anecdotal information. Skeptics deny that the only explanations for these experiences are paranormal and maintain that they are due to chance coincidences or can be given normal naturalistic causal explanations.

The second approach is the testing of mediums and psychics in séance rooms or in the laboratory. Again, the lack of rigor in these tests has been criticized. Skeptics maintain that almost invariably mediums and psychics have been found cheating or, at the least, have raised strong suspicions of fraud.

The third area of research has been experimental work in the laboratory with "normal" subjects. Although occasional fragmentary success has been reported, many researchers have had only negative results, even after years of trying to find an effect. For those researchers who claim to have achieved positive results, the protocol of the experiments or the grading techniques have often been questioned. Moreover, a "decline effect" has been noted—a subject who initially scores well in the laboratory is not able to maintain this success rate. Thus we are still without a clearcut demonstration of how to bring about a paranormal effect and whether indeed any exist. We are still unable to ascertain the conditions necessary to elicit an effect.

III

Skepticism is among the oldest intellectual traditions in philosophy, and it can be traced back to ancient philosophers like Carneades, Pyrrho, and Sextus Empiricus, and in modern thought to Descartes, Locke, Berkeley, Hume, and Kant. The term *skeptical* originally derived from the Greek *skeptikos,* which means "thoughtful," "reflective," "inquiring." Today skepticism is recognized as the very life-blood of scientific inquiry.

There are many varieties of skepticism. One form it may take is universal doubt, the attitude that the reality perceived by the senses and the validity of rational inference should be mistrusted. For this form of skepticism one must adopt an *epochē* in regard to all things; that is, assume the role of the agnostic and suspend judgment. Since one position is as good as the next, and all positions may be equally false, none can be said to be true. In philosophy, this has led to extreme solipsism, where one doubts not only the reality of the external world but one's own existence. In ethics, it has led to extreme subjectivism, a mistrust of reason, and a denial that there are any objective ethical standards; values, it is held, are rooted in personal taste and caprice. In science, universal skepticism has led to methodological anarchism, the view that all scientific positions depend upon the mere prejudices of the scientific community and the shifts in paradigms that occur. If this is the case, astrology would be as true as astronomy and psychic phenomena as real as subatomic physics. Such a form of skepticism is easily transformed into a kind of "neutralism"—since all positions may be equally true or false, we have no way of judging their adequacy.

Universal skepticism is negative, self-defeating, and contradictory. One cannot consistently function as a total skeptic but must follow certain principles of inquiry, some of which turn out to be more reliable than others. We must act upon the best evidence we have, as our beliefs confront the external world independent of our wishes. Moreover, we do have well-tested hypotheses with varying degrees of probability that may be incorporated into the body of knowledge. The skeptic's own universal principle that there is no reliable knowledge must apply to itself; and, if so, we are led to doubt its range of applicability. A universal skepticism is limited by its own criteria. If we assume it to be true, then it is false; since if it applies to everything, it applies to itself, and hence universal skepticism cannot be universal. We do not need to become impaled by the logic of types. The point is simply that the most meaningful form of skepticism is a *selective* one. Selective skepticism is *constructive*. It limits doubt to the context of inquiry. We cannot doubt all of our presuppositions at the same time, though we may in various contexts examine each in turn. The doubt that properly emerges is within a problematic context of inquiry and thus can be settled only by the relevant evidence—though perhaps not completely.

What this means is that the scientific community is always faced with new research problems, and it seeks solutions to these problems (a) in the theoretical sciences, through explanations of what is happening and why, (b) in the technological and applied sciences, by resolving questions of application. There are alternative theories or hypotheses that may be proposed and compete for acceptance. Some of them may fall by the wayside; those that win out seem to accord best with the relevant data and the conceptual framework at hand, though these may in turn be eventually modified.

Clearly, a researcher should suspend judgment until he can confirm his hypothesis and until it is corroborated by other inquirers. However, no one law or theory can be said to be final or absolute, or to have reached its ultimate formulation. Here Charles Peirce's famous "principle of fallibilism" plays a role, for we may be in error, we may uncover new data, or alternative hypotheses may be found to fit the data more adequately. Thus we must be prepared to admit new hypotheses, however novel or unlikely they may at first appear. Science is open to revision of its theories: The self-corrective process is ongoing. We must always be willing to entertain and not rule out new ideas. This applies to the established sciences, but also to newly emerging proto- or parasciences. And it also applies to skeptics, who must be careful not to allow their biases to intervene when appraising claims of the paranormal. One must keep an open mind about the possibility of new discoveries. One should never ignore or seek to suppress new data, however unsettling it may be to our preconceptions of how the universe operates. On the other hand, not every claim of a new discovery warrants equal attention.

The "Galileo principle" of course should command our respect; that is, do not reject a claim simply because it contradicts or overthrows basic or well-established principles held by the leading scientists of the day. In regard to a new field of inquiry, it may be a fledgling new science, a protoscience rather than a pseudoscience. Within the established fields, new theories may turn out to be correct and old ones may need to be rejected. Not all of the candidates for Galileo's mantle have the necessary credentials or are worthy of the honor, but there have been a sufficient number of cases in the history of science where this has proven to be true for us to be cautious in approaching novel ideas. This is the approach of selective or constructive skepticism as distinct from total or unlimited skepticism.

However, not every fanciful idea or theory deserves a fair hearing by scientific investigators and intellectuals. Some may be beyond the pale of comprehension, so unclear and confused that they do not lend themselves to any meaningful interpretation. Clearly, we need an open mind toward new departures. But the scientific revolution occurred only when investigators could move beyond vague, mystical, intuitive, or metaphysical speculations and frame meaningful questions and testable hypotheses. Science can only deal with coherent, internally consistent theories that are capable of some form of resolution. Many ideas that are presented may be frivolous or subjectivistic and incapable of verification. Presumably, we can deal only with those that allow for some methods of confirmation.

There is merit in questioning parapsychological claims: Precognition or psychokinesis may be true. We cannot rule it out on a priori grounds or on the basis of conceptual analysis. Yet if a phenomenon is to be accepted, then there must be a high probability that it exists. Surprising claims that overturn well-established observations and hypotheses require not simply fragmentary evidence but strong evidence that is incontestable. The evidence must be uncontaminated by experimental bias, bad protocol, sensory leakage, and grading errors. Before we can overthrow a basic limiting principle, the existence of contrary evidence should be so clear that a modification of our existing causal theories may be the only reasonable alternative.

A given hypothesis, idea, or theory may or may not conflict with the existing body of knowledge. Here Hume's famous principle concerning miracles is relevant. Hume argued that where a belief conflicts with a body of other, well-tested beliefs, if we are to accept it, then there must be a good deal of evidence in its favor. We simply have to weigh probabilities and accept the strongest. Now this cannot be taken as a decisive argument against paranormal claims, for there is always the danger that Hume's principle might be misused to ridicule or block novel ideas. We know that there are scientific prejudices and ingrained habits of thought that are difficult to overcome. Therefore, the existing body of accepted principles should not be taken as ultimate, nor function as a censor. Yet if Hume's argument cannot be used as an infallible basis for invalidating anomalous claims, it does provide some *prima facie* ground at least for being cautious about those claims that violate well-established principles or theories that are based on substantial evidence.

An important criterion in evaluating paranormal claims is the "burden of proof" argument. The skeptic maintains that the burden of proof is upon the claimant to first show that there is sufficient evidence for adopting a particular hypothesis. The burden is not upon the skeptic to disprove the claim, or to prove the negative—often a very difficult task. It is a mistake to argue that in principle one cannot prove a negative. Under certain conditions it is possible to do so. This depends upon the nature of the claim and the specificity of its range of application.

Whether psi or PK exist should not be framed as a universal or general question. For to solve the issue one must specify the particular circumstances and conditions under which such a phenomenon has been or can be observed. There is a fundamental difference between logical possibility and empirical probability. Some claims made may be logically impossible. Thus we cannot even speak intelligibly about square circles, let alone know where to look for them in the real world. Other concepts may be within the range of possibility, and antecedent logical questions raised against them are inadmissible. What is logically impossible is sometimes difficult to ascertain. Some skeptics deny, for example, that "a person can view his own funeral"; they reject any talk of discarnate spirits as unintelligible, for it violates our usual categories of linguistic discourse. Although it is difficult to conceive of how one might witness his own funeral without a retina, a brain, or a nervous system, one cannot foreclose the possibility on logical grounds. Dualists at least have long insisted that such talk makes sense. The real issue for most paranormal questions is whether the claims made are probable or improbable in light of the data or evidence brought forth in their behalf. Thus the burden is upon the claimant, not the skeptic, to demonstrate his case.

Skeptics have generally brought two kinds of criticism to bear on parapsychological claims. The first are analytic and logical objections to the conceptional framework of parapsychology, which seems to conflict with or contradict well-established principles of common experience and the natural sciences. Hume's famous argument against miracles has proven to be a powerful one. If a claim violates the regularities discovered by experience, then we ought to weigh the possibilities and accept the explanation that has the highest probability. At the very least, skeptics insist that extraordinary claims made by paranormalists should be supported by extraordinary evidence. If psi phenomena exist, then it is important that there be conceptually coherent hypotheses or theories to explain them. Perhaps this is not possible at the beginning stages of a science, but it is the ultimate goal. Parapsychology has not progressed in this area. Although it has postulated several constructs—e.g., ESP and PK—there is no developed theory, and what has been presented is in contradiction to the physical sciences.

The second and even more fundamental criticism concerns the data themselves. The crucial question is whether or not there is a sufficient degree of evidence to support the claim that ESP, psychokinesis, or any other psychic phenomenon exists. Parapsychologists maintain that there is; skeptics deny it. The key issue, therefore, is whether there is adequate data, objectively obtained and capable of replication in the laboratory by neutral and independent scientists. Before we can ascertain whether psychic phenomena exist, we need to carefully examine the fund of experiential and experimental data. And here is where the dispute rests, because skeptics deny that the evidence is strong enough and suggest that, where anomalies are uncovered, normal explanations can be given to account for them.

No doubt of great importance in this area is the argument from fraud. Unfortunately the field of psychic research has been replete with charlatans—individuals who claim to have special powers or gifts but are actually conjurers who have hoodwinked the public and scientists as well. The problem that puzzles skeptics is this: If one finds sleight-of-hand techniques being used some of the time by such individuals, then why should one accept anything else that is presented as genuine? Is not the evidence contaminated?

Eusapia Palladino is a good case in point. She was one of the most widely tested mediums of all time. A number of distinguished scientists submitted her powers to exhaustive testing in the early part of the century and were convinced by what they saw. But she was later caught in blatant acts of fraud by members of the Society for Psychical Research in Cambridge and by scientific committees at Columbia and Harvard universities. She was shown to be using a hand or a foot to move objects so that they appeared to be levitating. Even her defenders conceded that she cheated at least some of the time.

Similar doubts have been expressed about other psychics who were tested by numerous scientists and clearly shown to be using sleight-of-hand techniques. Some parapsychologists have argued that we ought to be concerned not with the ethics of the subject being tested but with the genuineness of the phenomena. The skeptic would reply that the alleged phenomena are in doubt once we know the subject will resort to cheating. One cannot use dirty test tubes in the laboratory.

Skeptics surely do not think that all paranormal data can be attributed to fraud, but they suggest that extreme caution is in order. This applies to experimenters as well, especially in the light of the Soal affair and Levy's work at Duke.

In spite of the need for caution, selective skepticism, not universal rejection, is essential in appraising the work of parapsychologists. Skeptics need to work cooperatively with them in designing, testing, and interpreting experimental projects. In the last analysis, the question of belief or nonbelief is irrelevant. An experimenter should play the role of neither a sheep (believer) nor a goat (disbeliever), but more appropriately should be a fox committed to careful and critical scrutiny of the hypotheses and the evidence. We need *neutral* investigators whose judgments are determined only by the evidence. Human beings are after all *human,* and it may be difficult to entirely abandon biases and preconceptions in the laboratory. Ideally, neutrality is the only legitimate position of a scientist qua scientist, whose higher loyalty must be to the furtherance of the aims of science and the quest for truth. By the same token, it is incumbent on those doing research in this controversial field to join with critics in exposing deceit and cant wherever they appear, including the popular exploitation of paranormal claims that have no basis in scientific fact.

A selective and constructive criticism is thus essential to the entire process of scientific inquiry. It should apply not only to parapsychology and other paranormal fields but to the established natural, social, and behavioral sciences as well. One surely should not reject all paranormal claims in a sweeping fashion. Nor can one refuse to investigate such claims fairly, objectively, and dispassionately. If rigorous standards of inquiry have been respected and if there is incontrovertible and replicable evidence to support a hypothesis or theory, then the only legitimate option for observers committed to the methods of science is to incorporate this hypothesis or theory into the body of established scientific knowledge. That parapsychology has discovered such evidence, or ever will, is still questionable.

In regard to psychical research and parapsychology, an important distinction must be made between the work of serious researchers who are committed to the best methods of science and the large number of extrapolated claims that seem to be proliferate in the public arena. Unfortunately, many of those who were involved in parapsychological research in the past did not conduct their work in a careful way and were beguiled by the call of the occult or the paranormal. The "transcendental temptation" is a strong human impulse and it has often stood in the way of objective inquiry. Those parapsychologists who painstakingly strive to adhere to scientific principles will find common ground with skeptics and a basis for dialogue and cooperative inquiry.

It is when the speculative theories of parapsychology are accepted uncritically by the broader public that skeptical criticism becomes vital: for the popularization of paranormal claims is often antithetical to scientific inquiry and assumes mystical and religious auras. From the days of the fraudulent mediums of the nineteenth century to the superpsychics and gurus of the twentieth, simliar psychological processes have manifested themselves in an unwary public. Here the skeptic moves out of the laboratory to become the debunker. There is an illustrious tradition of debunking in the world of ideas that includes the work of Socrates, Lucian, Montaigne, Hume, Voltaire, Nietzsche, George Bernard Shaw, Bertrand Russell, H. L. Mencken, Sidney Hook, and many others. It may be the only appropriate response to charlatans who seek to fleece a gullible public. Debunking and ridicule have no place within science proper, but it is relevant where hasty generalizations and irresponsible claims that have no foundation in fact are offered as scientific dictum.

Of considerable interest to the cause of skepticism is the formation in 1976 of the Committee for the Scientific Investigation of Claims of the Paranormal (CSICOP), which publishes the *Skeptical Inquirer*. This group is interested in the fair and unbiased examination of the wide range of paranormal claims. It is also interested in public education in the methods and aims of science, and this includes some debunking of those claims that are shown to be unfounded or false.

IV

The field of parapsychology and psychical research encompasses a wide range of ostensibly anomalous data. It is beyond the scope of this volume to treat all of the varieties of paranormal claims, but it does focus on the most important.

Part 1 presents some historical overviews of the field. Four psychologists, Ray Hyman, C. E. M. Hansel, and Edward Girden and Ellen Girden, all close students of parapsychology, review the entire field of psychic research from its beginning up to the present. All four conclude that neither ESP nor psychokinesis has been demonstrated in the laboratory. Part 1 also contains two review articles, by Simon Newcomb and Eric Dingwall, based on their personal investigations. Simon Newcomb (1835-1909), a distinguished astronomer, summarizes his skeptical reactions after fifty years of involvement in the field of occult research. Eric Dingwall was for many years involved in psychical research and expresses a similar skepticism after sixty years of active inquiry.

Part 2, "The Argument from Fraud," begins with this editor's analytical discussion of the problem of fraud, from the Fox sisters to the present. It is followed by the famous confessions of Margaret Fox Kane and Douglas Blackburn. Margaret Fox and her sister Kate, who made their debut as mediums in 1848, were the chief inspiration of the spiritualist movement in America. In 1888, her confession that she used trickery in order to bring about spiritualistic phenomena was first published in the *New York World*. Douglas Blackburn was believed by the SPR to have telepathic powers, and he and his partner, G. A. Smith, were tested for many years. In 1911, Blackburn published his confession, revealing how easy it had been to dupe the early members of SPR. John E. Coover, a noted psychologist in his day, reviews the history of psychical research from its beginnings through the late 1920s and provides numerous illustrations of the deception of mediums and psychics.

More recent work is also considered in Part 2. J. Fraser Nicol discusses the tendency of young children and adolescents to engage in trickery. Betty Markwick provides a detailed analysis of the Soal scandal, and D. Scott Rogo reviews the case of Walter J. Levy at Duke. Nicol, Markwick, and Rogo have been closely identified with parapsychological research, and Nicol and Rogo still have confidence in the reality of some psi phenomena. Trevor Hall's contribution to this section exposes the hauntings in the Borley Rectory in England, which many psychic investigators considered to be the "most haunted house in England." Part 2 concludes with a piece by James ("The Amazing") Randi and one by Martin Gardner, two veteran skeptical debunkers, about the need for conjurers and magicians in parapsychology laboratories to advise on protocol to prevent fraud and chicanery.

Part 3 provides the opportunity for some parapsychologists to reply to their critics. John Beloff pleads for a revaluation of the historical cases of mediums, in particular Eusapia Palladino, and he calls upon skeptics to give counter-explanations for what he believes were genuine psychic phenomena. Douglas Stokes carefully reviews the field of psi research, offering a qualified appraisal. Susan Blackmore, a parapsychologist who has had exclusively negative results, suggests important new departures for researchers interested in investigating ostensible anomalous phenomena. Gerd Hövelmann, Piet Hein Hoebens, and Marcello Truzzi, who believe that skeptics should work closely with serious scientific parapsychologists, have criticisms of some skeptics. They present an annotated quide to the skeptical literature. This is followed by a brief note by Ray Hyman.

Part 4, "Parapsychology: Science or Pseudoscience?" attempts to appraise the entire field of psychic research. Christopher Scott, Antony Flew, and the editor of this volume ask whether parapsychology is a genuine science. Is it like phrenology, a pseudoscience that has virtually disappeared from the scene, or is it a meaningful protoscience? Psychologist James Alcock discusses the strong religious motivation apparently present in much psi research and attributes this bias to the will to believe.

Part 5, "Some Methodological and Theoretical Issues," raises a number of epistemological and methodological issues. Persi Diaconis is concerned with the statistical questions of what constitutes chance or coincidence, and on what basis we may conclude an anomaly has occurred. Martin Gardner asks whether recent work in quantum physics can be used to support parapsychological claims as some recent advocates of paraphysics have maintained. Denys Parsons illustrates the importance of detective work in tracking down the facts behind anomalous claims and recounts some of his investigations. Charles Akers evaluates the use of meta-analysis to resolve the ESP controversy.

Part 6 provides some "Further Critiques." Piet Hein Hoebens analyzes the frequent claim that psychics are able to assist detectives in locating criminals or missing persons. Unfortunately, Hoebens died before completing his paper; Marcello Truzzi has edited it for publication. Next in his chapter on survival after death, Gerd Hövelmann reviews the recent literature in the field of near-death experiences. An important concluding paper in this section, by Leonard Zusne, interprets the role of magical thinking both in human experience and in parapsychology.

We hope that the *Skeptic's Handbook of Parapsychology* will be of use to both scientific researchers and the general public and that it presents fairly and objectively a wide range of points of view.

Contributors

CHARLES AKERS received his Ph.D. in psychology from the University of Texas in 1978. He was a research associate at the Institute for Parapsychology in 1978–79 and continued this research at Harvard University in 1984–85 under a grant from the Hodgson Fund. He is a member of the Parapsychology Subcommittee of the Committee for the Scientific Investigation of Claims of the Paranormal.

JAMES E. ALCOCK is a social psychologist on the faculty of Glendon College, York University, Toronto, Canada. His research interests include the study of belief systems. He is the author of *Parapsychology: Science or Magic* and many articles on parapsychological belief. Professor Alcock is on the Executive Council and chairman of the Education Subcommittee of the Committee for the Scientific Investigation of Claims of the Paranormal.

JOHN BELOFF retired in 1984 as senior lecturer in the Department of Psychology of the University of Edinburgh. He is a former president of both the Parapsychological Association and the Society for Psychical Research (London).

SUSAN BLACKMORE is at present Visiting Fellow at the Brain and Perception laboratory, University of Bristol, England. Dr. Blackmore is the author of *Beyond the Body* and numerous articles on parapsychology. She is a member of the Council of the Society for Psychical Research and editor of its newsletter.

JOHN E. COOVER (1872–1938) was professor of psychology at Stanford University. He is the author of *Experiments in Psychic Research* (1917).

PERSI DIACONIS is a professor of statistics at Stanford University. He spent ten years working as a professional magician and occasionally applies both fields of expertise to problems in parapsychology.

ERIC DINGWALL, a veteran psychical researcher, was for years associated with the British Society for Psychical Research. Among his many books are *Some Human Oddities, Very Peculiar People,* and *Ghosts and Spirits in the Ancient World.*

ANTONY FLEW is Emeritus Professor of philosophy at the University of Reading, England. He is the author of *Hume's Philosophy of Belief* and *Thinking Straight,* among many other books, and a Fellow of the Committee for the Scientific Investigation of Claims of the Paranormal.

MARTIN GARDNER is the author of *Science: Good, Bad, and Bogus* (1981) and *Fads and Fallacies in the Name of Science* (1952) and of some forty books in the fields of science, mathematics, philosophy, and literary criticism. The *Skeptical Inquirer* carries his regular column "Notes of a Psi-Watcher." He is a member of the Executive Council of the Committee for the Scientific Investigation of Claims of the Paranormal.

EDWARD GIRDEN is Professor Emeritus at Brooklyn College and was Distinguished Professor of Psychology at Florida International University. He is a fellow of both the American Association for the Advancement of Science and the American Psychological Association.

ELLEN R. GIRDEN is professor of psychology at Nova University and has taught at Northwestern University, Hobart & Smith College, and Yeshiva University.

TREVOR H. HALL, writer, historian, and lecturer, is president of the Leeds Library in England. He is the author of *The Strange Case of Edmund Gurney*, *The Search for Harry Price*, *The Enigma of Daniel Home*, *The Medium and the Scientist: The Story of Florence Cook and William Crookes*, and many other books.

C. E. M. HANSEL holds the Chair of Psychology at University College of Swansea, University of Wales. He is author of *ESP and Parapsychology: A Critical Reevaluation* and many other books and a Fellow of the Committee for the Scientific Investigation of Claims of the Paranormal.

PIET HEIN HOEBENS (1951-1984) was chairman of the Netherlands branch of the Committee for the Scientific Investigation of Claims of the Paranormal. He was chief editorial writer for *De Telegraaf,* the Netherlands' largest newspaper.

GERD H. HÖVELMANN, a Ph.D. candidate in philosophy of science, is a staff member of the Institute for Philosophy at Philipps University in Marburg/Lahn, West Germany, and has been an associate member of the Parapsychological Association since 1983. He is the author of numerous publications on methodological, philosophical, and sociological problems of parapsychology, as well as on the philosophy of language and the philosophy of the natural sciences.

RAY HYMAN is professor of psychology at the University of Oregon, with special interest in the psychology of belief systems and the analysis of parapsychological research. He is a member of the Executive Council of the Committee for the Scientific Investigation of Claims of the Paranormal and chairman of its Parapsychology Subcommittee. He has written extensively on parapsychology and is coauthor (with Evan Z. Vogt) of *Water-Witching USA.*

PAUL KURTZ is chairman of the Committee for the Scientific Investigation of Claims of the Paranormal and professor of philosophy at the State University of New York at Buffalo. He is editor of *Free Inquiry* magazine and author or editor of twenty books, including *Decision and the Condition of Man*, *The Fullness of Life*, *In Defense of Secular Humanism*, *Exuberance*, and *Humanist Manifesto II*.

BETTY MARKWICK, formerly a specialist in data correlation with a major engineering company, is a member of the Council of the Society for Psychical Research and an associate member of the Parapsychological Association. Her principal interests include statistical methods in parapsychology and in dream-ESP research.

SIMON NEWCOMB (1835-1909), the first president of the American Society for Psychical Research, was a distinguished astronomer and author.

J. FRASER NICOL has been engaged in psychical research in Britain and America for fifty years and has published many papers, some favorable to the subject, others critical, of which the paper included in this volume is an example.

DENYS PARSONS became a member of the Society for Psychical Research in 1942 and for many years was a member of its Council. His parapsychology projects have included research in ESP, PK, "radionics," and dowsing. He is a member of the British branch of the Committee for the Scientific Investigation of Claims of the Paranormal.

JAMES RANDI is an internationally known conjurer with forty years of experience in evaluating demonstrations of a purported paranormal nature. He is the author of *Flim-Flam* and *The Truth About Uri Geller* and a member of the Executive Council of the Committee for the Scientific Investigation of Claims of the Paranormal.

D. SCOTT ROGO is on the faculty at John F. Kennedy University in Orinda, California. He has written some twenty-five books on the paranormal and serves as consulting editor for *Fate* magazine.

CHRISTOPHER SCOTT is a psychologist and statistician with a lifetime interest in the paranormal. Starting as a reluctant believer, he became increasingly skeptical. In 1973 he contributed crucially to the uncovering of the S. G. Soal fraud. He is a member of the British branch of the Committee for the Scientific Investigation of Claims of the Paranormal.

DOUGLAS STOKES is a former parapsychological researcher and currently serves on the editorial staff of the *Journal of Parapsychology*. He holds a Ph.D. in experimental psychology and lives in Bryn Mawr, Pennsylvania, where he is chairman of the mathematics department of the Shipley School. He is a frequent contributor to the literature relating to parapsychology.

MARCELLO TRUZZI is professor of sociology at Eastern Michigan University and the director of the Center for Scientific Anomalies Research. He is the editor of the journal *Zetetic Scholar*, which seeks to promote dialogue between proponents and critics of claims of the paranormal.

LEONARD ZUSNE is professor of psychology at the University of Tulsa. In addition to books and articles in the fields of perception and history of psychology, he is the author (with W. B. Jones) of *Anomalistic Psychology* (the term is his coinage) and of many articles in this area. He also teaches the psychology of extraordinary behavior and experience and magical thinking.

Part 1

Historical Overviews

1

A Critical Historical Overview of Parapsychology

RAY HYMAN

Introduction

Robert Jahn, dean of engineering and applied sciences at Princeton University, began a recently published and much quoted paper on psychical research with the following words: "I venture to begin the most extraordinary writing task I have yet attempted: . . . a critical review of the status and prognosis of scientific research into so-called psychic phenomena" (Jahn 1982).

Jahn's prologue vividly depicts the elusive and intractible nature of the alleged phenomena:

> The world of psychic phenomena might be likened to a vast, fog-shrouded swamp, wherein are reported to dwell a bewildering array of bizarre phenomenological creatures, all foreign to our normal perceptual and analytical catalogs. . . . Some of these [creatures] are claimed to appear unexpectedly, erupting from the roily depths to flash momentarily in the sunlight of human experience, only to disappear again before any systematic calibration of their characteristics can be taken. Others are reportedly enticed to more replicable and controlled behavior, but only by persons of special talent or extensive training. Much invalid, even fraudulent evidence of such activity has been touted by exploiters of these mysteries, thereby casting deep suspicion on all other testimony. When fully sifted, only a very few legitimate specimens seem to have been captured, by tediously deliberate trolling of the brackish domain, or by more incisive invasion of its turbid interior, and even these have proven so incomprehensible and so delicate to exposure, and the imposed criteria for their credibility have been so severe, that they have not been fully persuasive. Yet the goal remains alluring, and the search continues.

Jahn's carefully balanced survey of the history and current status of psychical research captures, in my opinion, much of the paradox of this controversial activity. Based on this survey as well as on his own investigations of anomalous phenomena, Jahn concludes:

A shorter version of this paper will appear in the *Proceedings of the IEEE*.

3

Once the illegitimate research and invalid criticism have been set aside, the remaining accumulated evidence of psychic phenomena comprises an array of experimental observations, obtained under reasonable protocols in a variety of scholarly disciplines, which compound to a philosophical dilemma. On the one hand, effects inexplicable in terms of established scientific theory, yet having numerous common characteristics, are frequently and widely observed; on the other hand, these effects have so far proven qualitatively and quantitatively irreplicable, in the strict scientific sense, and appear to be sensitive to a variety of psychological and environmental factors that are difficult to specify, let alone control.

After examining the status of psychical research, Jahn obviously believes that, despite all its drawbacks, "further careful study of this formidable field seems justified, but only within the context of very well conceived and technically impeccable experiments of large data-base capability, with disciplined attention to the pertinent aesthetic factors, and with more constructive involvement of the critical community."

This is one of a number of justifiable reactions one can have as a result of fairly examining the case for psychical research. Jahn is willing to risk his time and reputation on the possibility that careful and diligent investigation will bring some lawfulness to this unruly area of inquiry. It will no doubt be several years before we know whether Jahn has managed to progress much beyond other attempts to bring scientific order into the field.

During the 130-year history of psychical research, many other scholars and scientists initiated investigations of psychic phenomena with equally high hopes of taming them. One was the philosopher Henry Sidgwick, who was the first president of the Society for Psychical Research founded in England in 1882. According to William James, Sidgwick and his colleagues "hoped that if the material were treated rigorously and, as far as possible, experimentally, objective truth would be elicited, and the subject rescued from sentimentalism on the one side and dogmatizing ignorance on the other. Like all founders, Sidgwick hoped for a certain promptitude of result; and I heard him say, the year before his death, that if anyone had told him at the outset that after twenty years he would be in the same identical state of doubt and balance that he started with, he would have deemed the prophecy incredible. It appeared impossible that the amount of handling evidence should bring so little finality of decision" (Murphy and Ballou 1969).

James, who made this observation in his last article on psychical research, in 1909, continued:

My own experience has been similar to Sidgwick's. For twenty-five years I have been in touch with the literature of psychical research, and have had acquaintance with numerous "researchers." I have also spent a good many hours (though far fewer than I ought to have spent) in witnessing (or trying to witness) phenomena. Yet I am theoretically no "further" than I was at the beginning; and I confess that at times I have been tempted to believe that the Creator has eternally intended this department of nature to remain *baffling*, to prompt our curiosities and hopes and suspicions all in equal measure, so that, although ghosts and clairvoyances, and raps and messages from spirits, are always seeming to exist and can never be fully explained away, they also can never be susceptible of full corroboration.

The peculiarity of the case is just that there are so many sources of possible deception in most of the observations that the whole lot of them *may* be worthless, and yet that in comparatively few cases can aught more fatal than this vague general possibility of error be pleaded against the record. Science, meanwhile, needs something more than bare possibilities to build upon; so your genuinely scientific inquirer—I don't mean your ignoramus "scientist"—has to remain unsatisfied.

Some 67 years after James's final words on the matter, philosopher Antony Flew (1978) summed up his 25 years of interest in parapsychology with remarkably similar sentiments:

My long-out-of-print first book was entitled, perhaps too rashly, *A New Approach to Psychical Research.* . . . When I reviewed the evidential situation at that time it seemed to me that there was too much evidence for one to dismiss. Honesty required some sort of continuing interest, even if a distant interest. On the other hand, it seemed to me then that there was no such thing as a reliably repeatable phenomenon in the area of parapsychology and that there was really almost nothing positive that could be pointed to with assurance. The really definite and decisive pieces of work seemed to be uniformly negative in their outcome.

It is most depressing to have to say that the general situation a quarter of a century later still seems to me to be very much the same. An enormous amount of further work has been done. Perhaps more has been done in this latest period than in the whole previous history of the subject. Nevertheless, there is still no reliably repeatable phenomenon, no particular solid-rock positive cases. And yet there still is clearly too much there for us to dismiss the whole business.

Sidgwick was assessing the first 50 years of psychical research. James was evaluating the same period with another 10 years or so added. Flew based his assessment on an additional 67 years of inquiry. Yet all three agree that they could detect no progress. In each case, after a quarter of a century of personal involvement, the investigator found the evidence for the paranormal just as inconclusive as it had been at the beginning. James openly conceded that *all* the claimed phenomena might be the result of self-deception or fraud. Yet he and the other two philosophers could not quite shake the conviction that, despite all this inconclusiveness, "there might be something there."

Over this same span of history, the critics have consistently insisted that "there is nothing there," that all the alleged phenomena of telepathy, clairvoyance, psychokinesis, levitation, spirit materialization, and premonitions can be accounted for in terms of fraud, self-delusion, and simple gullibility. The proponents have naturally resented such dismissals of their claims. They have argued that the critics have not fairly examined the evidence. They have accused the critics of attacking the weakest evidence and of ignoring the stronger and better-supported evidence in favor of the paranormal.

Unfortunately, as any reading of the history of psychical research quickly reveals, the psychical researchers are correct in their appraisal of their critics. Too often, the major critics have attacked straw men and have not dealt with the actual claims and evidence put forth by the more serious researchers. The fact that most of the criticism of psychical research has been irrelevant and unfair, however, does not necessarily mean that the psychical researchers have a convincing case.

Indeed, the message that we get from Sidgwick, James, Flew, and Jahn is that the evidential base for psychic claims is shaky at best. At most, these scholars, after carefully weighing all the evidence available to them, are claiming only that they cannot help feeling, despite the inconsistencies and nonlawfulness of the data, that "there must be something there."

As will be discussed later in this article, both the critics and the proponents subscribe to what I refer to as the False Dichotomy. When a scientist or a scholar, after investigating possible psychic phenomena, concludes that the phenomena are real, the assumption is that either his conclusion is justified or he is delinquent in some serious way—being either incompetent or subject to some pathology. When the critic denies that the claim is justified, the proponent feels that his integrity or competence is being challenged. And the critic, sharing in this assumption, feels that he must show that the claimant is incompetent, gullible, or deficient in some serious way (Hyman 1980).

I consider this a false dichotomy because competent and honest investigators can make serious judgmental errors when investigating new phenomena. Competence and expertise in any given field of endeavor is bounded. Cognitive psychologists, historians of science, and sociologists of knowledge have been gathering data that demonstrate how thinking is guided by conceptual frameworks and paradigms within which the thinker operates. Successful scientific thinking, for example, is successful not because it operates according to abstract, formal rules of evidence. Rather, it succeeds because the thinker is guided by the often implicit rules and procedures inherent within the specific content and practices of the narrow field of specialization within which the problem is being pursued. These "heuristics" or guidelines for successful thinking are not fool-proof and under changed circumstances they can trap the thinker into erroneous convictions. In other words, competence in a given scholarly or scientific disci-pline and high intelligence are no barriers to becoming trapped into asserting and defending erroneous positions.

I agree with Sidgwick, James, Flew, and Jahn in the most general sense that "something" is indeed going on. However, I do not see any need to assume that this "something" has anything to do with the paranormal.

I think we should not lightly dismiss the fact that for 130 years some of our best scholars and scientists have seriously carried out psychical research and have become convinced that they have demonstrated the existence of a "psychic force" or a supernatural realm occupied by intelligent and superior beings. As far as I can tell, these proponents were competent scholars, sane, and highly intelligent. They made every apparent effort to employ what they believed to be objective and scientific standards in observing, recording, and reporting their findings.

Yet, as I will argue, contrary to Jahn's assessment, the total accumulation of 130 years' worth of psychical investigation has not produced any consistent evidence for paranormality that can withstand acceptable scientific scrutiny. What should be interesting for the scientific establishment is not that there is a case to be made for psychic phenomena but, rather, that the majority of scien-tists who decided to seriously investigate *believed* that they had made such a case. How can it be that so many outstanding scientists, including several Nobel Prize winners, have convinced themselves that they have obtained solid scien-tific evidence for paranormal phenomena?

If they are wrong, what has made them wrong? Are weaknesses or limita-tions of scientific method and training indicated? And if these investigators have not actually encountered psychic phenomena, what is it that they have dis-covered?

I am not sure that I can provide satisfactory answers to these questions. But I believe that it will help to look at some selected cases in which investigators believed that they had obtained adequate scientific evidence for the reality of psychic phenomena. I will begin at the beginning by describing the sort of evi-dence that convinced the first scientists who took psychical claims seriously. Even some contemporary parapsychologists believe these early scientists may have been wrong, but their cases are still worth examining because in them we will find many of the same issues and problems that characterize contemporary parapsychological research. These early psychic investigators tested spiritualistic mediums who were noted for their ability to produce powerful psychic phe-nomena, such as levitations, materializations, and other physical feats.

Psychical research became transformed into what is now called parapsychology when the focus shifted, after the first half-century of investigation, to the study of extrasensory perception and psychokinesis in ordinary individuals by means of standardized testing materials and procedures. I will examine what was, at the time, considered to be the most rigorous and successful application of this form of parapsychological research—the now notorious investigations by S. G. Soal on Basil Shackleton and Mrs. Stewart. Again, the purpose is not to beat a dead horse but to abstract out principles and issues that still haunt contemporary parapsychology.

The card-guessing experiments begun by Rhine in the 1930s established the paradigm that dominated parapsychology for the next 40 years. New technology and interest in altered states resulted in departures from Rhine's paradigm beginning about 1970. Experiments with random-event generators, remote viewing, and the ganzfeld technique have been the strongest contenders for providing parapsychology with its long-sought-for repeatable experiment. I will argue that a fair and objective assessment of this latest work strongly suggests that, like its predecessors, it still does not stand up to critical scrutiny.

Table-Turning and Psychical Research

Modern spiritualism began in 1848, when unaccountable raps were heard in the presence of two teen-age girls, Margaret and Kate Fox. By using a code, the girls' mother was able to converse with the raps and concluded that they originated from the spirit of a peddler who had been murdered in the very house in which the Fox family now lived. Word of this miraculous communication spread quickly, and soon a variety of means for communicating with the unseen spirits via the "spiritual telegraph" were developed in the United States and then spread to Europe. The individuals through whom the spirits produced their phenomena and communicated with mortals were called mediums. The mediums at first displayed such phenomena as rapping sounds, movements of tables and objects, the playing of musical instruments by unseen agencies, and the occurrence of strange lights in the dark. Later, more elaborate phenomena were produced, such as the levitation of objects or of the medium; the disappearance of objects; the materialization of hands, faces, or even of complete spirit forms; spirit paintings and photographs; and written communications from the spirit world (Moore 1977; Podmore 1963).

By the early 1850s table-turning (also called table-tilting or table-rapping) had become the rage both in the United States and in Europe. A group of individuals, usually called "sitters," would arrange themselves around a table with their hands resting flat upon the table-top. After an extended period of waiting, a rap would be heard or the table would tilt upon one leg. Sometimes the table would sway and begin moving about the room, dragging the sitters along. On some occasions, sitters would claim that the table actually levitated off the floor under conditions in which all hands were above the table. Reports even circulated that sometimes the table levitated when no hands were touching it. Table-turning was especially popular because it could occur with or without the presence of an acknowledged medium. Any group of individuals could get together and attempt to produce the phenomenon in the privacy of their own living room.

Table-turning plays an important role in the history of psychical research because it was what first attracted the attention of serious scientists to alleged paranormal phenomena (Podmore 1963). The phenomenon had become so widespread in England by the summer of 1853 that several scientists decided to look into it. Although the prevailing explanation for the table's movements favored the agency of spirits, other explanations at the time were electricity, magnetism, "attraction," Karl von Reichenbach's Odylic force, and the rotation of the earth. Electricity, which in the public mind was then considered to be an occult and mystical force, was especially popular. Indeed, many spiritualists probably thought that the spirits operated by electricity.

In June 1853, a committee of four medical men held séances to investigate table-turning. They found that the table did not move at all when the sitters' attention was diverted and when they had not formed common expectations about how the table should move. They found that the table would not move if half the sitters expected it to move to the right and the other half expected it to move to the left. "But when expectation was allowed free play, and especially if the direction of the probable movement was indicated beforehand, the table began to rotate after a few minutes, although none of the sitters was conscious of exercising any effort at all. The conclusion formed was that the motion was due to muscular action, mostly exercised unconsciously (Podmore 1963). Other investigators came to similar conclusions.

But by far the most publicized and influential investigation was that by England's most renowned scientist, the physicist Michael Faraday. Faraday (1853) obtained subjects who were "very honorable" and who were also "successful table-movers." Faraday found that he could obtain movements at the table in a given direction with just one subject sitting at the table in the laboratory. His first tests were designed to eliminate as explanations well-known forces like magnetism and electricity. He demonstrated that such substances as sandpaper, millboard, glue, glass, moist clay, tinfoil, cardboard, vulcanized rubber, and wood did not interfere with the table-turning. He could find no traces of electrical or magnetic effects. "No form of experiment or mode of observation that I could devise gave me the slightest indication of any peculiar force. No attractions, or repulsion . . . nor anything which could be referred to other than the mere mechanical pressure exerted inadvertently by the turner."

Although Faraday suspected that the sitter was unconsciously pushing the table in the desired direction, the sitter adamantly insisted that he was not the agency but, instead, was pulled in the expected direction by some force within the table. Faraday created some ingenious arrangements to see if the sitter's claim was true. He placed four or five pieces of slippery cardboard, one over the other, on the table top. The pieces were attached to one another by little pellets of a soft cement. The lowest piece was attached to a piece of sandpaper that rested on the table top. The edges of the sheets overlapped slightly, and on the under surface Faraday drew a pencil line to indicate the position. The table-turner then placed his hands upon the upper card and waited for the table to move in the previously agreed upon direction (to the left). Faraday (1853) then examined the packet. "It was easy to see by displacement of the parts of the line, that the hand had moved further from the table, and that the latter had lagged behind—that the hand, in fact, had pushed the upper card to the left and that the under cards and the table had followed and been dragged by it."

In another arrangement, Faraday fixed an indicator to two boards on the table-top such that, if the sitter was pulled by the table, the indicator would slope to the right but, if the sitter pushed the table, the indicator would slope to the left. The table moved as before as long as the sitter could not see the indicator. But as soon as the sitter was able to watch the indicator, which gave him immediate feedback when his hands pushed in the expected direction, all movements of the table ceased. "But the most valuable effect of this test-apparatus . . . is the corrective power it possesses over the mind of the table-turner. As soon as the index is placed before the most earnest, and they perceive—as in my presence they have always done—that it tells truly whether they are pressing downwards only or obliquely, then all effects of table-turning cease, even though the parties persevere, earnestly desiring motion, till they become weary and worn out. No prompting or checking of the hands is needed—*the power is gone;* and this only because the parties are made conscious of what they are really doing mechanically, and so are unable unwittingly to deceive themselves" (Faraday 1853).

Faraday's investigation convinced several scientists that table-turning was the result of self-deception resulting from unconscious motor movements guided by expectation. His report is even credited with dampening the enthusiasm, for a few years, for spiritualism in England (Podmore 1963). But several spiritualists and table-turners were not convinced by Faraday's arguments. And this brings up another issue that invariably accompanies the controversy over paranormal claims. Whenever a skeptic demonstrates how an alleged psychic phenomenon can be duplicated by mundane means, the claimant usually responds, "It's not the same thing!"

To many spiritualists and those who had witnessed table-turning, Faraday's explanation appeared hopelessly inadequate. For example, while sitting at the table professional mediums could provide meaningful answers by means of table-rapping to questions that sitters put to their assumed spirit communicators. In addition, the table often moved in a variety of ways that seemingly could not be explained by simple muscular pressure applied by the sitters. For example, the table often levitated above the floor with all the sitters' hands resting on the top surface. And some reports claimed that the table moved and levitated when no human was in contact with it.

Faraday's explanation dealt with only one important cause of the table-turning. He did not attempt to account for the various ways in which the table could be moved and levitated by trickery. Nor did he refer to the problem of the notorious unreliability of eyewitness testimony. Nor did he and his fellow skeptics realize that an abstract, even if correct, explanation of table-turning was impotent when matched against the personal and powerfully emotional experience of a sitter who has been converted during an actual table-turning session. These same limitations on any attempt to "explain away" an alleged paranormal event by a mundane account continue to provide loopholes whereby the proponent can maintain the reality of a paranormal claim.

Two striking illustrations of the power of the experience that "it is not the same thing" can be found in the conversions to spiritualism of the next two major scientists to investigate psychic phenomena. Both Robert Hare and Alfred Russel Wallace were familiar with Faraday's research and explanation when they first investigated spiritualistic table-turning, and both were immediately convinced that their personal experiences could not be accounted for by Faraday's theory. In these instances, the forewarning, rather than serving to forearm, actually disarmed. And this, too, is a recurring theme in the history of psychical research.

Faraday, the first major scientist to seriously investigate spiritualistic phenomena, concluded that self-deception was sufficient to explain what he observed. As a result, he remained skeptical and critical of all further claims of paranormal phenomena. His scientific colleagues were obviously grateful for Faraday's investigation and conclusions. But within the next two decades three other major scientists also investigated paranormal claims and concluded, contrary to Faraday, that they had witnessed truly paranormal phenomena.

Robert Hare, the eminent American chemist, began his inquiry into spiritualistic phenomena in 1853, immediately after Faraday's investigation. Alfred Russel Wallace, the cofounder with Darwin of the theory of evolution by natural selection, initiated his investigations in 1865. And Sir William Crookes, the discoverer of thallium, began his investigations in 1869. All three had already achieved reputations as outstanding scientists before they surprised their scientific colleagues with their assertions of having witnessed psychic phenomena. Their colleagues were disturbed and puzzled by such assertions from obviously eminent scientists. Their reactions, unfortunately, were not always rational and tended to make a confusing situation worse rather than better.

I believe it is important to try to understand how these otherwise competent scientists became convinced that they had acquired evidence sufficient to justify the belief in paranormal phenomena. The investigations of these scientists can be credited with the initiation of psychical research as a field with scientific aspirations. And many of the same issues of scientific justification of claims for the paranormal that we find in their work are still with us today.

Robert Hare

Robert Hare was Professor Emeritus of Chemistry at the University of Pennsylvania and 72 years of age in 1853, when circumstances conspired to launch him on a new career as a psychic investigator. Hare, the author of more than 150 scientific papers, had invented the oxy-hydrogen blowpipe, which was the predecessor of today's welding torches (Shepard 1978). According to Isaac Asimov (1976), Hare was "one of the few strictly American products who in those days could be considered within hailing distance of the great European chemists."

When Faraday's conclusions on table-turning were published, Hare was asked his opinion. His reply appeared as a letter in the *Philadelphia Inquirer* on July 27, 1853. In his letter, he rejected the idea that some exotic force or electricity could produce movement in wooden tables. He ended his letter as follows: "I recommend to your attention, and that of others interested in this hallucination, Faraday's observations and experiments, recently published in some of our respectable newspapers. I entirely concur in the conclusions of that distinguished expounder of Nature's riddles."

Professor Hare died five years after writing this letter. If it had not been for a reply to this letter by a Mr. Amasa Holcombe and an invitation by a Dr. Comstock to "attend a circle," Hare might be remembered today as one of the first great American chemists, the inventor of the oxy-hydrogen torch, and a confirmed skeptic of psychical phenomena.

But Holcombe's letter convinced Hare that he might have been too hasty in his judgment, and his subsequent investigations of table-turning and other spiritualistic phenomena converted him to the cause of spiritualism. The result was an unusual book with the lengthy title: *Experimental Investigation of the Spirit Manifestations, Demonstrating the Existence of Spirits and their Communion with Mortals. Doctrine of the Spirit World Respecting Heaven, Hell, Morality, and God. Also, the Influence of Scripture on the Morals of Christians* (Hare 1855).

Upon accepting Dr. Comstock's invitation, Hare was taken to a private house. He described what happened as follows:

> Seated at a table with half a dozen persons, a hymn was sung with religious zeal and solemnity. Soon afterwards tappings were distinctly heard as if made beneath and against the table, which, from the perfect stillness of every one of the party, could not be attributed to any one among them. Apparently, the sounds were such as could only be made with some hard instrument, or with the ends of fingers aided by the nails.
>
> I learned that simple queries were answered by means of these manifestations; one tap being considered as equivalent to a negative; two, to doubtful; and three, to an affirmative. With the greatest *apparent sincerity*, questions were put and answers taken and recorded, as if all concerned considered them as coming from a rational though invisible agent. Subsequently, two media sat down at a small table (drawer removed) which, upon careful examination, I found to present to my inspection nothing but the surface of a bare board, on the under side as well as upon the upper. Yet the taps were heard as before, seemingly against the table. Even assuming the people by whom I was surrounded, to be capable of deception, and the feat to be due to jugglery, it was still inexplicable. But manifestly I was in a company of worthy people, who were themselves under a deception if these sounds did not proceed from spiritual agency.
>
> On a subsequent occasion, at the same house, I heard similar tapping on a partition between two parlours. I opened the door between the parlours, and passed that adjoining the one in which I had been sitting. Nothing could be seen which could account for the sounds. [Hare 1855]

Hare describes other phenomena that he could not explain on the basis of normal agency. During his first visit to the circle, for example, he held the table with all his strength, but was unable to keep it from moving to and fro when two female mediums sat opposite him and merely placed their hands on the surface of the table. In another circle, table-tilting was substituted for the sounds as a form of communication from the alleged spirit world. Messages could be spelled out by having a sitter pass his hand over an alphabetic pasteboard. A letter was selected when either the table tilted or rapped as the hand passed over it. A skeptical lawyer friend remarked that the coherent messages that resulted from this procedure must be due either to "legerdemain" on the part of the medium or to the agency of some invisible intelligent being.

Hare's reply is revealing: "But assigning the result to legerdemain was altogether opposed to my knowledge of his character. This gentleman, and the circle to which he belonged, spent about three hours, twice or thrice a week, in getting communications through the alphabet, by the process to which the lines above mentioned were due. This would not have taken place, had *they* not had implicit confidence, that the information thus obtained proceeded from spirits" (Hare 1855).

The preceding quotation suggests that Hare was already convinced that the phenomena he had witnessed were spiritual in origin. But Hare was too much the careful scientist to commit himself just yet. He "contrived an apparatus which, if spirits were actually concerned in the phenomena, would enable them to manifest their physical and intellectual power independently of control by any medium." Hare took a circular pasteboard disk of somewhat more than a foot in diameter. He attached around its circumference the letters of the alphabet in a haphazard order. By means of pulleys, cords, weights, and other mechanisms a medium could sit with her hands on a table, but not be able to see the letters of the alphabet on the pasteboard circle. Movements of the table would cause a pointer to move around the wheel and indicate various letters of the alphabet.

With an accomplished medium sitting at the table, Hare seated himself in front of the disk. Hare then began by asking if any spirits were present to indicate so by causing the letter Y to be under the pointer. Immediately the pointer moved to the letter Y. Hare next asked, "Will the spirit do us the favour to give the initials of his name?" The index pointed first to R and next to H. Hare immediately asked, "My honoured father?" The index pointed to Y. After a few more tests such as these, the onlookers urged that Hare admit the reality of spiritual agency. Hare must have still shown some hesitation, because the index spelled out, "Oh, my son, listen to reason!"

Hare's sense of scientific propriety kept him from prematurely committing himself. "I urged that the experiment was of immense importance, if considered as proving a spirit to be present, and to have actuated the apparatus; affording thus precise experimental proof of the immortality of the soul: that a matter of such moment should not be considered as conclusively decided until every possible additional means of verification should be employed."

Hare's companions accused him of extreme incredulity. His medium told him she "should not deem it worth while to sit for me again." But Hare managed to get her to relent and a few days later she came to Hare's house to try out an improved version of his apparatus. The results confirmed the preceding experiment. Hare's departed father, mother, and sister came through and said they were happy. Hare got similar results on the apparatus with other mediums.

Hare reports many other tests and observations. He claims to have seen a table continue its movements even when every person in the room had withdrawn to a distance of about a foot. He reports tables rising from the floor when hands were placed flat on the top surface. Many of the tests that Hare devised were suggested to him by the spirits who were communicating through the table raps and his alphabetical index.

Hare writes that the greatest difficulty he encountered in carrying out his research was the necessity of making every observation under conditions that guaranteed he was not being deceived by the mediums. But when he himself acquired the powers of a medium, sufficient to converse directly with his spirit friends, he no longer felt "under the necessity of defending media from the charge of falsehood and deception. It is now my own character only that can be in question."

Spiritualists, understandably, were delighted by Hare's conversion to their cause. His scientific colleagues, on the other hand, were outraged. The professors at Harvard University, of which Hare was a graduate, passed a resolution denouncing him and his "insane adherence to a gigantic humbug." When he tried to talk on his researches into spiritualism at the meetings of the American Association for the Advancement of Science in Washington, D.C., in 1854, he was shouted down by his colleagues, who refused to listen (Shepard 1978).

What are we to make of this? It is easy to dismiss Hare's conversion as simply the result of senility due to advanced age. But this is too simple and cannot explain equally startling conversions by later eminent scientists, most of whom were much younger and at the height of their careers. Hare obviously felt that he was behaving in the best traditions of science, in which he had spent the better part of his life. He was initially skeptical and supported Faraday's position. However, when he was challenged by a spiritualist to examine the evidence for himself, Hare felt obligated to give the proponent a fair hearing. He was impressed with what he saw, but he believed that he acted with proper scientific caution and did not commit himself until he had built special apparatus and conducted a variety of what he felt were controlled experiments to eliminate alternatives to the paranormal and spiritual hypothesis. When he eventually was able to receive communications from the spirits without the intervention of other mediums, he was sure that he had demonstrated his case.

Both Hare and his critics took it for granted that a competent scientist could carry out observations and experiments on a variey of phenomena and, as a result, come to trustworthy and sound conclusions. Until he announced his conversion to the spiritualistic hypothesis, Hare's colleagues did not doubt his competence as an observer and experimenter. When he announced his startling conclusions that he had not only experimentally verified paranormal phenomena but had been communicating with the spirits of his departed relatives and also with George Washington, John Quincy Adams, Henry Clay, Benjamin Franklin, Byron, and Isaac Newton, this placed his incredulous colleagues in a quandary.

For half a century, the scientific world had accepted Hare's scientific papers and conclusions with respect and admiration. His scientific competence was widely acknowledged, and he had received various honors as a result. But now this respected scientist, by using apparently the same observational and experimental skills that had earned him his renown, was claiming to have demonstrated the reality of phenomena that fellow scientists felt were just too preposterous to be true. Instead of examining Hare's arguments and evidence, his colleagues reacted emotionally and rejected his conclusions out of hand. Furthermore, they treated him as a traitor to the scientific enterprise and refused to allow him to present his case in the regular scientific forum.

From Hare's perspective this reaction was both unfair and unscientific. His arguments were being rejected without even being given a hearing. In his last few years he turned away from his scientific colleagues and confined his social interactions entirely to his spiritualistic associates. From the perspective of the scientific establishment, Hare had suddenly gone insane or had suffered some other form of pathology. Here we see the False Dichotomy in action. And this same False Dichotomy will be found throughout the story of psychical research right up to the present.

Alfred Russel Wallace

Wallace's conversion to spiritualism began in the same way that Hare's did—sitting at an animated table during a séance. Wallace's experience, just as Hare's, convinced him that Faraday's explanation of the table's antics would not do. Unlike Hare, however, Wallace was not 72 and at the end of his career. Instead he was 42 years old and in the middle of a long and productive career. It had been only seven years earlier that Wallace had independently conceived the theory of evolution by natural selection, the very same theory that Darwin had been secretly working on for many years. Here is how Wallace described his initial investigations:

> It was in the summer of 1865 that I first witnessed any of the phenomena of what is called Spiritualism, in the house of a friend,—a sceptic, a man of science, and a lawyer, with none but members of his own family present. Sitting at a good-sized round table, with our hands placed upon it, after a short time slight movements would commence—not often "turnings" or "tiltings," but a gentle intermittent movement, like steps, which after a time would bring the table quite across the room. Slight but distinct tapping sounds were also heard. The following notes made at the time were intended to describe exactly what took place:—"July 22, 1865.—Sat with my friend, his wife, and two daughters, at a large loo table, by daylight. In about half an hour some faint motions were perceived, and some faint taps heard. They gradually increased; the taps became very distinct, and the table moved considerably, obliging us all to shift our chairs. Then a curious vibratory motion of the table commenced, almost like

the shivering of a living animal. I could feel it up to my elbows. These phenomena were variously repeated for two hours. On trying afterwards, we found the table could not be voluntarily moved in the same manner without a great exertion of force, and we could discover no possible way of producing the taps while our hands were upon the table.

On other occasions we tried the experiment of each person in succession leaving the table, and found that the phenomena continued the same as before, both taps and the table movement. Once I requested one after another to leave the table; the phenomena continued, but as the number of sitters diminished, with decreasing vigour, and just after the last person had drawn back leaving me alone at the table, there were two dull taps or blows, as with a fist or the pillar or foot of the table, the vibration of which I could feel as well as hear. No one present but myself could have made these and I certainly did not make them. [Wallace 1875]

Wallace admits that deception by one or more of the sitters could possibly produce some of the phenomena. But he argues that, since the hypothesis of deception could not account for all of the various antics of the table, "we have no right to conclude that it was *ever* the case." Significantly, he quotes the following remark that occurred at the end of his notes: "These experiments have satisfied me that there is an unknown power developed from the bodies of a number of persons placed in connection by sitting round a table with all their hands upon it" (Wallace 1875).

Dr. W. B. Carpenter, an eminent physiologist of the day, bitterly denounced the pro-paranormal conclusions of Hare, Wallace, and Crookes in public lectures and articles. Carpenter had coined the term "ideo-motor action" to refer to the assumed unconscious muscular movement that underlay such phenomena as the divining rod and table-turning. It was only natural that Carpenter would explain Wallace's reported experiences with table-turning in terms of this concept and Faraday's experiments. Wallace (1878a) responded with what he felt were sound refutations:

We now come to the last part of Dr. Carpenter's lecture—table-turning and Spiritualism—and here there is hardly any attempt to deal with the evidence. Instead of this we have irrelevant matters put prominently forward, backed up by sneers against believers, and false or unproved accusations against mediums. To begin with, the old amusement of table-turning of fifteen or twenty years ago, with Faraday's proof that it was often caused by unconscious muscular action, is again brought to the front. Table tilting is asserted to be caused in the same way, and an "indicator" is suggested for proving this; and the whole matter is supposed to be settled because no one, so far as Dr. Carpenter is aware, "has ever ventured to affirm that he has thus demonstrated the *absence* of muscular pressure," and "until such demonstrations shall have been given, the tilting—like the turning—of tables may be unhesitatingly attributed to the unconscious muscular action of the operators." We suppose Dr. Carpenter will shield himself by the "thus" in the above sentence, though he knows very well that a far more complete demonstration of the absence of muscular pressure than any indicator could afford has been repeatedly given, by motion, both turning and tilting, of the table occurring *without any contact whatever.*

Wallace then describes several reports of individuals and committees who claimed to have witnessed such movements with no apparent human contact. Again we find a critic who unwisely attempts to dismiss a whole class of alleged phenomena with a single explanation that perhaps covers only some of the reported cases. And we find a proponent who seizes this opportunity to dismiss the criticism as irrelevant by maintaining "it is not the same thing."

In September 1865, Wallace attended his first séance. It was supervised by a professional medium, Mrs. Mary Marshall (Wallace 1875; Kottler 1974; Wallace 1906). Wallace (1875) claimed that he and his friends "made whatever investigations we pleased, and tried all kinds of tests. We always sat in full daylight in a well-lighted room, and obtained a variety of phenomena of a very startling kind. . . ." Among these phenomena were tables levitating and moving around the room. Wallace also received messages, purportedly from the spirit world, including the names, ages, and other information about departed relatives. Wallace was sure that such information could not have been known to Mrs. Marshall. Wallace wrote that he also tried to lay traps and insert tests to check on the possibility of deception. "However strange and unreal these few phenomena may seem to readers who have seen nothing of the kind, I positively affirm that they are the facts which really happened just as I have narrated them, and that there was no room for any possible trick or deception."

Wallace encountered his most dramatic phenomena a year later, in November 1866, when a young medium, Agnes Nichol (later Mrs. Guppy), was discovered by Wallace's sister. Miss Nichol produced phenomena in Wallace's own home that he considered to be conclusive. Wallace (1906) described one session to John Tyndall in a letter dated May 8, 1868:

> During the last two years I have witnessed a great variety of phenomena, under such varied conditions that each objection as it arose was answered by other phenomena. The further I inquire, and the more I see, the more impossible becomes the theory of imposture or delusion. I *know* that the facts are real natural phenomena, just as certainly as I know any other curious facts in nature.
>
> Allow me to narrate *one* of the scores of equally remarkable things I have witnessed, and this one, though it certainly happened in the dark, is thereby only rendered more difficult to explain as a trick.

The *place* was the drawing-room of a friend of mine, a brother of one of our best artists. The *witnesses* were his own and his brother's family, one or two of their friends, myself, and Mr. John Smith, banker, of Malton, Yorkshire, introduced by me. The medium was Miss Nichol. We sat round a pillar-table in the middle of the room, exactly under a glass chandelier. Miss Nichol sat opposite me, and my friend, Mr. Smith, sat next her. We all held our neighbour's hands, and Miss Nichol's hands were both held by Mr. Smith, a stranger to all but myself, and who had never met Miss N. before. When comfortably arranged in this manner the lights were put out, one of the party holding a box of matches ready to strike a light when asked. After a few minutes' conversation, during a period of silence, I heard the following sounds in rapid succession; a slight *rustle*, as of a lady's dress; a little *tap*, such as might be made by setting down a wineglass on the table; and a very slight jingling of the drops of the glass chandelier. An instant after Mr. Smith said, "Miss Nichol is gone," the matchholder struck a light, and on the table (which had no cloth) was Miss Nichol *seated in her chair*, her head just touching the chandelier.

I had witnessed a similar phenomenon before, and was able to observe cooly; and the facts were noted down soon afterwards. Mr. Smith assured me that Miss Nichol simply glided out of his hands. No one else moved or quitted hold of their neighbour's hands. There was not more noise than I have described, and no motion or even tremor of the table, although our hands were upon it.

You know Miss N.'s size and probable weight, and can judge the force and exertion required to lift her and her chair on the exact centre of a large pillar-table, as well as the great surplus of force required to do it almost instantaneously and noiselessly, in the dark, and without pressure on the side of the table which would have tilted it up. Will any of the known laws of nature account for this?

In addition to the usual standard fare of raps, table-tilting, levitation, and musical sounds, Miss Nichol often produced apports in the form of freshly cut flowers and other plants. Carpenter attacked Wallace's account of a session in which such plants were materialized by stating that "in Mr. Wallace's own case no precautions whatever had been employed!" Wallace (1878b) replied as follows:

I have never published a *detailed* account of this seance, but I have stated the main facts with sufficient care to show that the phenomenon itself was a test surpassing anything that could have been prearranged. The general precautions used by me were as follows: Five personal friends were present besides myself and the medium, among them a medical man, a barrister, and an acute colonial man of business. The sitting was in my own back drawing-room. No cloth was on the table. The adjoining room and passage were fully lighted. We sat an hour in the darkened room before the flowers appeared, but there was always light enough to see the outlines of those present. We sat a little away from the table, the medium sitting by me. The flowers appeared on the polished table dimly visible as a *something*, before we lighted the gas. When we did so the whole surface of the four-feet circular table was covered with fresh flowers and ferns, a sight so beautiful and marvelous, that in the course of a not uneventful life I can hardly recall anything that has more strongly impressed me. I begged that nothing might be touched till we had carefully examined them. The first thing that struck us all was their extreme freshness and beauty. The next that they were all covered, especially the ferns, with a delicate dew; not with coarse drops of water, as I have since seen when the phenomenon was less perfect, but with a veritable fine dew, covering the whole surface of the ferns especially. Counting the separate sprigs we found them to be forty-eight in number consisting of four yellow and red tulips, eight large anemones of various colors, six large flowers of *Primula japonica*, eighteen chrysanthemums, mostly yellow and white, six fronds of Lomaria a foot long, and two of a Nephrodium about a foot long and six inches wide. Not a pinnule of these ferns was rumpled, but they lay on the table as perfect as if freshly brought from a conservatory. The anemones, primroses and tulips had none of them lost a petal. They were found spread over the whole surface of the table, while we had been for some time intently gazing on the sheen of its surface, and could have instantly detected a hand and arm moving over it. But that is not so important as the *condition* of these flowers and their dewiness; and—Dr. Carpenter notwithstanding—I still maintain they were (to us) "demonstrably not brought by the medium."

This production of flowers, along with fruit as well, was repeated in many further séances. Wallace claimed that particular flowers or fruit were materialized upon request. "A friend of Dr. Alfred Wallace asked for a sun-flower, and one six feet high fell on the table having a large mass of earth about its roots" (Shepard 1978).

Again, I believe it is important to ask what is going on. To simply dismiss Wallace as excessively gullible hardly begins to account for such a report. F. M. Turner (1974) tried to account for Wallace's deviations from the beaten path in terms of the different sort of upbringing and education he had in comparison with his contemporary Victorian scientific colleagues: "Wallace was different from most of his scientific contemporaries because his life had been quite different from theirs."

Wallace had his own explanation. He denied that he had any prior bias toward a paranormal or spiritual belief. He insisted that since the age of 14 he had lost all capacity to be affected by either clerical influence or religious prejudice. Up to the time he encountered spiritualism he claimed to be a skeptic and a confirmed materialist. "Facts, however, are stubborn things. My curiosity was at first excited by some slight but inexplicable phenomena occurring in a friend's family, and my desire for knowledge and love of truth forced me to continue the inquiry. . . . The facts beat me. They compelled me to accept them, *as facts,* long before I could accept the survival explanation of them: there was at that time "no place in my fabric of thought into which it could be fitted" (Wallace 1875).

Elsewhere Wallace did admit to some early experiences that preconditioned him to be more open to anomalous claims. At the age of 21, when he was teaching in a boys' school, he and the students attended some lectures by a Mr. Spencer Hall on mesmerism. As a result, Wallace conducted experiments on both mesmerism and another popular topic of the day, phrenology. In his experiments on "phrenomesmerism," he observed phenomena that he felt could not easily be explained by contemporary science. For example, he would mesmerize a student and then touch, in turn, various phrenological areas of the boy's head. When his finger touched the area supposedly corresponding to "veneration," the student would drop to his knees and assume a religious posture. When his finger touched the area of "aggression," the student would display the corresponding emotion. Wallace claimed that he had controlled for inadvertent suggestion on his part by not looking to see what phrenological bump his finger was touching (Wallace 1906).

This early experience with two heresies that were under attack by orthodox scientists had a lasting effect upon Wallace. "Knowing by my own experience," he later wrote, "that it is quite unnecessary to resort to trickery to produce the phenomena, I was relieved from that haunting idea of imposture which possesses most people who first see them, and which seems to blind most medical and scientific men to such an extent as to render them unable to investigate the subject fairly, or to arrive at any trustworthy conclusions in regard to it." In addition, Wallace (1906) wrote:

> The importance of these experiments to me was that they convinced me, once for all, that the antecedently incredible may nevertheless be true; and, further, that the accusations of imposture by scientific men should have no weight whatever against the detailed observations and statements of other men, presumably as sane and sensible as their opponents, who had witnessed and tested the phenomena, as I had done myself in the case of some of them.

Wallace, although he was absolutely convinced of the reality of spiritualistic phenomena, did not expect his scientific colleagues to trust his word on so controversial an issue. Instead, he invited them to come to séances at his house and witness the phenomena for themselves. He first acquainted his scientific friends of his interest in spiritualism by sending them copies of his pamphlet *The Scientific Aspect of the Supernatural*, which he had written in 1866.

His friends were astonished that he should be taking spiritualism so seriously. Lewes, having convinced himself of the trickery of one medium, would not discuss it. Tyndall, who had already rebuked Thackeray for his public advocacy of spiritualism, took a later opportunity to rebuke Wallace. "I see the usual keen powers of your mind displayed in the treatment of this question. But mental power may show itself, whether the material be facts or fictions. It is not a lack of logic that I see in your book, but a willingness that I deplore to accept data which are unworthy of your attention." Darwin was upset. Huxley, who was a good friend of Wallace's, was vehemently opposed to spiritualism. He wrote, "The only good that I can see in the demonstration of the truth of 'Spiritualism' is to furnish additional argument against suicide. Better live a crossing-sweeper than die and be made to talk twaddle by a 'medium' hired at a guinea a seance." [George 1964]

During the two-year period of 1867 to 1868, Wallace tried hard to get Huxley, W. B. Carpenter, John Tyndall, and G. H. Lewes to attend séances with him and judge the phenomena for themselves. Because the phenomena were erratic and did not always occur with equal force at every séance, Wallace tried to get these scientific critics to commit themselves to attend at least six séances before making any judgments. He did succeed in getting Tyndall and Carpenter each to attend one session at his house. But either nothing occurred or the scientist in question refused to participate according to Wallace's plans. He failed to induce either Tyndall or Carpenter to return, and he never did succeed in getting any of the others to come even for one séance. After this missionary effort, Wallace finally gave up hope of getting his critics to examine the evidence at first hand (Kottler 1974).

Wallace was naturally disappointed in his failure to interest his skeptical scientific colleagues in examining the phenomena for themselves. But he was even more dismayed when these same colleagues later wrote debunking articles in which they asserted that the mediums would not subject themselves to true scientific tests.

Wallace's biographer, Wilma George (1964), sums up the price that Wallace paid for his venture into spiritualism as follows:

Wallace's spiritualism, regarded by his scientific friends with astonished tolerance, was less humanely respected by the scientific world in general, and it resulted in long-lasting damage to his reputation as a biologist. It is suggested that it is the reason why Wallace's scientific contributions are neglected among the works of the great nineteenth-century biologists.

Sir William Crookes

Critics have found it easy to dismiss Hare's psychical evidence on the basis of old age and Wallace's on the assertion that, while he was a great naturalist and observer, he was not an experimenter (George 1964). Neither criticism can be applied, however, to William Crookes, who was the next great scientist to investigate and endorse the reality of paranormal phenomena. Crookes was generally acknowledged, even by many who opposed his psychic beliefs, as one of the preeminent chemists and physicists of his day. Crookes—the discoverer of thallium, inventor of the radiometer, developer of the Crookes tube, pioneer investigator of radiation effects, and a contributor to photography and other fields—was elected a Fellow of the Royal Society at the age of 31, was later knighted, and received just about every honor available to a scientist of his time.

When Crookes began attending séances with Mrs. Marshall (the same medium who helped convert Wallace) and J. J. Morse in 1869, he was 37 years old. He had been devastated by the death of his youngest brother and apparently believed he had received spirit communications from him through the services of these mediums. In July 1870, Crookes announced his intention to conduct a scientific inquiry into spiritualistic phenomena. He wrote: "I prefer to enter upon the inquiry with no preconceived notions whatever as to what can or cannot be, but with all my senses alert and ready to convey information to the brain; believing, as I do, that we have by no means exhausted all human knowledge or fathomed the depths of all physical forces" (Medhurst 1972).

Although most of the scientific community assumed that Crookes was undertaking the investigation as a skeptic, according to his biographer, E. E. F. D'Albe (1924): "It is certain, at all events, that when in July 1870 Crookes, at the request, it is said, of a London daily paper, announced his intention of 'investigating spiritualism, so-called,' he was already much inclined towards spiritualism. What he really intended to do was to furnish, if possible, a rigid scientific proof of the objectivity and genuineness of the 'physical phenomena of spiritualism,' so as to convert the scientific world at large and open a new era of human advancement."

Crookes packed almost all his research in psychical phenomena into the four-year period 1870 to 1874 (Palfreman 1976). When he failed to sway his scientific colleagues—and as a result of bitter attacks by his critics—Crookes quietly dropped this work and devoted his scientific efforts from 1875 onward to more mainstream subjects. But he never gave up his beliefs and he never severed his ties with the field. In his final years, he began attending séances again and believed, near the end, that he had finally found proof of survival when he obtained a spirit photograph of his dead wife (Medhurst 1972).

By today's standards, the investigations that come closest to being "scientific" were those that Crookes carried out with the celebrated medium Daniel Dunglas Home. Home is probably the most colorful and enigmatic psychic in the history of spiritualism (Podmore 1963; Shepard 1978). In one session, which took place at Crookes's home on May 31, 1871, Home held an accordion (which had just been purchased by Crookes for this occasion) by one end so that the end with the keys hung down toward the floor. The accordion was placed in a special cage under the table, and this allowed Home's hand to be inserted to hold the accordion. Home's other hand was visible above the table. The individuals sitting on either side of Home could see his hand as well as the accordion in the wire cage. "Very soon the accordion was seen by those on each side to be moving about in a somewhat curious manner, but no sound was heard. . . ." After putting the accordion down, Home picked it up again. This time several notes were heard. Crookes's assistant crawled under the table and said that he saw the accordion expanding and contracting, but Home's hand was quite still (Medhurst 1972).

Crookes reported an experiment at the same session that he regarded as even "more striking, if possible, than the one with the accordion." A mahogany board, 3 feet long, with one end resting on a table and the other end supported by a spring balance, was in a horizontal position. Home, while "sitting in a low easy-chair" placed the tips of his fingers lightly on the extreme end of the board that was resting on the table. "Almost immediately the pointer of the balance was seen to descend. After a few seconds it rose again. This movement was repeated several times, as if by successive waves of the Psychic Force. The end of the board was observed to oscillate slowly up and down during the experiment" (Medhurst 1972).

To see if it were possible to produce an effect on the spring balance by ordinary pressure, Crookes stood on the table and pressed one foot on the end of the board where Home had placed his fingers. By using the entire weight of his body (140 pounds), Crookes was able to get the index to register at most 2 pounds. Home had apparently achieved a maximum displacement of 6 pounds.

Because of such results Crookes concluded that "these experiments appear conclusively to establish the existence of a new force, in some unknown manner connected with the human organisation which for convenience may be called the Psychic Force" (Medhurst 1972). The skeptics were not convinced. They raised a variety of objections to the experiment measuring the movement of the board. Crookes thought some of the criticisms were unfair and irrelevant, but others he felt were reasonable and could be answered.

He repeated the experiment with additional controls. To avoid direct contact with the board, he altered the apparatus slightly in a manner that had previously been used by Robert Hare in some of his experiments. A bowl of water was placed on the end of the board not supported by the spring scale.

Inside the bowl of water was lowered a "hemispherical copper vessel perforated with several holes at the bottom." The copper vessel was suspended from a large iron stand that was separate from the rest of the apparatus. Home placed his fingers lightly in the water in the copper bowl. Presumably, this prevented him from having direct contact with the board. Yet, under these conditions, Home managed to cause the other end of the board to sway up and down.

Finally, Home was removed a few feet away from the apparatus and his hands and legs were held. Even under these conditions, Crookes was able to record movements of the board, although the displacement was less the farther Home was from the apparatus. In further answer to critics, Crookes describes similar experiments carried out successfully by other researchers, including Robert Hare. Crookes also got similar results using in place of Home a woman who was not a professional medium.

This series of experiments is by far the most impressive, from a scientific viewpoint, of any that Crookes conducted. Indeed, so far as I can tell, although these were among the very first serious attempts by a scientist to test a psychic, they have not been exceeded in degree of documentation and experimental sophistication during the subsequent 114 years. This is despite the fact that, following Crookes's example, eminent scientists during almost every decade since Crookes's experiments have conducted tests of famous psychics.

The comments in the preceding paragraph should not be taken as an endorsement of Crookes's results. His experiments on the "Psychic Force" are superior *relative* to what has been reported by other scientists, including contemporary ones, in their tests of psychic superstars. On an absolute scale of judgment the experiments still leave much to be desired. A major problem is documentation. Crookes omits many details that, from today's perspective at least, seem important in assessing what might have taken place.

Responding to the accusation that his witnesses were not reliable, Crookes wrote: "Accustomed as I am to have my word believed without witnesses, this is an argument which I cannot condescend to answer. All who know me and read my articles will, I hope, take it for granted that the *facts* I lay before them are correct, and that the experiments were honestly performed, with the single object of eliciting *the truth*" (Medhurst 1972). Here Crookes raises an important issue. When he reported finding a green line in a spectrum where one had never been reported, and followed this up with various analyses and controls to support the assertion that he must have discovered a new element (thallium), his scientific colleagues did not insist that he import skeptical witnesses, nor did they question his observations. The reported observation was made by using standard apparatus and recording procedures. The necessary controls and possibilities of error in such a context were well known to workers in the field and it could be safely assumed that any trained chemist in this situation would behave according to both implicit and explicit rules.

But Crookes and his critics seriously err when they assume that similar confidence and trust can be placed in observations made in a field outside the investigator's training and one in which no standardization exists for instrumentation, making observations, instituting controls, recording the data, and reporting the results. The difficulties are compounded further when the observations are made not of inanimate and reasonably passive materials but of events involving humans who have a capacity to anticipate the experimenter's objectives and alter their behavior accordingly.

I recently discovered that Frank Podmore (1963), back in 1902, anticipated most of my reservations about Crookes's experiment on the movements of the balance:

> The experiment as it stands, even without the modifications introduced later by Mr. Crookes in deference to his scientific critics, seems, indeed, conclusive against the possibility of Home's affecting the balance by any pressure on his end of the board. But, tested by the canons laid down by Mr. Crookes himself at the outset of his investigations, we shall find the conditions of the experiment defective in one important particular. Mr. Crookes had shown that it is the province of scientific investigation not merely to ascertain the reality of the alleged movements and measure their extent, but to establish their occurrence under conditions which render fraud impossible. In the passage quoted on page 183 it is implicitly recognized that such conditions are to be secured by eliminating the necessity for continuous observation on the part of the investigator. The proof of the thing done should depend upon something else than the mere observation of the experimenters, however skilled.
>
> Now in the experiment quoted these conditions were not fulfilled. On the contrary, we are expressly told that all present guarded Home's feet and hands. It is pertinent to point out that a duty for which the whole company were collectively responsible may well at times have been intermitted. Moreover, Dr. Huggins and Mr. Crookes had to watch the balance also, and Mr. Crookes had to take notes. Again, the experiment described was not the first of the kind; it occurred in the middle of a long series. It is indeed stated that Home was not familiar with the apparatus employed. But as similar apparatus had been employed, probably at previous trials by Mr. Crookes himself, certainly by earlier investigators—amongst them Dr. Hare, with whose published writings on Spiritualism we cannot assume Home was unacquainted—the statement carries little weight. Further, a point of capital importance, there had apparently been many various trials with various modifications of the apparatus and many failures; in Mr. Crookes' own words, "the experiments I have tried have been very numerous, but owing to our imperfect knowledge of the conditions which favour or oppose the manifestations of this force, to the apparently capricious manner in which it is exerted, and to the fact that Mr. Home himself is subject to unaccountable ebbs and flows of the force, it has but seldom happened that a

result obtained on one occasion could be subsequently confirmed and tested with apparatus specially contrived for the purpose."

The real significance of this statement is that Home—a practised conjurer, as we are entitled to assume—was in a position to dictate the conditions of the experiment. By the simple device of doing nothing when the conditions were unfavourable he could ensure that the light (gas in the present instance) was such and so placed, the apparatus so contrived, and the sitters so disposed, as to suit his purpose, and that in the actual experiment the attention of the investigators would necessarily be concentrated on the wrong points. Under such conditions, as ordinary experience shows, and as the experiments described in the last chapter have abundantly demonstrated, five untrained observers are no match for one clever conjurer.

Podmore is referring, in the last sentence, to the dramatic experiment on eyewitness testimony conducted by S. J. Davey (1887). Davey had been converted to a belief in spiritualistic phenomena by the slate-writing demonstrations of the medium Henry Slade. Subsequently Davey accidentally discovered that Slade had employed trickery to produce some of the phenomena. Davey practiced until he felt he could accomplish all of Slade's feats by trickery and misdirection. He then conducted his well-rehearsed séance for several groups of sitters, including many who had witnessed and testified to the reality of spiritualistic phenomena. Immediately after each séance, Davey had the sitters write out in detail all that they could remember having happened during his séance. The findings were striking and very disturbing to believers. No one realized that Davey was employing tricks. Sitters consistently omitted crucial details, added others, changed the order of events, and otherwise supplied reports that would make it impossible for any reader to account for what was described by normal means.

Podmore has much more to say about this experiment. His reference to "untrained" observers is not meant to question Crookes's scientific competence. "But his previous training did not necessarily render him better qualified to deal with problems differing widely from those presented in the laboratory. To put it bluntly, if Home was a conjurer, Mr. Crookes was probably in no better position for detecting the sleight-of-hand than any other man his equal in intelligence and native acuteness of sense. Possibly even in a worse position; for it may be argued that his previous training would prepare the way for Home's efforts to concentrate attention on the mechanical apparatus, and thus divert it from the seemingly irrelevant movements by which it may be conjectured the conjurer's end was attained."

Finally, Podmore points out ways in which the report is incomplete. He then speculates about one possible way Home might have tricked Crookes. He describes a scenario in which Home could have employed a thread that he had attached to the apparatus, probably to the hook of the scale. Some further points could be mentioned, such as the fact that Crookes's unpublished notes suggest that the experiment was much more informal and involved many more distractions than the published version indicates (Medhurst 1972).

Crookes held many séances not only with Home but with almost every major spiritualistic medium who was in England during the years 1869 through 1875. He reported having observed a variety of phenomena that, he argued, could not have been produced by normal means: movement of heavy bodies with contact but without mechanical exertion; raps and other sounds; the alteration of weights of bodies; movements of heavy substances at a distance from the medium; the rising of tables and chairs off the ground without contact of any person; the levitation of human beings; the appearance of hands, either self-luminous or visible by ordinary light; direct writing; and phantom forms and faces (Medhurst 1972). His documentation for such phenomena, however, falls far short of what he has supplied us for the movements of the balance.

By far the most striking phenomena reported by Crookes emerged from his séances with Florence Cook. Crookes held these séances over a five-month period beginning in December 1873. Florence had just been "exposed" by a Mr. Volckman, who seized the materialized spirit form known as "Katie King" and discovered that he was holding, instead, the medium Florence Cook in costume. Florence, at that time, was being supported by a wealthy benefactor named Charles Blackburn. Blackburn, who had been present during the exposure, threatened to stop supporting Florence. Under these circumstances, Florence appealed to Crookes to help her convince Blackburn that she was, in fact, a genuine medium. Just why the young Florence believed that the famous William Crookes would respond to her pleas is not known. Even more puzzling is why Crookes would enter into such an arrangement, especially following upon the Volckman exposure (D'Albe 1924; Hall 1963b).

A typical séance in this series would be as follows: Florence would enter a cabinet and apparently become entranced. The cabinet was usually a curtained-off section of the room in which the sitters were located. After a while a white-robed, turbaned female would emerge from the cabinet claiming to be the materialized spirit "Katie King." Some skeptics pointed to the striking resemblance between Katie and Florence. Crookes admitted the resemblance but pointed out crucial differences. He observed that Katie was six inches taller than Florence; Katie's skin on her neck was smooth to touch while Florence had a large blister in the same place; Katie's ears were unpierced, while Florence wore earrings; Katie's complexion was very fair but Florence's was very dark; and Katie and Florence had markedly different mannerisms (Medhurst 1972).

The real proof that Katie King and Florence Cook were not one and the same person, however, would be to observe simultaneously Katie King and

Florence Cook. This Crookes claimed he was privileged to do on at least two occasions (Medhurst 1972).

The Florence Cook episode has created a dilemma for many psychical researchers. Some believers still cite the Katie King materializations as the strongest evidence for the reality of spiritual materialization. But many parapsychologists clearly find it difficult to believe in the reality of this particular case. For one thing, it has been frequently noted with regret by parapsychologists that such striking and powerful phenomena have not been reported since Crookes passed away. Also, Florence Cook was caught cheating not only before her séances with Crookes but also afterward. Furthermore, she learned her trade from the mediums Frank Herne and Charles Williams, who were notorious for their cheating. Yet William Crookes, one of the world's greatest scientists, insisted to his dying day that what he had reported about Katie King was true.

Trevor Hall (1963b) created quite a controversy by arguing at length that Crookes was having an illicit love affair with Florence and that the young medium used this affair to blackmail Crookes into collaborating with her in her false materializations. Some parapsychologists accept Hall's argument as compelling. Others sharply disagree. K. M. Goldney, for example, is among those who cannot believe that Crookes would have jeopardized his career and reputation by entering into such an affair. But Goldney and others find it difficult to believe that Florence was a true medium. The way they resolve this issue is to assume that Crookes did use rigorous scientific standards in his early experiments with Home but that when he was satisfied that Home really was genuine he relaxed his standards in his further inquiries. According to this view, by the time Crookes began his experiments with Florence Cook, he was so convinced of the reality of spiritual phenomena that it was easy for Florence to deceive him with the gross postures that apparently did not deceive other spiritualists of her day (Medhurst 1972).

As was the case with Hare and Wallace, Crookes was bitterly attacked for his views. Carpenter again led the opposition. He openly questioned Crookes's competence as a scientist, wrongly stated that Crookes's election to the Royal Society had been questionable, and made several other unwarranted accusations (D'Albe 1924; Palfreman 1976). Like Wallace, Crookes tried to get his scientific colleagues and critics to witness his experiments with Home and with other psychics, but none of them accepted his invitation.

Scientists and Psychics

Hare, Wallace, and Crookes were the first of many eminent scientists who investigated and endorsed psychics. Their work inspired many later scientists to also take time away from their regular scientific activities to investigate the paranormal claims of mediums and self-professed psychics. Yet I can imagine that many contemporary parapsychologists will object to my detailed examination of the work of these three psychic investigators as part of a general evaluation and critique of parapsychology. The objection would be based on two arguments: (1) Today most parapsychologists would not include the reports of Hare, Wallace, and Crookes in their case for the reality of *psi* (the current term for extrasensory perception and psychokionesis). (2) Even the reports by more recent scientists on psychics do not form part of their primary database. Instead, today's parapsychologists want to base their argument on evidence emerging from laboratory experiments with unselected subjects using standardized tasks.

However, I believe there are good reasons for focusing upon these three early investigators:

1. At the time they were reported, these investigations were considered to be the strongest evidence for the paranormal. From 1850 to 1866 Hare's research constituted practically the entire "scientific" case upon which proponents could base their claims. From 1870 until the founding of the Society for Psychical Research in 1882, it was the work of Crookes and Wallace that proponents put forth as the best scientific justification for their paranormal claims.

2. The psychical research of these three eminent scientists served as the model for all later investigations of psychics by scientists. No change in approach or improvements in methodology for such investigations has occurred during the 130 years since Hare first reported his findings. In terms of adequacy of documentation, for example, it is difficult to find any improvement over Crookes's reports on his experiments with Home in the subsequent accounts by psychic investigators such as Charles Richet, Sir William Barrett, Sir Oliver Lodge, C. Lombroso, Johann Zöllner, Jules Eisenbud, Russell Targ, Harold Puthoff, John Hasted, and the many others.

3. The work of this early trio served as an important impetus for the subsequent founding of the Society for Psychical Research. In his presidential address to the first general meeting of the Society on July 17, 1882, Henry Sidgwick (1882-83) went out of his way to acknowledge the importance and evidential value of the work of these pioneer researchers:

> I say that important evidence has been accumulated; and here I should like to answer a criticism that I have privately heard which tends to place the work of our Society in a rather invidious aspect. It is supposed that we throw aside *en bloc* the results of previous inquiries as untrustworthy, and arrogate to ourselves a superior knowledge of scientific method or intrinsically greater trustworthiness—that we hope to be believed, whatever conclusions we may come to, by the scientific world, though previous inquirers have been uniformly

distrusted. Certainly I am conscious of making no assumption of this kind. I do not presume to suppose that I could produce evidence better in quality than much that has been laid before the world by writers of indubitable scientific repute—men like Mr. Crookes, Mr. Wallace, and the late Professor de Morgan. But it is clear that from what I have defined as the aim of the Society, however good some of its evidence may be in quality, we require a great deal more of it. I do not dispute,—it is not now time to dispute,—with any individual who holds that reasonable persons, who have looked carefully into the evidence that has been so far obtained, ought to be convinced by that evidence; but the educated world, including many who have given much time and thought to this subject, are not yet convinced, and therefore we want more evidence.

Sidgwick makes it clear that he and the other founders of the Society for Psychical Research consider the findings of Wallace and Crookes as scientifically sound. Sidgwick has no doubt that Wallace's and Crookes's reports *should* convince reasonable members of the scientific community. But he pragmatically makes the distinction between what *should* and what *will* convince the critics. "What I mean by *sufficient evidence* is evidence that will convince the scientific world, and for that we obviously require a good deal more than we have so far obtained." In other words, Sidgwick does not aspire to improve the quality of the preceding scientific investigators. Rather, he wants to acquire more of the same quality.

4. The investigations of these original psychical researchers bring out many of the same issues of evidence, testimony, and proof that still characterize current controversies in parapsychology. Unfortunately not much in the way of further clarification or resolution of these issues has occurred since their efforts first stimulated the debate. I have already mentioned some of these issues in my discussions of the individual cases.

Many of the issues involve the problems of competency. To what extent, for example, does competency in one branch of inquiry transfer, if at all, to a different branch? Can a scientist, no matter how competent and well intentioned, initiate an inquiry into a previously unstructured and unstandardized area and single-handedly produce results that bear the same scientific status as the results he has produced in his original area of expertise? Elsewhere, I have given my reasons for answering this question in the negative (Hyman 1981).

One important issue is perhaps worth bringing up at this point. The scientists who have defended the trustworthiness of their psychical research have typically insisted that the observations and evidence of their reports of psychic happenings do not differ in quality from that which characterizes their more orthodox investigations.

Yet at the same time these same investigators acknowledge an important difference between their inquiries into physics and biology and their investigations of psychics. Hare, Wallace, and Crookes, as well as the later psychical researchers, insisted that the psychics being tested must be treated with proper respect and concern for their feelings. If the investigator is overly skeptical or otherwise betrays distrust of the alleged psychic, this could adversely affect the paranormal performance. Thus these scientists try to convey the impression that they conduct their tests using every precaution against fraud and deception but at the same time make sure not to take any step to include any condition that meets with the disapproval of the alleged psychic. Skeptics like myself, who have experience in conducting experiments with humans and have also been trained in conjuring, believe this is an impossible task. The twin goals of preventing trickery on the part of the alleged psychic and of ensuring that this same person will be satisfied with all the experimental arrangements are mutually incompatible.

But scientists who have testified to the paranormal powers of their subjects confidently insist they have simultaneously achieved both goals. A contemporary version of this theme has been eloquently put forth by a group of scientists, including two of England's outstanding physicists, in describing their experiments on the psychokinetic powers of Uri Geller (Hasted et al. 1976):

> We have come to realize that in certain ways the traditional ideal of the completely impersonal approach of the natural sciences to experimentation will not be adequate in this domain. Rather, there is a personal aspect that has to be taken into account in a way that is somewhat similar to that needed in the disciplines of psychology and medicine. This does not mean, of course, that it is not possible to establish facts on which we can count securely. Rather, it means that we have to be sensitive and observant, to discover what is a right approach, which will properly allow for the subjective element and yet permit us to draw reliable inferences. One of the first things that reveals itself as one observes is that psychokinetic phenomena cannot in general be produced unless *all* who participate are in a relaxed state. A feeling of tension, fear, or hostility on the part of any of those present generally communicates itself to the whole group. The entire process goes most easily when all those present actively want things to work well. In addition, matters seem to be greatly facilitated when the experimental arrangement is aesthetically or imaginatively appealing to the person with apparent psychokinetic powers.
>
> We have found also that it is generally difficult to produce a predetermined set of phenomena. Although this may sometimes be done, what happens is often surprising and unexpected. We have observed that the attempt to concentrate strongly in order to obtain a desired result (e.g., the bending of a piece of metal) tends to interfere with the relaxed state of mind needed to produce such phenomena. . . . Indeed, we have sometimes found it useful at this stage to talk of, or think about, something not closely related to what is happening,

so as to decrease the tendency to excessive conscious concentration on the intended aim of the experiment. . . .

In the study of psychokinetic phenomena, such conditions are much more important than in the natural sciences, because the person who produces these phenomena is not an instrument or a machine. Any attempt to treat him as such will almost certainly lead to failure. Rather, he must be considered to be one of the group, actively cooperating in the experiment, and not a "subject" whose behavior is to be observed "from the outside" in as cold and impersonal manner as possible. . . .

In such research an attitude of mutual trust and confidence is needed; we should not treat the person with psychokinetic powers as an "object" to be observed with suspicion. Instead, as indicated earlier, we have to look on him as one who is working with us. Consider how difficult it would be to do a physical experiment if each person were constantly watching his colleagues to be sure that they did not trick him. How, then, are we to avoid the possibility of being tricked? It should be possible to design experimental arrangements that are beyond any reasonable possibility of trickery and that magicians will generally acknowledge to be so. In the first stages of our work we did, in fact, present Mr. Geller with several such arrangements, but these proved to be aesthetically unappealing to him. From our early failures, we learned that Mr. Geller worked best when presented with many possible objects, all together on a metal surface; at least one of these objects might appeal to him sufficiently to stimulate his energies. . . .

Nevertheless, we realize that conditions such as we have described in this paper are just those in which a conjuring trick may easily be carried out. We understand also that we are not conjuring experts, so if there should be an intention to deceive, we may be as readily fooled as any person. Moreover, there has been a great deal of public criticism in which the possibility of such tricks has been strongly suggested. For this reason it has often been proposed that a skilled magician should be present to help to see that there will be no possibility of deception. It is in the nature of the case, however, that no such assurance can actually be given. For a skilled magician is able to exploit each new situation as it arises in a different and generally unpredictable way. . . . In principle, we would welcome help of this kind in decreasing the possibility of deception. It has been our observation, however, that magicians are often hostile to the whole purpose of this sort of investigation, so they tend to bring about an atmosphere of tension in which little or nothing can be done. Indeed, even if some magicians who were found were not disposed in this way, it does not follow that their testimony will convince those who are hostile, since the latter can always suppose that new tricks were involved, beyond the capacity of those particular magicians to see through them. Because of all of this, it seems unlikely that significant progress towards clearing up this particular question could be made by actually having magicians present at the sessions, though we have found it useful to have their help in a consultative capacity. . . . We recognize that there is a genuine difficulty in obtaining an adequate answer to criticisms concerning the possibility of tricks, and that a certain healthy skepticism or doubt on the part of the reader may be appropriate at this point. , , , However, we believe that our approach can adequately meet this situation.

These investigators close this discussion of the difficulties of carrying out such research with an optimistic prognosis, "We feel that if similar sessions continue to be held, instances of this kind might accumulate, and there will be no room for reasonable doubt that some new process is involved here, which cannot be accounted for, or explained, in terms of the laws of physics at present known. Indeed, we already feel that we have very nearly reached this point." These hopeful words were written in 1975. Neither they nor other scientists have yet managed to present scientific evidence that Uri Geller or his many imitators can bend metal paranormally. Although at least one major physicist continues his investigations of paranormal metal-bending (Hasted 1981), a decade of research on Uri Geller by scientists who adhered to the advice of treating the metal-bender as a respected colleague and catering to his aesthetic sensibilities has only succeeded in demonstrating that Geller can bend metal under conditions that allow him to do it by cheating (Hyman 1976).

Hare, Wallace, and Crookes, as well as subsequent psychic researchers, insisted they had guarded against the possibility of trickery while, at the same time, acknowledging the necessity to treat their subjects in the special way described by Hasted et al. Unfortunately, as Hasted et al. concede, this special treatment increases the difficulties of preventing deception. But, like their predecessors in psychical research, they express confidence that their scientific skills can overcome the difficulty. In fact, the suggested procedure gives the alleged psychic veto power over any arrangement that impedes trickery and also supplies a ready excuse for not producing phenomena when the dangers of detection suddenly seem too high. The conditions that the scientists report as ideal for the production of psychical phenomena are just those that are ideal for the production of the same phenomena by trickery.

5. As already discussed, Hare, Wallace, and Crookes were bitterly attacked by their skeptical scientific colleagues. And the same sorts of attacks and defenses have characterized subsequent cases. Both critics and defenders still implicitly subscribe to the same False Dichotomy. And neither the critics nor the defenders emerge as rational, objective, scientific, or otherwise admirable in their exchanges. Worse, no lessons from the past seem to have been either learned or carried over to the current controversies. If the critical exchanges had been more constructive and rational at the time of Hare, Wallace, and Crookes, today we might be closer to understanding what was really going on to make such eminent scientists put forth such seemingly outrageous claims.

Hare, Wallace, and Crookes had no success in inducing their critics to come and examine the evidence for themselves. It is possible that, if Huxley and Carpenter had accepted Wallace's invitation to attend at least six séances, no phenomena would have taken place. On the other hand, it would be useful to have the accounts of such skeptical observers before us if, say, Miss Nichol did produce the flowers in their presence. And it certainly would have helped if Carpenter and Stokes had accepted Crookes's invitation to watch his experiments with Home and the balance.

The Creery Sisters

For its first 30 years, psychical research consisted of individual and uncoordinated investigations by such scholars and scientists as Hare, Wallace, and Crookes. During this period some feeble and unsuccessful attempts were made to form investigating societies to coordinate the research (Gauld 1968). The first successful attempt to institutionalize psychical research was the founding of the Society for Psychical Research in London in 1882. Four of the principal leaders of this society—the philosopher Henry Sidgwick, the physicist William Barrett, the literary scholar Edmund Gurney, and the classicist Frederic Myers—had been encouraged not only by their own investigations of telepathy and mediums but by the research of such scientists as Wallace and Crookes. The founders of the Society clearly believed that they possessed solid scientific evidence for the reality of thought-transference. At the first general meeting of the Society in London on July 17, 1882, Henry Sidgwick (1882-83) ended his presidential address with the following words:

> We must drive the objector into the position of being forced either to admit the phenomena as inexplicable, at least by him, or to accuse the investigators either of lying or cheating or a blindness or forgetfulness incompatible with any intellectual condition except absolute idiocy. I am glad to say that this result, in my opinion, has been satisfactorily attained in the investigation of thought-reading. Professor Barrett will now bring before you a report which I hope will be only the first of a long series of similar reports which may have reached the same point of conclusiveness.

Before looking at the experimental results whose "conclusiveness" Sidgwick believes is beyond reasonable doubt, I would like to call the reader's attention to the use of the False Dichotomy in Sidgwick's strategy. The goal is to report evidence that is so compelling that the critic has to admit either that psychic phenomena have been demonstrated or that the investigator is deliberately lying, afflicted with a pathological condition, or incredibly incompetent. Sidgwick does not allow for the possibility that an investigator could be competent, honest, sane, and intelligent and still wrongly report what he believes to be "conclusive" evidence for the paranormal. Unfortunately, as seen in the cases of Hare, Wallace, and Crookes and as typifies the succeeding cases, the critics, in responding to paranormal claims, have implicitly accepted the False Dichotomy. When confronted with paranormal claims by otherwise competent investigators, many critics have taken the bait and have tried to discredit the offending investigator by questioning his competence, insinuating fraud, or suggesting pathology.

The "conclusive" evidence with which Sidgwick wanted to confront the objector came from a series of experiments on thought-transference conducted by his colleagues William Barrett, Edmund Gurney, and Frederic Myers (1882-83). The investigators introduced this series as follows:

> In the correspondence we have received there were two cases which seemed, upon inquiry, to be free from any *prima facie* objections, and apparently indicative of true thought-reading. One of these cases is given in the Appendix . . . but as we cannot from personal observation testify to the conditions under which the trials were made, we simply leave it aside. The other case was that of a family in Derbyshire, with whom we have had the opportunity of frequent and prolonged trials.
>
> Our informant was Mr. Creery, a clergyman of unblemished character, and whose integrity indeed has, so it happens, been exceptionally tested. He has a family of five girls, ranging now between the ages of ten and seventeen, all thoroughly healthy, as free as possible from morbid or hysterical symptoms, and in manner perfectly simple and childlike. The father stated that any one of these children (except the youngest), as well as a young servant-girl who had lived with the family for two years, was frequently able to designate correctly, without contact or sign, a card or other object fixed on in the child's absence. During the year which has elapsed since we first heard of this family, seven visits, mostly of several days' duration, have been paid to the town where they live, by ourselves and several scientific friends, and on these occasions daily experiments have been made.

The preceding quotation was taken from the "First Report on Thought-Reading," which was read at the first meeting of the Society. Several more experiments were conducted with the Creery sisters and the results included in the second and third reports (Gurney, Myers, and Barrett 1982-83; Gurney et al. 1982-83). Notice the emphasis placed upon the Reverend Creery's "unblemished character" and integrity. Within the Victorian society of Sidgwick and his colleagues this emphasis on character had a special significance. According to Nicol (1972), many flaws in the investigative reports of the Society were due to "a *double standard* of evidence":

The Society's double standard of evidence arose in the following way. The Society's leaders were members of the middle and upper middle strata of society. When faced with the problem of estimating the value of evidence, they divided the world into two classes: (a) Members of their own class (Ladies and Gentlemen in the Victorian sense) whom they tended to treat trustingly; (b) Members of the lower classes, whom for brevity we may call the Peasants: them they treated with suspicion.

The experiments with the Creery sisters were all variants of the popular Victorian pastime known as the "willing game."

The game admits of many variations, but is usually played somewhat as follows. One of the party, generally a lady, leaves the room, and the rest determine on something which she is able to do on her return—as to take a flower from some specified vase, or to strike some specified note on the piano. She is then recalled, and one or more of the "willers" place their hands lightly on her shoulders. Sometimes nothing happens; sometimes she strays vaguely about; sometimes she moves to the right part of the room and does the thing, or something like the thing, which she has been willed to do. Nothing could at first sight look less like a promising starting-point for a new branch of scientific inquiry. [Barrett, Gurney, and Myers 1882]

Barrett, Gurney, and Myers (1882; 1882-83) go to great lengths to assure their readers that they are aware of the many nonparanormal ways in which information from the senders can be communicated to the percipient. Subtle unconscious pushes by the "willer," for example, can guide the percipient to the correct place. And there is always the possibility of secret codes being employed. Nevertheless, they relate incidents from their own experience with the game that they believe cannot be handled by such obvious explanations.

In their typical experimental procedure, one child would be selected to leave the room. When she was out of the room, the remaining participants would select a playing card or write down a number or name. "On re-entering she stood—sometimes turned by us with her face to the wall, oftener with her eyes directed towards the ground, and usually close to us and remote from her family—for a period of silence varying from a few seconds to a minute, till she called out to us some number, card, or whatever it might be" (Barrett, Gurney, and Myers 1882). Before leaving the room, the child was always informed of the general category, such as playing cards, from which the target item was to be chosen.

The authors obviously felt that their knowledge of the various ways that inadvertent and deliberate signaling to the percipient could occur somehow made them immune from such errors. As an added precaution, however, they conducted several trials in which either members of the family were absent or only the experimenters knew the chosen object (unfortunately they do not distinguish among trials on which only the experimenters were informed of the target but the family was present and trials on which only the experimenters were present). The investigators claim that keeping the family uninformed did not appreciably lower the proportion of above-chance correct guesses.

The results were quite striking. Looking only at the results on those trials in which members of the committee alone knew the card or number selected, the investigators (Gurney et al. 1882-83) summarize their findings as follows: "260 Experiments made with playing cards; the first responses gave 1 quite right in 9 trials; whereas the responses, if pure chance, would be 1 quite right in 52 trials. 79 Experiments made with numbers of two figures; the first responses gave 1 quite right in 9 trials; whereas the responses, if pure chance, would be 1 quite right in 90 trials."

The experimenters also summarize the results of the much larger number of trials in which the family members were not excluded. Two points are worth noting about the results reported above. By ordinary statistical criteria the odds against such an outcome being due just to chance are enormous. But the calculation of such odds assumes that, in the absence of telepathy, we know the expected value and distribution of hits. The way experimenters can ensure the appropriate conditions for the application of the statistical tests is to include careful procedures for randomizing the targets on each trial such that each target has an equal chance of being selected and that the selected object on a given trial is independent of the selection on the next. But nowhere in the three reports do we find any mention of how the playing card or number was chosen on each trial. We do not know if the deck was shuffled even once, let alone between trials. The number selection is even more disturbing because if, as seems to be the case, a committee member simply thought of any two-digit number that came to mind, we know that some numbers are much more likely than others. And the same few numbers that are favored by the sender are likely to be those that come to the mind of the percipient. These most probable numbers, known as "mental habits" in the older literature, are called "population stereotypes" by Marks and Kammann (1980).

The second peculiarity, which was noted by Coover (1917), is that the proportion of successful hits in these experiments seems to be independent of the chance probability. Thus, the hit rate is 1 out of 9 trials regardless of whether cards or numbers are being guessed. To Coover this suggests the use of a code rather than the imperfect transmission of psychic signals.

As already indicated, the founders of the Society for Psychical Research believed that, with the experimental results on the Creery sisters, they had finally succeeded in scientifically establishing telepathy as a valid phenomenon.

As just one example of the importance attached to these experiments, Gurney's statement in the Society's first major monograph, *Phantasms of the Living* (Gurney, Myers, and Podmore 1886), can be cited: "I have dwelt at some length on our series of trials with the members of the Creery family, as it is to those trials that we owe our own conviction of the possibility of genuine thought-transference between persons in a normal state."

Despite this confidence in the conclusiveness of the Creery experiments, critics quickly pointed out perceived flaws (Coover 1917; G. Hall 1887-88; T. Hall 1964). It was charged that the experimenters grossly underestimated the extent to which sophisticated coding could be used by the girls in the experimental situation. The critics also suggested that the experimenters were naive in assuming that they could prevent inadvertent cueing just by being aware of the possibility.

Concerning the trials in which only the investigators knew the chosen object, the critics complained about inadequate documentation. The experimenters never state how the card or object was chosen; whether the members of the family were present during the selection (even though they were presumably kept ignorant of the choice); whose deck of playing cards was used; and so forth.

As can be seen, even on this brief account, we encounter a number of the issues that characterized earlier psychical research. The investigators assume that to be forewarned is to be forearmed. For example, they devote six pages of their first report to a discussion of the various types of errors that, if not excluded, could invalidate their research (Barrett, Gurney, and Myers 1882-83). The purpose is to assure the reader that because they are keenly aware of the possibilities of such errors they could not have occurred. As previously mentioned, one way the investigators tried to preclude giving the girl any involuntary muscular cue was simply for the investigator to be consciously aware of such a possibility and consciously prevent himself from displaying such cues. Not only is such a precaution useless (Pfungst 1911), but it was unnecessary since one could more directly prevent unwitting bodily cues by simply screening those who know the target from the percipient. This tendency to substitute *plausible* (to the investigator) reasons for discounting a possible source of error for actual experimental controls to guard against the error characterizes psychical research from its inception to the present.

A second theme is that prior experience in investigating paranormal claims automatically qualifies one as an expert who can be trusted not to make mistakes or be susceptible to trickery in future situations. This theme is closely related to the False Dichotomy issue.

The report on the Creery sisters also illustrates another recurring theme in psychical research—the "Patchwork Quilt Fallacy." As R. N. Giere (1979) points out, the Patchwork Quilt Fallacy gets its name because "the hypothesis, initial conditions, and auxiliary assumptions are pieced together in such a way that they logically imply the known facts." Telepathy or psi always seems to be just that mysterious phenomenon that produced all the peculiar patterns that we happened to observe in our data. On some days the Creery sisters performed no better than chance. This variability among days became, in the minds of the investigators (Gurney et al. 1882-83), a property of the phenomenon:

> It may be noted that the power of these children, collectively or separately, gradually diminished during these months, so that at the end of 1882 they could not do, under the easiest conditions, what they could do under the most stringent in 1881. This gradual decline of power seemed quite independent of the tests applied, and resembled the disappearance of a transitory pathological condition, being the very opposite of what might have been expected from a growing proficiency in code-communication.

The fact that alleged psychics inevitably seem to lose their powers under continued investigation has become known as the "decline effect," which can occur in a variety of patterns and guises. Gurney and his colleagues propose the decline as additional support for the genuineness of the telepathy because it is not what might be expected if the girls were becoming more proficient in using a code. The cynic, of course, views this decline in just the opposite way. Presumably the investigators are also becoming more proficient in knowing what to look for, especially in the face of continuing criticism and, as a result, have made it more difficult for the girls to get away with their tricks.

As it turns out, the investigators later caught the girls cheating. The girls, at least on this occasion, had used a simple code. This brings up an additional theme in psychical research, which we might, for short, label the "Problem of the Dirty Test Tube." Gurney (1888) revealed the deception in a brief note that appeared in the *Proceedings of the Society for Psychical Research* in 1888. Hall (1964) thinks it is very significant that Gurney's fellow investigators did not sign this revelation.

In the note, Gurney reminds his readers "that the earliest experiments in thought-transference described in the Society's *Proceedings* were made with some sisters of the name of Creery. The important experiments were, of course, those in which the 'agency' was confined to one or more of the investigating Committee. . . . But though stress was never laid on any trials where a chance of collusion was afforded by one or more of the sisters sharing in the 'agency,' nevertheless some results contained under such conditions were included in the records. It is necessary, therefore, to state that in a series of experiments with cards, recently made at Cambridge, two of the sisters, acting as 'agent' and 'percipient,' were detected in the use of a code of signals; and a third has confessed to a certain amount of signalling in the earlier series to which reference has been made." Gurney then describes both the visual and auditory codes used by the girls. He continues as follows:

> The use of the visual code was very gratuitous on the part of the sisters, since it had been explained to them that we did not attach any scientific value to the experiments in which they acted as agent and percipient in sight of each other, the possibility of success under these conditions having been abundantly proved. The object of our experiments at Cambridge on this occasion was, if possible, to strengthen the evidence for Thought-transference (1) when no members of the family were aware of the thing to be guessed, and (2) when the sister acting as agent was in a different room from the one acting as percipient. The experiments in which the codes were used were intended merely as amusement and encouragement with a view to increase the chance of success in the more difficult ones—which were all complete failures.
>
> The account which was given as to the earlier experiments, conducted under similar conditions, is that signals were very rarely used; and not on specially successful occasions, but on occasions of failure, when it was feared that visitors would be disappointed. But of course the recent detection must throw discredit on the results of all previous trials in which one or more of the sisters shared in the agency. How far the proved willingness to deceive can be held to affect the experiments on which we relied, where collusion was excluded, must of course depend on the degree of stringency of the precautions taken against trickery of other sorts—as to which every reader will form his own opinion.

This manner of treating the discovery of cheating illustrates a number of interwoven themes. The finding of a "dirty test tube" ordinarily implies that all the results of the experiment are brought into question. Gurney argues that only those results clearly attached to the "dirty test tube" should be discarded. Since the girls could not have used their code, in his judgment, in those trials in which only investigators knew the chosen object, those trials still retain their evidential value. Related to this is what the early psychical researchers called the problem of "mixed mediumship." Psychics and mediums are under constant pressure to produce results, yet they have little direct control over their fickle powers. Therefore, in order not to disappoint their followers or from fear of losing the attention that goes with mediumship, they learn to supplement their real powers with tricks to simulate the phenomena. Still another variant of this exploits the fact that many mediums and psychics are apparently in a trance or altered state when performing. In such a state they are highly suggestible and behave in ways expected of them. If skeptics are among the onlookers, they will sometimes cheat because this is what is expected of them. The onus for the consequent cheating is by this means placed upon the skeptic rather than the cheater.

The dirty-test-tube problem has been with psychical research from its beginning and, as we shall see, is still very much a part of the contemporary scene. The medium Eusapia Palladino's long career was noteworthy for the number of times she was caught cheating. She readily acknowledged that she would cheat if the investigators gave her the opportunity. Despite this record of cheating, many psychical researchers, including some of today's leaders in the field, have no doubt that on many other occasions she displayed true paranormal powers (Dingwall 1962). On the contemporary scene, parapsychologists are willing to admit that the controversial metal-bender Uri Geller often cheats, but that, on occasion, he exhibits real paranormal powers (Tart 1976). And parapsychologists blamed me, rather than Geller, for the fact that Geller cheated in my presence, because, as they put it, I did not impose sufficiently stringent conditions to prevent him from cheating (Hyman 1977b).

Despite this attempt to save some of the evidence from the Creery experiments, the leaders of the Society for Psychical Research quietly removed the experiment from their evidential data-base. But Sir William Barrett refused to go along with this demoting of the experiment. According to Gauld (1968), this incident sparked dissension between Barrett and the other founders:

> Barrett had been the first to experiment with these girls, and they were his special protégés. . . . Barrett would never agree that the later and crude cheating invalidated all the earlier results; he considered that his 1876 experiments, together with his experiments with the Creerys, had established his claim to be the discoverer of thought-transference, and he remained bitter toward the Sidgwicks for the rest of his life.

Not only did Barrett continue to defend the evidential value of the Creery experiments, but so did later parapsychologists. In his classic monograph of 1934, *Extra-Sensory Perception,* J. B. Rhine (1935) included this experiment as among the most evidential of the early research: "On the whole the early experiments in E.S.P. were admirably conducted . . . as one would expect from the array of highly impressive names connected with them. The experiments with the Creery sisters, for instance, were conducted by Professors William Barrett, Henry Sidgwick and Balfour Stewart, by Mrs. Henry Sidgwick, Frederic Myers, Edmund Gurney and Frank Podmore. . . . In all this work the results were sufficiently striking to leave no doubt as to the exclusion of the hypothesis of chance."

Despite these attempts to salvage something from the Creery experiments, I believe it is fair to say that today the experiments are not part of the case that parapsychologists would make in support of psi. Indeed, my perusal of several contemporary books and histories of parapsychology indicates that the experiments are rarely, if ever, mentioned.

The same fate befell the very next major experiment on telepathy conducted by the same investigators. In their "Second Report on Thought-Transference," Gurney and his colleagues describe the first of their experimental findings in which two young men, Smith and Blackburn, were apparently able to communicate telepathically under conditions that prevented normal communication. If anything, the investigators placed even more reliance upon these later experiments than on those with the Creery sisters.

As was the case with the Creery sisters, Smith and Blackburn soon lost their powers. Smith was then hired by the Society to assist in conducting several successful telepathic experiments. In 1908, Blackburn, thinking that Smith was dead, publicly confessed that he and Smith had tricked the investigators during the experiments. (See Chapter 8 of this volume.) Smith, who was very much alive and still employed by the Society, denied the charges. In the ensuing debate, the Society's leaders defended Smith. Good accounts of this amazing incident have been described by J. E. Coover (1917) and T. H. Hall (1964). Today, the Smith-Blackburn experiments are no longer considered part of the parapsychological case for psi.

J. B. Rhine

The founding of the Society for Psychical Research in 1882 was an attempt to organize and professionalize psychical research. Other societies, such as the American Society for Psychical Research quickly followed. Journals and proceedings were published and international congresses were held. Despite these steps toward institutionalization, psychical research continued for the next 50 years to be an uncoordinated activity of amateurs. No agreed-upon program or central body of concepts characterized the field.

During this period psychic researchers disagreed among themselves on issues involving subject matter, methodology, and theory. On one side were those, perhaps the majority, who supported the spiritist hypothesis that psychic phenomena reflected the activity of departed spirits or superintelligent beings. Opposed to these were psychic researchers like Nobel Laureate Charles Richet, who defended the position that the phenomena could be explained in terms of a "psychic force" without assuming survival of spirits (Mauskopf and McVaugh 1980).

Another division was between those who felt that psychical research should confine itself to mental phenomena, such as telepathy, premonitions, and clairvoyance. Opposed to these were those who felt that the physical phenomena, such as levitation, materialization, poltergeist events, and psychokinesis, should be the focus of inquiry. The majority of psychical researchers believed in telepathy but were dubious about clairvoyance. But a strong minority, led by Richet, believed that clairvoyance not only existed but was the basic phenomenon underlying telepathy.

Possibly the most divisive issue of all was the question of what sort of a research program was appropriate for psychical investigation. A small but vocal minority wanted psychical research to become a rigorous experimental science. A larger group felt that the natural-historical method was more appropriate because so many of the important phenomena were spontaneous and not observable in the laboratory. Opposed to both these groups were members of the societies who felt that the quantification and rigor of the natural sciences were irrelevant to the study of psychical phenomena.

The event that is credited with providing psychical research with a common focus and a coherent research program was the publication in 1934 of J. B. Rhine's monograph *Extra-Sensory Perception.* Mauskopf and McVaugh (1980) provide an excellent survey of the period from 1915 to 1940, which they treat as the period when psychical research made the transition from a preparadigmatic to a paradigmatic research program.

Rhine pulled together the various strands already existing in psychical research and coordinated them into a coherent program. He also coined the terms *parapsychology,* to refer to the new experimental science that descended from psychical research, and *extrasensory perception,* to refer to the basic phenomenon to be studied. In agreement with Richet, and in disagreement with the British parapsychologists, Rhine viewed clairvoyance to be on the same footing with telepathy. Later, precognition was also put under the rubric of extrasensory perception (ESP). ESP became defined as "knowledge of or response to an external event or influence not apprehended through known sensory channels" (Wolman 1977). This included telepathy, clairvoyance, precognition, and retrocognition. The psychic phenomena not involving reception of information were included under the term *psychokinesis* (PK), which is defined as "the influence of mind on external objects or processes without the mediation of known physical energies or forces" (Wolman 1977). Today both ESP and PK are included under the more general term *psi,* which is "a general term to identify a person's extrasensorimotor communication with the environment" (Wolman 1977).

Rhine's 1934 monograph deals only with clairvoyance and telepathy. In 1934 he also began research programs on precognition and psychokinesis. Apparently, he was reluctant to publicize these latter programs too soon for fear of making parapsychology too controversial and unacceptable to mainstream science (Mauskopf and McVaugh 1980). He waited until 1938 to publish anything on precognition and until 1943 to give the first reports on his PK results.

The major innovation introduced by Rhine was the use of the five target-designs: circle, cross, wavy lines, square, and star. These patterns were printed on cards and the standard ESP deck consisted of 5 cards of each symbol for a total of 25 cards. Rhine also introduced standard procedures for using these target materials. The two most common were the Basic Technique and the Down Through Technique. In the Basic Technique (BT), the deck is shuffled and placed face down and the percipient guesses the value of the top card; this is then removed and laid aside and the percipient guesses the value of the second card; the second card is then removed and laid on top of the first and the percipient now guesses the third card; and so on. This procedure is continued until all 25 cards have been used. At the end of such a "run," a check is made to see how many guesses were hits. If the procedure was supposed to test telepathy then an agent would look at each card at the time the percipient was trying to guess its symbol. If clairvoyance was being tested, no one would look at each card as it was placed aside. The Down Through Technique (DT) tested clairvoyance by having the percipient guess the symbols from top to bottom before any of them were removed for checking against the call. The DT technique is considered to be superior methodologically in that it better protects against inadvertent sensory cues from the backs of the cards.

Extra-Sensory Perception attracted the attention of both the psychical researchers and the skeptics for two reasons. Rhine's data-base consisted of 91,174 separate trials or guesses over a three-year period using a number of nonprofessional individuals as percipients. More important was the unprecedented level of success that he reported. Of the 85,724 guesses recorded using the five-symbol ESP decks, 24,364 were "hits." This was 7,219 more hits than the 17,145 that would be expected by chance alone. The odds against this being just an accident are calculated as being practically infinite. His subjects averaged 7.1 hits per run of 25 as against the chance expectation of 5. Although this is only 2 extra hits per 25, such consistency over this huge number of trials with different subjects had no precedent in the prior history of psychical research.

Rhine's best subject, Hubert Pearce, averaged 8 hits per run over a total of 17,250 guesses. As Rhine (1934) notes:

> Most people are more impressed by a spectacular series of successive hits than by lower but cumulative scoring. Pearce's scoring 25 straight hits under clairvoyant conditions, in my presence, and Zirkle's 26 straight hits in pure telepathy with my assistant, Miss Ownbey, are the best instances of these. Other subjects have approached these. Linzmayer scored 21 in 25 clairvoyance, in my presence; Miss Ownbey herself, unwitnessed, scored 23, pure clairvoyance. Miss Turner's score of 19 in distance P.T. [pure telepathy] work stands out because of the 250 miles between her and the agent. Miss Bailey scored 19 in P.T. in the same room with the agent, as did also Cooper. The odds against getting one series of 25 straight hits by mere chance would be 5^{25}, which is nearly 300 quadrillions—just one score of 25! A small part of our 90,000 trials.

Rhine's work provided the model for most parapsychological work from 1934 to around 1970. Using card-guessing with the five ESP symbols, an astonishing variety of questions about ESP were investigated (Wolman 1977). Because of its huge data-base, its claims to statistical and experimental sophistication, and its unprecedented rate of success, Rhine's research gained the attention of scientific and popular audiences. At first, scientists were at a loss about how to react. Many, as a result of reading Rhine's work, were encouraged to try to replicate the results. A few got encouraging results, but most failed.

The first attacks by the critics were aimed at Rhine's statistical procedures. As it turned out, some of Rhine's statistical procedures were technically incorrect, but for the most part his results could not be explained away as due to inappropriate statistical procedures. The critics turned out to be wide of the mark in many of their accusations. On the whole, however, the statistical debate led to constructive developments and improved clarification about the proper use of statistical procedures in such experiments (Mauskopf and McVaugh 1980).

Having essentially lost the statistical battle, the critics then turned to Rhine's experimental controls. Here, he was much more vulnerable. And, ironically, it was the British psychical research community that had anticipated the critics and that provided the sharpest critiques of Rhine's methods. The British parapsychologists were astonished both by Rhine's apparent ease in finding successful percipients and by his claims that clairvoyance worked as well as telepathy. With a few exceptions, they had found evidence only for telepathy. And their experience had convinced them that telepathic powers were very rare. While they welcomed Rhine's contribution, they were quick to point out many of its defects, especially Rhine's inadequate description of his procedures and the seeming casualness of his experiments.

During the 1930s, nevertheless, Rhine's work as reported in his *Extra-Sensory Perception* was hailed by parapsychologists as the best scientific case for ESP ever put before the world. Today, as I understand it, most parapsychologists, although they acknowledge its seminal influence on the development of the field, dismiss Rhine's early work as nonevidential because of its loose controls, poorly made target materials, and inadequate documentation. One parapsychologist set out to repeat Rhine's work, but with all the defects removed.

S. G. Soal

Rhine's strongest critic among the British parapsychologists was the mathematician S. G. Soal. Just prior to the appearance of Rhine's monograph, Soal had conducted a huge series of card-guessing experiments with only chance results.

To be sure, [Soal] found *Extra-Sensory Perception* incredible, particularly in view of his own laborious experiments on both telepathy and clairvoyance, which had given unequivocally negative results. A study of a very different sort carried out in early 1934, his investigation of the stage telepathist "Marion," had convinced Soal that Marion's remarkable feats were made possible by subconscious interpretation of subtle sensory indicia and were not truly telepathic—negative results again. In a private letter to Walter Franklin Prince in July 1934, Soal raised just those objections to ESP that would soon appear in Dingwall's review: unsatisfactory description of method, inadequate randomization of cards, bias towards positive results. In the same letter, he enclosed a list of particular criticisms of Rhine's procedure that he agreed could be sent on (anonymously) to Duke. He insisted that in psychical research the onus of proof was on the experimenter and that all normal explanations would have to be rigidly excluded before the supernormal could be entertained. Consequently, he felt, far more stringent precautions were required in preparing, shuffling, and presenting cards to the subject than Rhine appeared to have taken; and a committee of skeptical scientists would be far preferable to Rhine alone, or Pratt alone, as witness to the phenomena. [Mauskopf and McVaugh 1980]

Soal's career in psychical research is a strong mix of the bizarre aspects of this field as well as the most rigorous experimentation. His interest in psychical research was aroused by the reading of Sir Oliver Lodge's book *Raymond*. In this book, the noted physicist described how he became convinced he had communicated through the aid of spirit mediums with his son Raymond, who had been killed in World War I. As a result, Soal decided that he would try to communicate with his brother Frank, who had been killed in the same war. Soal published the results of a long series of sittings with the medium Blanche Cooper. During this series, Soal apparently received communications from his dead brother. The voice that emerged from the medium's lips, however, was not that of his brother, but of an old friend whom Soal believed was dead. It was not until a few years later that Soal discovered that his friend was alive. Nevertheless, Soal believed that the information coming from the medium displayed telepathic and paranormal aspects. Soal also discovered that he was an automatist. He could place himself in a dissociated state in which his hand would write long and coherent treatises. Soal's hand produced, for example, several passages purported to be written by the poet Margaret Veley. Soal did not attribute the scripts to actual entities or departed spirits. Rather, he considered them to be products of his own subconscious.

Soal eventually dropped his interest in mediums and automatic writing to concentrate upon experimental work and developed a reputation as a rigorous and critical experimentalist (Goldney 1975). The experiments for which Soal became most renowned began as a direct response to Rhine's monograph. After five years of heroic research, Soal was sure that he had succeeded in demonstrating only the laws of chance. A colleague, however, persuaded him to check for a certain trend in his data. And this resulted in a new series of experiments that for almost 25 years were hailed as the most convincing and fraud-proof demonstration of ESP ever achieved. Because the experiment and results seemed so impressive, some critics, in a way reminscent of Carpenter's attacks upon Wallace and Crookes and within the spirit of Sidgwick's False Dichotomy, openly accused Soal of fraud on no other basis than that his results were too good. Other critics attacked him on grounds that were irrelevant. As it turns out the critics were right, but for the wrong reasons!

As soon as Soal heard about Rhine's successful American research, he began an ambitious program to replicate Rhine's findings in England. Soal started late in 1934 and continued his experiments for five years. At the end he had accumulated 128,350 guesses from 160 percipients. This is almost 30 percent more guesses than Rhine had accumulated for his 1934 monograph. Soal was sure that he had removed all the flaws and weaknesses that had characterized Rhine's work. Unfortunately, Soal found that this enormous effort yielded "little evidence of a direct kind that the persons tested, whether considered as individuals or in the mass, possessed any faculty for either clairvoyance or telepathy" [quoted in Goldney 1974].

Soal reported these results to a stunned parapsychological world in 1940. At the same time another British parapsychologist, Whately Carington, reported his own card-guessing studies, which seemed to show a "displacement effect." Instead of achieving hits on the target card, his subjects seemed to achieve above-chance matches when their guesses were matched with either the immediately preceding card or the next card in the target series. Carington asked Soal to check his data to see whether he, too, might find such a displacement effect (Goldney 1974).

Soal was reluctant to do so. He told K. M. Goldney that he thought Carington's request was preposterous and that he wasn't going to waste his time going through his huge batch of records. But Carington persisted and Soal finally agreed. Soal found, among the records of his 160 percipients, 2 who seemed to show Carington's displacement effect. Although this finding was published, presumably Soal was realistic enough to realize that such a post hoc finding had to be replicated (Goldney 1974).

Fortunately, one of his two percipients, Basil Shackleton, was available for testing during the years 1941 through 1943. With the collaboration of Goldney, 409 sittings, which yielded a total of 11,378 guesses, were obtained with Shackleton during this difficult period when England was at war. As had been the case with the original testing, Shackleton's guesses were at chance level when compared with the actual target, but when compared with the symbol coming up immediately after the target (precognitive hitting), Shackleton's guesses yielded

2,890 successes, compared with the 2,308 expected by chance. The odds against this being a chance occurrence were calculated to be more than 10^{35} to 1 (Soal and Bateman 1954).

In 1945 Soal was able to begin experimenting on the second percipient who had displayed the displacement effect in the original data, Mrs. Gloria Stewart. He was able to accumulate a total of 37,100 guesses during 130 separate sittings. Unlike Shackleton or her own previous performance, her hitting this time was on the actual target rather than on the immediately preceding or following trial. She managed to achieve 9,410 hits, which was 1,990 more hits than would be expected by chance. The odds against such a result were calculated as 10^{79} to 1 (Soal and Bateman 1954).

Soal's stated objective was to make these experiments completely error free and fraud-proof. The basic procedure, which was varied slightly on occasion, was as follows. The percipient—Basil Shackleton or Gloria Stewart—sat in one room monitored by one of the experimenters (EP). In an adjoining room, the sender or agent sat at the table opposite the second experimenter (EA). The door between the rooms was slightly open so that the percipient could hear EA's call as to when to make his or her guess. The percipient, of course, could see neither the agent nor EA. A screen with a small aperture separated the agent from EA. For each block of 50 trials EA had before him a list of randomized numbers that determined the target for each trial. Each number could range from 1 to 5. If the target number for the first trial was, say, 3, EA would hold up a card with the number 3 on it so that it could be seen by the agent through the aperture. The agent had lying before him in a row, five cards. Each card had a different drawing of an animal on it: elephant, giraffe, lion, pelican, or zebra. Before each block of trials, the agent shuffled the order of the picture cards. If EA held up a card with 3 on it, the agent would turn up the third card and concentrate upon the animal depicted on it. The percipient would then try to guess which animal was being "sent" and write his guess for that trial in the corresponding place on the response sheet. After every block of 50 trials, the agent reshuffled the target cards so that, for that block, only the agent knew which animal corresponded with which number.

In addition to this rather elaborate number arrangement, independent observers were invited to attend many of the sittings. Several professors and a member of parliament were among the observers. On some blocks of trials, unknown to the percipient, the agent did not look at the symbols. This was a test for clairvoyance. Other variations were introduced from time to time. The experiments with Gloria Stewart, while following the same pattern, were admittedly not as carefully controlled. Special precautions were also introduced to ensure that the prepared target sequences could not be known to agent or percipient in advance. And careful safeguards were introduced during the recording of the results and the matching of the targets against the guesses. Duplicates of all records were made and posted to a well-known academic immediately after each session.

Never before had so many safeguards been introduced into an ESP experiment. With so many individuals involved, and with prominent observers freely observing, any form of either unwitting cueing or deliberate trickery would seem to be just about impossible. If fraud of any sort were to be suspected, it would seemingly require, under the stated conditions, the active collusion of several prominent individuals. Beyond these safeguards, Soal randomized his targets, instituted sophisticated checks for randomness, and used the most appropriate statistical procedures. Despite these elaborate precautions, the two subjects managed to consistently score above chance over a number of years.

Soal's findings were hailed as definitive by parapsychologists and were so good that the rest of the scientific community, including the skeptics, could not ignore them. Here was one of Rhine's severest critics—a man who had spent many years meticulously conducting enormous card-guessing experiments with only chance results, was by profession a mathematician, and was an experimenter who had seemingly taken every known precaution to guard against every loophole and possibility of error—who suddenly demonstrated highly successful telepathic and precognitive results over sustained periods of time with two percipients.

Whately Carington, the parapsychologist who convinced Soal to re-examine his seemingly unsuccessful results, wrote:

> Mr. Soal is a most remarkable man, for whose work I have the highest possible admiration. Possessed of a more than Jobian patience, and a conscientiousness, thoroughness which I can only describe as almost pathological, he worked in various branches of the subject for many years with nothing but a succession of null results to show for it. . . . Hoping to repeat Rhine's experiments in England, he tested 160 persons, collecting 128,350 Zener card guesses singlehanded, and using the most elaborate precautions against every possible source of error. . . . If I had to choose one single investigation on which to pin my whole faith in the reality of paranormal phenomena, or with which to convince a hardened skeptic (if this be not a contradiction in terms), I should unhesitatingly choose this series of experiments, which is the most cast-iron piece of work I know, as well as having yielded the most remarkable results. [Quoted in Goldney 1975.]

Similar sentiments were expressed by virtually every parapsychologist who commented on this work. As just one illustration, R. A. McConnell (1954) phrased it as follows: "As a report to scientists this is the most important book on parapsychology since the 1940 publication of *Extra-Sensory Perception After Sixty Years.* If scientists will read it carefully, the 'ESP controversy' will be ended."

Ironically, some critical scientists did read it carefully, but, contrary to McConnell's prognosis, the controversy did not end. Indeed, one of the first major reviews in a scientific journal raised the controversy to new heights. Although the Shackleton experiments had originally been reported by Soal and Goldney in the *Proceedings of the Society for Psychical Resesarch* in 1943, the scientific world did not become aware of those experiments until they were reported along with the later experiments with Gloria Stewart in the 1954 book *Modern Experiments in Telepathy* by Soal and Bateman.

What fueled the controversy was an unprecedented review article, nine pages in length, appearing in *Science,* the prestigious journal of the American Association for the Advancement of Science. On August 26, 1955, George R. Price's article "Science and the Supernatural" was the only feature article for that issue. Price, who as far as I can tell had never before written on parapsychology, was described as being a research associate in the Department of Medicine at the University of Minnesota.

Price (1955) began his controversial article by stating: "Believers in psychic phenomena—such as telepathy, clairvoyance, precognition, and psychokinesis—appear to have won a decisive victory and virtually silenced opposition." Price wrote that such a victory had seemed close in the past but that critics had always managed to find flaws. But Price saw the time at which he was writing as unique because practically no scientific papers had attacked parapsychology during the preceding 15 years.

> The victory is the result of an impressive amount of careful experimentation and intelligent argumentation. The best of the card-guessing experiments of Rhine and Soal show enormous odds against chance occurrence, while possibility of sensory clues is often eliminated by placing cards and percipient in separate buildings far apart. Dozens of experimenters have obtained positive results in ESP experiments, and the mathematical procedures have been approved by leading statisticians.
>
> I suspect that most scientists who have studied the work of Rhine (especially as it is presented in *Extra-Sensory Perception After Sixty Years*) . . . and Soal (described in *Modern Experiments in Telepathy*) . . . have found it necessary to accept their findings. . . . Against all this evidence, almost the only defense remaining to the skeptical scientist is ignorance, ignorance concerning the work itself and concerning its implications. The typical scientist contents himself with retaining in his memory some criticism that at most applies to a small fraction of the published studies. But these findings (which challenge our very concepts of space and time) are—if valid—of enormous importance, both philosophically and practically, so they ought not to be ignored. [Price 1955]

Price then elaborates upon a suggested scheme, using redundancy coding, that would make ESP useful, even if it is a very weak and erratic form of communication. He then presents his version of Hume's argument against miracles. He quotes Tom Paine's more succinct version of the same argument, "Is it more probable that nature should go out of her course, or that a man should tell a lie?"

To justify using Hume's argument as his only grounds for accusing the parapsychologists of cheating, Price first tries to show that if ESP were real it would violate a number of fundamental principles underlying all the sciences. Some of these principles are that the cause must precede the effect, signals are attenuated by distance, signals are blocked by appropriate shielding, and so forth. ESP, according to Price, if it exists, violates all of these principles. Then Price explains why he considers ESP to be a principle of magic rather than merely a previously undiscovered law of nature. "The essential characteristic of magic is that phenomena occur that can most easily be explained in terms of action by invisible intelligent beings. . . . The essence of science is mechanism."

These lengthy considerations back up Price's solution to coping with the challenge of parapsychological claims: "My opinion concerning the findings of the parapsychologists is that many of them are dependent on clerical and statistical errors and unintentional use of sensory clues, and that all extrachance results not so explicable are dependent on deliberate fraud or mildly abnormal mental conditions."

Actually, nothing is novel or startling about Price's opinion. The same opinion, stated in just about the same words, probably is held by all skeptics. Price has carried his opinion beyond skepticism, however. The thrust of his article is that the *best* research in parapsychology as exemplified in the work of Rhine and Soal *cannot* be dismissed on the basis of "clerical and statistical error and unintentional use of sensory clues." Therefore he concludes that the results of this otherwise exemplary research *must* be due to fraud. He does not feel that he requires any evidence of fraud. Hume's argument against miracles gives him sufficient license. Price's position, of course, no longer belongs to skepticism, but rather to dogmatism. His position seemingly is that no research, no matter how well done, can convince him of ESP.

But Price does not want to go to quite that extreme. He says that he still can be convinced *provided* that the parapsychologists can provide him with just one successful outcome from a truly fraud-proof experiment. "What is needed is one completely convincing experiment—just one experiment that does not have to be accepted simply on the basis of faith in human honesty. We should require evidence of such nature that it would convince us even if we knew that the chief experimenter was a stage conjurer or a confidence man."

But does not the Soal experiment with Shackleton and Stewart meet this criterion? No, says Price, because he can imagine scenarios in which cheating could have taken place. Price then presents a number of possible ways that he feels cheating *could* have occurred in the Soal experiments.

> I do not claim that I know how Soal cheated if he did cheat, but if I were myself to attempt to duplicate his results, this is how I would proceed. First of all, I would seek a few collaborators, preferably people with good memories. The more collaborators I had, the easier it would be to perform the experiments, but the greater would be the risk of disclosure. Weighing these two considerations together, I'd want four confederates to imitate the Shackleton experiments. For imitating the Stewart series, I'd probably want three or four—although it is impossible to be certain, because the Stewart sittings have not been reported in much detail. In recruiting, I would appeal not to desire for fame or material gain but to the noblest motives, arguing that much good to humanity could result from a small deception designed to strengthen religious belief.

After providing a sampling of scenarios in which cheating could have occurred, all involving the collusion of three or more of the investigators, participants, and onlookers, Price supplies some designs of what he would consider to be a satisfactory test. But the key to all of his designs involves a committee. "Let us somewhat arbitrarily think of a committee of 12 and design tests such that the presence of a single honest man on the 'jury' will ensure validity of the test, even if the other 11 members should cooperate in fraud either to prove or disprove occurrence of psi phenomena."

Perhaps if some enterprising group of scientists collaborated and conducted an ESP experiment with positive results according to one of Price's approved designs, the outcome might very well convince *him*. But I do not think it would, nor should it, convince the majority of skeptical scientists. Without going into all its other faults, a single experiment—no matter how elaborate or allegedly fraud-proof—is simply a unique event. Scientific evidence is based on cumulative and replicable events across laboratories and investigators. The rubbish heap of scientific history contains many examples of seemingly airtight experiments whose results have been discarded because later scientists could not replicate the results. The experiments on mitogenetic radiation would be just one example. No one has found fault with the original experiments. But since later experimenters could not replicate the results, the original experiments have been cast aside. Can anyone doubt that this would not also happen to a successful but nonreplicable ESP outcome from one of Price's "satisfactory tests"?

Price tells us that "I myself believed in ESP about 15 years ago, after reading *Extra-Sensory Perception After Sixty Years,* but I changed my mind when I became acquainted with the argument presented by David Hume in his chapter 'Of miracles' in *An Enquiry Concerning Human Understanding*." So Hume supplies him with his escape hatch.

But all this seems unnecessarily dramatic. Price has fallen into a particularly stark version of the False Dichotomy. He has been forced into the very position that Henry Sidgwick wanted for the critics. The best ESP evidence is so good that either the critic must admit the reality of psi or accuse the proponents of lying and fraud. In falling into this trap, one that critics from the days of Hare and Crookes right up to the present keep falling into, Price has needlessly attributed to the Rhine and Soal results a level of evidential value that they cannot carry. At the same time, Price has implied that he is sufficiently expert in parapsychological research that he can infallibly judge when a given outcome unquestionably supports the conclusions of the experimenters. In fact, I doubt that even the parapsychologists are ready to give such power to a single experiment, even one so seemingly well-conducted as Soal's.

Price writes as if, when confronted with experimental evidence for psi, such as can be obtained by reading *Extra-Sensory Perception After Sixty Years* (Pratt et al. 1940) or *Modern Experiments in Telepathy,* he must immediately (*a*) find ways to reject the findings on the basis of possible sensory leakage, statistical artifacts, or loose experimental controls; or (*b*) accept the outcome as proof of psi; or (*c*) accuse the investigators of fraud if he can imagine some scenario, no matter how complex and unlikely, under which fraud *could* have occurred. Price just does not understand either parapsychological research or scientific research in general if he truly believes these are the only alternatives open to him. Unfortunately, Price is behaving like many of the other outspoken critics of psychical research. To Price's credit, he has at least tried to make his basis for action explicit.

Both Rhine and Soal, in their responses to Price's critique, eagerly accepted Price's implicit endorsement of their experimental procedures. Soal (1956) commented: "It is very significant and somewhat comforting to learn that Price admits that 'most of Soal's work' cannot be accounted for by any combination of statistical artifact and sensory leakage." Soal also examined in detail Price's various proposed schemes for faking the experiments:

> Price goes to great length in devising variations on this theme, but they all depend on the Agent being in collusion with the chief Experimenter or with the Percipient. Now four of the Agents with whom Mrs. Stewart was highly successful were lecturers of high academic standing at Queen Mary College in the University of London. Two were senior lecturers and the other two were mathematicians who had done distinguished creative work. A fifth Agent who was brilliantly successful over a long period was a senior civil servant, in fact an assistant director of mathematical examinations in the Civil Service. Now is it plausible to suppose that I, as chief Experimenter, could persuade any of these

men to enter into a stupid and pointless collusion to fake the experiments over a period of years? What had any of them to gain from such deplorable conduct? If I had gone to any of them and suggested (as Price recommends) that in a good cause a little deception would do no harm, I know quite plainly that the result would have been a first-class scandal in university circles.

Rhine (1956) found even more solace in Price's attack: "Strange though it may seem, the publication of the George Price paper . . . is, on the whole a good event for parapsychology." For one thing, it was a way of getting a lot of instruction on parapsychology before the scientific community. Rhine also felt Price's vivid portrayal of the potential importance of ESP was valuable. He welcomed Price's effective rebuttal against the standard criticisms against ESP. And Rhine especially liked the fact that Price focused on the point that psi was incompatible with the materialism of science.

[Price], even more than any other critical reviewer, gives indication of having felt the force of the evidence for ESP. When he turns then—albeit a bit too emotionally—and says that, according to the current concept of nature, ESP is impossible and therefore the parapsychologists must all be fakers, he at least draws the issue where it can be squarely met. The answer of the parapsychologist is: "Yes, either the present mechanistic theory of man *is* wrong—that is, fundamentally incomplete—or, of course, the parapsychologists *are* all utterly mistaken." *One* of these opponents is wrong; take it, now, from the pages of *Science!* This recognition of the issue gives point to the findings of parapsychology in a way none can easily miss.

Notice that Rhine and Price agree on some aspects of this controversy. Both Rhine and Price believe that if the claims of parapsychology are correct the foundations of science come tumbling down. Rhine welcomes such a destruction of what he calls materialism. Price seems willing to take the most drastic measures to avoid this overthrow of what he calls the basic limiting principles. (Not all parapsychologists agree with Rhine that the acceptance of psi need be inconsistent with scientific materialism.) The issue of what it means for contemporary science to accept the reality of psi involves matters that are currently controversial among philosophers of science and so it is probably not fruitful to attempt to deal with it here.

Rhine and Price also agree that the standard arguments against parapsychological evidence do not hold up. According to reasonable scientific criteria, the evidence for psi is more than adequate. And so it is at this point that both Rhine and Price want to have the showdown. Price, as a defender of the materialistic faith, puts all his money on the hope that the parapsychologists have faked the data. He has no evidence to back this claim. But if he can invent possible scenarios whereby trickery *might* have been committed in a given experiment, then he believes he can, under license from David Hume, assume that fraud must have taken place. He is not completely dogmatic about this. If the parapsychologist can come up with positive results in at least one experiment conducted under what Price considers to be fraud-proof conditions, then Price has committed himself to accept the consequences.

Many issues are raised by Price's dramatic confrontational posturing. At this point, I will just mention one. Price goes beyond conventional scientific practice when he empowers a given experiment with the ability to prove the existence of psi. Once we realize that no experiment by itself definitely establishes or disproves a scientific claim, then Price's extreme remedies to save his image of science become unnecessary. No matter how well designed and seemingly flawless a given experiment, there is always the possibility that future considerations will reveal previously unforeseen loopholes and weaknesses.

Indeed, a careful analysis of the Soal experiment will reveal a variety of weaknesses. For example, in spite of the number of observers and experimenters, Soal always had control over the prepared target sequences or over the basic recording. And both Shackleton and Stewart produced successful results only when Soal was present. On one occasion, without informing Soal, his co-investigator Mrs. Goldney conducted a sitting with Shackleton. The outcome was unsuccessful. The American parapsychologist J. G. Pratt ran a series of experiments with Mrs. Stewart without Soal's presence. No evidence for psi was found. And whereas all Rhine's results showed no difference between telepathy and clairvoyance trials, both Shackleton and Mrs. Stewart produced successful results only on telepathy trials. Furthermore, in spite of the much vaunted measures to guard against sensory leakage, the actual experimental setup, when carefully considered, offered a variety of possibilities for just such unwitting communication.

None of the foregoing considerations, in themselves, account for Soal's findings. But they make superfluous, I would argue, the hasty assumption that the findings can only be explained either by psi or by some elaborate form of dishonest collusion.

The Discrediting of Soal

As previously mentioned, it now seems that Soal, in fact, had faked his data. This seemingly vindicates Price as well as C.E.M. Hansel (1966; 1980), who also insinuated that Soal had cheated. Price, as we have seen, made his accusations with no actual basis other than that, under the given conditions, ways to cheat could be imagined. Hansel at least tried to find evidence within the data itself.

As it turns out, if Soal did cheat—and it now seems almost certain that he did—he almost certainly did so in ways not envisaged by either Price or Hansel. The scenarios generated by these two critics involved collusion among several of the principals. Soal apparently managed the fraud entirely on his own or, at most, with the collusion of one other person. Furthermore, he probably used a variety of different ways to accomplish his goals.

If it had not been for a series of seemingly fortuitous events, Soal's experiment might still occupy the honored place in the parapsychologists' exhibits of evidence for psi. Because the Soal experiments were, for more than a quarter of a century, considered to be "a mainstay . . . of the evidence for ESP" (Markwick 1978), the various steps by which the confidence in the results became eroded are worth examining. Because the matter is complicated, I will examine the stages of the discrediting of this initially impressive experiment in chronological order.

As already described, Soal's experiments with Shackleton and Mrs. Stewart began in 1939, when he made the post hoc discovery, as a result of a suggestion from Carington, that two of his 160 subjects in a previous experiment had shown above-chance results if their guesses were matched against the card either immediately preceding or immediately following the intended target. Soal and Goldney initiated the experiments with one of the percipients, Basil Shackleton, in 1941 and published the results in 1943. After the war, Soal was able to carry out an even longer series of experiments with the second percipient, Gloria Stewart. Both the Shackleton and Stewart experiments were summarized and brought to the attention of the general scientific community in the 1954 book *Modern Experiments in Telepathy* by Soal and Bateman.

The preceding section described the high praise for this work by the parapsychological community. G. R. Price, as also previously described, brought the book to the attention of the general scientific community by his lengthy attack and his insinuations of fraud that were featured in a 1955 issue of *Science*.

In 1956, as part of a letter to the *Journal of the Society for Psychical Research,* Soal indicated that he had lost the original score sheets of the Shackleton experiments on a train in 1945. Although copies of the records existed, the original score sheets would have been needed to check accusations, which surfaced a few years later, of possible alterations. Christopher Scott and Philip Haskell (1974) apparently think it significant that Soal failed to indicate that his admission of having lost the records some 11 years earlier was forced upon him by a request from G. R. Price to examine them.

In 1959, C. E. M. Hansel, after scrutinizing the records of the Shackleton experiments, believed he had found a pattern for the hits to be more likely to appear on certain parts of the score sheets in a subset of the sittings. He republished his findings in his critical books on ESP, stating his belief that the pattern is difficult to explain on the basis of precognition but "it is quite consistent with the hypothesis that the subject was making prearranged 'guesses' at predetermined positions on the form or with the hypothesis that the forms had been marked in some way to signify positions at which the guesses had to be made" (Hansel 1966; 1980). Soal responded that the pattern that Hansel had pointed out was a previously undiscovered segmental salience effect. In treating this systematic pattern as a property of psi, Soal was using the patchwork-quilt fallacy. However, in the absence of any evidence for deciding the issue, a systematic periodicity in the data, unpredicted by either the believer or the critic, could just as well be the result of psi as the result of an artifact.

In 1960 Hansel published his scenario for how the percipient and the agent could have played a trick on Soal in producing the results. Hansel apparently dropped this particular charge of trickery when it was shown that it could not account for the results (Medhurst 1968). In its place, Hansel adopted the scenarios for possible trickery that had been suggested by Price (1955).

After the sixteenth sitting with Shackleton, a Mrs. Gretl Albert, who had acted as one of the agents, informed Mrs. Goldney that she had observed Soal altering numbers on the record sheets during the checkup. Later, she specifically indicated that she had seen him changing 1s into 4s and 5s. Mrs. Goldney did not immediately inform Soal of this, but instead asked him to bring the record sheets of the preceding session with him to the next sitting. She could not find evidence for such changes on the records. When she informed Soal of the accusation he was indignant and insisted that Mrs. Albert not participate in further sittings. He also convinced Goldney that there was no reason to publicize this accusation (Scott and Haskell 1974).

Apparently, however, rumors circulated. Christopher Scott was one person who heard about it. He interviewed Mrs. Albert in 1959. At that time, he also examined the records for the sittings in question and did not find anything to confirm Mrs. Albert's accusations. Nevertheless, he and Fraser Nicol insisted that Soal and Goldney should make Gretl Albert's charges public. They did this in a letter to the *Journal for the Society of Psychical Research* published in 1960.

Since neither Goldney's nor Scott's perusals of the score sheets had found any obvious evidence to confirm Mrs. Albert's charges, the matter seemed to end with the assumption that she must have mistaken some innocent touching up of some ambiguously written numbers as alterations. The issue was raised again when Hansel referred to it in his 1966 book. Medhurst (1968) refers to Hansel's treatment of the matter as follows:

> I cannot help regarding his handling of this episode as rather shabby. With no discussion or comment he says quite baldly that Mrs. Albert "stated after one sitting that when glancing through the hole in the screen, she had seen Soal, while acting as EA [i.e., the experimenter associated with the agent], altering

figures on the score sheets." Hansel made a similar statement on television, to an audience on the whole even less likely to check the full facts than readers of his book. Put in this unqualified way the statement, as I am sure Hansel appreciates very well, is not only extremely damaging to Soal but grossly unfair. If he had revealed to his readers and his television audience that this lady also asserted that she had smoked one of Basil Shackleton's cigarettes and found it to be drugged, though in fact many other people smoked Shackleton's cigarettes at this time and suffered no ill effects, it is certain that a different weight would have been put on the value of her testimony.

Christopher Scott, in the same year, in commenting on Medhurst's criticism, pointed out that "Mrs. Albert's allegation was suppressed for 17 years until Mr. Fraser Nicol and myself brought pressure on the authors concerned to publish it" (Scott and Haskell 1974).

Presumably stimulated by this controversy, Medhurst conducted a formal analysis of the scoring pattern during the questioned sittings and reported that he could find no confirmation of Mrs. Albert's accusations. More significantly, Medhurst programmed a computer to search through Soal's target sequences. As part of the apparent attempt to make this experiment as rigorous as possible, Soal had provided a detailed description of both the source of his prepared random numbers and his procedure for deriving the numbers from it. "If this had succeeded it would have settled once and for all any question of 'altering the figures,' at least as far as the targets were concerned. In fact, however, the search failed completely." Scott and Haskell (1974) extended Medhurst's search to every sitting in which Soal used prepared random numbers. They failed to find a single identifiable sequence.

Although this failure to find any matching between Soal's target sequences and his reported source of random numbers suggests that Soal was not the precise and careful experimenter he was reputed to be, it does not, of itself, prove he tampered with the target sequences. As Soal and his defenders indicated, there are many ways that investigators obtain lists of targets from prepared tables, and if Soal had varied his procedures slightly from what he reported it could have thrown the computer search off. It is this failure to find a match with the presumed sources, however, that was later to provide the stimulus for the major discrediting of Soal's data.

Medhurst's claim to have found no evidence to confirm Mrs. Albert's accusations also caught Scott's attention. He noted that Medhurst quoted some figures that apparently supported a pattern of tampering as suggested by the accusations with a significance level of $P = 0.014$. By conventional standards, this would be considered to be at least suggestive. Worse, Scott discovered that Medhurst had made an error in calculation and that the true probability of the result just being due to chance was only $P = 0.003$. Thus, Medhurst's analysis, contrary to his conclusion, seemed to support the possibility of tampering.

Stimulated not only by these suggestive indications in Medhurst's analyses but also by additional information concerning the precise nature of Gretl Albert's accusations, Scott and Haskell (1960) carried out a detailed examination of the data for the relevant sittings in terms of a model that would predict how the frequencies of both the targets and the hits should be distributed if Mrs. Albert's accusations were correct.

> From the above account it will be seen that the "GA allegation" had been widely noted and openly discussed for several years. It is surprising then to learn that none of the authors mentioned, nor any of those researchers who had elsewhere suggested loopholes in the experiments . . . took the trouble to examine the available copies of the experimental records to see whether the frequency of the different target/guess symbol pairs showed any evidence for the particular alterations which Mrs. Albert had reported. The present article reports such an examination. It will be shown that there is, in fact, definite evidence supporting Mrs. Albert's allegation for the sitting in question.

Scott and Haskell asked what would be expected if, as Mrs. Albert had charged, Soal had systematically changed 1s into 4s and 5s in the target list to create additional hits when the percipient's responses were being matched against the target? Four observable patterns would be expected: (1) an overall deficit of target 1s; (2) an overall excess of target 4s and 5s; (3) a deficit of target 1s in those trials in which the guess was 4 or 5; and (4) an excess of hits on 4 and 5.

Of these four predictions only the third and fourth actually showed up in the data. Scott and Haskell, in trying to make sense of this strange outcome, point out that a problem arises from the failure to discover a deficit of 1s and an excess of 4s and 5s. So they consider a second model in which Soal might be assumed to have stacked the original target lists in advance with extra 1s in preparation for the later transformation of some of them to 4s and 5s. Although this model is now somewhat post hoc, the authors derive some additional predictions from it of new patterns to be found in the data. They find that all the observations, including the significant hitting, can be accounted for by their second model. "The model is to some degree 'ad hoc,' but the significance levels are so overwhelming, and the consistency of the effects through the three sittings and the various subsittings is so clear, that it cannot seriously be dismissed as an after-the-fact construct based on chance irregularities. No such construct could hope to achieve such a close fit" (Scott and Haskell 1974).

Scott and Haskell, having found this pattern in the session at which Mrs. Albert had claimed having seen the tampering, looked for the signs of the same pattern in the other 40 sessions held with Shackleton. They found the same pattern in two other sittings. In other words, the specific manipulation that Gretl

Albert claimed to have observed seems to have been practiced in only a small portion of the total results. "Taking all this evidence together, we conclude that there is rather a strong case for accepting the essential truth of the 'GA allegation.' Further, if this interpretation is correct it seems unlikely that any significant proportion of the results in the Shackleton series was obtained by extrasensory perception" (Scott and Hansel 1974).

Some parapsychologists acknowledged that, as a result of Scott and Haskell's findings, Soal's research no longer could be considered part of the evidential case for ESP (Palmer 1978; Rogo 1975). But several, including some of the major leaders in the field, vigorously defended Soal's innocence and the credibility of his data (Barrington 1974; Goldney 1974; Wassermann 1975).

Soal's defenders used a number of arguments. Several tried to show that Gretl Albert was an unreliable witness based upon, among other things, her claim that she believed she had been drugged by one of Shackleton's cigarettes. The ad hoc nature of Scott and Haskell's analysis was questioned. The patchwork quilt was employed to argue that the particular patterns uncovered were simply further properties of psi. And, finally, the problem of the dirty test-tube arose when defenders made an issue out of the fact that the Scott-Haskell account could, at most, explain only 7 percent of the results. The implication is that the burden of showing that ESP is not the proper explanation for the large residue lies with the critics.

The final blow to the credibility of Soal's results came in 1978 when Betty Markwick (1978) published her article "The Soal-Goldney Experiments with Basil Shackleton: New Evidence of Data Manipulation." As with the previous revelations of peculiarities in the data, Markwick's stunning findings arose out of a series of fortuitous incidents. (See Chapter 11 in this volume for Markwick's account.)

Markwick informs her readers that her "enthusiasm for Parapsychology had been awakened [in 1960] through the chance reading of Soal and Bateman's *Modern Experiments in Telepathy*." When the controversy over the GA allegation came to her attention through reading about Medhurst's failure to find the source of Soal's target sequences, Markwick (1978) decided to see if she could vindicate Soal by carrying Medhurst's research further.

> I record here, for what it is worth, the fact that the initial motivation for the above piece of research sprang from a dream: a dream of a most intense quality in which Dr. Medhurst appeared in the role of tutor explaining a mathematical/graphical problem which he wished me to work upon. The dream occurred on 31 March 1971; five days later the *SPR Journal* arrived containing, to my astonishment, a posthumously-published paper by Dr. Medhurst, the subject matter of which seemed curiously linked with my dream. While shunning a survivalist interpretation, it was difficult to resist the feeling that an element of ESP might nevertheless be involved, impelling me to follow up certain ideas

suggested by the dream—with the outcome reported in this paper.

Incidentally, apart from attending (in 1969) two SPR lectures led by Dr. Medhurst, I met him only once, briefly in 1963.

Soon after reading about Medhurst's failure to find the source of Soal's random numbers, Markwick wrote a computer program to extend Medhurst's search to cover more possible ways that Soal might have chosen his targets from Chambers's Logarithm Tables. She was disappointed. All her efforts failed and she finally gave up.

Four years later, Markwick suddenly came up with a new way to possibly vindicate Soal. The idea came while she was wondering how to resolve the problem raised by the Scott and Haskell findings. These authors "presented an impressive statistical case in support of the GA allegation. Impressive . . . yet hardly *conclusive*. One longed for a conclusive settling of the matter—either way."

While rereading Medhurst's paper with this goal in mind, she recalled that the final digits of logarithms, when used as random numbers, generate sequences that are pseudo-random in a characteristic way. Presumably, if she analyzed Soal's target sequences and found this characteristic pattern this would constitute some evidence that he had generated the sequences, as he had indicated, from the final digits of Chambers's Tables.

The obvious step, at this stage, was to use a computer to check through the target sequences for these pseudo-random properties. Here, possibly, another of those fortuitous events that enabled the final discovery occurred. Markwick had to wait before she could get access to a computer. While waiting, she began examining the sequences by hand. During one of her hand-counts, she thought she recognized one of the target sequences cited in Medhurst's article. "On checking, however, I discovered that the sequences came from different sittings, *though matching to the extent of 19 digits*—far beyond what could reasonably be attributed to chance. Within the hour a second long repetiton (24 digits) had caught my eye, involving the same two sittings (Sittings 4 and 6)."

Eventually Markwick came across other repeated sequences. At first both Markwick, and J. G. Pratt, were encouraged by finding such repetitions. Although their existence suggested that Soal had been less than meticulous in compiling his target sequences, the existence of repeated strings of the same target sequences could have an innocent interpretation. In his carelessness, Soal could have inadvertently, on several occasions, re-entered Chambers's Tables at the same place he had entered them on a previous occasion when preparing target sequences. But at least replications of the same sequences would indicate that no tampering had taken place with the targets.

Markwick now used the computer to search for repetitions or approximate repetitions of larger sequences.

The duplication proved *not* to be extensive, but a very suspicious feature came to light. Some of the repetitions were not exact but exhibited occasional "extra" (or extraneous) digits, as though digits had been inserted into one of the pair of sequences (or omitted from the other), *and these extra digits showed a marked tendency to correspond to hits.* I first observed this effect in Sitting 2 (sheets 3, 5) through studying the *continuations* of the duplicated sequences: five single extra digits became evident at five-digit intervals. On checking the distribution of hits, I saw, to my dismay, that *every one of the five extra digits corresponded to a hit.* [Markwick 1978]

Markwick continued her examination of the target sequences and found other examples of either a partially duplicated sequence or the same sequence in reverse with inserted targets in one of the sequences. The inserted targets invariably corresponded with a hit and, in the sittings for which she found such duplications, the insertions accounted for the significantly above-chance hitting.

Although the interrupted duplications account for only 20 percent of the total data, Markwick suggested other ways, not detectable by her analysis, that Soal could have tampered with the other target sequences or, in some cases, with the percipient's guesses. Markwick considered possible ways that the patterns she uncovered might have arisen in innocent ways. Reluctantly, she was forced to conclude that only the hypothesis of deliberate tampering with the data could explain her findings.

Protestations to the effect that Soal, a respected scientist, would not have cheated in his own experiments—and that anyway the rigorous experimental conditions in the Shackleton series precluded fraud—seem to me to carry little weight in the face of the evidence. We can rarely fathom how conjurors achieve *their* feats, and perhaps Soal was as clever. It is futile to argue that the prison cell is escape-proof when the inmate has clearly gone. [Markwick 1978]

Scott and Haskell's discovery of patterns indicative of tampering in three sittings had weakened Soal's evidence only in the opinion of some parapsychologists. Several major parapsychologists were able to find sufficient loopholes in the Scott-Haskell argument to maintain their belief in the integrity of both Soal and his data. But the addition of Markwick's even more formidable case left parapsychologists no choice. Soal's experiments with both Shackleton and Stewart have been withdrawn from the evidential data-base.

Two immediate reactions by supporters and former co-investigators of Soal are of interest. Mrs. Goldney (1978) wrote:

Of those contributors defending Soal and his work, it was I who had had the closest knowledge of Soal in my long contact with him in experimental work since the 1930's and as co-author with him of the "Shackleton Report." . . . If Miss Markwick's findings are valid (and I have no reason to believe otherwise), I and others who replied to the Scott-Haskell paper were wrong, but justifiably so, in my opinion, in the light of the evidence then available. On page 81 of my reply I wrote: "Of course an adverse verdict, if established, will destroy individual hopes, even beliefs. So be it, if necessary. 'The world is wide' and the object of all our studies is to find and establish *the truth.*" This sentence summarised what I felt when I wrote it and what I feel now.

J. G. Pratt agreed with Markwick's conclusion that all of Soal's findings on Shackleton and Stewart must be discarded. Pratt (1978b), however, suggested that "some of the published findings from the Soal records [might provide] valid evidence of ESP in spite of the results that Miss Markwick has presented. Much of my own work with these records, particularly those from the Stewart series, brought to light position effects and displacement effects that I interpreted at the time as giving strong supporting evidence for paranormal processes at work in the tests."

This seems to me to be another example of the patchwork quilt. Pratt is referring to various secondary effects in the data. Because they had not been originally hypothesized, he believes that "such secondary effects as those mentioned above provide a kind of bedrock evidence for psi that is untouched even by accusations of fraud in the research." Pratt has apparently overlooked the fact that secondary effects can result from the primary effects introduced by the tampering and, as such, are just as much an indicator of tampering or other artifacts as they are of ESP.

Another revealing aspect of Pratt's statement is the way in which his belief in psi enabled him to suggest an alternative to cheating:

But those of us who have difficulty reconciling the idea of conscious fraud with the picture of an investigator who was totally absorbed in his research will not be compelled by Miss Markwick's findings to overcome that reluctance and agree that Soal was a hoaxer. I do not mind revealing that I am the person who suggested that Soal might have become his own subject on some occasions when preparing the lists of random numbers on the record sheets before the sittings were held. This explanation would require that he used precognition when inserting digits into the columns of numbers he was copying down, unconsciously choosing numbers that would score hits on the calls the subject would make later. For me, this "experimenter psi" explanation makes more sense, psychologically, than saying that Soal consciously falsified for his own records, but I do not argue that it should be accepted by others as the likely interpretation.

Pratt's account assumes that Soal was in an altered state or unaware of his insertions. One of Markwick's two hypotheses to explain Soal's behavior also made use of the well-known fact that Soal sometimes did automatic writing in a dissociated state. Markwick suggested the possibility that Soal may have had a split personality and that the cheating was done by his other self.

Markwick's second hypothesis involved data massage and has more universal psychological plausibility (although it is not necessarily inconsistent with her first hypothesis). She assumes that Soal's enormous accumulation of negative ESP findings were obtained legitimately. She also assumes that his post hoc finding of consistent displacement effects in the data of Basil Shackleton and Gloria Stewart was legitimate.

> Having embarked upon the Shackleton series, one may imagine the scoring rate begins to fade (as ESP scores are wont to do after the initial flush of success). Soal, seeing the chance slipping away of gaining scientific recognition for Parapsychology, a cause in which he passionately believes, succumbs to the temptation of "rectifying" a "temporary" deficiency. [Markwick 1978]

Markwick's second scenario is consistent with known patterns in which scientists have tampered with their data (Broad and Wade 1982; Hixson 1976). The components appear to be: (1) The investigator believes, on the basis of previous experience, that the phenomenon under investigation is "real." (2) For some unknown reason his current research fails to reveal the phenomenon. (3) If he reports negative results his readers might wrongly believe that the phenomenon does not exist. (4) As a result, the "truth" and assumed positive consequences of the phenomenon might be lost to humanity. Given these ingredients, it takes a very small step for the investigator to convince himself that he is helping both the truth and a good cause along by doctoring his data.

William James, with reference to his experiences in psychical research, suggested that cheating in order to convince others of the "reality" you know to be the case might be defensible. James discusses this matter in his last essay on psychical research. He referred to the policy of English investigators to consider a medium who has been caught cheating as one who always cheats. He indicated that he thought this had generally been a wise policy.

> But, however wise as a policy the S.P.R.'s maxim may have been, as a test of truth I believe it to be almost irrelevant. In most things human the accusation of deliberate fraud and falsehood is grossly superficial. Man's character is too sophistically mixed for the alternative of "honest or dishonest" to be a sharp one. Scientific men themselves will cheat—at public lectures—rather than let experiments obey their well-known tendency towards failure. [Murphy and Ballou 1969]

James gave two examples of such cheating. And then revealed the following about his own behavior:

> To compare small men with great, I have myself cheated shamelessly. In the early days of the Sanders Theater at Harvard, I once had charge of a heart on the physiology of which Professor Newell Martin was giving a popular lecture. This heart, which belonged to a turtle, supported an index-straw which threw a moving shadow, greatly enlarged, upon the screen, while the heart pulsated. When certain nerves were stimulated, the lecturer said, the heart would act in certain ways which he described. But the poor heart was too far gone and, although it stopped duly when the nerve of arrest was excited, that was the final end of its life's tether. Presiding over the performance, I was terrified at the fiasco, and found myself suddenly acting like one of those military geniuses who on the field of battle convert disaster into victory. There was no time for deliberation; so, with my forefinger under a part of the straw that cast no shadow, I found myself impulsively and automatically imitating the rhythmical movements which my colleague had prophesied the heart would undergo. I kept the experiment from failing; and not only saved my colleague (and the turtle) from humiliation that but for my presence of mind would have been their lot, but I established in the audience the true view of the subject. The lecturer was stating this; and the misconduct of one half-dead specimen of heart ought not to destroy the impression of his words. "There is no worse lie than a truth misunderstood," is a maxim which I have heard ascribed to a former venerated President of Harvard. The heart's failure would have been misunderstood by the audience and given the lie to the lecturer. It was hard enough to make them understand the subject anyhow; so that even now as I write in cool blood I am tempted to think that I acted quite correctly. I was acting for the *larger* truth, at any rate, however automatically. . . . To this day the memory of that critical emergency has made me feel charitable towards all mediums who make phenomena come in one way when they won't come easily in another. On the principles of the S.P.R., my conduct on that one occasion ought to discredit everything I ever do, everything, for example, I may write in this article—a manifestly unjust conclusion. [Murphy and Ballou 1969]

I wonder if James would have approved of the way William Crookes covered up the cheating of the medium Mary Showers in behalf of "the larger truth." Mary Showers, a young medium, conducted at least one joint séance with Florence Cook in Crookes's home. Apparently Crookes had several other sittings with Mary. Daniel Home presumably heard rumors that Crookes might be having an affair with the young Mary Showers. Crookes wrote a letter to Home explaining how the scandal had originated.

> According to Crookes he had obtained a complete confession from Mary Showers in her own handwriting that her phenomena were wholly dependent on

trickery and the occasional use of an accomplice, Crookes said, however, that he had undertaken not to reveal the fact that Mary was fraudulent even to her own mother, because of "the very great injury which the cause of truth would suffer if so impudent a fraud were to be publicly exposed." [T. Hall 1963b]

Plausible Alternatives and Scientific Acceptability

The controversy over the Soal experiments focused on issues of fraud. Unfortunately, all the preceding examples discussed in this paper have also raised issues of fraud, usually on the part of the subjects, but in at least the cases of Crookes and Soal, also on the part of the experimenter. Certainly fraud is an issue, but I would like to emphasize that I consider it, especially from the point of view of scientific evidence, not the most important issue in evaluating the arguments for psi.

Much of the controversy over claims for psi confuses two separate issues— scientific acceptability and plausible alternatives. The question of scientific acceptability is simply: Has the evidence of a particular claim been accumulated and reported in a manner that justifies the acquiescence of rational men of science? The question of plausibility of alternatives is: Has the critic supplied an alternative account (on the basis of, say, trickery by the percipient, unconscious cueing, etc.) that is consistent with the facts?

The decision that a given body of evidence does not meet acceptable standards does not obligate the decider to supply an alternative account. The skeptical scientist can reject Crookes's report on Home's moving the balance on the grounds that the documentation is incomplete and that it has not been independently replicated. It is then up to Crookes and his supporters to provide additional data that meet acceptable standards.

On the other hand, when Carpenter or other critics say that Home tricked Crookes by either hypnotizing him or using an invisible thread attached to the scale, they have taken upon themselves to demonstrate that their alternative account is plausible in terms of what is known about hypnotism and about the circumstances under which Home had to perform.

Almost all the controversy over the claims of Hare, Wallace, Crookes, Gurney, and Soal has dealt with the plausibility of the critics' charges. And, unfortunately, the critics' accusations have often been wide of the mark and easily challenged. As a result, much of the debate focused on the claims of the critics rather than on the claims of the proponents. The burden of proof was thus shifted from the proponents to the critics.

Both proponents and critics share the blame for this unfruitful history of controversy. Both have assumed, in line with Sidgwick's stated objective, that either the proponents' claims have to be accepted or the critics have to accuse the proponents of childish gullibility or fraud.

In my opinion, much of the controversy was unnecessary because the psychical researchers never put before the scientific community the sort of evidence that called for serious consideration. In many ways the cases that have been reviewed here, all of which were at one time put forth by proponents as scientific proof of psi, were unique and unreplicated events.

The scientific community should have responded to Crookes's evidence on Home's ability to move the balance by withholding judgment until independent investigators had replicated the experiment with Home and other mediums. To Crookes's credit, this is what he also hoped for. He invited his critics to come to his laboratory and observe the experiment. Unfortunately, none of them came. But more would have been needed than having the phenomena witnessed by critics in Crookes's laboratory. It would be important to produce the phenomenon in other laboratories in experiments controlled by independent investigators.

We see the necessity for this latter requirement in the Soal experiments. Soal's experiments with Shackleton and Stewart were unique in that they were witnessed by a large number of prominent observers. But, as John Beloff (1974) indicated in his defense of Soal against the GA allegation, Soal would have had a stronger case if he had allowed other investigators to independently test his two star subjects. And, in the aftermath of the Markwick revelations, D. J. West (1978) pointed out that before any ESP experiment be accepted it should have been conducted by independent investigators. For example, if instead of keeping full control of the sittings with Shackleton and Stewart, independent experimenters had had charge of alternate sittings—including preparing the targets and controlling all other aspects, and similar results had been obtained, there would have been no need for controversy over the findings.

What if Gretl Albert had not noticed and reported what she believed to be the alteration of targets by Soal? We would have no factual basis today for assuming that Soal had faked his data. And the parapsychologists might still be placing these experiments before us as solid proof of ESP.

But, I maintain, unless later parapsychologists had replicated Soal's results with the same sort of design, there would be no reason for the scientific community to take the results seriously. Nor would there be any need for the critics to try to "explain the results away." If parapsychologists had tried to insist that the results were replicable in the scientific sense because the findings held up over a number of sittings and were witnessed at different times by a variety of observers, then a number of objections could have been raised. Significant results were obtained only when Soal was present. When Shackleton was tested, without Soal's knowledge, by Mrs. Goldney, the results were nonsignificant. When Mrs. Stewart was tested in the United States by Pratt in Soal's absence, the results were consistent with chance. Furthermore, Mrs. Stewart's pattern of hitting was inconsistent with both Shackleton's and her own pattern in the preceding experiment. And, although Rhine and other parapsychologists hailed

Soal's findings as confirming previous reports of ESP (Rhine and Pratt 1957), Soal's findings departed strikingly from Rhine's in that his two percipients displayed significant hitting only on telepathy and not on clairvoyance trials. These inconsistencies do not disconfirm Soal's findings. But they do indicate that they have no scientific status until independently replicated.

This requirement for independently replicable findings is recognized by several of today's major parapsychologists. Beginning with the middle 1970s, parapsychologists have been claiming that they now have achieved the repeatable experiment. And it is this claim that we now will discuss.

The Post-Rhine Era

Rhine's card-guessing paradigm dominated experimental parapsychology from 1934 to at least the 1960s. Since the 1960s, card-guessing experiments have played a minor role. Contemporary parapsychologists have deviated from Rhine's paradigm in a variety of ways. In Rhine's paradigm both the possible targets and the possible responses are severely restricted. The targets consist of five deliberately neutral and simple symbols. And, on each trial, the percipient is restricted to calling out the name of one of these possible five symbols. From a strictly methodological viewpoint these restrictons have several advantages. Percipients have no strong preferences for any of the symbols; randomizing of targets is straightforward; scoring of hits and misses is unambiguous; and the statistical calculations are fairly standard.

But these same features have been blamed by contemporary investigators for the lack of impressive findings since the spectacular scoring reported by Rhine in 1934 (Rhine 1935). Because the symbols are relatively meaningless and uninteresting, the repetitive guessing over many trials is boring and, according to the parapsychologists, contributes to both a lack of motivation and emotional involvement that might be needed for the effective functioning of psi.

As a result, one break with the past is the increased use of more complex and meaningful targets, such as reproductions of paintings, travel slides, geographical locations, and emotionally laden photographs. In addition, instead of the forced-choice procedure of the card-guessing, experimenters allow free-responding on the part of their percipients. Percipients are encouraged, on a given trial, to free-associate and describe, both in words and in drawings, whatever comes to mind. The use of free responses complicates enormously the problems of scoring and statistical analysis. But parapsychologists believe the added complications are a small price to pay if the newer procedures produce better psychic functioning.

Along with free-response designs, parapsychologists have renewed their interest in the possibility that psychic functioning may be enhanced in altered states like dreaming, hypnosis, meditation, sensory-deprived states, and progressive relaxation. The basic idea is that these altered states greatly reduce or block attention to external sensory information while, at the same time, increasing attention to internal mentation. Under such conditions it is hypothesized that the psi signal is easier for the percipient to detect because it has less competition from sensory inputs (Honorton 1978). One survey of 87 experiments in which percipients were in an altered state found that 56 percent reported significant hitting of targets (Honorton 1977).

Another departure from the Rhine paradigm was stimulated by developments in electronic technology. Psi experiments employing random-event generators began in the 1970s. Electronic equipment could be used to generate random targets as well as automatically record the percipient's responses and keep running tallies of the hits. Although such equipment has been used to test ESP, the most widespread use has been in the study of psychokinesis. In such experiments an operator or "psychic" attempts to bias the output of a random-event generator by mental means alone. In 1980, May, Humphrey, and Hubbard (1980) found reports of 214 such experiments, "74 of which show statistical evidence for an anomalous perturbation—a factor of nearly seven times chance expectation."

A third major departure has been the so-called remote viewing paradigm (Hyman 1977a; 1984-85; Targ and Puthoff 1977; Puthoff and Targ 1976; Targ and Harary 1984). The claims made for the ability of this procedure to consistently demonstrate ESP with a variety of percipients are perhaps the strongest ever put forth by parapsychologists (Targ and Puthoff 1977):

> Our laboratory experiments suggest to us that anyone who feels comfortable with the idea of having paranormal ability can have it. . . . In our experiments, we have never found anyone who could not learn to perceive scenes, including buildings, roads, and people, even those at great distances and blocked from ordinary perception. . . . We have, as of this writing, carried out successful remote viewing experiments with about twenty participants, almost all of whom came to us without any prior experience, and in some cases, with little interest in psychic functioning. So far, we cannot identify a single individual who has not succeeded in a remote viewing task to his own satisfaction.

In a more recent assessment of remote viewing, Targ and Harary (1984) assert: "In laboratories across the country, and in many other nations as well, forty-six experimental series have investigated remote viewing. Twenty-three of these investigations have reported successful results and produced statistically significant data, where three would be expected."

In addition to the experimental programs on altered states, random-event generators, and remote viewing, contemporary parapsychologists have been actively doing research in other areas. The various chapters in the *Handbook of Parapsychology* (Wolman 1977) provide a good idea of the range of topics. The research on reincarnation, survival after death, paranormal photography, psychic metal-bending, poltergeist phenomena, hauntings, and faith healing, while admittedly colorful, does not deserve the serious attention of scientists—at least not in its current state. I suspect that most serious parapsychologists would also not want to rest their case on such research.

Today the parapsychologists who want the scientific establishment to take their work seriously do not offer for inspection the evidence that previous generations of psychic researchers believed was sufficient—the findings of Hare, Wallace, Crookes, Gurney, Rhine, or Soal. Nor do they offer up the reports on reincarnation, psychic healing, paranormal photography, spoon bending, psychic detection, and the related phenomena that so readily appeal to the media and the public. Instead, they ask us to look at the trends and patterns they find in research programs carried out in a variety of different parapsychological laboratories.

Two aspects of this new type of claim are worth noting. One is the admission that a single investigation, no matter how seemingly rigorous and fraud-proof, cannot be acceptable as scientific evidence. The idea of a single "critical experiment" is a myth. The second, and related, aspect is that replicability is now accepted as the critical requirement for admission into the scientific marketplace.

Both proponents and critics have previously assumed, either tacitly or explicitly, that the outcome of a single investigation could be critical. Sidgwick believed that the results of the investigation of the Creery sisters were of this nature. The evidence was so strong, he argued, that the critics had to now either accept the reality of telepathy or accuse the investigators of fraud (Sidgwick 1982-83). Carpenter, rather than withhold judgment until independent investigators had either succeeded or failed in attempts to replicate Crookes's experiments with Home, acted as if he had to either agree to Crookes's claim or prove that Crookes had been duped. Both Price and Hansel insisted that it would be sufficient for Rhine and Soal to convince them of ESP if a parapsychologist could perform successfully a single "fraud-proof" experiment.

The myth of the single, crucial experiment has resulted in needless controversy and has contributed to the False Dichotomy. Antony Flew (1978) is just one who has argued convincingly that a single, unreplicated event that allegedly attests to a miracle is simply a historical oddity that cannot be part of a scientific argument.

Apparently not all parapsychologists are convinced that the achievement of a repeatable psi experiment is either necessary or desirable for the advancement of parapsychology. The late J. G. Pratt (1978a) argued that "psi is a spontaneous occurrence in nature, and we can no more predict precisely when it is going to occur in our carefully planned and rigorously controlled experiments than we can in everyday-life psychic experiences. . . . Predictable repeatability is unattainable because of the nature of the phenomena."

Pratt argued that parapsychology should give up the quest for the replicable experiment—an impossible goal in his opinion—and concentrate upon accumulating enough data on anomalous happenings to convince scientists and the public that psi is real. Other parapsychologists, however, realize that scientists are not going to be convinced until some semblance of replicability has been achieved. The late Gardner Murphy, while noting that replicability was not necessary for scientific acceptability in some areas of science, argued that to support claims for such irrational phenomena as psi, replicability is necessary. And, speaking as one of the dominant figures in parapsychology Murphy (1971) made it clear that he felt that parapsychology had a long way to go before it achieved replicable results.

Perhaps Charles Honorton's (1981) position represents the contemporary position of the major parapsychologists:

> Parapsychology will stand or fall on its ability to demonstrate replicable and conceptually meaningful findings. Future critics who are interested in the resolution rather than the perpetuation of the psi controversy are advised to focus their attention on systematic lines of research which are capable of producing such findings.

Psi and Repeatability

As the preceding quotation indicates, Honorton believes that critics should focus on "systematic lines of research" that apparently display replicable and/or "conceptually meaningful" findings. And, as we have seen, contemporary parapsychologists have offered us a number of such systematic lines to demonstrate that they have, in fact, already achieved the goals of repeatability and conceptual meaningfulness. The claims put forth in behalf of the altered-state, random-event-generator, and remote-viewing paradigms have already been cited. Similar claims have been made for work on such correlates of psi as attitudes and personality.

What can we expect if a critic, in an effort to be open-minded and responsible, accepts the challenge of Honorton and his fellow parapsychologists to examine the accumulated evidence from one or more of the "systematic lines" of inquiry? A number of critics in recent times have mounted attacks upon parapsychology. But these examples supply us with inadequate guidelines to the answer because none of the critiques seems to have involved an examination of a systematic line of inquiry.

Price is one dramatic example. Price (1955) wrote that he had initially been converted to a belief in psi after reading *Extra-Sensory Perception After Sixty Years* and added, "I suspect that most scientists who have studied the work of Rhine (especially as it is presented in *Extra-Sensory Perception After Sixty Years*) and Soal (described in *Modern Experiments in Telepathy*) have found it necessary to accept their findings."

Price's position reveals one of the serious problems facing the critic. The two sources he mentions are secondary accounts. He does not tell us whether he has studied the primary reports upon which the two books were based. I suspect that, especially in the case of Rhine's work, Price's acquaintance with parapsychological research was limited to such secondary accounts. A serious and conscientious examination of the primary reports of Rhine's work up to that time would have required at least several months of careful study. In addition, there is no evidence that Price had had prior experience or gained expertise in parapsychological research.

No one would expect Price, whose Ph.D. was in physical and analytical chemistry, to be an effective critic of a line of research in astronomy, quantum mechanics, cellular biology, psychophysics, or some other branch of science outside his training and experience. Yet he and his editors apparently had no hesitation in relying upon his instant "expertise" in criticizing parapsychology.

In Price's case, he was apparently caught off guard by the fact that the evidence he encountered was embedded in a matrix of experimental and statistical sophistication for which his previous impressions had not prepared him. He immediately concluded that either the reported evidence proved the case for psi or that widespread cheating had occurred. Somehow it never occurred to Price that it would require both extended experience with the field and its peculiarities, as well as careful and detailed study of the experimental reports, before he could be in a position to properly weigh both the strong and weak points in the evidence.

Hansel, who followed Price in making the possibility of fraud sufficient grounds for rejecting an ESP claim, did in fact devote the time and effort to the study and reconstruction of primary reports (Hansel 1966; 1980). And his ability to dissect experimental arrangements and suggest possible scenarios for the occurrence of fraud is impressive. Yet he did not examine systematic lines of research. Instead, his strategy was to try to find the two or three "best" experiments in parapsychology and then analyze them in detail. His main efforts were focused upon two of Rhine's early and most successful experiments—the Pearce-Pratt experiment and the Pratt-Woodruff experiment—and Soal's experiment with Shackleton and Stewart. In each case he was able to demonstrate to his satisfaction how cheating could have taken place to account for the results. His account of how Pearce could have cheated has been challenged on the grounds that it depends upon a factually incorrect floor-plan of the experimental site (Honorton 1967). Hansel has never replied to this challenge. In the case of Soal's experiments, as we have seen, Hansel created scenarios that were much more involved and complicated than apparently was the case, but his suspicions of fraud did seem to be correct. Unfortunately, Hansel's approach assumes the possibility of settling matters on the basis of a single, crucial experiment. It also will enable the determined critic to reject any given experiment, because it is always possible to imagine some scenario in which cheating, no matter how implausible, could have occurred.

The alternative to trying to prove or disprove the case for parapsychology on the basis of a single experiment is, of course, to consider the evidence from several experiments. But this alternative opens up a variety of possibilities. One has to do with which experiments to include in the evaluation. It is impractical to consider *all* of the experiments in parapsychloogy, because even in this relatively sparsely populated area the number is by now enormous. In just considering a subset of experiments in the ESP area, John Palmer (1978), for example, covered approximatly 700 experimental reports. I would estimate that, today, a determined critic who wants to evaluate exhaustively all available experimental reports, including those on PK as well as on ESP, might have to cope with upward of 3,000 experiments. Given my recent experience in trying to do justice to just 42 experiments on the ganzfeld psi phenomenon (Hyman 1985), I would estimate that it would take a responsible critic more than five years of almost full-time effort to properly evaluate this material.

Another problem facing both the proponent and the critic is how, once a suitable sample of experiments has been selected, to make an overall judgment about what patterns, trends, strengths, and weaknesses characterize the sample. Up until recently, such a review of a body of literature has been an unstructured and highly subjective affair. Understandably, two individuals surveying the same body of literature could, and did, often come up with diametrically opposed conclusions.

As cognitive psychologists have emphasized, the capacity of humans to handle mentally a number of items is severely limited. What constitutes an "item" varies greatly with the structure of the material and the individual's previous familiarity and expertise in a given field of knowledge. Even within his specialty, a scientist would have great difficulty in trying to comprehend patterns in over a dozen or so reports without external aids and a systematic procedure.

When the nonparapsychologist critic tries to make sense of a large body of parapsychological literature, he is at a great disadvantage. His critical capacities have not been trained to pick out relevant from irrelevant details in seeking interrelationships. Lacking concrete experience with many of the experimental designs, he is at a decided disadvantage in knowing what things could go wrong and which sorts of controls would be critical. And when the number of separate reports is more than a dozen or so, he cannot be expected to be able to grasp the total picture without help from systematic and quantitative summarization procedures.

Yet, so far as I can tell, only two critical evaluations of "systematic lines" of parapsychological research have ever been made using systematic, explicit, and quantitative guidelines. Both of these were carried out fairly recently. One was by Charles Akers (1984), a former parapsychologist with both experience and publications in the field. The other one was my own, which I made as an external critic who accepted the parapsychologists' challenge to fairly evaluate a systematic line of research that they felt represented their strongest case for the repeatable experiment (Hyman 1985; 1983).

Akers's "Methodological Criticisms of Parapsychology"

Akers's (1984) evaluation represents a landmark in parapsychological criticism. Akers, who holds a Ph.D. in social psychology, once worked as a parapsychologist in Rhine's laboratory and knows the contemporary scene from the inside. He employed a systematic and explicit method both for the selection of experiments to include in his sample and for the grading of each experiment on each of his critieria. He chose both the areas of systematic research and the particular representatives of each area to represent the evidence at its best.

After his careful selection procedure, Akers arrived at a sample of 54 ESP experiments. These had all been cited in the *Handbook of Parapsychology* or other parapsychological literature as exemplars of the evidential data-base. The selection was restricted to studies in which significant results had been claimed for a sample of relatively unselected percipients. He excluded unpublished reports, studies that were reported only as abstracts or convention reports, and studies that were exploratory or preliminary to a stronger replication. He also excluded experiments that had produced scores in the wrong direction ("psi missing"): "The final sample of 54 experiments is fairly complete. If it is not inclusive, it is at least representative of findings in altered state and personality research."

Akers then screened all his 54 studies sequentially through each of his several criteria to see how many could pass all of them. On each criterion, Akers assigned a flaw only if, in his opinion, the defect was sufficient to account for the above-chance hitting actually reported. He then concluded: "Results from the 54-experiment survey have demonstrated that there are many alternative explanations for ESP phenomena; the choice is not simply between psi and experimenter fraud. . . . The numbers of experiments flawed on various grounds were as follows: randomization failures (13), sensory leakage (22), subject cheating (12), recording errors (10), classification or scoring errors (9), statistical errors (12), reporting failures (10). . . . All told, 85 percent of the experiments were considered flawed (46/54)."

In other words, only 8 of the 54 experiments—all of which were selected to be best cases—were free of at least one serious flaw on Akers's criteria. But he points out a number of reasons to be concerned about the adequacy of even these "flawless" studies. "There were eight experiments conducted with reasonable care, but none of these could be considered as methodologically strong. When all 54 experiments are considered, it can be stated that the research methods are too weak to establish the existence of a paranormal phenomenon."

Akers's conclusion is especially damaging to the case for psi because he leaned over backward to give the benefit of doubt to the experimenters. Akers was not judging whether the experiment had met standards of scientific acceptability but, rather, was assigning flaws if a given deficiency *by itself* was sufficient to have accounted for the results. And, finally, Akers did not consider the possibility that *combinations* of deficiencies, each in themselves being insufficient, might have been more than enough to account for the reported findings.

Hyman's Critique of the Ganzfeld Experiments

Although Akers's and my critiques were conducted independently, and although our samples and procedures differed in many important ways, we came to essentially the same conclusion. In spite of claims for both scientific confirmation of psi and repeatability within certain systematic lines of research, both Akers and I concluded that the best contemporary research in parapsychology does not survive serious and careful scientific scrutiny. Parapsychology is not yet ready to bring its case before the general scientific public.

My systematic critique began in the summer of 1981. I had been urged by a number of individuals, including both parapsychologists and nonparapsychologists, to critically assess the evidence for psi. I hesitated to undertake such a task. I had neither the resources nor the time (nor, for that matter, the inclination) to attempt to survey all the relevant published reports. Even if I restricted my sampling to the four major parapsychological journals, the total number of published studies, say, in the past 20 years, would be too much for one outside critic to read in any reasonable amount of time.

With further urging, I considered various possibilities for selecting a more manageable number of experiments to examine. I rejected, after some consideration, the alternative of taking a random sample from the major journals during the past 20 years. Such a sample would provide a sense of the average quality of the typical experiment, but this is not really what is required. I suspect the average experimental report in any area of scientific research is mediocre. At any rate, we do not judge the state of a given field of research by looking at the average or typical research report. Rather, we judge the field and the plausiblity of its claimed laws and phenomena on the basis of the best contributions.

My final decision was to look for a research program in parapsychology that consisted of a series of experiments by a variety of investigators and that was considered by parapsychologists as especially promising. I quickly discovered a systematic body of research that fit this requirement. This research program was based on the ganzfeld/psi paradigm.

The word *Ganzfeld* is German for "total field." It is used to describe a technique in the study of perception that creates a visual field with no inhomogeneities. The motivation for creating such a visual field stems from certain theoretical predictions of Gestalt psychology. A recently developed and simple procedure for creating such a ganzfeld is to tape halves of ping-pong balls over the eyes of subjects. A bright light is then directed to the covered eyes. The percipient experiences a visual field with no discontinuities and describes the perceptual effect as like being in a fog.

The parapsychologists became interested in the ganzfeld when it was reported that subjects who experience this procedure quickly enter into a pleasant, altered state. They adopted it as a quick and easy way to place percipients into a state that they felt would be conducive to the reception of psi signals. In a typical ganzfeld/psi experiment, the percipient has the ping-pong balls taped over his eyes and then sits in a comfortable chair or reclines on a bed. In addition to a bright light shining on the halved ping-pong balls, white noise or the sound of ocean surf is fed into the percipient's ears through earphones.

After 15 minutes or so in this situation, the percipient is presumed ready to receive the psi signal. An agent in another room or building is given a target that is randomly selected from a small pool, say, of four pictures (the pool of pictures has been selected, in turn, by random means from a large collection of such pools). The agent concentrates or studies the target during a predetermined time interval. At the same time the percipient, isolated in a relatively sound-proof chamber, freely describes all the associations and impressions that occur to him during the sending interval.

At the end of the session the halved ping-pong balls are removed. The pool of pictures for that trial, including the target, are brought to the percipient. The percipient then indicates, by ranking or rating, how close each of the items in the pool are to the impressions that occurred to him or her during the ganzfeld session. The most typical scoring procedure classifies the outcome as a "hit" if the percipient correctly judges the actual target as closest to the ganzfeld impressions.

In the typical experiment a pool of four target candidates is used on each trial. Over a number of trials, the percipients would be expected to achieve hits on 25 percent of the trials just by chance. If the actual rate of hitting is significantly above this chance level, then it is assumed, given that proper experimental controls have been employed, that ESP has probably operated.

Charles Honorton, the parapsychologist who first published a ganzfeld/psi experiment (Honorton and Harper 1974) and who also has strongly defended the paradigm as "psi conducive," responded to my request for cooperation by undertaking to supply me with copies of every relevant report between 1974, the date of the first published ganzfeld/psi experiment, and the end of 1981, the year I made the request. In January 1982, I received a package containing 600 pages of reports on the ganzfeld/psi experiment.

The experiments in the data-base given to me for examination were extracted from 34 separate reports written or published from 1974 through 1981. By Honorton's count, these 34 reports described 42 separate experiments. Of these, he classified 23 as having achieved overall significance on the primary measure of psi at the 0.05 level. This successful replication rate of 55 percent is consistent with earlier estimates of success for this paradigm, which ranged from 50 to 58 percent (Hyman 1985). Approximately half of these experiments had been published in refereed journals or monographs. The remainder had appeared only as abstracts or papers delivered at meetings of the Parapsychological Association. The studies were made by 47 different investigators, many of them prominent members of the Parapsychological Association.

Before beginning my systematic evaluation, I read through all of the papers. During my reading I noticed some obvious departures from the ideal design. Some experiments clearly had not guarded against sensory leakage because the percipient judged the pool of items that contained the actual target previously handled by the sender or agent. In some experiments, the randomization of all targets was done by a needlessly crude technique like hand shuffling and in others no explicit randomization was used at all. Despite such obvious defects, my overall subjective impression was that many of the experiments seemed to use sophisticated and careful procedures.

My next step was to devise relatively objective categories of flaws to which I could assign the experiments. Eventually I came up with 12 formal categories of flaws. I noted other flaws, but I did not try to systematically assign experiments to them because they were more subjective or difficult to assign unambiguously. I read through each study a second time, this time very carefully, and noted which flaws, if any, each contained.

The results of this systematic survey caught me by surprise. The situation was much worse than my first subjective perusal had led me to believe. My first difficulty came in trying to determine how Honorton counted 42 different experiments. I finally realized that he arrived at this number by using inconsistent criteria for what would count as a separate experiment.

The original ganzfeld/psi experiment had consisted of a single experimental condition. All 30 subjects had been treated in identical fashion, each having been put through the same ganzfeld induction procedure. One question that must be answered is how to treat a new ganzfeld/psi experiment in which there is more than one experimental condition? In one experiment, for example, the percipients were all put through the ganzfeld induction procedure but were assigned to four different experimental treatments. In this case Honorton treated each separate experimental condition as an independent replication. (Honorton actually counted two conditions as relevant and discarded the other two as involving an atypical treatment.)

The principle seems clear enough. Each group of percipients who undergo ganzfeld induction and are treated alike constitutes an independent replication of the original ganzfeld/psi experiment. However, Honorton was not consistent. Some other reports with multiple conditions were treated as one experiment by simply pooling the data over the separate conditions.

What difference does it make? It turns out quite a bit! By his original count, Honorton obtained 23 successful experiments out of 42, for a success rate of 55 percent. By applying his first principle consistently to the same reports, I come up with 24 successful experiments out of 66, for a success rate of 36 percent. And when we add to this total the additional experiments, which were apparently unknown to Honorton but had been reported during this same time period, we get a success rate of approximately 33 percent. Other considerations, such as unreported experiments, make it likely that the actual success rate is much less than 33 percent.

But even a success rate approximating one-third is impressive if the percentage of successes expected by chance is truly the advertised 5 percent. I supply several arguments in my critique that strongly indicate that the effective rate is much higher than 5 percent and probably is in the vicinity of 25 percent or higher (Hyman 1983). Many of these arguments are based on the fact that several of the studies used multiple analyses and options, which effectively increase their chances of coming up with "significant" results. If an experimenter, for example, uses several different statistical tests, each having a 0.05 probability of succeeding by chance, the probability of getting at least one "significant" result among the different tests is much higher than the individual significance levels. If several different tests are independent, the actual probability of at least one "significant" outcome can be calculated. In practice, most of the separate tests are not independent. For some cases, I was able to use computer simulations to estimate the actual probabilities of getting a successful result. In other cases, however, the best that I could do was to compute reasonable upper and lower bounds.

The problem of multiple analyses is compounded as the number of experimental conditions within an investigation increases. In my critique I illustrated how the various options for one of the experiments, not necessarily the worst case, produced an effective chance level of close to 0.85. In other words, the experimenters were claiming a significant outcome of one of their tests of significance as if the chance baseline was 5 percent. In fact, they had an approximately 85 percent chance to come up with a "significant" finding.

All told, I found six categories of flaws relating to multiple testing of data in these experiments. A flaw was assigned on each category if an experiment carried out the additional testing without compensating for it in the calculation of significance levels. Only 3 of the 42 studies were free of flaws in all six multiple-testing categories.

Implicit and uncompensated multiple options plague almost all scientific investigations. To some extent the biases and the tendencies to mistake accidental patterns as real, which is an all-too-human temptation, are diluted by the fact that the phenomena under investigation are robust, lawful, and easily replicable in other laboratories. But in parapsychology such robustness, lawfulness, and replicability do not exist. The problem is therefore much more serious, because the entire evidential base could possibly be the product of looking for psi to occur in a number of ways and places but not suitably taking into account how such degrees of freedom capitalize on accidental quirks of nature.

Multiple testing was just one of a number of defects characterizing this data base. I also found a number of what I will call procedural flaws. Now it is true, as parapsychologists often assert in their defense, that after the fact one can always dream up ways in which a given experiment has not met some ideal. Some critics, for example, have foolishly gone out on a limb and stated the criteria they would accept as a solid argument for psi. When Helmut Schmidt, for example, published his first experiments with random-event generators, many parapsychologists pointed out that his experiments had fulfilled the requirements specified by some of these critics. These same critics, who obviously were not about to announce their conversion to psi, promptly added additional criteria to their requirements. And, if Schmidt or some other parapsychologist now performs additional successful experiments that fulfill the new set of requirements, we can imagine these same critics generating additional criteria.

I have tried to avoid this tendency to generate criteria after the fact or to insist upon reasonable standards. In fact, in drawing up my formal list of flaws, I eliminated many from consideration only because, while desirable, they might appear post hoc and unduly demanding (such as insisting on having a skeptical magician observing each experimental trial). Instead, I deliberately used the standards that parapsychologists themselves have repeatedly insisted are the conditions that have to be met before they would accept the experiment as valid evidence for psi.

Some of the minimal standards that an adequate parapsychological experiment should meet can be derived form examining what the evidence for psi consists of. In all the laboratory experiments, this evidence consists of statistically significant deviations of the number of correct guesses (hits) from a chance baseline. Presumably, both parapsychologists and critics would agree that at least three elementary safeguards have to be met before such deviations can be attributed to psi:

1. Targets and conditions have to be randomized in such a way as to guarantee, on the chance hypothesis, that the resulting distribution of hits and misses will be consistent with assumptions underlying the statistical tests.

2. Given the underlying assumptions, the appropriate statistical tests have to be used in such a way as to guarantee that the assumed error rate is, in fact, the actual one.

3. Appropriate experimental controls have to be used to ensure that obvious possibilities for sensory leakage have been eliminated.

The first two safeguards are needed to make sure that apparent deviations are real rather than flukes of nature. The existence of multiple-testing options violates these safeguards. So does the use of inadequate randomization procedures, such as hand shuffling or relying upon intuitive arrangements. A number of subtle defects could also falsely inflate the assumed statistical significance. But I used only the most obvious categories in my scoring. Another defect would be the use of wrong statistical tests or making computational errors in applying the statistical procedures. Unfortunately such statistical mistakes could be detected in 29 percent of the experiments. And in only 26 percent was it clear that the randomization of targets was carried out by adequate means.

The possibility of sensory leakage can occur in a number of ways. Over half of the ganzfeld/psi experiments used a single target in such a way that either deliberate or unwitting sensory cues were available to the judge. In 24 percent of the experiments another clue might have been inadvertently provided by the order in which the pool of items was presented to the judge because no systematic procedure for randomizing the target among the other items was used. And 24 percent of the experiments were considered flawed on security grounds because they were conducted by a single experimenter or by inexperienced and unsupervised experimenters.

The standards I employed for judging the ganzfeld/psi experiments were neither esoteric nor subtle. The evidence for psi in parapsychological research is a statistically significant departure of the number of hits from the number expected by chance. And the standards I employed were those elementary and obvious safeguards that an investigator should use in order to ensure that the departures from chance are real and not due to ordinary sensory or physical causes. Yet not a single one of the 42 experiments in the ganzfeld/psi data base satisfied all of these elementary standards.

The existence of so many obvious flaws in the major systematic line of research in parapsychology is puzzling. I know that most of the authors of these studies not only are aware of the need to guard against such flaws but are certainly capable of conducting experiments that fulfill the minimum requirements one would expect of a parapsychological investigation. Certainly since the criticisms of the early Rhine experiments, every parapsychologist is aware that shuffling targets by hand is not only inadequate but unnecessary, because tables of random numbers and random-event generators are readily available. Yet, in this data-base, we find targets being shuffled by hand and other crude procedures being used to mix the targets among the foils. Even more disturbing is the seemingly casual disregard for the possibility of sensory cues.

My criticism in 1977 of the early ganzfeld experiments for inadequate randomization and the possibility of sensory leakage had no observable impact upon subsequent experiments in the same area (Hyman 1977b). This could be because I was an outsider and my criticism, although it was part of a dialogue with a parapsychologist, appeared in *The Humanist,* a publication not ordinarily read by parapsychologists. When J. E. Kennedy (1979a; 1979b), a parapsychologist, raised similar criticisms, however, his arguments did receive the attention of ganzfeld researchers.

Honorton (1979) defended the ganzfeld experiments in an interesting manner. He did not deny the existence of the defects that Kennedy and I had pointed out. Even though the possibility for sensory leakage existed in several ganzfeld experiments, Honorton argued that the critics had no right to claim that the experiments were "flawed" unless they could demonstrate empirically that the alleged defect actually accounted for the findings.

As just one example, Honorton examined the charge that the ganzfeld experiments that allowed for the possibility of sensory leakage were "flawed." According to his position, the critic does not have the right to call such experiments flawed unless he can demonstrate that this feature of the experimental design actually made a difference in the results. Honorton (1979) then reviews some experiments that suggested that subjects do not typically use subtle cues even when they are available. He then demonstrates that the degree of success among ganzfeld experiments that did not allow for sensory cueing is no different from the degree of success of those that did allow for such a possibility. "The handling cue hypothesis, therefore, must be rejected," he wrote.

Honorton's defense is interesting. A possible defect in the experimental design, according to this argument, can be charged against the experiment only if the critic can demonstrate that it could have accounted for the results. Here we have a confusion between supplying plausible alternatives and achieving scientific acceptability. Honorton's defense implies that a parapsychological experiment is licensed to depart from acceptable scientific standards as long as the critic cannot demonstrate that the departures are sufficient to account for the results. But this shifts the burden upon the wrong party. If the ganzfeld experimenter wants to claim scientific acceptability, he ought to be able to get results from experiments that are both designed and executed according to reasonable standards. The retrospective sanctification of poorly designed and executed experiments with plausible arguments as to why the departures from scientific practice should make no difference is hardly the way to achieve scientific respectability. The correct and only scientifically acceptable defense is to demonstrate that successful results can be obtained with properly designed experiments.

Honorton's defense is interesting also for its failure to explain why the ganzfeld experiments exhibited so many defects in the first place. Some internal evidence suggests reasons for the inadequacies of at least some of the experiments. These experiments are what I would call "retrospective experiments," because it appears that they were not originally intended to be formal investigations. One of the "experiments" was assembled, after the fact, from ganzfeld trials, each of which were originally conducted as demonstrations for the media. Another was originally a classroom demonstration that, admittedly, was published only because it had yielded interesting results. And some of the other experiments were initially begun as exploratory investigations.

Many of the investigators in this data-base probably considered their experiments as process-oriented rather than proof-oriented. And, when an experiment is conducted for examining the correlates of psi rather than trying to prove its existence, parapsychologists apparently believe that standards do not have to be as rigorous. K. R. Rao (1979) has stated this difference as follows:

> It might be appropriate at this time to clarify a situation that confuses many people. Those individuals who are neutral or skeptical about the existence of psi are primarily concerned about Type I errors and thus are interested only in the rigorous evidential value of each work. On the other hand, those of us who find the evidence convincing are more concerned with learning about the relevant variables. This leads us to be more concerned than skeptics about Type II errors and thus place more weight on work that may not be of the highest standards from an evidential point of view. The parapsychological literature should be evaluated with this in mind.

It could very well be that the ganzfeld/psi experiments "may not be of the highest standards from an evidential point of view" because the original investigators were conducting process-oriented research. Honorton and other parapsychologists who display the ganzfeld/psi paradigm as their major exemplar of the scientific case for psi make the mistake of trying to use exploratory and process-oriented research for purposes for which it was never intended. Somehow, by accumulating a number of individually defective experiments, Honorton and the other proponents believe they can create an ironclad proof of psi. This is an example of the "fagot theory," or bundle of sticks, that was once a mainstay of early arguments in psychical research.

What about Honorton's claim that an alleged defect cannot be called a "flaw" until it is shown to correlate with successful results? In agreement with Honorton's findings, I also found that the existence of possible sensory leakage was no greater among the successful than it was among the unsuccessful ganzfeld experiments. Nor did my other indicators of inadequate security correlate with significance of outcome. Most of the statistical and mutliple-testing indicators did not correlate with success either. However, inadequate randomization, incomplete documentation, errors in statistical tests, and inadequate safeguards during judging did correlate with successful results.

Does this imply that inadequate randomization contributes to the outcomes but inadequate security does not? Not at all. We cannot draw such conclusions from the correlations found among the assigned flaws and the results. Such findings, in themselves, can at best be treated as exploratory. And correlation, of course, does not always indicate causality. There are other reasons why, in this sample, neither absence nor presence of correlation can tell us if a given flaw did or did not contribute to the outcome.

Honorton's attempt to dismiss the flaws as irrelevant assumes that if a given defect, taken by itself, is insufficient to account for the results, then it cannot be called a "flaw." But defects do not occur in isolation. Typically others are present as well. And combinations of defects can possibly have large consequences even when the defects, taken individually, have almost none.

But the existence of the flaws, rather than taken as sufficient causes, can be looked upon as symptoms. When an experiment displays inadequate controls for sensory leakage and biased target sequences and uses inappropriate statistics, this strongly suggests that it was not originally intended to be a formal and confirmatory investigation. And it also suggests a casualness that is inappropriate for an investigation that is being asked to carry part of the burden for asserting the existence of phenomena that many scientists find difficult to believe.

As a result of my detailed examination of the claims for the ganzfeld/psi findings, I concluded my long report as follows:

The current data base has too many problems to be seriously put before outsiders as evidence for psi. The types of problems exhibited by this data base, however, suggest interesting challenges for the parapsychological community. I would hope that both parapsychologists and critics would wish to have parapsychological experiments conducted according to the highest standards possible. If one goal is to convince the rest of the scientific community that the parapsychologists can produce data of the highest quality, then it would be a terrible mistake to employ the current ganzfeld/psi data base for this purpose. Perhaps the Parapsychological Association can lead the way by setting down guidelines as to what should constitute an adequate confirmatory experiment. And, then, when a sufficient number of studies have accumulated which meet these guidelines, they can be presented to the rest of the scientific community as an example of what parapsychology, at its best, can achieve. If studies carried out according to these guidelines also continue to yield results suggestive of psi, then the outside scientific community should be obliged to take notice.

Conclusions

With the exception of the contemporary parapsychological literature, the evidence for psi reviewed in this paper comes from investigations that today's parapsychologists would not put before us as part of their strongest case for psi. Many of these parapsychologists may believe I was unfair in dwelling upon these castoffs from the past. But it is just the fact that the cases I have examined *are* now castoffs that brings up important questions about how to approach the contemporary evidence.

Each of the cases from the past that I have discussed was, in its own time, considered to be by the parapsychologists of that day an example of scientifically sound evidence for psi. It is only subsequent generations, for the most part, who have set the preceding exemplars aside. In some cases the reasons for the abandonment of what was once a foundation stone in the case for psi are clear. Subsequent investigators and critics found previously unrecognized defects in the studies or that strong suspicions of fraud were generated. Other experimental paradigms have disappeared from the data base for less obvious reasons.

Some previously successful paradigms have disappeared because they no longer seem to yield significant results. Others, such as the sheep-goats design, seem to have gone out of fashion. One major parapsychologist once told me that it seems to be the ultimate fate of every successful paradigm to eventually lose its ability to yield significant results. He believed this was related to the fact that psi depends both upon the novelty of the design and the motivations of the experimenter. At first a new paradigm generates excitement and optimism. But after it has been around for a while, the initial excitement and enthusiasm abates and the experimenter no longer communicates the original emotions that accompanied the paradigm when it was still relatively new.

But, whatever the reason, each generation's best cases for psi are cast aside by subsequent generations of parapsychologists and are replaced with newer, more up-to-date best cases. Not only does the evidence for psi lack replicability, but, unlike the evidence from other sciences, it is noncumulative. It is as if each new generation wipes the slate clean and begins all over again. Consequently the evidential data base for psi is always shifting. Earlier cases are dropped and replaced with newer and seemingly more promising lines of research.

The late J. G. Pratt (1978a), in challenging his parapsychological colleagues' hopes for a repeatable experiment, wrote:

> One could almost pick a date at random since 1882 and find in the literature that someone somewhere had recently obtained results described in terms implying that others should be able to confirm the findings. Among those persons or groups reflecting such enthusiasm are the S.P.R. Committee on Thought-Transference; Richard Hodgson (in his investigation of Mrs. Piper); Feilding, Baggally, and Carrington (in their Palladino investigations); J. B. Rhine (work reported in *Extra-Sensory Perception*); Whately Carington (in his work on paranormal cognition of drawings); Gertrude Schmeidler (in her sheep-goat work); Van Bussbach, and Anderson and White (in their research on teacher-pupil attitudes); the Maimonides dream studies; the Stepanek investigators; the investigators of Kulagina's directly-observable PK effects; researchers using the Ganzfeld technique; and the SRI investigators ("remote viewing"). One after another, however, the specific ways of working used in these initially successful psi projects have fallen out of favor and faded from the research scene—except for the latest investigations which, one may reasonably suppose, have not yet had enough time to falter and fade away as others before them have done.

When Pratt wrote those words in 1978, the "latest investigations" included the ganzfeld/psi experiments, the remote-viewing investigations, and the PK research using random-event generators. These would have been among the contemporary investigations that, given Pratt's pessimistic extrapolations, "one may reasonably suppose, have not yet had enough time to falter and fade away as others before them have done." Today, signs do seem to indicate that these seemingly "successful" lines of research may be much weaker than had been previously advertised.

However, as always, new and more promising lines of work seem to be ready to take their place. Honorton and his colleagues at the Psychophysical Research Laboratories (1983) in Princeton, New Jersey, seem to be developing a number of very promising lines of research. They have been developing a completely automated version of the ganzfeld experiment that eliminates many of the problems raised by my critique. They have also been perfecting a "transportable" experiment—one that can be carried out by any investigator who has access to an Apple personal computer. The experiment, also completely automated, is a variation of the random-event-generator paradigm but with a variety of built-in safeguards that apparently eliminate almost all the options for multiple testing.

Nearby, but completely independent of the work going on at the Psychophysical Laboratories, is the research on anomalous phenomena being carried out by Robert Jahn and his associates in the School of Engineering and Applied Science at Princeton University. For more than five years Jahn and his associates have been perfecting the instrumentation and experimental designs for conducting sophisticated variations of both the remote-viewing paradigm and the PK work with random-event generators. Although they have collected large data-bases for each of these paradigms, most of the work has been published only in technical reports (Nelson, Dunne, and Jahn 1984; Dunne, Jahn, and Nelson 1983). The reported findings do seem impressive, but they have yet to be described in sufficient detail for a full-scale evaluation. And, given both the scale of the effort and the sophistication of the methodology and instrumentation, it will be many years before adequate replications in independent laboratories will be possible.

As promising as this most recent work by Honorton and Jahn might seem to be, none of it has reached a stage where it is ready for a full-scale critical evaluation. Already, the sharp-eyed critic can detect both inconsistencies with previous findings in the same lines of research and departures from ideal practice. As the history of parapsychology teaches us, we will have to wait for several more years before we can adequately judge if somehow these latest efforts can avoid the fate that all their promising predecessors have suffered.

Perhaps, however, history does not have to repeat itself in all its depressing aspects. And I can see some encouraging signs of breaks with previous patterns in the way proponents carry out and defend their findings and the way critics respond.

Since its inception as an institutionalized undertaking, psychical research has suffered from the lack of relevant, informed, and constructive criticism. This particular deficiency seems to be changing. For one thing, the younger generation of parapsychologists have produced some internal critics who are both knowledgeable and effective. In addition to Akers, there are others, such as Susan Blackmore, Adrian Parker, Gerd Hövelmann, and J. E. Kennedy, who have recognized the current deficiencies of parapsychological research and have a strong commitment to raising the standards. Although it is still difficult to find external critics who are both informed and constructive, one can see some indications that this situation may also improve.

Another positive sign is the attempt to replace subjective, impressionistic evaluations of the parapsychological literature with more systematic, explicit assessments. Both Honorton and I have employed "meta-analysis" in our dispute over the adequacy of the ganzfeld/psi data-base. "Meta-analysis" is a term coined to describe the approach to reviewing a body of research that makes the various phases as explicit and quantitative as feasible (Glass, McGaw, and Smith 1981; Hedges and Olkin 1982).

> The approach to research integration referred to as "meta-analysis" is nothing more than the attitude of data analysis applied to quantitative summaries of individual experiments. By recording the properties of studies and their findings in quantitative terms, the meta-analysis of research invites one who would integrate numerous and diverse findings to apply the full power of statistical methods to the task. Thus it is not a technique; rather it is a perspective that uses many techniques of measurement and statistical analysis. [Glass, McGaw, and Smith 1981]

Meta-analysis is by no means a panacea. Much subjectivity remains on such matters as which studies to include in the sample, how to score the "effect size" or degree of success of a study, what variables to include, how to assign studies values on the variables, and what should be the sampling unit. In addition, many serious problems have to be resolved about how to cope with the fact that individual studies are not independent and the analyses are conducted "post hoc." Yet it has many advantages over the previously unstructured and subjective assessments. The reviewer is forced to make many more of his or her standards and procedures explicit. The resulting debate can be more focused and the specific areas of disagreement can be pinpointed. In addition, the use of quantitative summaries often brings out patterns and relationships that would ordinarily escape the unaided reviewer's cognitive limits.

Along with an increase in more informed and constructive criticism there are signs that the parapsychological community is responsive and willing to change both its procedures and claims in line with some of the criticisms. Although we still disagree strongly on many of the issues, Honorton has made many changes in his claims and procedures in a sincere effort to take some of my criticisms into account (Hyman 1985). At its 1984 annual meeting in Dallas, Texas, the Parapsychological Association formed a committee that will attempt to establish guidelines for the performance of acceptable experiments in various lines of parapsychological research. Along with Honorton and other major parapsychologists, the committee includes both internal critics like Akers and external ones like myself.

My survey of psychical research from the time of Hare and Crookes to the present has suggested that, although the specific evidence put forth to support the existence of psi changes over time, many of the key issues and controversies remain unchanged. The parapsychologists still employ similar strategems to seemingly enable them to stick to their claims in the face of various inconsistencies. And the critics, sharing many assumptions with the proponents, often behave in rather emotional and irrational ways. Indeed, the level of the debate during the past 130 years has been an embarrassment for anyone who would like to believe that scholars and scientists adhere to standards of rationality and fair play.

I suspect it is because the quality of the criticism has been so poor and its content so obviously irrelevant that parapsychologists have managed to live so long with the illusion that the quality of their evidence was so much better than it really was. Both Akers and I were surprised to find so many defects, relative to the most elementary standards, in the best of the contemporary parapsychological research. I know that some parapsychologists have been surprised at how far the current status of psi research departs from the professed standards of their field. And I would not be surprised to find that most of the rest of the parapsychological community, in the absence of systematic and critical surveys, has assumed that their data base was of a much higher quality than it in fact is.

All this suggests, as I have already indicated, that the parapsychological evidence, despite a history of more than 130 years of inquiry, is not ready to be placed before the scientific community for judgment. The parapsychologists' first priority should be to set their own house in order. They no longer can safely assume that the typical parapsychologist has the competence to correctly use statistical tools, design appropriate investigations, carry out these investigations correctly, and write them up properly. Indeed, the evidence suggests the opposite. Both the Parapsychological Association and the parapsychological journals have to establish explicit guidelines and minimal standards. Then they have to make sure that members of their profession become fully aware of these standards and recognize the necessity for living up to them.

At least two major parapsychologists have made statements that seem to reinforce the ideas I have expressed in the preceding paragraphs. John Beloff (1976) wrote:

> Positive results still largely depend on having the right subject, and a good card-guesser is no less of a rarity than a good medium in the bad old days of psychical research. Independent corroboration is still the exception rather than the rule, and it is now beginning to look as if we need not only the right subject but even the right experimenter. . . . I think that one thing we have got to recognize is that our field is so much more erratic, anarchic and basically subversive than we like to admit when we are engaged in one of our public-relations exercises.

And Martin Johnson (1976) put it in the following terms:

> I must confess that I have some difficulties in understanding the logic of some parapsychologists when they proclaim the standpoint, that findings within our field have wide-ranging consequences for science in general, and especially for our world picture. It is often implied that the research findings within our field constitute a death blow to materialism. I am puzzled by this claim, since I thought that few people were really so unsophisticated as to mistake our concepts for reality. . . . I believe that we should not make extravagant and, as I see it, unwarranted claims about the wide-ranging consequences of our scattered, undigested, indeed rather "soft" facts, if we can speak at all about facts within our field. I firmly believe that wide-ranging interpretations based on such scanty data tend to give us, and with some justification, a bad reputation among our colleagues within the more established fields of science.

Throughout this long chapter I have tried to give a feel for the sorts of arguments put forth in behalf of psychical phenomena during the preceding 130 years. At many points in this history, certain lines of research have been put before the scientific community as proof of psi. And, at each of these points, critics have rejected the evidence out of hand and have attempted to discredit the proponents by means that cannot be considered either fair or admirable. Both the proponents and their critics have worked within the framework of the False Dichotomy. Both have assumed that the evidence put forth either confirms psi or must be the product of either fraud or gross incompetence. The particular evidence put forth has changed with each new generation of parasychologists, but the False Dichotomy and its attendant drawbacks have persisted.

Probably the one most serious cause of the lack of progress in the ongoing debate has been impatience. Both proponents and critics want to resolve the major questions of psi now. This has led to the attempt to settle the matter once and for all with a single, crucial experiment. Such impatience has meant that the long years of controversy have actually settled nothing. If my assessment of the current situation is correct, there is no scientifically acceptable basis, as of today, for accepting the reality of psi. Today's most promising lines of inquiry have essentially begun from ground zero. We will have to wait patiently, and perhaps for several generations more, before we are in the position to judge if the parapsychologists have finally achieved their goal of finding and taming a phenomenon. As E. G. Boring (1955) put it in his assessment of parapsychology 30 years ago: "Parapsychology seems to me to be a normal ingroup phenomenon within that large body of activity that we call science. Of its importance in the developing scientific skein, posterity will be able to judge, and you cannot hurry history."

Perhaps the best comment I can make about the lack of cumulativeness and progress in this elusive quest is that these words are just as applicable today as they were 30 years ago.

References

Akers, C. 1984. Methodological criticisms of parapsychology. In *Advances in Parapsychological Research*, vol. 4, edited by S. Krippner, 112-164. Jefferson, N.C.: McFarland.

Asimov, I. 1976. *Asimov's Biographical Encyclopedia of Science and Technology*. New York: Equinox.

Barrett, W. F., E. Gurney, and F. W. H. Myers. 1882. Thought-reading. *The Nineteenth Century*, 2:890-900.

———. 1882-83. First report on thought-reading. *Proceedings of the SPR*, 1:13-34.

Barrington, M. R. 1974. Mrs. Albert's testimony: Observation or inference? *Proceedings of the SPR*, 56:112-116.

Beloff, J. 1974. Why I believe that Soal is innocent. *Proceedings of the SPR*, 56:93-96.

———. 1976. The study of the paranormal as an educative experience. In *Education in Parapsychology*, edited by B. Shapin and L. Colby, 16-29. New York: Parapsychology Foundation.

Boring, E. G. 1955. The present status of parapsychology. *American Scientist*, 43:108-117.

Broad, W., and N. Wade. 1982. *Betrayers of the Truth*. New York: Simon and Schuster.

Coover, J. E. 1917. *Experiments in Psychical Research*. Stanford, Calif.: Stanford University Press.

D'Albe, E. E. F. 1924. *The Life of Sir William Crookes*. New York: D. Appleton.

Davey, S. J. 1887. The possibilities of mal-observation and lapse of memory from a practical point of view: Experimental investigation. *Proceedings of the SPR*, 4:405-495.

Dingwall, E. J. 1962. *Very Peculiar People: Portrait Studies in the Queer, the Abnormal and the Uncanny*. New Hyde Park: University Books.

Dunne, B. J., R. G. Jahn, and R. D. Nelson. 1983. Precognitive remote perception. Technical Note, School of Engineering/Applied Science, Princeton University, August.

Faraday, M. 1853. Experimental investigation of table-moving. *The Athenaeum*, July 2: 801-802.

Flew, A. 1978. Parapsychology revisited: Laws, miracles and repeatability. In *Philosophy and Parapsychology*, edited by J. Ludwig, 263-269. Buffalo, N.Y.: Prometheus Books.

Gauld, A. 1968. *The Founders of Psychical Research*. New York: Schocken.

George, W. 1964. *Biologist Philosopher: A Study of the Life and Writings of Alfred Russel Wallace*. New York: Abelard-Schuman.

Giere, R. N. 1979. *Understanding Scientific Reasoning*. New York: Holt, Rinehart, and Winston.

Glass, G. V., B. McGaw, and M. L. Smith. 1981. *Meta-Analysis in Social Research.* Beverly Hills, Calif.: Sage Publications.

Goldney, K. M. 1974. The Soal-Goldney experiments with Basil Shackleton (BS): A personal account. *Proceedings of the SPR,* 56:73-84.

———. 1975. Obituary: Dr. S. G. Soal, M.A., D.Sc. *Journal of the SPR,* 48:95-98.

———. 1978. Statement [appended to B. Markwick's "The Soal-Goldney experiment with Basil Shackleton: New evidence of data manipulation"]. *Proceedings of the SPR,* 56:278.

Gurney, E. 1888. Note relating to some published experiments in thought-transference. *Proceedings of the SPR,* 5:269-270.

Gurney, E., F. W. H. Myers, and W. F. Barrett. 1882-83. Second report on thought-transference. *Proceedings of the SPR,* 1:70-89.

Gurney, E., F. W. H. Myers, and F. Podmore. 1886. *Phantasms of the Living.* London: Trubner's.

Gurney, E., F. W. H. Myers, F. Podmore, and W. F. Barrett. 1882-83. Third report on thought-transference. *Proceedings of the SPR,* 1:161-181.

Hall, G. S. 1887-88. Reviews of the *Proceedings of the English SPR,* July, 1882, to May, 1887, and of *Phantasms of the Living. American Journal of Psychology,* 1:128-146.

Hall, T. H. 1963a. Florence Cook and William Crookes: A footnote to an enquiry. *Tomorrow,* 11:341-359.

———. 1963b. *The Spiritualists: The Story of Florence Cook and William Crookes.* New York: Garrett Publications. Reprinted as *The Medium and the Scientist: The Story of Florence Cook and William Crookes.* Buffalo, N.Y.: Prometheus Books, 1985.

———. 1964. *The Strange Case of Edmund Gurney.* London: Duckworth.

Hansel, C. E. M. 1966. *ESP: A Scientific Evaluation.* New York: Scribner's.

———. 1980. *ESP and Parapsychology: A Critical Re-Evaluation.* Buffalo, N.Y.: Prometheus Books.

Hare, R. 1855. *Experimental Investigation of the Spirit Manifestations, Demonstrating the Existence of Spirits and Their Communion with Mortals: Doctrine of the Spirit World Respecting Heaven, Hell, Morality, and God. Also, the Influence of Scripture on the Morals of Christians.* New York: Partridge and Brittan.

Hasted, J. B. 1981. *The Metal-Benders.* London: Routledge and Kegan Paul.

Hasted, J. B., D. Bohm, E. W. Bastin, and B. O'Regan. 1976. Experiments on psycho-kinetic phenomena. In *The Geller Papers,* edited by C. Panati, 183-196. Boston, Mass.: Houghton Mifflin.

Hedges, L. V., and I. Olkin. 1982. Analyses, reanalyses, and meta-analysis [review of *Meta-Analysis in Social Research*]. *Contemporary Educational Review,* 1:157-165.

Hixson, J. 1976. *The Patchwork Mouse.* New York: Doubleday.

Honorton, C. 1967. Review of C. E. M. Hansel, *ESP: A Scientific Evaluation. Journal of Parapsychology,* 30:76-82.

———. 1977. Psi and internal attention states. In *Handbook of Parapsychology,* edited by B. B. Wolman, 435-472. New York: Van Nostrand Reinhold.

——. 1978. Psi and internal attention states: Information retrieval in the ganzfeld. In *Psi and States of Awareness*, edited by B. Shapin and L. Coly, 79-90. New York: Parapsychology Foundation.

——. 1979. Methodological issues in free-response psi experiments. *Journal of the American SPR*, 73:381-394.

——. 1981. Beyond the reach of sense: Some comments on C. E. M. Hansel's *ESP and Parapsychology: A Critical Re-Evaluation. Journal of the American SPR*, 75:155-166.

Honorton, C., and S. Harper. 1974. Psi-mediated imagery and ideation in an experimental procedure for regulating perceptual input. *Journal of the American SPR*, 68:156-168.

Hyman, R. 1976. Review of *The Geller Papers. The Zetetic (Skeptical Inquirer)*, 1:73-80.

——. 1977a. Psychics and scientists: "Mind-Reach" and remote viewing. *The Humanist*, 37 (May/June):16-20.

——. 1977b. The case against parapsychology. *The Humanist*, 37 (November/December):47-49.

——. 1980. Pathological science: Towards a proper diagnosis and remedy. *Zetetic Scholar*, 6:31-39.

——. 1981. Scientists and psychics. In *Science and the Paranormal*, edited by G. O. Abell and B. Singer, 119-141. New York: Scribner's.

——. 1983. Does the ganzfeld experiment answer the critics' objections? In *Research in Parapsychology*, edited by W. G. Roll, J. Beloff, and R. A. White, 21-23. Metuchen, N.J.: Scarecrow Press.

——. 1984-85. Outracing the evidence: The muddled "Mind Race." *Skeptical Inquirer*, 9:125-145.

——. 1985. The ganzfeld psi experiment: A critical appraisal. *Journal of Parapsychology*, 49(1):3-50.

Jahn, R. G. 1982. The persistent paradox of psychic phenomena: An engineering perspective. *Procedures of the IEEE*, 70:136-170.

Johnson, M. 1976. Parapsychology and education. In *Education in Parapsychology*, edited by B. Shapin and L. Colby, 130-151. New York: Parapsychology Foundation.

Kennedy, J. E. 1979a. Methodological problems in free-response ESP experiments. *Journal of the American SPR*, 73:1-15.

——. 1979b. More on methodological issues in free-response psi experiments. *Journal of the American SPR*, 73:395-401.

Kottler, M. J. 1974. Alfred Russel Wallace, the origin of man, and spiritualism. *Isis*, 65:145-192.

Marks, D., and R. Kammann. 1980. *The Psychology of the Psychic*. Buffalo, N.Y.: Prometheus Books.

Markwick, B. 1978. The Soal-Goldney experiments with Basil Shackleton: New evidence of data manipulation. *Proceedings of the SPR*, 56:250-277.

Mauskopf, S. H., and M. R. McVaugh. 1980. *The Elusive Science: Origins of Experimental Psychical Research*. Baltimore: The Johns Hopkins Press.

May, E. C., B. S. Humphrey, and G. S. Hubbard. 1980. Electronic system perturbation techniques. *SRI International, Final Report*, September 30.

McConnell, R. A. 1954. Review of *Modern Experiments in Telepathy*. *Journal of Parapsychology*, 18:245-258.

Medhurst, R. G. 1968. The fraudulent experimenter: Professor Hansel's case against psychical research. *Journal of the SPR*, 44:217-232.

————, ed. 1972. *Crookes and the Spirit World: A Collection of Writings by or Concerning the Work of Sir William Crookes, O.M.,F.R.S., in the Field of Psychical Research*. New York: Taplinger.

Moore, R. L. 1977. *In Search of White Crows: Spiritualism, Parapsychology, and American Culture*. New York: Oxford University Press.

Mundle, C. W. K. 1974. The Soal-Goldney experiments. *Proceedings of the SPR*, 56:85-87.

Murphy, G. 1971. The problem of repeatability in psychical research. *Journal of the American SPR*, 65:3-16.

Murphy, G., and R. O. Ballou. 1969. *William James on Psychical Research*. New York: Viking.

Nelson, R. D., B. J. Dunne, and R. G. Jahn. 1984. An REG experiment with large data base capability, III: Operator related anomalies. Technical Note, School of Engineering/Applied Science, Princeton University, September.

Nicol, F. 1972. The founders of the SPR. *Proceedings of the SPR*, 55:341-367.

Palfreman, J. 1976. William Crookes: Spiritualism and science. *Ethics in Science and Medicine*, 3:211-227.

————. 1979. Between scepticism and credulity: A study of Victorian scientific attitudes to modern spiritualism. In *On the Margins of Science: The Social Construction of Rejected Knowledge*, edited by R. Wallis, 201-236. Staffordshire, England: University of Keele.

Palmer, J. 1978. Extrasensory perception: Research findings. In *Advances in Parapsychological Research*, vol. 2: *Extrasensory Perception*, edited by S. Krippner, 59-243. New York: Plenum Press.

Panati, C., ed. 1976. *The Geller Papers: Scientific Observations on the Paranormal Powers of Uri Geller*. Boston, Mass.: Houghton Miffin.

Pfungst, O. 1911. *Clever Hans*. New York: Holt.

Podmore, F. 1963. *Mediums of the 19th Century*, 2 vols. New Hyde Park, N.Y.: University Books.

Pratt, J. G. 1974. Fresh light on the Scott and Haskell case against Soal. *Proceedings of the SPR*, 56:97-111.

————. 1978a. Prologue to a debate: Some assumptions relevant to research in parapsychology. *Journal of the American SPR*, 72:127-139.

————. 1978b. Statement [appended to B. Markwick, "The Soal-Goldney experiment with Basil Shackleton: New evidence for data manipulation"]. *Proceedings of the SPR*, 56:279-280.

Pratt, J. G., J. B. Rhine, B. M. Smith, C. E. Stuart, and J. A. Greenwood. 1940. *Extra-Sensory Perception After Sixty years*. Boston: Bruce-Humphries.

Price, G. R. 1955. Science and the supernatural. *Science*, 122:359-367.

Psychophysical Research Laboratories. 1983. Annual Report. Princeton, N.J.

Puthoff, H. E., and R. Targ. 1976. A perceptual channel for information transfer over kilometer distances: Historical perspectives and recent research. *Proceedings of the IEEE,* 64:329-354.

Rao, K. R. 1979. On "The scientific credibility of ESP." *Perceptual and Motor Skills,* 49:415-429.

Rhine, J. B. 1935. *Extra-Sensory Perception.* Boston, Mass.: Bruce Humphries. (Originally published in 1934 by the Boston Society for Psychical Research.)

———. 1956. Comments on "Science and the supernatural." *Science,* 123:11-14.

Rhine, J. B., and J. G. Pratt. 1957. *Parapsychology: Frontier Science of the Mind.* Springfield, Ill.: C. C. Thomas.

Roberts, F. S. 1975. An alternative theory. *Journal of the SPR,* 48:87-89.

Rogo, D. S. 1975. *Parapsychology: A Century of Inquiry.* New York: Dell.

Scott, C., and P. Haskell. 1974. Fresh light on the Shackleton experiments? *Proceedings of the SPR,* 56:43-72.

Shepard, L., ed. 1978. *Encyclopedia of Occultism and Parapsychology.* Detroit: Gale Research.

Sidgwick, H. 1882-83. Presidential Address. *Proceedings of the SPR,* 1:7-12.

Soal, S. G. 1956. On "Science and the Supernatural." *Science,* 123:9-11.

Soal, S. G., and F. Bateman. 1954. *Modern Experiments in Telepathy,* 2nd ed. New Haven: Yale University Press.

Stevenson, I. 1974. The credibility of Mrs. Gretl Albert's testimony. *Proceedings of the SPR,* 56:117-129.

Targ, R., and K. Harary. 1984. *The Mind Race: Understanding and Using Psychic Abilities.* New York: Villard Books.

Targ, R., and H. E. Puthoff. 1977. *Mind Research: Scientists Look at Psychic Ability.* New York: Delacorte.

Tart, C. 1976. Review of *The Magic of Uri Geller* by the Amazing Randi, *The Geller Papers,* edited by Charles Panati, and *My Story* by Uri Geller. *Psychology Today,* July: 93-94.

Thouless, R. H. 1974. Some comments on "Fresh light on the Shackleton experiments." *Proceedings of the SPR,* 56:88-92.

Turner, F. M. 1974. *Between Science and Religion: The Reaction to Scientific Naturalism in Late Victorian England.* New Haven: Yale University Press.

Wallace, A. R. 1875. *On Miracles and Modern Spiritualism: Three Essays.* London: James Burns.

———. 1878a. Dr. Carpenter on Spiritualism. In *The Psycho-Physiological Sciences and Their Assailants,* edited by A. R. Wallace, J. R. Buchanan, D. Lyman, and E. Sargent, 7-36. Boston: Colby and Rich.

———. 1878b. Psychological curiosities of skepticism: A reply to Dr. Carpenter. In *The Psycho-Physiological Sciences and Their Assailants,* edited by A. R. Wallace, J. R. Buchanan, D. Lyman, and E. Sargent, 37-55. Boston: Colby and Rich.

———. 1906. *My Life: A Record of Events and Opinions.* New York: Dodd, Mead.

Wassermann, G. D. 1975. The soul of Soal. *Journal of the SPR,* 48:89-91.

West, D. J. 1978. Letter to the editor. *Journal of the SPR,* 49:897-899.

Wolman, B., ed. 1977. *Handbook of Parapsychology.* New York: Van Nostrand Reinhold.

Zöllner, J. C. F. 1976. *Transcendental Physics.* New York: Arno Press. (Reprint of 1888 edition published by Colby and Rich, Boston.)

2

The Search for a Demonstration of ESP

C. E. M. HANSEL

Any act is conditional on underlying processes. Visual identification of an object requires both the use of the eyes and that light is reflected from the object. Parapsychologists claim that some people have the ability to perform such acts as identifying objects when the conditions normally assumed to be necessary for their execution are absent. Such behavior they call extrasensory perception, or ESP.

If people can act in this way new processes have to be admitted as underlying brain activity and the manner in which organisms interact with the environment. The existence of ESP would thus be of profound significance not only to the understanding of human behavior but also to science in general. It would signify that there are underlying processes in nature so far undiscovered that permit ESP to occur. ESP is possible or impossible depending on whether or not such processes exist.

Parapsychologists—or psychical researchers, as they were formerly called— started their inquiries by investigating unusual phenomena reported in everyday life and in the séance room. An early investigation of this nature was carried out by Michael Faraday in 1852.

Faraday was concerned with the supposed ability of people sitting around a table with their fingertips resting on it to receive messages from departed spirits. He accepted the fact that the table moved and created the taps, but he was suspicious of the theory advanced by the proponents of table tapping that the movements were due to the receipt of messages from the spirit world. He thought it more likely that those around the table caused the movement by exerting pressure with their fingertips.

Having ascertained that taps were produced when an acquaintance of his was sitting alone at the table, Faraday devised a method of detecting any force imparted by his friend's fingers to the table. He constructed a measuring device consisting of layers of wax between small pieces of card to indicate when pressure was exerted by the sideways displacement of one card on the other. When these were placed between the fingers and the table he found that pressure had been exerted on the table, although his friend said that he was unaware of having done so. Faraday thought that the pressure might have been exerted involuntarily. To investigate this possibility, he constructed a device whereby his friend could see when he was exerting pressure by watching the movements of a pointer. Under this condition movement of the table ceased and the taps were no longer heard.

Faraday's method of investigating this psychic phenomenon was to consider the obvious normal explanation to account for movements of the table. He then conducted his experiment to see whether this explanation applied. Having found that pressure had been exerted by the sitter, there were then two possibilities. Either the sitter had been giving the table a push, or he had applied pressure without having been aware of doing so in anticipation of its movement. In Faraday's second experiment, he eliminated one possibility and thus established a more likely cause of the table's movements.

Faraday was investigating movements of a table and seeking to find their cause. He did this by checking on more likely processes than communication from spirits. In an ESP experiment, what is observed may be high scores that are not likely to arise by chance. If the high scores disappear following removal of some likely everyday cause, in the manner that the table stopped moving when Faraday's sitter no longer applied pressure, then a likely explanation is available without invoking spirits. Experiments in which subjects fail to obtain high anti-chance scores following other experiments where high scores were present are thus of particular importance when seeking the cause of high scores in experiments.

ESP investigations have been of two main types. In the first type, the performance of a particular individual is studied. Here the subject has developed a procedure with which he claims to be able to demonstrate his psychic ability. He may not agree to modifications or alternative procedures required by the investigators. Any experimentation is then dependent on the extent to which the subject will do as he is asked by the experimenters.

The first two investigations reported by the Committee on Thought Transference set up by the Society for Psychical Research in 1882 were of groups of people who claimed to be able to demonstrate their psychic powers in this manner (Barrett, Gurney, and Myers 1882, 63). In each case confessions of fraud many years later indicated how easily investigators can be misled by simple tricks when they believe in the possibility of the processes under investigation (Blackburn 1908). They also indicate how the observations of critics are ignored.

The Smith-Blackburn investigation carried out in 1882 provided the main evidence for telepathy until Blackburn's confession of fraud in 1908. It appears that on two occasions when well-known critical scientists were invited to see

Smith and Blackburn in action precautions taken to prevent possible auditory or visual communication put a stop to the thought transference. Further tests showed "not the smallest response on the part of Mr. S to Mr. B's volitional endeavors. There was no more flashing of images into his mind. His pencil was idle. Thought transference was somehow interrupted" (Donkin 1907).

No mention was made of these observers, the tests they applied, or their effects in the report of the investigations. In the light of subsequent events, the fact that they introduced new safeguards and stopped thought transference should have been of greater significance to the Committee than the continued demonstration of telepathic abilities by Smith and Blackburn.

The second type of investigation takes the form of an experiment in which the design, method, and procedure are decided by the experimenters while the subject does as he is told to do and takes no other part in the experiment. The experiment may eventually lead to a set of conditions and a procedure with which a particular result is demonstrable. One fact evident in ESP experiments is that subjects are only successful in a fraction of their attempts. A satisfactory demonstration therefore requires a sufficient number of observations to ensure that failure is extremely rare.

For demonstrations of this nature, in the words of R. A. Fisher (1942, 16): ". . . We may say that a phenomenon is experimentally demonstrable when we know how to conduct an experiment which will rarely fail to give us a statistically significant result."

Such a demonstration has not been forthcoming. Rather, a large number of experiments have been reported that fail to be confirmed at the first attempt or as soon as obvious weaknesses are removed from them. The position has been clearly stated by John Beloff (1974, 9), of the University of Edinburgh, a former president of the Parapsychological Association:

> Before any claim, great or small, can be accepted definitely as a fact at least one or other of the following conditions must be met. Either we must be in a position to explain the phenomenon in question to an extent where we can predict when it should and when it should not occur or, failing any such theoretical understanding, we need overwhelming inductive grounds for believing that such and such procedures can be relied upon to produce such and such effects even though no one can say why this should be so. Only then can the particular observations and experiments upon which the claim is founded cease to have more than an historic interest and disputes about the honesty or competence of experimenters cease to be relevant. For at this point, it is open to any critic or doubter to try replicating the findings for himself.

A major investigation in which the investigators have made a large number of observations with a large sample of subjects and achieved a result that has astronomical anti-chance odds should be repeatable if the result has not been due to experimental error or trickery. If such an experiment fails to repeat, the cause of the original high scores must be sought.

In earlier surveys of the experiments the attempt has been made to isolate the best experiments for scrutiny (Hansel 1966; 1980). The best experiments in terms of anti-chance odds tend to be those in which tricks on the part of subjects or investigators are responsible for the results. If the experiments are rigorously designed to avoid experimental error and if ESP is nonexistent, trickery remains as the likely explanation.

While a satisfactory demonstration has not been forthcoming during a hundred years of research, there has been some agreement, first, on the manner in which the subject identifies targets and, second, on the ability of subjects to obtain high scores under clairvoyance and telepathy conditions. These two findings emerge in the research using symbols presented on cards as targets in clairvoyance and telepathy experiments.

Perception vs. Guesswork

Perception, in the normal sense of the word, denotes awareness of some object or event. Experiments on ESP almost invariably indicate that subjects are unaware of the symbol or object they are trying to identify and do not know when they are right or wrong. If this were not so, subjects would be able to demonstrate any ESP ability by achieving 100 percent successes on those targets that they attempted to identify and passing on the rest.

An exception to this has been reported by Russell Targ and Harold Puthoff, who tested the Israeli conjurer Uri Geller at the Stanford Research Institute (SRI). In their report published in *Nature* (Targ and Puthoff 1974), they describe tests under various sets of conditions in which Geller tried to make drawings similar to target drawings when either he or the target drawings were isolated in a Faraday Cage. Geller had some degree of success in 10 of 13 tests reported to have been made in this manner, but he passed in the 3 remaining tests, when for the first time each drawing was made by an independent scientist who made his drawing in private and kept charge of it until after Geller had been asked to make his attempt. These were the only tests among the 13 carried out in which a trick would have been impossible without the cooperation of the three independent scientists. On each of these three occasions, Geller declined to make an attempt.

In another of the experiments reported in *Nature*, Geller attempted to identify the uppermost face of a die after it had been shaken in a small box. The conditions were hardly experimental, as it is likely that Geller himself had had a say in the procedures to be adopted, but the investigators were presumably in a position to ask Geller to make a further attempt following a success and to take any further precautions that they thought necessary. They reported that Geller had 8 successes in 10 attempts and passed on the remaining 2 occasions. According to Targ and Puthoff, only the 10 trials were made. But Geller was present at SRI over an 18-month visit, and the tests with dice were said to have taken place at the start of his visit. It is difficult to believe that after such an astounding result the investigators should have lost interest and not asked Geller to make further attempts. If they did so and Geller refused to cooperate, that was an important feature and it should have been mentioned in the report.

Clairvoyance vs. Telepathy

A further feature of experiments on ESP at one time generally accepted was the ability of subjects to score equally well in clairvoyance and telepathy conditions. The research findings on these two processes leading to this conclusion will first be considered.

Clairvoyance is the simplest form of ESP, in that only a single individual is involved. It may be defined as the acquiring of information about some object or event without the mediation of the senses.

Experiments on clairvoyance were reported in 1884 by the French physiologist Charles Richet (1888). He enclosed playing cards in opaque envelopes and asked a subject who had been put under hypnosis to identify them. His subject is said to have been highly successful in a series of 133 trials, but when she performed before a group of scientists in Cambridge her powers deserted her. She is reported to have recovered her ability on her return to Paris (Rhine 1977, 26).

The following year J. M. Peirce and E. C. Pickering (1888) reported an experiment in which they tested 36 subjects over 23,384 trials under clairvoyance conditions, but they did not obtain significantly above-chance scores.

Following a gap of many years, in which the emphasis was on telepathy, in 1929 an experiment was reported by Ina Jephson (1929), a Council member of the Society for Psychical Research. Jephson used 240 subjects who tested themselves in their own homes. Instructions were sent by post asking each subject to complete 25 trials guessing the identities of playing cards, but making only 5 attempts on any one day. The subject was instructed to take a pack of playing cards, shuffle it, and draw out a card at random keeping it face down. He had to guess the card, record his guess, and then write against it the actual value of the card followed by the suit. He replaced the card in the pack and repeated the whole operation until he had recorded five trials. In this manner he completed five attempts on each of five days. The 240 subjects thus completed a total of

1,200 sets of 5 trials, giving 6,000 trials in all.

The results were assessed in terms of the chances of the card (1/52), its number (1/13), suit (1/4) and color (1/2) being correct. The 6,000 guesses produced 245 complete identifications as against the chance number of 115, giving enormous anti-chance odds. High above-chance scores were also obtained for number, suit, and color.

It was suggested by Dr. S. G. Soal, a lecturer in mathematics at London University and a member of the Society for Psychical Research, that three sources of error might have been present in Jephson's experiment: (1) the use by some subjects of old packs of playing cards, some of which the subject by constant use might have learned to recognize through markings on the backs; (2) careless manipulation of the cards, which may have resulted in the subject getting information on color or suit, possibly via reflections from a polished table; (3) the carrying out by some subjects of more than five sets of guesses on a particular day and then sending in the results of the best set.

Precautions were taken to exclude these forms of error in a further experiment (Besterman, Soal, and Jephson 1931) carried out by Jephson, Soal, and Theodore Besterman, the research officer of the Society for Physical Research. A large number of playing cards with plain backs were placed in blue envelopes that exactly fitted the cards. The envelopes were of such a nature that they could not be rendered transparent by strong light, X-rays, or solvents, such as alcohol, nor could they be opened without leaving traces. They bore on both sides the impress of the Society for Psychical Research's stamp. As an added precaution the whole operation of preparing targets and checking results was supervised by a fourth experimenter—Colonel Dick. The envelopes were sealed and sent to 559 percipients in batches of five in five successive weeks.

A total of 9,469 guesses showed no trace of any extra-chance factor. It was then clear that the original result obtained by Miss Jephson was not repeatable even though more than twice the number of subjects were tested in the repeat experiment.

The second experiment appears to have been sufficiently well designed to eliminate experimental error. It is then remarkable that no further use was made of this type of design. In terms of methodology, the conducting of the two experiments by members of the Society showed a definite advance on what had been done before and on most of what has gone on since. First, it indicated how data could be obtained from a large group of subjects using simple methods in an informal manner. Second, it tested the hypothesis that the investigators who were testing themselves were involuntarily affecting the scores. In the same way that Faraday had done, the investigators removed a possible cause of an unusual phenomenon, having thought of a more likely explanation for the high scores.

An important feature of the second experiment was the inclusion of the military gentleman, Colonel Dick, as a fourth investigator to supervise the other investigators and ensure that they followed in full the procedure as planned.

Until 1931, the main experimental evidence relating to clairvoyance indicated that subjects attempting to identify symbols on cards held at close range displayed no ability to do so in the absence of sensory information. A simple technique for testing subjects had been made available, but it was not considered necessary to continue the research in this manner.

Telepathy may be defined as a hypothetical process whereby one person receives information about another person's thoughts or experiences without the mediation of the senses. Thus in telepathy experiments a second person acts as agent or sender.

The first experimental investigation of telepathy using a group of subjects and playing cards for targets was reported by John E. Coover (1917), professor of psychology at Stanford University, in 1917. He used 105 guessers and 97 senders in a series of 10,000 trials. Coover sat with the sender in one room, and the guesser was situated in an adjoining room. The door between the two rooms was kept open. The targets consisted of playing cards 1 (ace) through 10 after the face cards had been removed. Before each guess was made Coover threw a die to decide whether the sender should see the card or not. The trials on which the card was not seen by the sender constituted a control series, in which telepathy was not possible. The remaining trials formed the experimental series, where telepathy was theoretically possible because a second person saw the cards. Sources of experimental error due to the manner in which targets were selected would be present equally in the experimental and the control series.

Coover had stated that he would require odds against chance of at least 50,000 to 1 to convince him that telepathy was possible. In the event, the difference in scores between the two groups was not significant at even the 0.05 level. From this it was concluded that no support was forthcoming for the hypothesis of telepathy.

A further experiment using playing cards was reported in 1927 by G. H. Estabrooks (1927), a graduate student in the Department of Psychology at Harvard. He used Harvard students as subjects, selecting those who were "positively interested." Estabrooks acted as experimenter and sender, with the guesser in an adjoining room. A total of 2,300 trials was conducted. In the initial three series, subjects were highly successful in terms of the suit of the card, but when they were sent to a more distant room with better insulation for a fourth series scores dropped to chance level.

Estabrooks stated at the end of his report that further tests were being made by his assistant at Springfield College, Springfield, Massachusetts. According to J. B. Rhine (1977, 31), who was in the Psychology Department at Harvard at that time, "Estabrooks' 'telepathy' experiment succeeded for him but was said to have failed the next year when repeated by an assistant."

Estabrooks (1927) made an observation regarding subjects that is of interest in relation to the experiments that Rhine started the following year. He wrote: "Another point is the very interesting fact that with practice a certain type of man can be weeded out beforehand. The very worst type of man for an experiment of this kind is the instructor in psychology; second only to him is the graduate student in the same subject. They simply cannot attack the problem in the proper spirit but insist on criticising the experiment and, much worse, reacting to it as they think it should be reacted to, and not as they are told to react."

The following year, Rhine accompanied William McDougall when he moved from Harvard to set up a department of psychology at Duke University. Rhine's first ESP experiment was concerned with a telepathic horse called Lady Wonder (Rhine and Rhine 1929). He then carried out tests on telepathy and clairvoyance using cards with symbols depicted on them. The experimenter acted as sender in telepathy experiments or merely held the cards face downward in clairvoyance experiments. Rhine tested children using numbers 0 to 9 as targets without discovering a single child whose performance warranted further investigation.

After that, in the fall of 1930, an experiment was conducted in collaboration with K. E. Zener, of the Department of Psychology. Three types of symbols were employed: numbers (0-9), letters of the alphabet, and cards containing five different symbols (star, square, circle, plus sign, and wavy lines) that had been suggested by Zener. A total of 1,600 trials was conducted with scores at chance level with each type of symbol (Rhine 1934).

It is remarkable that after this, when Zener dropped out of the research leaving Rhine to his own devices, results came in thick and fast. By 1934, Rhine had found that among the 14 graduate students in the Psychology Department, 6 had ESP ability to a marked extent; one had been reported to have the ability; and the remaining 7 had not been tested. The 6 high-scoring subjects achieved results indicating, without need for statistical analysis, that something other than guesswork was involved. These graduate psychology students at Duke were obviously quite different from those at Harvard.

Rhine found that in clairvoyance conditions it was unnecessary to isolate the target card from the pack. A pack of 25 Zener cards was shuffled, cut, and placed face down in front of the subject, who then recorded his guesses for the cards starting with the top card and proceeding down through the pack. After he had recorded his guesses they were checked against the targets and produced high above-chance scores.

It was discovered that a modification could be made when using the down-through technique. If the cards were shuffled after the subject had recorded his guesses, scores were still above-chance. This resulted in the discovery of "precognition" (Rhine and Pratt 1962, 57).

Rhine came to the conclusion that subjects did equally well under clairvoyance and telepathy conditions. R. H. Thouless (1935), noting this conclusion, suggested that a small overall above-chance score when combining the control and experimental series in Coover's experiment was due to clairvoyance operating in the control series. Since that time it has been supposed by many parapsychologists that Rhine's conclusion was correct. If the agent or sender is redundant and is omitted from ESP experiments it is far easier to arrange foolproof conditions owing to the ease with which targets can be kept secret.

Attempts to Repeat Rhine's Experiments

In his first book, *Extra-Sensory Perception,* published in 1934, Rhine produced what he claimed to be overwhelming evidence for ESP. In the following years, a number of psychology departments repeated his experiments in the attempt to confirm his results.

The first experiment of this nature was reported by W. S. Cox (1936) of Princeton University. His 132 subjects produced 25,064 trials when attempting to guess the suits of playing cards. Cox's conclusion was: "It is evident from the above results and computations that there is no evidence of extrasensory perception either in the 'average man' of the group investigated or in any particular individual of that group. The discrepancy between these results and those obtained by Rhine is due either to uncontrollable factors in experimental procedure or to the difference in the subjects."

Failure to confirm Rhine's findings was also reported from four other psychology departments in the United States (Adams 1938; Crumbaugh 1938; Heinlein and Heinlein 1938; Willoughby 1938). In Britain, S. G. Soal reported a similar failure to confirm the findings. Since Rhine had had little difficulty finding subjects and had voiced the opinion that about one in five of the population had ESP ability, the contrary findings using large groups of subjects were difficult to account for. Rhine came to the conclusion that the presence of critics affected the subjects and removed their ESP ability.

The 1940 Review of Experiments

In 1940, *Extra-Sensory Perception After Sixty Years* was published (Pratt et al. 1940). Its authors were Rhine and three other members of the Parapsychology Laboratory together with a professor of statistics at Duke. Experiments reported since 1882 were listed and those were isolated that could withstand all the counter-hypotheses to ESP put forward by critics. Three of the experiments carried out in Rhine's laboratory were included among those that survived this test: They were: (1) The Pratt-Woodruff experiment (Pratt and Woodruff 1939); (2) the Pearce-Pratt experiment (Rhine and Pratt 1954); (3) the Owmbey-Zirkle series (Pratt et al. 1940, 163).

The result of each of these experiments left no doubt that something other than guesswork was involved. Each of them resulted in above-chance scores having odds of a million or more to 1.

It is now known that each experiment contained serious flaws that escaped notice in the examination made by the authors of *Extra-Sensory Perception After Sixty Years.*

In the case of the Pratt-Woodruff experiment, the aim of the investigators to exclude any possibility of either experimenter affecting the result was not realized (Hansel 1961b). In addition, examination of the original records shows that it is likely that the carefully planned procedure was not adhered to by one investigator part of the time. This investigator had merely to rearrange the order of five Zener cards hanging on hooks before each run of 25 guesses was attempted by a subject. But the experimental record shows that on many occasions the cards were left in position from run to run. It emphasizes the importance not only of having a carefully planned procedure but also of ensuring that it is carried out.

The Pearce-Pratt experiment, among other things, indicated the importance of having a planned procedure and describing it accurately. Various reports of the experiment contain conflicting statements so that it is difficult to ascertain the precise facts (Hansel 1961a).

The Owmbey-Zirkle experiment indicated the importance of reporting any deviations from the stated procedure. The whole result was dependent on very high scores during the first three days of the experiment. It was not revealed in *Extra-Sensory Perception After Sixty Years* that there had been a lapse in the experimental conditions at the start that had been removed at the end of the third day (Hansel 1980).

During the period 1935 to 1940, a large number of experiments reported in the *Journal of Parapsychology,* published by the Parapsychology Laboratory, claimed to provide positive evidence for ESP. But, as criticism mounted and experiments were tightened up, high-scoring subjects disappeared from the scene and even large groups of subjects failed to be effective. As Beloff (1977, 19) comments: "With the virtual disappearance of the consistent scorer, the work of the Duke Laboratory might have ground to a halt had it not been for the discovery of the differential scoring effect."

The differential scoring effect was discovered in 1946. It was found that when a group of subjects was divided into two subgroups according to scores on a personality test, scores were high in one subgroup and low in the other. This led to the discovery of "psi-missing." Below-chance scores were attributed to "psi-missing," and it was claimed that ESP was responsible for them.

Group Experiments

The best-known of the group experiments is that of Gertrude Schmeidler (1945), who divided subjects into "sheep" and "goats" according to whether they believed in ESP or not. In subsequent tests, the sheep scored high and the goats scored low. This type of result has also been found when subjects are divided into subgroups according to their classification in personality tests.

As the overall score when the two subgroups are combined is usually at around the chance level, it is clear that special attention must be paid to the forming of the subgroups to ensure that there is no possibility of subjects being changed over from one group to the other in the course of the experiment. That errors might have arisen in this manner is supported by the finding that the experiments have not provided a repeatable demonstration and that investigators have failed to confirm their own results.

The sheep-goat effect was also not confirmed in extensive tests carried out for the U.S. Air Force (Smith et al. 1963). The four investigators—William R. Smith, Everett F. Dagle, Margaret D. Hill, and John Mott-Smith—approached the research having been impressed by the statement made by British psychologist Margaret Knight (1950, 20) that ". . . It is a waste of time to conduct further laborious studies merely to demonstrate the occurrence of ESP. This has now been established beyond reasonable doubt."

A special apparatus, VERITAC, was constructed that generated random targets consisting of the numbers 0 through 9, registered the subjects' guesses, compared them with the targets, and registered scores. The subject and agent were seated at consoles in different rooms with a third room separating them. Telepathy, clairvoyance, and precognition conditions were tested. Thirty-seven subjects completing 500 trials in each condition gave a total of 55,500 trials. Each subject had been given an indirect probing interview that classified him as a sheep or goat before the tests were carried out.

It was found that neither the group of subjects as a whole nor any member of it displayed any ability for ESP of any variety, and the differences between sheep and goats were not significant.

Animal Experiments

Two further developments were introduced at Duke. The first of these was to employ lower animals as subjects in experiments; the second was to use automated methods of testing, as had been employed with VERITAC. It is of interest that Rhine had had considerable experience in animal experiments. Before he started his ESP research, he and William McDougall had conducted tests with mice and claimed to have shown that learning was transmitted from parents to offspring. These experiments were similar in some respects to the later ESP work—large numbers of observations yielding a statistically "significant" result to provide evidence for a highly unlikely process disputed by orthodox science. It will be recalled that Rhine's first experiment at Duke had been with the horse Lady Wonder. Later Helmut Schmidt, who in terms of experimental sophistication may be regarded as the successor to Rhine, reported an experiment with his cat.

Schmidt's Cat: One winter night Schmidt placed his cat in a cold garden-shed heated only by a 200-watt lamp. The temperature was around zero in the shed, and the cat tended to settle down near the lamp. Schmidt thought that the cat's "feeling of pleasure" when the lamp was on might be utilized to affect a binary randomizer that put the lamp on and off. The aim of the experiment was to see whether the cat's feeling of pleasure might affect the binary randomizer so as to cause the lamp to light for more than the 50 percent of the time expected from theory. According to Schmidt, when the cat was in the shed the lamp tended to be on more than the theoretical 50 percent of the time. When the cat was not in the shed the lamp was only on 50 percent of the time. The experiment was discontinued when the outside temperature had risen, and no further attempts appear to have been made to confirm the original observations.

Other experiments have confirmed this result with lizards (Schmidt 1970b). Perhaps the most remarkable finding was published by W. J. Levy (1971). He found that fertilized chicken eggs tended to keep themselves warm by turning on a heat lamp by means of psychokinesis.

Schmidt also experimented with cockroaches and claimed that in two experiments he had results with odds against chance of 143 to 1 and 8,000 to 1 that they had affected his electronic randomizer. The cockroaches received an electric shock when the binary randomizer produced a 1 and no shock when it produced a 0. They displayed "negative scoring," however, affecting the machine so that they received more shocks than would be expected by chance.

Precognitive Clairvoyance in Mice: The experiments referred to above were not on ESP but on psychokinesis; but further investigations were claimed to provide evidence that, rather than affect the operation of a lamp or electronic apparatus, mice could precognize clairvoyantly that they might receive a shock and behave so as to avoid it. The first of these experiments, reported in 1968, was later claimed to be the first repeatable demonstration. It took the form of an automated experiment on clairvoyant precognition in mice (Duval and Montredon 1968).

A mouse was placed in a cage. The floor of the cage was separated into two halves by a barrier over which the mouse could jump. An electric shock would be given at one side of the cage or the other according to a binary number generator. The idea here was not that the mouse would affect the randomizer but that it would jump over the barrier to avoid shock. It was claimed that the mice avoided shock using precognitive clairvoyance, giving anti-chance odds of 5×10^4 to 1. Two further experiments in France produced a similar result with odds against chance of 25 to 1 and 8×10^7 to 1.

Nine additional experiments reported by W. J. Levy working in conjunction with various other investigators confirmed the earlier results with anti-chance odds in each case greater than 20 to 1. What was claimed to be the start of a repeatable demonstration came to a halt when Levy was caught tampering with the printout on the apparatus so as to achieve high scores (Rhine 1974).

Schmidt's ESP Experiments

The binary randomizer used in the above-mentioned experiments was constructed by Helmut Schmidt (1970a), who in addition constructed machines for testing ESP and psychokinesis. The failure of a machine system to prevent an investigator's rigging the results illustrates the fact that automation in itself is no substitute for experimental control. It may, on the other hand, simplify the task of the would-be trickster.

Various attempts had been made in the past to automate various aspects of ESP testing (Tyrrell 1936; Soal and Bateman 1954, 251; Kahn 1952). The first fully automated system using electronic apparatus was that of the team of VERITAC investigators mentioned above. Further experiments, using rather simpler machine methods, were conducted by Targ and Puthoff and by Schmidt. Schmidt's experiments have been claimed to provide the main evidence for ESP.

In 1969 Schmidt published details of research carried out at the Boeing Research Laboratories in which he found that subjects when tested on a machine were able to guess a target before its identity had been established by a process of random selection (Schmidt 1969a). His results were thus contradictory to those obtained by the VERITAC investigators. Schmidt's machine generated a random sequence of four targets. The subject had to predict which of the four targets would arise after he had pressed his button. The targets consisted of four lamps—blue, green, yellow, and red. Before each trial the lamps were unlit.

After the subject had made his choice and pressed the button, the lamp lit up, indicating whether he was right or wrong.

Random targets were produced by utilizing the unpredictability of quantum processes, in this case the unpredictability of the instant at which an electron would be emitted by a strontium-90 source. Following a delay of 1/1000th second, which lamp would light was decided by the length of time before the next electron was emitted. This stopped a free-running counter (1-4) operating at high speed. Thus the target had not been decided at the time the subject pressed his button.

Electromagnetic counters built into the machine recorded the numbers of trials and hits. Each counter was provided in duplicate, one counter being resettable before each test, the other being nonresettable and thus registering all trials that had been conducted on the machine when it was in circuit. These nonresettable counters provided the only safeguard on the machine to ensure that data was not selected by the experimenter. Thus, provided the machine was adequately sealed so that the counters could not be tampered with, anyone who wished to display precognition would have to "beat the machine" and produce a high above-chance score in relation to the total trials on the nonresettable counters. Means were provided for these counters to be switched in or out of circuit, but this would not enable above-chance scores to be obtained on them. This feature would have been useful when showing new subjects how to operate the machine.

Evidence that the machine could be beaten in this manner was not produced, owing to the fact that psi-missing occurred just about as frequently as psi-hitting. This was not so in the first preliminary experiment, but on this occasion no one appears to have made the necessary check of the counters. For the second experiment, there was a deficiency on the counters of only 23 hits in 20,000 trials. Here, one of the three subjects was a high scorer, getting +66 hits in 5,000 trials; the second, a low scorer, getting -86 hits in 5,000 trials; and the third subject scored +123 in 5,672 "high score" trials and -126 in 4,328 "low score" trials. He thereby had, according to Schmidt, 249 successes in 10,000 trials, making the overall score of "successes" for the experiment +401 in 20,000 trials.

In a further experiment on clairvoyance of the nonprecognitive variety, Schmidt (1969b) reported a deficiency of 44 hits in 15,000 trials. This consisted of 108 hits above chance from one group that was instructed to aim for high scores combined with 152 hits below chance from the same group of six subjects when instructed to aim for low scores. Further experiments on psychokinesis showed similar effects.

Even without the weaknesses outlined above, Schmidt's experiments could not provide evidence for ESP. The most important control required in any experiment is that of the experimenter. Replacing the Zener cards and scoring sheets used by Rhine with a machine makes little difference if the investigator is left to his own devices, since scores have to be transferred from the machine and used for further purposes. The experimental precaution eventually accepted by Rhine was that at least two experimenters each keep check on the other, and it is as essential with a machine as without it. The further precaution of having a supervisor taking the role taken by Colonel Dick in the Jephson experiments is also essential if note is taken of the ease with which one experimenter fooled others—not only in the Soal-Goldney series but also in the animal experiments and very likely in the Pratt-Woodruff and Pearce-Pratt experiments.

Experiments with Complex Targets

The experiments so far discussed use a fixed number of targets that are known to the subject and from which he makes his guess. In the animal experiments, there are two possible choices, owing to the fact that a binary randomizer is used. Other experiments with humans have used up to 52 choices with playing cards and down to 4 choices in the case of the machine experiments. This type of experiment has become less used in the past 20 years, while a method using complex pictures, such as art reproductions, has become more popular.

The investigations in 1882 on Smith and Blackburn used such materials. Smith attempted to reproduce simple objects and shapes drawn by one of the investigators and shown to Blackburn. In one test, the investigator drew a complex random pattern of lines, it being argued that it is a simple matter to communicate verbally about an object but almost impossible to describe verbally patterns of lines that cannot be named. But Smith was still highly successful. In this test, Smith's eyes were padded with cotton wool and a folded pair of kid gloves. These were bandaged with a thick dark cloth. His ears were filled with a layer of cotton wool and pellets of putty. His entire body and the chair on which he was seated were enveloped in two heavy blankets. Beneath his feet and surrounding his chair were thick, soft rugs to deaden and prevent signals by foot shuffles. Blackburn was brought back from the far end of a large room in which the drawing had been made and stood several feet behind the chair in which Smith was seated. Under these conditions, from beneath his shrouds, Smith was able to produce an almost line-for-line reproduction of the original drawing. Blackburn gave details of how he and Smith had carried out this trick in his confession. [See "Confessions of a Telepathist," Chapter 8 of this volume.]

The first full-scale attempt to use freely drawn objects in an experiment, permitting a statistical evaluation of the results, was made in 1938 by Whately Carington (1940), who held the Perrott Studentship at Trinity College, Cambridge University.

He used large groups of subjects who in their own homes attempted to make a drawing that would resemble a target drawing pinned to a door by Carington. He changed the drawing each night for ten nights in each series. A judge received the drawings and targets from more than 500 subjects without knowing the dates on which they had been drawn. Each drawing made by each subject was assessed against ten targets that included the target used on the day that the drawing was made, so that the result could be assessed statistically.

Carington thought that by using a large group of subjects and carrying out tests of this nature it would be possible to produce a repeatable demonstration. In fact, this was not so. From 1944 to 1945, four series of experiments similar to Carington's were carried out by the American Society for Psychical Research without success (Taves, Murphy, and Dale 1945). In 1946, Gertrude Schmeidler and Lydia Allison carried out another four experiments (Schmeidler 1948). Two of these tests used methods of assessing the drawings favored by Carington and gave chance results. One of the other experiments gave odds of 10,000 to 1 against chance.

Many years later, complex pictures were used in research at the Maimonides Medical Center, Brooklyn, New York, where a Dream Research Laboratory was set up in 1962 (Ullman et al. 1973). Since that time the techniques developed there have been employed extensively in other research, including ESP in dreams and in the ganzfeld situation.

Dream Research

The dream research experiments were of the telepathy type in which an agent viewed a complex picture—usually a postcard reproduction of a famous painting—while the subject was asleep in a laboratory some distance away. The subject was fitted with electrodes that enabled rapid eye-movements arising during dreaming to be monitored. An experimenter in an adjoining control-room awakened the subject when the rapid eye-movements stopped. The subject reported any dreams he or she had had. Then the subject might be questioned by the experimenter and allowed to go to sleep again and might be awakened several times in this way during the night. The whole operation was conducted on eight different nights using eight different target pictures.

The subject's performance was evaluated in two ways. The first method was for the subject to be given eight pictures, one of which was the target used. He then scored each of these pictures against his dream material. The pictures were then allotted ranks 1 to 8 depending on the scores achieved. Ranks 1-4 were then regarded as a hit and ranks 5-8 as a miss. Thus, although highly complex pictures were used rather than five known symbols as in the card experiments, the chances of getting a hit were 1 in 2 rather than 1 in 5.

The second method was to send the dream reports for the eight sessions together with the eight targets to an independent judge who ranked each of the eight targets against the set of dream reports and assessed hits and misses as in the first method.

The Ullman–Krippner Experiment: In this experiment (Ullman and Krippner 1970, 99), Dr. Robert Van de Castle, a well-known parapsychologist who had done well in exploratory tests, obtained hits on each of eight nights when assessed against the targets by an outside judge. The chances of such a result arising by chance are 1 in 256.

Before the sessions started, one member of the staff, designated the "recorder," prepared duplicate sets of targets by collecting 72 postcard-sized prints of famous paintings and dividing these into 9 target pools, each containing 8 pictures. Each target pool was given a code number and each picture was given a separate number. Each picture was then placed in an opaque envelope that the recorder signed across the flap. The signature was then covered with transparent tape. The eight envelopes in each pool were then randomly assigned numbers 1 to 8 and placed in a large opaque envelope.

The recorder then had, in duplicate, eight large envelopes each containing eight pictures, one set of which contained the targets that would be used on each of the eight nights. The other set of envelopes contained the duplicate set of pictures to be used when checking the subject's dream reports. The recorder had no contact with the subject.

The aim was to ensure that the target picture was not known to the subject or to the two experimenters until the subject had finished making his dream reports and that the agent would only learn the identity of the target after he had been isolated from all others taking part in the experiment.

The subject slept in the laboratory for eight successive nights. Each night one of the target pictures was seen by one of three female agents. The subject was allowed to choose the agent with whom he worked each night.

At each session, the subject was fitted with electrodes by an experimenter (E1) and then went to bed. Immediately afterward, the agent, together with another experimenter (E2), entered an office and selected a "random number." She counted down through the stack of large envelopes containing the large pools until she reached that number. She then selected another "random number" and counted down through the eight smaller envelopes inside the larger one to obtain the target. She gave the code number of the large envelope to the other experimenter (E2) so that the duplicate set of pictures could be located for judging purposes next morning.

The agent then went to her room 96 feet away from the subject, where she opened the envelope and obtained first sight of the target. According to the report, she was encouraged to write down her associations, to visualize the picture, to concentrate upon it, and to treat it in any other manner that would make its contents a dynamic part of her conscious processes.

During the night, the experimenters monitored the subject's sleep from an adjoining room and awakened him with a buzzer when his eye movements stopped. He then gave details of his dreams, after which he was asked questions about them by the experimenter. He might be awakened several times during the night.

After the final awakening, a "postsleep interview" was carried out in order to obtain any additional information. The subject was shown the set of eight pictures from the duplicate set left with E2 and asked to try to identify the target. He then ranked each picture with his dreams in the manner described above.

Tape recordings of the dream reports and interviews were mailed to a transcriber, and the transcripts were used by an outside judge for a supplementary evaluation. He ranked each of the eight target pictures used against the set of transcripts for the eight nights' dreams.

In this experiment it was found that the outside judge placed the target in the top half of the rankings for each of the eight nights, giving the 256 to 1 odds against chance occurrence.

One weakness in the design of this experiment was the manner in which the agent became aware of her target picture each night. It was important that only the agent should know the target and that no other person should be aware of it until the judging of targets had been completed. But an experimenter (E2) appears to have been with the agent when she opened her target envelope. In the report it states that before opening the envelope containing the target the agent was encouraged to write down her associations, etc., and then, "once this was done," there was no way that the agent could communicate with the experimenter or the subject without leaving the room and "breaching the conditions" of the experiment. If the experimenter (E2) had obtained knowledge of the target, the elaborate precautions to keep it secret were a waste of time.

There appears to have been little control over the activities of the main experimenter. It was essential that he had no contact with any other person until the material had been judged. The fact that the subject was questioned by the experimenter and that the experimenter could communicate in any way with the subject presented a further weakness.

Repetition of the Experiment: Confirmation of the results of this experiment was attempted by Edward Belvedere of the Dream Research Laboratory and David Foulkes of the University of Wyoming (Belvedere and Foulkes 1971). Foulkes was a psychologist interested in dream research who had not previously worked in parapsychology. For this experiment, 80 pictures were taken from magazines and formed into ten pools, which were arranged as in the first experiment. The small envelopes were numbered 1-8 and the large envelopes were now labeled A to J. This part of the procedure was carried out by E1, who handed over one set of ten envelopes (each containing eight pictures in smaller envelopes) to E2. E2 acted as "security officer." He stored the envelopes off the premises, and on the evening of the experiment randomly selected one of the large envelopes containing its eight pictures and took it to the laboratory.

At the laboratory the agent watched E3 attach the electrodes to the subject. E4 then conducted the subject to his bedroom. When the subject was in bed, E3 received the large envelope containing the large pool from E2—who had come to the laboratory after receiving a signal from E3 that the subject was in bed. E3 checked the signature and seal on the envelope and then retained the envelope for delivery to the agent after she had been locked in her room for the night. E3 conducted the agent to her room, where he gave her the large envelope containing the night's target pool. The agent was instructed not to open the envelope until E5 had delivered a slip bearing a randomly selected number indicating which of the pictures contained in the small envelopes was to be used as the night's target. E5 did not enter the room but pushed the slip under the door and then left the building. He retained a duplicate of each night's number, and it was later checked that the agent had opened the right envelope. E5 selected the number with replacement so that the same number could arise more than once. E2 selected his number so that a target pool would only be used once.

The agent was situated in a suite of rooms well away and on a different floor from the subject's room. The building was locked. The agent's door was locked. Tape seals were attached to the windows and door by E3. These precautions were made to ensure that the agent could not leave her suite and return without detection.

The subject was locked in his room and monitored continuously on a polygraph as well as through the intercom system by E3, who was in a control area next to the bedroom. The subject signaled the agent through a one-way buzzer when she was to start viewing the target. The agent indicated that she had received the signal by turning a switch that put a light on in the control room. At the end of a period of rapid eye movements, E3 signaled E4, who was in a room adjacent to the control area, so that E4 could awaken the subject. He also signaled the agent so that she would know that the dream period had ended. The agent indicated receipt of the message by turning off the switch that controlled the signal lamp in the control area. Details of dreams as reported by the subject were tape-recorded and postdream interviews were carried out by E4. After each report the subject was allowed to indicate any idea he had about the nature of the target picture.

The subject was awakened at 7:00 A.M., and E4 removed the electrodes. Meanwhile, E2 had delivered the duplicate pool of pictures to E3, who verified that the seal and signature were intact. E4 took these materials into the subject's room and placed the tape-recorder in position there. The subject then ranked the eight pictures for their similarity to his dreams. To do this he could play back the tape recordings that he had made during the night of his own reports of his dreams.

The agent was not released from her suite until the evaluations had been completed and were in E4's possession. E3 checked the seals of the agent's suite and also checked that only one of the eight envelopes in the target pool had been opened. He also checked that the envelope opened corresponded to the number on the slip delivered by E5 to the subject. He then conducted the agent to the subject's room, where, in the presence of E2, E3, and E4, the target was ascertained. E3 and E5 later verified that the agent's random number corresponded to that held by E5.

The correspondence between dreams and targets was assessed by the subject and by two independent outside judges, using the ranking procedure. The finding was that neither the subject nor the judges matched targets with dreams at significantly above the chance level. The subject assigned three hits and five misses (i.e., one hit less than expected by chance); judge 1 assigned three hits and five misses; judge 2 assigned two hits and six misses when judging only on the basis of dreams and four hits and four misses when also taking into account the subject's associations.

It will be noted that even the complicated procedure employed in this repeat experiment left some loopholes, e.g., the manner by which the agent turned a switch to signal back to the control room meant that the precautions to isolate her left a channel of communication open. But in fact, the precautions taken were enough to remove any supposed ESP.

Repeat of a Further Experiment: An attempt was made to confirm the result obtained in another experiment, reported by Krippner and Ullman together with three other investigators, in which Van de Castle had also obtained eight successes in eight nights.

In this case, Foulkes and Belvedere joined the original team of investigators and improved the experimental conditions. Again, the original result was not confirmed. The subject failed to score significantly above the chance level.

These experiments are of particular interest since, in the first case, a high-scoring subject was tested by independent investigators who improved the experimental conditions; in the second case, the original investigators were joined by additional investigators who had shown themselves to require sound experimental conditions, and again the original subject was used.

It might therefore be expected that further workers using this type of experiment would have learned something from the results and have attempted to produce reasonable conditions for avoiding experimental error in the future. This was not to be. Belvedere and Foulkes preferred to believe that extra precautions in their replication experiments inhibited the ESP powers of the subject rather than that they had removed a source of experimental error.

The Ganzfeld Experiments

It has been pointed out by H. J. Eysenck and Carl Sargent (1982, 81) that 20 experimenters have reported 55 ganzfeld type experiments, of which 27 "have given evidence of significant positive ESP scoring" and that only 2 have gone the "wrong way," significantly below chance. They write: "Once again, this massive majority in favour of positive ESP effects suggests that we are dealing with a 'lawful' phenomenon. Significant and positive ESP scoring has been reported by 12 different experimenters."

It is of interest to look at one of the 27 experiments that are claimed to give evidence of "significant positive ESP." This has not been selected as the weakest available from the literature, but it is one of the two experiments of this type for which the experimental report is available while this chapter is being written. It was carried out in the Psychology Department at Cambridge University by Carl Sargent together with Hugh T. Ashton, Peter R. Dear, and Trevor A. Harley (Ashton et al. 1981).

The experiment was remarkable in that the investigators also acted as subjects, and three of them also acted as agents in some of the sessions. Each investigator acted as subject for 8 sessions, in each of which he attempted one target. Three of the investigators also acted as sender or agent. Details are not given of who acted as experimenter but this was presumably one of the two investigators who was not occupied as subject or agent. From the description, it appears that a single experimenter and two of the other authors of the report were present, one of whom acted as subject and the other as agent. What the fourth person did or where he was located at the time is not stated. From the details given, the duties taken up by the four investigators are as shown in Table 1.

A plan of the rooms used is not provided, but it appears likely that one building contained a sound-attenuated studio with an adjoining control room and a further room down the corridor. This possibly was Carl Sargent's office. It will be referred to as the "office" in order to avoid confusion.

The second building contained a soundproof room that was used by the agent. This will be referred to as the "agent's room." In addition, a room is mentioned in the report to which the agent retired after completing his target

TABLE 1
Roles Taken by the Four Investigators

Subject	Agent	Number of Attempts	Experimenter	Ranks 1 2 3 4
HTA	CLS	8	TAH or PRD	4 2 1 1
TAH	CLS	6	HTA or PRD	3 2 2 1
	PRD	2	CLS or HTA	
PRD	TAH	4	CLS or HTA	2 3 1 2
	CLS	4	HTA or TAH	
CLS	TAH	8	HTA or PRD	5 0 3 0

viewing. This may have been in the second building.

The targets are referred to as "pictorial." Examples mentioned are: Manet's *Bar at the Folies Bergere,* Sheena McFall's *Water, Venus at her Toilet,* Botticelli's *Birth of Venus,* and a cartoon showing a fisherman who had just hooked a fish falling into a white-gray mountain stream. The targets were small enough to fit into an A4 envelope.

Twenty-four different sets of four pictures were "available for use in the experiment." The set to be used at each trial "was randomly determined with the constraint that no subject ever received the same set twice in the experiment."

Each of the 24 sets was in duplicate form. One set contained four pictures (labeled A, B, C, and D) in a single nonsealed A4 envelope labeled with the Set Number, e.g., Set 24. This set was later to be used for judging purposes. The other set, of identical pictures with identical labels, was employed by the agent. It is not clear whether these were also contained in an A4 envelope, but it would appear that each picture was individually sealed in an envelope labeled with the Set Number and its letter, e.g., 24A, 24B, 24C, 24D, and so on.

The reason for having these two sets of pictures was that the agent could take his set of four pictures to a distant room and there pick one of them at random to use as a target without other persons knowing which of the four pictures he had selected until after the subject had completed his report and the report had been assessed against each of the four pictures that were available in the envelope left behind in the office.

The subject was located in the sound-attenuated studio of its adjoining control room. The experimenter prepared the subject by fixing halved ping-pong balls with scotch-tape over his eyes and fitting him with earphones supplying white noise that had been passed through an amplifier using Slope and Bass filters. The experimenter and the agent then retired to the control room where the experimenter remained to view the subject through a one-way mirror and monitoring via headphones audible behavior as transmitted by a microphone feeding into a tape-recorder in the studio.

The precise instructions given to the subject are not stated, but presumably he had to report any imagery or thoughts that he experienced. When he started producing his report, it was recorded on a standard transcript sheet by the experimenter and during some sessions—not specified in the report—it was recorded on a tape-recorder.

The subject was allowed to decide his own time to produce his report. When he indicated to the experimenter that he had finished, the experimenter turned on the background lights. The subject was then given a post-session questionnaire to fill in. While he was occupied with this, the experimenter left the observation room and went to the office. He retrieved a set of four pictures in an unsealed A4 envelope that had been left there by the agent.

The experimenter brought this set to the subject together with the "session transcript" that he had written down. When he had completed his questionnaire, the subject had to judge each of the four possible targets to decide to what extent they matched the session transcript. For this purpose, each of the four pictures "was given an independent rating between 0 and 99." The experimenter appears to have been present during this part of the procedure, although this is not definitely stated in the report.

When judging was completed, the agent was summoned by telephone from a room to which he had retired after completing his target viewing. It is not stated where this room was located. It is possible that the agent had retired to the office, which was down the corridor from the studio. The agent then went to the experimental studio and "divulged the nature of the target."

At the start, after leaving the studio, the agent went to the office a little way down the corridor where he selected 1 of the 24 sets of cards. The actual procedure is not clear, but he is said to have used 1955 Rand Corporation tables subject to a nonrepetition proviso.

He then selected a small envelope from a set of 20 small envelopes, each of which contained either the letter A, B, C, or D. There were five of each variety of envelope. He cut the pack of small envelopes and then randomly selected a small envelope "using the Rand tables." If the report is complete, it would appear that the pack of small envelopes was at no time shuffled. It was merely cut. The letter contained in the small envelope drawn by the agent was later to decide which of the four pictures in the A4 envelope was to be used as the target.

The agent left the A4 envelope containing the four pictures in the office and took the duplicate set of "four sealed pictures" together with the small envelope containing the letter A, B, C, or D to an adjacent building where he took up a position close to a corridor telephone.

When the subject was ready to start, he gave the signal "Ready!" to the experimenter, who telephoned the agent and said "Go!" The agent then retired to the agent's soundproof room, opened the small envelope, extracted the slip of paper containing the letter A, B, C, or D, and opened the corresponding envelope from the set of four containing the pictures. He withdrew the target picture and viewed it for 20 minutes.

The method of judging the degree of success achieved by the subject was to rank the scores given to each of the four pictures in the envelope. The target then had a 1-in-4 chance of getting the highest score and being allocated rank 1. The total of 32 attempts—8 from each of 4 subjects—achieved 14 ranked 1 against the expected number of 8.

A further, more sensitive analysis was carried out that took into account all four rank positions.

Result of the Experiment: The report reads: "There were 24 [14?] direct hits in the experiment, a scoring rate of 44 percent (MCE = 25 percent) and a deviation of + 6 hits from the MCE value of 8. This deviation is significant (CR = 2.25, p = 0.012). Thus significant psi-hitting occurred in the experiment."

The value for direct hits appears to be a misprint since the total number of ranks 1 achieved according to the data given in the report and as reproduced in Table 1 above, was 14. The other values appear to be correct, however, giving odds against chance of about 80 to 1.

Weaknesses in the Design: (1) The Target Pictures. The report gives very little essential information about the manner of arranging the 24 sets of four pictures. Were these sets prepared specially for this experiment? Who prepared them? How were the contents of different sets decided? Was a record kept of the contents of the 24 envelopes and their serial numbers?

Each of the four investigators would become aware of the contents of most of these sets during the course of the investigation. He saw eight different sets of four pictures when he acted as subject, a further eight sets when he was experimenter, and eight single pictures when he was agent. If the same sets were used in earlier experiments, they are likely to have been known to at least some of those taking part.

The agent might also have felt tempted to take a look inside the unsealed A4 envelope containing the four pictures that were to be used when the subject's performance was judged. If they looked uninteresting, he might then have taken a different batch. It would no doubt be more interesting to gaze for 20 minutes at Manet's *Bar at the Folies Bergere* than at *Whistler's Mother*.

If we consider a particular set of four pictures, it will be clear that they will have different chances of scoring marks when assessed by the subject—even without any other assistance. A painting containing a large number of different namable features is likely to get more marks than a plain sheet of paper. A painting containing objects of interest to the subject may get more marks than one that is of little interest. Pictures containing nautical scenes might gain marks owing to the white noise that was being supplied to the subjects ears.

(2) Labeling of Pictures in Duplicate Set. The report reads: "Each of the 24 sets existed in duplicate form. One set contained all four pictures (labelled A, B, C and D) in a single non-sealed envelope. This set was used for judging purposes." It was unnecessary for the pictures to be labeled in any way, and the fact that they were labeled removed an essential security precaution.

(3) The Small Envelopes Containing the Key Letters. Each of the 20 small envelopes contained a slip marked with the letter A, B, C, or D. There were five of each letter. This meant that, after the agent had departed to view the target, inspection of the 19 small envelopes left in the office would reveal the identity of the letter being used by the agent to select the target.

No mention is made of any check of the key letter held by the agent against the letters in the 19 envelopes left in the office. The agent could have substituted some other letter, and as far as he knew the 20 envelopes may have each contained the same letter at the time he selected one of them.

(4) Judging the Pictures. The experimenter recorded the subject's utterances. He also appears to have been present when the subject went through the records to judge them against the pictures. A tape-recording was made during some of the sessions, but why not in all of them? It would have been far safer to have made tape-recordings throughout and for the subject to have judged the pictures for himself using the tape-recordings.

In a similar experiment reported by Sargent (1982) the following year, the description of the procedure when the pictures were being judged by the subject includes the following: "The subject and E1 went through the record of the subject's verbal utterances during the session and examined each response in relation to the four pictures, using an arbitrary but consistent scoring scheme to score points for each picture for each response. . . ."

If this is what happened, or if the experimenter was in any way able to intervene when the subject was making his decisions, it is clear that he could have had considerable effect on the outcome.

(5) Accessibility of the Key Letter. It is stated that after the subject had completed his attempts at the target he had to fill in a questionnaire. This part of the procedure is described more fully in the description of the later experiment. There it is stated that after the subject had been relieved from the ganzfeld situation he was given a questionnaire to complete while the experimenter "re-

trieved the duplicate set from my office which took approximately ten seconds."

Since the subject was occupied in another room with his questionnaire and the experimenter was unsupervised, the experimenter could have taken more than ten seconds if he had wished. He was then in a position to discover the letter taken by the agent by inspecting the remaining 19 envelopes. Since the four pictures, including the target, were in an unsealed envelope in the office, he was also in a position to inspect the target.

Owing to the fact that the duplicate set of four pictures and the 19 small envelopes were left in the office, it was essential that no other person could enter it during the experiment and that the subject and experimenter were isolated from other persons until the experiment was completed. No special precautions are mentioned in the report to ensure that other people in the building were not wandering around while the experiment was in progress.

(6) Accuracy of the Records. No mention is made of any precautions taken to ensure that the records were accurately recorded and maintained. The procedure was in sharp contrast to that of the Soal-Goldney experiment, where all record sheets were witnessed and signed by at least two experimenters and any observer present. In that experiment, duplicate records were made on the spot and one copy dispatched by post to Professor C. D. Broad in Cambridge. He kept them until the series of about 40 experiments was completed. It transpired that even those precautions were insufficient to stop Soal adjusting the score sheets. In the present experiments, all scoring and ranking should have been completed on standard forms, witnessed and signed by all present, copied and made public before the target was revealed by the agent.

(7) Checks on Procedure. No attention appears to have been paid to this important point. In the repeat experiments by Belvedere and Foulkes (1971) on ESP in dreams, the procedures were tightened up and checks were introduced to ensure that they were followed. There were no checks of this nature incorporated into the procedure of the present experiment. One of the three persons reported as being present acted as subject and was in no position to see or hear what was going on. A second of the three acted as agent and should have been locked in a room part of the time and isolated from all others taking part when he left it. But no check was kept of his activities. The third person acted as the main experimenter and was free to do more or less as he liked after he had prepared the subject and before he released him.

(8) Reference to Past Research. It is remarkable that the general design of this experiment was similar to that of the dream research, described earlier. Foulkes and Belvedere had improved the design of those experiments to eliminate possible sources of error. These necessary improvements were totally ignored and the investigators used a design that was more lax than that of the original dream experiment.

The Second Experiment: The other experiment reported the following year (Sargent 1982) used 20 visitors to the laboratory as subjects. Eight persons are mentioned in a footnote as co-experimenters. On three occasions the visitor supplied his own agent. An experimenter, E2, fitted up the subject and then took over the role of agent or accompanied the agent when he was supplied by the subject. A change seems to have been made in the preparation of the targets as the duplicate set of pictures in the unsealed envelope appear not to have been labeled. The description reads: "One copy of the set comprised the four different pictures contained in a single foolscap envelope (labelled, e.g., 'Set 20') and this was left in the office for judging purposes. The other copy comprised the four pictures individually sealed in A4 envelopes (labelled, e.g., '20A,' '20B,' '20C,' '20D'). This latter copy of the picture set was to be used by E2." In this case, however, evidence for ESP was absent. The report states: "The overall results were not significant by direct hit or by rank sum analysis."

Experiments of this nature are unlikely to provide a repeatable demonstration even if properly designed and executed. Although complex pictures are used as targets, the chances of getting a "direct hit," as it is called, are 1 in 4, owing to the method of judging results. If the target were mixed with ten others, as in Carington's experiment, there would be some possibility of achieving high anti-chance odds.

Difficulty in providing an adequate design arises from the fact that the agent has to know the identity of the target before judging takes place. If the agent is dispensed with and clairvoyance tests are used rather than tests for telepathy, most difficulties disappear, since pictures can be sealed up in such a manner that no one can know their identities until after the judging process is completed. If, as has been claimed in the past, subjects are as successful in clairvoyance conditions as in telepathy conditions, it is strange that such methods have not been employed.

It is not difficult to see why experiments of this nature should only be repeatable in about 50 percent of published cases, since parapsychologists adopt the 5 percent level for their criterion of significance. John Coover was wise when he decided that he would require odds of 50,000 to 1 to convince him that there was a case for telepathy. Had he achieved those odds, he might have expected that others would be able to confirm his findings.

Summary

In a hundred years of ESP research, a number of facts emerge: (1) In a small number of reported experiments, above-chance scores have been reported that are due either to ESP or to experimental error or trickery. (2) There has been a high incidence of trickery in parapsychology and a long history of inept experimentation. (3) A repeatable demonstration has not been forthcoming. (4) Results reported at low levels of confidence tend to be confirmed by parapsychologists at low levels of confidence.

The two main forms of experiment that have emerged from a hundred years of research are: (1) Machine experiments based on card-guessing with guessing against fixed odds at a small number of known targets. (2) Experiments with complex materials in which the subject has a free choice to report his experiences. Here he has fixed odds against his report being judged as having any resemblance to the target rather than to a small number of other pictures.

The first type of experiment enables a large number of observations to be made in a short space of time. It has been mainly successful under clairvoyance conditions, where psi-missing arises about as frequently as psi-hitting. Psi-missing was not present in experiments reported during the first 60 years of research, when machines were not used.

The second type of experiment has been used mainly under telepathy conditions. Psi-missing is not normally reported. Owing to the time taken for each trial and the method of scoring, results having very large odds against chance are not reported.

The main outstanding problem is to understand why experimental results as reported should be in disagreement with one another. Further understanding on this point is thought to require: (1) comparison of the design and procedures of experiments that fail to confirm a particular result with those that confirm it; (2) comparison of those experimenters who produce results claimed to be due to ESP with those experimenters who fail to do so.

Today ESP is no nearer to being established than it was a hundred years ago. The long history of trickery and inept experimentation, and the inability to confirm ambitious claims, serves to confirm the view held at the start by the majority of scientists that perception is mediated by the senses—that without sensory processes, perception is not possible. The parapsychologist should ensure, before publishing ambitious claims, that he has confirmed his own findings to such an extent that he can be reasonably certain others will be able to confirm what he has done.

References

Adams, E. T. 1938. A summary of some negative experiments. *Journal of Parapsychology,* 2:232-236.

Ashton, H. T., P. R. Dear, T. A. Harley, and C. L. Sargent. 1981. A four-subject study of psi in the Ganzfeld. *Journal of the SPR,* 51:12-21.

Barrett, W. F., Edmund Gurney, and F. W. H. Myers. 1882. First report on thought reading. *Proceedings of the SPR*, 1, Part 1:63.

Beloff, John. 1974. *New Directions in Parapsychology*. London: Paul Elek.

———. 1977. Historical overview. In *Handbook of Parapsychology*, edited by B. B. Wolman, 3-24. New York: Van Nostrand Reinhold.

Belvedere, E., and D. Foulkes. 1971. Telepathy and dreams—a failure to replicate. *Perceptual and Motor Skills*, 33:783-789.

Besterman, T. H., S. G. Soal, and Ina Jephson. 1931. Report of a series of experiments in clairvoyance conducted at a distance under approximately fraud-proof conditions. *Proceedings of the SPR*, 39:375-414.

Blackburn, Douglas. 1908. *John Bull*, December 5.

Carington, Whateley. 1940. Experiments on the paranormal cognition of drawings. *Journal of Parapsychology*, 4:1-134.

Coover, J. E. 1917. *Experiments in Psychical Research*. Palo Alto, Calif.: Stanford University Press.

Cox, W. S. 1936. An experiment in ESP. *Journal of Experimental Psychology*, 12:437.

Crumbaugh, J. C. 1938. An experimental study of extra-sensory perception. Masters thesis. Southern Methodist University.

Donkin, Horatio. 1907. *Westminster Gazette*, November 26.

Duval, P., and E. Montredon. 1968. ESP experiments with mice. *Journal of Parapsychology*, 32:153-166.

Estabrooks, G. H. 1927. A contribution to experimental telepathy. *Bulletin of the Boston SPR*, 5:1-30.

Eysenck, H. J., and Carl Sargent. 1982. *Explaining the Unexplained*. London: Weidenfeld and Nicolson.

Fisher, R. A. 1942. *The Design of Experiments*. Edinburgh: Oliver and Boyd.

Hansel, C. E. M. 1961a. A critical analysis of the Pearce-Pratt experiment. *Journal of Parapsychology*, 25(2):87-91.

———. 1961b. A critical analysis of the Pratt-Woodruff experiment. *Journal of Parapsychology*, 25(2):99-104.

———. 1966. *ESP: A Scientific Evaluation*. New York: Scribner's.

———. 1980. *ESP and Parapsychology: A Critical Re-evaluation*. Buffalo, N.Y.: Prometheus Books.

Heinlein, C. P., and J. H. Heinlein. 1938. Critique of the premises and statistical methodology of parapsychology. *Journal of Psychology*, 5:135-148.

Jephson, Ina. 1929. Evidence for clairvoyance in card guessing. *Proceedings of the SPR*, 38:223-268.

Kahn, S. D. 1952. Studies in extra-sensory perception. *Proceedings of the American SPR*, 25:1-48.

Knight, Margaret. 1950. Theoretical implications of telepathy. *Science News No. 18*. London: Penguin.

Levy, W. J. 1971. Possible PK by chicken embryos to obtain warmth. *Journal of Parapsycholgy*, 35:321.

Peirce, J. M., and E. C. Pickering. 1888. Appendices B and C. *Proceedings of the SPR*, 6:66-83.

Pratt, J. G., J. B. Rhine, Burke M. Smith, Charles E. Stuart, and Joseph A. Greenwood. 1940. *Extra-Sensory Perception After Sixty Years.* Boston: Bruce-Humphries.

Pratt, J. G., and J. L. Woodruff. 1939. Size of stimulus symbols in extra-sensory
perception. *Journal of Parapsychology,* 3:121-158.

Rhine, J. B. 1934. *Extra-Sensory Perception.* Boston: Bruce-Humphries.

———. 1974. A new case of experimenter unreliability. *Journal of Parapsychology,*
38:218-225.

———. 1977. History of experimental studies. In *Handbook of Parapsychology,* edited
by B. B. Wolman, 25-47. New York: Van Nostrand Reinhold.

Rhine, J. B., and J. G. Pratt. 1954. A review of the Pearce-Pratt distance series of
ESP tests. *Journal of Parapsychology,* 18:165-177.

———. 1962. *Parapsychology: Frontier Science of the Mind.* Oxford: Blackwell.

Rhine, J. B., and L. E. Rhine. 1929. An investigation of a mind-reading horse. *Journal
of Abnormal and Social Psychology,* 23:449-466.

Richet, Charles. 1888. Further experiments in hypnotic lucidity or clairvoyance. *Proceedings of the SPR,* 6:66-83.

Sargent, Carl. 1982. A ganzfeld GESP experiment with visiting subjects. *Journal of
the SPR,* 51:222-232.

Schmeidler, Gertrude R. 1945. Separating the sheep from the goats. *Journal of the
American SPR,* 39:47-50.

Schmeidler, Gertrude R., and Lydia W. Allison. 1948. *Journal of the American SPR,*
42:97-107.

Schmidt, Helmut. 1969a. Anomalous prediction of quantum processes by some human
subjects. Boeing Scientific Research Laboratories Document D1.82.0821, Plasma
Physics Laboratory, February.

———. 1969b. Clairvoyance tests with a machine. *Journal of Parapsychology,* 33:305.

———. 1970a. A PK test with electronic equipment. *Journal of Parapsychology,*
34:175-181.

———. 1970b. PK experiments with animals as subjects. *Journal of Parapsychology,*
34:257.

Smith, W. R., Everett F. Dagle, Margaret D. Hill, and John Mott-Smith. 1963.
Testing for extra sensory perception with a machine. Data Sciences Laboratory
Project 4610, May.

Soal, S. G., and F. Bateman. 1954. *Modern Experiments in Telepathy.* London: Faber
and Faber.

Targ, Russell, and Harold Puthoff. 1974. Information transmission under conditions
of sensory shielding. *Nature,* 251:602-607.

Taves, Ernest, Gardner Murphy, and L. A. Dale. 1945. American experiments on the
paranormal cognition of drawings. *Journal of the American SPR,* 39:144-150.

Thouless, R. H. 1935. Dr. Rhine's recent experiments in telepathy and clairvoyance
and a reconsideration of J. E. Coover's conclusions on telepathy. *Proceedings of
the SPR,* 48:24-37.

Tyrrell, G. N. M. 1936. Further research into extra-sensory perception. *Proceedings of
the SPR,* 44:99-166.

Ullman, Montague, and Stanley Krippner. 1970. Dream Studies and telepathy—an experimental approach. Parapsychology Monograph No. 12. New York: Parapsychology Foundation.

Ullman, Montague, Stanley Krippner, and Alan Vaughan. 1973. *Dream Telepathy*. New York: Macmillan.

Willoughby, R. R. 1938. Further card-guessing experiments. *Journal of General Psychology*, 18:3-13.

3

Psychokinesis: Fifty Years Afterward

EDWARD GIRDEN and ELLEN GIRDEN

Reliance upon the scientific method alone is the price of admissible evidence.
J. E. Coover, "Metapsychics and the Incredulity of Psychologists"

The controversy concerning experimental psychokinesis (PK), particularly at this time, requires some background about purported physical phenomena. The beginning of the modern period is associated with the organization of the Society for Psychical Research (London), which celebrated its one-hundredth anniversary in 1982. The issues are still highly controversial, dealing with such concepts as mediums, reincarnation, apparitions, poltergeists, telepathy, and telekinesis.

In the 1930s, when J. B. Rhine moved to Duke University, he used card tests for telepathy and then dice tests for telekinesis, which he renamed psychokinesis (PK). The experimental work was kept distinct from the qualitative purported psychical phenomena. The PK hypothesis, however unsophisticated, is psychological in nature. For Rhine, "There is a direct psychical effect on the fall of the dice . . . and [it] may be termed psychokinesis, or PK" (EG, 354). The variable was wishing, which is subjective, unobservable, and unmeasurable. For Rhine and J. G. Pratt, in everyday language, if ESP represents "mind to mind," PK refers to "mind to matter" (EG, 353). Rhine had noted that "PK implies ESP, and ESP implies PK" (EG, 354). These definitions are not precise and, in anticipation, can result in confusion—when dealing with animals, is it PK or ESP? One compromise was a statistical approach by McConnell, Snowden, and Powell: "The evidence for psychokinesis thus rests on two statistical effects . . . total deviation from chance expectancy of wished-for die faces, and the occurrence of extra-chance declines on scoring rates for these faces" (EG, 355).

In order to confine the references within reasonable limits, where possible citations will be quoted from the review (Girden, 1962a) from which the original sources can be obtained. The review will be identified in text as EG with the appropriate page reference.

Three periods can be roughly identified in the growth of PK studies. First, there was the rapid growth from 1934 through the 1950s with Rhine at Duke University. There was then a sharp drop in dice tests in the 1960s, as noted by C. E. M. Hansel (1980) and J. H. Rush (1977). R. G. Stanford (1977, 328) wondered, could "Girden's [1962a] negative review have taken a toll?" The review may or may not have been a factor, but there were other more serious events in the country at large that may have played a role. There were the discombobulated students and the sit-ins, symptoms of a time when collegial education was in disarray. These events were reflected in the decline in growth of psychology as measured in two of the colleges of the City University of New York (Girden 1985).

The 1960s were thus a transitional period, with a significant change in the 1970s concomitant with the deaths of the Rhines and Pratt. The major reduction in PK dice tests as such was replaced with an admixture of "psychics," "superstars," and experimental studies. It has been noted that studies with the superstars "have so far taught us little if anything about PK function, and the *supposed* [italics added] PK superstars have generally been difficult to get into the laboratory or keep there for systematic work" (Stanford 1977, 329). A marked increase in the psychics and qualitative phenomena coincides with the completion of the first century of the modern period. The wheel had completed a full circle. The early period has been covered in reviews in England by Denys Parsons (1945) and R. H. Thouless (1951). There has been the review by Girden (1962a; 1962b), with an intervening response by Gardner Murphy (1962). The review later formed the basis for a symposium (Girden et al. 1964). For a personalistic approach, see Pratt (1963).

Results

There has been considerable change since the earlier days, when dice guessing and placement tests predominated. In recent times, for example, there have been few dice PK tests. They have been replaced by game situations in relationship to luck, conscious effort as compared with intentions, and a variety of motivational and personalistic approaches. No attempt has been made here to obtain a representative sample. It is doubtful that it would be meaningful, for the period appears to be one of wide exploratory endeavors.

Mood

A random-number generator (RNG) was used to measure the possible influences of time of day or weather on the PK score of nine subjects. In neither of two experiments was a relationship obtained between PK and mood (André 1972). P. Wadhams and B. A. Farrelly (1968), testing themselves, used the same procedure with one of them obtaining a significant mood score in the morning, as had occurred in the earlier negative solo effort by Thouless (1951). However, S. W. Feather and L. E. Rhine (1969), acting as experimenters/subjects, in basically a "help-hinder test," reported that mood may have had a positive effect. This was a follow-up of Humphrey's report (EG, 367), but the overall test was insignificant. Of course, in these three tests, the unanticipated mood findings require independent replication.

Imagery

A. Levi (1979) made a preliminary report on the use of imagery with the goal to maximize hits on a Schmidt RNG. Subjects imagining high scores (goal oriented) did better than those imagining the tracking of the electronic impulses in the RNG circuit (process oriented). The control group scored close to chance. Similar results were reported by R. Morris, M. Nanko, and D. Phillips (1982) testing 16 subjects to bias a visual ring of lights produced by an RNG. The goal-oriented imagery subjects, visualizing only the final outcome, scored significantly above chance, whereas the process-oriented group was at chance level. An earlier reported study by Nanko (1981) indicated that subjects limited to goal-oriented instructions also obtained overall success.

A test of imagery attitude with 20 subjects was made by Stanford (1969). It consisted of a comparison of "visualization" and "associative activation of the unconscious." A careful test was conducted with an automatic die-casting machine. A vertical chute was interrupted by four rubber baffles, and there was a rubber floor on which the die landed. The subjects were divided into two groups of 10 each, and each group was given an opposite target sequence. For the visualization task, the first group thought of the chosen die face as it went down the chute. The other group freely associated in response to the desired die face. The latter group then was distracted from the PK situation by reading or looking at a book. There was some correlation between the different imagery attitudes of the subjects and the accuracy of their guessing. However, the score of 61 die hits for each of the two imagery groups was almost identical to the chance expectancy of 60 hits.

In a study by L. Braud and W. Braud (1979), visual feedback was the basic variable, and the subjects were to influence a Schmidt PK generator. For the first part, there was immediate feedback trial by trial, but there was no sensory feedback on the second half of the test. The "unexpected . . . absence of PK effect on feedback condition [was] inconsistent with a substantial body of experimental results . . . as well as the expectations of experimenters" (p. 28). There was also significant scoring in the absence of feedback on two repeated tests.

Relaxation and Concentration

J. Debes and R. Morris (1982), in an RNG PK test with continuous feedback, found that subjects given striving instructions scored significantly below chance, whereas those given nonstriving instructions scored above chance. Perhaps related is the significant calming reported for active (labeled "needy") persons but not for inactive persons. The PK calming effect was significantly greater for the active than for the inactive persons. It was concluded that nonstriving strategies are appropriate for both highly competitive and less competitive college subjects.

Charles Honorton and W. Barksdale (1972) tested muscle tension versus relaxation in an RNG PK situation, with reinforcement by appropriate suggestion. Six subjects were tested as a group by Honorton under the two conditions of tension and relaxation. The muscle tension set resulted in a significant positive score, whereas the relaxation suggestions resulted in an insignificant positive deviation. The second study, attempting to replicate the first one, with ten subjects tested individually, failed completely, the results being entirely insignificant. In a final test of Honorton alone, made by Barksdale, muscle tension "yielded a significant positive deviation," and the relaxation condition "yielded a significant negative deviation" (p. 212). The positive results in the first test were attributed to Honorton, who had been the experimenter. No subsequent study of these exploratory tests of Honorton or a repetition of the study itself has been carried out.

B. J. Steilberg (1975) compared the role of "conscious concentration" with that of "visualization" in forcing the dice to fall target-faces up in a PK task. In the first function, the subject attempted to "focus will power . . . inducing a tension of his muscles" to force the dice to fall with target faces up. The second attitude was one of relaxed "visualization" of the dice target-faces. The conditions appeared to be appropriate with precision-made dice, a die-casting machine, and controlled procedures for recording the data. Evidence for PK on the muscle-tension test was marginally negative, and the visualization test score was statistically insignificant in a total of 1,440 runs.

W. Braud and M. Schlitz (1983), using waking suggestion to measure muscle tension versus relaxation in a PK test, reported that a significant calming PK effect occurred for the active (needy) persons but not for the inactive persons. The authors acted as "influencers" with distant targets, as measured by reduction in skin resistance of the "needy" subjects. Using a single criterion, that is, skin resistance (the EDA; also known as the PGR), is very chancy as an index of the activity of the total autonomic nervous system. In the so-called "lie detector," the use of the PGR alone as an index of emotional excitement (e.g., lying) was discarded long ago. Unmentioned, but at the end of the scale, the extremely "withdrawn" are equally "needy." It might be more convincing were some other significant indices of autonomic function also employed. It is to be noted that the "individuals with excessive nervous system activity" would have a much wider range to change, whereas the moderate and especially the calm would change little or not at all. There is the likelihood that these extreme scores change because of statistical regression toward the mean; that is, extremely high scores are predicted to decline on retesting and extremely low scores are predicted to rise.

Hidden Targets

Stanford (1977) noted five studies that were involved exclusively, or in major part, with hidden targets, citing the reports by Fisk and West; Forwald, Mitchell and Fisk; Osis; and Thouless. The concern here is specifically with the actual conditions of the experiments. The report by Osis (1953) was considered a "minor report," and that by Thouless (1951) was a solo unwitnessed effort, "fitted into odd times when I happened to have a spare twenty minutes" (EG, 370 f.). Blundun, who could have been placed with the "solo efforts," was a "sensitive" studied over a period of years, by Mitchell and Fisk in 1953 and by Fisk and West in 1957–1958. Excerpting briefly from the earlier report, Blundun was first tested in a group of ten subjects, which was recognized as a pilot study, involving possible dice bias. In subsequent solo tests, which included optional stopping, Blundun became ill and the tests had to be abandoned. Some of the original data sheets with which she was working were lost in the confusion following her entry into the hospital. In the final two years, the targets were mailed to her and she did her own recording without witnesses. Fisk and West in 1957 concluded that the results of these five experiments spread over a period of six years did not provide a fairly satisfactory confirmation (EG, 374).

It should be emphasized most strongly that there is no reason whatsoever to suggest any possible contamination of the data. Indeed, Blundun offers "pertinent sources of error in one of the rare introspective reports as a subject" (EG, 374). In any case, no experiment is any better than the conditions under which it is carried out. A sort of variant of hidden targets is working for "doubles," that is, "highs and lows." The subject may usually be given one or a pair of dice, selecting as targets 1's or 6's, that is, lows or highs. A critique of Helmut Schmidt's solo PK studies for doubles is given by C. E. M. Hansel (1980, 224 ff.).

Games

D. Steen (1957), working at home with one subject in an "exploratory" test, scored dice throws in terms of baseball rules. R. J. Ratte and F. M. Greene (1960) adopted the dice mode to basketball, but the scoring was not simple. It involved four players and scores for the various procedures, such as baskets, fouls, and foul shots. A comparison was made of the self-ratings of 21 subjects on a lucky/unlucky scale with their success in the game. The analysis of the results was not simple, and the resulting positive correlation between the self-judged lucky and their scores in the game was questioned, the statistics being considered inappropriate. A study by Greene (1960) of the performance in a dice game of the lucky/unlucky subjects, rated by a lucky questionnaire, produced no evidence of a difference between the lucky and unlucky players. It is not clear whether there was a weakness in the questionnaire, in the design of the game, or in the subjects. A positive correlation between lucky/unlucky subjects with high and low scores was reported by Ratte and Greene (1960). Ratte (1960) reported that the scoring in competitive PK and noncompetitive basketball games, as well as between competitive and noncompetitive situations, favored the competitive situation. The differences, however, were not significant. When a simple situation is made complicated, the goal may get lost in the shuffle.

Odds and Ends

One of the few "pure" PK dice tests was reported by Charles Tart et al. (1972). A silver dollar was used with a coin-spinning apparatus, and 20 subjects were given 60 trials each, mentally wishing to influence the fall of the coin. The subjects chosen were only those who believed in PK and might demonstrate it. There was a significant level of scoring and a decline effect in the first experiment, with insignificant results in the final two tests. The differences among the three tests were insignificant, with 1,054 hits and a chance expectancy of 1,050. However, there were significant decline effects in the first halves of the three experiments.

In a study by Cox, Feather, and Carpenter (1966), subjects, by "willing," were to modify the speed of the sweep of a clock-hand. Visiting fellows serving as experimenters had to "unavoidably" terminate the tests, with their role taken over by two of the co-authors. All five series were "slightly" above mean chance expectation. Pooled results of three series were significant, but it is not clear whether this was part of the experimental design.

Humphrey (1947) had reported a help-hinder comparison in PK tests. The subject threw the dice for a given target, not knowing that an "observer" at times wished for the subject's target and at other times for a different face. There were positive scores when both wished for the same target, and insignificant differences when the two chose different targets. The study, however, was flawed in that all dice faces were not equally represented in the total number of throws (EG. 367).

Plants and Animals

The question arises whether the animal is affected by purported ESP or PK. Is it mind to mind, or mind to body? When one considers a fungus culture (Barry 1968) or plant leaves (Backster 1968), one is hard put to sort out the concepts. In one exploratory PK study, the object was to influence larvae to crawl to specific sectors of the experimental box (Metta 1972). The first larva demonstrated inconsistency in the individual run scores; it had a "strong psi influence but could not control its direction." The second larva score was at chance level. What of the control of bacterial growth with PK (Nash 1982); the study of cockroaches and cats; and the highly significant scores obtained by 12 human subjects, of which 9 were professed "psychics," whose goal was to arouse mice from ether anesthesia (Schmidt 1970b; 1971)?

Consider some of the experimental difficulties involved in the study by W. Braud (1976). In four of the experiments with the RNG, 34 aggressive fish were given 20 seconds with mirror presentations, constituting feedback or positive reinforcement. They were compared with an equal number of nonaggressive fish, without feedback. In the first two tests, aggressive fish showed "psi"-hitting (PK or ESP) only on one day. There was a decline effect over the four days, with varying scores of hits by the aggressive fish on the different test days. The nonaggressive fish were at chance performance on all four days and "a moderate amount of psychokinesis emerged. Decline occurred despite the presence of immediate feedback . . . in spite of hopes. It is, of course, not certain that the fish themselves were the active agents . . . the experimenters may have exerted some psychic influence on the results" (Braud 1976, 306).

Consider "Primary Perception in Plant Life" (Backster 1968), a study that has twice failed in replication (Johnson 1972; Horowitz et al. 1975). Backster has not repeated the study or responded to inquiries from Johnson. As a figure of speech, "This is no way to run a railroad." In the 1970s, Walter J. Levy, first a student then a colleague of Rhine, manipulated the data in a PK experiment and judgment has been suspended on all of Levy's publications until there is independent replication. This will include Levy's animal experiments before he was caught in fraud (Rhine 1974). Replication may be too much to ask—as did Rhine—since it has been generally marked by its absence.

Discussion

A range of psychological phenomena are to be noted in the reported studies, including imagery, mood, visualization attitudes, role of feedback, relaxation versus concentration, and striving. The vectors are not unequivocally demonstrated. In Debes and Morris (1982), passivity appears to score better, just as relaxation has the advantage over concentration (Honorton and Barksdale 1972). Steilberg (1975) reported that there was no evidence of PK on the concentration test, and the score on the visualization test was at chance level, yet the difference in scoring between the two tests was significant.

The use of games indicates the need to have a simple design, rather than the complications used in those studies. Tart had clear-cut PK scores in the first coin-spinning test, but the final two tests ended with negative results (Tart et al. 1972). The fault in Humphrey's study was omitted in recent overviews. The tests with animals and plants, at best, are a mixed bag. Certainly, the data in this area can be ignored until unequivocally confirmed data are available.

The range of the overall efforts is considerable, much wider than that of the earlier period. Not at all inconsequential is the failure to identify the weaknesses of earlier studies; e.g., the report on "hidden targets." The high PK score obtained by the experimenter Honorton in the last section of his study was inexplicably not followed up, as it would have been in the normal course of events in academic research. Some of the results in the motivatioal area remain puzzling. Passivity and relaxation are described as being inducive to evoking PK, in contrast to striving and muscle tension. There are studies with opposite results. In other studies motivation is not involved.

Before accurate replication is possible, it is necessary to have objective instruments, e.g., tests, paper and pencil or otherwise, to make some standardization of procedure. The wish must be replaced if there is to be any serious attempt to develop adequate measurement procedures. Additionally, studies have been reported in which an *unknowing* subject is identified as the source of the reported PK, even when unaware that an experiment was being carried out. This does not make sense. In many areas, especially in motivation and personality, it will be necessary to have constructed objective inventories to make experiments more regular. How much striving, or relaxation, did the subject express? The day of the wish, as such, is over and should have been discarded long ago.

Experimenter Effect

It is now generally recognized that the experimenter may so influence the subject or the interpretation of the data as to jeopardize the outcome of the research (Rosenthal 1976). In parapsychology, the implication is exactly the opposite. The experimenter, as well as the subject, is presumed to be a source of the influence, the "psi experimenter effect" (Kennedy and Taddonio 1976). But the Rosenthal experimenter effect is concerned with secondary, unconscious cues that can influence subjects unconsciously. The implication here is that without proper controls conscious, unrecognized secondary cues may improperly become susceptible to psi interpretation. This makes it mandatory that experimenters and subjects be completely protected from each other, physically and otherwise. Of course this procedure is impossible and the situation becomes more dangerous when the experimenter is also the subject. The "psi experimenter effect" is raised too frequently these days post hoc, with a complete absence of responsiblity in failing to perform control tests to determine its hypothetical role. As far as can be determined, there has never been a reported study in which the hypothetical psi experimenter effect has been tested under controlled conditions. The challenge of its occurrence in the Honorton and Barksdale (1972) study remains inexplicable.

Experimental Variable

The suggestion has been raised repeatedly, at one time or another, to skip the hocus-pocus with games and statistical procedures. In the middle nineteenth century, Michael Faraday proposed a simple and clear-cut test to determine whether a "sensitive" could "will" the movement of a delicately balanced wire. Sir William Crookes, a believer, attempted such a test with a delicate balance to no avail. Criticizing the very early Rhine PK dice-tests, Soal commented: "Unlike any other force of which we have any experience it [PK] is more successful in influencing 96 dice thrown together than a single die . . . [yet] it is incapable of moving a delicately suspended needle" (Soal 1948, 185). Old dog, but oh so pertinent.

Decline Effect

The case for PK was based on two criteria: an excess of the number of hits and/or a decline in hits. The second hypothesis was an unexpected postmortem finding of the "early dice tests." The most suitable decline was the quarterly decline (QD) of the distribution of the page score, from the first quarter to the final quarter of the page. It was then recognized, as McConnell, Snowden and Powell noted in 1955, that some methods of decline analyses were tailored to fit the individual experiment. This was the only thorough analysis in the "later dice tests" that supported the QD (cf. EG 377 ff.). As with the hit scores, the decline trends were not supported by the data of the early dice tests. Some reports supported the QD, but others did not. As Stanford (1977, 325) recognized, "spurious effects might occur in a number of ways, even unrelated to the PK hypothesis." In the more recent literature, declines are noted in some studies, somewhat like a passing remark rather than the result of a statistical test. In fact, more often than not, especially with an random-number generator, it is noted that there was no decline, which is usually attributed to the trial-by-trial feedback of information. Apparently, no specific tests of declines have been recently carried out, and it is possible that interest in the decline effect may further decrease and vanish.

Solos

In the earlier report, the category of solos was concerned with so-called sensitive psychics of which Blundun, who has already been considered, was one. Later, there were others who appeared: W. E. Cox, H. Forwald, and, more recently, H. Schmidt. Following a suggestion by J. G. Pratt, W. E. Cox, now a retired businessman as well as an amateur magician, introduced the placement test. Scores were made for hits on die faces and lateral placement areas, initially scoring for primary and secondary targets. In the first study, Cox (1951) recognized that essentially it involved "unwitnessed observations and recording" (p. 43). Over the years, a number of different variations developed as well as methods of scoring, using different objects, such as marbles, inclined planes, and chutes. There were 11 more studies by 1966, almost always solo and sometimes executed by an assistant. Others, including L. E. Rhine, have used the placement technique. The initial inadequacies of the placement criterion have been detailed in the earlier review (Girden 1962a).

The situation has not changed much in the past 25 years, and the criticisms of the weakness are even more relevant. The first of a long series of largely solo studies by H. Forwald was published by Rhine (1951). There were ten publications by 1961, of which only one involved a number of subjects (Pratt and Forwald 1958). Three joint studies with R. A. McConnell were concerned with checking implications of some of Forwald's earlier reports (McConnell and Forwald 1967a, 1967b; 1968). Forwald did a number of placement tests, and one of his claims was that the displacement of the wooden blocks was due to his PK. As C. C. L. Gregory argued, the sidewise scatter of the blocks "is not a sideways force, psychic or otherwise, it is determined by the horizontal distance between the cube's centre of mass and the point of contact on striking the floor."

Gregory's letter was rejected by Rhine, who was known regularly to refuse negative reports, but it was published elsewhere (cf. Hansel 1980).

Forwald's work began some years after publication of *Extra-Sensory Perception After Sixty Years* (Pratt et al. 1940), which was held to be one of the two most convincing documents in the field. By these standards, all of Forwald's solo reports would have been unacceptable. These standards were violated by Rhine (1951), when in publishing Forwald's initial report he said, "There is of course justification for the solo type of research in parapsychology since all other sciences use it" (p. 50). The statement merits reiteration: The solo scientific endeavor is an acceptable practice so long as the contingent clause is included: *replication of reported results*. But this procedure is noteworthy by its absence in parapsychology.

The first thorough application of automation was conducted by the U.S. Air Force Laboratories (Smith et al. 1963). A test with the tightest experimental controls was made with VERITAC for clairvoyance, precognition, and general extrasensory perception, using 37 subjects for a total of 55,500 trials. No significant test differences were obtained. The third consistent solo performer was Helmut Schmidt, who introduced the binary random-number generator for use in testing PK (1970a, 1970b; 1974; 1981). Criticisms have been directed at Schmidt's solo performances; and, in addition, the experimental conditions of Schmidt's reported ESP and PK data have been faulted. For some of the serious criticisms of experimental design as well as the inability to replicate Schmidt's results with Veritac, consult Smith et al. (1963) and Hansel (1980). Solo experimenters are now regularly testing themselves, with the absence of successful replication. Whatever else may be said of the solo performance, certainly apparatus per se does not guarantee good results. It is difficult enough to be an experimenter and obtain accurate observations. A reading of Blundun's account of trying to be her own subject and experimenter should be enlightening.

In the initial PK report, J. F. Nicol's (1954) criticism of solo performance had been applied to Soal's work: "At what state in the difficult history of psychical research it became permissible for sensitives to report their own results and expect them to be accepted as serious evidence in psychical research, I do not know. The number of such reports has grown disturbingly in recent years" (p. 355). And 30 years later, the point is increasingly pertinent to the continuing efforts by Cox and much of Forwald's and Schmidt's research. Wearing the hats of both experimenter and subject compounds the experimental fault.

A recent study by a parapsychologist indicates the low level of esteem of parapsychology in the eyes of established scientists. A questionnaire submitted to 497 Council members and selected committee members of the American Association for the Advancement of Science (AAAS) indicated that 62 percent of the AAAS scientists felt that, on the whole, parapsychological research had not been conducted in a competent manner: "71 percent of the responses had the highest level of skepticism regarding ESP of any major group surveyed within the last twenty years," and it is not surprising that this is "positively related to denial of legitimacy of the field of parapsychology" (McClenon 1982, 127).

Fallibilism

It has been a principle for many decades that a proper experimental design should be such that it will have *proved* the tested hypothesis; it must determine it to be right or wrong. The general principle, as put by Sir Karl Popper, requires that the inquiry or experiment can establish the correctness or incorrectness of the hypothesis. It must be capable of "falsifiability" (Perkinson 1978). When the experimenter is also subject in solo experiments, whatever other inherent limitations exist, the experiment is not "provable." This is especially irritating when it is often concluded that the experimenter may have been the source of psi. It is of interest that some parapsychologists recently have come to recognize the problem of fallibilism.

Hypothetical psi has resisted a satisfactory description that can be used as a hypothesis that can be properly *proven*. An inherent difficulty of the concept is that a test of it assumes that all known (knowable?) factors have been properly controlled. As an illustration, consider the problem of homing flights of millions of birds for thousands of miles. A number of environmental conditioning factors have been considered for land flight, but the flights over thousands of ocean miles resisted explanation. According to William Roll (1980), this problem was Pratt's strongest interest. Assuming psi to be involved, Pratt worked on this problem until a grant by the ONR ran out. The problem is a model demonstration of the marked limitations of psi as a hypothesis. It would be required first to rule out experimentally all known mechanisms; and in testing for psi one then faces the predicament of falsifiability.

It has now been demonstrated that birds deprived of the sun and equipped with bar magnets to disrupt their readings tend to become disoriented (Cooke 1984). In the past few years, material inferred to be magnetic has been detected in the tissue of several species, such as the honey bee and the homing pigeon. Also, magnetite crystals were isolated in the skull of the yellowfin tuna, and magnetic field information has been isolated as an operating factor in homing pigeons (cf. Walker et al. 1984). For those interested, an excellent overview of the phenomenon is offered by R. R. Baker (1984). Nature provides a magnificent range of variables susceptible to experimental proof and repeatability, but the paras will be "psiing" for the unknown. To each his, or her, own.

Fraud

Fraud is a practice traceable to antiquity. It is to be found at all levels of society world-wide. The turn of the century was a time of psychics and much fraud, and it appears to recur as a generational cycle. In the 1920s, there was considerable concern with regard to mediumistic fraud. Houdini, the famous magician, became intimate with the psychic literature and spent much of his time exposing fraudulent mediums. His comment at that time is still most pertinent: "It is not for us to prove that mediums are dishonest, it is for them to prove that they *are* honest" (Houdini 1924, 270). Arthur Conan Doyle, a close friend of Houdini, believed that Houdini possessed supernatural powers, which Houdini, who believed in the hereafter, strongly denied. And now there is Ted Serios, discovered by Jules Eisenbud who still believes in Serios's psychic abilities, although the latter confessed that he had been caught cheating. For collateral discussions, the same applies equally to Uri Geller, another recent phenomenon (cf. Houdini 1924 and Randi 1975). Notwithstanding, these superstars are supported in the psychic literature (cf. Krippner 1977; Wolman 1977).

Triggering the issue in the recent period in parapsychology was George Price's argument (1955) that, in the absence of a foolproof experiment, the most likely explanation was that of fraud. The Levy case in Rhine's laboratory has already been noted (Rhine 1974). In response to the serious charges by Hansel (1980), the answer has been that "successful repetition of experiments by independent investigators seems the best course of action" (Martin 1979, 139). This problem is becoming increasingly serious in academic and other, even medical, research areas (cf. Fisher 1982). There is an important consideration here.

As a principle, an experiment should stand on its own right. It is good when independent studies come to the same conclusion. But J. E. Coover (see Chapter 9 of this volume) warned a long time ago, "A reliance upon the corroboratory testimony of others often increases the confidence of a scientist in his own observations to the extent of weakening the rigour with which he may reasonably be expected to guard against fraud" (p. 234 f.). In discussing a Forwald experiment, Thouless commented: "It remains, of course, true that, as in such outstanding tests for ESP as the Soal-Goldney experiment, this Pratt-Forwald [1967] result would be of little scientific interest if it stood alone" (Thouless 1972, 150). The Soal-Goldney study, listed as a classic ESP experiment, has now been shown to have demonstrated fraudulent manipulation in the target sequences (Markwick 1978). In an addendum to that report, Mrs. Goldney, who assisted Soal, forthrightly accepted these findings. In an accompanying statement, Pratt also acceded to the fact of Soal's manipulations in this experiment for which Soal had received a doctorate. There are also critical assessments of other highly regarded psychic studies (cf. Hansel 1980).

There is a contingent relation with respect to the area of magic. Scientists lack the special skills of magicians to know what to look for when a conjurer is performing. Scientists' observations, and even those of amateur magicians, leave much to be desired. (See Persi Diaconis, Chapter 24 of this volume.) This is most relevant, for the parapsychologists have a deep-seated drive to believe and more readily accept a range of purported psychical phenomena. Indeed, in some of the investigations, it was necessary to have several investigators concentrating on given aspects of a skilled fraudulent performance. After all is said, the bottom line is independent replication.

Summary

In the century of modern psychic research, the development of sound conclusions was not readily forthcoming. The psychic search has been a long one, and perhaps William James's perception was correct; a century may be the required time unit. With respect to the current scene, answers are not yet readily available. The Soal-Goldney tests with Shackleton, beginning in 1941, were under continuous examination for decades until Markwick (1978) clearly demonstrated that the data had been manipulated. That was a time interval of almost four decades, and it may require another generational interval before satisfactory conclusions can be drawn about the more recent studies. With respect to the specific issue of PK, the modern period of study has covered a half-century.

At this time, it is relevant to quote again a statement from Gardner Murphy, an eminent, respected, and admired believer, not at all a "hard-line" experimentalist. Murphy noted that "the fundamental rule in laboratory science is that you truly have captured a phenomenon only when you can so fully specify the conditions which engender it, that you can yourself make it happen again and again, and other qualified workers can do the same. We do not, for the most part, even attempt this in parapsychology" (Murphy 1958, 233). Another respected figure has noted: "There is still no repeatable experiment on the basis of which any competent investigator can verify a given phenomenon for himself . . . the scientific community has preferred to stay aloof" (Beloff 1977, 759). This was applicable a century ago and, if William James is right, it may still be applicable a century from now.

A number of observers have commented on a deep strain of religiosity among parapsychologists. It is, for example, clearly discerned in the writings of William James, Henry Sidgwick, Gardner Murphy, and J. B. Rhine. If this observation has merit, it lends some insight into the deep, and perhaps irreconcilable, differences between the psychic and experimental interests. There is, at present, a paucity of solid and replicable PK data, and there is no suggestion of a sudden breakthrough. It will be a long hard road. The earlier conclusion is pertinent now, a judgment that Pratt (1963) entirely misconstrued. In response to the comments of Gardner Murphy (1962), it was concluded (Girden 1962b), having "no strong opinion, pro or con but, on the basis of the available evidence, the soundest judgment is a Scottish verdict: *not proven*" (Jury 1911).

References

André, E. 1972. Confirmation of PK action on electronic equipment. *Journal of Parapsychology*, 36:261-282.

Backster, C. 1968. Evidence of a primary perception in plant life. *International Journal of Parapsychology*, 10:329-348.

Baker, R. Robin. 1984. *Bird Migration: The Solution to a Mystery?* New York: Holmes & Meier.

Barry, L. 1968. General and comparative study of psychokinetic effect on a fungus culture. *Journal of Parapsychology*, 32:237-243.

Beloff, J. 1977. Parapsychology and philosophy. In *Handbook of Parapsychology*, edited by B. B. Wolman, 757-768. New York: Van Nostrand Reinhold.

Braud, L., and W. Braud. 1979. Psychokinetic effects upon a random event generator under conditions of limited feedback to volunteers and experimenter. *Journal of the SPR*, 50:21-32.

Braud, W. 1976. Psychokinesis in aggressive and non-aggressive fish with mirror presentation feedback of hits: Some preliminary experiments. *Journal of Parapsychology*, 40:296-307.

Braud, W. and M. Schlitz. 1983. Psychokinetic influences on electrodermal activity. *Journal of Parapsychology*, 47:95-120.

Cooke, P. 1984. How do birds find where they are going? *Science 84*, 5:26.

Cox, W. E. 1951. The effect of PK on the placement of falling objects. *Journal of Parapsychology*, 5:40-48.

———. 1974. PK tests with thirty-two channel Balls machines. *Journal of Parapsychology*, 38:56-68.

Cox, W. E., S. R. Feather, and J. C. Carpenter. 1966. The effect of PK on electro-mechanical systems. *Journal of Parapsychology*, 30:184-194.

Debes, J., and R. Morris. 1982. Comparison of striving and nonstriving instructional sets in a PK study. *Journal of Parapsychology*, 46:297-312.

Feather, S. W., and L. E. Rhine. 1969. PK experiments with same and different targets. *Journal of Parapsychology*, 33:213-227.

Fisher, K. 1982. The spreading stain of fraud. *Monitor*, 13:1 ff. Washington, D.C.: American Psychological Association.

Girden, E. 1962a (EG). A review of psychokinesis. *Psychological Bulletin*, 59:353-388.

———. 1962b. A postscript to "A review of psychokinesis (PK)." *Psychological Bulletin*, 59:529-531.

———. 1985 (in press). Recollections of psychology at Brooklyn College. *American*

Psychologist.

Girden, E., G. Murphy, J. Beloff, A. Flew, J. H. Rush, G. Schmeidler, and R. H. Thouless. 1964. A discussion of "A review of psychokinesis (PK)." *International Journal of Parapsychology,* 6:26-137.

Greene, F. M. 1960. The feeling of luck and its effect on PK. *Journal of Parapsychology,* 24:129-141.

Hansel, C. E. M. 1980. *ESP and Parapsychology: A Critical Re-evaluation.* Buffalo, N.Y.: Prometheus Books.

Honorton, C., and W. Barksdale. 1972. PK performance with waking suggestions for muscle tension versus relaxation. *Journal of the American SPR,* 66:208-214.

Horowitz, K. A., D. C. Lewis, and E. L. Gasteiger. 1975. Plant primary perception: Electrical unresponsiveness to brine shrimp killing. *Science,* 189:478-480.

Houdini, H. 1924. *A Magician Among the Spirits.* New York: Harper & Row (reprinted by Arno Press, New York, 1972).

Johnson, R. V. 1972. To the Editors. *Journal of Parapsychology,* 36:71-72.

Jury. 1911. *Encylopaedia Britannica* (11th edition), 15:592. New York: Encyclopaedia Britannica.

Kennedy, J. E., and J. L. Taddonio. 1976. Experimenter effects in parapsychological research. *Journal of Parapsychology,* 40:1-33.

Krippner, S. 1977. *Advances in Parapsychological Research.* New York: Plenum Press.

Levi, A. 1979. The influence of imagery and feedback on PK effects. *Journal of Parapsychology,* 43:275-289.

Markwick, B. 1978. The Soal-Goldney experiments with Basil Shackleton: New evidence of data manipulation. *Proceedings of the SPR,* 56:250-281.

Martin, M. 1979. The problem of experimenter fraud. A re-evaluation of Hansel's critique of ESP experiments. *Journal of Parapsychology,* 43:129-139.

McClenon, J. 1982. A survey of elite scientists: Their attitudes towards ESP and parapsychology. *Journal of Parapsychology,* 46:127-152.

McConnell, R. A., and H. Forwald. 1967a. Psychokinetic placement, I: Re-examination of the Forwald-Durhamm experiment. *Journal of Parapsychology,* 31:51-69.

———. 1967b. Psychokinetic placement, II: A factorial study of successful and unsuccessful series. *Journal of Parapsychology,* 31:198-213.

———. 1968. Psychokinetic placement, III. *Journal of Parapsychology,* 32:9-38.

Metta, L. 1972. Psychokinesis on lepidopterous larvae. *Journal of Parapsychology,* 36:213-221.

———. 1972. Confirmation of PK action on electronic equipment. *Journal of Parapsychology,* 36:289-293.

Morris, R., M. Nanko, and D. Phillips. 1982. A comparison of two popularly advocated visual imagery strategies in a psychokinetic task. *Journal of Parapsychology,* 46:1-16.

Murphy, G. 1958. Progress in parapsychology. *Journal of Parapsychology,* 22:229-236.

———. 1962. Report on paper by Edward Girden on psychokinesis. *Psychological Bulletin,* 59:520-528.

Nash, C. B. 1982. Psychokinetic control of bacterial growth. *Journal of the SPR,* 51:217-221.

Nicol, J. F. 1954. The design of experiments in psychokinesis. *Journal of the SPR*, 37:355-357.

Parsons, D. 1945. Experiments on PK with inclined plane and rotating cage. *Proceedings of the SPR*, 47:296-300.

Perkinson, H. 1978. Popper's fallibilism. *Et cetera: A Review of General Semantics*, 35:5-19.

Pratt, J. G. 1963. The Girden-Murphy papers on PK. *Journal of Parapsychology*, 27:199-209.

Pratt, J. G., and H. Forwald. 1958. Confirmation of the PK placement effect. *Journal of Parapsychology*, 22:1-19.

Pratt, J. G., J. B. Rhine, B. Mott-Smith, C. E. Stuart, and J. A. Greenwood. 1940. *Extra-Sensory Perception after Sixty Years*. New York: Holt.

Price, G. R. 1955. Science and the supernatural. *Science*, 122:359-367.

Randi, J. 1975. *The Magic of Uri Geller*. New York: Ballantine (revised as *The Truth About Uri Geller*, Prometheus Books, Buffalo, N.Y., 1982).

Ratte, R. J. 1960. A comparison of game and standard PK testing techniques under competitive and noncompetitive conditions. *Journal of Parapsychology*, 24:235-244.

Ratte, R. J., and F. M. Greene. 1960. An exploratory investigation of PK in a game situation. *Journal of Parapsychology*, 24:159-170.

Rhine, J. B. 1951. The Forwald experiments with placement. *Journal of Parapsychology*, 15:49-56.

———. 1974. A new case of experimenter unreliability. *Journal of Parapsychology*, 38:215-225.

Roll, W. G. 1980. J. Gaither Pratt: 1910-1979. *Journal of Parapsychology*, 44:3-8.

Rosenthal, R. 1976. *Experimenter Effects in Behavioral Research*. New York: Irvington.

Rush, J. H. 1977. Problems and methods in psychokinesis research. In *Handbook of Parapsychology*, edited by B. B. Wolman, New York: Van Nostrand Reinhold.

Schmidt, H. 1970a. PK experiment with electronic equipment. *Journal of Parapsychology*, 34:175-181.

———. 1970b. PK experiment with animals as subjects. *Journal of Parapsychology*, 34:255-261.

———. 1971. Possible PK influence on the resuscitation of anesthetized mice. *Journal of Parapsychology*, 35:257-272.

———. 1973. PK tests with high speed random number generator. *Journal of Parapsychology*, 37:105-118.

———. 1974. Comparison of PK action on two different random number generators. *Journal of Parapsychology*, 38:47-55.

———. 1981. PK tests with pre-recorded and pre-inspected seed numbers. *Journal of Parapsychology*, 45:87-98.

Smith, W. R., E. F. Dagle, M. D. Hill, and J. Mott-Smith. 1963. Testing for extra sensory perception with a machine. Data Sciences Laboratory Project 4610, May.

Soal, S. G. 1948. The reach of the mind by Rhine (review). *Journal of Parapsychology*, 34:183-185.

Stanford, R. G. 1969. "Associative activation of the unconscious" and "visualization" as methods for influencing the PK target. *Journal of the American SPR*, 63:338-351.

――――. 1977. Experimental psychokinesis: A review from diverse perspectives. In *Handbook of Parapsychology*, edited by B. B. Wolman, 324-381. New York: Van Nostrand Reinhold.

Steen, D. 1957. Success with complex targets in a PK baseball game. *Journal of Parapsychology*, 21:133-146.

Steilberg, B. J. 1975. "Conscious concentration" versus "visualization" in PK testing. *Journal of Parapsychology*, 39:12-20.

Tart, C. T., M. Boisen, V. Lopez, and R. Maddock. 1972. Some studies of psychokinesis with a spinning silver coin. *Journal of the SPR*, 46:143-145.

Thouless, R. H. 1951. A report on an experiment in psychokinesis with dice, and a discussion on psychological factors favoring success. *Proceedings of the SPR*, 49:107-130.

――――. 1972. *From Anecdote to Experiment in Psychical Research*. London: Routledge and Kegan Paul.

Wadhams, P., and B. A. Farrelly. 1968. The investigation of psychokinesis using B-particles. *Journal of the SPR*, 44:281-289.

Walker, M. M., J. L. Kirschvink, and A. Edizon. 1984. A candidate magnetic sense organ in the yellowfin tuna. *Science*, 224:751-753.

Wolman, B., ed. 1977. *Handbook of Parapsychology*. New York: Van Nostrand Reinhold.

4

Modern Occultism

SIMON NEWCOMB

Simon Newcomb (1835–1909) was the first president of the American Society for Psychical Research, founded in 1885. One of the most distinguished astronomers of his day, Newcomb was a skeptic who spent many decades investigating psychical research. The following paper was published in the journal Nineteenth Century, *in January 1909, and expresses his conclusions about the field after a lifetime of study.— ED.*

When eminent men of science announce discoveries of great interest it is an obvious general rule that their conclusions receive respectful consideration and, in the absence of strong reasons to the contrary, are accepted without serious question. But there is an exception to this rule so curious that it may well deserve our attention. Among the most important questions with which thought has been engaged are those of the possible modes of interaction between mind and mind. Coupled with this is the question of the direct action of mind upon matter, or of matter upon mind without physical agency. Ideas of this subject are older than civilization and arise so naturally that nothing but suggestion is necessary to implant them in the mind of the child. Discredited by the general trend of modern thought, the affirmative view has very generally been classed with superstition as belonging to a stage of intellectual development that the world has now left behind it. Belief in witchcraft vanished from the minds of civilized men more than two centuries ago, and with it disappeared the belief in every form of mental interaction otherwise than through the known organs of sense. But now men of eminence, whose opinion is entitled to the greatest respect, are informing us that the instincts of our ancestors did not err so greatly as we have supposed and that beliefs that our fathers called superstitious are well grounded in the regular order of nature. At least three scientific philosophers of the highest standing have placed themselves on record as accepting this view. Two of them, Sir Oliver Lodge and Professor William Barrett, have, during the past year, informed us that, not only is the direct transference of impressions from one mind to another a fact, but the spiritual world, which the thought of our time has been removing further and further from our everyday experience until it seemed likely to vanish from intellectual sight, is a reality knocking at our doors.

If these are truths, we can scarcely exaggerate their importance. Our most cherished aspirations and the consolations that religion offers to the dying and the bereaved are taken from the realm of sentiment and placed on the sure pedestal of science. A new view of mind is opened out, to the development of which we can set no limit. Accepting it, a system of conveying impressions from mind to mind at great distances, and of reading the secret thoughts of our fellows, seems more likely than it would have seemed a century ago that electricity would enable us to communicate with our antipodes. With such prospects opened out to us by scientific authorities so high, it certainly seems more appropriate that the skeptic, if such there be, should make known his reasons for the faith that is in him—perhaps we should say for his lack of faith—than that the doctrines should be treated as unworthy of attention.

A glance at the state of public opinion upon the subject will serve to guide the course of our thoughts. The class that fully accepts the views in question, notwithstanding its eminent respectability, is probably small in numbers. Between this class and those who entirely reject the views, as at least groundless, if not unworthy of consideration, there is an intermediate class holding that phenomena known as "occult" are exhibited that science has not yet satisfactorily explained. Their view has recently been happily stated by an able writer in the *Saturday Review:* "The existence of abnormal phenomena which science is only beginning to take notice of, a dim region of strange things which, even if they can be proved not to be supernatural, are at any rate outside the limits of organized experience," has been proved by the work of the Society for Psychical Research. "There are more things in heaven and earth than are dreamt of in your philosophy" has never ceased to express a feeling of the same general nature in the minds of intelligent men, and is at least one article of a creed always lending hope to the inquirer after the occult. This middle class, which thinks that there is something to learn in occultism, is certainly large, and perhaps makes up a majority of the intelligent community. It is to this class, as well as to that of believers, that the writer desires to address himself.

The personal element necessarily plays so large a part in any discussion of occultism that it may not be wholly out of place if the writer ventures on a brief statement of his own experience. The idea that the emotions of beloved relatives, sometimes at a great distance, might be agents in directing the various currents of feeling that run through the mind was imbibed in early childhood. Just how the idea originated he cannot say, but it is probably more common among children than we suspect. More than once, when hurrying home, he intently fixed his mind upon his mother with a strong desire that she should expect his coming, think about him, and prepare herself accordingly. But all these efforts proved failures. Another idea prevalent at a later period was that, by fixing the attention on someone sitting at a distance in front of you in church, you could move him to turn and look around him. But no systematic experiments in this direction were seriously attempted. When, in the early fifties, the great wave of spiritualism, with its rappings, table-movings, and communications from the dead, was reaching its height, he naturally took an interest in the subject. But what little he could see of these performances seemed so silly as to prejudice him against the whole subject.

About 1858 an agent of prime importance in the history of spiritualism is worthy of being recalled. A warm discussion of the pretensions of certain mediums in the columns of the *Boston Courier* ended with the offer, by an anonymous writer (understood to be Professor Felton, afterward president of Harvard University), to pay a large reward to any mediums who would, in the presence of a committee to be named by himself, perform any of their pretended feats—move a table without touching it, read a paper in a closed envelope, or produce a rap the cause of which could not be traced. The offer was promptly accepted by the leader of the Boston spiritualists, and several of the most famous mediums were brought from different parts of the country. The committee was three in number. At its head was Professor Louis Agassiz, and his coadjutors were two eminent scientific men of Cambridge. The séances were held in the room of a Boston hotel. The result was a failure so complete that the professors felt humiliated to sit hour after hour and see nothing to enliven the proceedings. Some cabinet feats of tying and untying were attempted, but nothing was done in this line except very elementary tricks of legerdemain. The mediums could assign no better reason for their failure than the contempt of the spirits for men who disbelieved in their existence. A large measure of abuse was heaped upon the committee by the spiritualists, but no argument better than this was adduced in explanation of their failure.

After this the general attitude of the writer toward the subject was this: "I have no time to engage in the search after wonders. But tell me in any special case when I can go to a séance with any reasonable chance of seeing something out of the usual order of nature, and I will avail myself of the opportunity with alacrity." What has especially struck him ever since has been the absence of any such opportunity. When he was told of wonderful phenomena, and inquired as to details, the stories were always about things that had happened long before. An inquiry where a medium of special power could be found elicited no answer but that her whereabouts was unknown and she had probably left the city.

But after many years of waiting, an opportunity was at last presented. The most wonderful performer yet seen came to Washington, and her feats were vouched for by a party of intelligent gentlemen who had been invited to a private exhibition of her powers. She was a Miss Lulu Hirst, of Georgia. It must be said that spiritualism, as well as any other theory, was ignored by her;

but this was a minor matter, as the feats were of the same kind as those essayed by the professional spiritualists. A day or two later arrangements were made for another series of tests, in which the writer took part. Without going into details, which were published fully at the time, it will suffice to remark in the present connection that nothing was shown but what was obviously produced by the efforts of a muscular and dexterous young woman. She was quite frank and honest, without pretenses to be investigated or trickery to be exposed. Every surprising element in the narrative proved to be based on imperfections of observation and misconception of what was seen. Only one feature was needed to complete the picture. When the public performance of the "wonder-girl" came off, the press reporters were, of course, present, and their accounts of her feats as narrated in the journals rivaled or outdid the performances of the most celebrated mediums.

After the English Society for Psychical Research was organized by a body of men eminent in various fields of thought and action, the past failures of the writer did not prevent his taking part in the formation of an American society of the same kind, of which he had the honor to be elected the first president. Two years of experiment, study, and reading confirmed his ideas on the subject, but he remained for some time longer in occasional communication and cooperation with Dr. Hodgson, a well-known member of the English Society, then resident in Boston. He now invites the courteous consideration of the reader to the views of the subject that he has reached after a half-century of occasional study coupled with reading the best he could find in support of occultism.

II

We may approach the heart of our subject in the easiest way by recalling two lines of research in which Sir William Crookes took a prominent part. The name of this eminent investigator has become a household word in science from his discovery that a singular radiance may be produced at the cathode of a vacuum tube through which an electric current is passing. He also observed curious phenomena of motion among material objects in his laboratory for which he could not assign any physical cause. Several years elapsed after these discoveries before either of them seemed destined to develop into an important branch of science. Then the one first mentioned suddenly assumed importance.

In 1895 Professor Röntgen made the astounding discovery that certain rays from a Crookes tube were capable of passing through opaque substances and imprinting themselves upon a photographic plate beyond. About the same time it was shown by Becquerel that rays of similar properties, but different in kind, could be produced from uranium. All the physical laboratories of the world were at once actively engaged in testing these discoveries and following up the lines of research they suggested. The result was the discovery of radium and the development of a new branch of physics—radioactivity, which has gone on expanding until it bids fair to revolutionize our views of matter, ether, and their relations. Works on radioactivity are multiplying, and physicists are looking for new theories of light and electricity that are to grow out of this field of research.

With this outcome in mind, let us trace up the lines of the other observation. More than ten years before Röntgen's work the Society for Psychical Research had been organized. The special purpose was the critical investigation of occult phenomena in general, especially those that seemed to show the passage of impressions from mind to mind without material agency. A discovery that seemed to inaugurate a revolution in science of mind was soon announced in the form of an experiment equally remarkable for its simplcity and its importance. A blindfolded person, called a "percipient," was seated at a table with pencil in hand and paper before him, while his senses, especially those of sight and touch, were protected so far as possible from the action of all external agencies. His mind was to be quite free from all prepossession and his will to be reduced as nearly as possible to a state of quiescence. The only action allowed was that of drawing geometrical figures on the paper quite at random, without intent to produce any special forms. Behind him, but not in contact or communication, was seated an "agent" with a miscellaneous collection of geometrical figures. While the agent concentrated his vision and attention as intensely as possible upon one of these, the percipient was instructed to allow his pencil to move on the paper without any prejudice in favor of any special form of motion. The process was repeated with one figure after another. When the drawings of the percipient were compared with the originals, a resemblance was found sufficient to show an undoubted relation between the reproduced figures and those on which the attention of the agent had been fixed.

The experiments were not confined to geometric forms. Others were devised with the common object of showing that the random actions of one mind were affected by the action of another mind in its neighborhood, without the use of words or signs. When the agent drew cards from a pack one by one, and at each drawing the percipient named a card at random, it was found that the proportion of correct guesses was much greater than it should have been as the result of chance, which would, of course, be 1 out of 52.

In one point these experiments had a great advantage over those of the physicists. Crookes tubes and other apparatus required for experiments in radioactivity demand so much care and expense in their production that their use is confined to professional workers in physical laboratories. But the apparatus necessary to the demonstration of thought-transference abounds in every household. Men, women, paper, pencils, tables, screens, handkerchiefs for blindfolding, and cards make up a fairly complete list of essentials. The results to be ultimately expected from the experiments transcend in practical importance all that we can expect from the development of radioactivity. Such being the case, the natural anticipation was that thought-transference would become a branch of experimental psychology, the laws of which would form an important chapter in every treatise on this subject, and that apparatus for showing it would be as well known in every psychological laboratory as that for experimenting in X-rays is in every physical laboratory.

Twenty-five years have elapsed since the announcement, and what has been the outcome? Scientifically, nothing at all. The science of psychology has been behind few others in the extent of its development since the experiments described were begun. But if thought-transference is seriously treated in any treatise on this science the writer has not noticed it. The reason is not far to seek. No result relating to thought-transference has yet been reached that belongs to the realm of science. Science properly so called comprises the statement of laws or general facts. No collection of isolated events, however large it may be, forms a part of it. Radioactivity is a science because it is a general fact that everyone can verify that, if you organize a certain system of experiments, you can take a photograph through many opaque substances. That coal will burn when brought into contact with fire is a proposition belonging to the same domain. But if we could only say that someone in England had at some time made coal burn, then, a few years later, someone in Russia, then someone in America, and so on, such facts, though they mounted into the hundreds or the thousands, would not establish the law that coal was combustible, and therefore would not belong to science. The question of how the supposed burning came about in the special cases cited might be interesting, yet the process of investigation would be difficult if no careful experimenter were ever able to bring the combustion about.

So with thought-transference. In order that a scientific conclusion as to its reality may be reached, it is necessary to show under what conditions it takes place. The Psychical Society tried to determine, by a repetition of the experiments under various conditions, whether the action of the agent upon the percipient would pass through a screen, and how it varied with the conditions. When these questions could be answered, the first step would be taken toward placing the subject upon a scientific basis. But no result could ever be reached that was general in form. The nearest approach to a general proposition that could be formulated from all the experiments was: If you make the experiment you may possibly see what seems to show thought-transference, and you may not. The probability of success cannot be stated because we have no record of the failures, the number of which defies estimation. I have tried to learn whether during the past ten years the Psychical Society has done anything toward elucidating the subject. But nothing bearing on the case is found in its recent published proceedings. Would it be altogether unfair to put the conclusion in the form: Possibly you may succeed, but the more pains you take to avoid all sources of error, the less likely success will be?

During the past 15 years interest has been transferred from thought-transference to telepathy. The question of how, if an impression cannot be conveyed through a space of a few feet, it can yet dart from one city to another is one that, how strongly soever it may present itself, may rest in abeyance while we inquire about the seeming facts. These, as found in the fine volumes *Phantasms of the Living,* by Gurney and Myers, and in the publications of the Psychical Society, are too numerous to be summarized. But a typical example that will answer our present purpose is easy to give. A person is struck by a sudden hallucination, or has a vision or dream of a friend or relative, generally in distress. This impression is so vivid that some anxiety may be felt lest it correspond to a reality. Next morning, or as soon as the mail or telegraph can bring the news, it is learned that the friend or relative has either died at the time of the vision or has suffered some violent emotion. Great pains were taken to verify the authenticity of stories of this kind, and none were accepted unless deemed "veridical." Taking the hundreds of coincidences as they stand, and regarding each narrative as complete in itself, the conclusion that there must have been some causal connection between the distant event or emotion and the vision looks unavoidable. But may it not be that causes already known are sufficient to account for the supposed coincidences without introducing telepathy or any other abnormal agency? If such is the case, then the hypothesis of telepathy is purely gratuitous and un-called-for, on the general principle that we never attribute events to new and unknown causes when we see that they are the natural results of known conditions. This is especially the case when the new causes deduced are so improbable and so far outside the line of our general experience as telepathy must be. The strongest believer in this agency must admit that its acceptance is not without difficulty. Everyone who sleeps in London is surrounded by several millions of minds within a radius of three or four miles. Among these are hundreds in a state of violent action or emotion. Scores are constantly in the throes of death. How do the inhabitants of London sleep on undisturbed by the spiritual tumult? How is it that in the ordinary experience of life one person cannot divine the most intense feeling of another, even though he be near or dear, except by sight, touch, or hearing? So far as the writer is aware, the advocates of telepathy have evaded rather than grappled with these difficulties.

The question we shall now consider is whether there are not known causes at play that we should naturally expect to result in phenomena that seem to indicate telepathy. Those that I shall adduce are not all of one kind, but are made up of complex elements, each of which is familiarly known to all who carefully think and observe. First to be mentioned is the element of truth. Then will come the omission of important features from the narrative. I believe that Bacon remarked that men score only the hits, and ignore the misses. We also have unconscious exaggeration; the faculty of remembering what is striking, and forgetting what is not; illusions of sense, mistakes of memory; the impressions left by dreams; and, finally, deceit and trickery, whether intentional or unconscious. Before reaching a conclusion we must inquire as to what we should naturally expect as the combined result of these agencies in the regular course of experience.

As to the first: error finds support in so entwining itself with truth that it is difficult to separate the two. Double personality, hypnotism, and especially the action of one mind on another by hypnotic suggestion, have been confused with telepathy through a supposed power of the operator to influence the will of his subject at a distance. The mystery that has very generally enveloped the subject of "animal magnetism" is so fertile in vague theories of abnormality that now, when the whole subject is placed on a scientific basis, the elimination of traditional and baseless ideas is by no means an easy task. The belief that a hypnotic operator influences his subject by telepathy is widely diffused through all classes of the community except professional psychologists. The latter are, I believe, practically unanimous in holding that no influence is exerted on the subject except through the medium of the senses, and that, if the subject is to act in a certain way in the absence of the operator, the latter must make known in advance the time and nature of the expected action. I am aware that Richet and perhaps other operators have found cases that seem telepathic, but a critical reading of their evidence shows it to be wholly inconclusive.

A course of events may appear ever so wonderful and incomprehensible by well-known agencies by mere omission, without deviating from the truth in any particular. I once examined an interesting case of this kind at the request of Dr. Hodgson. A naval ship had been wrecked in a storm off Cape Hatteras some years before, and most of those on board, including the captain, had perished. Before she sailed on her voyage one of her officers was seized with so strong and persistent a presentiment that the ship would be lost that he formally requested to be detached from her. This being refused, he left his post of duty and was tried by court martial for desertion. Dr. Hodgson desired me to see whether this story could be verified by the official records.

This was easily done, and the narrative was found to be substantially correct so far as it went. But it omitted to state that the officer had exhibited symptoms of mental aberration before his presentiment, that the latter was only one of a great number of wild fears that he had expressed to various parties, including his superior officer, and that several months elapsed after this before the ship sailed on her fateful voyage, she having in the meantime made several trips on the coast. When thus completed the story became altogether commonplace.

A coincidence between an emotion experienced by a distant person and the impression of that emotion in another at a distance can indicate a causal relation only when the coincidence is real and the impression unusual. In establishing the facts there is wide ground for error. We are all subject to errors of memory, especially if we have to state the exact time and circumstance of an act or impression. Probably few of us could tell all that we did the day before yesterday, hour by hour, without either some erroneous statement, the omission of some act, or the introduction of an event that belonged to a different day. The longer the time that elapses, the greater the liability to error. Writers on telepathy take too little account of these errors of memory. In the vast majority of cases the correction cannot be made, and the error goes on record as truth, when it becomes the basis for some remarkable coincidence. When this is not the case it passes into oblivion. If we set a net for errors that we cannot distinguish from truth, how shall we know that our catch is anything but error? It is only by having some independent test of the accuracy of a remembered event that we can be sure of its correctness. A written and dated document, if genuine, would always suffice for this purpose. But such support is almost if not quite universally wanting in the narratives of wonderful coincidences.

I only recall a single case in which the correctness of a telepathic narrative was tested by independent and conclusive authority. In the *Nineteenth Century* for July 1884, an article, "Apparitions," by Edmund Gurney and Frederic W. H. Myers, appeared that was justly regarded as affording the most indisputable evidence ever adduced for the reappearance of a dead person. Sir Edmund Hornby, a judge of the Consular Court at Shanghai, had been visited during the night by a reporter desiring a copy of a decision that he was to deliver on the following morning. He rose from his bed, dictated what he had to say, and dismissed the reporter with a rebuke for having disturbed him. Next morning, on going to court, he was astounded by learning that the reporter, with whom he was well acquainted, had died suddenly during the night. Inquiring after the hour of the demise he found it to coincide with that of the nightly visitation. The authors also informed us in the article that the story was confirmed by Lady Hornby, who was mentioned in it and was cognizant of the circumstances.

This narrative was almost unique in that it admitted of verification. When it reached Shanghai it met the eyes of some acquainted with the actual facts. These were made known in another publication and showed that several months must have elapsed between the reporter's death and the judge's vision. The latter was only a vivid dream about a dead person. When the case was brought to the judge's attention he did not deny the new version and could only say he had supposed the facts to be as he had narrated them.

I cite this incident not merely to show how the most conclusive case of telepathy ever brought to light was invalidated when the facts were made known but to elucidate the further fact that a wonderful story may lose the element of surprise by quite natural and easily admitted additions and explanations. All the interest of such stories depends upon the element of wonder.

> The looker-on feels most delight
> Who least perceives the juggler's sleight.

It is positively humiliating to allow an amateur juggler to explain his extraordinary tricks. It humiliates one that he did not himself see how the thing was done. Why should we hesitate to ascribe any number of seemingly supernatural occurrences to the innumerable blunders that we know nearly every one of us is making in memory every day?

The statistical onesidedness of all evidence in favor of telepathy, apparitions, and other forms of supernormal mental action must be considered, and so far as possible corrected, before any conclusion can be reached. The principle involved and the ease with which we may reach a false conclusion may be illustrated by a very simple example. If a bag of corn contains a million normal grains and a single black one, the probability that a grain drawn at random from the bag would be the black one is so minute that we should justly regard the drawing as practically impossible in all the ordinary affairs of life. If a blindfolded boy, dipping his hand into the bag, drew the black grain on the first trial, we should justly claim that there was some unfairness in the proceeding, or, if we wish to deal in mystery, some attraction between his hand and the black grain. If on a thousand trials of this kind the black grain was drawn several times our suspicion would ripen into practical certainty. And yet, if every inhabitant of Great Britain made such a trial, it is practically certain that there would be about 30 drawings of the black grain without abnormality. In fact, did such drawings number only 20, the suspicion would be on the other side. We should be sure of some defect in the enumeration or of some instinct toward evading the black grain. The whole question turns on the number of unrecorded failures.

Through inquiries made under the auspices of the Psychical Society it would seem that about one person in every ten is more or less subject to hallucinations of some kind. Probably a large majority of people have occasional dreams so vivid that in Great Britain alone there must occur annually many millions of cases in which people, during their waking or dreaming hours, see before them images of distant relatives or friends. If, as may well be the case, the chances are millions to one against the illusion coinciding with the death or distress of the person seen, we should still have in all probability many such cases in a year. Thus, when the eminent members of the Society instituted their inquiries for such cases, it might have been predicted in advance that, without any bias whatever, they would have been discovered by the hundred.

But the concession of exactness is one of great improbability. Visions and dreams are in all ordinary cases dropped from the mind and speedily forgotten. But let one be connected in any way with a death or other moving event, and the memory, instead of being effaced, grows in the mind, month after month. The event associated with the vision may have occurred days or weeks before or after it, but the general tendency will be to bring them into coincidence and weave them into a story, as we have seen in the case already quoted.

The following case, cited by Mr. Beckles Willson in his recent work, *Occultism and Common Sense,* may be chosen for study because it is among the most remarkable of its kind. A traveler in a railway carriage is quoted:

> One week ago last Tuesday, at eleven o'clock at night, my wife, who had just retired to bed upstairs, called out to me, "Arthur! Arthur!" in a tone of alarm. I sprang up and ran upstairs to see what was the matter. The servants had all gone to bed. "Arthur," said my wife, "I've just seen mother," and she began to cry. "Why," I said, "why, your mother is in Scarborough." "I know," she said; "but she appeared before me just there" (pointing to the foot of the bed) "two minutes ago as plainly as you do." Well, the next morning there was a telegram on the breakfast table—"Mother died at eleven last night." Now, how do you account for it?

I will try to answer this question. I would not be at all surprised, could the facts be made known, if the wife had said something of the kind to her husband every day or night for a week, especially if the mother were known to be very ill. If any night had been missed, I would not be surprised if it were the fateful Tuesday. Then the problem would have been reversed, and we should have had to explain why it was that the vision failed on the night of the death. The memory of the narrator had more than a week in which to cultivate the wonder. The quotation, it will be noticed, purports to be verbatim, though, from what the author says, many years had probably elapsed. During this time the wonder, as it came from the lips of the original speaker, had ample time to develop still further in the mind of the narrator. What limit can we set to its possible growth, first in one mind and then in another? I cannot but feel that the more experience the reader has had in observing this form of growth, the less he will be inclined to set any limit to it.

Considering the natural processes of adaptation and exaggeration, from which no mind is so well disciplined as to be absolutely free, we conclude that the annual number of seeming but groundless telepathic phenomena in Great Britain alone is probably to be counted by thousands. The volumes of *Phantasms of the Living* might be continued annually without end could all the cases be discovered. The few hundred cases published are actually fewer than what we should expect as the result of known conditions. There is therefore no proof of telepathy in any of the wonders narrated in these volumes, and in the publications of the Psychical Society.

III

We have considered the evidence for the various forms of telepathy with some fullness because the theory is, in form at least, a scientific one, and the evidence admits of being treated by the established methods of logical inference. But telepathy is only the beginning of the wonders collected by modern inquirers into the occult, who find so many phenomena unexplainable, even by this agency, that they regard the latter as only a first step in the science they are trying to construct. Our conclusion from all these supposed phenomena are so much matters of individual judgment, not admitting of being readily reduced to first principles, that they must be disposed of quite briefly. The belief in specially gifted persons—doers of miracles and practitioners of witchcraft—was once almost universal. Our modern students of occultism have revived what seems very like these discarded beliefs, though the word "witchcraft" is no longer used to express the abnormal powers in question. These powers are not merely those possessed by men in general and heightened in degree, like the faculty of the lightning calculator or the muscular dexterity of the acrobat; but they are powers of which men in general are absolutely devoid. Examples of them are "levitation," clairvoyance, ability to make one's self seen in distant places, to move objects without touching them, to put one's head into the fire or walk over burning coals without injury, and as many others as ingenuity can suggest. Men are still living who testify to having seen a medium rise in the air and waft himself around a room, or disappear through a window.

Now, if we admit the existence of gifted individuals having such abnormal powers as these, why not equally admit the existence of men having the faculty of seeing, or thinking they remember having seen, the nonexistent? The latter certainly seems much easier to suppose than does the former. It is a familiar fact of physiological optics that, in a faint light, if the eyes are fixed upon an object, the latter gradually becomes clouded and finally disappears entirely. Then it requires only a little heightening of a not unusual imagination to believe that, if the object that disappeared was a man, he wafted himself through the air and went out of the window.

What are we to say of the performances of mediums, tiers and untiers of hands, table-rappers, slate-writers, cabinet-workers, materializers, and the whole class of performers to which they belong? May we not adduce the general principle that similar phenomena are to be attributed to similar causes? These performances are quite similar to those of legerdemain, which we may witness for a few shillings in broad daylight at any exhibiton of the juggler's art. The principal point of difference is that they are less wonderful and, being generally seen in a faint light, give much greater opportunity for trickery than do those of the professional operators on the stage. Is it logical to attribute them to occult causes when we regard the professional performers as mere mystifiers? This question seems to the writer to answer itself.

I have not considered the supernatural knowledge supposed to be possessed by the "trance-medium" because the data for reaching any conclusion on the subject are too vague to admit of precise statements. The careful examination of Mrs. Piper made by the Psychical Society several years ago is unique in that the proceedings were reported stenographically. A few of her expressions did seem to show supernatural knowledge of, or impression by, facts with which she could not have been acquainted by any natural process. But the relation was wanting in that definiteness on which alone a positive conclusion could be based. The balancing of the probabilities on the two sides can well be made by everyone for himself.

In reaching a general conclusion upon all the evidence for the occult I would lay special stress on a feature already mentioned in narrating my personal experience. Almost all the narratives I have seen or heard relate to experiences of years previous, and scarcely ever to the present, so that the wonder has plenty of time to grow in the memory. The latest work on occultism with which I am acquainted is that of Mr. Willson, already cited. Turning over its leaves I fail to find any occurrence, in England at least, of later date than 1896, 12 years before publication. There are a few dubious-looking reports from other countries of a little later date than this, but nothing of the present time. Except the trance-mediums and fortune-tellers, who still ply their trade, and an occasional "materializer," the writer has heard nothing of mediumistic performances for ten or even twenty years. Why do

> Peor and Baalim
> Forsake their temples dim?

Is it not because in the course of years a wonder grows in the memory, like an oak from an acorn? The writer fails to see how a sane review of the whole subject can lead to any other conclusion than that occultism has no other basis than imperfect knowledge of the conditions, or how a wide survey of the field can leave any room for mystery.

We live in a world where in every country there are millions of people subject to illusions too numerous to be even classified. They arise from dreams, visions, errors of memory that can rarely be detected, and mistakes to which all men are liable. It is unavoidable that when any of these illusory phenomena are associated with a moving event at a distance, there will be an apparent coincidence that will seem more wonderful every time it is recalled in memory. There is no limit to devices by which ingenuity may make us see what is unreal. Every country has ingenious men by the thousands, and if a willingness to deceive overtly characterizes only a small fraction of them, that fraction may form so large a number of individuals, always ready to mystify the looker-on, that the result will be unnumbered phenomena apparently proving the various theories associated with occultism and spiritualism. Nothing has been brought out by the researches of the Psychical Society and its able collaborators except what we should expect to find in the ordinary course of nature. The seeming wonders—and they are plentiful—are at best of the same class as the wonder when a dozen drawers of the black grain of corn out of a million are presented to us. We are asked to admit an attraction between their hands and the black grain. The proof is conclusive enough until we remember that this dozen is only a selection out of millions, the rest of whom have not drawn the black grain. The records do not tell us, and never can tell us, about the uncounted millions of people who have forgotten that they ever had a vision or any illusion, or who, having such, did not find it associated with any notable occurrence. Count them all in, and nothing is left on which to base any theory of occultism.

5

The Need for Responsibility in Parapsychology: My Sixty Years in Psychical Research

E. J. DINGWALL

Since I gave up nearly all active work in psychical research, I have often been asked why, after more than sixty years' work in the field, I have finally lost most of my interest in it. There are two answers to the question. First, I have come to the conclusion that the present immense interest in occultism and in the grosser forms of superstition is due, to a certain extent at least, to the persistent and far-reaching propaganda put out by the parapsychologists. In this they have, I think, a very grave responsibility. With the gradual decline in the West of belief in Christianity has come not, as one might have hoped, a leaning toward the rational way of looking at the world but a decided tendency to adopt the magical way. Thus Christianity, unbelievable as it may be to the rational mind, has been supported by the occult superstitions of darker ages. One reason, therefore, for my ceasing work is that I do not wish to be associated with persons who actively support such superstitions as are today everywhere apparent. I cannot accept such responsibility.

The second reason is that, even if I wished, with increasing age I have neither the energy nor the capacity to check, substantiate, and attempt to verify the reports of cases I receive that either are already printed or are submitted to me with a view to publication. For example, some years ago certain experiments were undertaken in England under the auspices of the Society for Psychical Research (SPR) into an alleged telepathic communication between a mother and her child. Year after year I pressed for a report on the results. Finally a paper was published by the Society in 1968 giving an account of the work and its results. The record started with a trial at guessing seven letters. It stated that at the first trial there were four successes; but the table showed that there were five. These learned parapsychologists could not even take the trouble to count the success or failure of seven guesses. Presumably all must have read the

Reprinted from *A Century of Psychical Research*, edited by Allan Angoff and Betty Shapin (Parapsychology Foundation, 1971), by permission of the copyright owner, Parapsychology Foundation, Inc., and the author.

proofs, and the editor, a professional psychologist, had let it pass as it stood. If this kind of material, where the simplest calculations are erroneous and can be checked in five minutes, is passed by all concerned, what becomes of the elaborate statistical work submitted by parapsychologists in paper after paper in their journals? To speak bluntly, I no longer believe the stories I read or that are reported to me. They may or may not be true, but I have no longer any inclination to test their accuracy myself. You may well ask me why this is so. You will not, I think, much like the answer, but I intend giving it.

After sixty years' experience and personal acquaintance with most of the leading parapsychologists of that period I do not think I could name half a dozen whom I could call objective students who honestly wished to discover the truth. The great majority wanted to prove something or other: They wanted the phenomena into which they were inquiring to serve some purpose in supporting preconceived theories of their own.

Let me give an example, such as thought-transference, which is as good as any. When the British SPR was founded, the public was led to believe that at least a scientific survey was to be made, and I have no doubt that even some of those closely associated with the early days thought so too. But Myers, among others, had no such intention and cherished no such illusion. He knew that the primary aim of the Society was not objective experimentation but the establishment of telepathy. To understand why this was so it is necessary to realize the position in which so many educated and intelligent people found themselves during the 1870s and later in Victorian England. With the emergence of new scientific concepts touching the origin of man and his place in the universe, the very foundations of their religious beliefs began to give way. I myself am a Victorian, and I saw it happen in my own family. Swept hither and thither in the eddying currents of increasing unbelief, they looked about for straws to clutch at, straws that would do violence neither to their intelligence nor to their integrity.

It was then some years since the Hydesville knockings of the Fox sisters had promised a new revelation, but the dancing tables and miracles of materialization were hardly spiritual enough for the founders of the SPR. What was wanted was proof that mind could communicate with mind apart from the normal avenues, for if mental sharing was a fact when the persons concerned were incarnate it could plausibly be suggested that the same mechanism might operate when death had occurred. Thus the supernatural might be proved by science, and psychical research might become, in the words of Sir William Barrett, a handmaid to religion.

In the ears of every thinking rationalist the alarm bell was clearly audible. Occultism was to be brought back from the limbo into which it had been cast and, nicely arranged in a pseudoscientific setting, it was to be employed to buttress the mass of crude superstitions from which man, during so many centuries, had been struggling to free himself. The two ways of looking at the world were again to be brought face to face. The magical and the rational again confronted each other, but the magical had taken on a new appearance. No longer were its adherents criminals in red hats or ignorant priests driving devils out of sick people, but ladies and gentlemen in white coats performing what they called experiments in what they called their laboratories. Following their lead, the rest soon followed, and the sight of bishops supporting the latest occult nonsense became as familiar as the viewing by thousands on television of bad spirits being exorcised. We are drifting back into the Dark Ages, and it is to those times that I now propose to direct your attention. Perhaps from a brief survey it may be possible to draw some conclusions from the past and present state of occultism and parapsychology in Europe and America.

It now seems almost impossible to realize the extent of human suffering that had to be endured before man was able partially to free himself from the mass of crude occult teaching carried out by the Christians and others in their endeavor to stifle all independent thought that did not conform to their point of view. Rivers of blood flowed. Marketplaces were lighted up by the burning bodies of the hapless victims of these ruthless superstitious savages. Let me take a few examples of how the belief in the unseen world permeated society.

Consider the weather. From pagan times the gods were thought to be responsible for storms and tempests, and Christians, as in so many other matters, continued to hold many of these gross superstitions and made them articles of faith. The Fathers of the church thought that demons caused meteorological phenomena, and this was not confined to the few or to the ignorant. St. Thomas Aquinas believed it and so did St. Bonaventura, the Seraphic Doctor who died in 1274. In literature and art the idea was common, and in Bordone's picture of Venice you can see the demons bringing a storm to the city. Century after century passed but the idea was still kept alive, and it is said that Luther believed that if a stone was thrown into a certain pond a frightful storm would develop since the stone would release the devils sitting under the water. A somewhat similar idea seems to have been held in Tibet before the Chinese entered the country and began to influence the people to forsake their magical and occult beliefs and look at the world from a rational standpoint. Here devils were supposed to live underground, and mining operations, it was thought, might release them. Few countries illustrate better the unfortunate influence of occultism in restraining human progress. But even in Tibet the lamas would, I think, have hesitated before admitting beliefs that modern parapsychologists have no compunction in publishing in their pseudoscientific journals.

These harmful operations on the weather could be dealt with by exorcism, and as late as 1628 Locatelli gave a list of exorcisms that had been found most useful in this respect. Sometimes methods were simpler. The great German

Jesuit, Jakob Gretser, who died in 1628, stated that sometimes all that had to be done was to make the sign of the cross, speak a few words, and the storm would pass away. If exorcism failed, then other means were adopted. The Agnus Dei, a lump of wax blessed by the Pope, proved very valuable and lucrative, since in Paul II's Papal Bull of 1470, Paul II reserved to himself the distribution of the miraculous piece of wax.

The power of the demons in influencing the weather was questioned by a few bold men who were gradually beginning to see the enormity of the witchcraft persecutions. Such were Pomponazzi and Agrippa, but their suggestions were soon disposed of by writers of the caliber of Jean Bodin who relied on the supposed authority of the Bible and the pronouncements of the Popes. In this connection we are reminded that one of the critics of Jean Bodin and of the others with such views was Reginald Scot, whose great book *The Discoverie of Witchcraft* was first published in 1584.

Scot, who had little patience with the occultists and demonologists, was, as might be expected, bitterly assailed by the believers, among whom was numbered King James I, who described Scot's views as damnable. It was Scot who tried to show that conjurers were able to demonstrate what seemed to be examples of the paranormal whereas, when explained, they were clearly simple tricks. Neither the occultists of the sixteenth century nor modern parapsychologists of the twentieth have ever been able to grasp the fact that, because they did not then and do not now understand how these tricks were and are done, this does not mean that the effects are paranormal. Our modern occultists have apparently learned nothing since the sixteenth century, since they are still assuming that, because they do not understand how certain tricks are done, these must be paranormal. I need hardly mention such examples as Sir Oliver Lodge and the Zancigs and Sir Conan Doyle and Houdini. Even as I write these words I have received a leading journal dealing with parapsychology that is largely devoted to the amazing paranormal phenomena exhibited by a performer who, from the accounts, would seem to be an ordinary playing card manipulator and card location expert.

It might have been thought by some that influencing the weather by psychic means was an idea common in the Middle Ages but hardly one likely to be practiced in the twentieth century. Far from it. I could refer you to a number of so-called parapsychologists who have claimed to do just this and whose performances have been thought worthy of being discussed at length in the publications of the British SPR and shown on television. Instead of priests commanding spirits to depart, we have learned scientists and technicians exercising their powers of PK, mental concentration, and so forth. Such nonsense is always news and provides a sensation for a public whose mental faculties have been dulled by the ceaseless propaganda of the parapsychologists and who are perhaps even more credulous than their predecessors in the Dark Ages.

It would be too tedious and indeed too painful to describe the ghastly history of the witch delusions, based as they were on the pathetic view of occult influences on human life. Very gradually the belief that demons controlled the weather faded. God took their place and thus the lightning conductor was bitterly assailed, although some thought it a little strange that God permitted so many church spires to be struck and destroyed. However, in the eighteenth century a church in Brescia, in the vaults of which explosive mixtures had been stored, was struck and portions of the city were destroyed and thousands lost their lives. This event may have been responsible for the believers in demonic and divine influences at last consenting to the use of the conductor, because since then attacks on ecclesiastical buildings appear largely to have ceased. Occult meteorology, as we have seen, only reappeared in force in the twentieth century.

From occult influence on the weather I pass to similar influences on disease. Just as the early Christians carried over pagan beliefs in demonic influences and incorporated them into their own peculiar ideas, so similar views on the nature of health and disease prevailed among them. Sometimes the unfortunate patient was being punished by God; at other times he was possessed by spirits. In the same way as the study of meteorology was stifled so was medical work condemned unless it conformed with the crazy notions of these early occultists. Disease had to be dealt with by supernatural not natural means. This was a part of the magical way of looking at the world, and until Europe freed itself from its poisonous influence no advance was possible. Thus spiritual healing through relics, candles, and holy bones was widespread, and it made no difference if some of the bones, as was said to be the case with the relics of the holy Saint Rosalia of Palermo (+ c. 1160), were found to be those of a goat. Such details have never worried the believers in occult matters, then as now.

The struggle to free medicine from occult superstition was intensified by the objection to the study of anatomy. Had it not been through the courageous work of men like Vesalius, progress would have been even slower since the extraordinary idea of the resurrection of the body hindered the dissection of corpses.

Not only did the magical way of looking at the world hinder anatomical and medical research. It continued right up to modern times to oppose inoculation, the use of anaesthetics, and even ordinary standards of bodily hygiene and simple sanitation. To believers in spirits and demons such measures were useless, irreverent, and to be condemned. Thus thousands died who might have survived, and to be filthy and unwashed was a sign of sanctity. St. Abraham is said not to have washed his hands or feet for fifty years, while as to St. Simeon Stylites, the less said the better. His close association with the spiritual world was such that when the worms fell off his stinking ulcers he put them back to enjoy the food with which God had provided them.

The admiration that dirt inspired was not conducive to good health; but since diseases were thought by Christians to be due to demonic and occult influences so those who remained fairly healthy through their better regard for sanitation immediately became suspect, and many of these unfortunate people were burnt alive as a result of the magical way of looking at society. Similar events accompanied the treatment of lunacy. In the early centuries in Greece and Rome madness was regarded as a disease of the brain, and it was only after the emergence of deep-seated occult ideas regarding demons that insanity was regarded in the same way as other complaints. For example, one day a nun ate some lettuce, became ill, and was regarded as possessed. When ordered to leave the patient, the evil spirit declared that it was not his fault as he was sitting on the lettuce and the nun, not having made the sign of the cross, which would have been sufficient to make him jump off, swallowed him along with the lettuce. This rubbish, directly due to the belief in occult influences on human life, is credited to Pope St. Gregory the Great, who flourished about 590 C.E. and who was one of the four doctors of the Western Church. Indeed, it was thought that the demons often got into the body through eating, sometimes perhaps disguised as flies, and when the mouth was shut they found less guarded entrances. One priest, when attempting to drive a devil out, was so kind as to offer the demon asylum in his own body, and when that night he had a stomach ache he firmly believed the demon was running amok in his intestines.

Now and then persons who had not succumbed completely to the occult theories of the church ventured to make a few experiments. For example, in the famous late-sixteenth-century case of the possessed woman Marthe Brossier, Bishop Miron submitted her to a few simple tests, such as deceiving her in various ways and thus testing her reactions. Very gradually with the gathering strength of a growing rational outlook the occult delusion weakened, although it was active in Europe until 1853, when the Morzine epidemic broke out. Tests similar to those to which Marthe Brossier was subjected were applied and the same results followed. Little was heard of demonic possession until parapsychology began to flourish and the age-long occult superstitions were revived in modern dress. This refers not only, be it said, to the simple belief in the occult influences on human life, the weather, and the crops, but even to the more fantastic phenomena of the Holy Roman Church, such as the translation of the Holy House at Nazareth or the odd performances of the Holy Bambino of Bari.

As I have said, occultism—or psychical research, as it was then called in its modern form—began in the nineteenth century. As early as 1875 a commission was appointed by the University of St. Petersburg, and Mendeleyev wrote a long account of his experiences. It was this commission that dealt with the phenomena of spiritualism generally and did not confine itself to the alleged paranormal phenomena of mesmerism as did the much earlier French commissions, whose work and conclusions I described in my volume on France in the recently published four-volume work *Abnormal Hypnotic Phenomena*, which was sponsored and issued under the auspices of the Parapsychology Foundation.

It seems clear that Mendeleyev was not at all impressed by what he had seen and came to the conclusion that these practices made people lose their attitude of common sense, spread mystical ideas, and reinforced superstition. Thus as early as 1876 one eminent European scientific man realized the danger of occultism and issued a warning. It was in vain. The British SPR was founded in 1882 in order to establish telepathy, and from that date to the present day has issued thousands of cases and reports, some of very great interest and psychological value. Gradually its standards began to decline, until today its publications contain material that would not have been considered during the first 25 years of its existence. From the first, its activities were regarded with suspicion by the spiritualists, whose propaganda was every year becoming more shrill and more persuasive. The SPR in its early days was anxious to obtain good evidence, since its aim to establish thought-transference was in order to convince the Victorian intellectuals that their religious beliefs could be supported by scientifically proven facts. They were generally careful to avoid accusations of sensationalism that might make people think they were of the same way of thinking as the little group of eminent and thoroughly respectable persons who, before the foundation of the Society, described the miracles of the séance room and the extraordinary behavior of Sir William Crookes when confronted by such spiritualist stars as Florence Cook and Mary Showers. An attitude of aloofness was adopted, although in later years they did not hesitate to elect Crookes as their president, while apparently never taking the opportunity to ask him to explain his attempt to hush up the alleged fraud of Mary Showers so as not to damage the cause. Indeed, the Society had already begun its policy of suppressing evidence that might damage the work they had set their hearts on. In the 1870s occultism was flourishing in Europe and only a few saw the dangers inherent in its progress. As the years went by spiritualism made rapid progress, and the various societies and institutions began to attract persons who did not really understand what was involved. The SPR was busy with its renowned cross-correspondences, which have proved impossible to investigate since we are not yet permitted to examine the original documents. In France, Germany, Italy, and elsewhere the attention of parapsychologists was directed rather toward the physical than the mental phenomena, and the enigma of Eusapia Palladino seemed as difficult to solve as that of D. D. Home.

The First World War caused renewed interest in the question of survival, and Sir Oliver Lodge and Sir Arthur Conan Doyle became the chief propagandists of the New Revelation. The interest in occultism rapidly increased: thousands of séances were held and spiritualism began to be popular with persons who previously had been unmoved by its claims. Spirit photography became a subject of so-called "scientific" examination, and a society was founded with an extremely intelligent secretary in charge. I knew him well, and year after year I tried to point out the weakness of his case. It was as useless as to argue with a Capuchin about the devils on the lettuce. He was firmly convinced that occult action had been demonstrated. It was to me at least a striking example of what a deadly effect occultism could have on the mind of the parapsychologist. However, at long last and as sometimes happens when all the critical faculty has not been lost, the rational prevailed over the magical, and he realized that all his work had been in vain, that the evidence he had so stoutly defended was worthless and all the results he had had were probably fraudulent. At his death the whole of his vast collection passed into my possession, eventually, when catalogued and arranged, to add to the fine occult section of the Department of Printed Books in the British Museum.

As the years went by interest increased, and the years between the two world wars provided abundant material for the student. The magical way of looking at the world was getting stronger, and the kind of crazy beliefs I have described again emerged. Fairies and the little people were believed in, and I once attended a lecture where they were described and where photographs were shown of them sitting on a cabbage. But it was left until 1954 for a book to describe how a lady was possessed by a devil who apparently had forced her to swallow a piece of pork some time previously. Exorcisms proved of little help, but after a final attempt she vomited up what seemed to be the offending morsel, horns complete.

As long as occultism was of a type that consisted mainly of anecdotal evidence and ghost stories generally, there was little hope of attracting the attention of scientific men working in other fields. What was wanted, the parapsychologists clearly saw, was something that seemed learned, profound, and preferably something that the general public would not understand but that at the same time would attract the attention of more serious people. Statistics were the answer. Theories of probability were aired. The guessing of cards could be used and the results shown to be above chance. As all sources of error were excluded, what remained was clearly extrasensory perception. Thus in 1934 ESP in its modern fashionable attire was born, and tens of thousands of people started guessing cards and getting extraordinary results. Indeed, the American universities seemed to become full of sensitives, and ESP private circles began to be formed, and they too provided excellent evidence for the new occultism.

I was, I admit, wholly unmoved by the flood of propaganda put out by the parapsychologists in support of these claims. I did not believe in their stories, since the conditions seemed to me to be far from adequate and allowed plenty of scope for normal methods to operate. However, I was hardly prepared for what one day I found lying on a table in New York. It was, it appeared, one of the famous cards used in certain card-guessing experiments that were supposed to suggest ESP. This card was so crudely made that a mere glance at the back was sufficient to determine what was on the front. Although I knew that the cards used in the early experiments at Duke were so badly made that they were not in some cases even of the same shape, it was an additional shock to discover that some of the cards were almost transparent. Evidently some, at least, of the astonishing beyond-chance successes could easily be explained.

On my return to England I made known my findings and, as was to be expected, I met the usual attacks by those who sincerely believed that another Revelation was being born in the United States. In reply to my critics, I pointed out that they need not take my word for it since all they had to do was to go to the rooms of the SPR in London and look at the latest patented set of cards used at the parapsychology laboratory at Duke and see for themselves the kind of cards that were thought to be suitable for demonstrating ESP. Please note that this was seven *years* after the experiments had begun.

In parapsychology, when exposures of this kind are made, the defense usually follows a familiar pattern, just as it did when a few bold people in the Middle Ages ventured to question the believers' findings. In medieval times such objections were dangerous; it meant probably prison, torture, or even the stake. Today, thanks to the rational way of looking at life being a little stronger and more widespread, I could not be threatened with such dire penalties. All that the faithful could be promised by a leading British parapsychologist was a champagne dinner "after that man has died." Alas, he has predeceased me, but others will doubtless subscribe to the happy event that cannot now be much longer delayed. I hope I am there to see them enjoy it, but (may I venture to say it?) I doubt it.

It might have been thought that after an exposure of this sort the ESP propagandists would have quietly repaired the damage and seen to it that no such scandal again arose. The officials of the SPR in London were, it is true, somewhat disconcerted by these discoveries and succeeded in having cards made that could not be read from the back, which at least removed one source of error. Later, however, the Society, having apparently sold their stock of the opaque cards, began selling again the packs patented by J. B. Rhine in 1937. During tests in 1960 by an SPR working group, remarkable hits in clairvoyance runs were obtained; but it soon emerged that the transparent nature of the cards offered an easy solution. The handbook supplied with the cards in 1937, which was arranged and edited by members of the Duke University Parapsychology Laboratory, is quite clear as to how the cards were to be used, and in the single card-calling test the amateur is instructed to test his ESP by having the pack in front of him and calling the cards one after another.

After the lapse of 30 years, the transparent cards are still being sold and the instructions clearly state that all handling of the cards should be screened from the subject. But on the card of instructions provided with the deck of cards it is said that in the BT (Before Touching) clairvoyance card tests the experimenter can see the cards and thus clues might unwittingly be given to the subject during a series of tests of this kind.

In May 1969 Dr. R. A. McConnell stated in *American Psychologist* (24:533) that he now regarded these cards as "a museum piece," yet thinks that they can be "a lot of fun and can be used in preliminary testing." It may seem to be a lot of fun to test extrasensory perception by guessing what is on the front of a card when it is visible from the back, but it is certainly not a scientific experiment and must have led many interested people astray, as it did in the SPR 1960s group experiments. And yet Dr. McConnell still wonders why psychologists are not interested in ESP. In my view the experimental work of many modern psychologists is poor enough, but it can hardly compete with the early Duke experiments in which one of the grossest sources of error is still being perpetuated 30 years after it was pointed out.

I have now mentioned one indubitable fact in regard to ESP, which may provide a warning to beginners as to the kind of confidence to be placed in parapsychologists working in this field. Now I have to give another warning. It is common practice among parapsychologists to offer the most fantastic tales of the occult and then refuse to permit any adequate investigation by other people. The British SPR carried out this policy with relation to the cross-correspondence. Even the identity of some of the mediums was secret, and the public was only permitted to know who Mrs. Willett was after she was dead. It was then too late to ask her a few questions. The student will find that every kind of obstruction, evasion, and refusal will meet his request to be allowed to verify the details of the stories in question. Here is an example.

In 1959, the British SPR published an extraordinary tale of a luminous apparition containing a number of extremely unusual and interesting details. It was written by a member of the Council and was said to have been experienced by a distinguished scientist and his wife, who was a member of the SPR. It was also stated that they only consented to have their experience reported on condition that their identity could not be traced. One reason they gave for this was that they feared "curious friends." Does this not sound very odd? Curiosity about nature had, I thought, a place in science, and as Mrs. X was a member of the SPR one might be pardoned for supposing that she had some curiosity about apparitions and would understand that others felt the same. Suspecting that there was something very odd indeed about this case and the profound secrecy surrounding the persons involved, I did all I could to discover the facts, but I was met as usual by a wall of evasion and obstruction. No independent inquiry was to be allowed. The distinguished scientist and his SPR wife were said to be adamant in their refusal. In parapsychology you are constantly treated in this way if you seriously want to discover the truth. What the truth was in this case may never be known. It is, I think, possible that the whole story was a hoax designed to test the credulity of those willing to publish such tales in a supposedly scientific journal. Such seems to have been the case with the reports of two marvelous telepathic subjects in Czechoslovakia that were featured in a journal called the *New Scientist* in England. The editor had apparently accepted the tales as coming from a reliable source, but finally I had to explain to him that the whole case was a hoax and that nothing coming from parapsychological sources could be believed without the most rigorous and searching corroboration from impeccable sources.

An example of what is necessary can be seen in the recently published scripts of the late Miss Geraldine Cummins purporting to emanate from the famous SPR automatist Mrs. Willett. This book was supported by at least three ex-presidents of the SPR, one of whom wrote a long preface to it of over 70 pages. In the course of the communications two odd and startlingly evidential items of information, involving a word and a phrase, were given by the medium, and the editor of the book assured us both that these were actually in the diaries left by the deceased communicator. Fortunately, in this case the original diaries had been preserved. They were examined, and their owner stated that neither the word nor the phrase was to be found in them.

One additional recent example will suffice. It illustrates the attempts made by well-known and highly respected parapsychologists to suppress the truth when this is likely to harm what they call "the cause." This was an inquiry into what was described as a watertight case for survival, the pamphlet in question being placed on the bookstall of the Churches' Fellowship, with which the Bishop of Southwark is associated. The investigator, a prominent member of the Council of the SPR, made a thorough inquiry, assisted by myself and others, into the case. After the most laborious investigation it emerged that the data were based on a highly organized and complex fraud. It was considered desirable, therefore, to suppress it, and the Churches' Fellowship quietly withdrew the pamphlet from their bookstall. The chief investigator concerned has just died, and I was not surprised to hear that instructions had been given to destroy the whole of the dossier that had been built up over five years. I raised this matter at the annual general meeting of the British SPR. One member of the Council rose to defend the suppression of the case and the destruction of the documents. Only one ordinary member of the Society rose to express her surprise and disapproval. The other members preferred to remain silent.

I have chosen these recent cases simply as examples of what is going on today. During the past 60 years I have noted similar incidents in which leading parapsychologists and their propagandists have been shown to be barefaced liars. After but a few years in psychical research Frank Podmore, who was one of the few senior members of the British SPR who almost consistently rejected the magical way of looking at the world, became gradually more and more disillusioned. As early as 1880 he expressed his unbelief in many of the phenomena reported, including the alleged materialized form of Katie King. Although he spoke of the extravagance, grotesqueness, and absurdity of spiritualism, he at that time remained convinced that he had personally witnessed phenomena that he could not explain and that he regarded as paranormal. Hoping, doubtless, to be in a position to meet more mediums, he joined the National Association of Spiritualists and, surprisingly enough, was accepted and became a member of their Council. Some 20 years later his attitude had hardened. "Is it credible," he asked, "that there is anything of value behind this fifty years' record of quibbling and chicanery?" Perhaps Andrew Lang, who, although always near to credulity, yet managed to retain his sanity, was right when he was reported as saying that sometimes it looked as if psychical research does somehow change and pervert the logical faculty of scientific minds. It may be he was right. How otherwise can be explained the blind belief of Mrs. Sidgwick, who after years of experience with the subject accepted almost without question the alleged telepathic phenomena demonstrated by the late Gilbert Murray? With such credulity nothing can be done. As a seventeenth-century author was said to have written: "When men have once acquiesced in untrue opinions and registered them as authentic records in their minds, it is no less impossible to speak intelligently to such men as to write legibly on a paper already scribbled over."

I am often told by my critics that the progress of parapsychological studies is hindered by the skepticism with which the alleged discoveries are regarded by so many scientific men. So long as the methods of research and presentation adopted by modern parapsychologists continue, this is bound to be so. A glance at the stories published quarter by quarter by the British Society for Psychical Research and the mode of presentation there adopted would amply suffice to make any sane man approaching the subject for the first time take second thoughts. I am in complete agreement with Dr. Henry Margenau when he said that the field of parapsychology is "largely avoided by scientists because of the loose treatment of serious matters that prevails in it." It is clear that he, at least, has not been deceived by the tale so frequently told by the parapsychologists that orthodox scientists refuse to consider their results because they are afraid that, were they to do so, their whole picture of the world as they see it would be upset. What is perhaps the most damaging aspect is that few protests are made by serious officers of the Society. Year by year the same kind of tales and experiments are published and money urgently required for other work is frittered away on articles of not the smallest scientific value. Little is done to show disapproval or publish criticism of the more extreme vagaries of the spiritualist press, which week by week publishes stories of the miraculous that would hardly have found support in medieval times. For example, in a single issue of one of these periodicals with a wide circulation, I read that a carved wooden African head caused any amount of misfortune to those who possessed it and that it was finally sent to a cabinet minister. Within a week the Profumo scandal broke, presumably caused by the head. In the same issue I learn that apports used to come tinkling down from the small end of Mrs. Estelle Roberts's trumpet; that a gentleman in Puerto Rico, a deaf mute since birth, speaks and sings in perfect English; that a full-form materialization of a person just dead appeared before 20 witnesses; and that in England a rector stated that two pigs had been reduced to skeletons through the evil eye. Nothing from the 1870s could really approach this miscellany of marvels.

Again, organizations are functioning in England that have the support of large numbers of bishops and other presumably sane individuals who have so fully adopted the magical way of looking at the world that they easily accept the tales sponsored by these bodies and think nothing of senior members going around exorcising alleged haunted houses, driving demons out of mentally disturbed persons, and advertising themselves and their performances on television. Years ago one of the occult magazines published a fantastic tale. I mention it merely as an example of the kind of story put out by so-called parapsychologists and the difficulty experienced by any critic anxious to discover the facts. In an English quarterly magazine, *Beyond,* edited by a prominent member of the Churches' Fellowship, occurs an article in 1961 said to be a translation of a paper originally published in a French journal. It was considered of such interest that it was also published in the Fellowship's quarterly review. This story purported to show that the power of prayer had been scientifically proved. It stated that a Mr. N. J. Stewel, an atomic scientist, tried with his colleagues to discover what happened in a human brain when its owner was at the point of death. A woman who was an earnest Christian was chosen for the experiment. It was thought that she had but a short time to live. Measuring apparatus was installed in her room in order to record movements and oscillations of her brain. Five well-known scientists conducted the experiment. At the moment of death the needle moved violently as the cerebral waves affected the instruments. There was apparently no contact between the apparatus and the dying woman.

I determined to look into this case as I suspected that it was fiction being circulated by the parapsychologists to assist their propaganda. I started by inquiries that included a lengthy correspondence with the Chairman of the Churches' Fellowship early in 1962. As I expected, no kind of corroboration of the story was available. I discovered that the French journal in which it originally appeared was a French version of a paper called *Herald of His Coming,* published in California. The editor of the French paper refused to answer any letters as did the editor of *Herald of His Coming.* The inquiry, after hours of wasted time, had to be abandoned. So I returned to where I started.

I do not intend to waste any more time over the hoaxes and fictional reports put out by parapsychologists. The Churches' Fellowship is one of the leading Christian occult organizations in England today and has an impressive list of bishops and distinguished clerics supporting it. It is abundantly clear that before publishing these tales those responsible made no attempt whatever to obtain any kind or sort of corroboration. The revival of occultism under the name of psychical research has been accompanied by nearly all the follies that were so striking a feature in medieval times and, masquerading as science, has succeeded in attracting the attention of many who have little idea of what lies below the surface. Most of Europe appears to be infected, and it is, in my view, one of the signs of the disintegration of Western culture. Horoscopes appear in most newspapers every day, and the state of the public mind in England at least can be measured by a statement made to me by a well-known worker in the BBC. He told me that today, if a man was shown falling off a chair and the viewers were told that he was in a trance, they would be thrilled. In Germany, a society has been formed to try to combat the growing superstitious attitudes that are so common in the population, but throughout Europe charms and amulets are on open sale, and, as far as I can see, leaders of European and American parapsychology do little or nothing to show their disapproval. In my view such silence on their part is almost tantamount to approval, but it has nearly always been a feature of the parapsychological scene.

In the issue of the *American Psychologist* for May 1969, already mentioned, R. A. McConnell, in an admirable summary of some difficult questions, asks why psychologists are not interested in ESP. Has it ever struck him that their lack of interest is because they do not want to be associated with the parapsychologists whose reputation for the pursuit of truth is not of the highest and who are linked with a crowd of dubious and half-baked seekers after marvels. Were it to rid itself of these people instead of suffering them and appointing them to positions of prestige and authority, it might have a great future. But I doubt if the purge will come in my time.

In my view parapsychologists have a grave responsibility in these matters. Modern mass means of communication pick up these tales of the occult world, and the general public is led to believe that the paranormal can be observed almost anywhere at any time. Children in England are holding ouija board séances, believing that they can get in touch with the spirits, and on several occasions the results have not been happy. An attitude of skepticism is deplored and the public is led to believe that anybody who throws doubts on the alleged discoveries of the parapsychologists is sunk in a morass of outdated materialism. Little do they know what lies beneath the surface of the new occultism and the new witchcraft. Anyway, I have finished with it.

Part 2

The Argument from Fraud

6

Spiritualists, Mediums, and Psychics: Some Evidence of Fraud

PAUL KURTZ

The spiritualist movement, which first developed in the mid-nineteenth century in the United States and Great Britain, was the precursor of modern interest in psychical research and parapsychology. It was a movement that was regrettably full of fraud and deceit. The spiritualists claimed that certain individuals possessed special paranormal powers and that this enabled them, among other things, to communicate with discarnate spirits.

The basic premise was that human personalities survived death and were able to communicate through specially selected persons. The spirit world manifests itself in many ways: by mental communication, such as telepathy, visions, and apparitions, and in physical phenomena, such as poltergeists, levitation, table tappings, ectoplasmic emissions, materializations, the playing of musical instruments, and automatic writing. The most convenient method of communication was in a special séance in a darkened room, where the discarnate person would communicate through a medium by verbal or physical manifestations.

The spiritualist movement was religious, or quasi-religious, in motivation and function, for it pointed to a hidden realm, transcending this world. And it gave the promise of an afterlife. Hope for survival was one of its main inspirations. There soon developed two camps: (1) believers, who accepted the existence of another dimension of reality and the ability of certain mediums to communicate with it, and (2) skeptics and disbelievers, who rejected the phenomena as self-deceptive nonsense.

Belief in spiritualism has been common to all ages of human history. The Bible is full of reports of supernatural phenomena, including visitations from the dead and apparitions in the dream or waking state. And, in the third century, the skeptical philosopher Porphyry investigated the alleged movements of untouched inanimate objects, the levitation of mediums, the apparitions of spirits, and other unusual manifestations. Similar accounts of spiritualistic phenomena are found in the lives of the saints, in the accounts of witch trials, and in reports of poltergeists and haunted houses and castles. In the eighteenth century, the Swedish mystic Emanuel Swedenborg gave much impetus to spiritualism when he claimed to possess clairvoyant and precognitive powers.

The Fox Sisters

Modern spiritualism literally began in 1848, when the members of a poor and isolated family living in Hydesville, a small town in upstate New York, became convinced that their house was haunted by the spirit of a man who allegedly had been murdered and buried in their cellar.

The story of the Fox sisters reads like fiction. It involved the Foxes' two young daughters, Margaretta (age 11, later called Margaret), and Kate (age 9), and their much older sister, Leah.* The only thing that was real was the gumption of the sisters in perpetuating this fraud and the unbelievable receptivity manifested by the public in swallowing it whole.

It all began when the Fox family heard unusual noises in the house. On March 31, 1848, after Kate and Margaret had gone upstairs to bed, strange rappings were heard by their parents downstairs. They rushed upstairs to be greeted by knockings and rappings throughout their daughters' bedroom. When Kate snapped her fingers, rappings would follow. The raps "counted" to ten and even gave the ages of the children. When Mrs. Fox, who was prone to believe in spiritualistic forces, asked: "Is this a disembodied spirit that has taken possession of my dear children?" the answer was a sharp rap, which was taken to be an affirmative response. Mrs. Fox ran to tell the neighbors, and they flocked to the house. One of them, William Duesler, later reported that on another evening 12 or 14 people were in the house too frightened to enter the bedroom. Duesler went in and heard Mrs. Fox ask questions and heard the rappings in response. Various neighbors also got answers to their questions. The "spirit" gave the ages of those present—one rap for each year—and the number of children in each family.

The news of these remarkable occurrences swept the area surrounding Hydesville, and new visitors appeared day after day. The ability of the Fox sisters to interpret the spirit world was enhanced when their older brother David suggested that they spell out words. He would name the letters of the alphabet, and the spirit would rap when the proper letter was reached. Although a slow and laborious process, in this way messages were received from the beyond. The careers of the Fox sisters took a dramatic turn when their older sister, Leah Fox Fish, appeared on the scene. She lived in Rochester and had heard about the foregoing events. She immediately took Margaret and Kate aside and had them show her how they were able to produce the mysterious noises.

In subsequent months, hundreds of curious people visited the Foxes in

*There are conflicting accounts of the ages of the girls. Arthur Conan Doyle says they were 14 and 11 when the hauntings began. The Fox sisters themselves, later in life, made themselves younger by claiming that they were only 8 and 6 at the time. I have used the ages provided by the *Encyclopaedia Britannica* (11th ed.).

Hydesville and in Rochester, where they visited Leah; many came away believers.

At the behest of Eliah Wilkinson Capron, a newspaper editor, and George Willets, a large hall was rented in Rochester for three performances. They evidently saw the money-making potential of the phenomena, and they were right—nearly 400 people turned up the first night, each paying 25 cents admission, a goodly sum in those days. The audience was treated to the rappings and then heard a lecture delivered by Capron. Each night a committee of five persons was selected from the audience to investigate the strange doings. Curiously, no longer confined to the haunted house in Hydesville, the rappings followed the Fox sisters wherever they went, and they were able to invoke any number of departed spirits.

Each night the crowd increased. None of the three appointed committees was able to detect any evidence of fraud. There was audience opposition, however. On the third evening a riot ensued, led by Joseph Bissell and others, who insisted that the whole thing was full of "humbug" perpetrated on the unwary in order to fleece them of their money. The local newspapers were also critical of the Fox sisters and ridiculed the notion of spirit communication. But the sisters' powers soon received national attention when Horace Greeley's *New York Weekly Tribune* reported on the three meetings after receiving a letter from Capron and Willets. Greeley was one of the most powerful and respected journalists of the time. The response to the reports in his paper was immediate.

Margaret and Kate were invited to New York City, where they held séances in Barnum's Hotel. They were visited by great throngs of people, many of them hopeful of making contact with dead relatives and loved ones. They were not disappointed. Spirit communication was constantly displayed. Many of those who asked questions were stunned at the accurate replies they received.

Greeley became a staunch believer. He said he was confident of the "perfect integrity and good faith" of the Fox sisters. Indeed, they were invited to stay at his mansion. Other New York City newspapers, however, were highly skeptical, and they accused the girls of "jugglery" and "outright fraud." Yet belief in the Fox sisters grew rapidly. Many distinguished persons were won to the cause, including Judge Edmonds, of the New York Supreme Court. Many made pilgrimages to the séances and were duly impressed: James Fenimore Cooper, the famous novelist; George Bancroft, the historian; William Cullen Bryant, the poet; Governor Tallmage of Wisconsin; General Bullard; and others. Moreover, hundreds of other mediums came forth who were able to manifest similar powers, and spiritualism swept the country like a prairie fire. Séances were convened all over the United States. The Fox sisters went on a money-making western tour, and wherever they went a new circle of spiritualists was established. The concept of spiritualism was now strongly implanted in the popular imagination. Dozens of magazines and newspapers were founded to proclaim the new faith.

George Templeton Strong, a prominent New York attorney, deplored the popularity of spiritualism and pronounced it an ominous development. He had attended several séances but could not figure out how the things he witnessed had occurred. He nevertheless thought the spiritualist explanations were unacceptable and particularly decried their easy acceptance by otherwise sensible people. "What would I have said six years ago," Strong wrote in 1855, "to anybody who could have predicted . . . that hundreds of thousands of people in this country would believe themselves able to communicate daily with the ghosts of their grandfathers?" (Nevins and Thomas 1952, 244–245). And he observed that the believers included "ex-judges of the Supreme Court, senators, clergymen, and professors of physical science" who even lectured and wrote books touting spiritualism. There were then millions of Americans who apparently accepted spiritualism, and it was estimated that some 30,000 mediums were conducting séances, though it was no doubt difficult to get an accurate census of believers.

Interestingly, from the earliest days critical exposés of the Fox sisters were available. But these had little effect on those who wished to believe. Dr. E. P. Langworthy, a Rochester physician, reported on February 2, 1850, in the *New York Excelsior* that his investigation had indicated that the rappings invariably came from under the girls' feet or from objects, such as tables or doors, with which they were in physical contact. He concluded that the noises were produced by Margaret and Kate themselves. Others came to a similar conclusion. The Reverend John M. Austin wrote to the *New York Tribune* that the knocking could be produced by cracking the toe joints. And in December 1850, the Reverend Dr. Potts demonstrated to an audience in Corinthian Hall in Rochester that he could replicate the raps in the same way.

That same year, the Reverend Charles Chauncey Burr and his brother published a book, *Knocks for the Knocking,* in which they maintained that they had investigated the Fox sisters and other mediums in five states and attributed the alleged phenomena to "fraud" and "delusion." Burr said that he could produce the rappings in seventeen ways, his favorite being toe cracking.

In February 1851, a committee of three doctors from the University of Buffalo, Austin Flint, Charles A. Lee, and C. B. Coventry, investigated Margaret and Leah (who by now was also able to produce knocking sounds). They concluded that the raps were voluntarily produced by the sisters. They had observed their facial expressions and inferred that the sounds were produced by the cracking of their bones, probably their knee joints. The semi-dislocation of the bone joints, they said, caused distinct jarrings of doors, tables, and other objects with which they had contact. Using a controlled test, the doctors had Margaret and Leah sit on a couch, extending their legs so that their heels rested on cushions. The sisters sat in this manner for 50 minutes, urging the spirits to communicate. But there were no rappings—that is, until they were again able to put their feet on the floor. Leah admitted that the spirits did not manifest themselves when their feet were on cushions. She offered the lame excuse that her friendly spirits had retired when they saw "the harsh conditions imposed by their persecutors" and that they could do nothing to detain them. This is a pretext often encountered in the psychical field: that the presence of skeptics prevents the effect from happening.

Another decisive indication that skulduggery was afoot was that Mrs. Norman Culver, David Fox's sister-in-law, admitted in 1851 that the girls had confessed to her how they did the trick. Mrs. Culver gave her testimony in the form of a deposition. "The girls have been a great deal in my house," she said, "and for about two years I was a sincere believer in the rapping." But she went on to say that she eventually began to suspect they were deceiving people. She offered to assist Kate, who then told her how they did the trick. "She revealed to me the secret. The raps are produced with the toes. All the toes are used. After nearly a week's practice with Catherine [Kate] showing me how, I could produce them perfectly myself" (Capron 1855, 421). Margaret had also told her that, when people insisted on observing her feet and toes, she could produce raps with her ankles and knees.

Given these exposés, the Reverend Burr predicted that the "reign of these imposters is nearly at an end" (Isaacs 1983, 95). How wrong he was. Exposés continued to be offered by critical scientific bodies, but to no avail. The effect of challenging the faith of believers is often only to strengthen their beliefs. In 1853, Professors Henry and Page of the Smithsonian Institution concluded that the raps were produced not by the spirit world but by the Fox sisters themselves, as did a committee of three Harvard professors in June 1857. In 1884 the Seybert Commission at the University of Pennsylvania also attributed the rapping sounds to foot pulsations.

There were of course defenders of the Fox sisters. Of particular note was the famous British scientist Sir William Crookes, who held séances with Kate in London in 1871. His tests led to the following emphatic conclusion concerning the Fox sisters' powers (Crookes 1874, 88):

> With a full knowledge of the numerous theories which have been started, chiefly in America, to explain these sounds, I have tested them in every way that I could devise, until there has been no escape from the conviction that they were true objective occurrences not produced by trickery or mechanical means.

In time the Fox sisters became world-famous celebrities, giving séances even at the White House and for Queen Victoria in London. Large sectors of the public remained enthralled. Yet the mediums had their permanent critics.

The Bar Association of New York City decided to do what it could to clear the city of mediums, whom they considered to be con artists. With this in mind, they engaged the Academy of Music for the night of October 21, 1888, in order to expose the spiritualist movement. Margaret Fox Kane was signed on as the main speaker. What a coup to have one of the leading exponents of spiritualism denounce it! After 40 years of deception, and apparently disenchanted, Margaret now made a complete confession, with her sister Kate in the audience to cheer her on. (Her written confession was published in the *New York World.* See Chapter 7 of this volume.) Margaret began her talk:

> There is no such thing as a spirit manifestation. That I have been mainly instrumental in perpetrating the fraud of spiritualism upon a too-confiding public many of you already know. It is the greatest sorrow of my life. . . . When I began this deception, I was too young to know right from wrong.

She blamed her sister Leah (with whom she had had a bitter feud) for using her and Kate in order to make money and for sucking them into a grand deception. Beginning with toe crackings, her sister Leah later added other spiritualistic attractions to the repertoire, including levitation, the plucking of musical instruments, and the appearance of ghosts made out of luminous paper. Kate Fox Jencken, in an interview published in the *New York Herald,* concurred with Margaret in the need to expose spiritualists. She insisted that "Spiritualism is a humbug from beginning to end . . . the biggest humbug of the century."

Doctors in the audience were invited onto the stage to observe close up. Margaret came forward in her stocking feet and mounted a low pine table. The audience listened raptly. One could hear a pin drop. Margaret repeatedly snapped her big toe against the top of the table, and loud distinct rappings were heard reverberating throughout the auditorium. Here was the woman who helped to launch the spiritualist movement now contributing to its denouement. Margaret was highly excited and agitated; she danced, clapped her hands, and exclaimed: "Spiritualism is a fraud from beginning to end! It's a trick. There's no truth in it!" (Rinn 1954, 61).

Could spiritualism survive this crushing exposé? Spiritualists later denied that the sisters had ever made a confession; they said that they were alcoholics (which was true), that they entered into the exposé game for money, and that their testimony was unreliable.

After the Academy of Music meeting, both sisters took to the road, giving numerous other demonstrations wherever they went. Their elder sister, now Mrs. Leah Underhill, denied their entire story. The spiritualists fought back, and they attempted to have Margaret's children taken from her. A year later, Margaret recanted her confession, saying that she had been misled by unscrupulous men. In desperate financial straits, she found that there was far less money in the debunking business than she had anticipated. Arthur Conan Doyle, a dedicated proponent of spiritualism, was typical of those who accepted this retraction, saying that Margaret had been led astray. Moreover, Doyle (1926, 113) postulated that "ectoplasmic rods" had protruded from her feet and in some way were responsible for the raps but that this was still a "psychic force." Histories of spiritualism are written today by sympathetic paranormalists who still consider that the Fox sisters were genuine. They either fail to mention the confession of fraud or discount it. (For example, see Inglis 1977.)

Nevertheless, the Fox sisters had revealed other tricks of the trade. They said that at a séance they would watch the facial movements of a questioner as he or she recited the alphabet for clues as to the meaningful letters. This technique, known as "muscle reading," is widely employed by spiritualists. They also revealed how they were able to make rapping sounds appear to come from different parts of the room. By placing a foot at the bottom of a table or a door, they could make the sound seem to emanate from the top. If they wished to make the sound seem to resound from a distant wall, they simply had to make the raps louder and look earnestly at a spot on the wall. By putting a toe on the footboard of the bed, the sound would reverberate throughout the room (Brandon 1984, 7). They were not above using accomplices either and, when it suited their purposes, someone would rap in the cellar or under the stage at the signaled time.

Much of this is detailed in a book written by Reuben Davenport (1888) entitled, *The Death Blow to Spiritualism*. Both sisters contributed a preface authorizing the book and testifying to its veracity. But, although it may have momentarily weakened the spiritualist movement, it did not lead to its demise. For after the death of the Fox sisters other mediums and spiritualists came forth to take up the cudgels and to lead the unwary into a further quest for discarnate spirits.

Other famous mediums, many of them highly controversial, were abundant in the late nineteenth century and continued their performances well into the twentieth century. Many were tested by committees of distinguished scientists. Some were found to be blatant frauds, and others were thought to possess spiritistic powers. A curious impasse developed. There were those who insisted that, once a medium was caught cheating, all of his or her other alleged manifestations were to be discounted and taken as unreliable. Proponents of a spiritualistic paranormal universe insisted, however—and still do—that although some of the testimony on behalf of a medium or a psychic may be tainted by obvious cheating there may still be other well-observed and well-documented evidence for the existence of genuine anomalous phenomena.

Nevertheless, the number of outright cases of fraud were numerous. For example, Jonathan Koons, a farmer from Dover Village, Ohio, had built a log house and locked it tight. But he discovered that reams of spirit messages were received in the locked interior. He brought in various musical instruments and phosphorous solutions for the spirits to dip their hands in and manifest themselves. Word spread quickly that the spirits of departed persons would play the instruments and that this would lead to pandemonium.

Another medium, Henry Gordon, developed the power of levitation. He was allegedly raised from the floor by spirit forces and carried to the ceiling of an adjacent room. Since the séance room was always dark, people could believe he was levitating only from his cries that he was "going up" or "floating in air," and actual confirmation of such events was never made.

A kind of religious fervor swept large regions of the land. The Reverend C. Hammond claimed that he had received a spirit communication from Tom Paine. In Columbus, Ohio, a Miss Vinson, a medium, and an elderly Methodist minister gave public sittings. Musical instruments were suspended from the ceiling on strings; when the lights were turned off the spirits played the instruments. One evening two men turned on the lights in the midst of the concert to find the clergyman and the medium playing the instruments.

Thus, if the general public was able to debunk such blatant chicanery, why didn't scientists? In 1857, after suffering the criticism that orthodox science was unwilling to examine the claims of spiritualism, three professors from Harvard University—Louis Agassiz, Benjamin Peirce, and Eben Horsford—agreed to test the authenticity of mediumship; and the *Boston Courier* offered $500 for proof of any genuine spiritualistic ability. Leah Fox Brown, Kate Fox, and four other mediums had been brought to Boston to be tested, but they were unable to demonstrate any powers under the stringent conditions laid down by the professors.

Other mediums volunteered to come forth to be tested by scientists, believing that they could outwit them. Indeed, they often were able to do so, for many scientists were convinced of spiritualistic phenomena and were easily hoodwinked. Others were more skeptical, and many mediums were shown to be cheating. Henry Slade was caught cheating by John W. Truesdell in 1872 in New York. In 1876, he was also unmasked by Professor Lankester and Dr. Donkin and was convicted and sentenced to three months in jail, though he was able to abscond to the Continent before the sentence was carried out. He had been caught substituting a slate upon which a "spirit" message had been written. He was again caught in Ontario, Canada, in 1882, and again and again.

Robert Owen, the famous utopian socialist, was a believer in spiritualism, and in 1860 he reported having seen a luminous figure of a woman walk through the room during a séance led by Leah Fox Brown Underhill. These materializations soon became common. Often religious overtones were present. Sometimes the participants would begin the séance by singing hymns. Many of those who visited mediums did so in the expectation that they would hear from a dead relative or lover. They would enter the séance room with high expectations and were often drained by the experience. In this emotionally charged atmosphere, as they sat around a table in a dimly lit room, all sorts of occult phenomena were manifested.

To aid mediums in their efforts, a "Blue Book" was circulated among the mediums in the United States. It contained a pool of personal information that the mediums had gathered about the people who frequented their séance parlors. And, when arriving in a strange town, the medium or an accomplice might pay a visit to the local cemetery to take down names and dates of death. In this way it was not difficult to unnerve an unsuspecting client by providing information "that could not have been known from any other source."

In spite of the audacity of the mediums, their trickery was often detected by the wary, and so the general public was alerted to possible dupery. However, true believers who wished fervently to believe in an afterlife did so in spite of the evidence to the contrary. The passion for overbelief, particularly concerning matters of life and death, is so powerful that the critical defenses that are normally put up can often be broken down, particularly in the face of a glimmer of hope about future immortality.

D. D. Home

Many consider Daniel Dunglas Home to have been the most awesome medium of the era. Home performed miraculous feats that few were able to explain. Even today spiritualists and paranormalists look back on Home with respect. Although he was on occasion tested by scientists—notably Sir William Crookes, who vouched for his "remarkable powers"—Home was never caught in the act of cheating. However, there is some evidence that he engaged in deception.

The Home case is important because we do not have a massive amount of negative tests, as with the Fox sisters and Eusapia Palladino, whom we will discuss later. But we are at least close enough in time to Home that we may surmise and possibly reconstruct how he operated.

There is always some risk to the fraud thesis, of course, for Home may have been genuine; the phenomena that were reported to have occurred in his presence may have in fact occurred, and perhaps only a supernormal explanation for them will suffice. Scientific skeptics cannot, as do religious believers, refuse to examine the evidence, nor can we simply believe a priori that fraud is involved in all such cases. If the will to believe tends to cloud the perception and judgment of true believers, who are inclined to accept paranormal matters readily, then, conversely, it can also bias the observation and interpretation of skeptics, who might refuse to accept the existence of anomalous events no matter what the evidence, or who might believe that in all cases something untoward must be present. It is clear that in the paranormal areas as elsewhere objectivity is essential.

What are the facts of Home's career? Daniel Home was born in Edinburgh in 1833. He claimed descent from the tenth Earl of Home, a distinguished Scottish family, and he assumed the middle name of Dunglas. No proof is given for his aristocratic lineage, and some commentators, such as Trevor H. Hall (1984), have attempted to demonstrate that Home fabricated this heritage in order to make his way into the uppercrust of society. While quite young, Home was adopted by an aunt and taken to the United States. In his autobiography, *Incidents in My Life,* Home (1864) reported that he had "second sight," or spiritual powers: he claimed that when he was only 13 he was able to foresee the death of a school chum and that he thereafter communicated with his friend's spirit. He also said that, in 1850, he clairvoyantly saw the death of his mother in Scotland. Loud raps and moving furniture disturbed his aunt's quiet household, so much so that she turned him out.

From that time onward Home assumed the role of a professional medium, as did so many others following the great success of the Fox sisters. His style was different from that of other mediums, however, in that he did not charge fees for his séances, though he apparently was able to exist on the largesse of those influenced by his personal charm. He was not unlike the man who came to dinner and stayed on indefinitely as a house guest. His friends in America—and there were many famous personalities who came under his spell—raised funds to send him to England in 1855, and he soon acquired the reputation there of being a talented medium. He said that he considered his mission in life to be "a great and holy one": not to make money but to prove the existence of immortality, which would "draw us nearer to God."

In spite of Home's professed lack of greed, his grateful admirers showered him with gifts—as did Mrs. Jane Lyons, who presented him with £33,000 and other emoluments. But she changed her mind mid-stream, declaring that Home had unduly influenced her. Home had delivered "spirit messages" to Mrs. Lyons in which her dead husband bade her to adopt Home as her son and to make a will giving him the family arms and name and all her property. Mrs. Lyons took Home to court, and he was required to make full restitution. Later in life he was married twice to women with considerable fortunes, one of Russian nobility, which enabled him to live in affluence thereafter.

Home gave spiritual advice and séances to a host of distinguished personalities, and it was largely on their testimony that his reputation was based. Among these were Sir David Brewster, Lord Brougham, Sir E. Bulwer Lytton, T. A.

Trollope, Viscount Adare (who became the fourth Earl of Dunraven), and Lord Lindsay (later Earl of Crawford). He also gave séances on the Continent for the French, German, and Dutch crowned heads, and even for the Czar of Russia.

Home's séances were similar to those performed by other mediums of the day. At first there were knocks, raps, and vibrations of the table. Next the séance table levitated, and the hands and clothing of the sitters under the table were touched, presumably by a spirit. More complicated phenomena were then produced: Hands and arms and other luminous objects would manifest themselves, and pieces of furniture would suddenly move toward the séance table. But Home added other specialized features to his act: He made an accordion float in the air; or he held it with one hand, and without any apparent touching of the keys it played a tune (invariably "Home Sweet Home" or "The Last Rose of Summer"). More astonishing to his bewildered guests were the occasions when his body would become elongated and when he plunged his hands into the fireplace and walked around carrying a glowing piece of coal. Considered even more remarkable was Home's ability to levitate his body above the heads of the sitters, sometimes touching them as he floated by (Podmore 1902; 1910). His most famous feat was his supposed levitation out one window of a London apartment and in at another.

Home's great reputation was based on the hearsay of those who attended his séances. He very rarely was tested by scientists under rigorously controlled conditions. During his performances, very few controls were applied. Neither his hands nor his feet were held or bound, as was the case in testing other mediums. Home himself decided who was to sit next to him at a séance. At the beginning of a sitting, when raps and knocks were heard, the light was fairly decent. Before the more complex manifestations occurred, such as the appearance of spirit hands or the movement of articles of furniture, the lights were usually turned off and only a fireplace, often screened, or an open shutter emitted any light. Under such conditions there were few, if any, safeguards against trickery, such as the possible use of wires, hooks, pulleys, ventriloquism, or other forms of conjuration. This was before the time of the Society for Psychical Research and the available reports hardly sufficed as a basis for scientific judgment.

Home used suggestion effectively, as in his levitation sequence. When he would declare, "I am now going up," no one would see him, yet they believed him. Or he would say, "I am being elongated," when he might have been simply stretching, contorting, or even standing on his toes. Perception in a dim light could always be influenced by suggestive remarks by Home. Some critics postulated that he caused hallucinations in some of his visitors; others thought that he was an outright imposter. Robert and Elizabeth Browning, the noted poets, watched Home at a séance, and Browning later accused him of being a "cheat." He even composed a poem to defame Home, calling it, "Mr. Sludge, the

Medium."

It is said that Home, unlike virtually all other mediums of his day, had never been caught in the act of outright cheating. Frank Podmore indicates, however, that there was some evidence of fraud, and he cites a letter from a Mr. Merrifield, written in 1855, giving an account of a sitting he witnessed conducted by Home. Merrifield reported that the only light in the séance room was that coming in the window from the stars, since the moon had already set. He described the séance, which took place about 11 o'clock in the evening. Home sat at one side of the table, the participants on the other side. His hands were under the table. After hearing some raps, someone suddenly reported that they saw a "spirit hand," and an object resembling a child's hand with a long, wide sleeve attached to it appeared in the dim light. The object appeared at one of two separate distances from the medium, either that of his foot or his outstretched hand; and, said Merrifield, "I noticed that the medium's body or shoulder sank or rose in his chair accordingly." Then, he said, "I saw the whole connection between the medium's shoulder and arm, and 'the spirit hand' dressed out on the end of his own" (Podmore 1910, 45–46). He reported that the trick was so plain to his eyes and the company present so reverential and adoring that he was seized with a strong impulse to laugh.

The journalist Delia Logan reported on a similar séance held at the home of a nobleman in London. The nobleman observed Home groping his way through the darkened room, while every now and then luminous hands would appear. According to Logan, the nobleman saw Home surreptitiously place a small bottle on the mantle. The nobleman thereupon covertly took the bottle and later discovered that it contained phosphorated oil, which was responsible for the luminosity. Everyone in the room nevertheless had been impressed by Home's "spiritualistic marvels." The nobleman never confronted Home directly with his discovery. (See Chapter 9 of this volume.)

Home was generally very cautious in conducting his séances, and thus he never suffered direct exposure. He always prepared his performance with consummate skill. Much has been made of the fact that Home had been tested by Sir William Crookes. Crookes's first séance with Home took place in 1871 and was attended by Crookes and his personal friends. Various phenomena appeared: the partial levitation of Home, the plunging of his hands into the fire, the levitation of the table, the appearance of luminous hands, and the playing of the accordion without any apparent fingers touching the keys. How did Home accomplish these things? Did he use black string? Did he carry a harmonica in his mouth in order to play the tune, as has been suggested, or did he use a music box? Was Crookes taken in by conjuration? It is difficult today to reconstruct the full sequence of events or to explain how they occurred (Crookes 1889; Podmore 1902; 1910).

Three things all too often stand out in the history of psychical research and its relation to science: First, psychical phenomena more readily tend to occur when the conditions for testing it are fairly loose and informal. Second, as test conditions are tightened up the effect tends to disappear. Third, great men of science, if they are predisposed to believe in paranormal or spiritual phenomena, may be as easily duped as the ordinary person. Indeed, many conjurers believe that some scientists who accept the ethical standards of science and trust the honesty of their test subjects are often, because of their naiveté, easier to fool than others. Magicians who have learned the art of deception often find it easier to distract the mind of an adult, even a logical scientist, than that of a child. There is no guarantee that because a scientist is qualified in one field of science he will be able to bring the same standards of trained observation and interpretation to other fields, particularly where his subject is a hoaxer dedicated to deceiving the experimenter and misdirecting his attention.

Was this true of William Crookes? He contrived an experiment with Home using a cage in which he placed an accordion. According to Crookes, Home could not touch the keys, yet Crookes reported that the accordion played and even hovered inside the cage. The séance room of course was somewhat darkened. One may ask: Was there sufficient light to determine whether it was a spirit hand or whether some material explanation could account for the musical sound? Various contrivances have been used by other mediums to achieve a similar effect: A concealed loop of catgut is attached to a hook, which then is used to pull the lower end of the accordion and produce notes. If the séance room is very dark, the medium can, by means of a rubber tube, blow air into the accordion. His lungs take the place of the bellows, and air produces some notes. In addition, we might ask, was Crookes's perceptive ability influenced by Home's powers of suggestion? Was he accurately reporting what occurred? Given the fact that Crookes had vouched for the Fox sisters when others found them fraudulent and testified that Florence Cook was able to materialize a spirit form provides considerable ground to question his judgment in the Home case.

Perhaps the most famous spiritualistic phenomenon on record is the alleged levitation of Home over a London street. This has been cited in the annals of spiritualism as a near-miraculous event. Arthur Conan Doyle, who maintained that during his career Home had levitated more than a hundred times before reliable witnesses, gives an account of this most famous of all levitations. It reportedly occurred on December 16, 1868, at Ashley House, the apartment of Lord Adare. The witnesses were Lord Adare, Master Lindsay, and Captain Wynne. According to Doyle (1926, 196), Home put himself into a trance state and then "floated out of the bedroom and into the sitting room window, passing seventy feet above the street." Lord Adare was amazed and remarked that he could not understand how Home could have done this; at which point Home allegedly told Adare "to stand a little distance off. He then went through the open space head first quite rapidly, his body being nearly horizontal and apparently rigid. He came in again feet foremost." Doyle insisted that the three eyewitnesses were "unimpeachable." Sir William Crookes (1874) maintained that "no fact in sacred or profane history is supported by a stronger array of proofs." If one were not to allow the admission of this testimony, Doyle insisted, then the possibility of verifying any facts by human testimony must be given up.

The circumstances surrounding this supernormal event, however, are far more cloudy than Doyle allows and hardly meet the standards of objective impartial inquiry. The actual account of the event was written up by Lord Adare in his *Experiences in Spiritualism with Mr. D. D. Home,* which he privately published. Apparently only 50 copies were printed, and most of these were later withdrawn by Adare, who may have had second thoughts. He sent still another description of the strange event to his friend Sir Francis C. Burnand. Lord Lindsay also related his version of the story on two different occasions: before the Committee of the London Dialectical Society, which was interested in investigating spiritualistic phenomena, and in a letter to *The Spiritualist,* a weekly newspaper. The Dialectical Committee later held four controlled séances with Home, but without any significant results. There is also a letter from Captain Wynne to Home testifying to the event.

Trevor Hall (1984) made a painstaking investigation of Home's "levitation." His book on Home shows a photograph of the building (which has since been torn down) where the event was said to have occurred, showing the windows and ballustrades. Hall demonstrates that it could have been possible for Home to make his way from one balcony to the next by normal means. He further shows that Adare and Lindsay were unreliable witnesses, that they were given to seeing apparitions, and that Adare in particular was under the influence of Home's strong personality. Interestingly, Home and Adare lived together for a period of time and even shared the same bedroom, so that Adare's so-called impartiality has hardly been demonstrated. Hall hypothesizes that Adare's state of mind could have made him prone to Home's suggestive influences. In any case, on that fateful evening, according to Adare's account, Home began to walk about the room. "He was both elongated and raised in the air. He spoke in a whisper, as though the spirits were arranging something." Adare next reports that before Home left the room to enter the passage he told them, "Do not be afraid, and on no account leave your places" (Hall 1984, 109–110). This statement by Home had effectively precluded any scrutiny of his subsequent behavior.

According to Adare, Lindsay heard a spirit voice tell him that Home was going out of one window and coming into the next. Then, says Adare, "We heard Home go into the next room, heard the window thrown up, and presently Home appeared standing upright outside our window. He opened the window and walked in quite coolly. 'Ah,' he said, 'You were good this time,' referring to our having sat still and not wished to prevent him. He sat down and laughed" (Hall 1984, 124). Lindsay, who confirmed the fact that he heard the window go up but could not see it as he sat with his back to it, said that he "saw his [Home's] shadow on the opposite wall" (p. 125). He said that he saw Home floating in the air outside the other window.

But, according to Hall, Home could have left the window in one room, made his way along the ledge of the building and climbed into the next window. He could even have placed a board between the two balconies (as an earlier critic had suggested), which Hall estimated were only about 4 feet 2 inches apart (not 7 feet 4 inches, as Adare said). Moreover, the height of the third floor was not 85, 80, or even 70 feet above the street, as different versions of the incident have alleged, but approximately 32 feet. Hall maintains that it was possible for Home to move from one balcony to the next without much trouble; at least it was not impossible. Thus, instead of levitating, Home could have climbed out one window and come in the next while the three men were seated.

Home's levitation has never been corroborated by anyone who viewed it from the street below or from an adjacent or opposite apartment. Since the stories of Lindsay and Adare differed in many details, and since the only light in the room was the moonlight coming through the window, critics have a legitimate basis for skepticism. It is Hall's view that Home's principal secret was his ability to influence those who came in contact with him and to suggest supernormal interpretations for the phenomena. Hall's explanation seems more plausible than the spiritualistic account. It is more in accordance with David Hume's principle that we should not accept an event as miraculous unless we have extraordinary and reliable testimony about it, which is hardly the case in this instance.

Interestingly, the London levitation occurred only a few months after Home had lost his court case with Mrs. Lyons. Home shortly withdrew (in 1871) from the active practice of mediumship. He moved to France, where he married a wealthy woman, and little was heard from him again. In 1877, he published *Lights and Shadows of Spiritualism*, in which he devoted his attention to exposing the fraudulent practices of other mediums, particularly those who claimed that they were able to materialize departed spirits in the séance room. Home died in 1886. His critics maintain that he was a fraud; his defenders, that his powers were genuine.

Numerous other mediums, however, came forth to proclaim and manifest their marvelous abilities. They were often able to evoke a positive response from the general public and from some members of the scientific community as well.

The Society for Psychical Research Tests Mediums and Psychics

The intense public interest in spiritualism no doubt was responsible for helping to stimulate a cognate interest in psychical research among scientists and philosophers. Part of this scientific interest was motivated by a genuine desire to prove the existence of paranormal phenomena. Darwin's *Origin of Species,* published in 1859, had dislodged the human species from the center of the universe, and this was viewed with alarm as a blow to spirituality. If it could be demonstrated that human nature had other psychic or spiritual dimensions and that these transcended the limits imposed by materialistic science, what a boon this would be to religious faith. One could again have the "right to believe," and on evidential, scientific grounds. In 1882 the Society for Psychical Research was founded in England, headed by Henry Sidgwick, the noted British philosopher. Three key investigators, Richard Hodgson, Edmund Gurney and Frederic W. H. Myers, worked assiduously for many years to place the examination of psychical phenomena on a scientific footing. And they were able to enlist a number of other distinguished scientists and men of letters in their cause, such as Sir Oliver Lodge, Sir William Crookes, Charles Richet of France, and Sir W. F. Barrett. This led to the establishment of the American Society for Psychical Research shortly thereafter under the creative tutelage of philosopher-psychologist William James.

There is some evidence that the original founders of the SPR entered into the examination of psychical research not simply in the spirit of impartial or neutral inquiry but in order to demonstrate the reasonableness of religious belief. It is therefore remarkable to have both Sidgwick and James say, 25 years after the founding of the Society, that they were surprised that they had made so little progress toward this end and that they found the field so full of fraud. James ended up with only one possible "white crow," Mrs. Piper, and most of the other mediums were rejected as untrustworthy or unproven. The stated aims of the Society were certainly high-minded. It was to make ". . . an organised and systematic attempt to investigate that large group of debatable phenomena designated by such terms as mesmeric, psychical, and spiritualistic" (*Proc. SPR,* vol. 1). According to the Society's organizers: "From the recorded testimony of many competent witnesses, past and present, including observations recently made by scientific men of eminence in various countries, there appears to be, amidst much delusion and deception, an important body of remarkable phenomena, which are *prima facie* inexplicable on any generally recognised hypothesis, and which, if incontestably established, would be of the highest possible value." They go on to state that the task of examining such residual phenomena had previously been undertaken by individuals but "never hitherto by a scientific society organised on a sufficiently broad basis."

The Society focused on the survival issue, including the evaluation of reports of apparitions, trance-states, automatic writing, and the role of mediums in communicating with discarnate spirits. But it also dealt with other paranormal phenomena, such as telepathy, precognition, clairvoyance, and psychokinesis.

Six committees were appointed to take over different parts of this inquiry. Among their tasks would be:

An examination of the nature and extent of any influence which may be exerted by one mind upon another apart from any generally recognised mode of perception.

The study of hypnotism, and the forms of so-called mesmeric trance, with its alleged insensibility to pain; clairvoyance, and other allied phenomena. . . .

A careful investigation of any reports, resting on strong testimony, regarding apparitions at the moment of death, or otherwise, or regarding disturbances in houses reputed to be haunted.

An inquiry into the various psychical phenomena commonly called Spiritualistic; with an attempt to discover their causes and general laws. [*Proc. SPR,* vol. 1]

The early work of the members of the SPR was infused with enthusiasm, and often they were duped in their investigations by unprincipled charlatans. An especially graphic illustration of this was the telepathic tests conducted with Douglas Blackburn and G. A. Smith. These tests were cited for many years as evidence for thought transference. It was only after the death of the principle figures in the SPR that Blackburn revealed that he and Smith were frauds. This is all too typical of the history of psychical research. Often news of a remarkable psychic or medium is reported in the press. The person may then be tested by psychical researchers, and often his powers are uncritically accepted and heralded as genuine. Sometimes after many years, and usually only after meticulous and diligent investigation, some fatal flaw in the experiment is uncovered or the presence of fraud is demonstrated. This is what happened with Blackburn and Smith. They were first discovered by Edmund Gurney and F. W. H. Myers and then introduced to other members of the SPR, including Mrs. Sidgwick, Alice Johnson, and Frank Podmore. Some SPR members became so excited about their alleged abilities that they published an account of the Blackburn-Smith tests in the first volume of the *Proceedings of the SPR*. Smith was later hired as secretary of the Society and worked in this capacity for many years.

It was not until some 30 years later that the full story of what had happened was revealed by Blackburn in a story in the London *Daily News* of September 1,

1911. (See Chapter 8.) According to Blackburn, he had been editing a weekly journal called *The Brightonian,* and he had begun a campaign to expose fraudulent mediums, for Brighton, a seaside resort, had become the hunting ground for mediums of every kind. In 1882, he came across Smith, a 19-year-old youth who gave an exceptionally versatile psychic performance. The two struck up a friendship and entered into a compact, said Blackburn, to "show up" some of the professors of occultism who were then holding forth unchallenged. They thus began their own thought-reading act. Their exhibition was described enthusiastically in *Light,* a spiritualistic magazine. According to the article, Smith was able by strong concentration to read in an uncanny fashion the thoughts and mental images of Blackburn. It was on the strength of this article that the SPR contacted Blackburn and Smith. Blackburn described these learned gentlemen as "superior types of spiritualistic cranks." He reported incredulously that they accepted the results of their private séances with them without hesitation and without taking reasonable precautions. According to Blackburn, both he and Smith were highly amused; but they were determined to show "how utterly incompetent were these 'scientific investigators.'" Their plan was to bamboozle them thoroughly.

They employed a rather simple set of signals, such as the jingling of pince-nez or sleeve links, breathing, and even blowing. Blackburn maintains that Myers and Gurney were so anxious to get corroboration of their pet theories that they were extremely gullible and very lax in their testing procedures. Time and again they gave the benefit of the doubt to experiments that were complete failures. They allowed Blackburn and Smith to impose their own conditions, and they accepted without demur their subjects' explanations for failures. For example, reports Blackburn, in describing one of his experiments they maintained emphatically that "in no case did B. touch S., even in the slightest manner." Yet, says Blackburn, "I touched him eight times, that being the only way in which our code worked." Blackburn was amazed that two young men, with only a week's practice and mischief in their hearts, could so inveigle Gurney and Myers (and later Podmore and Sidgwick) to accept them as genuine psychics. What, he asked, would a more experienced cheat be able to do with the same investigators?

When Smith read Blackburn's 1911 confession, he emphatically denied that he had cheated. Blackburn said in response that, when he made his confession, he was totally unaware that Smith was still alive and that he regretted embarrassing him. But he insisted that they *had* cheated and he went on to describe in great detail how they were able to hoodwink the SPR. The SPR committee, he said, often tried to get them to transmit "irregular things," for these could not be easily signaled by code. Blackburn and Smith had failed so often in communicating irregular things that the committee had abandoned the use of these tests.

One test was devised, however, in which Blackburn and Smith acquitted themselves successfully. It involved the transmitting of "irregular patterns." The SPR considered this test to be a confirmation of telepathy. According to Blackburn, it was "pulled off" in an ingenious way.

In this test, Smith would sit at a large table. His eyes were padded with wool and bandaged with a thick dark cloth. His ears were filled with cotton wool and covered with putty. Seated on a chair, he was completely covered by two heavy blankets. Underneath his feet and the chair was a thick soft rug, which was intended to prevent any sound signals from being transmitted by his feet. Blackburn was standing at the opposite side of the room. Myers showed him a drawing, the image of which he was supposed to transmit to Smith. It was of a triangle intertwined with lines and curves and could not easily be described in words or conveyed by a signal. Blackburn reported that he gazed on the irregular figure for several minutes, pacing back and forth, but always keeping out of touching distance of Smith. During this time, Blackburn openly drew and redrew the figure several times in front of the observers, in order, he told them, to better fix his mind on it. He then describes how he was able to convey the message directly to Smith by sleight of hand:

I also drew it, secretly, on a cigarette paper. By this time I was fairly expert at palming, and had no difficulty while pacing the room collecting "rapport," in transferring the cigarette paper to the tube of the brass projector on the pencil I was using. I conveyed to Smith the agreed signal that I was ready by stumbling against the edge of the thick rug near his chair.

Next instant he exclaimed: "I have it." His right hand came from beneath the blanket, and he fumbled about the table, saying, according to arrangement: "Where's my pencil?"

Immediately I placed mine on the table. He took it and a long and anxious pause ensued.

This is what was going on under the blanket. Smith had concealed up in his waistcoat one of those luminous painted slates which in the dense darkness gave sufficient light to show the figure when the almost transparent cigarette paper was laid flat on the slate. He pushed up the bandage from one eye, and copied the figure with extraordinary accuracy.

It occupied over five minutes. During that time I was sitting exhausted with the mental effort quite ten feet away.

Presently Smith threw back the blanket and excitedly pushing back the eye bandage produced the drawing, which was done on a piece of notepaper, and very nearly on the same scale as the original. It was a splendid copy.

This test is one of those that had been cited as incontrovertible evidence for telepathy. It also indicates that gullible scientists are sometimes easy targets for sharpshooters intent on deceiving them.

The scientists and philosophers associated with SPR in time, however, became aware of the widespread presence of fraud, if not in the Blackburn-Smith case, in others. And they did their part in exposing some of it. Richard Hodgson was sent to India to investigate the reported occult and psychic powers of Madame Blavatsky, founder of Theosophy.

Helena Petrovna Blatavsky was the daughter of a German nobleman named Hahn, who had settled in Russia, and a granddaughter of a Russian princess. She was married in 1848 at the age of 17 and shortly afterward left Russia to visit India, the United States, and Canada. In 1873 she visited New York, and two years later in collaboration with various well-known individuals interested in spiritualism she founded the Theosophical Society. She left for India in 1878 and established her headquarters in Madras. She allegedly was capable of many supernormal powers, which her followers considered to be miracles. Hodgson went to India with an open mind. He came back to issue a blistering report in 1885, accusing Blavatsky of brazen fraud. Sidgwick, president of the SPR, and others had been impressed by Blavatsky and considered her a "remarkable" woman. Yet they were persuaded by Hodgson that her alleged marvels were based on fraud from beginning to end (Brandon 1983, 23). Basic to the teaching of Theosophy were some letters that were supposedly written by a Tibetan mahatma; but Hodgson reported that these were penned by Madame Blavatsky herself. The shrine at which she performed her miraculous feats was situated next to her bedroom, and Hodgson discovered a fake panel between the two rooms. This exposure by the SPR, however, had little effect on those true believers who accepted Madame Blavatsky and the weird philosophical-theological underpinnings of her system. When she died in 1891, there were, it is said, approximately 100,000 Theosophists.

The SPR investigated other mediums, notably Eusapia Palladino in Great Britain and Mrs. Leonore Piper in America. Mrs. Piper went into a trance state, and she claimed that by means of her control, Mr. Phinuit, to be able to convey messages from the "other side." Curiously, Phinuit, a Frenchman, never spoke in French, and although he was supposed to have lived in Marseilles, there is no record of such a person having lived there. Yet William James was impressed by Mrs. Piper's alleged powers. No doubt the most thoroughly tested medium of her time was Eusapia Palladino. Her story perhaps best illustrates the curious human tendency even of scientists to be charmed by the call of the supernormal.

Eusapia Palladino

Eusapia Palladino was born in the province of Bari, Italy. The daughter of peasants, she had little or no formal education and was unable to read or write.

She had been married off at a young age to a traveling magician, who no doubt taught her the art of legerdemain. After the death of her father, she was employed as a domestic in the household of a family that practiced spiritualism. While taking part in a séance, she pronounced herself to be a medium and, according to her account, was able to stimulate spontaneous manifestations. Although she claimed to be fearful of her powers, she was persuaded to develop her spiritualistic talents further and went through an extended apprenticeship in the mediumistic circles of Naples.

Eusapia was tested by the famous Italian criminologist and psychiatrist Professor Cesare Lombroso, who although a skeptic thought her powers were genuine. In 1892, Lombroso invited a group of scientists, including Professor Charles Richet of Paris (who later became president of the SPR), to participate with him in various sittings. Richet at first expressed uncertainty about Eusapia. Nevertheless he found many of the phenomena produced in her presence impressive and difficult to attribute solely to deception. This included the levitation of tables, the movement of nearby objects, the alteration of the medium's weight on a balance, the appearance of "spirit hands," and so on. In these séances Eusapia was in constant contact with her "spirit guide and control," John King. Richet admitted that he could not provide assurance that no fraud was being perpetrated by Eusapia or that simple illusion was not present.

In 1893–94, 40 sittings were held in Warsaw by Dr. Ochorowicz, in which three experimenters participated. The results were mixed, some attested to her paranormal powers, others expressed doubt and claimed they saw Eusapia using her hands and feet to evoke manifestations.

Under the auspices of Professor Richet in 1894, various British researchers were invited to take part in four sittings. These included Sir Oliver Lodge (a noted physical scientist) and F. W. H. Myers. Professor and Mrs. Sidgwick later took part in the sittings. A report of these séances appears in the *Journal of the SPR* (vol. 6, 1894). Lodge and Myers, strong believers in such phenomena, were convinced that they had observed authentic supernormal manifestations. The Sidgwicks, who did not attend as many séances as Lodge where truly extraordinary things allegedly occurred, nevertheless maintained that, if the medium's hands were well controlled, there was no way that the phenomena could be accounted for except by non-natural means.

The general conditions at the sittings were to some extent dictated by Eusapia. She insisted that they be followed, and if they were not she would fly into a rage and refuse to continue. The séances were generally held in darkness or semi-darkness, usually at night when many of the sitters were tired. Eusapia was usually a late riser and came well rested. Invariably wearing a long dress or skirt, she would sit at a small table at one end of the room. Behind her, black curtains were hung to enclose a small corner of the room (about three feet deep) which was called a "cabinet." Inside was a table and various musical instruments. Eusapia sat only one or two feet from the cabinet curtains. Two of the sitters would sit beside her, one on each side. One sitter would hold one of her hands, and Eusapia would hold a hand of the second sitter with her other hand. Eusapia would place each of her feet on a foot of each sitter; or they would put their shoes against hers or encircle her feet with theirs. She would begin by going into a trance; her body would twist and writhe. In the course of the séance, rappings would be heard, the table would levitate, objects, such as a small table, would emerge from the cabinet and rise. Musical instruments would play, and strange hands would appear, as if materialized. Sitters would at times be pinched on their arms and legs.

Serious doubts were expressed, particularly by Richard Hodgson, about the adequacy of the controls: Were Eusapia's hands and feet held securely, or did she manage to produce phenomena by sleight of hand—or foot? A sufficient number of questions were raised for the SPR to invite Eusapia to Cambridge University for 21 additional sittings. Eusapia again imposed serious restraints on the proceedings. She determined the conditions of lighting. She was insistent that her hands be held only in a certain way. She would not permit the witnesses to feel about in the darkness, and they were expressly forbidden to grab hold of a materialized hand or any of the objects that levitated or moved about.

Those who participated concurred that Eusapia was sometimes seen to be using her hands and feet. She would, for example, release one hand so that one or both of the sitters might hold a different portion of the same hand or even each other's, so that Eusapia then had a free hand to invoke marvelous phenomena. The light in the séance room usually was so poor that Eusapia's hands were rarely completely visible, and they could not be held very well because of her contortions. For experimental purposes the committee had given Eusapia ample latitude to cheat so that she could be observed; and she indeed took advantage of these opportunities. They concluded that she was engaged in blatant fraud, systematically developed over the years by arduous practice, and that this accounted for some of the phenomena; and they inferred that it applied to the others as well. Spiritualist critics of the Cambridge sittings nevertheless said that, although she evidently did on occasion resort to fraud, not all of her manifestations could be so explained and that some of them were supernormal. The SPR, however, was so convinced of her roguery that they decided not to have anything to do with her henceforth.

However, Eusapia had so intrigued the world of science that she continued to be tested in subsequent years by distinguished scientists and scholars, such as Henry Bergson and Pierre and Marie Curie. Eusapia received handsome fees for her sittings. Though highly controversial, she became a celebrity. Some scientists, such as Professor Enrico Morelli of the University of Genoa, declared unreservedly that Eusapia Palladino possessed paranormal powers. Other, more skeptical scientists insisted that she was an outright fraud. The scientific world thus was divided in their verdict.

After many years, the SPR in 1908 again decided to investigate Eusapia's powers. A committee of three was appointed, composed of Everard Feilding, Hereward Carrington, and W. W. Baggally. Albert Meeson, an employee of the American Express Co., was engaged to take notes of the sittings. Mrs. Eleanor Sidgwick, president of the SPR, explained why their Council decided to endorse the new tests. She said that the Society had a policy of not concerning itself with mediums who had been detected in deliberate fraud. To do so would encourage, she said, "a mischievous trade" and stand in the way of scientific inquiry. Although the SPR wished to discourage the flowing of fees with "unabated abundance" into the hands of tricksters, said Mrs. Sidgwick, it was important that an exception be made in the case of Eusapia; for it had been repeatedly alleged that she manifested genuine powers. In spite of the fact that she had been caught cheating by the SPR, enough scientists of distinguished reputation had testified to her powers, said Mrs. Sidgwick, that it was important that their claims be reexamined, particularly since they affirmed that not all of the phenomena could be explained by detected methods of trickery (Sidgwick 1909).

The three sitters, although dedicated psychical researchers, were amateur conjurers; they had been involved in exposing the trickery of others and had published accounts of how the tricks were done. Everard Feilding came from a distinguished aristocratic family. A committed religious believer, intent on discovering whether immortality existed, he nonetheless was dedicated to careful methods of investigation. Carrington (1907), an American, had written a book showing in detail how tricks were actually perpetrated by fraudulent mediums. He was himself able to reproduce by conjuring techniques many of the miracles of the mediums; indeed, the three investigators had declared that they had never met a medium who could produce supernormal phenomena that could not be explained by trickery. Feilding had found so many blind alleys in his investigations that he had reached a state of complete skepticism concerning the possibility of ever finding clear examples of a genuine spiritualist force. He had investigated one case in which a well-known lawyer amazingly had materialized and apported small objects seemingly out of nowhere. He and his accomplice were carefully searched but to no avail, until it was discovered that he had adroitly concealed screws, pins, and sealing wax in a suppository tube, seven inches in length (Feilding 1963).

The Palladino sittings took place from November 21 to December 19, 1908, in the Victoria Hotel in Naples. The séance room was similar to those used before. Detailed notes of 11 séances, now known as the Feilding Report, were published in the *Proceedings of the SPR* (Feilding 1909). Feilding was involved in all eleven séances, Carrington in all but the last, and Baggally in seven. In addition, other people took part, including Italians known to Eusapia at the time. Some evidence of trickery was discovered. Mr. Baggally reported that Eusapia used an arm or leg by substitution at least three times, and that a kiss allegedly made through the curtains seemed to be made by a thumb and finger pinching him. Nonetheless they all declared that in many instances there was no discernible evidence of trickery on her part.

The degree of control permitted by Eusapia varied according to her mood. If she was in a good mood, she allowed her feet and hands to be well controlled. If she was in a bad temper, she was irascible. However, the committee found that in spite of the controls, even when they were severe, Eusapia was able to manifest genuine spiritualistic phenomena. During the séance, she would slip into a deep trance and be in communion with her spirit control, John King. Sometimes she would talk in a deep voice, as if under his influence; at other times she became passive. Yet time and again the committee reported that physical phenomena appeared. In addition to raps, levitations, and table tippings, other extraordinary phenomena were observed: hands materialized, Eusapia's dress ballooned forth, a bulge appeared in the cabinet curtains, and cold air was emitted from a scar on her forehead.

The Feilding Committee reached the conclusion that "some force was in play which was beyond the reach of ordinary control, and beyond the skill of the most skilled conjurer" (Feilding 1909). The conditions of the séance were such, they added, that it was inadmissible to suppose that there were any accomplices. The question had been raised as to whether the sitters were collectively hallucinating. This hypothesis they also emphatically rejected. Alice Johnson, a skeptical member of the SPR, wondered whether Eusapia was able to influence their perception in some way so that they imagined that they saw the phenomena. No, they replied. The only conclusion they could draw, and with "great intellectual reluctance," was "that there does actually exist some hitherto unascertained force liberated in her presence."

Hereward Carrington added a note to Feilding's report summing up his attitude:

> I have to record my absolute conviction of the reality of at least some of the phenomena; and the conviction, amounting in my own mind to certainty, that the results witnessed by us were not due to fraud or trickery on the part of Eusapia.

Carrington was a key sitter. Participating in ten of the séances, he was responsible for holding Eusapia's hand and foot on one side. Was Carrington a bad observer, or was there some other explanation for Eusapia's powers?

Carrington on occasions even lay on the floor, claiming that he held her ankles and that they did not move. Curiously, the next year, after publication of the Feilding Report, Carrington served as Eusapia's agent and took her on a tour of America. He became the strongest defender of Eusapia and her chief apologist. Did he profit from heralding her powers to the world? Carrington's entire life was devoted to spiritualism and psychical research. He wrote dozens of books and evidently made his living in this field.

Some of the critics of Eusapia in the SPR were not fully satisfied with the Feilding Report. Frank Podmore (1910, 42) analyzed it with great care and speculated that virtually all of the major phenomena reported could have been produced normally if Eusapia had been able to get a hand or leg free. He wryly observed that the expressed conviction of Messrs. Baggally, Carrington, and Feilding "that their senses were not deceived" is irrelevant to the scientific issue. If a man knows that he is deceived, the deception is incomplete. If he believes that he is not deceived, then it is effective. In any case, Podmore observed, the matter is not to be decided by argument but by experiment.

Science, Deception, and the Predisposition to Believe

In the history of religion gurus, shamans, prophets, and saints performed their wonders with few, if any, detailed controls. Most of what we know about the founding of the great religions is so veiled in obscurity that post hoc scientific or historical analysis is difficult or impossible. It cannot be done by analogical reconstruction and interpolation from what we now know of human behavioral processes. Most of the supernormal feats that have been proclaimed in the great sacred books are now immune to careful skeptical scrutiny, and millions of devout believers have gone to their graves expressing a steadfast faith in the occurrence of such miraculous events and convinced that the only interpretation that could be placed on these events was a supernatural one.

Today we are able to submit mediums and psychics to careful experimental investigation. What an advance over accepting the uncritical "eyewitness testimony" of credulous believers. Yet, surprisingly, a new obstacle has been encountered. For one should not assume that religious superstition has been cultivated only by untrustworthy and uneducated people and that sophisticated intellectuals are immune to infection by gullibility or willful belief. It is false to assume that, simply because a person calls himself a scientist or claims such credentials, he or she will be open-minded and impartial. Often we simply do not know what the cause of an event might be. To discover it may involve a slow and laborious process. The term *miracle* thus is a mask for our ignorance of natural causes. Unable to discover a natural explanation, some investigators are prone to invoke some supernormal, occult, or paranormal one. All too often this willingness is the product of a passionate predisposition to invest some hidden meaning to existence, based upon a glimmer of hope that there may be an after-life. Some scientists are more easily deceived than the proverbial "man in the street." The ordinary person who is busily engaged in the day-to-day tumble to earn a livelihood and survive may be much less likely to fall for a con game than would an aristocrat of impeccable lineage or a distinguished professor or scientist who lives in a cloistered tower and is unable to imagine that there are charlatans out there ready to ensnare the unwary for ignoble motives like fame and fortune.

Might something similar be said of skeptics? Do they have closed minds concerning the possibility of supernatural phenomena? Do they refuse to accept anomalous events because they do not fit into the natural scheme of things? Does not bias enter both ways—willful belief for believers, but also willful dis-belief for skeptics? There is some danger of dogmatism on both sides. It is clear that a full commitment to open and free inquiry is needed, wherever it leads us.

A perplexing factor confronting the scientific investigation of the super-normal, however, is the persistence of widespread and willful fraud. This is not the judgment of skeptics alone. Even devoted disciples of psychical research have come to the same realization, and often with considerable dismay. Indeed, it is rare to encounter mediums or psychics so pure in motive and sincere in interest that they are willing to cooperate fully with scientific inquiries into the quest for truth. If the supernormalists' claims were demonstrated to be true, what profound and far-reaching implications this would have for our under-standing of the universe and human life. Yet in virtually every case either (1) the medium is found to engage in fraud, or (2) the experimental conditions of observation and control are unreliable. In spite of the prevalence of fraud, there is always a rationalization offered to discount it. Thus many believers will expostulate that, though a medium may be caught cheating on some occasions, they do not cheat all of the time. And, until the skeptic can prove in every case how cheating occurs, believers will continue to insist that there are some genuine phenomena mixed in with the fraudulent. There are still glimmering psychic gems, we are told, that stand out in the shoddy rough. (See John Beloff, Chapter 16.)

How are we to cope with this curious argument, which is still being offered up today? It is, I submit, the last vestige of a deep-seated faith, a kind of intransi-gent will-to-believe in someone or something in spite of evidence to the contrary. It illustrates the persistence of magical thinking in human psychology. One may ask: Is the moral character of the subject and the experimenter relevant in evaluating the evidence for the supernormal? Surely any defects in character, as evidenced by chicanery, would make chinks in their impregnable armor—or at least it should—though believers would no doubt invent new rationalizations for their continued belief.

Now Eusapia Palladino was no saint, and we do not hope to derive a moral system from her performances; but whether she had any genuine ability to break through the barriers of the natural universe and to unlock a transcendent spiritualist one is of momentous import for those who desire it. The question is this: If a person cheats some of the time, a few times, half the time, or most of the time, is it still possible that, in those instances where there is no clear proof of cheating, genuine phenomena occurred? If we cannot figure out how a medium cheated, should we assume that no cheating was going on? We have two possible options: (1) to adopt the stance of the agnostic and admit that we cannot say how or whether he or she cheated, or (2) to admit the position of the believer and maintain that since we cannot tell how the medium cheated *in every instance,* we therefore have a right to infer that at least some of the phenomena were genuine. Believers in psychic powers insist that the second option is justifiable, especially when distinguished investigators were involved in the sittings or experiments and could not fathom how the medium might have tricked them. Ergo, they insist that the only solution to the quandary is a spiritualist one. Skeptics who refuse to accept this are accused of being closed-minded.

But does the burden of proof rest with the skeptic, present or absent at the séance? Must the skeptic show in complete detail how a medium cheated? Is it the case that, unless a skeptic can reconstruct the historical situation post hoc and indicate how the cheating was done, the believer is entitled to believe that a genuine effect was present? I think not. The only sensible position to take is that of the agnostic or the *a*spiritualist.

Two test cases will illustrate my argument. First, let us say that we go to a magic show, that the performer does not tell us that he is a magician, and that we cannot figure out how he did his act. Let us say that the magician controls the conditions of his performance, that he is given free reign, and that the light in which he performs is not the best. Because we cannot figure out his clever act, are we entitled therefore to believe that magic is "real"? What may be at stake here is the status of magical thinking. Do things suddenly go bump in the night without cause? Or are there natural causes at work, even if we do not know what they are? Magic fascinates us because the magician is able to make things happen that are contrary to our normal expectations. We surely are not entitled to infer on the basis of our inability to explain how he did it that the cause is supernormal.

Second, let us imagine for the moment that money is missing from a bank vault, and we discover that a bank teller has concealed the money in his brief-case. Let us say that the teller pleads innocence, admits that it was an absent-minded mistake, and expresses profound remorse. Let us say that, since the teller has worked for the bank for many years, the bank president decides to give him the benefit of the doubt. A month later, a considerable sum of money is again missing. This time you discover that the teller was the only one to have entered the vault. He is thoroughly searched and the money is found hidden in his lunch box. When confronted, the teller says that he has special psychokinetic powers, that money sometimes mysteriously disappears when he is around, and that he cannot always control this power. Should we assume that the teller is honest and take him at his word? Let us stretch the case beyond the limits of forbearance and say that he is given still another chance, and that a third time money is missing but that, when the teller is searched, it cannot be found. Are we entitled to then conclude that the cause was "supernormal"? Or has the teller this time really outsmarted us? (*Cherchez le suppositoire!*) To maintain that the cause is here "supernormal" would be a violation of all of the principles of common sense and logic. Yet this kind of reasoning seems to be acceptable in the world of psychical research.

Many psychic investigators were apparently impressed by the Feilding Report. Here at long last, they said, hard-nosed skeptics had taken precautions against cheating, and they had witnessed phenomena that could not be explained by normal means. Were some of Eusapia Palladino's manifestations genuine? Do we at least have a white crow? Or may we surmise that possibly Eusapia was far more clever than Feilding and his associates? Did Eusapia have an accomplice, perhaps a scientist or friend who had attended several séances, or even Carrington? Did she use every trick in the book, changing them to suit her purpose? Being a woman, voluptuous and erotic to boot, were her male sitters taken in by her charms and did they fail to take all of the proper precautions? Eusapia was obviously a skillful illusionist, well versed in her craft; and perhaps those who sat with her, though skilled in their specialties, were outsmarted. The Feilding Report denies the possibility of accomplices or prearranged props in the hotel room, but should we accept this denial?

The decisive exposure of Eusapia occurred on her visit to America. Here the results were totally negative. Moreover, she was caught flat-footed in one of the most blatant acts of chicanery. The advice of professional magicians, however, became essential in ascertaining *how* she cheated.

As mentioned earlier, Carrington arranged Eusapia's trip to the United States and acted as her impresario. He declared that he was bringing her to America so that other scientists could test her. There was great fanfare and intense public interest. Numerous stories appeared in the newspapers. Two series of tests were held. In November and December 1909 a number of scientists participated in séances, but with no apparent results. The most revealing sitting was held on the night of December 18. Hugo Münsterberg, a Harvard professor of philosophy and psychology, had carefully laid a trap. Eusapia was thoroughly searched, including every article of her clothing, before the séance began. Münsterberg sat on Eusapia's left side; on her right sat another scientist. There were strict controls: Her right hand was clasped by the scientist and her left hand by Münsterberg. Her right foot was covered by the foot of the scientist and her left foot rested on Münsterberg's. For an hour, Palladino carried on her performance. Carrington implored John King, the spirit control, to touch Professor Münsterberg's arm and to lift the small table in the cabinet behind Eusapia. And sure enough John King complied. Münsterberg reported that first "he touched me distinctly on my hip and then on my arm and at last he pulled my sleeve at the elbow, I plainly felt the thumb and the finger. It was most uncanny" (quoted in Hansel 1980, 62). They waited in anticipation for John King to lift the table in the cabinet, and, indeed, the table began to scratch the floor, as if to move. Suddenly, there was "a wild, yelling scream. It was such a scream," reported Münsterberg, "as I have never heard before in my life, not even in Sarah Bernhardt's most thrilling scenes. It was a scream as if a dagger had stabbed Eusapia right through the heart" (quoted in Hansel 1980, 62). What had happened, unknown to Carrington or Eusapia, was that by prearrangement a man had been lying on the floor and had managed to slip very quietly under the curtain into the cabinet. Once behind the curtain he was shocked to see Eusapia remove her right foot from her shoe and with a backward thrust of her leg move it into the cabinet and begin fishing with her toe for the little table. At that point, the man on the floor seized her foot and held onto her heel. With her loud and piercing scream, Eusapia knew that at long last she had been detected and that her method was now uncovered. Münsterberg later reconstructed what had happened at the séance. Eusapia apparently freed her foot and lifted it to his arm and pinched him with her toes. Just before penetrating the cabinet she had leaned forward heavily over the séance table, and in doing so she was able to stretch her foot backward and reach into the cabinet. Münsterberg thought he had felt her foot on his all during the sequence, but it was only her empty shoe. Eusapia had clearly indulged in fraud and had been caught, but what about the other times? Were any of the various phenomena induced in her presence authentically supernormal?

    In a second series of ten séances, conducted at Columbia University between January and April 1910, a specially appointed committee of ten professors could not reach a decision and were unable to detect any trickery. At that juncture they decided to invite in experts in conjuration. Joseph F. Rinn, a noted conjurer and magician, was brought in with others well versed in the craft: W. S. Davis, James L. Kellog, and John W. Sargent. Rinn (1954) provided a detailed account of what ensued. A controlled test was carefully arranged, and a dress rehearsal was held beforehand. Rinn and a Columbia student, Warner C. Pyne, were to dress in clothing the same color as the carpet, to secretly crawl into the room and position themselves on the floor beneath the chairs of the sitters, again unknown to Eusapia or Carrington.

On the evening of the séance, Eusapia arrived dressed in black. Since she spoke no English, an interpreter was brought in. The sitters, Davis, Kellog and Sargent, were introduced to her as professors. Standing about two feet away were a group of other professors and their assistants. Eusapia sat down at the séance table, her back to the curtains of the cabinet. The séance table, noted Rinn, weighed only 11 pounds and could easily be lifted by one finger. The room was put into semi-darkness, and Eusapia began to moan, as if beginning her trance. At that point Rinn and Pyne crawled furtively into place. The plan was to allow Eusapia to go through her act in the first part of the séance so that they could see exactly what she did. Kellog, seated on the right of Eusapia, held her right wrist, and she placed her left hand in Davis's. Her right foot was on Kellog's left foot, and her left on Davis's right foot. As the séance continued, she began to writhe and to slap her feet up and down on the feet of Kellog and Davis. She also began slapping her hands above the table. Under the table Rinn saw Eusapia give a slap with the foot that was resting on Davis's, and at the same time she twisted her right foot sideways. As it came down, she allowed her toe to rest on Davis's toe and her heel on Kellog's toe. Her left foot was now free. Rinn and Pyne had devised a code informing Davis and Kellog what was happening. As they lay there they saw her make the curtain bulge out, as if by a spirit breeze, and also play the musical instruments on the table behind the curtain—all with her foot and toes. She was able to release one hand in a similar way and was able to make the table wobble to and fro with her left hand. She tilted the table, her toe under one of the legs to give it a boost, and with the use of her hand she caused the table to rise, as if by levitation. She again put her foot into the cabinet by stretching it back and played the musical instruments.

Thirty minutes had passed, while Eusapia was given free reign to perform. At an agreed upon signal, Davis and Kellog tightened the controls. They shifted position. Eusapia's free hand and foot were now completely controlled, and they would not allow her to shift or free either of her hands or feet. She cursed and shrieked. As a result, however, nothing occurred during this period of tight control. Again at an agreed-upon signal, the controls were loosened, and she was given 30 minutes of freedom to do as she pleased. Manifestations were again produced by the skillful use of a free hand or foot. During this period, Kellog and Davis reported that they felt touches and their hair was pulled, not by a spirit, but by Eusapia's fingers and toes. Again they tightened controls and again nothing happened. Thus a kind of conditional relationship was established: Whenever the controls were loosened, phenomena occurred. When they were securely tightened, there were no manifestations. Rinn observes that it was truly remarkable to see how many stunts Eusapia was able to do with a free hand or foot. Like a trapeze artist or juggler, her skills were well-honed and highly developed, and she used them with abandon.

In the Feilding Report, it had been claimed that a cool breeze was emitted from a scar on Eusapia's forehead. As the séance neared its end, Eusapia sat on a chair moaning. Her face was covered by her hands as she gulped in air and exhaled through them. Supposedly, she was coming out of her trance state. Some of the professors present noticed that a breeze was being emitted above her head. Evidently, as she sucked in air and breathed it out, an air current was blown over her forehead. This readily explained how she was able to produce the "mystical breeze" that so stunned her sitters in Naples. Eusapia was able to fool many astute scientists with this trick for many years.

The séance was concluded without either Eusapia or Carrington being aware that detailed observations of her performance had been recorded by Rinn, Kellog, and Davis. Even some of the professors at the test were totally unaware of the controls and believed that genuine paranormal phenomena had occurred. Only Professors Jastrow and Miller knew beforehand what the plan was. After Eusapia and Carrington left, Davis and Kellog took the same positions as they had earlier, and Rinn took the place of Palladino. Rinn was able to replicate everything that she had done. The professors present were satisfied that Rinn's phenomena, though brought about by trickery and equally as baffling, were similar to those produced by Eusapia and that she was a fraud.

The following day the full exposé was published in the press. Professor Dickenson S. Miller (1910) of the Columbia University Philosophy Department published a letter in *Science* magazine in which he described what had happened at the ten sittings. Various phenomena had been observed, he said, including levitations, rappings, touchings, breezes, lights, materializations, and movements in and about the cabinet. Miller wrote, however, that "conclusive and detailed evidence was gained as to the method by which typical specimens of them were repeatedly produced. . . . When the medium was securely held, they were not produced at all." He concluded that "no substantial evidence remains that her feats were spiritualistic."

Carrington (1910), still the defender of Eusapia, responded in a letter to the *New York Times,* insisting that he remained "quite unaltered" in his belief that Eusapia Palladino produces "genuine phenomena." "Why do I continue to believe in her?" he asked. And he replied, "Because I have seen levitation when both the medium's ankles were held beneath the table." (Note: Carrington was the only one to have done so.) He went on to say that "Eusapia herself says that she will cheat if allowed" but that her powers still are real.

Carrington proposed that further tests be held and that stringent conditions be set forth by those who were to do the testing. These were arranged. Eusapia balked but finally agreed to them, but she never turned up for the tests. She eventually returned to Italy, her American trip having ended in disaster.

However, one final series of five sittings was conducted in Naples, in December 1910, this time by Everard Feilding, whom she had deceived before. By then, Feilding was well aware of the findings in the American tests and the methods of cheating that Eusapia used. Carrington was not present at these tests. Feilding, W. Marriott, and Count and Countess Petovsky-Petrovo-Solovovo were present and found only negative results. In their report to the SPR, they concluded that "all the sitters are agreed that the . . . phenomena were entirely fraudulent." At the termination of the séances they informed Eusapia of their negative results. She did not dispute the justice of these conclusions, but stated that she could not remember anything that had occurred while she was in the trance state. She pleaded "ill health" as an excuse for her failure to give satisfaction. She accepted her full fee, however (Feilding and Marriott 1911). The career of Eusapia was now virtually over. Although she did occasional séances thereafter, she was able to evoke little scientific interest in testing her again. She died in 1918, in Italy, with a number of scientists convinced that she was a fraud and many believers still willing to testify to her supernormal powers.

In the latter category fits Hereward Carrington. In a book he wrote many years later, he summarized his attitude toward Palladino (Carrington 1954). If Eusapia can produce spiritualistic phenomena, he asked, then why did she need to resort to fraud? He replied that in a really *good* séance practically no trickery was used, but that at a *poor* séance some 50 to 90 percent of the phenomena might be spurious. To the question, Why was this necessary if she was genuine? he responded that Eusapia depended for her production of the phenomena on an "inner energy" over which she had very little control. Sometimes this energy was very strong. When it was weak, however, she "would endeavor to produce [the phenomena] artificially rather than disappoint her sitters." If she found that her trickery was undetected, said Carrington, she would continue the fraud throughout the rest of the séance. Moreover, he added, Eusapia "took a mischievous delight in seeing how far she could hoodwink her sitters." Eusapia had a good deal of vanity and felt duty bound to produce the phenomena. But genuine phenomena "exhausted" her; hence she resorted at times to trickery. What a lame excuse for her outrageous behavior; yet, incredibly, many believers accepted it at face value. This pretext appears over and over again in the literature.

Eusapia was a highly skilled conjurer, and she was able to dupe team after team of scientists without being detected—particularly if there were poor lights. Carrington explained that the bright lights demanded by skeptics inhibited the phenomena! Carrington also stated in the conclusion of his book that his own conviction in Eusapia's supernormal powers had "remained unshaken" over the years, ever since the first tests in Naples. But he added that his conviction also rested upon "certain unofficial sessions" with the medium. According to Carrington, Eusapia often invited some of her sitters to remain behind after the séances for informal sessions. And, said Carrington, it was at these meetings that "the most startling phenomena developed." He reports that she could, for example, develop a "psychic waterspout," a vortex of forces that would hover over the center of the séance table, and that everyone present would feel it. However, more important, Carrington reported that on several occasions Eusapia "transferred her telekinetic powers" to him and that he then had the power to move objects himself without any physical contact. Eusapia could in bright light cause a small stool to move simply by placing his hand over it. Then, when she would touch Carrington's shoulder, he could himself get the stool to move as if some magic or occult force was being transmitted through him. He also reported that on at least one occasion he held a "materialized hand" in his and that he "felt it dissolve" within his grasp!

Carrington's testimony is totally uncorroborated by other witnesses. We only have his word for it. Was Eusapia's chief disciple in America a true and naive believer, or was he, like her, a fraudulent hoaxer? Either or both explanations have some rationale, though the latter no doubt seems especially compelling.

Uri Geller

We now jump ahead some 60 years to examine a twentieth-century "psychic," a person whom many people believe to be the most sensational. Uri Geller has traveled throughout the world and has been widely seen or read about by hundreds of millions of people, and he has been extensively tested by numerous scientists.

The Uri Geller story has a good deal of romance and legend associated with it. A strikingly handsome, charming, flamboyant individual exuding great charisma, he is able to bend and break keys, spoons, and rings, to make stopped watches start up again, jam computers, divine the contents of sealed envelopes and boxes, materialize objects, and even teleport himself. People are convinced that his powers are extraordinary, even miraculous. A consummate showman, he displays childlike wonder at his own feats.

Geller was born in Tel Aviv, Israel, on December 20, 1946. In his book *My Story,* Uri claims that he was "born with these powers" and that he "was actually given them from some source. . . . I don't want you to think that I'm a Moses or a Jesus, but according to the Israeli account, Jesus was born on the 20th of December. Maybe it is a coincidence," he says. "I believe that Jesus had powers and so did Moses, and so did all those others in history" (quoted in Wilhelm 1976).

According to Uri's uncorroborated testimony, his psychic mission manifested itself when he was only three or four years old, when he was visited by a flying saucer while alone in a garden near his home:

It was late afternoon but still light. . . . Suddenly there was a very loud, high-pitched ringing in my ears. All other sounds stopped. And it was strange, as if time had suddenly stood still. The trees didn't move in the wind. Something made me look up at the sky. I remember it well. There was a silvery mass of light. . . . This was not the sun, and I knew it. The light was too close to me. Then it came down lower, I remember, very close to me. The color was brilliant. I felt as if I had been knocked over backwards. There was a sharp pain in my forehead. Then I was knocked out. I lost consciousness completely. I don't know how long I laid there. . . . Deep down, I knew something important had happened. [Geller 1975, 95-96]

At six or seven years old, Uri discovered that he could move the hands of his wristwatch by 10 or 15 minutes solely by the power of his mind. Similarly, he relates, his mother knew that he had strange gifts because he was able to tell her after she came home from a cardgame exactly how much she had won or lost. At the age of nine, silverware began to break in his hands. He said that he kept these strange occurrences quiet because of fear of ridicule.

In 1967, Uri was wounded while fighting with the Israeli Army in the Six-Day War. While recovering, he met Shipi Shtrang, a lad seven years younger, and Shipi's sister Hannah. They became Uri's intimate friends and were with him during his meteoric rise to fame. Shipi and Uri apparently came across a book that dealt with magic and magicians and began working together to develop a night-club act. Under the direction of a personal manager, Uri was booked into theaters throughout Israel and became an instant star. He performed his one-man act innumerable times and with great success. His routine began with his asserting that the mental energy of his audiences was essential to his success and that he could not perform with negative vibes. Uri's show, according to his critics, was standard magic, with the psychic dimension thrown in to heighten the drama. He followed the same routine employed by other mentalists—such as Kreskin and Dunninger—though with some clever new twists. He would usually begin by asking someone from the audience to write the name of a color on the blackboard, which the audience observed but which Uri presumably could not see. Similarly, he guessed the names of foreign capitals. It is possible to do these tricks with an accomplice in the audience, providing the proper signals have been prearranged, or it can be done merely by finding an opportunity to quickly peek at the blackboard where the words are written. Next Uri would bend or break metal objects—razors, keys, nails, or spoons—by sleight of hand, or make stopped watches go again. All of these tricks can be easily duplicated by magicians without any pretense that they are supernormal.

Uri's career took a different turn when he and Shipi met Dr. Andrija Puharich, an American psychic researcher and physician who, having heard of Uri's gifts, went to Israel to investigate them. Puharich was duly impressed by

Uri's powers. Hypnotized by Puharich, Geller identified himself as "Spectra," a computer aboard a spaceship from a distant galaxy. Under the control of "Hoova," he was sent to intervene on earth and Puharich was to assist Geller. How much of this was due to Puharich's or Geller's fantasies and how much was a result of pure fabrication on the part of both is difficult to say.

The "intelligences" that Uri drew upon were from outer space. For many, UFOlogy has become a new religion, replete with science-fiction imagery of the post-modern world. And Uri, like countless others, has embellished his mission with fanciful space-age symbols. Just as the metaphors and symbols of transcendent revelation of previous ages have been clothed in the imagery and metaphors of their times, the paranoral revelations and powers of the present day are charged with scientific technology and space-age gadgetry. However, these fanciful accoutrements can today be more easily investigated and refuted. Although there have been millions of reports of UFO sightings and hundreds of cases of alleged abductions or direct visitations, after decades of intensive scrutiny not one case stands up as clear evidence of an extraterrestrial vistation. Virtually all sightings can be given a normal pedestrian explanation (meteors, planets, weather balloons, swamp gas, helicopters, and so on), and no case of abduction has been shown to be reliable, even though in many instances the abductee actually believed that he or she had been kidnapped by outer-space aliens.

John Wilhelm, a science writer, interviewed Geller and Puharich after they had arrived in America. Puharich claimed that his own tests with Geller convinced him that Uri was genuine. He told Wilhelm that both he and Uri were in contact with extraterrestrial beings who used various channels to communicate, and he claimed to have taped Geller's "transvoice" and that it sounded as if it was synthesized by a computer. Moreover, he said, the tapes often vanished (Was Geller hiding them from Puharich?) and it was all due to the intelligences from Hoova, who would intervene. In Uri's presence, Puharich said, many inexplicable things would happen: radar jammed, computers reprogrammed, motors shut off in cars, and gears shifted—all without any physical intervention. Puharich even claimed that "the voice" would at times speak to him on the phone (Wilhelm 1976, 32).

Geller seemed at times to wish to distance himself from some of Puharich's speculative ideas. Yet he also went along with the story. Thus Geller related that there were several instances in which he and Puharich witnessed UFOs. As with vanishing tapes, no one else could corroborate their account. One night Geller rushed from his Tel Aviv apartment, taking Puharich and a female friend with him. Driving into the suburbs, Geller stopped the car; he saw flashing blue lights in the distance. Cautioning the others not to accompany him, he approached the lights just behind a dip in the terrain. After a few minutes Geller returned carrying Puharich's pen, which according to Puharich had mysteriously "dematerialized" a few days earlier.

Geller also relates the incredible story that one day he teleported himself virtually instantaneously from the streets of Manhattan some 30 miles north to Puharich's home in Ossining, New York, coming right through the upper portion of the screened porch (Geller, 1975, 266 ff.). Uri claimed that he didn't think the powers that he evinced were coming from him but that they were being channeled through him. "What I am able to do," he confides, "is maybe part of a much greater plan which concerns more than the earth and mankind."

No doubt the most dismaying development in the Uri Geller story was his ability to convince many scientists that his powers were genuine. Geller had become an international media personality, transfixing audiences world-wide. Famous television and radio personalities were impressed at his ability to bend keys and read the contents of sealed envelopes. They became convinced of his reliability. But, skeptics asked, are his powers real or fraudulent? Has a modern-day superpsychic emerged, one who clearly demonstrates the paranormal powers of the mind and has been tested in objective controlled laboratory situations?

Geller learned that there were many scientists who were willing to test him to confirm his psychic credentials: the "Geller Effect" was the name given by scientists to the strange contra-causal or even anti-causal phenomena that appeared in Geller's presence.

Geller agreed to be tested at the Stanford Research Institute (SRI) in Menlo Park, California, by Harold Puthoff and Russell Targ, two physical scientists. Puthoff was identified with Scientology, which presupposes astro-projection, reincarnation, space travel, and other psychic powers. Targ and Puthoff have tested other Scientological psychics, such as Pat Price and Ingo Swann, who they claimed also manifested psychic powers, especially clairvoyance, telepathy, and the ability to identify objects outside the laboratory and transmit this knowledge to a psychic within. They called this "remote viewing," as if a television camera in the mind could pick up a distant signal by some strange means. The SRI experiments with Geller were carried out at various times between November 1972 and August 1973. They were supposed to test Geller for clairvoyance, telepathy, and psychokinesis. The results of the clairvoyance and telepathy experiments (Targ and Puthoff 1974) were published in *Nature*, Britain's most prestigious scientific magazine, though the editors expressed numerous doubts about the experimental design and the lack of rigor. The paper was published, we were told, in order to allow parapsychologists and other scientists to assess the quality of the SRI research and to see how much it contributed to the field of parapsychology.

One of the tests reported on dealt with Uri's ability to telepathically read target pictures chosen at random by the experimenter or others. Of 13 targets, Targ and Puthoff maintained that Uri had scored well on 6 and fair on 2 of his guesses. According to them the probability of this happening by chance was one in three million. Skeptics have criticized the test for lacking stringent controls. They have pointed out that the pictures drawn by Geller did not match what they were supposed to correspond to but appeared, rather, to be responses to verbal cues. What constituted a "hit" is open to dispute. The conditions under which the experiments were conducted were extremely loose, even chaotic at times. The sealed room in which Uri was placed had an aperture from which he could have peeked out, and his confederate Shipi was in and about the laboratory and could have conveyed signals to him.

The same was true in another test of clairvoyance, where Geller passed twice but surprisingly guessed eight out of ten times the top face of a die that was placed in a closed metal box. The probability of this happening by chance alone was, we are told, one in a million. Critics maintained that the protocol of this experiment was, again, poorly designed, that Geller could have peeked into the box, and that dozens of other tests from which there were no positive results were not reported.

Geller failed a third test, in which he was supposed to draw his impression of target pictures that had been placed inside of sealed envelopes. Targ and Puthoff also reported in *Nature* that, although metal bending by Geller had been observed in their laboratory, they had not been able to combine such observations with adequately controlled experiments to obtain data sufficient to support the paranormal hypothesis.

The Targ and Puthoff tests apparently helped to catapult Geller's career—for now he had been "tested" by science. Wherever Geller went he repeated his act. The "Geller Effect" took on psychological dimensions; for if people were predisposed to believe that he exuded psychic powers, the slightest suggestion that anything unusual was going on was taken to be a psychic phenomenon. In his many broadcasts and telecasts throughout the world, Uri would ask his listeners and viewers to concentrate on bending metal. After the program, hundreds, even thousands, of calls would pour into the station reporting miraculous psychokinetic effects: spoons, keys, locks, and watches all displayed seemingly mysterious effects.

Geller (1975, 4) describes the psychokinetic effect that he was able to produce on metal:

> What happens is very simple but also very startling. The key begins to bend slowly as I either rub it lightly with my fingers or hold my hand over it. Then it continues bending after I take my hand away. Sometimes it bends only slightly and stops. Other times, it continues up to a 45 degree angle, or even to a right angle. Sometimes it will seem to melt, without heat, and half the key will drop off.

Now all of these feats can be easily duplicated by magicians without any pretense that they are supernormal. James Randi, the professional conjurer, has demonstrated that he can perform similar tricks by sleight of hand. He has bent keys by physical manipulation or pressure, undetected by observers; then, holding them in his fingers and turning them gradually, they appear to bend. Similarly, he is able to exert metal fatigue on a specially prepared spoon or key, which after gently stroking seems to melt and then break off. He is able to advance or retreat the minute or hour hands on watches by deft flicking of the winder. He has also been able to divine the contents of sealed envelopes either by surreptitiously holding them up to a light or by peeking into them when no one is about.

On some occasions, before Geller was tested (as on the Johnny Carson show), Randi was consulted to ensure that the tests were foolproof. When he did so, Geller invariably failed to produce results. It is when Geller controls the conditions of the performance or experiment—as was the case with Eusapia Palladino—that he is successful. If he is unable to succeed, he blames the negative vibes of nearby skeptics and scoffers and is then able to loosen conditions and heighten the effect.

Two psychologists, David Marks and Richard Kammann (1980, 107), carefully monitored Geller's visit to New Zealand. Marks was permitted to test Geller in his hotel room. He had placed a previously prepared drawing of a sailboat in a sealed envelope and handed it to Uri. Marks was surprised when Geller was able to duplicate the figure. Later Marks retrieved the discarded envelope and found that Geller had evidently peeled it open when Marks was in the bathroom and the other observer was distracted by a phone call. He apparently peeked into the envelope to see the drawing. Richard Kammann also tested Uri's ability to "divine" drawings, and he found that Uri would succeed if he could observe the movements of the top of the pencil, but if the pencil top was concealed he could not. In testing their students Marks and Kammann also demonstrated that an astute person could perceive the outlines of a folded drawing through the envelope if allowed to put it up to the forehead (the light) as Geller had done. As to the thousands of reports of bent cutlery that radio and TV stations had received, Marks observed that virtually anyone can find a bent fork or spoon in their house if a thorough search is made. Marks and Kammann (1980, 107) also performed an interesting test of watches that needed repairs. If a watch or clock is held in the palm of the hand for a few minutes, the heat from the body is able to warm the watch, and it often begins to tick. They examined watches awaiting repair in seven jewelry stores, and they found that 60 out of 106 started ticking again when held in a warm hand for a few minutes. The success rate was 57 percent. However, there is no evidence that Uri can repair watches by the mind alone, not when the mainspring is broken or some other structural mechanism is in need of repair.

It is the uncanny ability of Geller to convince scientific observers of his powers that deserves special attention. A number of them have attested to his psychic abilities, and this is especially the case where there is a predisposition to believe in such powers, an unawareness of how trickery or conjuration can be done, and an implicit trust that the person under observation is honest and reliable.

A remarkable collection of papers was assembled by Charles Panati (at one time a science editor for *Newsweek* magazine) and published under the title *The Geller Papers: Scientific Observations on the Paranormal Powers of Uri Geller* (Panati 1976). These papers, by 14 scientists and 3 magicians, might convince an impartial reader that the "Geller Effect" has been carefully confirmed in the experimental laboratory. The book includes the *Nature* paper by Targ and Puthoff already discussed and three other papers, by Wilbur Franklin, Eldon Byrd, and John Taylor, that seem to indicate some kind of physical confirmation of Geller's psychokinetic powers.

John Taylor, professor of applied mathematics at King's College, University of London, and a physicist, has a brief report in *The Geller Papers* on Geller's visit to his laboratory. He details how Geller had apparently caused objects to "fly through the air" or disappear, how a "compass needle had been caused to rotate without the intervention of a visible mechanism," and other strange phenomena (Panati 1976, 217). These events he deemed impossible to comprehend, and they left him in a state of "mystification." Taylor had observed Geller perform on a television program. He was so baffled that he became convinced of his paranormal gifts. He was apparently unaware of conjuring techniques at that time. In pursuing his research, Taylor had also tested a number of young children who he claimed were able to bend metal spoons and forks. He devised an experiment whereby an aluminum rod six inches long was placed in a transparent plastic tube sealed at both ends by red rubber stoppers, which were held in place by screws covered in wax. Much of this was written up in Taylor's (1975) *Super Minds*. (See also Taylor 1980.) Curiously, Taylor noted that there was a "shyness effect"; that is, children could not perform their feats when they were under direct observation. But Taylor always saw evidence of disformation after the fact. He attributed these phenomena to unknown causes.

James Randi once visited Taylor incognito at his office, and he was able to perform psychokinetic feats that Taylor could not explain. Randi found that he could easily break open the seal of the plastic tube, bend the aluminum rod, and return it apparently undetected. Apparently Taylor had been taken in by simple conjurer tricks; he could not believe that young teenagers could possibly cheat. Two scientists at the University of Bath tested the "shyness effect." They allowed six metal-bending children an opportunity to perform. An observer in the room did not note anything unusual, but a secret television camera showed that the children cheated when the observer was not looking. Geller may have worked the same way. To his credit, Taylor has since withdrawn his views on psychokinetic effects, admitting to his former errors, and now claims that the existence of psychic phenomena is doubtful. However, Taylor rejected the idea because he could not find any known physical theory to explain it; but the crux of the matter is that what he had observed was most likely due to conjuring tricks.

The paper by Eldon Byrd in the Panati volume has been cited as giving strong evidence for psychokinesis. Many were impressed by what seemed to be independent physical corroboration that Geller was capable of bending metal by non-normal means. Byrd used a sample of an unusual alloy, nitinol. This metal wire has a physical memory for the shape in which it was formed at the time of manufacture. Only by heating the wire to a very high temperature could it be reshaped. Geller rubbed the nitinol wire in Byrd's presence. When he removed his fingers the wire had a definite bump or kink in it. When Byrd placed it in boiling water, instead of snapping back to its original straight shape, it began to form a right angle. The bends that Geller had produced, reports Byrd (1976, 82), had "permanent deformations." How had Geller achieved this, asks Byrd? He has been quoted as saying "Geller altered the lattice structure of a metal alloy in a way that cannot be duplicated. There is no present scientific evidence as to how he did this" (quoted in Gardner 1981, 160). Byrd's paper has been cited by parapsychologists as a decisive verification of the "Geller Effect."

Martin Gardner (1981), however, has refuted these claims. He attempted to replicate Byrd's experiments, and much to his surprise he got the same effect, but by normal means. He bent the wire using pliers. Then bending it back into shape, he caused a bump in it by pressing it with his thumb nail. He then placed the wire into a bowl and poured boiling water on it. Lo and behold! The wire took on the form of an angle, similar to that described by Byrd. It was entirely possible, said Gardner, that Uri had done what Gardner did when Byrd was not watching, or had even come with a prepared wire, whose properties were incidentally well known to magicians.

In another paper, "Fracture Surface Physics Indicating Telenural Intraction," Wilbur Franklin, chairman of the Department of Physics at Kent State University, also seemed to provide proof that Geller was able to cause changes in physical objects by unknown means. In this case, Franklin reported that a platinum ring had spontaneously developed a fissure in its surface in Geller's presence, "without his having touched the ring" (Panati 1976, 75 ff.). Franklin submitted the fractured ring to metallurgical analyses. He found that the surface of the fracture on the ring and also a needle broken by Geller were "distinctively different" from known types of nontelenural fracture surfaces. He concluded that "it would have been extremely difficult to fabricate these surfaces by known laboratory techniques" (p. 80). He also said that such "telenural interaction with

matter" points to the necessity of developing new theoretical constructs to account for the "Geller Effect." In the Panati book there are photographs of the
various fractured metals—all presented as impressive verification.

Since that time, Franklin has withdrawn his conclusion entirely and admitted to his error. The circumstances were as follows. As Chairman of the Committee for the Scientific Investigation of Claims of the Paranormal (CSICOP), I
invited Wilbur Franklin to Buffalo, New York, in 1977 to appear on a television
program I was moderating on the paranormal and parapsychology. Also participating were three skeptics, James Randi, Ray Hyman, and Ethel Romm. Mrs.
Romm expressed her dismay that Franklin did not include a picture of the
normal fractured ring along with the Geller ring so that we could compare the
similarities and differences. Franklin insisted that the Geller fracture was not
standard. He later went back to his laboratory and fractured a platinum ring by
physical means and compared it with the photo of the Geller fracture. He found,
much to his embarrassment, that they were virtually identical! So the last major
piece of physical corroboration was now withdrawn.

No doubt one factor in Franklin's decision to reexamine the evidence was
Randi's performance of "paranormal tricks" in his presence. He bent Franklin's
key, broke a spoon, correctly guessed the contents of a sealed envelope, and
moved a watch-hand ahead. He even had Franklin pull out a book from his own
briefcase, asked him to open it to a page, and then told him a word on the top
line. All of this flabbergasted Franklin. He said that he was shaken, for he had
witnessed Geller do similar things and was convinced then that they were "telenural" and "paranormal." But now a professional conjurer had duplicated the
"Geller Effect."

Conclusion

The point of this discussion of mediums and psychics should now be evident: It
is a fairly simple matter to be able to deceive people, especially (a) if someone is
intent on perpetrating a fraud, (b) if no known or apparent cause is readily
observable, and (c) if there is a predisposition to belief. This tendency may even
apply to skeptics who are not ordinarily given to gullibility or self-deception.

I will conclude this chapter by citing two other cases. They both involve
James Randi, the conjurer, and are based on his first-hand testimony and
intimate detailed observation of what occurred. Randi is a skilled practitioner.
Like other magicians, he practices deception. He has specialized in duplicating
what "psychics" have done, but he has never claimed that he has exactly replicated the feats of psychics, only that by conjuring techniques he has been able to
evince similar effects.

Suzie Cottrell, a teenage coed from Kansas, claimed to have "the gift of ESP." She appeared on the Johnny Carson show. She shuffled a deck of cards and dealt hands to four persons. She was able to tell who had the lowest card and what it was. Millions of viewers saw her amazing "mind reading" ability. Suzie Cottrell's father contacted me, saying that although he was a skeptic he was impressed by her abilities and wanted to know if CSICOP could test her. Suzie had already been tested for several months by a parapsychologist in Kansas who attested to her powers. We were curious ourselves. How did she do it?

We invited her to the State University of New York at Buffalo for a series of tests. Assembled in a room with her were approximately fifty people—her father and manager, several professors from the university, skeptical members of CSICOP, a five-man ABC-TV crew, the renowned skeptic Martin Gardner, and James Randi. Suzie was seated at a table in the middle of the room. Opposite her sat a young woman to whom she dealt the cards. On either side of Suzie were Gardner and Randi. Before the test began—as a warm-up—we asked her to show us what she could do. She shuffled the cards, spread them out on the table, and then had the woman pick up five. Suzie was able to correctly guess one of the cards the woman selected. And she did this three times. Gardner and Randi sat quietly observing her. Everyone in the room, including the many skeptics, were impressed.

At that point we declared that the official test would begin. There would, however, be one change. Suzie would not be permitted to shuffle the deck or handle or touch any of the cards. We proceeded through many trials. Suzie's powers had suddenly disappeared. The "decline effect" had set in with a vengeance. Her results were negative. Gardner and Randi were the only ones present who saw exactly what she did and how. Suzie had used the forced-deal card-trick perfected by Matt Shulein, a Chicago card shark. In shuffling, Suzie had managed to peek at the bottom card and to "force it" on the recipient by positioning it on the table where it would most likely be selected.

In order to see her in action again, we took a temporary break and announced that the tests would resume in ten minutes. Immediately after we resumed, Suzie scored a hit in the next deal. Unknown to her, however, there was a hidden TV camera that recorded her surreptitiously peeking at the top card during the intermission. Playing the tapes backward afterward, we clearly saw her cheat.

The last of the tests were then carried out. Suzie had claimed that she could guess almost all the cards in a deck of 52. We ran through the deck several times; the cards were shielded as she sat behind a screen. Again she failed. The session eventually ended in disarray, for we brought in Edward Fechner, a well-known magician, who did far better than Suzie. He was able to palm five cards and to read the entire set of cards dealt to the receiver! Suzie broke into tears. "That's not the way I did it," she cried, and the testing session broke up.

In going over the published results of the tests one parapsychologist (Jule Eisenbud) insisted that the tests were significant in support of ESP after all, because Suzie had scored below chance in many of the tests. Wasn't this evidence for psi-missing! Later she was tested by Eisenbud in Colorado, who found that she had demonstrated ESP. Had she demonstrated genuine ESP or had she hoodwinked the experimenter? Apparently our early discovery that she had cheated had no effect on those who were determined to believe that Suzie had psychic powers (Eisenbud, 1980).

The second case to illustrate this point concerns Tina Resch and the alleged poltergeist manifestation in her home in Columbus, Ohio. It illustrates the central conflict between skeptics and believers concerning evidence and the will to believe.

Strange events suddenly began to happen in the home of John and Joan Resch when their adopted daughter Tina was present. It was reported that lights and faucets went off and on without any apparent cause and that objects flew through the air as if possessed by some psychic force. A reporter for the *Columbus Dispatch,* Michael Hardin, who had written an earlier story about Tina, was called in, and he brought with him Fred Shannon, a photographer. They reported that eerie events were taking place in the house. Eggs, lamps, and telephones would suddenly fly through the air and fall to the floor. Fred Shannon photographed a telephone in mid-air, and this photo appeared in newspapers worldwide. An avalanche of press people descended on the house, and many astute journalists and cameramen attested that they too had witnessed paranormal events.

Called upon by a skeptical journalist in Boston to provide another point of view, CSICOP sent a three-man scientific team to Columbus for an on-sight investigation. (This included professors Nicholas Sanduleak and Steven Shore, astronomers from Case Western University, and James Randi). They were denied admittance to the house, though they were able to question many of the key figures and to piece together the circumstantial evidence. Two parapsychologists, William Roll and an associate, however, were allowed into the house. Roll promptly announced that psychokinetic activity had occurred.

Reports of poltergeists (which literally means "rumbling spirit") have abounded throughout history. These strange rappings and moving objects are attributed to a spiritualistic agency. Roll has investigated numerous reports of poltergeist phenomena. In an article in the *Handbook of Parapsychology,* Roll (1977) attributes genuine cases to psychokinetic energy often released, he says, by an adolescent in the vicinity. He surveyed 116 cases and estimated that approximately one-third of the cases were genuine, one-third fraudulent, and one-third uncertain in interpretation. In the Tina Resch case he maintains that he observed a picture and the picture-hook fall to the floor. When he went to get a pair of pliers lying nearby to nail the hook back in, a tape-recorder on the other side of the room flew through the air. As he went to pick that up, the pliers that he had put on a table also took off. Tina was the only one present in the room with him.

Our investigators came up with the following explanation: Tina Resch is a disturbed fourteen-year-old who has dropped out of school and is being tutored at home. Her fosterparents had provided a home for more than 250 children over the years. Tina was intent on finding her natural parents. She had also seen a movie on poltergeists and had learned how to hurl objects into the air unobserved. These feats brought her the attention she apparently craved. Here was another patent case of fraud being perpetrated on the gullible public.

Could this skeptical solution be corroborated? It was, and in spite of it believers persisted in their convictions that supernatural events had occurred. First, a TV camera-crew planted itself in the house in order to photograph flying objects. Though they waited hours, nothing occurred when they had the camera on Tina and were observing her directly. On one occasion, they left the room but left the camera on, unbeknownst to Tina, who thought that it had been turned off. Suddenly a lamp came crashing to the floor, and it did so twice. People in the room with Tina thought it was a poltergeist. When the camera crew returned to the studio to develop the film, they were astonished to discover that Tina had furtively yanked the lamp to the floor. No one in the room saw her do it. But the videotape, if played in slow motion, showed incontrovertible evidence. The film was played on the evening TV news for everyone in Columbus to observe. Tina's mother's explanation was that Tina was tired by all the commotion and wanted everyone to leave so that she could visit with a friend. She accordingly knocked the lamp down so that everyone would be satisfied and leave.

Believers in psychic miracles accepted the story at face value. Even Mike Hardin and Fred Shannon believed it, thus supporting the psychological principle that, if people are strongly predisposed to believe in a supernatural event, there is often little that can be done to dissuade them. Were Tina's powers genuine? Was this incident an isolated exception? There is a principle of caution that seems eminently sensible: If a person is once caught cheating, then the further display of his or her powers should be highly suspect. Alas, many resist this implication in regard to psychics and other miracle workers. When thrown into retreat by a clear case of trickery, they may attempt to take another stand further back. Yes, said the defenders of Tina, she may have cheated on this one occasion, but at other times her powers were genuine.

Was there additional evidence of fraud? If we go back to the original photographs taken of the flying phones we find that the photographer, Fred Shannon, said that if he looked at Tina directly the "force" would not manifest itself. Only if he turned his head and squinted out of the corner of his eye would it take off. Then he would suddenly turn and photograph it directly while in the air. It turned out that under careful questioning no one could testify to having seen an object first standing at rest and then take off; they had seen the objects only after they were airborne. It is not difficult to imagine the following sequence of events: Carefully observe the people nearby. As soon as they are not looking, quickly shoot an object into the air. If you tell them that it is a poltergeist, and they can't easily see how it could have taken off, then they may accept the claim as genuine. If there is a predisposition to believe and the situation is charged with drama and emotion, it is more likely to arouse an affirmative response. This would explain Roll's misperception and that of other reporters in the house.

Is this skeptical critique unfair to Tina? Perhaps she does have these marvelous powers and perhaps it is the skeptics' will to disbelieve that causes them to refuse to accept the testimony of others.

In the case of Tina, we have at least four other incidences of chicanery. Fred Shannon had taken a long series of photographs of other kinds of poltergeist or kinetic manifestations besides the flying telephones. A careful analysis of these photographs reveals the following facts: In one case a sofa seems to be rising in the air. People on the scene swore that it was a case of a paranormal manifestation. A close inspection of the photograph, however, clearly shows Tina's foot under the couch and apparently responsible for lifting it. Another photograph of a moving chandelier shows a hand striking it—though it is not clear if the hand is Tina's or that of a collaborator (Randi 1985). The last two instances are the testimony of Joel Achenbach, a reporter later sent to investigate Tina Resch in North Carolina. Tina was taken by William Roll to his parapsychological laboratory there for further testing. While there, she broke her leg and was admitted into the hospital to have it set in a cast. The reporter visited her in the hospital. While in the room her plastic wrist band suddenly flipped through the air; later a bottle of nail polish did the same. In both cases the reporter saw her hurl them through the room. When confronted with this she simply giggled and apologized. "Sorry," Tina said smiling. (Achenbach 1984.) Since that time the Columbus poltergeist case has become part of the literature. The skeptics have published their critiques. Numerous publications—including the *Reader's Digest* —have since presented the account of what took place in the house with a clear implication that genuine psychic events had occurred. Thus another paranormal manifestation has become part of folklore and legend.

Tina Resch and Uri Geller are like Eusapia Palladino and D. D. Home of earlier generations. The Tina Resch case is not unique. It duplicates almost blow by blow what happened to the Fox sisters in the nineteenth century and elsewhere. The same psychological processes seem to be present in our age and earlier ages. There is often willful deceit and fraud on the part of psychics or mediums, and the hunger to believe in a spiritualistic or paranormal universe and super psychics on the part of credulous believers. *Plus les chose changent, plus c'est la même chose!* (The more things change, the more they stay the same!)

References

Achenback, Joel. 1984. The teen-ager and the poltergeist. *Buffalo Magazine.* Oct. 28.

Brandon, Ruth. 1984. *The Spiritualists.* Buffalo, N.Y.: Prometheus Books.

Byrd, Eldon. 1976. Uri Geller's influence on the metal alloy nitinol. In *The Geller Papers,* edited by Charles Panati. Boston, Mass.: Houghton Mifflin.

Capron, E. W. 1855. *Modern Spiritualism, Its Facts and Fanticisms, Its Consistencies and Contradictions.* Boston.

Carrington, Hereward. 1907. *The Physical Phenomena of Spiritualism.* London: Werner Laurie.

———. 1910. *New York Times.* May 13.

———. 1954. *The American Séances with Eusapia Palladino.* New York: Garrett.

Crookes, William. 1874. *Researches in the Phenomena of Spiritualism.* London: Burns and Oates.

———. 1889. *Proceedings of the SPR,* 6:98-127.

Davenport, Reuben B. 1888. *The Death Blow to Spiritualism: Being the True Story of the Fox Sisters.* New York.

Doyle, Arthur Conan. 1926. *The History of Spiritualism.* London: George H. Doran.

Eisenbud, Jule. 1980. Examination of the claims of J. Randi and S. Cottrell. *Skeptical Inquirer,* 4, no. 3:74-78.

Feilding, E., W. W. Baggally, and H. Carrington. 1909. Report on a series of sittings with Eusapia Palladino, *Proceedings of the SPR* 23:306-569 (reprinted in E. Feilding, *Sittings with Eusapia Palladino and Other Studies* [with an introduction by E. J. Dingwall], University Books, New Hyde Park, N.Y., 1963.)

Feilding, Everard, and W. Marriott. 1911. Report on a further series of sittings with Eusapia Palladino at Naples. *Proceedings of the SPR,* 25.

Gardner, Martin. 1981. *Science: Good, Bad and Bogus.* Buffalo, N.Y.: Prometheus Books.

Geller, Uri. 1975. *My Story.* New York: Praeger.

Hall, Trevor H. 1984. *The Enigma of Daniel Home: Medium or Fraud?* Buffalo, N.Y.: Prometheus Books.

Hansel, C. E. M. 1980. *ESP and Parapsychology.* Buffalo, N.Y.: Prometheus Books.

Home, Daniel Dunglas. 1864. *Incidents in My Life.* New York: Carlton.

Inglis, Brian. 1977. *Natural and Supernatural.* London: Hodder and Stoughton.

Isaacs, Ernest. 1983. The Fox sisters and American spiritualism. In *The Occult in America: New Historical Perspectives,* edited by Howard Kerr and Charles L. Crow. Urbana: University of Illinois Press.

London Daily News. 1911. September 1.

Marks, David, and Richard Kammann. 1980. *The Psychology of the Psychic.* Buffalo, N.Y.: Prometheus Books.

Miller, Dickenson S. 1910. *Science* Magazine. May 20.

Nevins, Allan, and Milton H. Thomas., eds. 1952. *The Diary of George Templeton Strong,* vol. 2, New York: Macmillan.

Panati, Charles. 1976. *The Geller Papers.* Boston: Houghton Mifflin.

Podmore, Frank. 1902. *Modern Spiritualism,* 2 vols. London.

———. 1910. *The Newer Spiritualism.* London: T. Fisher Unwin.

Randi, James. 1980. Examination of the criticisms of J. Eisenbud. *Skeptical Inquirer,* 4, no. 3:78-80.

———. 1985. The Columbus poltergeist case. *Skeptical Inquirer,* 9, no. 3:221-236.

Rinn, Joseph F. 1954. *Searchlight on Psychical Research.* London: Rider.

Roll, William G. 1977. Poltergeists. In *Handbook of Parapsycholgoy,* edited by B. B. Wolman, 382-413. New York: Van Nostrand Reinhold.

Sidgwick, Eleanor. 1909. *Proceedings of the SPR,* 23.

Targ, Russell, and Harold Puthoff. 1974. *Nature,* 252, no. 5476. October 18.

Taylor, John. 1975. *Super Minds: A Scientist Looks at the Supernatural.* New York: E. P. Dutton.

———. 1980. *Science and the Supernatural.* New York: E. P. Dutton.

Wilhelm, John L. 1976. *The Search for Superman.* New York: Pocket Books.

7

Spiritualism Exposed:
Margaret Fox Kane Confesses to Fraud

The following article containing the confession of Margaret Fox Kane was published in the New York World *on October 21, 1888. In her confession, Margaret reveals how she and her sisters Kate and Leah perpetrated the fraud.*— ED.

On many occasions THE WORLD has been able to expose the fraudulent practices of so-called spirit mediums and turn the bright light of careful investigation upon the secret methods of these social vampires. Several times have WORLD reporters torn the white robes from the mediums as they groped about their darkened parlors deceiving their dupes into the belief that the returned spirits of their friends were before them. Besides this many persons have been saved from the clutches of these soulless impostors just as the mediums were about to hold them within their avaricious grasp.

But the severest blow that Spiritualism has ever received is delivered to-day through the solemn declarations of the greatest medium of the world that it is all a fraud, a deception and a lie. This statement is made by Mrs. Margaret Fox Kane, who has been able, through long training and early muscular development, to produce peculiar rappings and knocks which were affirmed to be spiritual manifestations, and which were so skillfully done as to baffle all attempts at discovery. It was this woman, then Miss Margaret Fox, and the most expert of the world-famed "Fox sisters," who was first brought before the public as a medium. Her tour of the great cities of the Unted States is historical. She was seen by most of the prominent theologians, physicians and professional men, but there was not one who could solve the mysterious power that seemed to possess her nor imitate her alleged spiritual rappings.

The Exposure is Complete

The unparalleled excitement caused by these young girls suggested to the minds of many unscrupulous persons the vast financial field that lay before anybody who should pretend similar mediumistic powers. At once there were hundreds of mediums in all parts of the country and the number of these impostors has increased year by year. Now the Fox sisters have come forward and as a matter of long-neglected duty to the public and for their own peace of mind say boldly that theirs has been a life of deception and fraud. As the first and greatest of all mediums the weight of their evidence can not fail to sound the death knell of the abominable business which they, at an age when they knew not what they did, began and have seen flourish into one gigantic world-wide fraud.

The statement which THE WORLD gives was prepared by Mrs. Margaret Fox Kane, the widow of the famous arctic explorer, Dr. Kane. This she will repeat to-night at the Academy of Music, and she will demonstrate to all, as she has to a WORLD reporter, exactly how she performs the tricks which have deluded 8,000,000 people in this country alone. At the same time Dr. C. M. Richmond and Mr. Frank W. Stecham will expose the many other tricks and illusions commonly practiced by mediums at their séances. The admission to the Academy to-night has been placed at such a figure as to merely pay the expenses of the exposure, which is made purely in the interest of the public.

The Medium's Statement

Mrs. Margaret Fox Kane Tells the Story of Her Remarkable Life

I think that it is about time that the truth of this miserable subject "Spiritualism" should be brought out. It is now widespread all over the world, and unless it is put down soon it will do great evil. I was the first in the field and I have the right to expose it.

My sister Katie and myself were very young children when this horrible deception began. I was eight, and just a year and a half older than she. We were very mischievous children and we wanted to terrify our dear mother, who was a very good woman and very easily frightened. At night, when we went to bed, we used to tie an apple to a string and move the string up and down, causing the apple to bump on the floor, or we would drop the apple on the floor, making a strange noise every time it would rebound. Mother listened to this for a time. She could not understand it and did not suspect us of being capable of a trick because we were so young.

Childish Mischief at First

At last she could stand it no longer and she called the neighbors in and told them about it. It was this that set us to discover the means of making the raps. I think, when I reflect about it, that it was a most wonderful discovery—a very wonderful thing that children so young should make such a discovery, and all through our mischief. Children will always find means to accomplish mischief. And to the thought of spirits, this never entered our brains. We were too young to know anything about that.

Our eldest sister, Mrs. Underhill, was twenty-three years of age when I was born. She was in Rochester when these tricks first began, but came to Hydesville, the little village in Central New York where we lived and were born, shortly after. My father and mother were very good, honest people and great friends with the Hyde family for whom the village was named and who lived near. They took a great fancy to us and we were especial favorites of the Hydes, both before and after the notoriety that our rappings made became widespread. All the people around, as I have said, were called into witness these manifestations. My sister, now Mrs. Daniel Underhill—she was Mrs. Fish then—began to form a society of spiritualists. There were so many people coming to the house that we were not able to make use of the apple trick except when we were in bed and the room was dark. Even then we could hardly do it so that the only way was to rap on the bedstead.

And this is the way we began. First as a mere trick to frighten mother, and then, when so many people came to see us children, we were frightened ourselves and kept it up. We were then taken by Mrs. Underhill to Rochester. There it was that we discovered how to make the other raps. My sister Katie was the first one to discover that by swishing her fingers she could produce a certain noise with the knuckles and joints, and that the same effect could be made with the toes. Finding we could make raps with our feet—first with one foot and then with both—we practiced until we could do this easily when the room was dark. No one suspected us of any trick because we were such young children. We were led on by my sister purposely and by my mother unintentionally. We often heard her say, "Is this a disembodied spirit that has taken possession of my dear chidren?"

Convinced That Murder Had Been Done

That encouraged our fun, and we went on. All the neighbors thought there was something, and they wanted to find out what it was. They were convinced some one had been murdered in the house. They asked us about it, and we would rap one for the spirit answer "Yes," not three, as we did afterwards. We did not know anything about Spiritualism then. The murder, they concluded, must have been committed in the house. They went over the whole surrounding country, trying to get the names of people who had formerly lived in the house. They found finally a man by the name of Bell, and they said that this poor innocent man had committed a murder in the house, and that these noises came from the spirit of the murdered person. Poor Bell was shunned and looked upon by the whole community as a murderer. As far as spirits were concerned, neither my sister nor I thought about it.

I am the widow of Dr. Kane, the Arctic explorer, and I say to you now, as I hold his memory dear and would call him to me were it possible, I know that there is no such thing as the departed returning to this life. I have tried to do so in every form, and know that it cannot be done. Many people have said to me that such a thing was possible, and seemed to believe so firmly in it that I tried to see if it were possible. While in London, some years ago, I went to the sexton of a churchyard and asked him if I could go among the graves at 12 o'clock at night. He consented when I told him that I wanted to do this for a certain purpose. I left my servant at the gate outside. I went to each grave and stood over it, and called upon the dead, alone there in the dark, to come and give me some token of their presence. All was silent, and I found that the dead would not return. That is how I tested it. There is no test left that I have not thoroughly sifted. Mediums I do not visit. They are too low and too illiterate. Dr. H. Wadsworth, of 91 Queen Anne street, London—a very dear friend of mine—sent me money for my expenses to go over to London. I said to him when I arrived: "I think too much of you to have you deceived, and there is nothing in Spiritualism. It is a fraud."

He answered me: "I thank you for telling me about it, Maggie. I know all the rest to be humbug. I thought I would have you to come in last." I said: "There are no dead or departed spirits that have ever returned." He said: "If you say so, Maggie, it must be true, because I have always believed in you." But still he seemed incredulous.

How the Séances Were Held

To return to the story of my childhood: I said I had gone with my sister Katie and Mrs. Underhill, my oldest sister, to Rochester. It was here that Mrs. Underhill gave her exhibitions. She took us there and we were exhibited to a lot of Spiritualist fanatics. We had crowds coming to see us and Mrs. Underhill made as much as $100 to $180 a night. She pocketed this. Parties came in from all parts to see us. Many as soon as they heard a little rap were convinced. But as the world grew wiser and science began to investigate, my younger sister and myself began to adapt our experiments to our audiences. Our séances were held in a room. There was a centre-table in the middle, and we all stood around it. There were some who even believed that the spirits of living people could be materialized. There are many different forms of Spritualism. To all questions we would answer by raps. When I look back upon that life I almost say in defense of myself that I did not take any pleasure in it. I never believed in the spirits and I never professed to be a Spiritualist. My cards always say: "Mrs. Kane does not claim any spirit power, but people must judge for themselves." Nobody has ever suspected anything from the start, in 1848, until the present day as to any trickery in our methods. There has never been a detection.

How the Rapping Is Done

Like most perplexing things when once made clear, it is astonishing how easily it is done. The rappings are simply the result of a perfect control of the muscles of the leg below the knee which govern the tendons of the foot and allow action of the toe and ankle bones that are not commonly known. Such perfect control is only possible when a child is taken at an early age and carefully and continually taught to practise the muscles which grow still in later years. A child at twelve is almost too old. With control of the muscles of the foot the toes may be brought down to the floor without any movement that is perceptible to the eye. The whole foot, in fact, can be made to give rappings by the use only of muscles below the knee. This, then, is the simple explanation of the whole method of the knocks and raps.

Some very wealthy people, formerly of San Francisco, came to see me some years ago when I lived in Forty-second street, and I did some rapping for them. I made the spirit rap on the chair, and one of the ladies cried out, "I feel the spirit tapping me on the shoulder." Of course that was pure imagination. A great many people, however, when they hear the rapping imagine at once that the spirits are touching them. It is a very common delusion. One fanatic gives Sunday services at the Adelphi Hall yet. He is called the "Old Patriarch." He said to some one the other day: "If Mrs. Kane says that she can make these rappings without the aid of the spirits, she lies." This person will be one of those who will see that I speak the truth.

The Meeting with Dr. Kane

As I have said before, my sister Katie and myself continued in this business until she was twelve years old and I thirteen and a half. After we left Rochester we travelled all over the United States. I was thirteen years old when Dr. Kane took care of me and took me out of the miserable life we began in 1848, and it was in 1853 that he took me away from this thing. It was at Philadelphia he met me. He sent me to a seminary and my vacations were spent with Mrs. Waters, a sister of Senator Cockrell. She lives now at No. 7 East Sixty-second street. She was a little inclined to believe in Spritualism herself, although she never let Dr. Kane know it. I was taken away from all "spiritual" influences and for a long time did not see any of my old associates. When Dr. Kane came into the room at Philadephia I told him that I hated this thing, that I had been pushed into it. I explained to him that it was a trick, that I had been forced into it and did not want to go on with it. I think now that if my brain had not been very round I should have been a maniac. Spiritualists say that I am mad now, that if I attempt to expose these tricks I am mad. I have had a life of sorrow, I have been poor and ill, but I consider it my duty, a sacred thing, a holy mission to expose it. I want to see the day that it is entirely done away with. After my sister Katie and I expose it I hope Spiritualism will be given a death blow.

Every morning of my life I have it before me. When I would wake up I would brood over it, and Dr. Kane has said to me more than once, "Maggie, I see that the vampire is over you still." Dr. Kane was certainly not a believer in Spiritualism. He was often horrified at the blasphemy of those fanatics. One day he came into the room, at Philadelphia, and an old fanatic asked me to call up St. Paul. The doctor hurried in and took me out. He was shocked beyond measure. If those we love who have passed away before us can look down upon us from heaven—if we are ever to meet again—I know my dead husband is looking on me now and blessing me for my work.

I remember one time before my marriage the death of Mr. Brown, the second husband of my sister Mrs. Fish, now Mrs. Underhill. Although Dr. Kane had no great devotion to Mr. Brown, he had respect for death. He sent his body servant Morton to sit up with the corpse. When he was laid out he asked me to come and look at the dead and to see how dreadful it was to trifle with death. There were several champagne bottles in the room, I suppose for the refreshment of Morton—and as I entered the room a cork popped with a dreadful noise, and I made for the door horrified. My sister forced me to wear mourning for Mr. Brown and to go to the funeral in state. This is an example of how entirely under the influence of Mrs. Underhill I was during that dreadful time. Katie and I were led around like lambs. We went to New York from Rochester, than all over the United States. We drew immense crowds. I remember particularly Cincinnati. We stopped at the Burnett House. The rooms were jammed from morning until night and we were called upon by these old wretches to show our rappings when we should have been out at play in the fresh air. We made the tour of the States, and came back to New York where Mrs. Underhill left us. Mother went on to Philadelphia and took me and that is where Dr. Kane met me and brought me away from this life.

Living Only to Make Atonement

All during this dreadful life of deception I had been protesting. I have always rebelled against it. I have been going to expose it time and time again. After I married, Dr. Kane would not let me refer to my old life—he wanted me to forget it. He hated the publicity. When I was poor, after his death I was driven to it again. I have told my sister, Mrs. Underhilll, time and time again: "Now that you are rich, why don't you save your soul?" But at my words she would fly into a passion. She wanted to establish a new religion and she told me that she received messages from spirits. She knew we were tricking people, but she tried to make us believe that spirits existed. She told us that before we were born spirits came into her room and told her that we were destined for great things. But we knew when to rap "yes" or "no" according to certain signs she made us during the séance. After my marriage, my sister Katie still kept up the séances. She had many wealthy patrons here in New York—Mr. Livermore, a wealthy banker, and a Dr. Gray, a well-known homeopathic physician. They used to have regular meetings privately and Katie was the medium.

I have seen so much miserable deception that I am willing to assist in any way and to positively state that Spiritualism is a fraud of the worst description. I do so before my God, and my idea is to expose it. I despised it. I never want to lay eyes on any Spiritualists again, and I wish to say clearly that I owe all my misfortune to that woman, my sister, Mrs. Underhill. The last act of treachery she did—she has been persecuting me all along until recently—was to take my boys from me. Her hand has been felt in all my sorrows and misfortunes.

Now I am, I hope, a Christian and a sincere one. I am a Catholic, baptized in the Roman Catholic Church by the Rev. Father Quinn in St. Peter's, in Barclay street. I want to do honor to my faith. Father Quinn said to me that as long as I was in this business and did not believe in it and had to support myself, to charge very high prices, so that it would at least limit the number of my patrons; that I should not give any free exhibition and never claim supernatural powers.

When Dr. Kane died he left only $5,000 in trust for me. There was a suit over the possession of some of the doctor's letters which I wanted to publish. These letters have been in the care of a Catholic priest, and also of my lawyer. Afterwards some of these letters were published, although Dr. Kane's family strongly objected. The book was called "The Love-Life of Dr. Kane." I received but little income from the book and have had few sources of revenue. I now am very poor. I intend, however, to make the exposé of Spiritualism because I think it is my sacred duty. If I cannot do it, who can?—I have been the beginning of it. I hope to reduce at least the ranks of the 8,000,000 Spiritualists now in this country. I go into it as into a holy war. I do not want it understood that the Catholic Church has advised me to make these public disclosures and confessions. It is my own idea, my own mission. I would have done it long ago if I could have had the necessary money and courage to do it. I could not find any one to help me. I was too timid to ask.

My oldest sister, Mrs. Underhill, has gone to the country, and this exposé will be a severe blow to her, and perhaps kill her. I am waiting anxiously and fearlessly for the moment when I can show to the world, by personal demonstration, that all Spiritualism is a fraud and a deception. It is a branch of legerdemain, but it has to be closely studied to gain perfection. None but a child taken at an early age would have ever attained the proficiency and wrought such widespread evil as I have.

I trust that this statement, coming solemnly from me, the first and most successful in this deception, will break the force of the rapid growth of Spiritualism and prove that it is all a fraud, a hypocrisy and a delusion.

Margaret Fox Kane

A Seance

Mrs. Kane Shows "The World" Reporter How Perfect the Deception Is

When a WORLD reporter called on Mrs. Margaret Fox-Kane at the hotel, where she has been closely guarded from the attempts of certain mediums to kidnap her, a private séance was arranged to demonstrate the mysteries of the supposed spiritual knockings. Mrs. Kane was not aware that it had been arranged to have the rappings, and she came from her room to the hotel parlor expecting only an interview. She expressed herself as in the best of spirits and said that she felt thankful for having an opportunity to tell the story of deceit and sorrow through THE WORLD. If there was anything she could do to complete the exposure she would be only too glad to do it, and leave no stone unturned in her effort to undo the wretched work she was led into when a thoughtless child. To demonstrate the utter absurdity of the claim made by mediums that she was possessed by a spiritual power in spite of her denials, she desired to give the WORLD reporter some evidence of how the tricks were done.

Producing the "Spirit" Rappings.

"Now," said Mrs. Kane, "I will stand up near these folding-doors, and you may stand as near as you please and I will call up any 'spirit' that you wish and answer any question. One rap means 'No'; three raps mean 'Yes.' Are you ready?"

"Is Napoleon Bonaparte present?" the reporter asked, watching Mrs. Kane closely.

Three raps (yes).

"Does he know me? I mean, did he ever meet and converse with me?"

Three raps.

"That is strange, isn't it?" remarked Mrs. Kane, smiling. "In view of the fact that he must have died before you were born. Try again."

"Is Abraham Lincoln present?"

Three raps.

"Well, you see the 'spirits' are very obliging."

"Will Harrison be elected?"

One loud rap (no).

"Will President Cleveland get another term?"

Three raps.

For half an hour Mrs. Kane continued the "spirit rappings" in all parts of the hotel parlor in the broad daylight. At times the knocking was faint and at others loud, and she had the power of making the sounds come from under chairs and tables at a short distance—a sort of expert ventriloquism of the feet. The closest watching gave no evidence of even the slightest muscular effort. She remained perfectly quiet to all appearances and produced the rappings with ease and rapidity.

It was plain to see how even the strongest skeptics failed to understand or detect the secret of the rappings and, after many attempts to fathom the mystery, settled down to the belief that they had really seen manifestations from the "spirit world."

8

Confessions of a Telepathist: Thirty-Year Hoax Exposed

DOUGLAS BLACKBURN

The following article appeared in the Daily News *(London), September 1, 1911. It was written by Douglas Blackburn, who along with G. A. Smith was extensively tested by the Society for Psychical Research. The tests with Blackburn and Smith were taken as scientific evidence of the existence of thought transference, or telepathy. Smith, who had been employed by the SPR, denied the allegations.—ED.*

For nearly 30 years the telepathic experiments conducted by Mr. G. A. Smith and myself have been accepted and cited as the basic evidences of the truth of Thought Transference.

Your correspondent "Inquirer" is one of many who have pointed to them as a conclusive reply to modern skeptics. The weight attached to those experiments was given by their publication in the first volume of the proceedings of the Society for Psychical Research, vouched for by Messrs. F. W. H. Myers, Edmund Gurney, Frank Podmore, and later and inferentially by Professor Henry Sidgwick, Professor Romanes, and others of equal intellectual eminence. They were the first scientifically conducted and attested experiments in Thought Transference, and later were imitated and reproduced by "sensitives" all the world over.

I am the sole survivor of that group of experimentalists, and as no harm can be done to anyone, but possible good to the cause of truth, I, with mingled feelings of regret and satisfaction, now declare that the whole of those alleged experiments were bogus, and originated in the honest desire of two youths to show how easily men of scientific mind and training could be deceived when seeking for evidence in support of a theory they were wishful to establish.

And here let me say that I make this avowal in no boastful spirit. Within three months of our acquaintance with the leading members of the Society for Psychical Research, Mr. Smith and myself heartily regretted that these personally charming and scientifically distinguished men should have been victimized, but it was too late to recant. We did the next best thing. We stood aside and watched with amazement the astounding spread of the fire we had in a spirit of mischief lighted.

Showing Up Occultism

The genesis of the matter was in this wise. In the late [eighteen-]seventies and early eighties a wave of so-called occultism passed over England. Public interest became absorbed in the varied alleged phenomena of Spiritualism, Mesmerism, and thought-reading. The profession of the various branches abounded, and Brighton, where I was editing a weekly journal, became a happy hunting ground for mediums of every kind. I had started an exposure campaign, and had been rather successful. My great score was being the first to detect the secret of Irving Bishop's thought-reading. In 1882 I encountered Mr. G. A. Smith, a youth of 19, whom I found giving a mesmeric entertainment. Scenting a fraud, I proceeded to investigate, made his acquantance, and very soon realized that I had discovered a genius in his time. He has since been well known as a powerful hypnotist. He was also the most ingenious conjurer I have met outside the profession. He had the versatility of an Edison in devising new tricks and improving on old ones. We entered into a compact to "show up" some of the then flourishing professors of occultism, and began by practicing thought-reading. Within a month we were astonishing Brighton at bazaars and kindred charity entertainments, and enjoyed a great vogue. One of our exhibitions was described very fully and enthusiastically in "Light," the spiritualistic paper, and on the strength of that the Messrs. Myers, Gurney, and Podmore called on us and asked for a private demonstration. As we had made a strict rule never to take payment for our exhibitions, we were accepted by the society as private unpaid demonstrators, and as such remained during the long series of séances.

It is but right to explain that at this period neither of us knew or realized the scientific standing and earnest motive of the gentlemen who had approached us. We saw in them only a superior type of the spiritualistic cranks by whom we were daily pestered. Our first private séance was accepted so unhesitatingly and the lack of reasonable precautions on the part of the "investigators" was so marked, that Smith and I were genuinely amused, and felt it our duty to show how utterly incompetent were these "scientific investigators." Our plan was to bamboozle them thoroughly, then let the world know the value of scientific research. It was the vanity of the schoolboy who catches a master tripping.

Telepathic Rapport

A description of the codes and methods of communications invented and employed by us to establish telepathic rapport would need more space than could be spared. Suffice it that, thanks to the ingenuity of Smith, they became marvellously complete. They grew with the demands upon them.

Starting with a crude set of signals produced by the jingling of pince nez, sleeve-links, long and short breathings, and even blowing, they developed to a degree little short of marvellous. To this day no conjurer has succeeded in approaching our great feat, by which Smith, scientifically blindfolded, deafened, and muffled in two blankets, reproduced in detail an irregular figure drawn by Mr. Myers, and seen only by him and me.

The value of a contribution such as this should lie not so much in describing the machinery as in pointing out how and where these investigators failed, so that future investigators may avoid their mistakes.

I say boldly that Messrs. Myers and Gurney were too anxious to get corroboration of their theories to hold the balance impartially. Again and again they gave the benefit of the doubt to experiments that were failures. They allowed us to impose our own conditions, accepted without demur our explanations of failure, and, in short, exhibited a complaisance and confidence which, however complimentary to us, was scarcely consonant with a strict investigation on behalf of the public.

That this same slackness characterized their investigations with other sensitives I am satisfied, for I witnessed many, and the published reports confirmed the suspicion. It is also worthy of note that other sensitives broke down or showed weakness on exactly the same points that Smith and I failed—namely, in visualizing an article difficult to describe in words signalled by a code. A regular figure or familiar object was nearly always seen by the percipient, but when a splotch of ink, or a grotesque irregular figure, had to be transferred from one brain to the other, the result was always failure. We, owing to a very ingenious diagram code, got nearer than anybody, but our limitations were great.

Startling Hits

Smith and I, by constant practice, became so sympathetic that we frequently brought off startling hits, which were nothing but flukes. The part that fortuitous accident plays in this business can only be believed by those who have become expert in the art of watching for and seizing an opportunity. When these hits were made, the delight of the investigators caused them to throw off their caution and accept practically anything we offered.

I am aware it may be reasonably objected that the existence of a false coin does not prove the non-existence of a good one. My suggestion as the result of years of observation is that the majority of investigators and reporters in psychical research lack that accurate observation and absence of bias which are essential to rigorous and reliable investigation. In fine, I gravely doubt not the bona fides, but the capacity, of the witnesses. I could fill columns telling how, in the course of my later investigations on behalf of the Society for Psychical Research, I have detected persons of otherwise unimpeachable rectitude touching up and redressing the weak points in their narratives of telepathic experiences.

Mr. Frank Podmore, perhaps the most level-headed of the researchers—and to the end a skeptic—aptly puts it: "It is not the friend whom we know whose eyes must be closed and his ears muffled, but the 'Mr. Hyde,' whose lurking presence in each of us we are only now beginning to suspect."

I am convinced that this propensity to deceive is more general among "persons of character" than is supposed. I have known the wife of a Bishop, when faced with a discrepancy in time in a story of a death in India and the appearance of the wraith in England, [to] deliberately amend her circumstantial story by many hours to fit the altered circumstances. This touching up process in the telepathic stories I have met again and again, and I say, with full regard to the weight of words, that among the hundreds of stories I have investigated I have not met one that had not a weak link which should prevent its being accepted as scientifically established. Coincidences that at first sight appear good cases of telepathic rapport occur to many of us. I have experienced several, but I should hesitate to present them as perfect evidence.

Biased Principles

At the risk of giving offense to some, I feel bound to say that in the vast majority of cases that I have investigated the principals are either biased in favor of belief in the supernatural or not persons whom I should regard as accurate observers and capable of estimating the rigid mathematical form of evidence. What one desires to believe requires little corroboration. I shall doubtless raise a storm of protest when I assert that the principal cause of belief in psychic phenomena is the inability of the average man to observe accurately and estimate the value of evidence, plus a bias in favor of the phenomena being real. It is an amazing fact that I have never yet, after hundreds of tests, found a man who could accurately describe ten minutes afterwards a series of simple acts which I performed in his presence. The reports of those trained and conscientious observers, Messrs. Myers and Gurney, contain many absolute inaccuracies. For example, in describing one of my "experiments," they say emphatically, "In no case did B.

touch S., even in the slightest manner." I touched him eight times, that being the only way in which our code was then worked.

In conclusion, I ask thoughtful persons to consider this proposition: If two youths, with a week's preparation, could deceive trained and careful observers like Messrs. Myers, Gurney, Podmore, Sidgwick, and Romanes, under the most stringent conditions their ingenuity could devise, what are the chances of succeeding inquirers being more successful against "sensitives" who have had the advantage of more years' experience than Smith and I had weeks? Further, I would emphasize the fact that records of telepathic rapport in almost every instance depend upon the statement of one person, usually strongly disposed to belief in the occult.

9

Metapsychics and the
Incredulity of Psychologists:
Psychical Research Before 1927

JOHN E. COOVER

In a recent article suggesting an admirable metapsychic experiment, Dr. W. F. Gehrhardt (1926) reiterates "the wonder with which one must regard the opposition of official science, particularly psychology, to the new field." The opposition of the psychologist is probably stronger than that of his fellow scientists because much of the detail in his particular field of knowledge has an especial pertinence to the evidence and methods of metapsychics. To understand his position, however, it is necessary first to examine the opposition of "official science," which he shares, and which springs from a persistent, sometimes described as an "obstinate," incredulity.

It is a fact that official science regards the phenomena of metapsychics with incredulity. It is an old fact. Official science was incredulous in 1848 when the Rochester Knockings began with Catherine and Margaret Fox; it was still incredulous 34 years later, when Professor Henry Sidgwick in the first presidential address before the Society for Psychical Research said, "I say it is a scandal that the dispute as to the reality of these phenomena should still be going on, that so many competent witnesses should have declared their belief in them, that so many others should be profoundly interested in having the question determined, and yet that the educated world, as a body, should still be simply in an attitude of incredulity." There followed the further accumulations of evidence for a period of 44 years, and René Sudre (1926) in an address delivered in the Amphitheatre of Medicine (College of France, in Paris), under the auspices of the School of Psychology, on March 22, 1926, exclaimed:

Reprinted from *The Case For and Against Psychical Belief*, edited by Carl Murchison, pp. 229-264. Worcester, Mass.: Clark University Press. 1927.

Now the facts of metapsychics are reported by scientists who, from Crookes to Richet, are entirely accustomed to observe natural phenomena. Why, then, does their incorporation into academic science meet such resistance?

Thus the results of all the researches in metapsychics during the past three-quarters of a century have failed to break down the incredulity of official science. Still more definitely, official science does not accept a single phenomenon of any one of the three or four classes of metapsychic phenomena, notwithstanding that some men of science who have engaged in metapsychic investigation claim for many of the phenomena of the several classes "irrefragable and incontrovertible proof."

What is the cause of this persistent incredulity of official science? Interested metapsychists have repeatedly faced this question, and offered answers; for they know that "the final test for truth is the agreement of experts," that the standard of evidence must be drawn from the recognized sciences, and that to prevent a miserable failure metapsychics must produce evidence that will convince the scientific world. To remove this incredulity, its cause must be found and removed. Until this is done, metapsychics stands without the pale of the accredited sciences. This is the most serious problem of metapsychics. It has always been its most important problem, whether fully recognized or not, and as the years of opportunity have passed, and the incredulity of official science has remained persistent, it has become more and more serious, acute, menacing. For half a century, there has been earnest and persistent, individual and collective, effort to adopt and maintain scientific standards in metapsychic research, to make metapsychic research indistinguishable from scientific research, in the hope of solving this problem, of winning an honored place among the established sciences—without avail.

Various causes of the incredulity of official science are suggested by recent writers. René Sudre says that:

the skeptics' negation is an *a priori* one; a state of mind arising out of no conscientious examination of the facts. . . . Telepathy and clairvoyance are no longer seriously denied by anybody. . . . We wish a scientific audience. We demand but a simple effort of good will—yes, let us say it, of honesty; for it is not honest to deny without trying to examine fairly.

He thinks official science is incredulous because, (1) it fears miracles, fears facts refractory to accepted principles; (2) its philosophy is materialistic, regarding mind as epiphenomenal, and the laws of material science as inviolate and alone competent to explain all the phenomena of the universe; and (3) its repugnance for phenomena long associated with superstition, arising from his knowledge (*a*) of the role of illusion and fraud, (*b*) of the will to believe, (*c*) of the concomitant variation between precautions against fraud and sparsity of phenomena, (d) of the uniform failure of noteworthy decisive tests.

He discounts these reasons for incredulity, on the grounds that new phenomena are being constantly assimilated by official science, that biological and psychological phenomena are granted principles that range beyond the laws of material science, that the disputed phenomena have been witnessed by eminent scientists, such as Crookes and Richet. The causes of incredulity he is able to find do not seem to him adequate. There is an element of culpable negligence in the attitude of official science; a taint of dishonesty. His cure would be persuasion, further exposition of results of metapsychic experiments of the same character as those past and current.

Charles Richet (1923), the eminent physiologist, in a recently published treatise on metapsychics, presents the arguments of official science against objective metapsychics: The more latitude for fraud the more apparent are the phenomena; all mediums have been caught in conscious or unconscious deception, hence fraud is always possible; unless one is versed in legerdemain he cannot imagine how completely an observer can be duped; no observer can maintain continuous attention during the two or three hours of a séance; etc., and he says, "These doubts have occurred to me hundreds of times, and I know, better than anyone else, the full force of these arguments. Nevertheless, I do not think them well founded, and I am firmly convinced that there are real physical metapsychic phenomena."

Richet confesses that the innumerable experiments published by eminent men of science would not have convinced him if he had not himself been a witness of the four fundamental facts of Metapsychics. He says he was an unwilling witness, very critical, distrustful of the facts that forced themselves upon him. That he, nevertheless, was able to verify those facts under exceptional conditions and despite his desire to disprove them. They determined his belief, "and that not at once, but after long consideration, meditation, and repetition." The phenomena to which Richet gives credence, because he has verified them, are:

1. *Cryptesthesia:* A faculty of cognition that differs radically from the usual sensorial faculties. A sample of evidence: Stella, in the presence of G., whose family she does not know, and *cannot* have known, gave the first names of his son, of his wife, of a deceased brother, of a living brother, of his father-in-law, and of the locality where he lived as a child.

2. *Telekinesis:* Raps and the movement of objects without contact. While Eusapia's head and hands were held, a large melon weighing six pounds was moved from the sideboard to the table, the distance between them being over a yard.

3. *Ectoplasms:* Hands, bodies, and objects seem to take shape in their entirety from a cloud and take all the semblance of life. Eusapia was in half-light, her left hand in my right, and her right in my left tightly held, and before Lodge, Myers, and Ochorowics, a third hand stroked my face, pinched my nose, pulled my hair, and gave a smack on my shoulder heard by Ochorowics, Myers, and Lodge.

4. *Premonitions:* That cannot be explained by chance or perspicacity, and are sometimes verified in minute detail. Alice, at 2 p.m. told me, for the first and only time, that I should soon give way to violent anger before one, two, three persons whom she designated with her hand as if she saw them. At 6 p.m. the unlikely and unforeseeable impertinence of a person absolutely unknown to Alice provoked me to one of the strongest and most justifiable fits of anger of my whole life before two other persons, an anger that led to my receiving a challenge to a duel, the only one I have ever received.

Richet in his treatise on metapsychics has brought together the tremendous amount of evidence that has accumulated during the past three-quarters of a century, organized it, and indexed it with approximately 1,800 names. He says he "tried to extricate the sciences anathematized as occult from chaos, and to put in a clear light knowledge that official science, in its pride of reputation, has refused to consider. It has seemed to me that the time has come to claim for metapsychics a place among the recognized sciences by making it conform to the rigor and the logical treatment which have given them their authority."

He recognizes that "scientific men will be surprised, and perhaps indignant," but he thinks that a study of the evidence he presents will shake their incredulity. Since the facts are very strange, however, "and clash with current scientific dogmas, the affirmations made will give rise to strongly adverse criticism and to mocking incredulity." He then presents strong argument for the acceptance of metapsychic phenomena:

There are too many well-verified facts and rigorously conducted experiments that chance, illusion, or fraud should always be attributed to all these facts and experiments without exception. [p. 595]

It is not possible that all these observers [200 competent scientists, and a thousand others] should never have made mistakes, but the whole constitutes a sheaf of testimony so large and homogeneous that no criticism of details, however acute, will be able to disintegrate and disperse. [p. 599]

To suppose that all metapsychics are an illusion is to suppose that [twenty named eminent scientists] were all, without exception, liars or imbeciles; it is to suppose that two hundred distinguished observers less eminent, perhaps, but persons of high and acute intelligence, were also liars or imbeciles. [p. 600]

I shall refer later to the sheaf of testimony as the "fagot theory," and consider the possibility of complete and wholesale delusion.

Richet is candid and forceful. He points out that the Business of Science is to establish positive facts, not to formulate negations, that at every moment she is confronted with profound mysteries.

> Therefore when new facts supported by many irrefragable proofs are brought forward, the new facts being positive facts that do not contradict old positive facts, lovers of truth ought to bow before them and receive them joyfully. [p. 600]

> To admit telekinesis and ectoplasms is not to destroy even the smallest fragment of science; it is but to admit new data, and that these are unknown energies. . . . That a hand having all the attributes of a living hand should be formed from a whitish cloud in no way nullifies the laws of circulation, nutrition, and structure of a normal hand. It is a new fact but not a contradictory one. [p. 601]

Richet freely grants that these phenomena are not understood; that "the more we try to analyze Cryptesthesia the less we undersand it" (p. 614); "its modalities and its mechanism escape us entirely" (p. 615). And, "as regards the substance of materializations our ignorance is painful" (p. 476). He is sanguine, however, of important contributions to scientific knowledge and declares, "We must advance resolutely, using exact scientific methods" (p. 624).

Richet pleads for the acceptance of the phenomena on the grounds of the evidence for their occurrence, not because they are in any way understood. This appears to be a curious position and raises a question concerning the quality of the evidence. If the evidence for occurrence is sound, scientific results are already obtained and no anxiety should be felt lest they be disregarded by official science. Resolute advance, by "using scientific methods," would make important contributions to scientific knowledge, and the incredulity of official science would gradually disappear. But is the evidence for a phenomenon really sound if nothing concerning the phenomenon is revealed but its occurrence? Is this not the essential characteristic of illusion and hallucination? Official science quite probably takes this stand.

II

Whatever the causes the metapsychists find responsible for the obstinate incredulity of official science, they are weighed and found wanting, and it is possible either that undiscovered causes remain or that there is some error in estimating the weight of those found.

The conservatism of official science in its admission of new facts is a natural precaution against error and the waste of time and energy. The evidence for the new phenomenon will have had to meet the requirements for rigorous proof. It is a curious fact that during the past half-century many new facts have been presented with proper credentials and have been admitted; some of them were very strange and were revolutionary in their effects upon current laws of nature, but none of them were metapsychic. Conservatism cannot be an unjust cause of the incredulity.

General indifference of official science to metapsychic phenomena may be granted, but the indifference has not been complete. For three-quarters of a century distinguished men of science have given occasional professional attention to them and have investigated them—with negative results. And many other intelligent observers have from time to time seen and reported natural methods of producing what were currently accepted as supernormal phenomena.

The persistence of this stream of negative evidence has had the effect of strengthening the incredulity of official science:

1. Fraud is not only frequent and general, but it is witnessed and published.

2. Astute, and sometimes eminent, observers—even scientists—witness the same phenomena and pronounce them metapsychic.

3. Some of the more eminent scientists have persisted in maintaining the validity of their observations at the same time that they were cognizant of the adverse reports of other observers upon the same phenomena and cognizant of the disabilities of observation and reporting of phenomena produced under the identically restricted conditions, pointing with confidence to the corroboration of their observations by independent witnesses in other places at other times.

4. A reliance upon the corroboratory testimony of others often increases the confidence of a scientist in his own observations to the extent of weakening the rigor with which he may reasonably be expected to guard against fraud.

The application of each of these four points may be shown in the investigation of "raps," for which eminent scientists have presented "irrefragable proof," and which of all telekinetic phenomena Richet wisely suggests are most worthy of study. The observations upon raps will also illustrate the effect of the stream of negative evidence upon the incredulity of official science.

It will be recalled that raps started the movement known as Modern Spiritualism, in Hydesville, New York, in March 1848, in a family consisting of John D. Fox, his wife Margaret, and their two younger daughters, Margaret aged 14, and Catherine aged 12. Owing to the annoyance of curious crowds that swarmed the premises, Kate was sent to the neighboring city of Rochester to stay with her sister Leah Fish, and Maggie was sent to her brother's farm. The raps followed the girls, and the Rochester Knockings soon became the object of public investigation. Three public meetings were held in Corinthian Hall, in

November 1848, to receive the reports of investigating committees appointed from the floor. With each report confessing failure to determine a natural cause for the raps, the excitement grew until it flared into a sensation that spread over the world and, much abated, has continued to the present time.

1. The chairman of the last Committee was Dr. E. P. Langworthy, a young physician in Rochester, who took further opportunity to investigate these raps and reported his results to the *New York Excelsior,* February 2, 1850. The knockings were always under the Fox girls' feet, or if upon doors or tables their dresses were in contact with the objects rapped. He concluded that the mysterious rapping was so intimately connected with the persons of these girls that they voluntarily produced them.

2. John W. Hurn, of Rochester, wrote a number of articles to the *New York Tribune,* during January and February 1850. He related that the Fox girls could get no sounds when they were completely isolated from the floor, claimed that the whole affair was the most miserable imposition ever attempted upon a civilized community, that he had entered into an agreement with the girls to procure ink to use on walls that would appear visible after a short time, and to deliver spirit blows to the heads of sitters.

3. The Rev. John M. Austin, of Auburn, wrote to the *Tribune,* March 27, 1850, saying that he had been three times to hear the sounds, but thought they were made by human agency. He had reliable information that "persons in Auburn" could make all these knockings with the cracking of toe joints, without any movement the eye can detect.

4. The Rev. Dr. Potts delivered a lecture in Rochester in December 1850, announcing the toe-joint theory. He stood upon the stage in Corinthian Hall and demonstrated the raps by cracking his toes.

5. The Rev. C. Chauncey Burr wrote to the *New York Tribune,* January 2, 1851, saying that he not only discovered how their rappings are produced, but by much practice he learned to produce them himself, in a manner that no person could detect, if he chose to impose upon his credulity, and so loud that they were heard in every part of a hall crowded with an audience of a thousand people. He made the raps by snapping the toe-joints.

6. Three Buffalo University professors, Austin Flint, M.D., Charles A. Lee, M.D., and C. B. Coventry, M.D., investigated the raps of Margaret Fox in the Phelps House and reported their results to the *Buffalo Commercial Advertiser,* February 18, 1851, and the *Buffalo Medical Journal* for March. They immediately saw by observing the countenance that the raps were the result of voluntary effort and concluded that they were made by the dislocation of bones at the joint: knees, ankles, toes, or hips. They studied the mechanism in a patient who could make the raps with her knee-joints and made a medical report. They observed that the anatomical and physiological books had neglected articular

sounds—which allowed the Fox girls' deception to gain headway.

7. At another sitting at the Phelps House, for the purpose of resisting the damaging report of the Buffalo professors, Mrs. Fish and Margaret Fox produced phenomena in profusion for the gratification of friends and believers. But that sitting is listed here because a frank reason was given for a cardinal principle of control in the séance: Question: What is the use of these demonstrations? Answer: They are made to prove the mediums have no agency in it. Mr. Stringham: May I leave the table whilst the others remain that I may look under and see the bells ring? Answer: What do you think we require you to sit close to the table for? When spirits make these physical demonstrations they are compelled to assume shapes which the human eyes must not look upon.

8. Mrs. Culver, a relative by marriage to the Fox girls, made a signed statement before witnesses April 17, 1851, explaining the fraud. She had helped Catherine by touching her when the right letters came in the calling of the alphabet, and Catherine showed her how to make the raps by snapping her toes. She also said that Margaret told her that, when people insisted on seeing her feet and toes, she could produce a few raps with her knees and ankles.

9. Professor Henry and Professor Page, of the Smithsonian Institute, visited the Fox sisters when they were in Washington, in February 1853. Professor Page published the results of his observations in a book issued later in the year. He remarked that he was surprised to notice how the scrutinizing powers of the most astute fail as soon as they entertain the remotest idea of the supernatural in these cases. After many experiments, he concluded definitely that the sounds were entirely at the control of the girls. Every rap was attended with a slight movement of the person of the rapper. A very distinct motion of the dress was visible about the right hypogastric region. He declared that there was no necessity for wonderment on account of the rapping sounds so long as one is excluded from a personal examination of the rappers.

10. Rev. H. O. Sheldon, of Berea, Ohio, spent some time investigating the subject. The mediums that he detected rapped by snapping their toes.

11. Three professors of Harvard College, Agassiz, Peirce, and Horsford, were part of an investigating committee appointed to pass upon phenomena offered to win a prize of $500 put up by the *Boston Courier,* in June 1875. Mrs. Leah Fox Fish Brown and Catherine Fox were the first mediums to be employed. Agassiz declared with emphasis that there was an easy physiological explanation of all the effects that the Fox sisters, or any other rappers, produced. The editor, Mr. George Lunt, issued a report in a pamphlet dated 1859. Whenever conditions were favorable for observation, the raps did not come, when they were not, they came in profusion. Mr. Clark, assistant to Agassiz, produced raps on a box with his knuckles in a way that could not be detected. Agassiz said the taps of the mediums were produced by the bones of the feet.

12. The Seybert Commission of the University of Pennsylvania investigated the raps produced through Margaret Fox Kane, in November 1884, and "Dr." Henry Slade, in February 1885. Professor Furness placed his hand upon one of the feet of Margaret Fox and distinctly felt pulsations in her foot, but no movement, while the raps were being produced. Both Miss Fox and Slade knew when other raps than their own were produced, no matter how similar in sound.

13. In May 1888, Margaret Fox Kane sent from London a letter to the *New York Herald,* in which she said, "Spiritualism is a curse. . . . Fanatics like Mr. Luther R. Marsh, Mr. John L. O'Sullivan, ex-minister to Portugal, and hundreds equally as learned, ignore the 'rappings' (which is the only part of the phenomena that is worthy of notice) and rush madly after the glaring humbugs that flood New York. . . . Like old Judge Edmonds and Mr. Seybert, of Philadelphia, they become crazed, and at the direction of their fraud 'mediums' they are induced to part with all their worldly possessions as well as their common sense. . . ."

14. After coming to New York, Margaret Fox Kane granted an interview to the *New York Herald,* in August 1888, in which she said she was going to expose spiritualism from its very foundation. She loathed the thing she had been during her years of deception. She proposed to expose the raps to the public and produced raps for the reporter on the floor near his feet, under his chair, under a table, on the other side of the door, on the legs of a piano.

15. On October 21, 1888, Margaret appeared at the Academy of Music in New York before a large audience, enunciated her solemn abjuration of spiritualism: "That I have been chiefly instrumental in perpetrating the fraud of spiritualism upon a too confiding public, most of you doubtless know. . . . The greatest sorrow of my life has been that this is true and, though it has come late in my day, I am now prepared to tell the truth, the whole truth and nothing but the truth—so help me God!". . . A plain wooden stool, resting upon four short legs, was placed before her. Removing her shoe, she placed her right foot upon this table. The entire house became breathlessly still, and was rewarded by a number of little short, sharp raps—those mysterious sounds that for more than forty years frightened and bewildered hundreds of thousands of people in this country and Europe. A committee, consisting of three physicians taken from the audience, then ascended to the stage and, having made an examination of her foot during the progress of the "rappings," unhesitatingly agreed that the sounds were made by the action of the first joint of her large toe.

16. In this confession Margaret Fox Kane had the support of her sister, Kate Fox Jencken, who had recently returned from Europe and who sat in a box during the abjuration and demonstration.

17. Kate Fox Jencken also granted an independent interview to the New York papers in which she said: "Spiritualism is a humbug from beginning to

end. . . . The manifestations at Hydesville in 1848 were all humbuggery, every bit of them. . . . *I certainly know that every so-called manifestation produced through me in London or anywhere else was a fraud.* The time has come for Maggie and me to set ourselves right before the world . . . and not leave this base fabric of deceit behind us unexposed."

It is true that these mothers of spiritualism were declared completely un-balanced, that fast living had destroyed their judgment and blunted their moral sense, and that their confessions were fraudulent. But there is a completely corroborative fact that is decisive in its support of the confessions, and it has been almost wholly overlooked. When Margaret Fox and her mother were in Philadelphia, engaged in "spiritualistic manifestations," in 1852, Margaret met Dr. Elisha Kent Kane, the intrepid arctic explorer. He was much struck with her naiveté and her danger. Margaret was eighteen and beautiful. In a letter to her he described his first impression of her: "A little Priestess, cunning in the mysteries of her temple, and weak in everything but the power with which she played her part. A sentiment almost of pity stole over his worldly heart as he saw through her disguise." He sought to remove her from her life of deception and from the influence of her elder sister Mrs. Leah Fox Fish Brown Underhill. He wrote many letters to both Margaret and Kate, warning them of the dangers ahead of them, pleading with them to turn to a good life before the shackles became too strong, and offering them help. They agreed, and he put Margaret in school; Katie had promised to live with them after Dr. Kane married Margaret. He was especially fearful that the "rappings" would be found out and adjured them to remain faithful to their promise not to have anything to do with séances anymore. He returned from his second expedition, married Margaret, and died.

18. Margaret Fox Kane, in 1888, said: "From the first of our intimate acquaintance, Dr. Kane knew that the 'rappings' which I practiced were fraudu-lent. . . . I simply obeyed the impulse of my candid regard for him, when the knowledge of his devotion grew upon me, and confided to him the whole secret of the fraud, together with my increasing repugnance to the life I was living."

Here was an early confession not only made but acted upon. The Fox girls only repeated it to the public 45 years later in New York.

This is a part of the stream of negative evidence that undoubtedly supported the incredulity of official science concerning the supernormal nature of spiritual-istic raps. And it might well extend to other telekinetic phenomena or to any "manifestations" through the Fox sisters, the greatest mediums of the early days, in spite of the eminence of the witnesses.

In the statements of Kate Fox Jencken quoted above she explains that *all* the phenomena (including raps) ever produced anywhere through her were fraudulent. Let us now examine the records of observations of her phenomena written by an eminent man of science who made "Researches in the Phenomena of Spiritualism" (Crookes 1874, 86-88) during 1871-74:

> With mediums, generally it is necessary to sit for a formal séance before anything is heard; but in the case of Miss Fox it seems only necessary for her to place her hand on any substance for loud thuds to be heard in it, like a triple pulsation, sometimes loud enough to be heard several rooms off. In this manner I have heard them in a living tree, on a sheet of glass, on a stretched iron wire, on a stretched membrane, on a tambourine, on the roof of a cab, and on the floor of a theatre. Moreover, actual contact is not always necessary: I have heard these sounds proceeding from the floor, walls, etc., when the medium's hands and feet were held, when she was standing on a chair, when she was enclosed in a wire cage, and when she had fallen fainting on a sofa. I have hard them on a glass harmonica, I have felt them on my own shoulder and under my own hands. I have heard them on a sheet of paper, held between the fingers by a piece of thread passed through one corner. *With a full knowledge of the numerous theories which have been started, chiefly in America, to explain these sounds, I have tested them in every way that I could devise, until there has been no escape from the conviction that they were true objective occurrences not produced by trickery or mechanical means.* [pp. 86-88]

Crookes's observations on Ectoplasm through Kate Fox:

> The first instance which I shall give took place, it is true, at a dark séance, but the result was not satisfactory on that account. I was sitting next to the medium, Miss Fox, the only other persons present being my wife and a lady relative, and I was holding the medium's two hands in one of mine, whilst her feet were resting on my feet. Paper was on the table between us, and my disengaged hand was holding a pencil.
>
> A luminous hand came down from the upper part of the room, and after hovering near me for a few seconds, took the pencil from my hand, rapidly wrote on a sheet of paper, threw the pencil down, and then rose up over our heads, gradually fading into darkness. [p. 91]

Crookes's observations on Telekinesis through Kate Fox:

> Miscellaneous occurrences of a complex character.—Under this heading I propose to give several occurrences which cannot be otherwise classified owing to their complex character. Out of more than a dozen cases, I will select two. The first occurred in the presence of Miss Kate Fox. To render it intelligible I must enter into some details.
>
> Miss Fox had promised to give me a séance at my house one evening in the spring of last year. Whilst waiting for her, a lady relative, with my two eldest sons, aged fourteen and eleven, were sitting in the dining-room, where

the séances were always held, and I was sitting by myself, writing in the library. Hearing a cab drive up and the bell ring, I opened the door to Miss Fox, and took her directly into the dining-room. She said she would not go upstairs, as she could not stay very long, but laid her bonnet and shawl on a chair in the room. I then went to the dining-room door, and telling the two boys to go into the library and proceed with their lessons, I closed the door behind them, locked it, and (according to my usual custom at séances) put the key in my pocket.

We sat down, Miss Fox being on my right and the other lady on my left. An alphabetic message was soon given to turn the gas out, and we thereupon sat in total darkness, I holding Miss Fox's two hands in one of mine the whole time. Very soon a message was given in the following words: "We are going to bring something to show our power;" and almost immediately afterwards we all heard the tinkling of a bell, not stationary, but moving about in all parts of the room; at one time by the wall, at another in a further corner of the room, now touching me on the head, and now tapping against the floor. After ringing about the room in this manner for fully five minutes, it fell upon the table close to my hands.

During the time this was going on no one moved, and Miss Fox's hands were perfectly quiet. I remarked that it could not be my little hand-bell ringing, for I left that in the library. (Shortly before Miss Fox came I had occasion to refer to a book which was lying on a corner of a book-shelf. The bell was on the book, and I put it on one side to get the book. That little incident had impressed on my mind the fact of the bell being in the library.) The gas was burning brightly in the hall outside the dining-room door, so that this could not be opened without letting light into the room, even had there been an accomplice in the house with a duplicate key, which there certainly was not.

I struck a light. There, sure enough, was my own bell lying on the table before me. I went straight into the library. A glance showed me that the bell was not where it ought to have been. I said to my eldest boy, "Do you know where my little bell is?" "Yes, papa," he replied, "there it is," pointing to where I had left it. He looked up as he said this, and then continued, "No—it's not there, but it was there a little time ago." "How do you mean?—has anyone come in and taken it?" "No," said he, "no one has been in; but I am sure it was there, because when you sent us in here out of the dining-room, J. (the youngest boy) began ringing it so that I could not go on with my lessons, and I told him to stop." J. corroborated this, and said that, after ringing it, he put the bell down where he had found it. [pp. 96-98]

Why should official science be expected to accept the fact of telekinesis, upon the basis of "irrefragable proof" of rapping or other phenomena produced through the mediumship of Kate Fox? William Crookes does not stand alone in disclaiming the *possibility* of a natural agency. Very probably the larger proportion of the 13,000 signers of the Memorial to Congress, in 1854, could have testified to the raps through this same medium—producing "a sheaf of testimony" unexampled by any other. Is it not possible that all of the witnesses for their supernormal nature have been wrong in each and every instance? The fagot theory is dangerous.

If such is the case with the phenomena of the Fox sisters, can the phenomena of other mediums be regarded free from suspicion, even though "irrefragable proof" is offered by eminent scientists for them?

In most of the summaries of evidence, phenomena of "Dr." Henry Slade, Florence Cook, Daniel Dunglas Home, and Eusapia Palladino are included. Official science has some negative evidence on all of them.

It is well known that the great Slade was a notorious and resourceful imposter, and we may record a few of the counts against him:

1. In 1872, Henry Slade was caught in fraud in New York by John W. Truesdell, who had two sittings with him. Clasping the medium's hands at the small séance table, and being held close to it, Truesdell felt something touching him and pulling at his clothing as if there was someone under the table; directly, the thing came up into his lap. Slade said it was a materialized spirit-hand. A surreptitious glance, hardly won, indicated a foot. Watching his opportunity, when the "spirit-hand" was playing its most venturesome tricks, Truesdell suddenly recoiled from the table . . . just in time to see the "Doctor's" left foot withdraw from his lap to the medium's slipper. He saw plainly the movements of the cords in the medium's wrist when the "spirits" were producing slate-writing. At the second sitting, that took place months later, T. refused to give his name, but left in his overcoat the name of Samuel Johnson. While waiting for the medium he noticed a slate hidden under a low sideboard, covered with a stock message, and upon it he wrote a second message in a bold hand: "Henry! Look out for this fellow—he is up to snuff! Alcinda" (the name of Slade's deceased wife). In the sitting, T. got a message from "Mary Johnson" on the first slate. The next slate fell to the floor, and, when regained, presented the double message on the substituted slate: Slade was at first furious, but he quickly recovered, acknowledged T. as a great medium, and they exchanged tricks.

2. In 1876, Henry Slade was unmasked in London by Professor Lankester and Dr. Donkin. They caught him in the act of substituting a slate upon which a "spirit message" had been prepared. Criminal prosecution followed. After a trial at Bow Street Police Court lasting three days, Slade was sentenced to three months' hard labor. He took appeal, which was sustained, on the ground

that the words "by palmistry or otherwise" had been omitted in the indictment. Before he could be arrested on the new summons, Slade fled to the continent, in 1877, and presented himself to Professor Zöllner at Leipzig.

3. In 1882, Henry Slade was caught in fraud in Belleville, Ontario. Dr. Abbott saw Slade's heel making the raps against the rung of his chair. Mr. James Starling, when touched under the table by an ectoplasmic hand, suddenly raised his right foot; the "hand" felt like the calf of a leg, and on Slade's countenance there was an expression of pain. Mr. A. McGinnis saw the slate passing under the table on Slade's left foot. Chief McKinnon detected Slade causing telekinetic phenomena on a chair with his toe. They saw him writing "spirit messages" and saw him substituting slates. They confronted him with his fraud, and upon his confession and his accommodatingly showing them his tricks, they permitted him to catch the noon train for the East.

4. In 1885, Henry Slade was caught in fraud by the Seybert Commission. They saw his slates with prepared messages, they saw him substituting the slates, they saw him making scratching motions with his thumb to simulate spirit writing. At the moment a slate had been substituted, in preparation for the long process of getting spirit writing, Professor Sellers asked: "Dr. Slade, will you allow me to see that slate?" The reply was, "No, not now; the conditions are not favorable." Professor Furness, the great Shakespearian scholar, had seen the prepared message on that slate. At the close of their investigation Professor Sellers said: "The methods of this medium's operations appear to me to be perfectly transparent, and I wish to say emphatically that I am astonished beyond expression at the confidence of this man in his ability to deceive, and at the recklessness of the risks which he assumes in his deceptions, which are practiced in the most barefaced manner."

5. In 1886, Slade created a furor in Hamburg among the spiritualists. But he balked at tests, and was out-conjured there. Dr. Borchert wrote to Slade offering him one thousand marks if he would produce writing between locked slates, similar to the writing alleged to have been executed at the Zöllner séances. The medium took no notice of the professor's letter. Slade could do nothing in the presence of the conjurer Carl Wilmann, and the conjurer Schradieck eclipsed Slade in his own tricks, making use of a "spirit hand" by means of his left foot, just as Slade did.

Daniel Dunglas Home is said never to have been publicly exposed in fraud, which may have been owing to the special protection afforded him by his peculiar social relations that made his observers his hosts. Nevertheless, there are reported charges of suspicious circumstances against him:

1. A spirit hand that could be seen against the faint light of the window appeared and disappeared at the edge of the table. It was observed to be

continuous with Home's body: "The situation at this point struck me so forcibly—the trick so plain to my eyes and the reverential and adoring expression of the company . . . that I was seized with a strong impulse to laugh."

2. Delia Logan, the journalist, in writing of one of Home's séances at the house of a nobleman in London, says that the medium failing to produce balls of fire tried for luminous hands. In the darkened house Home groped his way alone to the head of the broad staircase where every few minutes a pair of luminous hands were thrown up. The audience was satisfied generally. But the host stood near the mantel piece and had seen Home abstractedly place a small bottle upon it; he slipped the bottle into his pocket, and upon examination found it to contain phosphorated oil. He had seen Home's marvels and had testified to them freely, but after the discovery of the phosphorous trick he dropped him at once.

3. Solovovo wrote that it had always seemed to him that action by Home's feet was often not a very improbable hypothesis, and that detailed descriptions, even those of Sir William Crookes, were extremely faulty in this particular respect. That the spirit hand was not a stuffed glove, at least when it worked under the table, is seen from Aksakoff's description: "Tender but firm fingers began to work, trying to take off the ring . . . and I was fully convinced these were living, warm, thin human fingers." There was no mention of the control of Home's feet, however. All these omissions are very unfortunate.

4. In the action brought by Mrs. Jane Lyon, in 1867, against Home, for the recovery of some £30,000, the testimony convicted him of culpable fraud. Through "spirit messages" from the deceased husband, Home induced the lady to (a) adopt him as her son, (b) set aside £24,000 to yield him an annual income of £700, (c) make a will giving him the arms and name of Lyon and all the property, and (d) make him a birthday gift of £6,800. After ten days of trial, Vice-Chancellor Giffard decreed that the gifts and deeds were fraudulent and void.

5. Home refused Mr. Addison's offer of £50 to float in the air in his presence; and he declined the Emperor Napoleon's proposal for Robert Houdin, the conjurer, to be present at one of his séances.

Miss Florence Cook and Miss Showers appear to have given séances together that permitted Sergeant Cox to study their materialized spirits and led to the consequent exposure of Miss Showers in April 1874.

1. Cox studied the "spirits," "Katie" and "Florence," moving about together in a lighted room; he saw that they could breathe, talk, perspire, and eat; and that in face, complexion, gesture, and voice, they precisely resembled the two mediums who were asserted to be lying entranced behind the curtains. When the form of "Florence" appeared in the aperture between the curtains, Mrs.

Edwards opened the curtains wider. In the spirit's struggles to prevent this, the head-dress fell off, and revealed the spirit's head as that of Miss Showers. The chair where the medium should have been sitting was seen to be empty. The medium was masquerading as a spirit.

2. At one of Florence Cook's séances, Mr. W. Volckman scrutinized the form, features, gestures, size, style, and peculiarities of utterance of the so-called spirit. He grasped the spirit form and found he held the medium. [Crookes, who studied the phenomena of Miss Cook, referred to this incident as a "disgraceful occurrence" that cast unjust suspicion upon an innocent young woman.]

3. At another sitting, in a dark séance with Miss Cook, one William Hipp seized the hand of the spirit that was sprinkling him with water, and when a light was struck found himself grasping the hand of the medium.

4. Some half a dozen years later, in 1880, Sir G. Sitwell and Carl von Buch seized the spirit and found it to be the medium, Mrs. Corner (formerly Miss Cook).

Podmore says:

> Reading between the lines, we are forced to recognize that the confidence expressed by scientific witnesses in the genuineness of these "materializations" is inextricably bound up with their confidence in the personal integrity of the medium, and Miss Cook's later career, at any rate, scarcely allows us to suppose that such confidence was ever well founded.

It is well known that Eusapia Palladino has been frequently caught in fraud, and it is said that her early training included legerdemain. Sitters have recognized in her an adept in conjuring. Those scientists who report favorably upon her phenomena recognize that the weight of their evidence depends upon the *impossibility* of fraud.

The illustrations of suspicious circumstances of fraud that are brought together here constitute but a very small fraction of the stream of negative evidence that without doubt supports the persistent incredulity of official science. They are not intended to offer a means of estimating the full weight of all the negative evidence. Rather, they were chosen for the purpose of explaining why official science hesitates to accept the favoring results of investigations in metapsychics carried out by the most eminent scientists—such as Crookes, Lodge, and Richet—and of providing some concrete material for use in the constructive intimations of this exposition.

What weight has Crookes's report on the phenomena of Kate Fox? Of Home? Of Miss Cook? The rating by official science is probably just zero. The Zöllner report on Henry Slade is also, even more positively, rated at zero. The various reports on Eusapia Palladino probably receive no higher rating.

The stream of negative evidence warns official science that all metapsychic phenomena may be illusory; may be but physiological, psychological, or simple legerdemain.

III

Another cause for the incredulity of "official science" is to be found in the prevalent methods of metapsychic investigation, and this cause perhaps has much greater weight than the stream of negative evidence.

"Unless the 'conditions' are observed, the phenomena will not appear." But since this is true in all science, why does it have special significance in metapsychics? Because in science the experimenter controls the conditions and in metapsychics the medium controls the conditions. In case the medium is not satisfied with the conditions proposed by the investigator, who in fact is only a sitter, she need not produce the phenomena, and she is excused on the grounds of their uncontrollability.

The reports of metapsychic investigations do not always show how completely the control of the conditions under which the phenomena occur lies with the medium, and many earnest students of the literature will be ready to dispute the fact. We can do no better than to examine one of the best possible cases: the classic report by Crookes on the phenomena of D. D. Home. It reads like a laboratory report, and the natural presumption of the reader would be that the experiments followed laboratory procedure.

Eighteen years after the research, Crookes, in response to earnest entreaty for the long promised amplified report of his investigations, published his notes that were written while the phenomena were going forward and sometimes copied or expanded immediately after. Curiously enough, the heading for these "Notes" carries the term "séances" instead of "experiments."

The Séance of June 21, 1871, at Mr. Crookes's house is described in the "Notes" as follows (Crookes 1889-90, 110-112):

Wednesday, June 21st, 1871.—Sitting at 20, Mornington-road.—From 10:45 to 11:45. (This séance was held shortly after the previous one [8:40 to 10:30 on the same evening].) We all got up, moved about, opened the windows, and changed our positions.

Present: Mr. D. D. Home (medium), Mrs. Wr. Crookes, Mr. Wr. Crookes, Mrs. Humphrey, Mr. C. Gimingham, Mr. Serjt. Cox, Mr. Wm. Crookes, Mrs. Wm. Crookes.

In the dining room. The table and apparatus the same as before.

The light was diminished, but there was still light enough to enable us to distinguish each other plainly and see every movement. The aparatus was also distinctly visible.

The automatic register was pushed up close to the index of the balance.

We sat in the following order: [Cut of rectangular table, with positions labeled—Mrs. Wm. C. sat between Home and the apparatus (mahogany board, etc.), and Mr. Wm. Crookes sat by the apparatus.]

A lath was lying on the table. [A foot from the edge at which Home sat.]

Almost immediately *a message came, "Hands off."* After sitting quiet for a minute or two, all holding hands, we heard loud *raps on the table;* then *on the floor* by the weight apparatus. The *apparatus was then moved* and the spring balance was heard to move about strongly. We then had the following *message:*

"Weight altered a little. Look."

I then got up and looked at the register. It had descended to 14 pounds, showing an additional tension of (14 – 5 =) 9 pounds.

As this result had been obtained when there was scarcely light enough to see the board and index move, I asked for it to be repeated when there was more light. The gas was turned up and we sat as before. Presently the board was seen to move up and down (Mr. Home being some distance off [sitting or standing?] and not touching the table, his hands being held), and the index was seen to descend to 7 pounds, where the register stopped. This showed a tension of 7 – 5 = 2 pounds.

Mr. Home now told us to alter our position. We now sat as follows: [Cut of positions; Mr. Wm. Crookes is moved two places further from the apparatus, and *Home sits by it.*]

Mr. Home thereupon moved his chair to the extreme corner of the table and turned his feet quite away from the apparatus close to Mrs. H. Loud *raps were heard on the table* and then *on the mahogany board,* and the latter was shaken strongly up and down. The following message was then given:

"We have now done our utmost."

On going to the spring balance it was seen by the register to have descended to 9 pounds, showing an increase of tension of 4 pounds.

The apparatus was now removed away from the table, and we returned to our old places (see first diagram).

We sat still for a few minutes, when *a message came:*

"Hands off the table, and all joined."

We therefore sat as directed.

Just in front of Mr. Home and on the table, in about the position shown on the first diagram, was a thin wooden lath 23¼ inches long, 1½ inch wide, and ⅜ inch thick, covered with white paper. It was plainly visible to all, and was one foot from the edge of the table.

Presently the *end of this lath*, pointing towards Mr. Wr. Crookes, *rose up* in the air to the height of about 10 inches. The other end then rose up to a height of about five inches, and then the lath floated about for more than a minute in this position, suspended in the air, with no visible means of support. It moved sideways and waved gently up and down, just like a piece of wood on the top of small waves of the sea. The lower end then gently sank till it touched the table and the other end then followed.

Whilst we were all speaking about this wonderful exhibition of force the lath began to move again, and rising up as it did at first, it waved about in a somewhat similar manner. The starting novelty of this movement having now worn off, we were all enabled to follow its motions with more accuracy. Mr. Home was sitting away from the table at least three feet from the lath all this time; he was apparently quite motionless, and his hands were tightly grasped, his right by Mrs. Wr. Crookes and his left by Mrs. Wm. Crookes. Any movement by his feet was impossible, as, owing to the large cage being under the table, his legs were not able to be put beneath, but were visible to those on each side of him. All the others had hold of hands. As soon as this was over the following *message was given:* "We have to go now; but before going we thank you for your patience. Mary sends love to aunt, and will play another time."

The séance then broke up at a quarter to twelve.

This sample indicates that the "spirits" directed the seating, the order of the phenomena, and the time to inspect the phenomena or read indicators. Looking over the rest of the notes, the reader learns that they regulated the amount of light. The behavior of the mahogany board was irregular, sometimes swaying sideways. And the experiments of a single type were not generally repeated consecutively. Always much else went on: movement of furniture, playing of accordion, passing flowers, clothing tugged, and persons touched by a "spirit hand," elongation or levitation of Home's body, movement of planchette, tumbling and ringing of a bell, knotting of handkerchiefs, the jumping of the table in keeping time with the accordion music, writing of messages on paper, the movement of curtains, trembling of the table, heavy knockings, innumerable raps, and many "messages." In general, we have a multiplicity of phenomena produced in confusion, very similar to those Slade provided Zöllner; and we know that Home kept up an incessant chatter. Home was the only person free to move about.

Metapsychic investigations are not experiments, they are séances. The phenomena come unexpectedly, not just at the moment the observer is prepared to examine them carefully. Rarely are the phenomena of the decisive kind, that are asked for and prepared for, produced.

Crookes, before the researches, had reproved the spiritualists for their extravagant evidence, such as the levitation of pianos, and said that what the scientist yearns for is the exercise of a force of one-ten-thousandths of a gram on the pan of a balance that is confined in a closed case, the swinging of a pendulum in a glass case, the passing of a thousandth part of a grain of arsenic into a sealed glass tube. He did not get these phenomena. He does imply that an enclosed pendulum was set in motion, but nowhere does he describe the experiment.

Zöllner (1880) asked for: (1) The linking of two solid rings of different kinds of wood. (2) The reversal of the twist in snail shells. (3) A knot in an endless bladder band. (4) The placing of a paraffin candle in a hollow glass ball, without melting the edges.

What he obtained was: (1) The placing of the rings on a jointed centre-post of a table. (2) The removal of the snail shells from the top of the table to a slate held beneath. (3) The entangling of the bladder band with a cord having sealed ends. He regarded these as such an improvement upon what he had requested that the paraffin candle was neglected.

Even when scientific instruments are used in metapsychic investigation, the control of the conditions of experiment remains in the medium's hands.

In 1907, assistants of Professor Mosso, Doctors Herlitzka, Charles Foa, and Aggazzotti, held sittings with Eusapia Palladino in Turin:

[They saw some of the usual phenomena] but the tests they had specially prepared in order to render physical intervention on the part of Eusapia impossible unfortunately miscarried. At the first sitting a clockwork cylinder, covered with blackened paper, was placed inside a bell-glass, secured from interference by sealed tapes. The object of the test was to obtain a vertical mark on the cylinder, and the key of the electric circuit through which end could be accomplished was enclosed in a securely fastened and sealed cardboard box. In the event the sealed tapes were torn off the bell-glass; the lid of the cardboard box was forcibly removed, and the key then depressed. The test was thus rendered useless. Eusapia explained, however, that if woven material instead of cardboard had been used to protect the key, it could have been moved without interference with the apparatus. Acting on the hint the experimenters prepared for the next séance a new apparatus. Inside the cabinet was placed a manometer—a U-shaped tube of mercury with a floating pointer which would automatically register any movements of the mercury on a scale. The tube was in connection with a vessel full of water, and closed with a rubber capsule. Pressure on the capsule would, of course, force up the mercury in the tube. The vessel of water was enclosed in a wooden box, the sides of which rose high above the capsule. The top of the capsule was blackened. In place of a lid the box was covered with cloth, so as to prevent pressure on the capsule by normal means. At the close of the séance the mercury was found to have risen; but the cloth covering was torn. [Podmore 1910, 100-101]

In the same year another series of investigations was made with Eusapia by Professor Botazzi of the University of Naples:

> No trouble was spared to test the phenomena and ascertain the conditions. At the beginning of each sitting the barometric pressure, the temperature, and the atmospheric saturation were recorded. Several pieces of apparatus—a letter balance, an electrical metronome, a commutator, a rubber ball in connection with a manometer—were placed on a table in the cabinet behind Eusapia, in connection with automatic registering machinery in another room; and in the course of the séance several movements were registered of which the tracings are published. Other inexplicable phenomena were observed, such as a mandolin moving about by itself on the table, whilst Eusapia's hands lay in her lap. But again the only really conclusive test failed. A telegraph key had been securely enclosed in a wire cage, and this Eusapia and her spirit control 'John' were uanble to move. [Podmore 1910, 110 f.]

Forty-three sittings with Eusapia were held under the auspices of the Institute General Psychologique in Paris:

> The investigators loyally complied with the conditions imposed, but sought in various ways to devise tests which should still be valid. The really valuable part of their report is the history of the successive rejections or evasions of their tests by Eusapia. At one time they suggested that the sleeves of the medium should be sewn to the sleeves of the controllers' coats by tapes four inches long. She accepted this method of control on three occasions only—one in each year—and then refused to have anything more to do with it, giving as her reason that she had seen lunatics fastened together in this manner in an asylum, and that the recollection was unbearable. [Podmore 1910, 105]
>
> They tested Eusapia's alleged power of affecting the balance without touching it. At first a small machine, like a letter weigher, designed by M. Yourievitch, was employed. It was surrounded with a wooden frame, with linen or wooden panels to fit in the frame, so as to prevent the use of a hair or other fraudulent device. Eusapia tried it with the wooden covering and failed; tried it with the linen covering and failed; tried it with the frame alone and failed. All the protecting apparatus was then removed. Eusapia put her hands on either side of the scale and it went down, and the onlookers could not find out how it was done. Nothing daunted, M. Yourievitch then procured a more delicate balance (pèse-cocon) and surrounded it with a panelled glass lantern. M. Yourievitch further isolated the balance on a cake of wax, and put it in connection with a charged electroscope, so that if Eusapia touched the balance the fraud would be instantly detected. No result. All the glass panels were then removed except the one next Eusapia. Still no result. The last panel was then taken away, a handkerchief being placed over Eusapia's mouth to prevent her breath affecting the sensitive balance. She stretched out her hands as before, and once more the scale moved; but the electroscope was not discharged. Twice more the

same results followed. Then—in consequence of some suspicious movement observed by Madame Curie and another member of the Committee—the light was raised (our first intimation that the previous experiments took place in partial obscurity), and an arch of thick wire was placed in front of the balance. The balance moved no more, and Eusapia said she was tired.

Now, Madame Curie and her colleagues had suspected from the position of Eusapia's hands that she might have affected the movement by means of a fine thread, and in fact, on experimenting afterwards, it was found that the scale could be depressed by means of a hair without discharging the electroscope. After this experience M. Yourievitch coated the scale with lamp-black, on which even the pressure of a hair would leave a mark—and the balance moved no more.

Then they tried again with the other balance, replacing the metallic scale by a disc of paper in a wooden frame. If a pin were used, the paper would be pierced; if a hair, it would crackle. In fact, the balance moved once, when Eusapia's hands were held—but the paper crackled!

On another occasion Eusapia asked that her hands might be held and in this position she placed her hands on either side of the leaf of an india rubber plant, and the leaf was seen to move. Unfortunately for her she had forgotten her usual precaution; an isolated observer saw the hair between her hands. She was detected on another occasion moving the balance by the same means. [Podmore 1910, 108-109]

The investigator who introduces instruments of precision meets special difficulties when the medium retains control of the laboratory. He is merely a sitter in a séance.

The distinction must be made between (A) parlor observations under séance conditions, which yield at best but anecdotal evidence, and (B) scientific observations under laboratory conditions, which yield evidence acceptable to "official science." We must regard scientific method.

A. Under séance conditions, proper observation is precluded by the (a) multiplicity of phenomena, (b) unexpectedness of each event, (c) distraction of synchronous phenomena or discourse, (d) demand on attention for several hours continuously, (e) dim light, (f) lack of essential instruments, (g) lack of control of the conditions, (h) emotional atmosphere, (i) taking of inadequate notes while phenomena are occurring.

The observer cannot be prepared to observe a specific occurrence, for he doesn't know what is coming next; any observation is consequently incidental, out of the tail of the eye, or in peripheral vision. Incidental observation in poor light for two continuous hours, amid distractions addressed to both eyes and ears, and attention often misdirected, favors inference in description and becomes malobservation. With the medium in control of the conditions, no instruments to assist the senses can be used to certain advantage. The report at best can be but anecdotal.

B. Under laboratory conditions, proper observation is carefully provided for by (*a*) selecting as simple a phenomenon as possible, (*b*) providing a definite moment for its occurrence, (*c*) excluding as much distraction as possible, (*d*) limiting the time for concentrated attention, (*e*) adapting most favorable lighting, (*f*) utilizing all essential instruments, (*g*) keeping complete control of the conditions, (*h*) excluding emotional elements, (*i*) recording correctly after the phenomenon has occurred.

The experimenter is prepared to observe the specific event at the moment it occurs. He gives concentrated attention, and his attention is directed to it. Immediately after he "observes accurately," he "records correctly" by taking care to exclude inference from his description. With the conditions of experiment under his control, he can vary them at his pleasure and repeat the experiment as often as is necessary to reach a decisive, reliable result. His report is scientific.

The attitude in the séance is that of blind faith; in the laboratory, of precaution. The closer the scrutiny, in the séance, the less you learn; in the laboratory, the more you learn. Cooperation in the séance is simulated; in the laboratory, effected. The purpose in the séance is to conceal causes; in the laboratory, to reveal them.

The charge has often been made, and in itemized detail, that the rules of the séance enforce the conditions precisely favorable for fraud. And it is a curious fact, briefly suggested in the contrasted lists above, that if all the requirements in scientific method are formally set down in a list, and their opposites are then formally set down, the second list gives the method of the séance. Whereas the rules of the séance grew up empirically in the course of the practice of years, it is certainly suggestive that they may be logically deduced by the principle of negation from the method upon which we depend to acquire knowledge in all the fields of science.

The "obstinate incredulity" of "official science" must be largely attributed to the séance method of investigation to which metapsychics has been almost wholly confined.

For three-quarters of a century, evidence has been accumulating in metapsychics, and many eminent scientists have contributed to this evidence. The most constant factor in the investigations, whether by laymen, public committees, academic committees, metapsychists, or scientists, during all this time, is the method of the séance. There is no agreement upon the nature, or the description, of a single phenomenon in metapsychics; there is nothing constant in the "how" of any of the phenomena. There is agreement only "that" phenomena occur that no one can yet describe or explain. The full yield of the séance is the conviction in the minds of metapsychists that unknown phenomena occur.

"Official science" without doubt will refuse to recognize even the "fact" that the alleged phenomena occur until it is established by the scientific method, which at the time of revealing the fact of occurrence will also reveal something of the nature of the phenomena. The eminence of men of science will not outweigh the disabilities of the séance method.

IV

The incredulity of the experimental psychologist is probably more obstinate than that of his fellow scientists. All of these metapsychic phenomena seem to be associated with the mind of a medium, and the reports are dependent upon the mind of the observer. A large proportion of the evidence offered for metapsychic phenomena can be immediately written off in accordance with the psychology of deception and the psychology of testimony. The liability of error in séance observations is very great, much greater than is generally granted. An eminent scientist may be wrong in his observation, even repeatedly wrong, as Crookes certainly was, without being "either a knave or a fool"; and to charge him with error is by no means to call him "either a liar or an imbecile."

The ease and completeness of deception have been amply illustrated by séances held for the purpose of studying the extent and nature of malobservation. David J. Halstead, proprietor of the *Syracuse Daily Courier,* reported to that paper what he saw at a sitting with Truesdell, a prominent young businessman of Syracuse (Truesdell 1892, 160-169):

> The table cloth was removed from the table; upon the table were placed a plain slate with a bit of pencil, and some writing paper also with a bit of lead pencil. Two tureen covers were brought, one placed over the slate, the other over the paper. A sitter went to another room and wrote names of deceased persons on slips of paper which he brought back tightly folded into pellets.
>
> The medium placed these pellets to his forehead, and called out signals at letter after letter, to be recorded, while the sitter repeated the alphabet. In this way the name "Adelbert" was communicated. The selected pellet was unfolded and revealed that name on it.
>
> After writing-sounds, located under the tureen cover on the slate, had ceased, the cover was removed and a message of twelve or more lines, pertinent to the evening's experiment, was found on the slate, and it was signed "Adelbert."
>
> The medium rubbed his arm, rolled up his sleeve, and showed glowing flesh upon which was recorded in pale skin the name "Adelbert."
>
> All occurred under full gas light (and by legerdemain).

Mr. L. W. Chase, a spiritualist, reported to the *Syracuse Daily Courier*, of December 7, 1872, the results of a sitting with Truesdell (Truesdell 1892, 184-203). Chase went into an adjoining room to write down names of deceased friends, on slips of paper to be folded into pellets. "On reentering the room he [T.] called out, 'This is all fraud; Caroline C. is not dead, but your sister Charlotte is. If you wish to get anything at all, you must deal honestly with me. . . .' Imagine my chagrin. . . . I am entirely satisfied that no mortal eye save my own rested upon the names I had written, and still held tightly folded in my hand, nor did a live soul in the city of Syracuse know the relations of these individuals to myself."

He received on the under surface of a slate lying on the table, in the full glare of gaslight, a message: "My dear Brother: You strive in vain to unlock the hidden mysteries of the future. No mortal has faculties to comprehend infinity. Charlotte." The message was characteristic of his sister, and the handwriting "so closely resembled her's that, to my mind, there cannot be a shadow of doubt as to its identity." He also received a message from his mother in her own hand-writing on a piece of paper. The time is not far distant when "to doubt upon this subject will not only evince greater credulity than to believe, but will necessarily destroy all confidence in our senses. . . . I think, Mr. Editor, if men of science are anxious to investigate (in an honest manner) . . . here is an excellent opportunity. . ."

Mr. Chase was a stranger; he appeared to be an honest, earnest, seeker after spiritual knowledge. He called upon Truesdell at the moment the latter was closing his office for the day, and requested an appointment for a sitting. Mr. Truesdell tried to dissuade him, protesting that he was merely an amateur investigating for amusement and instruction, that all reports about him were greatly exaggerated, and that science would probably reveal the true origin of the phenomena to be of a material, instead of a spiritual, nature. The more he protested, the more earnestly Chase begged for a sitting, and when Truesdell noticed the large diary in which Chase made one or two memoranda, he reluctantly made an appointment for a sitting in the evening at his home. Before they left the office, however, Truesdell turned on the draft of the coal-stove, compelling the perspiring visitor to remove his overcoat, and examined that diary and a letter from Chase's sister (while Chase was engaged with a book in the adjoining room).

Truesdell explains the phenomena of the sitting at his home: The ballots were exchanged for blanks by palming, and were read; the message was prepared and the slate substituted; the movement of the slate was effected by a thread tied to a vest-button; the sound of the writing was produced by the rubbing of a slate-pencil, held by silk loops to the knee, against another pencil clamped to the flange of the table.

Richard Hodgson had some sittings with Eglinton, in 1884, and endeavored to make detailed records of the phenomena. For the first time, he said, he appreciated the difficulties of observation and of recollection of such events; they seemed so great as to effectually prevent a full and accurate description (Hodgson 1886-87, 382). He arranged with S. J. Davey to give séances to ascertain exactly how much reliance could be placed upon the reports of even acute and intelligent observers.

Mr. Davey, who was first attracted to séance phenomena by reports of Eglinton, was so amazed at the ease with which the medium deceived his sitters that he set to work at séance technique to see how much he could perform by legerdemain that would be recognized as supernormal. Spiritist reports were so glowing that he was accepted as one of the great mediums. After the Hodgson-Davey investigation, Alfred Russel Wallace declared that the findings of that investigation could not be accepted until it was proved that Davey was not a genuine medium pretending to use legerdemain.

The reports of séance phenomena produced by Davey were written by educated and intelligent witnesses immediately after the séance. A single small sample follows:

> Mrs. Y.: This test seemed to me *perfect*. The slate was under my own eye, on top of the table, the whole time, and either my daughter's hand or my own was placed firmly upon it without the intermission of even a second; moreover, we closed and opened it ourselves. [JSPR 1891, vol. 5]

Nevertheless, the substitution occurred, and Hodgson saw it. Hodgson also saw Davey write the message on the slate in the morning.

The results completely discredit the reliability of records of séance phenomena, upon the grounds of malobservation. In addition to these illusions of perception, Hodgson emphasizes illusions of memory that affect descriptions written weeks or months after the events (Hodgson 1886-87; 1892).

Henry Sidgwick and Mrs. Sidgwick's sister attended a séance by Haxby, in 1878, and observed phenomena that created a complete illusion of perception in Mr. X. (Sidgwick 1886-87, 61-62):

> Mrs. Sidgwick's sister said: Abdullah professed to dematerialize before us once as at the previous séance. My head was only about 1½ feet from him, and I saw him go through the same processes as he did then. I saw his arms plainly till he was right down on the floor. Then he put up his hands to the cloth on his head bringing the part hanging behind over the top and front, to hide the tiara, and then pulled the whole off his head, the white cloth remaining as the last bit of Abdullah for a few moments. I saw his hair plainly as the cloth came off, and also his back inside the curtains.

Before this séance all the members of the circle, including an enthusiastic spiritist [Mr. X.] had been told what to expect.

Mr. Sidgwick said: I was seated at the farthest point in the circle; at the same time in witnessing Abdullah's disappearance I was uanble even to imagine it anything else than the medium withdrawing gradually into the cabinet, having first fallen on his knees, and then gradually lowering his head. But Mr. X, who sat nearly as far off, but certainly not farther than I did, remarked when the performance was over that "All our doubts must now be removed," and afterwards to Mr. H., on going away, that our materializations were better than theirs in Paris.

Experiences like this make one feel how misleading the accounts of some completely honest witnesses may be. . . . And after all it appears that those marvelous séances [in Paris] were no better than this miserable personation by Haxby.

Many illustrations of the illusion of memory may be found in the literature. But three will be quoted. The first two relate to the phenomena of D. D. Home.

Sir David Brewster, with Lord Brougham, attended a sitting with Home in Cox's Hotel, in 1855. In his diary he recorded:

A small hand-bell was then laid down with its mouth on the carpet; and after lying for some time, it *actually rang when nothing could have touched it*. The bell was then placed on the other side, and it came over to me and placed itself in my hand. . . . Could give no explanation. . . .

Four months later he wrote a letter to the *Morning Advertiser,* October 12, 1855:

Round table covered with copious drapery beneath which nobody was allowed to look. The spirits were powerless aboveboard. . . . A small hand-bell, to be rung by spirits, was placed on the ground near my feet. I placed my feet round it in the form of an angle, to catch any intrusive apparatus. *The bell did not ring;* but when taken to a new place near Mr. Home's feet, it speedily came across and placed itself in my hand. . . . Conjecture it was done by Home's feet. [Podmore 1902, vol. 2, 142-143]

An alternative explanation of the contrast between the two accounts of the same phenomena, given above, is that, upon reflection, the sensorial memory responsible for the first account was discredited. Whatever the explanation, the reliability of testimony remains impaired.

In the "Researches," William Crookes (1874) reports the behavior of the wooden lath as follows:

A small lath . . . moved across the table to me, in the light, and delivered a message to me by tapping my hand; *I repeating the alphabet, and the lath tapping me at the right letters.* The other end of the lath was resting on the table, some distance from Mr. Home's hands.

The taps were so sharp and clear, and the lath was evidently so well under the control of the invisible power which was governing its movements, that I said, "Can the intelligence governing the motion of this lath change the character of the movements, and give me a telegraphic message through the Morse alphabet by taps on my hand?" (I have every reason to believe that the Morse code *was quite unknown to any other person present*, and it was only imperfectly known to me.) Immediately I said this, the character of the taps changed, and the message was continued in the way I had requested. The letters were given too rapidly for me to do more than catch a word here and there, and consequently I lost the message; but *I heard sufficient to convince me that* there was a good Morse operator at the other end of the line, wherever that might be.

Crookes (1889-90, 123-124), in his "Notes" published eighteen years later, but recorded on the spot, reported as follows:

The wooden lath now rose from the table and rested one end on my knuckles, the other end being on the table. It then rose up and tapped me several times. *Questions which I put were answered "Yes" or "No" in this manner.* I said, "Do you know the Morse alphabet?" "Yes." "Could you give me a message by it?" "Yes." As soon as this was rapped out the lath commenced rapping my knuckles in short and long taps, in a manner exactly resembling a "Morse" message. My knowledge of the code and of reading by sound *is not sufficient to enable me to say positively that it was a message;* but it sounded exactly like one; the long and short taps and the pauses were exactly similar, and *Mr. C. Gimingham, who has practice with the Morse code,* feels almost certain that it was so.

Sir Edmund Hornby, formerly Chief Justice of the Supreme Consular Court of China and Japan, at Shanghai, provides the third illustration of illusion of memory. In this case dream elements very probably enter to alter the events as experienced (Gurney and Myers 1884, 89-91).

He [Hornby] described events occurring on the night of January 19, 1875. It had been his habit to allow reporters to come to his house in the evening to get his written judgments for the next day's paper.

On the day of the event he went to his study an hour or two after dinner and wrote out his judgment.

"I rang for the butler, gave him the envelope, and told him to give it to the reporter who would call for it. I was in bed before twelve . . . I had gone to sleep, when I was awakened by hearing a tap at the study door, but thinking it might be the butler—looking to see if the fires were safe and the gas turned off—I turned over . . . to sleep again. Before I did so, I heard a tap at my bedroom door. Still thinking it the butler . . . I said, 'Come in.' The door opened, and, to my surprise, in walked Mr.———. I sat up and said, 'You have mistaken the door; but the butler has the judgment, so go and get it.' Instead of leaving the room he came to the foot of the bed. I said, 'Mr.———, you forget yourself! Have the goodness to walk out directly. This is rather an abuse of my favor.' He looked deadly pale, but was dressed as usual, and sober, and said, 'I know I am guilty of an unwarrantable intrusion, but finding that you were not in your study I have ventured to come here.' I was losing my temper, but something in the man's manner disinclined me to jump out of bed to eject him by force. So I said simply, 'This is too bad, really; pray leave the room at once.' Instead of doing so he put his hand on the footrail and gently, and as if in pain, sat down on the foot of the bed. I glanced at the clock and saw that it was about *twenty minutes past one.* I said, 'The butler has had the judgment since half-past eleven; go and get it!' He said, 'Pray forgive me; if you knew all the circumstances you would. Time presses. Pray give me a précis of your judgment, and I will take a note in my book of it,' drawing his reporter's book out of his breast pocket. I said, 'I will do nothing of the kind. Go downstairs, find the butler, and don't disturb me—*you will wake my wife;* otherwise I shall have to put you out.' He slightly moved his hand. I said, 'Who let you in?' He answered, 'No one.' 'Confound it,' I said, 'What the devil do you mean? Are you drunk?' He replied quickly, 'No, and never shall be again; but I pray your lordship give me your decision, for my time is short.' I said, 'You don't seem to care about my time, and this is the last time I will ever allow a reporter in my house.' He stopped me short, saying, 'This is the last time I shall ever see you anywhere.'

"Well, *fearful that this commotion might arouse and frighten my wife,* I shortly gave him the gist of my judgment. . . . He seemed to be taking it down in shorthand; it might have taken two or three minutes. When I finished, he rose, thanked me for excusing his intrusion and for the consideration I had always shown him and his colleagues, opened the door, and went away. I looked at the clock; it was on the stroke of *half-past one.*"

(Lady Hornby awoke, thinking she had heard talking; and *her husband told her what had happened, and repeated the account when dressing the next morning.)*

"I went to court a little before ten. The usher came into my room to robe me, when he said, 'A sad thing happened last night, sir. Poor ——— was found dead in his room.' I said 'Bless my soul! dear me! What did he die of, and when?' 'Well, sir, it appeared he went up to his room as usual at ten to work at his papers. His wife went up about twelve to ask him when he would be ready for bed. He said, "I have only the Judge's judgment to get ready, and then I have finished." As he did not come, she went up again, about a quarter to one, to his room and peeped in, and thought she saw him writing, but she did not disturb him. At *half-past one* she again went to him and spoke to him at the door. As he didn't answer she thought he had fallen asleep, so she went up to rouse him. To her horror he was dead. On the floor was his note-book, which I have brought away. She sent for the doctor, who arrived *a little after two,* and said he had been dead, he concluded, about an hour.' I looked at the note-book. There was the usual heading: 'In the Supreme Court, before the Chief Judge: The Chief Judge gave judgment this morning in this case to the following effect'—and then followed a few lines of indecipherable shorthand.

"I sent for the magistrate who would act as coroner, and desired him to examine Mr. ———'s wife and servants as to whether Mr. ——— had left his home or could possibly have left it without their knowledge between eleven and one on the previous night. The result of the *inquest* showed he died of some form of heart disease, and had not and could not have left the house without the knowledge of at least his wife, if not of the servants. Not wishing to air my 'spiritual experience' for the benefit of the press or the public, I kept the matter at the time to myself, only mentioning it to my Puisne Judge and to one or two friends; but when I got home to tiffin *I asked my wife* to tell me as nearly as she could remember what I had said to her during the night, and I made a brief note of her replies and of the facts."

[*Lady Hornby has kindly confirmed the* above facts to us, as far as she was cognizant of them.]

"As I said then, so I say now—I was not asleep, but wide awake. After a lapse of nine years my memory is quite clear on the subject. I have not the least doubt I saw the man—have not the least doubt that the conversation took place between us.

"I may add that I had examined the butler in the morning—who had given me back the MS. in the envelope when I went to the court after breakfast—as to whether he had locked the door as usual, and if anyone could have got in. He said that he had done everything as usual, adding that no one could have got in even if he had not locked the door, as there was no handle outside—which there was not. . . . The coolies said they opened the door as usual that morning—turned the key and undid the chains."

A communication to the *Nineteenth Century,* November 1884, by Frederick H. Balfour, points out some discrepancies between the narrative above and the facts:

1. Mr.——— is the Rev. Hugh Lang Nivens, editor of the *Shanghai Courier.* He died not at *one* in the morning but between eight or nine a.m. after a good night's rest.

2. There was no Mrs. Hornby at that time. Sir Edmund's second wife had died two years previously, and he did not marry again till three months *after* the event.

3. No Inquest was ever held.

4. The story turns upon the judgment of a certain case to be delivered the next day, January 20, 1874. There is no record of any such judgment.

Before printing the letter from Balfour, the Editors sent it to Judge Hornby for his comment:

[My vision] must have followed the death (some three months) instead of synchronizing with it. At the same time this hypothesis is quite contrary to the collection of the facts both in my own mind and in Lady Hornby's mind. . . . If I had not believed, as I still believe, that every word of it [the story] was accurate, and that my memory was to be relied on, I should not have even told it as a personal experience.

All these discrepancies are concordant with the results of psychological research on testimony and are to be attributed to psychological law rather than to either dishonesty or culpable carelessness.

The readiness of metapsychists to rely upon observations of séance phenomena, their insistence that illusion can be avoided, and their quick condemnation of the competence of an observer who is tricked, clearly indicate that they do not understand that error is inevitable. Consequently the psychologist remains incredulous in the face of all the accumulating "evidence."

Perception is not the photographic process the layman and elementary textbooks take it to be. We do not perceive with our senses. We perceive with our minds. What we perceive is represented in part by (a) immediate sensations (through our special senses) and in part by (b) mental stuff (imagery) contributed by our past experience. A perception, we might say, is a process compounded of sensation and imagination; it is the result of sensory impressions being assimilated by memorial material. The ratio between sensation and imagination varies greatly in what we call perception, depending upon the definiteness of the sensory component and upon the definiteness, or readiness, of the memorial elements—which is often referred to as "expectancy." When the sensorial component is definite but overridden, illusions occur; when it is negligible, hallucinations occur. Thus perception is not different in its constitution from illusions or hallucinations. The observer himself is unable to distinguish the difference; nor can the trained observer in the psychological laboratory by introspection separate the memorial component from the sensory component in a perception, so thoroughly fused are they in the unitary psychical process.

The method of the séance is precisely adapted to produce illusions and hallucinations, and it strains credulity to imagine that any trustworthy observations come from it. All of the evidence is suspect, and no "sheaf of testimony" is more cogent than its weakest component. The "fagot theory" is fallacious. It is not universally true that "where there is so much smoke, there must be some fire," for the "smoke" may be but dust stirred up by artful deceivers for artless perceivers. It is useless to fagot séance evidence.

It thus becomes clear why evidence for phenomena observed under séance conditions cannot be accepted by the experimental psychologist, and why his refusal does not reflect upon the honesty or the general scientific competence of the séance observer.

The disability of the evidence for metapsychic phenomena can be removed only by the adoption of the laboratory method. That the phenomena are extremely variable and difficult to control is no more a reason for avoiding the scientific method in metapsychics than in physiology or psychology where similar difficulties are met.

Memory is not the recovery of a block of experience that has lain in a pigeonhole. Physical analogy is hopelessly inadequate to illustrate the way the mind works. Memory is a process, and a process that never repeats itself exactly. A block of experience has no more existence before it is recalled than the North wind has in a calm and cannot be pigeon-holed. Its recollection is another mental process, a new one in itself, reproducing elements identical or similar to the elements in the original experience. In the representative repetition, however, the mutation of the elements in the original experience is characteristic and is often very great. It is not so much of a surprise, therefore, that flagrant errors in testimony occur as it is that conditions can be devised by which testimony may be accurate. The method of experiment in the laboratory provides these conditions by requiring the record on the spot.

Perhaps another circumstance bearing upon the incredulity of the psychologist should be given consideration. In the psychological laboratory the study of mental processes, dependent upon an adult person, is a cooperative enterprise. The experimenter and the observer, when the information sought must be obtained by introspection, have each their definite respective parts to play. The experimenter and the subject, when the information sought is accessible to the experimenter, must likewise assume their respective roles. In either case, thorough understanding and complete cooperation are essential.

Now any record of séance phenomena reads like a contest between the medium and the sitters. There is the matching of wits, with the great advantage in favor of the medium, who retains control of the phenomena. When scientific instruments are brought into the séance room, they must first be "magnetized," and later they are almost invariably misused, so that all crucial tests fail and the investigators are forced to return to the usual séance phenomena.

If the relation becomes experimenter and subject, and the experimenter retains control of the conditions of the experiment, the nature of the phenomena need not depend upon the immediate control of the medium's body. The use of scientific instruments will reveal the exact relation of her body or her movements to the phenomena. And, should phenomena new to science appear, the conditions favoring them could be determined, and headway could be made in the further study of their nature and the laws governing them.

The use of scientific method and instruments of precision does not constitute a threat to the medium, as is sometimes intimated, and neither she nor her manager should demur at their use. To do so implies a fear lest the phenomena will be found to be normally produced. Sincerity on the part of those in charge of the phenomena should inspire not only a willingness to cooperate in the only method of research fitted to advance knowledge, but an earnest request to be allowed to do so. This attitude would immediately disarm many a priori critics, and recommend the medium to the psychologist as a suitable subject for his laboratory.

Research could then begin on two simple but fundamental types of metapsychic phenomena: (a) telekinesis, and (b) cryptesthesia. The experimental problems might be, (a) What are the raps? and (b) Is there supernormal knowledge?

The incredulity of the psychologist does not spring from an a priori judgment that metapsychic phenomena are not possible; it comes from his knowledge of psychological causes of error and the resulting conviction that reliance upon the scientific method alone is the price of admissible evidence.

References

Crookes, William. 1874. *Researches in the Phenomena of Spiritualism.* London: Burns.
———. 1889-90. Notes of séances with D. D. Home. *Proceedings of the SPR,* 6.
Gerhardt, W. F. 1926. A metapsychic experiment. *Journal of the American SPR,* 20:502.
Gurney, E. and F. W. H. Myers. 1884. Visible apparitions. *Ninetheeth Century.* July 16.
Hodgson, Richard. 1886-87. The possibilities of mal-observation and lapse of memory, from a practical point of view. *Proceedings of the SPR,* 4:381 ff.
———. 1892. *Proceedins of the SPR,* 8:253 ff.
Podmore, Frank. 1902. *Modern Spiritualism.* London: Methuen.
———. 1910. *The Newer Spiritualism.* London: Unwin.
Richet, Charles. 1923. *Thirty Years of Psychical Research.* New York: Macmillan.
Sidgwick, Mrs. Henry. 1886-87. Results of a personal investigation into the physical phenomena of spiritualism, with some critical remarks on the evidence for the genuineness of such phenomena. *Proceedings of the SPR,* 4:45 ff.
Sudre, René. 1926. Psychical research and scientific opinion. *Journal of the American SPR,* 20:333-342.
Truesdell, John W. 1892. *The Bottom Facts Concerning the Science of Spiritualism.* New York: Dillingham.
Zöllner, J. C. F. 1880. *Transcendental Physics: An Account of Experimental Investigations.* London: C. C. Harrison. (Trans. by C. C. Massey.)

10

Fraudulent Children in Psychical Research

J. FRASER NICOL

The Right Honorable Arthur James Balfour, later Earl of Balfour, philosopher, psychical researcher, and future president of the Society for Psychical Research and prime minister of the United Kingdom, was in his Cambridge youth arrested by the police for mischievous doorbell-ringing one night. Hauled before the Cambridge magistrates, he was warned by the chairman (mayor of Cambridge) that if he did not regulate his conduct he would one day find himself in prison and was fined £1 (Young 1963, 22).

The mischief young people will engage in for the purpose of annoying or, more often, amazing their elders and glorifying themselves is a common psychological phenomenon. And in the production of paranormal or pseudoparanormal occurrences, it has a history going back hundreds of years. In this chapter I will try to give a small selection of the psychic mischief of boys and girls through the ages, leading of course to the recent outbreak of boy and girl spoon-benders imitating the mysterious performances of the Israeli Uri Geller.

The production by children of bogus psychical phenomena was common in the witchcraft scares from the fifteenth to the eighteenth centuries, when many convictions of innocent women were obtained on the perjured or delusive evidence of adolescents; and, so, hundreds of harmless women were tortured, hanged, and burned. In Germany in 1628 the fantastic stories told by 13-year-old Peter Roller were responsible for 24 persons being burned at the stake. In the Salem, Massachusetts, cases of 1692 most of the accusations came from teenage girls. Thirteen women and six men were hanged and one man was pressed to death. Afterwards, one of the girls sought to excuse herself and her friends because they felt at the time that they "must have some sport" (Robbins 1959, 94-95).

In poltergeist history, much of the continuing skepticism can be attributed to the fact that so many of the wild occurrences were hoaxes perpetrated by children. Daniel Defoe spent much of his life investigating paranormal phenomena, which he reported in several volumes. At about the age of 11, Daniel

Reprinted from the *Parapsychology Review* with permission of the Parapsychology Foundation, Inc., and the author. Copyright 1979 by the Parapsychology Foundation, Inc.

was a pupil in a boys' boarding school near Dorking, south of London. Nearby was a vacant mansion house that had been occupied by an old lady, recently deceased. Banging sounds began to be heard from the house, to the great mystification of neighborhood residents. And at night the old woman could be seen carrying a candle as she walked about a nearby field; and "though the wind blew ever so hard it would not blow the candle out." Sometimes the ghostly woman with the candle would be seen "up in the trees."

The whole thing was a practical joke by the schoolboys. Gaining entry to the house, they had tied a rope to the chair in an upper room, dropping the other end to the ground, where in a place of concealment a boy pulling the rope caused the chair to rise and fall repeatedly, creating a din. The neighbors hearing the alarming noise gathered "in the courtyard," presumably at the other side of the house, "where they could plainly hear it, but not one would venture to go upstairs." As for the inextinguishable candle, wrote Defoe in his recollections, one of the boys "had gotten a dark lanthorn, which was a thing the country people did not understand"; and of course it could be turned off and on at will and protected from the winds (Defoe 1840, 371-373).

A recent Defoe authority (Moore 1958, 30-32) has suggested that young Daniel himself participated in the foolery. I am not so sure; but, in any case, knowing all the facts, it must have been a valuable lesson to Defoe concerning the risks of malobservation, fallacious inferences, and errors of memory when he came to investigate more mysterious claims in his adult life.

Some poltergeist activities involving children may be genuine, history's most famous case being that of the teen-aged Daniel Dunglas Home (1863, 23-27). When he lived with his aunt in Connecticut, things were inexplicably tossed about the rooms, so alarming his aunt that she put the boy out of the house. But the Homes of the psychic world are rare, and mischievous children are common. Spiritualism was born in 1848 out of the mysterious percussive sounds heard in the presence of the Fox children, Catherine (aged 11) and Margaretta (14). Greater marvels developed through the years—spirit messages, telekinesis, full-form materializations. Catherine eventually moved to London, where she gave many sittings for Sir William Crookes, who was greatly impressed. She married the Anglo-German international lawyer Henry Jencken, by whom she had two children. When he died she was left penniless and sank into alcoholism (like her father before her). Margaretta also became a habitual drunkard. Catherine returned to New York where the law stepped in and deprived her of her children. To raise the wind the two women toured the halls to confess that all their séances had been fraudulent. Later they recanted. Catherine died in 1892 and Margaretta's death came a few months later (apparently at 456 West 57th Street, New York). So ended the lives of the two pretty children who mothered modern spiritualism. How much of their performances were genuine it is impossible to say. Perhaps none at all. Even their confessions have been discounted as fraudulent (Pond 1947).

Out of a list of about 420 physical mediums, it is safe to say that 400 cannot be considered authentic—either because the mediums were proved frauds or because the printed narratives were so lacking in necessary details that they afforded no true evidence.

Willie Eglinton

The most important bogus medium in history was William Eglinton, who began his corrupt activities in adolescence. Important because the ultimate effect of his slate-writing trickery was to revolutionize psychical investigations. When Willie was 17, his father, becoming curious about spiritualism, gathered some friends together to see whether, sitting around a table, they could evoke psychic phenomena. Willie, saying that spiritualism was "all humbug," refused to join the company and stuck a notice on the séance-room door: "There are lunatics confined here; they will shortly be let loose; highly dangerous." After several empty séances, the father warned the boy he must either participate or leave the house. Willie chose the former (Eglinton 1878, 1-2). In his presence the table tilted and tapped out messages. It rose in the air and descended. Then he gave the appearance of passing into a "trance" in which he delivered psychic messages.

His fame spread and his pseudo-mediumship developed variety, including the protection of materialized phantoms (handsomely dressed) in darkened rooms in half a dozen countries. More significant for our interest, he also developed the art of slate-writing. Séances were held in normal lighting—like the mini-Geller affairs nearly a century later. Sitters having examined a fresh pair of slates and placed a piece of slate pencil between them, Eglinton held the slates under the table, perhaps for a long time, until the sitters' watchfulness had relaxed. A scratching would be heard, perhaps produced by Eglinton's fingernail. He might become agitated, swaying about, uttering exclamations, and perhaps dropping the slates on the floor, where there was often a pile of supposedly clean slates. When the slates were opened there was a message from the Other World.

Numerous scientists and intellectuals wrote tributes to Eglinton's powers. Four conjurers who had sittings at different times were convinced of his miraculous gifts. A visiting American geologist, H. Carvill Lewis (1886-87) was not so easily convinced as the malobserving conjurers. Pretending to divert his attention, he watched Eglinton out of the corner of his eye and moment by moment he discovered how the "spirit warning" was fraudulently produced.

S. John Davey (Hodgson and Davey 1886-87; Hodgson 1892), a young and almost unknown member of the Society for Psychical Research, had been deeply impressed by his sittings with Englinton, but afterward realized that his powers of observation may have failed him. He began to practice slate-writing by prestidigitation (like Eglinton in fact) and a new friend, Richard Hodgson, arranged for séances, the sitters not knowing it would be trickery, but agreeing to provide reports of their experiences. Those reports are among the most sensational in the history of psychical research; on matters of accurate observation and report they revolutionized the subject; and now in the days of Geller and mini-Gellers they are essential reading. In none of the numerous séances did any sitter notice anything wrong. They failed to report essential incidents; they reported "events" that never happened. To take only two items: A Japanese marquess was astounded to read on the slate a message addressed to him in his native language. A conjurer noticed no tricks at all.

Imogene Kirkup

Seymour Kirkup (Cust 1909) was a well-known British painter and art scholar of substantial private means, who early in his career moved to Florence, where he spent most of his very long life and won the friendship of other British residents, including the Brownings, Walter Savage Landor, the Trollopes, and D. D. Home. Having discovered the long forgotten fresco portrait of Dante, he was awarded by the Italian king the honor of cavaliere. Kirkup mistakenly supposed this was a barony, and so he became known as Baron Kirkup.

In 1854, when he was 66, he became the father of a child, Imogene, the mother being a Florentine young lady, Regina Ronti, to whom he was not married. The mother died two years later. In 1868, Kirkup wrote in a letter to the artist Joseph Severn: "I am now living with a little daughter. She is now fourteen. Her maid is an ex-nun—very good and glad to be free. They are both mediums, the former ever since she was two years old." Kirkup was a kindly man, but credulous; Mrs. Browning called him "incautious." He could not foresee the trap that the bogus mediumship of his daughter would lead him into.

The sham phenomena of Imogene and her maid probably included the usual pseudo-clairvoyance and table-turning, and certainly fake materializations and apports. In 1871, when Imogene was 17, Kirkup was "favored" (as he bitterly recalled years later) "with materialization, and two 'spirits' walked through my rooms, and shook hands with us. . . . My English and American friends were taken in like myself."

Imogene married, probably before 1875. In that year Kirkup himself married. He was 87, his bride, 22. The marriage no doubt dismayed Imogene, who presumably had assumed she would have been his sole heir. The "spiritual" phenomena now took the form of letters teleported between two séance-rooms many miles apart. Later, Imogene and her Italian husband stole the teleported letters, and, as Kirkup reported to his friend Home (1877), "deposited [them] in the tribunate to prove me insane." The conspirators' purpose was to obtain control of Kirkup's property. He was forced to accept a compromise by which his daughter and her husband agreed "to sell me my liberty for a ransom . . .

and I have paid a part of my small fortune to save the rest. From the day they left my house I have heard or seen no more of spirits."

The girl medium did not long survive her fraud, dying in 1878 at the age of 23 or 24. Her father died in 1880 in his ninety-second year.

Master Watkins

Children have sometimes been lured into the production of spurious phenomena by their elders. One ridiculous case concerns the famous American slate-writing medium Charles E. Watkins, whose son was made to perform at the age of one year. At the end of a sitting in Boston, attended by an English pharmacist, Robert Cooper (1887), Watkins, "calling to his wife, who was at the other end of the room nursing the baby, then about 12 months old, to come to the table, placed the child's hands on the slate as it sat on its mother's lap. Master Watkins, however, could not be induced to hold his hands still for even the fraction of a minute, whereupon Watkins said [as Cooper reported], 'We will try another plan,' and, taking the slate from the table, placed it on a chair and sat the baby on it. In a very short time writing was found on the slate; being an appropriate answer to my query relative to the previous communication. I was thus satisfied of the genuineness of Watkins' mediumship."

Six years later the boy Watkins was entertaining his young friends with the wonders of slate-writing. It should be added that Robert Cooper had had many years of experience investigating psychical phenomena, yet it never occurred to him that his powers of observation vis-à-vis Watkins and the baby may have been inadequate to the task.

Hugh Moore's Daughters

A man who, without a pang of conscience, drew his own children into the practice of cheating was the notorious physical medium the "Rev. Dr." Hugh Moore, who early this century was the talk of New York City. He employed eight or nine confederates who acted the parts of materialized spirits. Their wages, derived from admission fees paid by credulous sitters, amounted to $60 a week. Two of Moore's daughters participated in the deceptions.

I have some Moore séance photographs—undoubtedly posed for the occasion—taken in 1905. One shows a little girl, about 12 years old and dressed in a beautiful white robe and heavenly crown, faking the part of the child guide "Pansy" as she sweetly gazes up at an elderly woman sitter. Nearby sits the "Rev. Dr." Hugh Moore, looking the very soul of spiritual piety.

Not long afterward, Moore was accused of imposture and made a hurried departure from New York. Eventually he returned to New York, where Eric J. Dingwall (1922) and Walter F. Prince saw through his pretenses, but other sitters accepted the show as perfectly genuine.

The Cottingley Fairies

The so-called "fairy photographs" allegedly obtained by two girls in a woodland at Cottingley in Yorkshire in 1917 caused an international sensation when Sir Arthur Conan Doyle (1971) published a favorable account of them in 1920. The girls were Elsie Wright, 16 years old when the pictures were taken, and her little cousin Frances Griffiths, aged ten. The photographs showed fairies dancing in the air beside one or other of the girls, and in another instance a gnome apparently trying to leap on to Frances's knee as she sat on the grass.

Among many criticisms was one by C. Vincent Patrick (1921), who pointed out that the illumination of the girls and the fairies came from different directions. Also the photographs did not look like "snapshots," but pictures carefully posed. And "one would have expected to see some blurring, due to movement, in the fairies' wings and feet at any rate, with a 1/50th of a second exposure at a distance of four feet. None is visible in the reproduction." Patrick concluded that the photographs were faked.

A year after Conan Doyle published his story, the *Star* newspaper (December 20, 1921) reported that "Messrs. Price and Sons, the well-known firm of candle makers, informs us that the fairies in this photograph are an exact reproduction of a famous poster they have used for years to advertise their night lights. 'I admit on these fairies there are wings, whereas our fairies have no wings,' said a representative of the firm to a *Star* reporter, 'but with this exception, the figures correspond line for line with our own drawing'" (quoted in Houdini 1972 [1924], 124).

Even some spiritualists were embarrassed, including Miss Mercy Phillimore (1959), for many years secretary of the London Spiritualist Alliance, who wrote of the pictures as "photographs of two teen-age [*sic*] girls gazing at small figures, resembling paper cutouts of fairies and gnomes."

The Creery Sisters

Telepathy experiments under laboratory conditions have frequently produced favorable evidence. But with children professing to demonstrate telepathy there have often been serious doubts, and in some cases plain evidence of fraud.

In 1881, the Rev. A. M. Creery, of Buxton, England, had five daughters aged 10 to 17. Creery informed the physicist Professor W. F. Barrett that four of his children, also a servant girl, could demonstrate thought-reading. Barrett experimented with them and was convinced. When, in the following year, the Society for Psychical Research (*Proc. SPR* 1882a; 1882b) was founded, the Society's leaders continued the investigation of the girls, who were free from "morbid or hysterical symptoms, and in manner perfectly simple and childlike." Usually one girl functioned as percipient and was sent out of the room, while the investigators, together with other members of the family, decided on the targets, which were usually playing cards from a shuffled deck, or names, or solid objects. The girl was brought back into the room and made her guess. The successes of all the children were phenomenal.

The SPR observers realized that, under such conditions, a code might be used. So, in some playing-card trials one investigator drew a card from the pack, and he alone knew the target. Success was considerable. But here the two published reports lack essential details. Did the cards belong to the Creerys and, if so, could they have been identifiably marked on their backs? We don't know. While the agent was looking at the card could its face have been reflected on some shiny surface, such as a mirror, a framed picture, a window?

Six years later when two of the girls were re-investigated at Cambridge, they were detected using visual and auditory codes. They also confessed that signals had been used in the previous tests "on occasions of failure, when it was feared that visitors would be disappointed" (Gurney 1888-89).

With the benefit of a hundred years of history behind us, we know that consistently high-scoring subjects are extreme rarities. In the Creery affair there were alleged to be five living in the same house.

"Amy Joyce"

A 13-year-old girl, who did not hesitate to cheat if she could get away with it, is known in the literature by the pseudonym "Amy Joyce." Though her father, a clerk of works, had done many telepathy tests with his child, he did not realize that the cards he looked at could be reflected in his thick glasses. Amy, like many other children, did not disillusion him.

Half a dozen SPR members investigated her over a period of months. Sir Oliver Lodge (1913-14) obtained fairly impressive results. He did not wear glasses and apparently excluded the risk of corneal reading. But significantly enough, Amy did best when her father, wearing his glasses, was co-agent. In clairvoyance trials, when Lodge did not know the target, Amy failed.

The Hon. Everard Feilding brought her to London, where she spent a week in his Mayfair house and was watched by several SPR leaders. Feilding and Alice Johnson (1913-14) tested her with drawings and reported: "One very definite conclusion was ... reached by the experimenters, namely, that ... Amy Joyce habitually and very cleverly availed herself of any opportunity of normal 'vision' which might present itself, and also that she as habitually and as cleverly tried to conceal the fact of her having done so." Feilding and Johnson added that Amy was "abnormally quick of vision and clever at seeing things without appearing to see them."

The girl resisted strict conditions and took every opportunity to circumvent them. She would not sit still, "but was constantly finding excuses to get up and walk around the room, which made it more difficult to keep the drawing hidden from her." When Feilding accused her of cheating, she at first denied, but afterward admitted it.

Other persons tested her, and there was a general impression that she probably did have some telepathic gift. The most interesting sequel is that she was dropped and never heard of again.

Lillian

Lillian was a nine-year-old girl at the Wright Refuge in Durham, N.C., in 1936, where she and other children were tested for card-guessing in the school playground. The experimenter was Margaret Pegram (later Reeves), who sat on the ground at a very low table, with Lillian opposite. Pegram placed on the table five ESP cards showing the symbols Cross, Circle, Rectangle, Star, and Wavy Lines. She handed Lillian a pack of shuffled cards face down. Those were not the commercially printed cards of later times but rectangles of white cardboard with the symbols hand-stamped on one side. Lillian's task was to identify each card paranormally and place it opposite the appropriate symbol on the table. Usually other children looked on, or played around, and Pegram had to keep them in order—a somewhat tricky setup for a scientific investigation.

Small prizes were awarded to children who got good scores. Lillian's scores were usually not far removed from chance expectation. But one day she scored 23, and on another day guessed an entire pack of 25 correctly.

In the report of Mrs. Reeves and J. B. Rhine (1942), six years later, they stated with admirable candor that "it should be frankly recognized" that the experimental procedure was "not secure against the possibility of error." But we are also assured about the quality of the cards and also that Lillian, as she removed a card from the deck, could not have seen its face reflected on the table top because the latter was "dull and unpolished."

The authors were not well acquainted with the literature of psychical research or they would have known of Mrs. Margaret Verrall's (1895) card-guessing experiences in 1890. Mrs. Verrall was a classical scholar and became a lecturer at Newnham College, Cambridge. She also had an undoubted psychic gift, as reports of her evidential automatic writing attest. If she made a mistake, she reported it in print without trying to make excuses.

Her card-guessing experiments, in which she often held the card deck, like Lillian, included some attempts to discover normal explanations. She knew, of course, that a polished wood table would reflect a card face; but she also found the same effect when she used "an ordinary leather-covered writing table."

More instructive for the Lillian case, Mrs. Verrall discovered that in suitable lighting she was "able to see enough of the cards reflected on a well ironed white linen tablecloth to enable me to distinguish with certainty between picture and non-picture cards, black and red, and so on. I could not distinguish 3 of Hearts from 3 of Diamonds, but I dare say I should soon have acquired the skill, had I persevered "

The Lillian experiments were somewhat different, taking place out of doors "in the spring of 1936." Spring continues until June 21. She lifted a card a little from the top of the deck. Though open to correction, I doubt whether the sun, however bright, would create a reflection of the target card on the back of the card underneath. But in bright sunlight it is possible that the light would shine through the card and transmit its image to the white back of the next card. With only five possible pictures, perfect images would be unnecessary. A line down the center would mean a cross, one near the edge a rectangle, etc.

Mrs. Verrall also found she could detect playing cards by simply passing the sides of her thumbs "rapidly" over the surface of the cards. With 52 different cards, she could not always be right; but, as an example, in 400 trials the expected score would be 7.7; Mrs. Verrall by touch scored 34. The odds against chance are hundreds of billions to one. Mrs. Verrall had the skin of her hands tested and found that it was "not more than normal," but the sensitiveness "along the inner edge of the left thumb . . . was as high as at the point of the index finger, which is unusual."

In the Lillian case the authors did not consider the possibility of the girl seeing shadows of the card faces or identifying them by touch.

The Mini-Gellers

All the child adventurers in the past have been surpassed by the uncountable number of boy and girl spoon-benders imitating the mysterious performances of the Israeli Uri Geller. If Geller is in any respect genuine it is a pity he has never been tested by competent psychical researchers.

A scientist strongly devoted to the children is John Taylor, professor of applied mathematics at King's College, University of London, who narrates in his book *Superminds* (Taylor 1975b) that on seeing Geller in action he "felt as if the whole framework with which I viewed the world had suddenly been destroyed. I seemed naked and vulnerable. . . ."

"Naked and vulnerable" indeed, not because his world had been destroyed but because he had stepped into a world of which he had little or no knowledge. His innocence is shown when he ventures outside the metal-bending to publish old photographs of other alleged phenomena that he never saw. One is a flashlight photograph of the medium Colin Evans being perpendicularly levitated in the dark. Professor Taylor in his profound lack of knowledge is evidently unaware that exactly the same effect can be obtained by a person jumping, as was proved by a former SPR research officer, C. V. C. Herbert (now Earl of Powys), by a series of experimental photographs in 1938 (Herbert 1938-39).

Many other examples of the professor's lack of knowledge and experience mar his book, especially when he deals with boy and girl cutlery-benders. In one section there are 14 boys and 20 girls, all between 7 and 17 years of age, and 7 of them are "severely retarded."

A case that Taylor surprisingly accepts as "well authenticated" happened at a luncheon for young and older spoon-benders given at the London Hilton Hotel by the tabloid *Daily Mirror*, which he quotes: "Fourteen of us sat around the table . . . our eyes closed in deep concentration. After two minutes it happened. A silver-plated coffee spoon engraved London Hilton 73, curled itself round a saucer. No one touched it. The coffee spoon apparently bent of its own accord." If 14 people had their "eyes closed," how could they know that "no one touched" the spoon? A woman Gellerite was "considered responsible," but, in another incident, two children caused a reporter's watch that hadn't gone for two years to start again (Miller 1975).

Taylor tells of one child "who silently swears 'bend, damn you, bend,'" and of a 13-year-old girl who "found herself unable to bend a spoon during an interview with reporters from a local newspaper, yet immediately they had gone she had no trouble in doing it." Taylor takes such stories seriously.

He also used thin metal strips inside glass tubes or wire mesh. In the laboratory, all his subjects failed to bend the strips; but when allowed to take them home for a week two subjects succeeded in bending the metal. Doubts, however, have been raised about Taylor's method of sealing.

Reviewing Taylor's *Superminds* in *New Scientist*, David Berglas (1975), a conjurer, pointed out that on page 165 there is "a photograph which author John Taylor describes as 'metal sculptures created by psychokinetic powers of a 10-year-old boy.' I was with John Taylor when this boy was creating similar sculptures, and it seems much less clear to me that they are psychokinetic. We went to this boy's house, where the father kept the boy well supplied with aluminum rods. For half an hour, the boy tried unsuccessfully to bend the rods. Then John Taylor suggested that the boy go upstairs with the rods as usual. He explained that the boy would go to his room without us and that while playing with his model airplanes, 'things happen.' When he came back sure enough the rods had bent. What kind of scientist accepts this as evidence of the paranormal?"

Replying, Taylor (1975a) said the "episode . . . in a different part of the house 'as usual' was never used in the text, though [the boy's] powers have been validated in the way described there." Taylor does not give the page number in which the ten-year-old's powers were "validated," but if he means small items on pages 163-166, the vague stories have no claim to validation.

David Berglas, associated with the *Daily Express*, offered £5,000 to anyone who could bend metal by "inexplicable supernatural means." Half the money would go to the successful person, half for research on that person. A dozen children were selected for "semi-final" trials in London and Birmingham. This was scientific research in the style of Fleet Street. Joseph Hanlon's (1975) account in the *New Scientist* tells us that the children—seven in London, five in Birmingham—were crowded into one room, with four "observers," including Hanlon and some parents. "Virtually all the children" bent a spoon and/or fork. "It was not possible to watch all the children constantly [!], and some bent cutlery in a way not readily explicable by the observers." But "the subtlety, perceptiveness and gall of children as young as seven came as a rude shock."

"When attention was diverted to a child at one end of the room, a boy at the other end glanced around the room; confident that no one was watching, he used two hands and all his strength to bend a fork. So sure was he of his deception that he did not even attempt to shield his effort.

"Another boy, after an hour of furtive glances showed him that he could never be totally unobserved, slowly moved the spoon down beside him in the chair, hidden from observers. As he pressed it against the chair seat with maximum pressure, several observers clearly saw him grimace. Yet he displayed the then bent spoon with pride, confident that no one saw him use force."

At Bath University in England, two psychologists tested six mini-Gellers who, however, did not know that their activities were being videotaped through two-way mirrors. As part of the investigative scheme, after 20 minutes the observer in the room relaxed his vigilance. After that, "*A* put the rod under her feet to bend it; *B*, *E*, and *F* used two hands to bend a spoon. . . . We can assert that in no case did we observe a rod or spoon bent other than by palpably normal means" (Gardner 1975).

The cases above are only a sampling of many instances of cunning children trading on the credulity of their elders whose sense of awe surpassed their sense of sight. How often have psychical researchers been earnestly assured by inexperienced witnesses: "Of course it's true—I saw it with my own eyes." In most cases they saw only what they were intended to see and then they misinterpreted what they so briefly observed. We began this article with an experience of the wayward A. J. Balfour in his youth; we may end with a warning he spoke in his mature years: "Our perceptions are habitually mendacious."

References

Berglas, D. 1975. Review of J. Taylor, *Superminds*. *New Scientist*.

Cooper, R. 1887. Letter to the editor. *Light*, 7:502.

Cust, L. 1909. In *Dictionary of National Biography*. London: Smith and Elder, s.v. Kirkup, S. S.

Defoe, D. 1840. *The History and Reality of Apparitions*. London: Thomas Tegg.

Dingwall, E. J., ed. 1922. A versatile medium. *Journal of the American SPR*, 16:41-50.

Doyle, A. C. 1971 [1921]. *The Coming of the Fairies*. New York: S. Weiser.

Eglinton, W. 1878. The career of Mr. Eglinton as a medium: Personal statement. *Spiritual Notes*, 1.

Feilding, E., and A. Johnson. 1913-14. Report on some experiments in thought-transference. *Journal of the SPR*, 16:164-173.

Gardner, M. 1975. Paranonsense. *New York Review of Books*, October 30 (quoting *Nature*, September 4, 1975.

Gurney, E. 1888-89. Note relating to some of the published experiments in thought-transference. *Proceedings of the SPR*, 5:269-270.

Hanlon, J. 1975. But what about the children? *New Scientist*, June 5.

Herbert, C. V. C. 1938-39. Short exposure photographs of a jumping model. *Proceedings of the SPR*, 45:196-198.

Hodgson, R. 1892. Mr. Davey's imitations by conjuring of phenomena sometimes attributed to spirit agency. *Proceedings of the SPR*, 8:253-310.

Hodgson, R., and S. J. Davey. 1886-87. The possibilities of mal-observation and lapse of memory from a practical point of view. *Proceedings of the SPR*, 4:381-495.

Home, D. D. 1863. *Incidents in My Life*. New York: Carleton.

———. 1887. *Lights and Shadows of Spiritualism*. New York: Carleton and Company.

Houdini, H. 1972 [1924]. *A Magician Among the Spirits*. New York: Arno.

Lewis, H. C. 1886-87. Account [of seance with Eglinton]. *Proceedings of the SPR*, 4:352-375.

Lodge, Sir O. 1913-14. Report on a case of telepathy. *Journal of the SPR*, 16:102-111.

Miller, T. 1975. Geller twists Britain. In *The Amazing Uri Geller*, edited by M. Ebon, New York: New American Library.

Moore, J. R. 1958. *Daniel Defoe: Citizen of the Modern World*. Chicago: University of Chicago Press.

Patrick, C. V. 1921. The fairy photographs. *Psychic Research Quarterly*, 1:341-344.

Phillimore, M. 1959. Sir Arthur Conan Doyle: Champion spiritualist. *Tomorrow*, 7(4):65-75.

Pond, M. B. 1947. *The Unwilling Martyrs*. London: Spiritualist Press.

Proceedings of the SPR. 1982a. Report of the committee on thought reading, 1:13-46.

———. 1982b. Second report of the committee on thought reading, 1:70-78.

Reeves, M. P., and J. B. Rhine. 1942. Exceptional scores in ESP tests and the conditions, I: The case of Lillian. *Journal of Parapsychology*, 6:164-173.

Robbins, R. H. 1959. *The Encyclopedia of Witchcraft and Demonology*. London: Peter Nevill.

Star (newspaper). London, December 20, 1921. Quoted in Houdini, H., 1924. *A Magician Among the Spirits* (reprint). Arno Press, 1972, p. 124.

Taylor, J. 1975a. Letter to the editor. *New Scientist*. May 8.

———. 1975b. *Superminds*. New York: Viking Press, May 8. [Taylor has since recanted these views. See *Science and the Supernatural*, E. P. Dutton, New York, 1980.]

Verrall, M. de G. 1895. Some experiments on the supernormal acquisition of knowledge. *Proceedings of the SPR*, 11:174-193.

Young, K. 1963. *Arthur James Balfour*. London: Bell.

11

The Establishment of Data Manipulation in the Soal-Shackleton Experiments

BETTY MARKWICK

Historical Background

The Discovery of Basil Shackleton

The series of experiments carried out in the early 1940s by S. G. Soal with the percipient Basil Shackleton had a curious origin. Although scathingly critical of J. B. Rhine's card-guessing experiments, Soal embarked, in November 1934, on an extensive series of experiments in an endeavor to replicate Rhine's results under tighter conditions. Soal tested 160 individuals, amassing a grand total of 57,450 telepathy trials and 70,900 clairvoyance trials (Soal 1937; 1940). In July 1939, in a letter to Dr. Gibson (quoted in Thouless 1974), Soal declared: "I have delivered a stunning blow to Dr. Rhine's work by my repetition of his experiments in England . . . there is *no evidence* that individuals guessing cards can beat the laws of chance."

Soal (1940, 152) relates how, a few months later, his growing skepticism received a shock. During 1939, Whately Carington (1940) had been engaged in a series of experiments with drawings, in the course of which he noted that his subjects' hits tended to cluster around, rather than on, the intended target. Carington urged Soal to re-examine his data, comparing each guess with the card before and the one after the intended target card. Soal (1940, 153) continues: "It was, however, in no very hopeful spirit that I began the task of searching my records for this 'displacement' effect. And yet within a few weeks I had made two quite remarkable finds, which fully confirmed Carington's conjectures." Soal looked first at the 2,000 trials of the most promising GESP subject, Mrs. Gloria Stewart, and found significant above-chance scoring on both the precognitive "+ 1" and postcognitive "– 1" cards. The second discovery was Basil Shackleton, a man whose confidence in his ability to demonstrate telepathy had impressed Soal in 1936. Shackleton's 800 GESP trials, apparently null, showed significant above-chance scoring on the "+ 1" and "– 1" cards in almost equal degree. For the "+ 1," "0," "- 1" results pooled, odds against chance were estimated to be of the order 10^8 to 1 in the case of Gloria Stewart and 10^5 to 1 in the case of Shackleton. Soal went on to examine all his GESP records without finding any further instances of a significant displacement effect.

In December 1940 Soal sought out Shackleton, a photographer by profession and recently invalided out of the Army. Thus began the main Shackleton series, conducted under difficult wartime conditions from January 1941 until April 1943. As his co-experimenter Soal chose Mrs. K. M. Goldney, who had previously assisted him in the investigation of the stage "telepathist" Marion (Josef Kraus). The Shackleton series, comprising 40 sittings and some 12,000 trials, was reported in Soal and Goldney (1943), the "Soal-Goldney Report." In 1945, Soal undertook a further series with Gloria Stewart, accumulating some 50,000 trials before her "powers failed" four years later. An account of both the Shackleton and Stewart series duly appeared in Soal and Bateman (1954).

It is not clear why the experiments with Shackleton ceased when they did. He was said to have found the experiments an increasing strain, and a few further sessions proved unsuccessful. Shackleton emigrated to South Africa in 1946, where he resided until his death in May 1978. On visits to England in 1954 and 1960-61 he participated in a variety of experiments at the Society for Psychical Research, but the results were entirely null.

Experimental Procedure and Conditions

In the Shackleton series the expressed aim of the experimenters was to design a watertight experiment, and "stringent precautions were taken to eliminate the possibilities of normal leakage, fraud, and collusion" (Soal and Goldney 1943, 35). They endeavored to render the conditions "proof, so far as was humanly possible, against even the possibility of fraud, on the part of percipient and experimenters alike" (p. 80). Special emphasis was placed on the role of independent witnesses. There is not space here to do justice to the "precautions"; the question of their efficacy is, in any case, no longer a crucial issue. However, it will be necessary to state the basic features of the experimental procedure. For details of the many variations in procedure and personnel, and of the precautions, the reader is referred to the Soal-Goldney Report; Soal and Bateman (1954) provide a more readable, though less comprehensive, description.

The agent and the main experimenter (EA) sat on either side of a table separated by a screen in which there was a three-inch-square aperture. Shackleton sat in an adjoining room, usually supervised by an experimenter (EP). The agent had before her a row of five cards, each bearing a picture of an animal: an elephant, giraffe, lion, pelican, or zebra (or E, G, L, P, or Z). In advance of the session, lists of random digits 1 to 5 were prepared, usually by Soal, on printed score sheets, each accommodating two columns of 25 entries. Before each set of 50 calls, the agent or an observer shuffled the five animals cards (out of sight of EA) and laid them face down in front of the agent; after Sitting 6 the cards were shielded in a box. On each trial EA presented a card at the aperture in the screen, bearing a number 1 to 5 according to the next random digit on the list. The agent glanced at the face of the corresponding animal card in the row counting from the left. The target was thus determined by a double-randomization procedure. Shackleton, on hearing the serial number of the trial called by EA, wrote down his guess (E, G, L, P, or Z) in pencil on the score sheet, or EP recorded Shackleton's spoken (or otherwise indicated) guess.

On completion of 50 calls the order of the animal cards—the "code"—was recorded on EA's score sheet. The "check-up" took place at the end of the session, or (in the early experiments) more frequently. Shackleton's guesses were decoded into digits and entered on EA's score sheet in columns to the left of the random digits. The number of hits in the "0" (direct), "+ 1" (precognitive), and "– 1" (postcognitive) categories were counted, double-checked, and entered on the score sheet. At the end of each session handwritten copies were made of the record sheets and posted to C. D. Broad (C. E. M. Joad in the case of Sitting 1). Soal re-checked the score sheets at home and counted the hits in the "+ 2" and "– 2" categories.

At the "normal" rate a run of 25 calls would take about 60 to 70 seconds; "rapid" and "slow" rates were also tried, roughly double and half the normal rate, respectively. In clairvoyance runs, the agent merely touched the back of the appropriate animal card. On some occasions the random digits were generated during the run by EA drawing colored counters by touch from a bag or bowl.

Until the latter part of Sitting 18, Soal took the role of EA or "Recorder for Counters"; thereafter he changed his role to EP. The principal agent until Sitting 30 was Miss Rita Elliott, who had assisted in the 1934-39 series of tests, and who married Soal in October 1942. The sole agent for the remaining sittings was Mr. J. Aldred, a friend of Soal's of 20 years' standing. With the agents Rita Elliott and Gretl Albert, Shackleton scored significantly in the "+ 1" mode, whereas with J. Aldred he was successful in both the "+ 1" and "– 1" modes. Shackleton scored at chance level with eight other agents. Chance-level scoring was also associated with the clairvoyance condition, and with the slow rate. At the rapid rate significant scoring became displaced on to the "± 2" modes.

Of the 40 sittings, 31 yielded significant results. Overall, 2,890 hits were recorded in 11,378 "+ 1" trials, with odds against chance exceeding 10^{35} to 1. The published totals do not include the results of Sittings 39 and 40 (having become available too late): if included, one gets 3,017 hits in 11,762 "+ 1" trials, which is even more significant.

The Criticisms of Price and Hansel

The phenomenal results of the Soal-Goldney experiment, obtained under allegedly watertight conditions, inevitably attracted the attention of critics who sought to establish an explanation in "normal" terms.

In his famous onslaught on parapsychology, "Science and the Supernatural," G. R. Price (1955) challenged the validity of research findings with special emphasis on the work of Soal. Price considered such normal explanations as experimental error, sensory leakage, and statistical artifact to have been effectively eliminated in some of Rhine's work and most of Soal's. Fraud remained the only alternative to the ESP hypothesis. Invoking David Hume on miracles, Price argued that the "magical" quality of psi is incompatible with science, whereas the "knavery and folly of men" are commonplace. Which hypothesis, then, was more reasonable? Price accordingly advanced six hypothetical tricks illustrating how the Shackleton and Stewart experiments *could* have been faked, all involving collusion. To fabricate the Shackleton series, Price suggested that Soal would have required four confederates. Soal's experiments had thus *not* been conducted "with every precaution that it was possible to devise," and therefore did not constitute a satisfactory test of ESP. Finally, Price specified his design for a fraud-proof experiment.

A fierce controversy ensued in the pages of *Science.* Soal (1955) reacted with great indignation, arguing the implausibility of the implied accusation of fraud. Rhine's response was more constructive. The *Journal of Parapsychology* carried an extensive review of the controversy (Rhine 1955). Rhine evidently also engaged in private correspondence with Price. Years later Price (1972) issued a cryptic little note of apology, retracting what he now considered had been an unfair attack on Rhine and Soal. In a subsequent letter to C. E. M. Hansel it emerged that the 1955 article had been directed primarily against supernatural *religion* and that the "unfairness" consisted in the assumption that ESP researchers would be motivated to fabricate evidence in support of religious belief.

The possibility that a loophole existed in the design of the Soal-Goldney experiment, whereby the agent (if not properly supervised) could have operated a card substitution trick in collusion with Shackleton, was suggested to Soal by Hansel in 1949 following a discussion with R. C. Read (Soal and Bateman 1954, 193; Hansel 1960, 14). In the hypothesized trick the agent, who saw the random digits displayed during the run, was in a position to alter the order of the five animal cards to secure hits on prearranged guesses. In a simple application of the technique, with five calls (say, G, L, P, Z, E) arranged at predetermined positions on the score sheet, an average of 3.36 spurious hits would be secured; this could be improved by elaboration of the technique up to a maximum of 5 substitutions per sheet. Soal (1955) argued that such a trick was precluded by the experimental conditions; nor could it account for certain secondary effects in the scoring.

R. C. Read (1950) had carried out a prolonged scrutiny of about half the Shackleton data with the object of ascertaining whether clues to a normal explanation might be found in any nonrandom features in the target and guess sequences. Read made various frequency counts but found nothing amiss. During the course of this investigation, Hansel raised the question of card substitution. Read then went on to examine this possibility, but considered that such a trick would not necessarily be detectable in the data. Soal (1950) misleadingly stated that Read had found no evidence of card substitution, while Hansel (1960) neglected to mention Read's conclusion, based on further considerations, that the card-substitution trick did not provide a viable explanation of the Soal-Goldney experiment.

In the early part of 1959, *New Scientist* carried a dispute touched off by an article by Hansel. The article, essentially a precursor of Hansel's (1960) critique, included a presentation of the card-substitution hypothesis. Some months later Hansel (1959), this time in *Nature,* drew attention to a periodicity effect in Shackleton's rapid trials. The Soal-Goldney Report (p. 139) lists the total number of hits corresponding to each of the 23 "+ 2" positions on the score sheet. By dividing the 23 totals into groups of five blocks and summing over corresponding positions in the block, Hansel showed the resulting five quantities to have a nonuniform distribution, with odds against chance exceeding 100 to 1. Hansel proclaimed this effect as evidence in support of his card-substitution theory, since prearranged guesses might tend to favor certain positions in the blocks of five as ruled on the score sheet. However, Soal (1960a) interpreted the anomaly as a "segmental salience" effect of ESP. Moreover, the normal trials, constituting the bulk of the data, did not exhibit the periodicity effect.

Christopher Scott (1960) reported a demonstration in 1958 of the practicability of Hansel's postulated card-substitution trick, with Hansel, Scott, Goldney, and D. J. West, respectively, taking the roles of agent, percipient, experimenter, and observer. Soal (1960c) responded in some derision to the meager scores obtained. Scott also reported, in the same article, his examination of the Shackleton data in respect of some criticisms made by Rudolph Lambert in 1953: specific predictions made by Lambert were not borne out in the data.

Hansel (1960) presented a critique of the Shackleton and Stewart experiments, based on two papers read in 1955 at meetings of the British Psychological Society. Hansel's stated objective was to evaluate the experimental design. The incidence of trickery and error in the psychical research field was by no means negligible, and would—in a flawed experimental design—constitute a more likely hypothesis than precognitive telepathy with its high a priori improbability. Starting with a provisional assumption of the impossibility of ESP, Hansel pointed to various weaknesses in the design of the Soal-Goldney experiment: the possibilities of the agent changing the order of the cards, of the transmission of information by voice cues, of the substitution of score sheets, and so on. His main attack was concentrated in the development of his card-substitution theory. Soal's earlier objections (Soal and Bateman 1954, 193-194) were shown to be largely unfounded. Hansel went on to demonstrate that card substitution could account for the main result of the Shackleton series, and the secondary effects also (notably, the reinforcement of "± 1" and "± 2" scoring associated with multiply determined guesses). To account for the characteristic secondary effects in the Stewart data, Hansel developed a technique of consecutive (rather than spaced) substitution. Hansel concluded that the experimental results could have been brought about by collusive trickery involving the two percipients, some of the agents, and (probably) the main experimenter. Since a normal explanation was not excluded by the experimental design, the experiments did not provide conclusive evidence for ESP, whether or not a trick actually occurred.

In his reply to Hansel's critique, Soal (1960b) pointed out that Hansel and Read had illegitimately "watered down" the Shackleton data by including irrelevant groups of data. Soal demonstrated that the postulated card-substitution trick, even had the maximum five substitutions per sheet beeen achieved, would be hopelessly inadequate to account for the magnitude of the extra-chance effect. Soal also argued that interchanging the cards would not have been feasible in the presence of an observer. Further, the techniques proposed by Hansel for the Stewart series would have led to consequences at variance with the data.

A chapter on the Soal-Goldney experiment appeared in Hansel's book *ESP: A Scientific Evaluation* (1966, Chap. 9). The inadequacy of the card-substitution trick was conceded. Hansel then illustrated the application of Price's six hypothetical tricks to successive sittings of the Shackleton series and also advanced some further methods. R. G. Medhurst's (1968a) critique of Hansel's book, while not unfavorable to Hansel's declared methodological position, took him to task on numerous points. In regard to the Soal-Goldney experiment, Medhurst pointed out—with justification—that Hansel had misrepresented the· situation at Sittings 17 and 28; he also queried the relevance of the periodicity effect. A heated discussion ensued between Scott and Medhurst (Scott 1968a; 1968b; Medhurst 1968b; 1968c). An updated (but otherwise unrevised) version of the Soal-Goldney chapter duly appeared in Hansel's book *ESP and Parapsychology* (1980, Chap. 12).

The Gretl Albert Allegation

The course of events, as extracted from the literature and set in chronological order, appears to have been as follows:

Mrs. Gretl Albert (a friend of Mrs. Goldney's) was invited to act as agent at Sittings 15 and 16. After Sitting 15, Mrs. Albert complained to Goldney that she had felt drugged after starting to smoke one of Shackleton's cigarettes. At Sitting 16, which took place on May 23, 1941, Mrs. Albert participated in an "agents in opposition" experiment (sheets 5, 6, 7). Goldney was unavoidably absent from Sitting 16, but on her return, during a suppertime conversation on May 29, Mrs. Albert made a serious allegation. She claimed that she had seen Soal, through the aperture in the screen, altering figures (in ink) on a score sheet. During further conversations on June 5 and 10, she was more specific, emphasizing that she had seen Soal changing the figure 1 to the figure 4 or 5, four or five times; also, she thought the alterations had been on the first sheet.

Goldney wrote full notes of the conversations in documents dated May 30, June 6, and June 11 (quoted in Medhurst 1971). On the pretext of wishing to see the results of the interesting double-agent experiment, Goldney asked Soal to bring her the record sheets for Sitting 16. She examined the figures with a magnifying glass but could find nothing suspicious, nor could a trusted colleague. Following Sitting 17, on June 6, Goldney informed Soal of Mrs. Albert's allegation. He was extremely indignant, particularly since no steps had been taken at the time to clear up the matter, and threatened legal action if he heard any more of it.

Goldney subsequently urged Soal to include an account of the incident in the Soal-Goldney Report. He refused, on the grounds that he was unwilling to create suspicion when there was no supporting evidence, nor was he ready to jeopardize his university position as senior lecturer in mathematics. (Soal fails to state unambiguously what, if innocent, would be the most cogent reason of all: that he *knew* the allegation to be erroneous.) Goldney nevertheless prepared a detailed account of the incident and deposited it at the Society for Psychical Research; she also showed the document to several friends on both sides of the Atlantic, including Scott.

In January 1956 Soal reported (by way of an aside) that in 1945 he had lost all the original record sheets of the Shackleton series. (With the possible exception of Sitting 1 [Palmer 1984]. It is an unresolved mystery that these few sheets display a variant of Soal's normal handwriting.) The sheets were said to have been left late at night in a train full of soldiers in Cambridge railway station (Soal 1956; Goldney 1974, 75). The admission was forced following a request from G. R. Price (who had evidently got wind of Mrs. Albert's allegation) to consult the original record sheets 5, 6, 7 from Sitting 16. It appears that on getting out the sheets for photocopying only the Broad duplicates were found to be available. After much prevarication and in great distress, Soal wrote to Goldney confessing what had happened. The occasion also gave rise to the curious case of "the error that wasn't." D. J. West, misinterpreting Soal's decoding procedure, drew attention to a supposed error in the order of recording of the three columns of figures. Incredibly, Soal acquiesced in the misinterpretation until, months later, Betty Humphrey Nicol pointed out that there had been no error.

Scott interviewed Mrs. Albert in June 1959 regarding her allegation. Under pressure from Scott and Fraser Nicol, with the active (though covert) cooperation of Goldney, Soal withdrew his objection to publication. The result was a statement by Soal and Goldney (1960) explaining the circumstances. Notes by Goldney (1968) and Soal (1968) further explained why publication had been withheld for 17 years. (See also: Medhurst 1968a, 224; 1968b, 305; Scott 1968a, 300-301; Scott and Haskell 1974, 43-45; Goldney 1974, 77-79. Other details can be found in the personal correspondence of Goldney and Scott. Curiously, Hansel made only a passing reference to the Albert allegation in his 1966 book, *ESP: A Critical Evaluation.*)

Miss M. R. Barrington (1974) visited Mrs. Albert in 1971, by which time (not surprisingly) her recollections had become confused in certain respects and incorporated details from the 1960-61 series of experiments. In particular, Mrs. Albert described seeing Soal alter a 3 into a 5. Ian Stevenson (1974) visited Mrs. Albert in 1973 and heard a similarly revised story.

The Evidence of Data Analysis

The Medhurst Paper

In his paper "The Origin of the 'Prepared Random Numbers' Used in the Shackleton Experiments," R. G. Medhurst (1971) made public for the first time the specific nature of the Albert allegation: namely, the altering of 1's into 4's and 5's. Medhurst first examined sheets 5, 6, and 7 of Sitting 16 to see whether there was an excess of hits on targets 4 and 5—as might be expected if the Albert allegation was true. He did find an excess, with $P = 0.014$ (subsequently amended to 0.003 by Scott [1971]). However, although consistent with Mrs. Albert's reported observation of "four or five" alterations, the anomaly was insufficient to account for the huge deviation (28.2) from above-chance expectation.

Medhurst argued that the allegation clearly referred to the check-up, probably the second stage at the end of the sitting; further, any manipulation must have been in the target sequences, not in Shackleton's guesses or decoded guesses. In the hope of settling the question once and for all, Medhurst devised an ingenious scheme for identifying the target sequences in the source cited by Soal. Soal had specified in detail how he had compiled the target lists from the final digits of 7-figure logarithms at intervals of 100. Medhurst acccordingly attempted to reconstruct the target sequences using a computer in order to demonstrate that they were free from manipulation. Medhurst selected several sequences from Sitting 16 and also from a few other sittings, but in every case the computer search failed. Soal, on being informed, thought he might have used intervals greater than 100. Medhurst repeated the search on two of the sequences with intervals up to 600, without success. Tragically, Medhurst died in January 1971 before he could carry the search further.

Reactions to the Medhurst Findings

The failure of the computer search caused some consternation. Although not necessarily suspicious, the failure indicated that Soal's precise statement of how he had compiled the target lists was inaccurate and cast doubt on the reliability of Soal's work in general. Soal (1971) now claimed that he may not have used logarithm tables in preparing the Shackleton target lists, but a book of random numbers borrowed for the purpose.

J. G. Pratt (1971) suggested that Soal might conceivably have constructed an intermediate pool of pseudo-random digits and read them in another direction when entering them on the score sheets. This was a highly plausible idea, one which had occurred independently to the present writer.

I had set about extending Medhurst's computer search in April 1971, exploring a variety of ways in which Soal might legitimately have used the logarithm tables. The search failed, even though my program made provision for occasional discrepancies in an attempt to identify the target sequences *whether manipulated or not*. I also made a preliminary analysis of two-step procedures, assuming various dimensions for the supposed intermediate pool. This proved a prohibitively time-consuming task, even for a computer, and the quest had to be abandoned at that time.

The Scott-Haskell Paper

Christopher Scott and Philip Haskell (1974) reported having extended Medhurst's computer search to all sittings involving prepared random numbers without identifying a single sequence.

The substance of the paper, first reported in *Nature* (Scott and Haskell 1973), presents impressive statistical evidence in support of the truth of the Gretl Albert allegation. Scott and Haskell started by examining the records of Sitting 16, to see whether the frequencies of the target-guess pairs showed any evidence for the specific alterations alleged. They wrote a computer program to print out the "+ 1" target-guess matrices (by numbers and by letters) for every sitting or sub-sitting. On the basis of the allegation, four predictions were made about the scoring pattern in Sitting 16: (1) An overall deficit of target 1's. (2) An overall excess of target 4's and 5's. (3) A deficit of target 1's in those trials in which the guess was 4 or 5. (4) An excess of hits on 4 and 5. Effect (3) was strikingly obvious in the matrices for both parts of Sitting 16; effect (4) was also present. On the assumption of ESP operating in a "noneccentric" manner, P-values were estimated: $P = 0.00002$ for effect (3), $P < 0.001$ for effect (4). Tests (1) and (2) showed small deviations of no significance, in the wrong direction in the case of test (2).

The partial confirmation, with two of the predicted effects demonstrated at a high level of significance, suggested a simple modification to the model: that the targets might have been stacked in advance with an excess of 1's and a deficit of 4's and 5's in anticipation of the planned manipulation. The modified hypothesis led to two further predictions: approximately equal frequencies of guesses 1, 2, 3 on target 1, combined with an intermediate excess of hits on target 1; chance-level scoring on target 2 and 3. Both predictions were confirmed in the data. Scott and Haskell then showed, by means of an example involving the change of 41 target 1's into 4's and 5's, that all the observations in Sitting 16 could be accounted for, including most of the above-chance score, leaving an insignificant "ESP effect."

In view of the somewhat ad hoc nature of the modification to their original model, Scott and Haskell sought confirmation in the rest of the data, using the highly specific effect (3) as a search criterion. The effect was found to be present, at a high level of significance, in Sitting 8 and in the first part of Sitting 17. In each case the whole constellation of effects as found in Sitting 16 was reproduced. Again, an example gave a good fit to the data and accounted for most of the above-chance deviation.

Scott and Haskell considered an alternative explanation in terms of ESP operating differentially in respect of the number-symbols but dismissed this model as implausible. They also discussed the experimental and psychological conditions and found no serious contra-indication to the manipulation hypothesis. Scott and Haskell concluded that the evidence presented pointed to manipulation in the three sittings concerned and that it was more plausible to assume that the rest of the data was counterfeited by some unspecified method rather than that ESP and manipulation coexisted in the same series.

An appendix reported the presence of some 57 discrepancies between the computed scores, based on the Broad duplicates, and the scores listed in the Soal-Goldney Report.

Reactions to the Scott-Haskell Findings

A number of leading parapsychologists sprang to the defense of Soal, and their comments were published simultaneously with the Scott-Haskell paper. The ad hoc nature of the modified hypothesis was perhaps the principal focus of criticism, and various alternative explanations were offered for the statistical anomalies. The reliability of Gretl Albert's observation was widely questioned, and almost all the defenders of Soal raised psychological objections. (Soal died in February 1975, apparently in ignorance of the furor.)

Goldney (1974) wrote of her long association with Soal, of the circumstances of the experiments and Mrs. Albert's allegation, and of the inconceivability of Soal's being a cheat. She summed up her attitude thus: "Of course an adverse verdict, if established, will destroy individual hopes, even beliefs. So be it, if necessary. 'The world is wide' and the object of all our studies is to find and establish *the truth*."

Pratt (1974) questioned the validity of Scott and Haskell's attempt to confirm, in the rest of the data, their modified model based on Sitting 16. He pointed to weaknesses in the "web of evidence," notably the absence of instances where the supposed trick had failed to carry through, leaving an excess of target 1's. In explanation of the statistical anomalies, Pratt considered an ESP model of consistent missing to be viable. Pratt also demonstrated at length that the Scott-Haskell Appendix grossly misrepresented the situation regarding the accuracy of the published scores (cf. Scott and Haskell 1975, 225-226; Markwick 1976).

Thouless (1974) acknowledged that the conjunction of the statistical anomaly in Sitting 16 with the Albert allegation made a strong case for supposing that *some* manipulation had occurred, but he favored a hypothesis of genuine ESP supplemented by manipulation. He pointed to weaknesses in the case and suggested that the principal anomaly could be explained as an ESP effect of consistent missing.

John Beloff (1974) offered A. E. Roy's (1972) finding in some nonrandom runs as evidence of an ESP effect in the Shackleton data that Soal could not have faked; likewise Pratt's findings of secondary effects in the Stewart data. Beloff also considered that Scott and Haskell had dismissed too lightly their ESP model of positional bias.

C. W. K. Mundle (1974) questioned the reliability of Mrs. Albert's testimony and the assumption that the remaining sittings had been falsified. Ian Stevenson (1974) discussed at length his doubts about Mrs. Albert's testimony in the light of his 1973 interview. M. R. Barrington (1974) hypothesized malobservation as a *consequence* of the scoring pattern, based on inference. F. S. Roberts (1975) offered a similar theory. G. D. Wassermann (1975) pointed to evidence that Soal habitually tidied up figures—an allusion to his own role in

1941-42 in touching off a heated exchange with Goldney.

Scott and Haskell (1975) replied to the various points raised by their critics. In answer to the ad hoc objection, they restated their statistical procedure, stressing that they had used one effect as a search criterion and three independent criteria for confirmation. They argue that the various alternative explanations underestimated the extent of the evidence, that the question of the reliability of Mrs. Albert's testimony was irrelevant, and that tricks could produce unplanned secondary effects.

J. Palmer (1978, 67-68), taking a harder line among the parapsychologists, expressed the opinion that "none of [the defenders of Soal] was able to refute the heart of the [Scott-Haskell] argument. . . . Nonetheless, the case against Soal cannot, at this point, be considered conclusive."

The impact of the Scott-Haskell case, even among critics of parapsychology, fell surprisingly flat, perhaps because of the complexity of the statistical argument. Hansel (1980, 161-164) summarized the findings, commenting: "Mrs. Albert's observations led to testable hypotheses about the record sheets and these were confirmed." However, Hansel's "improved" fit to the data is invalid, since he failed to take into account the actual guess frequencies.

My reaction to the evidence may be indicated briefly. I found the coincidence between the statistical anomaly and Mrs. Albert's allegation compelling but hardly *conclusive*. Various ambiguities became apparent on further study of the target-guess matrices, raising subtle statistical questions, which (in my view) weakened the claimed confirmation in the data of a specific manipulation hypothesis. Moreover, the statistical peculiarities admitted of alternative explanations in terms of ESP. The conclusion that the Shackleton series was wholly fabricated was, in any case, unwarranted. The parapsychologists' defense of Soal against the charge of fraud thus seemed reasonable at that time. But the seeds of doubt had been sown.

The Markwick Paper

The story of how I became involved in the controversy is recounted in Part 1 of my "Soal-Goldney Experiments with Basil Shackleton" (1978). The new findings reported therein are summarized below.

The initial finding, in 1975, concerned the discovery of duplicated sequences in the target lists of up to 25 digits in length. At a later stage reversed duplicated sequences came to light. The duplication was not suspicious in itself, and could have arisen from repeated use of a pool of random digits. At least it could be said that the *repetitions* must be free from manipulation (else they would not appear as repetitions). Nor was there anything suspicious about the distribution of hits in the duplicated sequences. Nevertheless, the finding cast further doubt on the accuracy of Soal's experimental reports.

It became apparent, from perusing the *continuations* of certain duplicated sequences, that the continuations sometimes resembled each other—apart from the occasional intrusion of an "extra" digit. *And these extra digits showed a high tendency to correspond to hits.* Subsequent computer analysis revealed some 40 clear cases of extra digits (mostly in the later sequence of the pair), with about three in four of them corresponding to hits. The probability of this "interpolated hits" effect occurring by chance is of the order $P = 10^{-10}$. On removal of the suspect trials the scoring rate in the regions concerned falls to chance levels. Sheets 1, 3, and 5 of Sitting 25 exhibit a systematic near-reversal with respect to sheets 1, 2, and 3 of Sitting 24: Some 18 extra digits are evident, all but 3 of them corresponding to hits. Sheets 3 and 5 of Sitting 23 show direct duplication: Sheet 3 has 5 extra digits, at 5-digit intervals, all of them corresponding to hits. Sittings 3, 16, 26, and 36 contain 8 more suspicious hits. Sittings 1 and 2 of the Stewart series also show the effect, with 5 possible instances.

Contrary to a misconception that has arisen, the anomalies in the target sequences—duplication, reversed duplication, and the associated extra digits—were uncovered, not by computer analysis, but in the course of intensive scanning of the data by eye. Ironically, had computer time been initially available for carrying out certain frequency counts, the anomalies would never have come to my attention. Computer analysis subsequently made possible an objective assessment.

The computer assessment of the interpolated hits effect was achieved by a systematic search for "interrupted" duplicated sequences, direct and reversed. An objective criterion, based on combinatorial considerations, was developed and applied to the results of the search.

Curiously, the "interruptions" were found to occur almost exclusively in the form of *extra* digits, not as mismatches. This feature is inconsistent with the Scott-Haskell model, where 1's belonging to the true target-sequence would be subject to alteration. Moreover, 1's, rather than 4's and 5's, tend to predominate among the interpolated hits. Different techniques could, of course, have been operative in different sittings.

Some other features of the duplication may be mentioned. The prepared random numbers alone, not the counters data, exhibit duplication. Extra digits sometimes occur in null experimental conditions (clairvoyance or slow rate), but the scoring rate on these trials is at chance level. Some very unexpected duplications were found between sequences *allegedly* prepared from different source books, between sequences *allegedly* prepared by Soal and by Wassermann, and between the Shackleton series and the start of the Stewart series. Multiple duplications also occur.

The new evidence thus presented the manipulation effect directly, pinpointing specific digits. The effect in Sitting 25 is particularly striking, with the suspect trials accounting for virtually the whole of the above-chance deviation. I conjectured that Soal might have succumbed to "data massage" as genuine results began to fade: This seemed to me more plausible than outright fabrication. In view of Soal's mediumistic personality, I also considered the possibility of "dissociated manipulation," with the falsification of the data carried out in a less than fully conscious state. I concluded that manipulation had been established in some sections of the Shackleton data and that all Soal's card-guessing experiments must therefore be discredited.

Reactions to the Markwick Findings

In view of the reaction of parapsychologists to the Scott-Haskell findings, I anticipated a measure of resistance even to my more direct evidence. However, the previous defenders of Soal were unanimous in declaring themselves now convinced that manipulation had taken place in at least part of the data. No longer were psychological objections raised as to motivation.

Statements by Goldney (1978) and Pratt (1978), published simultaneously with my paper, magnanimously acknowledged the validity of the new evidence. Goldney commented: "I and others who replied to the Scott-Haskell paper were wrong, but justifiably so, in my opinion, in the light of the evidence then available." Pratt, who had invested an immense amount of time and effort during the fifties and sixties in analyzing secondary effects in the Shackleton and Stewart data, set aside Soal's work with understandable reluctance. He considered that an innocent explanation might yet emerge and speculated that Soal, in a dissociated state, might conceivably have produced the interpolated hits precognitively (not to be confused with my non-psi version mentioned above).

R. H. Thouless (1978) commented that, although the Scott-Haskell evidence had given grounds for suspicion, he had not been wholly convinced. The new findings removed any doubts, and the Shackleton experiments could no longer be claimed as evidence for psi. Thouless nevertheless argued for the genuineness of the displacement effect in the preliminary (1936) data, and in the early stages of the main series.

Scott (1978) pointed up the lesson that no reliance could be placed on supposedly fraud-proof experiments. Beloff (1979a) endorsed this, urging that the best security lay in independent replication of research claims. Stevenson (1979) also considered the hope of a fraud-proof experiment to be illusory. Beloff and Stevenson both emphasized that their previous defense of Soal had been justified at the time. D. J. West (1978) advocated contemporaneous checks on ESP experimenters. Other reactions included: a fanciful "psi-evasiveness" theory from J. L. Randall (1978) and some pertinent general observations from Charles Akers (1979) in response to a critique by Edward Girden.

Carl Sargent (1979; 1980) considered that fraud was not necessarily the correct interpretation of the data anomalies and that fudging was in any case more likely than outright faking. He believed it might be possible to demonstrate ESP effects in portions of the Shackleton data and in some of Soal's other experimental series. He drew attention (Sargent 1979) to some tests carried out with Shackleton by psi-inhibitory experimenter Denys Parsons (1946; 1947): The GESP data yielded a P-value of 0.032 (one-tailed, not two-tailed as assumed by Sargent) in respect to above-chance "– 1" scoring, while the clairvoyance results were at chance level. An ingenious re-analysis (Sargent 1980) of Soal's 1928-29 free-response data (Soal 1932), for which Soal had never claimed any significance, yielded a strong extra-chance effect; however, this proved to be almost certainly artifactual.

Fraser Nicol (personal communication 1976) considered my findings to be "devastating evidence against the genuineness of the research." Critics of parapsychology inevitably hailed the new evidence as conclusive proof of fraud. Thus Martin Gardner (1981, 129) referred to my having "proved beyond any shadow of a doubt that Soal had deliberately cheated." Hansel (1980, 165), apparently confusing the "extra digit" anomaly with the "interpolated hits" effect, ascribed manipulation to 17 sittings instead of (at most) 6. Among the more fanatical critics, H. B. Gibson (1979), of the British Psychological Society, reacted by launching a scornful attack on parapsychology, with a rejoinder by Beloff (1979b). The Soal scandal also provided John Wheeler, the eminent physicist, with added ammunition in his (abortive) attempt to get parapsychology ousted from the AAAS.

A comment by Michael Grosso (1979, 199) is most apposite: "It is useless to deny that this exposure of Soal is an occasion for the most acute embarrassment for parapsychology. One imagines the fanatical skeptic leaping with irrepressible glee. However, before leaping too high, one should study Markwick's report."

Discussion

The Case for Data Manipulation

Until the end of the 1960s, criticism of the Soal-Goldney experiment had been almost exclusively conjectural in character. Investigation of the data was predominantly concerned with whether statistical features supported, or contraindicated, various speculations as to the use of trickery. Little *hard* evidence emerged, except perhaps for the periodicity effect pointed out by Hansel in a minor section of the data. Medhurst seems to have been the first to take a direct approach by examining the scoring pattern in relation to Mrs. Albert's allegation and by attempting to reconstruct the target sequences using a computer. The sophisticated analyses that became feasible with the advent of computers could hardly have been foreseen at the time of the experiments. Grounds for suspicion intensified with the discovery by Scott and Haskell of a striking statistical anomaly in support of Mrs. Albert's allegation, constituting strong presumptive evidence of fraud. Ironically, the final dénouement, in the form of clear-cut evidence of data manipulation, was brought about by a parapsychologist whose research on the data had been initiated by an ESP-like dream (Markwick 1978, Coda).

In Sittings 23 and 25 the "interpolated hits" effect is virtually conclusive; in a few other sittings suggestive only. The Scott-Haskell case for manipulation in Sittings 8, 16, and 17, generally regarded as inconclusive, may be said to have been vindicated in the light of the later, more decisive evidence. The two independent lines of evidence point to distinct techniques of manipulation in the two groups of sittings concerned—perhaps not unconnected with Soal's change of role after Sitting 18. It should be remarked that the Scott-Haskell model does not follow *uniquely* from the Albert allegation and the target-guess distribution in Sitting 16. Mrs. Albert reported seeing "four or five" alterations. But there are more than 40 alterations to be accounted for in Sitting 16: there is no reason to assume that they *all* involved changing 1's to 4's and 5's. The easiest alteration to make would be a guess L into E. It so happens that there *is* a significant anomaly in the target-guess matrices for Sitting 16 consistent with a considerable number of L's having been converted into E's. By "spreading the load" over targets and guesses, the heavy (and risky) advance stacking of the target lists, as postulated by Scott-Haskell, would be obviated.

The question arises: How *extensive* is the manipulation? Of the 31 significant findings, 5 have been implicated by the evidence of data analysis. The "duplicated sequences" method allowed analysis of only some 10 percent of the Shackleton data, and about a quarter of that 10 percent exhibits interpolated hits. My 1978 paper evidently failed to bring out this point clearly enough, to judge from the misinterpretation of my findings by Hansel and others. One may reasonably *surmise* that the manipulation is more widespread, but this could only be demonstrated by identification of the source of the prepared random-number sequences. The failure of the Medhurst computer search, it should be noted, cannot be attributed to the presence of manipulation since even duplicated sequences manifestly free from manipulation (otherwise they would not appear as repetitions) cannot be identified.

The fraud hypothesis needs more stretching than seems generally to be realized to make it explain the whole of the Shackleton data. Hansel's card-substitution theory, his preferred trick, collapsed because of its inadequacy to account for the magnitude of the extra-chance effect. The Scott-Haskell model required an additional assumption, that a target 1 was occasionally changed into a 2 or 3, in order to achieve a close fit: otherwise the model, as applied, leaves a marginally significant ESP effect in the 16 sheets concerned ($P = 0.038$, binomial test). My findings included long, *exact* repetitions in the target sequences exhibiting high above-chance scoring—although the repetitions must be presumed manipulation-free, at least as far as the target digits are concerned.

If outright fakery is the true explanation of the main Shackleton series, then the dramatic discovery of the displacement effect in the Stewart and Shackleton records of 1936 must also be assumed fabricated. It may be argued that Soal's skeptical stance until 1939 was an act, that the obscure ESP effect was planted, that Soal was in collusion with several agents *and* with Joad. In an interim report on the 1934–39 series, Soal (1937) stated that duplicate record-sheets were posted to Joad at the conclusion of each session: Subsequent tampering with the record sheets would thus have risked exposure from that source. One may speculate, and counterspeculate, but it cannot be denied that the necessity for including the 1934–39 series in the plot further decreases the plausibility of the outright-fraud hypothesis. Again, it is difficult to reconcile the null series of 1954–58 (with university students) with the hypothesis that Soal was wholly fraudulent: Why did he persist so long without falsifying that series?

Conceivably, the displacement effect in the 1936 data, and in the early stages of the main Shackleton series, may have been genuine. Then, as the ESP effect began to decline, one may imagine that Soal resorted increasingly to boosting the scores. In science generally, the development of fraudulent behavior in initially genuine research is recognized to be more common than outright fraud. In Soal's case, it is likely that the gaining of scientific and academic acceptance for parapsychology, a cause to which his writings frequently testify, would have constituted a more powerful motive than material reward or prestige. (For some inside information regarding Soal's doctorate, see Thouless [1969].) Some illuminating insights into the psychology of fraud, in relation to the case of Sir Cyril Burt, are provided by Anita Gregory (1979).

It is of interest to ask: Did Shackleton succeed with any other experimenter? During the course of the Soal-Goldney experiment Soal did not permit other experimenters access to Shackleton, which admittedly looks suspicious. However, the Parsons experiment with Shackleton, undertaken only two months after the conclusion of the Soal-Goldney experiment, may be regarded as an independent (albeit small) replication. The marginal significance of the result, while not comparable with Shackleton's previous scoring rate, is consistent with his having some degree of ESP ability. Likewise, a marginally significant effect in the clairvoyance runs of the Soal-Goldney experiment (Foster 1956): Soal regarded clairvoyance as a "null" condition, and consequently those runs would not have called for a trick. Shackleton's interest in the paranormal subsequently turned toward the healing aspect, although he occasionally participated in ESP experiments, notably the 1960–61 series conducted by Goldney and others. There are no reports of Shackleton ever again achieving significant results.

There is another dimension to be considered in the case of Soal. How *conscious* was the manipulation? The question is not as fatuous as it may at first appear. Soal had a mediumisic personality, subject to severe bouts of dissociation and capable of producing automatic writing of outstanding quality. On occasion, a secondary personality would manifest in his unconscious writing. It *may* be relevant that Soal was wounded in the head in 1917 at the Battle of the Somme. R. A. McConnell (1983, 216) considers that Soal may have been a classic case of multiple personality; his discussion of multiple personality (Chaps. 3, 4) makes interesting and relevant reading. Even in the absence of a full-blown secondary personality, it is conceivable that the manipulation was carried out in an abnormal state of consciousness: an extreme form of unconscious experimenter bias. The "dissociated manipulation" hypothesis appears to be gaining favor with other parapsychologists, too (West 1983; Palmer 1984; Grosso 1979)—not in order to exculpate Soal but in an endeavor to make psychological sense of a complex case.

The supposedly rigorous experimental safeguards were manifestly *not* wholly effective, but the question of how exactly the manipulation was achieved is probably unanswerable. It scarcely seems necessary to invoke wholesale collusion, as Price did and Hansel (1980, 166) evidently still does. No experimental report can record *every* minute detail. Apparently insignificant deviations from protocol, or momentary lapses in control, could conceivably have allowed the working of single-handed manipulation—especially if the aim was to enhance, rather than create, the ESP effect. Again, misdirection of observers' attention may have been used in the manner of a conjurer. Single-handed manipulation *during* the run seems ruled out by the experimental format; for one thing, a guess and a random digit cannot be spuriously matched without knowledge of the code. The actual entering-up of the decoded guesses appears to have been strictly supervised, but the danger could lie in the intervals *preceding and following* that operation. Thus, during the counting of hits, Soal might have been able to alter figures under cover of the routine task of placing ticks against the direct ("0") hits. Perhaps he worked one sheet behind, or (if able to glimpse the next guess sheet) one sheet ahead. Perhaps he substituted false score-sheets or false guess-sheets. Further opportunities for tampering with the figures may have arisen during the making of the Broad duplicates.

Following Mrs. Albert's allegation, and a sitting that yielded only chance results, Soal changed his role and thereafter took charge of the guess sheets rather than the score sheets. The move seems to have been designed to allay suspicion—and yet the access to the guess sheets *could* have opened up new loopholes if, for example, he were to memorize information from the target lists using mnemonic aids. A hypothetical scenario, consistent with the interpolated-hits effect in Sitting 25, may be outlined. Suppose that, when entering the random number sequences in advance of the session, Soal first writes in (say) five extra digits per sheet and secretly marks the corresponding positions on the intended guess-sheets. During the run Soal records Shackleton's guesses, in pencil, perhaps writing ill-formed L's (for ease of alteration to E, G, P, or Z) in the marked positions. Soal contrives to learn the letter-to-digit codes during the prelude to check-up and alters the marked guesses in accordance with the memorized extra digits. Writing on the guess sheets *before* comparison with the target lists need arouse no suspicion. The method would not have been feasible at Sitting 28, for which the target lists were prepared by an outsider and observation was unusually stringent. Arguably, other loopholes existed. Arguably, Soal resorted to collusion on occasion. The *bona fides* of the principal agent, Rita Elliot, inevitably comes under suspicion, since she became Soal's wife. Incidentally, it has emerged that she *resented* the experiments and Soal's interest in psychical research generally, even (it is rumored) to the point of destruction of his papers: The imagination runs riot.

To summarize, as the evidence stands manipulation has been established in some sections of the Soal-Shackleton data. How extensive and how conscious was the manipulation and how precisely it was accomplished under the conditions of the experiment remain open questions. Outright fraud is the obvious explanation. However, on statistical, circumstantial, and psychological grounds, it has been argued that a small, but genuine, ESP effect boosted by data massage constitutes a plausible alternative hypothesis. Of course manipulation established in any part of the data renders the whole evidentially worthless.

Future Prospects: A Personal View

The once-celebrated Soal-Goldney experiment lies in ruins, with Soal's work as a whole discredited. This may not be the end of the story, however, for some mysteries remain. If the source of the target sequences were, after all, to be identified, a more extensive analysis of the data would become feasible. In the Stewart series, a nonrandom feature (the notorious "ABA" deficit) in the target lists may point the way to the identification of those sequences, and a similar data analysis could be undertaken. In some quarters work goes on in the forlorn hope of exonerating at least some of Soal's data. Thus E. F. Kelly (1982, 104n) writes: "... particularly in the light of a recent conversation with Evan Harris Walker, I am not convinced that the controversy over the Soal-Shackleton data has been resolved conclusively and against Soal." (Palmer 1984) speculates that Soal might have been "framed."

The exposé is not an isolated case in the history of parapsychology. In 1974, W. J. Levy, director of Rhine's prestigious Institute, was detected in fraud by his fellow researchers and actually admitted to bolstering his results (Rhine 1974). Should one conclude that all apparently significant psi experiments are flawed by error or fraud? Not necessarily. The field of parapsychology may be particularly vulnerable, but orthodox science has its share of malpractice. To quote Martin Gardner (1981, 123): "Yet the sad fact is that the history of science swarms with cases of outright fakery and instances of scientists who unconsciously distorted their work by seeing it through lenses of passionately held beliefs." The fields of science concerned are not thereby invalidated. Moreover, some cases appear to solve an *underlying basis of truth*: for example, Mendel, Burt, Summerlin (on the latter case, see Wingerson 1981). So may it be with Soal and Levy.

To postulate a residuum of real psi must strike the skeptical reader as perverse and unnecessary. Have we not plausible counterexplanations in terms of such commonplace phenomena as error, fraud, and delusion? Certainly in the absence of first-hand experience of psi, a thoroughgoing skepticism is appropriate and reasonable. For the concept of psi is *outrageous*—to common sense and science alike. The concept of psi is *subversive*—threatening to undermine the very foundations of science and bring about a Copernican Revolution in our understanding of matter and mind. The essential "magical" quality of psi, too often glossed over by parapsychologists, is the rock on which all arguments aimed at convincing the skeptic ultimately founder; it is the reason that extreme evidence is demanded.

To urge greater open-mindedness on the part of the skeptic is no answer. The likely rejoinder is that in some matters one *should* be narrow-minded. Price (1955) defined a criterion for the adoption of a narrow-minded attitude; but the criterion, couched in mechanistic terms, is surely too short-sighted. It is extremely unlikely that no further laws of nature remain to be discovered. Our understanding of mind, in particular, is still at a comparatively rudimentary stage, and increased knowledge may well bring radical changes to our conceptual framework. Suppose that the nature of mind is such that individual minds are linked at some deep level, as are islands in the ocean. By this simple, albeit fundamental, extension to the concept of mind the idea of telepathic infusion at once becomes conceivable. By a further extension, paranormal mind–matter interaction (clairvoyance and psychokinesis) could be accommodated. Precognition invokes quite another order of miraculousness. Suffice it to say that instances of apparent precognition, when analyzed in depth, are often reducible to contemporaneous psi (although most parapsychologists would contest this). Soal's so-called "precognitive telepathy" experiments are a case in point: A. C. Garnett (1965) offers an interesting explanation in terms of contemporaneous psi.

The extreme skeptic is implicitly asserting that *every* paranormal claim ever made, experimental or spontaneous, must be fallacious; for a single manifestation of psi would falsify his or her position. The question is: If psi is real, how can the skeptic identify an instance? There exists one situation permitting such an identification: a personal encounter with psi. The encounter is liable to induce a painful state of cognitive dissonance in the skeptical mind. In any case, the new insight cannot be communicated to another skeptic—the "enlightened" skeptic will merely be presumed to have fallen prey to self-deception. However, if such insight be valid, then the extreme skeptic is as the native of the "country of the blind," denying the existence of light and deriding reports of visual experience. The rational skeptic will at least grant that some individuals have anomalous, or psilike, experiences—even if the interpretation be in question. For my part, I cannot discount the claim of the "enlightened" skeptic: It is my own.

The case of Soal has brought full realization that there is no such thing as a fraud-proof experiment. However watertight parapsychologists may make their experimental designs, it is always open to the critic to allege that any significant results *could* have arisen form a trick, specified or unspecified. The way out of this impasse lies in the independent replication of successful research. Above all, replication needs to involve skeptics and magicians. Moves in this direction have typically come up against resentment on the part of parapsychologists at what they see as intrusion into their field and unrealistic demands on the part of critics who naively overlook vital psychological factors. Greater tolerance and understanding are called for on both sides—*and* a new breed of percipient who does not go into psi-shock at sight of a skeptic! Skeptics themselves might try the role of percipient—not in the arid rapid-guessing tests of yesteryear, but in today's more powerful and illuminating "altered states" techniques: dreams (natural and hypnotic), ganzfeld, and so on. First-hand experience alone is likely to convince the skeptic: either directly, as percipient, or indirectly, as experimenter in full control of an experiment.

The question of whether psi exists or does not exist is both fascinating and crucially important in its implications. It may be that anomalous phenomena—from subjective experience to laboratory evidence—will yield progressively to normal explanation, as in the case of hypnosis; a situation would eventually be reached *tantamount* to disproof of psi. It may be that the long-sought repeatable experiment will be developed through improved techniques in the elicitation and detection of a delicate psychological faculty. Either way, parapsychology presents an ongoing challenge.

Paul Kurtz urges parapsychologists "to bring their findings to the most thoroughgoing skeptics they can locate and have them examine their claims of the paranormal under the most stringent test conditions." John Beloff (elsewhere in this volume) urges critics to adopt a responsible role by forgoing rhetoric, examining the evidence, and suggesting specific counterexplanations. In a synthesis of the two strategies, I here entreat and challenge all readers involved in the controversy over psi: Abandon the fruitless rounds of attack and counterattack, exhilarating though such confrontation can be. Truth, our common quarry, will be more effectively pursued as parapsychologists respond to the restraining rein of constructive criticism and skeptics recognize the value of an expanded vision. Let us seek, then, to engage in constructive dialogue and to collaborate in experimental research—for how else shall the enigma of psi be resolved?

Acknowledgements

I am indebted to Dr. Christopher Scott for commenting upon the above article in draft, leading to clarification of certain points in the exposition. [See Scott's note, page 497.]

References

Akers, C. 1979. A reply to Edward Girden. In *Research in Parapsychology,* edited by W. G. Roll, 1979, 180-181. Metuchen, N.J.: Scarecrow Press (reply to a critique in vol. 10 of the *Handbook of Perception*).

Barrington, M. R. 1974. Mrs. Albert's testimony: Observation or inference? *Proceedings of the SPR,* 56:112-116.

Beloff, J. 1974. Why I believe that Soal is innocent. *Proceedings of the SPR,* 56:93-96.

———. 1979a. Correspondence. *Journal of the SPR,* 50:126.

———. 1979b. The importance of parapsychology: A reply to H. B. Gibson. *Bulletin of the British Parapsychological Society,* 32:244-246.

Carington, W. W. 1940. Experiments on the paranormal cognition of drawings. *Proceedings of the SPR,* 46:34-151.

Foster, E. B. 1956. A re-examination of Dr. Soal's "clairvoyance" data. *Journal of Parapsychology,* 20:110-120.

Gardner, M. 1981. *Science: Good, Bad and Bogus.* Buffalo, N.Y.: Prometheus Books (reprinted 1983 by Oxford University Press.)

Garnett, A. C. 1965. Did Shackleton demonstrate precognition? *Journal of the SPR,* 43:195-200. (Reply by S. G. Soal and counter-replies [1966]; *Journal of the SPR,* 43:250-252.)

Gibson, H. B. 1979. The "Royal Nonesuch" of parapsychology. *Bulletin of the British Psychological Society,* 32:65-67.

Goldney, K. M. 1968. Correspondence. *Journal of the SPR*, 44:308-312.

——. 1974. The Soal-Goldney experiments with Basil Shackleton (BS): A personal account. *Proceedings of the SPR*, 56:73-84.

——. 1978. Statement. *Proceedings of the SPR*, 56:278.

Gregory, A. 1979. Review of "Cyril Burt—Psychologist," by L. S. Hearnshaw. *Journal of the SPR*, 50:247-257.

Grosso, M. 1979. Review of "Philosophy and Parapsychology," edited by Jan Ludwig. *Journal of the American SPR*, 73:195-203.

Hansel. C. E. M. 1959. Experimental evidence for extra-sensory perception. *Nature*, 184:1515-1516.

——. 1960. A critical review of experiments with Mr. Basil Shackleton and Mrs. Gloria Stewart as sensitives. *Proceedings of the SPR*, 53:1-42.

——. 1966. *ESP: A Scientific Evaluation*. New York: Scribner's.

——. 1980. *ESP and Parapsychology: A Critical Re-evaluation*. Buffalo, N.Y.: Prometheus Books.

Kelly, E. F. 1982. On grouping of hits in some exceptional psi performers. *Journal of the American SPR*, 76:101-142.

Markwick, B. 1976. Correspondence. *Journal of the SPR*, 48:287-288.

——. 1978. The Soal-Goldney experiments with Basil Shackleton: New evidence of data manipulation. *Proceedings of the SPR*, 56:250-277.

McConnell, R. A. 1983. *An Introduction to Parapsychology in the Context of Science*. Pittsburgh: R. A. McConnell.

Medhurst, R. G. 1968a. The fraudulent experimenter: Professor Hansel's case against psychical research. *Journal of the SPR*, 44:217-232.

——. 1968b. Correspondence. *Journal of the SPR*, 44:303-308.

——. 1968c. Correspondence. *Journal of the SPR*, 44:424.

——. 1971. The origin of the "Prepared Random Numbers" used in the Shackleton experiments. *Journal of the SPR*, 46:39-55. (Editor's Note [Corrections]: Ibid., 203.)

Mundle, C. W. K. 1974. The Soal-Goldney experiments. *Proceedings of the SPR*, 56:85-87. (First published in 1973, in *Nature*, 245:54.)

Palmer, J. 1978. Extrasensory perception: Research findings. In *Advances in Parapsychological Research Findings*, Vol. 2: *Extrasensory Perception*, edited by Krippner, pp. 59-243.

——. 1984. The great trial reconvened: The frame theory. Unpublished manuscript.

Parsons, D. A. H. 1946. Attempts to detect clairvoyance and telepathy with a mechanical device. *Proceedings of the SPR*, 48:28-31.

——. 1947. Correspondence. *Journal of the SPR*, 34:58-59.

Pratt, J. G. 1971. Correspondence. *Journal of the SPR*, 46:199-202.

——. 1974. Fresh light on the Scott and Haskell case against Soal. *Proceedings of the SPR*, 56:97-111.

——. 1978. Statement. *Proceedings of the SPR*, 56:279-281.

Price, G. R. 1955. Science and the supernatural. *Science*, 122:359-367. (Summarized by C. Scott in *Journal of the SPR*, 38:175-179).

——. 1972. Apology to Rhine and Soal. *Science*, 175:359.

Randall, J. L. 1978. Correspondence. *Journal of the SPR*, 49:968-969.

Read, R. C. 1950. Report on an investigation of the Soal-Goldney experiment in precognitive telepathy. Unpublished manuscript.

Rhine, J. B., ed. 1955. The controversy in *Science* over ESP. *Journal of Parapsychology*, 19:236-271.

————. 1974. A new case of experimenter unreliability. *Journal of Parapsychology*, 38:215-225.

Roberts, F. S. 1975. A comment on *Proceedings* volume 56, part 209: An alternative theory. *Journal of the SPR*, 48:87-89.

Roy, A. E. 1972. Note on a series of Shackleton non-random experiments. *Journal of the SPR*, 46:181-191.

Sargent, C. L. 1979. The Parsons experiment with Basil Shackleton: Some neglected data. *Journal of the SPR*, 50: 174-179.

————. 1980. A Re-analysis of some GESP test data reported by S. G. Soal. Unpublished manuscript.

Scott, C. 1960. Notes on some criticisms of the Soal-Goldney experiments. *Journal of the SPR*, 40:299-308.

————. 1968a. Correspondence. *Journal of the SPR*, 44:299-302.

————. 1968b. Correspondence. *Journal of the SPR*, 44:422-423.

————. 1971. Correspondence. *Journal of the SPR*, 46:252-253.

————. 1978. Correspondence. *Journal of the SPR*, 49:969-970.

Scott, C., and P. Haskell. 1973. "Normal" explanation of the Soal-Goldney experiments in extrasensory perception. *Nature*, 245:52-54.

————. 1974. Fresh light on the Shackleton experiments? *Proceedings of the SPR*, 56:43-72.

————. 1975. Fraud in the Shackleton experiments: A reply to critics. *Journal of the SPR*, 48:220-226.

Soal, S. G. 1932. Experiments in supernormal perception at a distance. *Proceedings of the SPR*, 40:165-362.

————. 1937. A repetition of Dr. J. B. Rhine's work in extra-sensory perception. *Journal of the SPR*, 30:55-58.

————. 1940. Fresh light on card-guessing—Some new effects. *Proceedings of the SPR*, 46:152-198.

————. 1950. The Shackleton experiments: A comment by S. G. Soal on an investigation by R. C. Read. *Journal of the SPR*, 35:309-310.

————. 1955. Reply to "Science and the Supernatural." *Journal of the SPR*, 38:179-184 (also printed in *Science*, 123 (1956):9-11).

————. 1956. The Shackleton report: An error discovered. *Journal of the SPR*, 38:216. (Related correspondence by S. G. Soal, D. J. West, B. Humphrey Nicol: Ibid.: 216-219, 341-347.)

————. 1960a. Experimental evidence for extra-sensory perception. With a reply by C. E. M. Hansel. *Nature*, 185:949-950.

————. 1960b. A reply to Mr. Hansel. *Proceedings of the SPR*, 53:43-82.

————. 1960c. Correspondence. *Journal of the SPR*, 40:376-377.

————. 1968. Correspondence. *Journal of the SPR*, 44:312-313.

————. 1971. Correspondence. *Journal of the SPR*, 46:202-203.

Soal, S. G., and F. Bateman. 1954. *Modern Experiments in Telepathy.* New Haven: Yale University Press.

Soal, S. G., and K. M. Goldney. 1943. Experiments in precognitive telepathy. *Proceedings of the SPR,* 47:21-150.

———. 1960. Correspondence. *Journal of the SPR,* 40:378-381.

Stevenson, I. 1974. The credibility of Mrs. Gretl Albert's testimony. *Proceedings of the SPR,* 56:117-129.

———. 1979. Correspondence. *Journal of the SPR,* 50:191-192.

Thouless, R. H. 1969. Correspondence. *Journal of the SPR,* 45:91-92.

———. 1974. Some comments on "Fresh Light on the Shackleton Experiments." *Proceedings of the SPR,* 56:88-92.

———. 1978. Correspondence. *Journal of the SPR,* 49:965-968.

Wasserman, G. D. 1975. A comment on *Proceedings* volume 56, part 209: The soul of Soal. *Journal of the SPR,* 48:89-91. (Reply by K. M. Goldney and counter-replies: Ibid., 91-94 and 245-247.)

West, D. J. 1978. Correspondence. *Journal of the SPR,* 49:897-899.

———. 1983. Thoughts on testimony to the paranormal. In *Research in Parapsychology 1982,* W. G. Roll, J. Beloff and R. A. White, 27-30. Metuchen, N.J.: Scarecrow Press.

Wingerson, L. 1981. William Summerlin: Was he right all along? *New Scientist,* 89:527-529.

12

J. B. Rhine and the Levy Scandal

D. SCOTT ROGO

The field of parapsychology faced one of its greatest crises on June 12, 1974. That was the day that Dr. J. B. Rhine of the Institute for Parapsychology (in Durham, North Carolina) learned that his own director of research was falsifying the results of his experiments. Between 1970 and 1974, Dr. Walter J. Levy had become a genuine *Wunderkind* in the field, by reporting a phenomenal string of successful experiments. These experiments primarily demonstrated that small rodents possess ESP. It seemed to be a promising line of research, and Rhine had long been nurturing Levy to take complete control of the Institute. Levy's research was achieving prominence not only within the parapsychological community but also in the scientific press in general. The reason was simple. Parapsychology had long bemoaned the fact that it possessed no repeatable experiment, but Levy seemed to be on to one—until the evening of June 11, 1974, when three of his own associates caught him faking one of his key experiments.

The Background of the Scandal

The background of Levy's meteoric rise within the field dates back to 1968. Two talented French scientists reported a novel experiment that year that purportedly demonstrated that mice possess precognitive ability. Dr. Remy Chauvin and Dr. J. P. Genthon (both writing under pseudonyms) reported that they had placed mice in a box divided by a barrier over which they could jump. Each side of the box could be independently fed an electric shock, and the experimenters wanted to determine if the mice could detect (paranormally) which side was about to be given a jolt on any given occasion. The mice, of course, jumped over the barrier as soon as they received a shock, but the researchers paid particular attention to those times when the mice jumped the barrier for no discernible reason *before* a shock was delivered. These movements were called "random behavior trials." The original report showed that more than 50 percent of these movements coincided with jumps *away* from the side of the box about to receive a shock.

This suggested to the scientists that the mice were using precognition to determine which side of the box to avoid (Duval and Montredon 1968).

This interesting line of research generated considerable attention within the parapsychological community. Not only were the strong results reported by Chauvin and Genthon impressive, but the test was completely automated. This innovation conveniently diminished the role of human error to a minimum.

Walter J. Levy appeared on the parapsychology scene shortly after the French work was published. He was finishing medical school in Georgia at the time, and commencing in 1970 began spending more and more time at the Institute for Parapsychology. Weekends would invariably find him there, and he decided to devote himself full time to parapsychology after his graduation. He did not pursue an internship but moved instead to Durham.

It was soon apparent that Levy's special interest was in pursuing small-rodent ESP research, and it wasn't long before he was attempting to replicate the French work. His first tests were not too significant, but gradually he began isolating a small but significant effect using the random behavior trial criterion. Levy then went on to revise and extend the scope and nature of the small-rodent work. One of his chief innovations was to replace the electrified box with a running wheel, thereby forcing the rodents to regulate their pace in order to avoid shocks to randomly determined sides of the wheel. But precognition was not the only aspect of parapsychology that caught Levy's interest. He also conducted research to see if chicken embryos could use psychokinesis on a random-event generator to receive warmth from a lamp, tested (human) volunteer subjects to see if they would use ESP to work through a maze; and tested to determine whether rats could use psychokinesis to receive stimulation to the pleasure centers of the brain. Levy was nothing if not industrious and often spent the night on a cot at the Institute while engaged in his research.[1]

The sheer energy Levy brought to his work was considerable. Between 1969 and 1974 he authored twenty studies (some published only as abstracts) of which most focused on experimental research (see Rhine 1975b). J. B. Rhine was impressed by this young and talented researcher. It should be remembered that Rhine was in his seventies at the time and was looking for an eventual successor. Levy struck him as a good choice, and in 1973 Rhine made him director of the Institute for Parapsychology. Rhine even moved out of the main building of the Institute to a residence a few blocks away. This, too, was owned by the Foundation for Research on the Nature of Man (FRNM), which controls the Institute.

But there were signs of trouble brewing in paradise. Levy was an ambitious and politically astute young man, but he soon made enemies as well as friends. Some of the FRNM staff openly disliked him and felt that he was manipulating Rhine—who, in the past, had shown himself to be more than a little myopic when enthusiastic over a new and gifted researcher. The situation grew worse during 1973, when it was first suggested that Levy might be misrepresenting his data or even falsifying them. Most of these rumors were vague and possibly unfounded, but it wasn't long before several members of the parapsychological community became suspicious of Levy and his unheard of string of successful experiments. (I personally first heard these suspicions voiced during the summer of 1973 while visiting New York City en route to Durham, when a prominent parapsychologist there took me into his confidence. He explained that he had heard rumors that Levy was simply making up his data and that the editorial staff of the Institute's *Journal of Parapsychology* had to clean up Levy's papers before publishing them.)

There is evidence that some researchers tried to warn Rhine that Levy was unreliable and should not be given free reign at the Institute. Dr. José Feola, a former FRNM worker then living in Minneapolis, tried to warn him that Levy's results made no biological sense and therefore appeared spurious. He was also critical of Levy's methodology and cautioned Rhine about it several times (Feola 1984).

Despite these warnings, only one direct allegation of fraud was brought to Rhine's personal attention. Mr. Graham Watkins, an FRNM staff member who was engaged in professional and personal rivalry with Levy, met with Rhine early on during Levy's tenure and charged his colleague with direct fraud. He charged that the equipment Levy had used for a recent experiment was faulty and was producing false readings. Levy, he claimed, had reported positive data from the read-outs anyway, despite the fact that he knew them to be unreliable. Rhine later apparently discussed the Watkins allegation with another staff member, but neither of them followed it up. Though perhaps this was negligent on Rhine's part, the truth was that Watkins had provided no hard data that Rhine could have acted upon. But Watkins personally felt that Rhine was ignoring his warning.

In retrospect, it is of course difficult to determine just how wary Rhine should have been of Levy and his string of successes. Based on my own personal interactions with Levy during the summer of 1973, I think Rhine should have been more cautious. I stayed in Durham for six weeks while working at the neighboring Psychical Research Foundation and had the opportunity of getting to know Levy fairly well. It took me very little time to conclude that he probably *was* guilty of falsifying his research. I based my opinion on several facts, including tip-offs I had received from several talks with Watkins when I first arrived. I also grew suspicious when, during our first meeting, Levy showed me some of his unpublished work that reported unbelievably high (90 percent) success rates. I grew even more suspicious later in my stay when Levy fed me false information about the security precautions built into the FRNM computer to control for experimenter fraud and when he asked me *not* to broach the subject of experimenter fraud with other FRNM staff members! I certainly felt at the time that Rhine should have been suspicious of him, too. Several other researchers who were employed at the Psychical Research Foundation that summer shared my feelings about Levy. We grew even more concerned when one of our own staff members, Mr. Jerry Levin, was offered a job to work as Levy's assistant at FRNM. Mr. Levin was a bright young researcher with a promising career ahead of him, and we certainly didn't want to see it ruined should he become too close to Levy. So with no other options from which to choose, two of us took Levin aside one afternoon and explained our trepidations. Levin explained that he was aware of the rumors about Levy and promised that he would be careful.

The Scandal at FRNM

The final proof that Levy was faking his research was not to come until the summer of 1974. By that time he was working on a new project to see whether rats with electrodes implanted in the pleasure center of the brain could use psychokinesis to obtain stimulation. This experiment, like most of Levy's, was thoroughly automated. The suspicion that he was helping his experiments along came gradually during the course of these tests. During some of the early runs, two FRNM staff members—James Davis and James Kennedy—became suspicious of Levy's behavior but failed to obtain any hard evidence that he was engaged in fraudulent activities. The final damning proof came in June, when Jerry Levin noticed that Levy tended to linger around the computer that was monitoring the tests. Since the experiments were automated, Levin knew that there was simply no reason for Levy to be so attentive and concerned about them or the computer. His misgivings were aroused further when, on one occasion, he caught Levy in the computer room manipulating the equipment while a run of successful results were being simultaneously recorded. Levin immediately shared his observations with Davis and Kennedy, and they set a careful trap for him on the evening of June 11. This entailed running hidden duplicate leads from the computer into another room, where they were able to get an independent read-out of the scoring on the ongoing rat experiments. Davis hid in the computer room to see what might happen should Levy visit the room. The plan paid off. Their general suspicions were confirmed later that night when Davis watched Levy enter the room and deliberately manipulate the equipment so that the computer generated a string of "hits." The independent read-outs received in the other room showed only chance scoring, and the three researchers instantly realized that Levy was resorting to fraud.[2]

Levin, Davis, and Kennedy found themselves placed in a curious dilemma. They realized that they had to go to Rhine with what they knew, but they didn't know what to expect from him. Rhine could be a very difficult man to deal with, and in the past he had been hesitant to admit the failings of his personal favorites—even in the face of opposition from his staff. (See Brian 1982, 272-280.) The young men knew there was a possibility that *they* would be fired when they confronted Rhine. But they decided to proceed the next day anyway.

On June 12, they began by speaking with Dr. Louisa Rhine, J. B. Rhine's wife, at the Rhines' offices in the residence where they had recently moved. It was not rare for Mrs. Rhine to mediate problems between her husband and the staff, and she immediately recognized the importance of the data the researchers had collected. She agreed to take them to Rhine herself. Dr. Rhine was, in fact, meeting with Levy at that very time in his office. Mrs. Rhine and the three researchers waited for Levy to leave, went upstairs, and then showed Rhine their data and told him about their observations. It was a stunning blow to Rhine, and he questioned them carefully about the procedures they had used to catch Levy. He then thanked them for their candor and immediately called for Levy to return to his office.

The critical meeting between Rhine and Levy occurred immediately after the charge of fraud had been leveled. Rhine explained the situation to Levy, who confessed to the fraud on the spot. His only excuse was that he was working under extraordinary self-imposed strain and that he had committed the fraud for the good of parapsychology. Rhine questioned him further, but Levy asserted in no uncertain terms that he had committed no fraud during the course of any of his earlier work. The current fraud, he maintained, was only a single unfortunate lapse of judgment stemming from overwork. He offered his verbal resignation nonetheless, which Rhine took under advisement—"officially" neither accepting nor rejecting it. (Rhine later [1974] claimed that he accepted the resignation on the spot, but this does not technically seem to be the case.)

Despite these unfortunate events, it was clear that Levy wished to salvage his reputation and his job. Rhine was somewhat ambivalent about just what steps should be taken under the circumstances—a situation no doubt nourished by his own personal and emotional investment in his protégé, whom he had sometimes treated more like a son than a colleague. From the time he learned of Levy's fraud until a staff meeting the next day, Rhine toyed with several options. He was impressed by Levy's claim that overwork was the cause of his "lapse," so at one point he considered merely giving him a leave of absence to recover from his "breakdown." Rhine apparently discussed this possibility directly with Levy, although it is not clear who actually came up with the idea—nor for how long Rhine actually entertained it. It was an option he soon rejected, though.

The critical decisions regarding the Levy matter came the next day, June 13, when Rhine chaired a staff meeting at FRNM to discuss the situation. He was still vascillating on what steps to take, and Levy was still hoping to salvage his position. Levy finally suggested that a committee should be formed to investigate the charges against him. This of course would have stalled Rhine from taking action on Levy's (now formal) resignation. Rhine seemed willing to entertain the notion but was advised against it by his wife. He then rejected the suggestion and officially "fired" Levy.

Later that day, Rhine drafted the first version of his letter about the affair to FRNM's board of trustees. He revised it the next day (June 14), circulated it among the FRNM staff, and finally mailed it on Monday, June 19. It was also during this time that he tried to dissuade the council of the Parapsychological Association (parapsychology's professional organization) from asking Levy for his resignation. Some parapsychologists felt at the time that this was a ploy on Rhine's part to keep Levy professionally associated with the field, perhaps with the intent of bringing him back to FRNM at some future time. But it is also possible that he merely wanted to give Levy a chance to quietly resign (which was actually what happened) to avoid further embarrassment to himself and to the field of parapsychology. For, despite the betrayal, Rhine *was* still concerned about Levy and his future. This was evident by the way in which the Levy situation was publicly announced by Rhine both in his letter to his colleagues and in his own *Journal of Parapsychology*.

Rhine's official letter of June 19 to all interested parties was, in fact, filled with euphemisms and excuses on Levy's behalf. It was a poor communication by any criteria. Rhine did not explain how Levy had been caught in cold-blooded fraud but, instead, wrote that Levy had been caught relying on "unreliable procedures" and had "resorted to improper methods to keep his research going." He even went on to partially excuse his protégé, writing that the researchers who had exposed Levy's fraud "regarded this utterly foolish action as so much unlike him that he must have been 'out of his head,' that he must have been working too hard."

This was indeed Dr. Levy's version of the lapse, but it rather went against the facts. No mention was made of the fact that the researchers who caught him were acting on long-standing suspicions, nor that Levy's fraud was premeditated. It would seem that, even at this time, Rhine could not admit to himself that his trust in Levy had been misplaced and preferred to put some credence in the idea that Levy had broken down under the stress of overwork.

Rhine also ended up at loggerheads with his staff and with other Durham parapsychologists over how the situation should be reported in FRNM's own *Journal of Parapsychology*, where much of the Levy work had been published. He was reluctant to identify Levy by name, even though this was his duty and responsibility. His plan was to write up the affair by referring to Levy completely anonymously. Rhine explained to his staff that he didn't want the incident to be a permanent blot on Levy's record—that is, a ghost that might come back to haunt him years in the future. He felt that the regular readers of the *JP* would know exactly whom he was writing about, while outsiders would not.

It need not be emphasized how strongly opposed some of the FRNM staff were to this course of action. They felt that a complete disclosure was not only called for but imperative. Rhine stood his ground but capitulated to the extent that he agreed to identify Levy by his first initial. He would go no further. So the many readers of the *JP* learned in the June issue (published several months later) only that a "Dr. W." had been caught cheating at the Institute (Rhine 1974). Rhine pointed out in his *JP* editorial, however, that all of this researcher's work now had to be considered suspect, a pointed reference to Levy.

Levy, in the meantime, vacated the FRNM premises and prepared to return to medicine. He spent the next few weeks clearing up matters in Durham in order to move back to Georiga. It didn't take long, however, before the FRNM staff began uncovering evidence that his fraud was certainly *not* restricted simply to the rat experiments.

The Aftermath of the Scandal

By the end of that summer, Rhine knew that all of Levy's research had to be examined for evidence of fraud, even though he would have preferred to let the matter simply drop. He also knew that all of Levy's previous work had to be independently replicated. So he sent James Davis to the 1974 annual meeting of the Parapsychological Association at St. John's University in New York City to announce some of his plans. It was the beginning of even more problems for Levy's credibility and more controversies for Rhine.

By the middle of the next year, it was no secret that Levy's fraud was extensive. While Rhine himself was diffident about reanalyzing Levy's old data, some of his staff members were more enterprising. James Kennedy, in particular, devoted himself to checking the computer records of Levy's maze experiments. The records revealed purely chance results even though Levy had reported significant positive scoring. It was clear to the FRNM staff that Levy had invented the data he had published. Kennedy next examined data taken from Levy's research on PK in chicken embryos, and there he found more evidence of fraud. Phenomenally long and highly suspicious strings of "hits" similar to those he was caught faking during the rat implantation research were evident in the read-outs.[3] Rhine made these findings public in 1975, at which time he wisely dropped the questionable practice of identifying Levy only by his initial (Rhine, 1975b). It was during this same time, though, that another controversy was brewing at the Institute. This disheartening affair accompanied the return of one of Levy's former assistants to the lab.

James Terry had been a highly regarded staff member at FRNM, and he had collaborated with Levy on some of the early replications of the French small-rodent work. (He was the coauthor of three papers published by Levy in 1973.) When the Levy scandal broke, Terry was working in Brooklyn at the division of parapsychology at the Maimonides Medical Center. Since he was working toward his doctorate at the time, he was naturally alarmed when he learned of the developments in Durham. Since it appeared that some of the work on which he had collaborated was suspect, Terry determined to get to the root of the matter. By reviewing the procedures he and Levy had used, Terry came to a series of conclusions about the possible extent of Levy's fraud. He could not figure out how their first replications could have been falsified, because he himself had been in charge of collecting the data. He finally decided that Levy's critical error was in replacing the electrified box with the running wheel in the small-rodent work. Terry considered it likely that these later experiments probably failed for some psychic or methodological reason, causing Levy to panic and to initiate his fraudulent activities (Terry, c. 1976).

With all these thoughts in mind, Terry wrote to Rhine and Davis in the summer of 1974 asking to see the data tapes from the early Levy work to check them for signs of fraud. The official response from FRNM was to put Terry off somewhat, and by March of the next year they had still not sent out the data (which required some computer reprogramming to be made understandable). Terry eventually came to the conclusion they were not going to send him the data. He then wrote to Rhine suggesting that he return to Durham to replicate Levy's early box experiments. Rhine agreed, and Terry began preparing to make the move. Rhine was no doubt eager to see Terry return to Durham, since by this time researchers there were finding that they couldn't replicate *any* of the Levy work. So many failures were cropping up, in fact, that some of the staff reached an informal consensus that all the failed replications should be reported as a package and not independently. This course of action was not explained to Terry and was not included in the terms of his employment.

The results of Terry's return to FRNM constitute another unfortunate chapter in the history of parapsychology. During the months of June and July (1975) both he and Jerry Levin attempted to replicate the early "box" experiments, but they failed time and time again. They both also realized the important implications of their failures and concluded that it was imperative that they report their findings to the scientific community. They fully expected to report them at the upcoming convention of the Parapsychological Association scheduled for August in Santa Barbara. Rhine encouraged their plan and twice, while the research was still in progress, agreed to allow them to report their work there. A bombshell exploded, however, in July, when Levin completed his research and submitted his brief, which made clear that his attempted replication of the small-rodent work had produced nonsignificant results. Rhine studied and then rejected the brief, explaining to Levin that he didn't want it reported to the Parapsychological Association. He told the researcher that there was no reason to report an experiment showing such minimal results. When Terry heard the news, he was shocked by Rhine's attitude and explained at the staff meeting that it was necessary that the status of the Levy replications should be immediately made known. But Rhine would not budge.

Terry was thoroughly alarmed. He was beginning to realize that Rhine would probably not allow him to report on his *own* failed replications and that he would minimize or "hide" the importance of all the failed replications while promoting any positive ones that might be forthcoming. Rhine continually stood his ground in the face of Terry's repeated protests and finally explained to Terry that all the replication work should be reported together and that this was a "house" policy—which was certainly news to Terry at the time. He felt that Rhine was simply going back on his word and that the Levin brief had been rejected solely because it reported a failed replication.

The situation grew worse during the week of July 14, as Terry prepared to formally submit his own brief. By this time he had also reported the situation to Charles Honorton, who was then the president of the Parapsychological Association and his former boss at the Maimonides laboratory. The final showdown came later that month when Rhine refused to discuss the matter any further with Terry, who finally submitted his brief on July 28. The brief did not go directly to Rhine, since he had placed Dr. B. K. Kanthanani (a veteran FRNM staff member) in charge of handling such submissions. She immediately rejected the brief, explaining that Rhine had made it clear to her that no briefs dealing with the Levy replication or showing anything but positive results could be reported to the upcoming conference. This situation was really not surprising since it was well known that Rhine did not like to call too much attention to insignificant findings under any conditions (Rhine 1975a). But Terry quickly concluded that Rhine was hiding behind his "policies" to camouflage the poor status of the Levy replications.

Things probably could have been resolved even at this point had not Rhine been so immobile in his position. When Terry learned that his brief was being rejected, he immediately went to confront Rhine, who refused point-blank to see him. Nor could the young researcher marshal much support from the rest of the staff, who were well aware that Rhine tended to explode when faced with impertinence. Most members of the staff sided against Terry, and some of them accused him of being a "spy" for Charles Honorton.

This was, of course, a perfectly ridiculous charge. But Terry *was* keeping his former boss informed. Since Honorton was in charge of accepting research briefs for the upcoming convention, there was nothing underhanded in Terry's action. But it was also true that Honorton had long been critical of Rhine's policies regarding nonsignificant findings.

The climax of the controversy came on July 30, when Terry decided to go over Rhine's head by submitting his brief directly to Honorton. He was not acting out of malice but took this course of action to meet the PA's deadline for submissions, feeling that he could always retract it if Rhine was willing to work out a compromise with him. Rhine didn't learn about this development until the following week, and he was furious when he heard the news. He responded by ordering Terry to withdraw his brief, and two FRNM staff members went through Terry's desk without his permission to see what he was reporting to Honorton. Terry stood his ground and refused to retract his brief, and on August 7 he was fired by Rhine and ordered out of the FRNM building. Rhine also threatened to destroy Terry's career and cause him "financial hardship" unless he capitulated, but Terry refused to be intimidated. He left town soon after, fearing that Rhine would try to serve him with a court injunction to keep him from reporting on his research.

The upshot of the situation extended far beyond Durham, however. Rhine—to stop the Terry brief from being publicly aired—immediately called Honorton in Brooklyn to retract the brief and keep it from being accepted.[4] But Honorton wasn't about to be intimidated either, and he forcefully sided with Terry. He had accepted the brief, he told Rhine, and he wanted it read in Santa Barbara. This aggravated the hostilities between Rhine and Honorton, and Honorton finally decided to reject all research briefs being submitted by FRNM on the grounds that they represented "selective" reporting. The official response from FRNM was to "withdraw" their briefs, protesting that Honorton had acted unethically in accepting an "unauthorized" one from Terry.[5] The Terry brief was eventually delivered on the opening day of the Santa Barbara conference (Terry 1976), while Rhine later published a brief resume of all FRNM's failed replications of the Levy work in the *Journal of Parapsychology* (Rhine 1975b). Some successful work carried out at other laboratories was also reported, and these primarily concerned experiments on ESP in small rodents.

Some Concluding Remarks

The Levy scandal, in itself, was and is of little importance to the scientific case for parapsychology. Levy was only one researcher, at one laboratory, following one highly specific line of research. But two important questions that arise from the Levy affair *do* bear on the field. The first of these is fairly obvious: Just what factors compelled Levy to systematically fake his research in the first place? The second is whether the fraudulent nature of Levy's research undermines the whole case for ESP in animals in general. Each of these questions will be addressed in turn.

It has been generally assumed that Levy faked his research simply because he was a "bad" and "corrupt" scientist. This is not the whole answer by any means, for the situation is actually much more complex. There were probably several factors that laid the foundation for his fraudulent actions. It is my feeling that the blame for Levy's behavior can, in some respects, be placed on the way Rhine ran FRNM during these years. It was Rhine's position that the only truly *good* parapsychologist was one who could achieve successful results. (He told me in 1973 that there was not a single good young parapsychologist actively working in the field at the time. He rejected several researchers I specifically mentioned in protest.) He therefore put constant pressure on his staff to keep turning out successful experiments, even though such successes in parapsychology tend to be few and far between. Rhine simply had very little time for researchers who didn't meet his expectations or couldn't obtain good results. It was this mind-set that prompted Rhine's practice of publishing only experimental reports that gave positive results. FRNM, under Rhine's direction, was simply a laboratory that rewarded good results and punished poor ones. Furthermore, it was no secret at FRNM that he could be ruthless when it came to getting rid of staff researchers who fell from his favor for just about any reason. Levy arrived at the laboratory when Rhine was still in strict charge of things, and he soon realized that he had to keep cranking out significant results or face the probability of being booted out. This turned into a vicious circle of sorts; for the more successes he reported, the more pressure Rhine placed on him to keep up the good work. His lapse into fraud could be considered, in one sense, a predictable response to such pressure.

So there really was no single or *simple* reason for Levy's fraud. It resulted from an unfortunate defect in his character, complicated by self-imposed overwork, but also as a response to the social pressures that existed at Rhine's lab at the time. It is even possible that Levy genuinely achieved some limited early success but panicked when he saw that his subsequent research was failing to corroborate it.

The worst drawback of the Levy affair was the dampening effect it had on "anpsi" research (research on psi in animals) in general. Research into the possible existence of animal ESP did not originate either with Levy or with the earlier French precognition research. It dates back to the 1950s and early 1960s, although it did not come to the forefront of parapsychology until the 1970s along with Levy's rise to fame (Morris 1970). Levy's successful replications of the original French research had encouraged researchers in other laboratories to pursue similar lines of inquiry. Despite the fact that the Levy work must be rejected, the fact remains that other researchers were able to report very similar findings both before and after his unmasking. Successful research employing small rodents as subjects has been reported from the University of Waterloo (Craig and Treurniet 1974); from Holland (Schouten 1972); and even by Terry himself (Terry and Harris 1975). More provisional success has been reported from the University of Edinburgh (Parker 1974), and by Dr. Hans Eysenck in England (1975). These reports represent a significant body of successful research.

The Levy scandal, however, left a bad taste in everybody's mouth, and anpsi research, so popular in the 1970s, eventually faded from the forefront of parapsychology and has not been reactivated. This is probably the real tragedy of the Levy scandal. It influenced researchers around the world to drop an area of ESP research that seemed to be fruitful—and which in fact did not fully rely on the successes reported by Levy.

Endnote

The damage the Levy scandal could have had on parapsychology was probably minimized by similar events reported from the Sloan-Kettering Institute for Cancer Research that same summer. This controversy revolved around a researcher employed there who was also caught falsifying his research. This unfortunate affair merely went to prove that experimenter fraud is a problem in every science. Since that time, the problem of experimenter fraud has come up for renewed examination by the scientific community (Broad and Wade 1982).

Dr. Walter J. Levy did not go into medical practice, as everyone had expected. He completed an internship in Georgia and then embarked on a career in medical research, specializing in neurology. He eventually took a research post at a university in the Midwest, where he continues to publish in the field of neurosurgery.

Acknowledgments

The material published in this report is drawn primarily from interviews with those involved in the original scandal, as well as from their written (though unpublished) reminiscenses. I would like to thank FRNM for placing some of this material in my hands. The viewpoints expressed are solely those of the author, however.

Notes

1. Considerable play has been given to the fact that Levy literally lived and slept at the Institute, thereby proving his devotion to the field. The fact of the matter was that Levy was one of those rare people who needed only a few hours of sleep a night. He was a workaholic to boot, and it was often simply more convenient for him to stay at the Institute than any place else.

2. In his book *The Whys of a Philosophical Scrivener*, Martin Gardner (1983) writes of the Levy scandal: "I have it on good authority that his crime was detected not because of careful controls in Rhine's laboratory, but because older staff members, jealous of the younger man, set a careful trap for him." These remarks are wholly false. The three researchers were all newcomers to the field and didn't plan to remain in it permanently. Nor were they jealous of Levy but considered him a close friend. Levy had even been an usher at the wedding of one of the young men. [Accepting Rogo's account of the Levy affair, Gardner has altered the latter part of his sentence in all later prints of *Whys* to: "because suspicious young staff members set a careful trap for him."—ED.]

3. It has always struck me as puzzling that these analyses were not secretly done while Levy was still at the lab. Several people there were aware of the rumors about Levy's possible fraud, and these simple analyses could have laid the matter to rest. Failing to make an analysis of the hit patterns in the PK research can be excused, since previous to the summer of 1974 no one could have suspected just how he was manipulating his experiments. But the scores from the maze work could have been easily checked against those Levy was reporting and should have been a routine procedure. While not a damning criticism of the way in which Rhine ran FRNM by any means, this indicates that the security precautions at his laboratory during the 1970s were not what they should have been.

4. Some commentators on the Levy matter believe that Rhine's action stemmed from his possible desire to cover up the status of the Levy replications. However, by this time, the issue at stake was whether Rhine could tolerate his authority being undermined. His action at this point was probably more a matter of principle than anything else.

5. A motion was later submitted to the council of the Parapsychological Association to censure Honorton for his actions. The motion was defeated and, in fact, the PA went further by adopting a policy against the reporting of only positive results. This policy states that experiments resulting in insignificant results should not be barred from being published or publicly reported.

References

Brian, Denis. 1982. *The Enchanted Voyager: The Life of J. B. Rhine*. Englewood Cliffs, N.J.: Prentice-Hall.

Broad, William, and Nicholas Wade. 1982. *Betrayers of the Truth*. New York: Simon & Schuster.

Craig, James, and W. Treurniet. 1974. Precognition as a function of shock and death. In *Research in Parapsychology—1973*. Metuchen, N.J.: Scarecrow Press.

Duval, Pierre, and E. Montredon. 1968. ESP experiments with mice. *Journal of Parapsychology*, 32:153-166.

Eysenck, Hans. 1975. Precognition in rats. *Journal of Parapsychology*, 39:222-227.

Feola, José. 1984. Private communication: September 3.

Gardner, Martin. 1983. *The Whys of a Philosophical Scrivener*. New York: William Morrow.

Morris, Robert. 1970. Psi and animal behavior: A survey. *Journal of the American SPR*, 64: 242-260.

Parker, Adrian. 1974. ESP in gerbils using positive reinforcement. *Journal of Parapsychology*, 38:301-311.

Rhine, J. B. 1974. A new case of experimenter unreliability. *Journal of Parapsychology*, 38:215-225.

———. 1975a. Publication policy regarding non-significant results. *Journal of Parapsychology*, 38:135-142.

———. 1975b. Second report on a case of experimenter fraud. *Journal of Parapsychology*, 39:306-325.

Schouten, Sybo. 1972. Psi in mice: Positive reinforcement. *Journal of Parapsychology*, 36:261-282.

Terry, James. c. 1976. *A Time with Rhine*. Unpublished manuscript.

———. James. 1976. Continuation of the rodent precognition experiments. In *Research in Parapsychology—1975*. Metuchen, N.J.: Scarecrow Press.

Terry, James, and Susan Harris. 1975. Precognition in water-deprived rats. In *Research in Parapsychology—1974*. Metuchen, N.J.: Scarecrow Press.

13

A Note on Borley Rectory:
"The Most Haunted House in England"

TREVOR H. HALL

The writer of nonfiction books on unusual subjects is frequently asked how his interest was first aroused. I have been a Sherlock Holmes enthusiast since my schooldays, and it was as a schoolboy that my father, who was acquainted with the late Sir Arthur Conan Doyle, introduced me to the creator of my hero. The meeting took place in Sir Arthur's psychic bookshop in Westminster, and we were invited to inspect the curious exhibits in the basement museum. The impression made upon a small boy by the greatest exponent and champion of spiritualism in its history was clearly formidable, and my father, who was a wise man, decided that an immediate antidote was necessary.

We went to Maskelynes, where I saw that greater miracles than those described by Sir Arthur could be accomplished in full light by normal means. An enthusiasm for amateur conjuring was a natural development, leading after many years to an Hon. Vice Presidency of the Magic Circle of London and to an interest in the historical bibliography of the subject, on which I wrote the standard work in 1972. That afternoon in London so long ago also accounts for my contributions to the published literature of critical psychical research. Old houses, supposedly haunted, have always been of great interest to me for more than one reason. First, I happen to live in one, and during the whole of my years of occupation I have never heard so much as a solitary tap not due to natural causes. Second, it was during my investigation of a case of this kind that I met the lady who is now my partner in a particularly happy marriage.

During a period of nearly thirty years eight books on critical psychical research by me (two in collaboration) have been published. The first was *The Haunting of Borley Rectory*, 1956, of which my joint authors were Dr. E. J. Dingwall and Mrs. K. M. Goldney. The purpose of the book, based on a five-year investigation, was to establish the facts in regard to the supposed "psychic phenomena" alleged to have occurred in the notorious Essex rectory. It was written in the public interest to correct the sensational and inaccurate presentation of the case by the late Harry Price (1881–1948) in his two books, *The Most Haunted House in England* (1940) and *The End of Borley Rectory* (1946). It is, in my opinion, a matter for regret that the legend has now been revived and that an attempt has been made to rebuild what Professor Antony G. N. Flew, then professor of philosophy at the University of Keele, described in his review of our book in *The Spectator* of January 27, 1956, as "the house of cards which Harry Price built out of little more than a pack of lies."

In 1975, a 240-page book, *The Ghosts of Borley*, by the late Paul Tabori and Peter Underwood, was published. It was dedicated to "Harry Price, the man who put Borley on the map." The authors specifically stated in their introduction that they "believe that at least some of the phenomena were genuine" and that they "reject the indictment brought against the author of *The Most Haunted House in England* and *The End of Borley Rectory*." They "believe that the Borley hauntings represent one of the most interesting, most cohesive and varied chapters in the history of psychical research and that they contain, as if in a microcosm, the whole range of psychic phenomena."

The publication of *The Ghosts of Borley* has proved that the later paragraphs of the review of our exposure of 1956 in *The Economist* of April 7, 1956, were prophetic, despite the compliments paid to the three authors:

> The record of cumulative suggestion, embroidery, misrepresentation, practical joking and downright fraud painstakingly analysed by the authors of this book, is as good in its way as the ghost story itself. . . . But the build-up of the legend and the psychology of the witnesses is a much more interesting affair; and the authors' level-headed and patient unravelling of incident after incident, discrepancy after discrepancy, does the subject full justice.
>
> Entertaining as the book is, it leaves a slightly nasty taste in the mouth. Not because the late Harry Price emerges unmistakably as a rogue, a falsifier and manufacturer of evidence; not because certain other persons with motives less material though understandable enough, faked a bigger volume of evidence than he did; but because the whole long drawn-out Borley affair at once constituted a debasement of popular opinion and thought. Everything that was shoddy, muzzy, slipshod and anti-rational in the public mind responded to, and throve on, the Borley sensation. It will take more than this antidote to counter so massive and thoroughly assimilated a dose of dope.

According to Harry Price's two books on Borley, psychical phenomena took place at the rectory during the occupation of all the four incumbents who lived there from its building in 1863 to its final demolition, i.e., the Rev. Henry Dawson Ellis Bull, his son the Rev. Harry Foyster Bull, the Rev. G. Eric Smith, and the Rev. Lionel Algernon Foyster. Price made it clear, however, that it was during the period from 1930 to 1935, when Foyster and his wife

Marianne were the final occupiers of the rectory, that the most numerous, violent, and varied manifestations occurred. Tabori and Underwood echoed Price's opinion with enthusiasm, but offered no supporting evidence of their own that will stand examination. It seems to me remarkable (particularly in view of what follows) that the authors of *The Ghosts of Borley* should assert on page 36 of their book: "Certainly the Reverend Henry D. E. Bull and his wife knew about the legend of the ghostly nun. They built the large pavilion [the summerhouse] in the garden for the express purpose of watching for her appearances. During their lifetime the walk bordering the lawn became known as the 'Nun's Walk.'"

There is no possible doubt that Underwood and Tabori were familiar with a long featured article on Borley by the late Kenneth Allsop, illustrated by Godfrey Thurston Hopkins, published in *Picture Post* on January 1, 1955, for they refer to it on pages 213-214 of *The Ghosts of Borley*. The authors confine their account of this article, however, entirely to a descripton of a photo of the old gateway of the Rectory taken by Hopkins, which when developed showed two black, cloudlike shapes (looking very much like the wings of a moth close to the camera and therefore much out of focus) that Hopkins had not noticed in the view-finder. It seems to me inexplicable that Underwood and Tabori made no mention of the very revealing interview, recorded in the same article by Allsop, with the late Ethel Bull and the late Alfred R. G. Bull, the daughter and son of the late Rev. Henry D. E. Bull. Alfred Bull said to Kenneth Allsop: "I was astounded when I saw Price's book was called *The Most Haunted House in England*—all the years we lived there I saw nothing."

Allsop continued: "The Bulls had several more comments to make about statements by Price; their father did *not* have the dining-room window bricked up to prevent the nun staring in, but to stop the view of ordinary nosey passersby; that he did *not* build the summer-house as a grand-stand for the nun's perambulations, but for use during tennis parties; and the title, the Nun's Walk, must have been given by Price, because they never knew it as that."

In their long chapter in *The Ghosts of Borley* on the tenancy of Borley Rectory by the Rev. Lionel Algernon Foyster and his wife Marianne from 1930 to 1935 (pp. 46-87), Tabori and Underwood make it clear that they believe that during that period the alleged phenomena "reached an extraordinary intensity and developed a considerable variety" (p. 46). They say that Mr. Foyster was not "the kind of man who could be hood-winked for five long years. His writing, too, suggests an honorable man and we see no reason to refuse acceptance of his testimony" (pp. 63–64). As Foyster, who was 20 years older than his wife, was willing to pose as her father to enable her to trick a man called Henry Francis Fisher into a bigamous marriage in a Roman Catholic church in 1935 (I have the certificate of this ceremony), we may have our doubts about the eulogy of the Rev. Foyster by Underwood and Tabori.

Reverting to my collaboration with Dr. Dingwall and Mrs. Goldney in publishing *The Haunting of Borley Rectory*, I was invited to write four of the eight chapters of the book. These were "II. Borley Rectory. Its Topography and Legends," "III. The Bull Incumbencies," "V. The Foyster Incumbency," and "VII. Later Borley". Of these, Chapter V was by far the most important and interesting. Price's files of correspondence had been handed over with his books to the University of London Library before his sudden and unexpected death in 1948 and were placed at our disposal by the then Goldsmiths' librarian, Dr. J. H. P. Pafford. From these and other sources I found that Price believed that Mrs. Foyster had produced the alleged phenomena during her husband's incumbency at Borley, in direct contradiction of his accounts in his two books, and had said so in letters to friends that were available for quotation. I decided that in fairness I must interview Mrs. Foyster if possible and, if she were willing, obtain a statement from her that I could quote in juxtaposition with the surprising evidence discovered in Price's papers.

My difficulty lay in the fact that after Foyster's death in April 1945, his widow seemed to have disappeared without trace. I was a serving officer until September of that year, and my first acquaintance with the alleged Essex haunting was in 1946, when I bought and read the newly published *End of Borley Rectory*. It was not until 1951 that I was invited to join in the Borley investigation, originally suggested by the Society for Psychical Research. I began the search for Marianne Foyster at the beginning of 1953, which was conducted mainly but not wholly in East Anglia. This inquiry, although resulting in an assembly of information that could justifiably be described as incredible had it not been supported throughout by official documentary evidence, ended in failure in 1955 when it finally became clear that the woman I was seeking had left England in 1946 and was living at an address, which I ultimately discovered, in America. She had persuaded an American GI that she had become pregnant by him during the last months of the Rev. Foyster's life, and in 1945, while the commercial traveler she had bigamously married was away on a long journey, she married her American lover. He went home with his battalion in due course, while Marianne, after adopting a baby of convenient age, managed to get through the transit camp and sailed for America as a "GI bride." Through American friends I ultimately obtained Marianne's address, and for some years have corresponded with her to enable my forthcoming book *Marianne Foyster of Borley Rectory*, now ready for publication, to be as accurate as possible.

After the publication in 1956 of *The Haunting of Borley Rectory* my interest in the life of Marianne continued. The use made in that book of the information I had obtained about her was limited to three footnotes on pages 88 and 89. These notes merely gave the date and place of her birth, the basic facts of her marriages to the Rev. L. A. Foyster and R. V. O——, her addresses in Suffolk after she left Borley in 1935, and the name by which she was generally known at that time, which was neither Foyster nor O——. In 1958, through the cooperation of the Parapsychology Foundation of New York, I was able to arrange for Marianne to be interviewed by a very able lawyer armed with a number of questions suggested by me that I hoped would clear up once and for all the matter of the supposed violent haunting of Borley Rectory during her sojourn there. "S," as I shall call the legal interrogator, not only recorded the questions and answers on tape, but also recorded privately his views of the sessions, not in the presence of Marianne. It was made quite clear from the report of S that Marianne would not have agreed to this interrogation if she had not been aware of the information I had already obtained about her.

I should explain that the Foysters were poverty-stricken during their period at Borley, owing to the very low stipend of the living, plus the fact that such private income as Foyster had inherited from his family had disappeared before he left St. John, New Brunswick, where he had been living for a year—out of work since he lost the living of Sackville—to take the living of Borley. Foyster's net income at Borley was £219 per annum, with a very large rectory to maintain. After his retirement in 1935, crippled by arthritis, his income was reduced to a pension of £125 per annum, plus £16 from rents. Foyster died on April 18, 1945, at Rendlesham, a hamlet in East Suffolk about four miles from Woodbridge, forever associated with Edward Fitzgerald. A plain stone marks his grave in the nearby village churchyard of Campsey Ash. His total estate at his death, left to Marianne, was £818-8-1d.

Lionel Foyster became acquainted by correspondence with my friend Sidney H. Glanville, a distinguished engineer who had been one of the observers who spent nights in the empty rectory after the departure of the Foysters, when Price rented the empty house for a year for £30. He prepared all the plans used in Price's two books on the case and compiled the famous Locked Book, *The Haunting of Borley Rectory. Private and Confidential Report*, consisting of 162 typed pages and many photographs. It is beautifully bound in three-quarter calf and fitted with a Braman lock. It bears Glanville's book-plate, but while it was on loan to Price the latter included it in a gift of books to the University of London Library. It was retrieved by Glanville, who most kindly presented it to me in July 1953, six months before his death from a heart condition. That he shared my views on Borley and Price is implicit in the inscription: "To Trevor with my kindest regards and appreciation of his help and encouragement at a time when the making of a re-statement of the history of Borley Rectory seemed to be beyond my capacity. Sidney."

Sidney told me that in 1937 he had naturally been most anxious to meet Marianne Foyster for the same reasons that had actuated me in 1953. As I had been, he was unsuccessful. Sidney was acquainted with the Rev. Foyster's brother, the late Arthur Henry Foyster of Pinner, Middlesex, and wrote to him with the object of finding where the Foysters were living, following the retirement of the former Rector of Borley two years previously. Arthur Foyster did not reveal the address but said that he would write to his brother to ask if he would care to communicate with Sidney Glanville. It was clearly a delicate situation, since Marianne was living at 102 Woodbridge Road East, Ipswich, with her partner in her bigamous marriage, Henry Francis Fisher, who had been tricked into believing that Lionel Foyster was her father, who was supporting her in this deception and was living with them.

Foyster wrote to Glanville, and the correspondence between the two men is preserved in the Locked Book and can be summarized:

1. Foyster insisted that he believed in the "phenomena" at Borley, although "not being psychic myself I never did see anything, though present with people who could." Mrs. Foyster was "very psychic."

2. Foyster wrote of Marianne and himself as if the household at Ipswich was an entirely normal one.

3. Foyster was most anxious to interest a publisher in a book he had written, *Fifteen Months in a Haunted House* (of which more anon) and sent the typescript to Glanville with this stated object in mind. Before returning it ("I am keeping it for the moment, pending your reply"), Glanville tried very hard to persuade Foyster to allow him to drive over to Ipswich to see him (and, more importantly, Marianne) but without success. "I am sorry it does not seem possible for us to meet, as letter-writing, at which I am a poor hand, does not allow for the expression and interchange of ideas which are essential if a subject of this sort is going to be properly examined." Foyster avoided this and other overtures in his replies, for obvious reasons.

4. Two sentences in Glanville's letter accompanying the return of the typescript to Foyster formed an interesting comment on the "observer period" of the Price tenancy. "I must say that it is the most astounding document I have ever read. Compared with my own experiences of a few mild taps, it is simply astounding" (*Locked Book*, p. 79). This can be compared with his letter to Price of December 6, 1937. "Dr. Bellamy, Roger and I went down to the Rectory on Friday evening, arriving about 7 o'clock. We left again about 10 o'clock on Saturday morning. During the whole period nothing whatever happened. We seem fated to draw blank days and nights."

A word should be said about Foyster's *Fifteen Months in a Haunted House*, which consists of 184 typescript pages, crudely bound in cloth. Pseudonyms are used throughout, but it is clearly a narrative based on the Borley "haunting" written by Foyster during the time when his arthritis made him more or less immobile, with the object of making some money, which was sorely needed, as we have seen. It is, however, of great interest for another reason. After the American interviews were over, and the tapes had been presented to me, I received a letter from the late Mrs. Eileen Garrett of the Parapsychology Foundation dated July 20, 1958, which reads in part:

> I suppose Borley was a game to her. A diversion, perhaps, and yet how did she hear of spritualism enough to practice it for the entertainment of all and sundry? I asked her this question but she denied that she knew anything about the subject, and despised mediums and all their works, not to mention psychical researchers. In fact, she was adamant that nothing happened at Borley that the various visitors and boys of the village were not responsible for.

There is some evidence to suggest that while Foyster was Rector of Sackville in New Brunswick from 1927 to 1929, or more likely when he was unemployed for a year before coming to Borley and living in St. John, New Brunswick, he and Marianne had read a book that described what was supposed to happen in a very much haunted house and would know that its publication had been extremely successful and profitable to its author. The first edition of Walter Hubbell's *The Haunted House: A True Ghost Story. Being an Account of the Mysterious Manifestations that have taken place in the presence of Esther Cox . . . The Great Amherst Mystery*, was marketed by a publisher in St. John, New Brunswick, in 1879. It was an account of a well-known (and fraudulent) case in which, as at Borley, messages were alleged to have appeared on the walls of a house in Amherst in the adjoining province of Nova Scotia. Other features of the Amherst haunting were (as with Marianne Foyster at Borley) that Esther claimed to see apparitions visible to nobody else and that mysterious voices were alleged to have been heard, which was the very first manifestation at Borley when the Foysters arrived. As at Borley during the Foyster incumbency, household objects were transported from place to place and sometimes temporarily lost, while another common feature of both affairs was the violent throwing of small objects and the upsetting of beds and other furniture. Other precise similarities with what was alleged to have occurred during the Foyster period at Borley included manifestations concerned with Esther's bed and bedclothes, together with small outbreaks of fire that were always extinguished before any damage was done.

Hubbell's book was remarkably successful, running into at least ten editions, with sales totaling over 50,000 copies, which was a remarkable feat in a thinly populated part of the world. It may be thought that the book would be very well known in St. John and in Sackville, the last two locations of the Foysters before their return to England and Borley. Esther Cox, indeed, used to visit her married sister in Sackville. If, as seems very possible, the Foysters had read one of the many editions of Hubbell's book in St. John or Sackville, this would explain two matters. One was the almost precisely similar pattern of the "phenomena" at Borley, and the other was a very considerable coincidence. In making up the names for the characters in his *Fifteen Months in a Haunted House*, Foyster gave the name "Mr. Teed" to one of the leading members of the group of spiritualists who visited "Cromley Hall" to investigate the haunting. That Teed is an uncommon name can be confirmed by a glance at an English telephone directory. It was, however, the name of Esther Cox's sister and brother-in-law, who occupied a central position in Walter Hubbell's *The Haunted House: A True Ghost Story*, since it was in the Teeds' house in Amherst, where Esther lived, that the manifestations occurred.

Earlier in this essay, I have explained how Marianne was questioned in America by a lawyer who was armed with the results of my long inquiry into her extraordinary life in England, which were not included in the book published in January 1956. The questions and answers were recorded on tape, now in my possession, and I have chosen a number for reproduction in this account—using "S" and "M" to represent the interrogator and Marianne—which throw a flood of light on the alleged haunting of Borley Rectory. The location of the two hotels (the second in New York) where Marianne was questioned is given, together with the identification of the private reports made by "S" not in the presence of Marianne. The reader will need to know that the man referred to as François d'Arles, whose real name was Frank Pearless and who is now dead, became the tenant of the cottage at Borley Rectory (the rent was no doubt welcome to the Rev. Foyster) but spent much time in the Rectory. A reference to his intimacy with Marianne is essential to the story.

> S. How soon after d'Arles arrived at Borley did you have sexual relations with him?
>
> M. D'Arles brought his son down one Saturday leaving him there. He didn't return for about a month or six weeks. I am not positive about the time. I think it was several weeks before we had sex relations.
>
> S. You felt that you liked him when he first arrived?
>
> M. Not particularly. [*Gladstone Hotel*, 1958]
>
> S. This afternoon you told me that Lionel prepared a manuscript concerning the haunting of Borley Rectory which was strictly to be a mystery story—a fictional and not a true story. Is that correct?
>
> M. Yes. When he first became ill and in order to amuse himself, he made up mystery stories. He decided to write one based on Borley. I knew it was a fictional story.

S. According to your conversations with Lionel concerning the manuscript, would you say that he made up certain stories in order for the book to be attractive to the reading public?

M. Very definitely, because the happenings at Borley were Halloweenish and silly, and there would be nothing attractive to the reading public. They just wouldn't buy it. [*Gladstone Hotel*, 1958]

S. Now, in Price's *MHH*, p. 79, "Leaves from the Foyster Diary" it states: "March 28, 1931. Marianne sees a monstrosity (seen by her on other occasions) near kitchen door. It touches her shoulder with an iron-like touch." What have you to say to that?

M. I don't recall any such incident at all. The only time I ever recall anything around the house was Guy Fawkes night, kids coming around and I know that would not be in the interior passage. I may have been startled and squealed because I came on these kids on Guy Fawkes night, but I knew immediately that they were just children. I don't know whether Lionel dramatised that incident or not. [*Governor Clinton Hotel*, 1958]

Foyster himself recorded repeatedly that although his wife was "very psychic" he himself was not, and therefore he did not share her experiences of seeing apparitions in the Rectory. According to Foyster's written account, however, d'Arles had independent experiences that confirmed Marianne's stories. On three occasions he saw a figure in one of the bedrooms, and after the last of these encounters he appeared at the breakfast table with a black eye. He alleged that this had been inflicted upon him by a phantom with whom he had endeavored bravely but unsuccessfully to grapple. No first-hand account of these remarkable experiences is available, but Marianne had an explanation that at this stage omitted d'Arles's black eye, inflicted by herself:

Marianne said that d'Arles was always snooping about the Rectory and playing ghosts. She said that Lionel was a sick man while they were at Borley; the blood in his body did not go to his brain properly causing loss of memory. Lionel would start talking about one subject, and then suddenly talk about something else. D'Arles took advantage of Lionel's condition by leaving articles or hiding them from Lionel, and then saying that the ghosts were at it again. D'Arles used to say that he had seen monstrous apparitions in the Rectory, which he admitted to her he had never seen at all. Marianne said that she positively knew that d'Arles was playing ghosts with Lionel. If Lionel mislaid things about the house through loss of memory, d'Arles would say that the ghosts had taken them away. Marianne said that d'Arles loved to be cruel to Lionel in this way. Lionel would believe him and tell Marianne about it." [S— Report, 1958]

Marianne's general explanation of the phenomena at Borley, the subject of a taped report by S, was that it was a mixture of natural causes, major and minor trickery (always by others), and the dishonest writings of Price:

> Marianne told S. that she had not read the books written by Price on Borley Rectory. She said that she had been advised by friends in England not to read them, as they were full of lies and would make her unhappy. Marianne said that she does not believe in ghosts, and that Borley was not haunted when she was living there. The Rectory was in bad condition and draughty, so that if there was a wind outside it came through the house causing ghostly noises. Marianne said that the village boys were often in the remoter parts of the Rectory unknown to Lionel and herself, so that their noises and visits were often mistaken for ghosts. Marianne said that the Rectory had a reputation as a haunted house before she and Lionel moved into it. The village boys would throw stones at the "haunted house" as they passed. She said that the old boards and doors creaked in the Rectory, and that if one was quiet for a short period one could imagine anything from the various creaks heard, or the running of rats and the flying of bats in the house.
>
> Marianne said that at times tramps sought shelter in the Rectory simply by walking through the back doors and occupying one of the unused rooms. She said that she would often see one of these men walking away from the house in the morning. Marianne said that the small fires that sometimes occurred in the Rectory were probably started by tramps trying to keep warm, or by the village boys who were always playing around the house. She said that d'Arles and Price were very close and that d'Arles played ghosts in the Rectory for Price. Price depicted false occurrences at Borley simply to write a sensational book. Marianne said that she never saw any apparitions at Borley, or anywhere else.
> [S— Report, 1958]

Marianne's statement in regard to the presence in the house of bats and rats has confirmation from the wife of the Rev. G. Eric Smith, who preceded Lionel Foyster as Rector of Borley but had to leave as a result of the discomfiture caused by the publicity in the *Daily Mirror* precipitated by Price's first visit to Borley in 1929. Mrs. Smith made a statement she allowed us to print in *The Haunting of Borley Rectory*:

> Admittedly we had a terrible experience at Borley, but not from haunts or poltergeist phenomena, but from the publicity which brought hordes of sightseers who trampled down our lawn and flower-beds, broke our windows, and so disturbed our peace that we had to get police to disperse them. Ghosts would never have frightened us, as we believed in Higher Protection. I have gone upstairs in the dark at Borley and watched in the supposed haunted room and looked from the windows: the result has always been "NIL"—only bats and the scratching of rats.

On the other hand, there is the curious story of Ian Greenwood in regard to the bell-ringing. Greenwood approached the authors of *HBR* shortly after its publication, and I entertained him at the Waldorf Hotel in London to hear his story. He was Marianne's son by a man named Harold Giffard Greenwood. They were legally married in Ireland in 1914, when Marianne was 15, in order to regularize the situation, but Greenwood disappeared in a matter of months after the marriage. His death was not recorded in Great Britain or Ireland, and it was thought that he had gone to Australia or New Zealand. No divorce had taken place. The baby was brought up by Marianne's parents and passed off as Marianne's brother when she went out to New Brunswick in 1922 to marry Foyster, who paid for the child's education.

Greenwood told me that he rang the Borley house-bells himself by accident while staying at Borley with his "sister" and her husband early in 1933. Marianne had sent him into the courtyard to fetch coal and pump water. It was raining and blowing at the time, and he was wearing an old raincoat without buttons, which he could not keep closed in the wind. He saw a piece of string half hidden in the ivy in the corner of the yard and thought this would be useful to tie his coat around him. He gave the string a sharp tug to break it from the nail upon which he thought it hung. To his astonishment the bells in the kitchen passage rang furiously, and he rushed into the Rectory shouting that he had found the ghost. Marianne came out from her room and told him to keep quiet. She called out to Foyster that Greenwood was having a joke by trying to frighten them all. According to Greenwood, the string was tied to a group of exposed bell wires in the floor of the landing between the upper rooms of the disused wing and the kitchen passage.

> S. Concerning the phenomena at Borley, Greenwood found a string which he pulled and the bells started ringing. He rushed to you to tell you about it and you said "Oh, shut up," indicating not to say anything about it. How do you explain this?

> M. I can't explain it except that Greenwood did find a string, but so did I and other people. The wires were bent and pulled down. As far as Greenwood saying that I instructed him not to say anything about it—I just said "Oh, shut up"—well, I didn't mean anything by it. [*Gladstone Hotel,* 1958].

Greenwood said that Foyster believed in the Borley ghosts. According to Greenwood it was d'Arles who finally told Marianne that the deception was getting out of hand and must stop. D'Arles said to Greenwood cynically that the spiritualistic group who were coming to Borley to hold a séance and cleanse the house of spirits (and thus provide a convenient explanation for the cessation of the supposed phenomena) would "take the poltergeist away in a paper bag."

The reader of these stories of the fantastic events that were taking place behind the scenes during Mr. Foyster's tenancy of "the most haunted house in England" may well reach the conclusion that the whole of the alleged phenomena can be attributed partly to natural causes or to fraud and lying, partly to cover-up for other nocturnal activities, and partly, perhaps, simply to an attempt to alleviate boredom.

In conclusion, it is interesting to record Marianne's extreme dislike of the late Harry Price, revealed during her questioning in America, despite the fact that he had been dead since 1948 and that she had only met him on a single occasion. On May 12, 1958, at the Governor Clinton Hotel in New York, she recorded on tape: "I wished to have nothing to do with Harry Price. The only living person that I can ask to bear this out is Mr. Foyster's sister, who knew how greatly I dislike Harry Price, and would have nothing to do with him."

The tape of an earlier interview with her at the Gladstone Hotel, Jamestown, on February 28, 1958, included the following: "Mr. Price was a magician and a member of the Magicians' Society. At one time he conducted an experiment on a black mountain, trying to turn a goat into a man. He indulged in all these kinds of public stunts. Anyway, he thought he was going to make a lot of money out of Borley."

The late Mrs. Eileen Garrett wrote to me on March 25, 1958: "The mention of Price's name is almost too much for her. She regards him as a faker, and one who would readily have produced the effects for his own purpose."

At the close of the American interviews, Marianne prepared a signed statement about Harry Price in her own hand, which Mrs. Garrett sent to me with the tapes: "At my stay at Borley Rectory I became acquainted with Harry Price, the head of a psychical research society. He was a man who blew hot and cold—he said sometimes he believed in a future state, and sometimes that death ended all, and that he could prove both points. He obtained by fraud and false pretence the manuscript written by the Rev. Foyster. He said that he only wanted to read it. He said that he would never show it, use it or print it. He broke his word. He told me he had lost it. He was not an honourable man."

On page 83 of *The Haunting of Borley Rectory*, in my chapter on "The Foyster Incumbency," I recorded that Price wrote to Dr. E. J. Dingwall, whose friend he had been since 1920, in a letter dated October 17, 1946, "I have now acquired Foyster's complete *Fifteen Months in a Haunted House*." Poor Foyster's laboriously typed book of 184 pages was included in Price's library when it was transferred to the University of London. I am happy to say that when I produced the correspondence, the Goldsmiths' Librarian agreed that it belonged to Foyster's widow and released it.

14

The Role of Conjurers in Psi Research

JAMES RANDI

Science-fiction author Lester Del Rey is accustomed to declaring authoritatively on every subject from oenology to onomancy. He has been so bold as to have his business card imprinted with the single modifier "Expert." And I suspect he can support that claim upon demand.

We all have need of expert advice and assistance in our daily lives, on both a personal and a professional level. As highly trained and experienced as he is, I have known my dentist to step to the telephone and ask a distant colleague about some aspect of his craft—while I recline in his chair with a mouth full of tubes, cotton wads, and assorted bits of hardware. But I respect his need and his wisdom in reaching out for help in order to function more efficiently.

Consider: I doubt that many readers recognized the words *oenology* and *onomancy*, which I used above. To resolve that small problem, you can turn to a dictionary. You need not feel like a simpleton in order to do so. Very well educated and intelligent people have quite thick, comprehensive, and well-thumbed dictionaries available to them. Such reference tools—and the recognition that they are necessary—enable us to live and work effectively.

A little boy once went to the public library and asked the librarian for a book about penguins. He was given a book, took it away with him, and returned the next day. The librarian asked him if it had served his purpose. "This book," said the boy, "taught me more about penguins than I needed to know." Obviously, there is a need for discrimination in seeking out and accepting expertise. One need not know the life history of Henry Ford in order to adjust an Edsel carburetor. But without reference to the appropriate manual such an adjustment becomes hit or miss where it could be a straightforward procedure.

Parapsychologists are very much in need of a certain type of expert help. Involved in tests for ESP, precognition, psychokinesis, and other unlikely—but not impossible—abilities, they are frequently faced with human subjects who are sometimes able to deceive them by bypassing controls and outwitting understandably inexperienced and inexpert observers. The field is chock full of examples of this problem, and it is still an active factor in paranormal research.

In the 1920s, when Dr. Joseph Banks Rhine introduced a statistical approach to the very new study of parapsychology, orthodox scientists were able at least to express their willingness to consider the paranormalists' claims. But the dramatic impact of such conjurers as the now-faded psychic nova Uri Geller was far too tempting for incautious parapsychologists and bumbling amateurs. They saw Nobel prizes in the breakthroughs revealed by one individual exhibiting marvelous supernatural abilities, and they abandoned the statistical, systematic methods introduced by Rhine. High-profile members of the parapsychological elite began agitating for a return to the study of "gifted subjects" and set the entire movement back decades.

By now, even Rhine's work was beginning to lose its former luster. Critics were able to show that his findings were somewhat less than compelling and that his protocols had not only been bypassed but had been insufficiently developed to guard against a number of now-obvious pitfalls. But his basic premise—that a statistical approach was the only valid one—is still widely accepted among responsible parapsychologists.

(Recent work at Princeton University is strongly oriented in this direction, and if these findings can withstand the close examination of skeptics, can be replicated by neutral experimenters, and are not the result of some artifact of the protocol—intentional or otherwise—ESP may at last have been established as a fact. But it would be well to hold back on the fanfare; very attractive new proofs often have a way of suddenly collapsing.)

In 1978, I set in motion an experiment that I named "Project Alpha." For years I had been urging parapsychologists to recognize that the expert advice of a qualified conjurer is an absolutely necessary part of designing an experiment in which there is a possibility of deliberate trickery on the part of either the subject or the experimenter. This message had been ignored. Several researchers had firmly declared that (to quote one of them) "magicians must not be put in charge of experiments!" Of course I had not suggested that at all, because I firmly believe that a conjurer's participation in any scientific endeavor must be limited to his narrow—but important—spectrum of expertise.

At that time, I had in my files letters from two young would-be conjurers who had expressed their availability should a situation arise in which I might demonstrate that scientists can be easily deceived. When an Associated Press news release announced that a physics professor/parapsychologist at Washington University in St. Louis, Missouri, had been given $500,000 to study "spoon-bending children," I realized that the ideal opportunity had arrived.

First I wrote to the parapsychologist to advise him that I was available to him for consultation on any experimental design or implementation, free of any obligation of payment or acknowledgment. I was informed, in effect, that he could manage quite well without a conjurer. I then set out to prove him wrong.

The two boys—17 and 18 years old at the time—contacted the "spoon-bending" laboratory in St. Louis and provided stories to fit the expectations of the scientists there. Parapsychologists prefer to believe that "gifted subjects" become psychic when exposed to trauma of some sort. Each "mole" said he had received an electric shock (one while still *in utero!*) after which his psychic powers became evident. They were accepted into the lab and tested for a total of 160 hours over the next three-and-a-half years on week-ends and during school holidays.

Fooling the scientists proved very easy. Using as a guide the general tactics employed by Uri Geller when he was tested by scientists, both Alpha subjects produced "spirit" photos on Polaroid film; bent spoons, keys, and coat-hangers; turned tiny propellers inside bell-jars; moved objects around on a table; traced cryptic messages in ground coffee sealed in an upturned fish tank; caused ghostly inscriptions to appear on paper sealed in glass jars; and in general convinced the researchers that they were bundles of psychic energy. They did it by bullying the experimenters into doing things their way or not at all. The mice were running the experiments.

When the Washington University staff initially reported to their colleagues on this remarkable series of miracles, they wrote that many varieties of psychokinetic results had been obtained in their lab. They even presented a slide show and a videotape to prove their case. But when I was at last allowed to participate by showing a videotape of admittedly faked psychic trickery—some of which had been used by the Alpha subjects in the Washington University tape—the written report was hastily recalled and modifiers like "purportedly" and "apparent" were inserted in the formerly naive account.

Most important, following my initial participation, I was able to demonstrate to these researchers certain weaknesses in their control techniques. At this late date, they implemented my recommendations and the Alpha boys were no longer able to fool them. The experiments ceased.

Finally, we terminated our experiment by exposing the ruse, and Looking-Glass Land was in a turmoil. After things settled down, the official organization of psychic researchers, the Parapsychological Association (PA), issued an advisory to its members stating that, in cases where subjects might be able to affect test results by some sort of subterfuge, the use of an experienced conjurer as an advisor would be a wise move. Almost immediately, two prominent parapsychologists contacted me, and I suggested adequate protocol for an upcoming experiment. A few weeks later, they reported that this amendment to their protocol had resulted in exposure of a psychic faker in one lab. Project Alpha had paid off, and continues to do so.

My Alpha experiment was remarkably well received by the PA members. It had consisted of planting two "moles" in an exceedingly well-funded parapsychology lab to see if the researchers were really as naive as they seemed. They were. As a result, we can hope that future experiments will be better controlled.

Now it must be recognized that not all involvement of magicians in parapsychology has proven useful; there have been minor disasters in this regard. Wide-eyed psientists in Europe have in several cases called in amateur (and professional) conjurers to witness "psychics" at work, only to hear from their "experts" that the phenomena exhibited are genuine—when other magicians saw quite obvious and well-established trade methods being employed.

What, then, is the definition of a "qualified conjurer"? Since conjuring is essentially (of necessity) a "closed" profession, it is not readily obvious to observers what criteria should be sought in an advisor. First, let us define our terms. A "magician" is one who performs "magic." My preferred definition of "magic" is: "Using spells and incantations to control the forces of Nature." Let me assure you that all the spelling and incanting you can muster will not find a chosen card in a deck, nor will it materialize a bunny in an empty hat. For those ends, we employ chicanery and allied methods. The dictionary tells us that the correct term for my profession is *conjuring*. Properly, then, I am a conjurer, "One who uses trickery to simulate magic."

As a professional conjurer for many decades, I can tell you that there are three general classes of persons associated with my calling. They are: (1) amateur conjurers, (2) people who do tricks very, very well, and (3) master conjurers.

The first group, to me, are welcome colleagues so long as they remain aware of the meaning of the word *amateur*. It derives from the French and means, in this connection, "one who loves conjuring." But, with rare exceptions, I would not consider amateurs as suitable advisors in parapsychological matters. One faulty conception they have is that their duplication of a "psychic" trick proves that the faker used the same means. Of course it does not. It merely demonstrates that such a trick is easily done. That fact is of limited value.

Admittedly, the second category includes some of the very finest, most convincing and entertaining performers. Most are full-time artists and make up the largest proportion of what the public recognizes as professional magicians. Their repertoires, however, are often strictly limited to the requirements of their performances. They have what the trade calls "an act." It is usually a finely honed and highly professional presentation. But the artist, in many cases, does not go beneath the surface to understand the psychology or even the sometimes esoteric technology of the art—nor is such knowledge needed. Such an artist performs by instinct, learned from long experience. Does a virtuoso violinist need to design or construct violins?

I must make one further comment to prepare you for my eventual point. My students are always taught one important fact: Audiences do not go to see "the tricks," though they may have that initial intention. They go to see "the person." It is the Wizard, the Magician, the Personality that they enjoy. And that conjurer performs a trick. To continue my analogy, I go to see and hear Itzhak Perlman playing the Mendelssohn Violin Concerto, Opus 64; I do not go primarily to see and hear Mendelssohn's Concerto.

The third class I have designated above—the Master Conjurers—are such persons as Dai Vernon, Charles Reynolds, Jay Marshall, Fr. Cyprian, Mel Stover, and a host of others who you may never have heard of but who not only can perform (in some cases, with such diabolical dexterity that it makes my eyes water with jealousy!) but also understand thoroughly the nuances of the art, down to the almost subliminal perception of the movement of a spectator's eye. But they are aware of their perception; it is not merely an instinctive reaction. They, and they alone, are qualified to serve as advisors to responsible parapsychologists who earnestly wish to impose strict controls over their subjects. I am proud to know that many of those in my profession include me with Conjurers of the Third Kind.

Mind you, I have found that many parapsychologists seem to believe that a positive result obtained under loose conditions is vastly preferable to a negative one resulting from proper controls. The scientific method calls for the gathering of evidence, the examination of that evidence, the formulation of a theory to explain it, and the testing of that theory. It does not permit the gathering of evidence to prove a favorite idea.

The three general classes of conjurers I have specified above are, of course, not necessarily distinct from one another. Harry Blackstone, Jr., for example, is most certainly a paramount name in my profession. He is, as the son of one of the greatest performers who ever lived, highly knowledgeable and thus belongs in both latter classes. Charles Reynolds, with his encyclopedic expertise in conjuring, belongs there too—but from the opposite direction; he does not perform professionally. Reynolds advises and designs for leading pros in the trade.

Unfortunately, though for reasons that are obvious to astute observers, the PA specified in their directive that consultant conjurers must be chosen from among members of certain fraternal organizations in the United States that claim the vast majority of their members from the first class of conjurers I have designated. Since, at that time, I did not—by choice—belong to those organizations, it was felt that I thus would be excluded from consideration by any serious investigators. However, as reported above, two prominent parapsychologists had asked for my assistance. Then, within two weeks, three more applied. It is encouraging to see that some parapsychologists are responding to the suggestion that they may need expert assistance. There are at present some notable researchers who have ignored the PA advisory and believe they are simply too smart to be deceived. This is a dangerous philosophy. Such thinking leads to many spurious sales of the Brooklyn Bridge every year.

There is, however, a form of deception against which the combined talents of scientists and conjurers may be powerless. It is self-deception. Benjamin Franklin remarked, "There are no worse liars than quacks—except for their patients." Substitute "frauds" for "quacks" and "victims" for "patients" and you will see my point. The victims of so-called psychics are prone to lie or waffle about the miracles they have seen, often believing what they say either because they have reconstructed the events incorrectly or because they feel that a little gloss cannot hurt the story of their experimental results. In either case, they are fooling themselves. This tendency can go to extreme lengths. In a recent best-selling book, two parascientists (one was a member of the Stanford Research Institute [SRI] team who was fooled by Geller, and the other believes that he himself has magic powers) said that Martin Gardner, a "well-known critic" of parapsychology, was "motivated mainly by [his] own private fear of the unknown." Concerning some very damning evidence against the SRI researchers that Gardner had reported, they said that he had admitted that "he had just made it up." The evidence in question involves data tapes. The SRI scientists offered to validate some 1974 research with an "ESP teaching machine." Gardner discovered that they had torn apart the data tapes and kept the successful ones in order to prove the case. The "ESP teaching machine" actually taught that no ESP was present. Yet it is not at all impossible that these authors have fooled themselves into believing that there was no deception in that experiment.

This tendency to self-deception is pervasive. For example, one dupe of Project Alpha continues to believe that those "moles" performed genuine miracles, even after their detailed confessions. There is no protection against such masochism.

The recent and continuing preoccupation with parapsychology of certain scientists and the public was given strong impetus in the early 1970s when the conjurer from Israel named Uri Geller arrived at SRI (now known as Stanford Research International) in Palo Alto, California, to dazzle researchers there with some basic and well-used standards of his profession, as well as show them a few new wrinkles that even experienced conjurers like myself had never seen before. His new routines were of such a nature that they could not stand by themselves as entertainment but were remarkably effective when presented as genuine phenomena.

To illustrate that last point: One of the basic tricks for the card manipulator has always been the find-the-chosen-card effect. In essence, a spectator selects a card (by physically drawing it from the pack, mentally choosing it, naming one at random, or by other means) and it is discovered by the conjurer (by being named, physically located, found in a pocket, etc.). The process is generally recognized as a conjuring trick, especially if the performer is dressed in a tuxedo and is known as "The Great Balsamo" or another euphonious title. However, it is evident that if someone who does not claim any manipulatory skill were to be able to perform the find-the-chosen-card effect without resorting to trickery, it would upset every notion of the universe as we know it.

But suppose that person were only able to demonstrate an ability to divine—with a degree of statistical significance—the color (red or black) of a playing card. As entertainment, that routine is a loser; as a laboratory project, it's a big winner. The Geller spoon- and key-bending tricks were of that nature. Unless you believe they are genuine examples of supernatural powers, they are pretty poor theater. Geller was able, in his heyday, to draw huge crowds of people who would never have paid to see the Great Balsamo bend a spoon but who trampled one another to witness Geller doing it. And some scientists were drawn into that net as well.

When this ex-fashion-model-turned-conjurer arrived at SRI to begin what turned out to be one of the greatest deceptions of science ever to be carried out, he found a minor hurdle in his way. An amateur magician, who in spite of his exposure to methods of deception believed—and still believes—in paranormal powers, was asked by the SRI scientists to design a foolproof procedure for testing Geller. He gave them what he believed to be a suitable protocol. Geller immediately rejected it and demanded that the conjurer be excluded from the experimentation entirely. This is the mice-running-the-experiment procedure that we saw was used by the Alpha subjects when they were emulating Geller. We will never know how effective the amateur's precautions might have been, for he now refuses to discuss the matter.

Amid a welter of hamburger wrappers, spilled soft drinks, cigarette butts, and other debris, the SRI researchers worked through weekends when their lab facilities were otherwise unused. What should have been tightly controlled and monitored experiments ended up as disconnected, informal examples of demonstrations done at the whim of the performer. Yet a film was produced by SRI that purported to document their research, and it was shown to a rapt audience at Columbia University in New York City. At that moment, Geller's reputation was established. He has never tired of reminding detractors that he was tested and proven at SRI, and when *Nature* magazine—a prominent and respected British scientific journal—featured a report by SRI on the Geller wonders, it was taken as official scientific validation of the SRI findings. Few readers of that account noticed the cautious *Nature* editorial that prefaced the article, saying essentially that the article had not met their standards and that the referees were not at all satisfied with it, but that it was printed so that readers could judge for themselves the quality of research being carried on in parapsychology.

Geller performed all manner of standard tricks for the SRI people. His spoon-bending was so unconvincing that even the commentary accompanying the film told viewers that they had not been able to establish that this part of Geller's act was genuine. But they included it. Why? We'll never know. But it seems safe to assume that they had to bolster a very weak case.

There is an episode at the very beginning of that film that would give any observant conjurer a fit of giggles. In that sequence, where the two SRI researchers are shown beaming at the Israeli psychic's act, the inexperienced observer will see Geller write something (not shown) on a pad of paper. Geller then asks the SRI publicity director to "think of a number" and to write it on his own pad. Crossing the room, Geller then shows that he has written the very same number! This is a perfectly standard, recognized routine of the conjuring trade. As seen by the layman—and, obviously, by these scientists—it becomes a miracle that is impossible to explain by anything short of paranormal powers. As seen by the conjurer, it is quite well understood as a trick.

Later in that same film, SRI portrayed Geller doing a demonstration with a steel file-card box that concealed a single six-sided die. Though Russell Targ said that "at no time did Geller touch the box," we now know that not only did he touch it but he also was the one who shook it to randomize the die, he actually held it in his hands while "concentrating" to see which side of the die was uppermost; and, on at least one occasion, he himself was the one who opened the box and announced the upper face! These "experiments" appear to have been filmed consecutively, but they were not. They were performed over a period of several days, when Geller "felt" like doing them. As with much of the work shown in the film and reported by SRI, we can never know what really took place in the free-for-all that Geller put on for the two rather naive scientists.

Now, can we say that those who reported these results were actually lying? No, I don't think so, not from my point of view as a magician. Rather, the experimenters were merely showing that they were out of their depth when confronted with a shark, which Uri Geller proved to be. Unreported facts and distortions of those that are reported are commonly encountered when laymen describe a conjurer's performance. Seeing a magician pluck a rabbit from a hat, would you know enough to observe whether he paused to roll up his sleeves before or after the hat was shown to be empty? Failure to know that and to report it makes your account incomplete—and you have no reason to know that such an observation is absolutely essential to a solution of the modus operandi. Did the magician return his handkerchief to his inner pocket after wiping out the inside of the hat—or did he even wipe out the hat? You don't know, and there is no reason that you should know, or that you should report it. But—and this is most important—*you presume far beyond your expertise when you later declare confidently that you observed and reported every detail correctly.* Worse, you can justifiably be labeled a bare-faced liar if and when you reconstruct your memories of the event to fit the needs of your conclusions.

Geller's performances on television—out of the laboratory—are transparent hoaxes. The "moment of truth" occurs either while the commercial announcement is on the screen or while the camera is busy elsewhere. On rare occasions, the camera captures the "move"—which simply cannot be seen by the layman unless he is informed of what to look for and when to look. When Geller appeared on the Johnny Carson show, I was consulted before the program, and gave them instructions on how to control the conditions so that only a *real* wizard could perform. The result was 20 minutes of Geller's fussing about and making excuses peppered with comments on his nervousness at being on such a prestigious program. I believe that Geller was nervous, but for quite a different reason. Absolutely nothing happened. But the Carson show was determined that, if Geller used trickery, he would be unable to do so on their program. As Johnny Carson himself has said, anyone is welcome to appear there as a performer, but if he or she professes genuine powers they must be proved under proper conditions. On more than one occasion, magicians have attempted to fool Carson and have failed, only to be revealed as tricksters. Johnny Carson shares my total delight with an honest performance of conjuring, and he presents such prodigious performers as Lance Burton with great enthusiasm. But he will not be a party to flim-flam, and he earns my total respect for that. I wish that other television hosts shared that with him.

Though television has provided Uri Geller with some very bad moments, in personal appearances he is even more vulnerable. In Madison, Wisconsin, he was scheduled to appear before a convention of well-seasoned and gullible believers who were there to be dazzled by my Alpha subjects as well. I had sent in my check to register for this great event, but it was refused. Undaunted, I dyed my beard, donned a red wig from Woolworth's and dark contact lenses, slipped in grotesque false teeth to fit over my own, and attended as "Adam Jersin, documentary film maker, auragrammist, dowser, and researcher." My registration was accepted under that name, and in that get-up I sat in the front row and saw Geller and my Alpha boys perform on stage. Geller made little attempt to cover his moves, and the trickery was very evident to us. In fact, the Alpha boys were startled to see just how bold Geller was. He seemed to be showing his disdain for those assembled by blatantly bending spoons with both hands, right before their eyes, without much effort to conceal the process. It was a bizarre experience indeed.

But Geller saw to it that a team from BBC-TV that was there to capture metal-bending on film, missed doing so. They ran out of film seconds before the "move" was made. I must mention that this group had previously asked me to design a protocol that would effectively control against cheating in two kinds of metal-bending experiments they proposed to do. One kind was the "sealed-sample" type in which the metal object has been enclosed securely in such a manner that it cannot be tampered with. The other is the "open-sample" type where the metal object is available for handling by the performer. Provided with my system, they tested Masuaki Kiyota, a highly-touted Japanese trickster, and my two Alpha boys—who were not told by me that they were going to be subjected to such a test. All of them failed, because the protocol was firmly applied by the BBC-TV team. But, as I had predicted, Geller refused to allow them to tell him how he was to do the tests. (After all, he had always had his way, and he expected to continue that way!) He bamboozled them by managing to keep his moves from the cameras.

Though the TV folks had failed to get around Geller, I was more successful. That night I managed to obtain Uri's autograph in a book and had my photo taken with him. The great psychic failed to recognize his nemesis. This is just another of those strange facets of psychic forces that we may never understand.

Had the SRI scientists, as well as the many other professional and amateur observers of Uri Geller, followed proper procedure by calling in appropriate advisors, much waste of money and time, and needless embarrassment, might have been avoided. But they chose to make the same error that many of their colleagues—in other fields of science, as well—have made. They said: (1) I am intelligent. (2) I am well-educated. (3) I am a good observer. Therefore: Anything I see and do not understand is supernatural.

Wrong. What they regard as supernatural may very well be the result of using those three facts against them. This is in accord with the very basics employed by the conjurer to deceive his audience. The smarter they think they are, the harder they fall. Children, as has often been said, are very difficult for the conjurer to fool. They simply lack the sophistication of adults, and they are therefore not prepared to presume the simple, basic facts that we must presume every day. Their experience of the world is not sufficient for them to be fooled! The conjurer can casually drop a cardboard box upon a chair and, because it sounds empty, he need not show that it is empty—for the adult audience. The child, not yet familiar with the sound of an empty box in contrast to the sound of a box containing something, needs to be shown. It is also a fact that the audience, subconsciously assuming the box to be empty, is more convinced of that fact than if they had been directly *shown* that it was empty. Adults tend to believe what they are allowed to assume for themselves, much more than what is specifically pointed out to them. ("Methinks he doth protest too much . . .")

I recall that, when I was a child in Canada, a certain company who made baking powder adopted a rather clever ruse to degrade the competition. They announced, "Our product is made without the use of alum!" and they immediately won over my mother as a customer. When I asked her if the other manufacturers put alum in their baking powder, she was a bit puzzled by my question. She had merely made an unconscious assumption that they did. This very gambit is well known to conjurers—and to "psychics" as well. One popular American "mentalist" is heard to declare, "Why, if I wanted to, I could perform *all* of these demonstrations by trickery!" And the audience jumps into the trap by assuming that at least some of the items are *not* performed by trickery. Wrong.

A parapsychologist, by my definition, is one who, seated in the park near a riding academy and hearing hoofbeats approaching, expects a unicorn to round the corner. He is surprised and disappointed when he sees a horse come into view. No matter how well motivated, these researchers cannot afford to entertain such expectations. They must follow the rather unglamorous procedures their colleagues in other disciplines insist upon. Otherwise, their complaints about a lack of acceptance by their peers cannot be heard.

Expert advice and involvement is available to serious researchers in the field of paranormal research. They would do well to take advantage of it; if they do not, they may find themselves in the company of the rather large number of academics who have learned, too late, of their own vulnerability.

15

Magicians in the Psi Lab: Many Misconceptions

MARTIN GARDNER

Harry Collins, a University of Bath sociologist, is best known for his extreme relativistic philosophy of science and for having caught a group of spoon-bending children at cheating. The *New Scientist* (June 30, 1983) printed his "Magicians in the Laboratory: A New Role to Play," in which he discusses what he calls the "vexed relationship" between magicians and psi researchers. His article contains many misconceptions about magic; but, before detailing them, first a sketch of his views.

James Randi's recent Project Alpha, Collins writes, has reminded us again of how easily psi researchers can be hoodwinked. Because the history of para-normal research has been riddled with fraud, Collins wisely recommends that, no matter how innocent a subject may appear, experiments must be designed on the assumption that the subject is "a notorious cheat." Unfortunately, he adds, completely fraud-proof tests are impossible because there is no way to anticipate new methods of cheating. Since magicians know standard ways, they can be enormously useful as advisors. But because they are not much better than nonmagicians in spotting new methods they are of little value as observers.

He feels that magicians should not be allowed to monitor experiments because they are usually unfriendly toward psi research and have a vested interest in seeing psychics discredited. Collins doesn't mention the belief of most parapsychologists that hostile observers inhibit psi phenomena, but even aside from this he thinks magicians would have a damaging effect on experiments if they were allowed to monitor them.

How, then, can conjurers help? One way, Collins says, is by breaking their code of secrecy and explaining to reserchers how cheating can be done. If magicians are unwilling to do this, they should serve as "protocol breakers," by demonstrating the same paranormal phenomena under the same controls applied to the psychic. If they fail to break the protocol, this "would act as a certificate

Reprinted from the *Skeptical Inquirer*, vol. 8, no. 2, Winter 1983-84, pp. 111-116, with permission.

of competence in experimental design."

Misconception 1: Collins fails to distinguish stage performers from magicians who specialize in close-up magic. Throughout his article he repeatedly refers to "stage magicians" and "illusionists." The distinction is vital, because the methods used by psychic charlatans have almost nothing in common with stage magic. Although psychics like Uri Geller and Nina Kulagina may use a few concealed "gimmicks" (magnets, "invisible" thread, nail writers, palmed mirrors, and so on), for the most part they perform close-up magic that requires no apparatus.

Some stage magicians are knowledgeable about close-up magic, but not necessarily so. A stage performer is essentially an actor playing the role of a magician, relying for his miracles on costly equipment designed by others. Any good actor could easily take over Doug Henning's role in the Broadway musical *Merlin,* for example, and the stage illusions would work just as well. It is important for psi researchers to know this. Otherwise they might seek the help of a prominent stage performer who has less knowledge of close-up magic than thousands of amateurs.

Misconception 2: Collins is persuaded that magicians are not much better than scientists in spotting new ways to cheat. He concedes that "skilled practitioners of deception" may be better than scientists in seeing loopholes develop in an experiment, but he adds, "I think it would be hard to demonstrate this."

On the contrary, it is easy to demonstrate. Collins could convince himself of this simply by accompanying someone like James Randi to a magic convention at which dealers demonstrate new tricks for the first time and see how he compares with Randi in figuring them out. It is true that magicians sometimes fool other magicians, but not often and not for long. The "magician's magician" who enjoys inventing tricks to fool his colleagues bears no resemblance to the psychic charlatan. The charlatan is usually a mediocre performer who has hit on some crude methods of deception all his own—methods that are transparent almost at once to any knowledgeable close-up magician who sees the charlatan perform.

When new tricks come on the market, dealers like to advertise them in magic periodicals with glowing descriptions that seem to rule out all standard methods. Magicians are often extremely good in guessing the modus operandi from the ad, without even seeing the trick performed. Of course, if they actually saw the trick demonstrated, it would be enormously easier. And if they saw it more than once, it would be a rare trick indeed that would resist unraveling.

A few years ago Persi Diaconis, a statistician who is also a skilled card magician, telephoned to say that a certain Oriental conjurer was appearing that night on television and would be performing a sensational new trick with a silk. The silk is twisted like a rope, cut in half, the halves rolled into a ball, and when unrolled, the silk is restored. Persi had not yet seen the trick, but had heard it described by puzzled magicians. After discussing several methods, we finally agreed on what we thought was the most probable technique. When we watched the show that night, our hypothesis was verfied. The point is that we guessed the method before we even saw the trick.

Sometimes it is impossible to guess from a description. When I was a young man in Chicago, Joe Berg's magic shop advertised a miracle called the "none-such ribbon effect." A ribbon, the ad said, is cleanly cut in half and the ends widely separated. After the restoration, the ribbon is the same length as before. No ribbon is added or taken away, and no adhesives, magnets, or other secret aids are needed. I was unable to guess the method. A few days later, in Joe's shop, I asked him to demonstrate the trick. As soon as he did, I understood. I am free to give away the secret because this clinker of a trick has never been performed by a magician, and never will be. The "ribbon" proved to be crepe paper. It was genuinely cut, the halves folded into a parcel, one half palmed away, then the other half was pulled out of the fist in such a manner that it stretched to twice it's original length!

New methods of deception are invariably based on ancient general principles that any experienced conjurer knows in his bones. No magician could have witnessed the none-such ribbon effect without seeing at once how it worked, even though no one had ever before thought of restoring a ribbon in this peculiar way. Scientists are helpless in the hands of a clever charlatan, whether he uses old or new methods, but knowledgeable magicians are far from helpless regardless of how unorthodox the new methods may be. Their ability to detect fraud by novel techniques is vastly superior to that of any investigator without a magic background, even if he has a high I.Q. and a Nobel Prize.

Misconception 3: The suggestion that magicians should advise but not observe is naive. Until a magician actually sees a clever psychic perform, he is in a poor position to know what controls should be adopted. It is no good to rely on a scientists's memory of what he saw, because such memories are notoriously faulty. Good magic is carefully designed to conceal a trick's most essential aspects, and even what a magician says is planned to make a spectator forget crucial details. The medium Henry Slade, for example, was once tested by a group of scientists. No one recalled afterward that a slate had "accidentally" slipped out of Slade's hands and dropped on the rug. Yet it was at just this instant that Slade switched slates. Magicians are alert to such misdirection. Non-magicians are not. Incidentally, in Slade's day many scientists were totally convinced that his slate writing was genuine. Is it not curious that chalked messages appearing on slates have disappeared from the repertoire of modern psychics?

Conjurers obviously can be of great help in designing protocols, but if a charlatan is using new methods, or performing a feat never performed before (such as Ted Serios's trick with Polaroid cameras), it is almost essential that he be observed initially by a magician. True, in many cases a committeee of magicians may, on the basis of a careful, accurate description of a psychic's performance, figure out how the psychic could be cheating and suggest adequate controls. In some cases, however, the memories of psi researchers are too vague and flawed to permit such reconstruction. Only by seeing the psychic do his or her thing can the magician make intelligent guesses and not waste the researcher's time by suggesting twenty different ways the psychic could have cheated. Of course it is essential that a psychic not know a magician is present. Psi powers have a way of evaporating even if the psychic only suspects a magician may be present. The reason D. D. Home was never caught cheating was that Home took extreme precautions to perform miracles only in the presence of persons he knew to be untrained in magic.

Suppose a club suspects a member of cheating at card games. How should members go about catching him? It is folly to ask an expert on card-swindling to design precautions, because there are thousands of ways to cheat. I can show you fifty ways to false-shuffle a deck, and as many ways of getting secret peeks at top and bottom cards. Persi can demonstrate twenty different ways to deal the second card instead of the top one, some by using only one hand. There are dozens of subtle ways to mark certain cards in the course of a game. Nor is it feasible for a card "mechanic" to give club members an adequate course in cheating. It would require many months. Obviously nothing is gained by having the mechanic sit in on the games if the hustler knows who he is. And how can club members be sure that the hustler doesn't know?

The fact is that there is only one good way to settle the matter. A trap must be set. Let the expert observe a game secretly, either through a peephole or a carefully constructed two-way mirror. This is such a simple way to trap a cheat that one of the great marvels of modern psi research is that the only researchers of recent decades who have used it seem to be Collins and the parapsychologists in Dr. Rhine's laboratory who set a peephole trap for their director, Walter Levy.

Consider the case of John Hasted, a Birkbeck College physicist who firmly believes that children can paranormally bend paperclips inside a glass sphere, provided the sphere has a hole in it and the children are allowed to take it into another room and do their psychic bending unobserved. A ridiculously easy way to settle this hypothesis would be to videotape the youngsters secretly, the way Collins did. If Hasted ever tried this, I haven't heard of it. It is passing strange that parapsychologists who become convinced that psychics can bend metal seem absolutely incapable of devising a simple trap. This augurs ill for the hope that they will ever seek the aid of magicians in any significant way.

Misconception 4: It is naive to suppose that most researchers are capable of setting up controls for a magician that are identical to those imposed on a psychic in the past experiment. If a videotape of an entire experiment is made, without breaks, it might be possible; but even here there are major difficulties. Take the case of Ted Serios. Suppose a tape had been made that showed Ted holding his "gizmo" (rolled piece of paper) in front of the camera lens and a picture of the Eiffel Tower appearing on the film. A magician asked to break protocols would ask: Was the gizmo examined immediately before the event was recorded? The researcher may honestly say yes; but unless a magician had been there, there is no way to rule out the possibility that Ted palmed an optical device into the gizmo *after* it had been examined. Even if the tape showed the gizmo being examined, if Ted were careful of camera angles nothing on the film would reveal palming. Similarly, an adequate tape would have to show the gizmo examined immediately after the camera snapped, and in such a way that it ruled out Ted palming a device out of the gizmo.

Jule Eisenbud, who wrote an entire book about Ted, has repeatedly challenged Randi to break his protocols. Why has Randi refused? Because Eisenbud, having learned from magicians how Ted could have cheated, now wants to impose on Randi controls that were never imposed on Ted. Magicians think Randi has already broken Eisenbud's protocols; but Eisenbud does not think so, and neither do many top parapsychologists. Researchers typically demand of magicians that they repeat past miracles under conditions radically unlike those that prevailed when the "psychic" produced them. The fact is that there is no way to make sure controls are identical unless a magician has been there to see the psychic perform. Memories of researchers untrained in magic are far too unreliable. Of course one could ask that a magician and a psychic produce a paranormal event under identical controls, supervised by outsiders, but what psychic charlatan would ever agree to such a test?

Misconception 5: Collins makes much of his belief that magicians refuse to give away methods used by psychics. They do indeed refuse to give away secrets of tricks by which professional magicians earn a legitimate living, including entertainers like Kreskin who pose as psychics; but at the low level of prestidigitation on which psychics operate, magicians have never hesitated to give away secrets.

As Collins knows, Houdini constantly exposed the methods of fraudulent mediums. Randi has tirelessly explained the methods of Uri Geller and other mountebanks. The three magicians who investigated Serios for *Popular Photography* (October 1967) explained in detail how to produce all of Ted's effects with an optical gimmick. One of the three, Charles Reynolds (who designs illusions for Doug Henning and other stage performers) is certainly not going to tell Collins how Doug vanished an elephant or how David Copperfield made the Statue of Liberty disappear, but he minds not at all telling any parapsychologist willing to listen how Geller bends keys. Surely Collins knows about my *Science* article (reprinted in *Science: Good, Bad and Bogus*) that exposes the secrets of eyeless vision, except for Kuda Bux's method—and that was because Kuda made his living with it. Surely Collins knows of the two books by Uriah Fuller, on sale in magic stores, that give away all of Geller's basic techniques. Randi and I will happily tell anyone how Nina Kulagina uses invisible threads to move matches and float table-tennis balls, and how Felicia Parise could have moved a pill bottle for Charles Honorton. How Collins got the impression that magicians are reluctant to explain secrets of psychic fraud is beyond me. Even the secrets of legitimate magic are readily available to any psi researcher who cares to buy a few dozen modern books on the subject.

Misconception 6: Collins actually thinks that if magicians were routinely asked to observe psychic wonders it would wreck science. It is not just that fraud is possible in all experiments and there aren't enough magicians to go around; but psi research, like all research, is a vast social enterprise extending over long periods of time. It simply would not work, says Collins, if hostile magicians were perpetually underfoot.

What Collins ignores here are two all-important distinctions. One is between the operations of nature and human nature; the other is between ordinary and extraordinary phenomena. As I like to say, electrons and gerbils don't cheat. Even among psychics, very few claim such fantastic powers as the ability to bend metal by PK, translocate objects, and levitate tables. It is only when exceedingly rare miracles like these are seriously investigated that it is essential to call in an expert on the art of close-up cheating. And it is essential in many cases that the expert be there to watch, not just give advice at some later date to researchers who, more often than not, in the past have paid not the slightest attention to such advice.

Some of the most widely heralded miracles are one-time events that the psychic never does again, such as the time Geller translocated a dog through the walls of Puharich's house, or Felicia moved a pill bottle, or Charles Tart's sleeping subject guessed the number on a card that Tart had put on a shelf above her line of vision. Since no expert on fraud was there as an observer, no one should take seriously the claims of Andrija Puharich, Charles Honorton, and Charles Tart that those events were genuine. Who can take seriously today J. B. Rhine's claim that Hubert Pearce correctly guessed 25 ESP cards in a row? Only Rhine observed this miracle, and there are 20 ways Pearce could have cheated. When a psychic produces events this extraordinary, it is impossible to imagine that he or she would ever submit to retesting under controls recommended by a magician, let alone being observed by a magician during the retesting.

In sum: if parapsychologists seeking the aid of magicians tried to follow Collins's naive guidelines, it is easy to predict the outcome. In a word—zilch.

Part 3

Parapsychologists Reply

16

What Is Your Counter-Explanation?
A Plea to Skeptics to Think Again

JOHN BELOFF

I say it is a scandal that the dispute as to the reality of these phenomena should still be going on—that so many competent witnesses should have declared their belief in them, that so many others should be profoundly interested in having the question determined, and yet the educated world as a body should still be simply in the attitude of incredulity.

Henry Sidgwick (Presidential Address to the Society
for Psychical Research, June 17, 1882)

Belief is not a matter of choice. In the end, either one is convinced by the evidence of the arguments or one is not. Long before that stage is reached, however, there is ample room for dialogue. Perhaps the evidence on which we based our belief was inadequate. Perhaps the arguments on which we relied were unsound. At all events, I think it is important that the dialogue between parapsychologists and their critics should continue. There will always be those who will say that controversy is a waste of time, that the two sides will never see eye to eye, that time spent in this way would be better spent on research. But, while I have some sympathy with this view, I regard it as short-sighted. So long as incredulity remains the typical response of the scientific community to parapsychological claims, parapsychology will be accorded a low level of priority in the competition for funding and resources, and this, in turn, will retard its progress, thereby reinforcing the initial incredulity. Is there any way out of this impasse?

There are, I suggest, two assumptions skeptics habitually make that should not go unchallenged. The first is that only the strict experimental evidence needs to be taken seriously, that any other kind of evidence can be dismissed as anecdotal and unscientific. The second assumption is that, given the antecedent improbability of the phenomena, nothing short of their becoming commonplace—which means, in effect, finding a way of producing them on demand, could ever justify our accepting them at face value. The two assumptions go hand in hand. Thus, if there were, at the present time, some unequivocally

This chapter is dedicated to the memory of Piet Hein Hoebens (1951-1984).

repeatable psi effect, there would be every reason to emphasize the experimental evidence because it alone would allow us to satisfy ourselves as to its validity without having to take anyone else's word for it. But, of course, if such were the case, parapsychology would no longer be the controversial science that it now is. The present controversy takes as its point of departure the fact that the disputed phenomena are too unstable and elusive to permit such an outcome. We cannot even say at the present time whether such an outcome is even theoretically possible. In these circumstances the experimental evidence takes on a very different complexion. For an unrepeatable experiment is just another unique historical event; it no longer represents a recipe for obtaining similar results as experiments ordinarily purport to do.

Hence, to rely exclusively on the experimental evidence to settle the question of the basic existence of psi is to betray a profound misunderstanding of the role of experimentation in science. Scientists do not carry out experiments with the aim, primarily, of making converts, though every successful experiment strengthens the credibility of the phenomenon under investigation. They carry out experiments in order to test hypotheses and thereby advance our understanding of the phenomena. And, if a truly repeatable experiment should prove possible, it is precisely by increasing our knowledge of the phenomena that we shall arrive at it. That is why most parapsychological researchers at the present time are avowedly "process-oriented" rather than "proof-oriented" in their work, even when their original belief in the reality of psi may have sprung from some personal experience and not from their work in the laboratory. But, however important such process-oriented research may be in the long run, I do not think we have yet reached the stage where it can be made to bear the weight of the controversy directed at the proof issue.

Meanwhile, there is a danger that exclusive preoccupation with the experimental evidence may lead us to overlook the fact that what we may be getting in the laboratory is no more than a weak, fitful, or degenerate manifestation of psi. After all, no one would ever have had recourse to the laboratory in the first instance had there not been a strong presumption that psi occurs in the outside world and has done so in every age and in every society of which we have knowledge. Obviously the laboratory affords a degree of security, rigor, and control in a way that is hardly possible in the field, but such advantages must be set against the disadvantages of dealing with psi effects whose very presence can only be detected by means of statistical analysis. Should the skeptic's attention, then, be redirected to the spontaneous evidence?

The snag is that it is then that the second assumption comes into its own. The argument is essentially that which David Hume first propounded in his famous essay on miracles.[1] A miracle, he pointed out, is, by definition, a singular exception to some law of nature. But, since the laws of nature are daily confirmed in our experience, no mere human testimony, however imposing, could ever suffice to outweigh the reason we have for doubting it. The fatal weakness of this argument, as I see it, is that it is bound to fail when put to the test. Thus we would have no difficulty envisaging a *hypothetical* situation where we would be left in no doubt whatsoever that a paranormal event had occurred. To take a concrete, if jocular, example, we could imagine a press conference in the White House at which the President of the United States, in full view of audience, security officers, and television cameras, were suddenly to vanish and, as suddenly, reappear elsewhere. Whether any *actual* event similarly rules out the element of doubt is, of course, quite another matter, although Hume, to his credit, does try to make his argument proof against such a contingency. Thus he goes out of his way to remind the reader that, only shortly before the time he was writing, a whole series of miraculous cures had been reported from the cemetery of St. Medard in Paris. (For an account of these events, which puzzled not only Hume but even Voltaire, see Dingwall 1947, Chap. 4.) He then concedes that, other things being equal, the evidence for their authenticity must be acknowledged as overwhelming. But, precisely because they are miraculous, a rational person has no option but to reject them as spurious But, in saying this, Hume is surely mistaken. A point may be reached, as our hypothetical example showed, where no one, rational or otherwise, had any option but to believe. What, in fact, Hume has done, all unwittingly, is to furnish a *reductio ad absurdum* of his own argument. If the evidence he cites for the events in question were indeed so overwhelming, we would have to accept it, miracles or no miracles. Actually, few skeptics are content these days to base their case on the a priori impossibility of psi phenomena. We have witnessed so many upheavals in science that we are much less prone to suppose than were Hume's contemporaries that either science or common sense can tell us in advance what can or cannot be the case. Perhaps we are more ready these days to agree with St. Augustine when he pointed out that a miracle was not so much contrary to nature as contrary to what we know of nature.[2]

Let us assume, anyhow, that we are not all Humean skeptics and that we are willing to consider the possible existence of phenomena that do not meet the strongest criterion of validation, production on demand. How then are we to set about deciding rationally between belief and doubt? The main aim of this paper is to suggest an appropriate strategy. It is the following. Whenever one is confronted with a claim, from whatever source, that has certain paranormal implications, one should ask oneself what normal explanation there could be that would obviate the necessity of invoking anything of a paranormal nature. The question, then, is whether this alternative explanation is more or less plausible than the original paranormal claim. This strategy will not solve the controversy, if only because what to one person may seem a perfectly reasonable scenario may strike another as wildly implausible and far-fetched. Nevertheless, such a strategy can, I maintain, serve to sharpen a controversy that is always liable to get out of focus.

The Problem of the Counter-Explanation

The significance of the counter-explanation was brought home to me some years ago when, in answer to a challenge, I wrote a paper for the *Zetetic Scholar* in which I discussed seven classic experiments in the parapsychological literature that I regarded as strong evidence of the existence of psi (Beloff 1980). Of the four well-known skeptics whose commentaries were also published, only one, Christopher Scott (1980), offered a specific counter-explanation for any of my seven experiments. The other critics were all content to disagree with me on general grounds. The particular experiment that Scott elected to probe was the so-called "Brugmans Experiment," which took place at the University of Groningen in Holland in 1921 (perhaps the earliest parapsychological experiment to be conducted under university auspices). Only a single special subject was involved in this experiment, and the task on each trial was to point to a square on a checkerboard of 48 squares that corresponded with the square designated as a target for that trial. Scott's suggestion was that the instructions might have allowed a certain ambiguity as to when a trial was concluded and so which square had been chosen. In that case, an overzealous observer might consistently misread the signals, and this could have accounted for the highly significant scores obtained. I am not by any means convinced that this is what *did* happen. On the contrary I would have thought it inconceivable that any experimenter (and here there were three) could be so foolish as to carry on a lengthy experiment that ran to many sessions when, all the time, there was some doubt about what response the subject was actually making—which is, after all, the one critical item of any experiment. Nevertheless, I had to concede that Scott's counter-explanation was compatible with the account we have of the experiment, and I gladly acknowledge its ingenuity and the spirit in which it was offered.[3]

Some readers may suspect that, by insisting on a counter-explanation, I am attempting to shift the burden of proof from the claimant, where it rightly belongs, onto the critic who contests the claim. I must therefore point out that, once he has published his claim, the claimant has already done everything that is initially required of him. If someone then wishes to query it, it is up to that person to state his objections. Of course no one needs to set up as a critic. There are many situations in life when the wisest course of action is simply to admit ignorance or bafflement and leave it at that. But anyone who enters the arena of controversy cannot shirk the consequences. Too often critics of parapsychology are content to use mockery and ridicule in their efforts to bring the field into disrepute. And, since the literature of psychical research is full of fraudulent and farcical incidents, they are assured of an easy time. But in the interests of truth this temptation should be resisted. My demand for counter-explanations is a plea to forgo rhetoric and examine the facts. Even so, is it reasonable to expect a critic to be able to come forward with a counter-explanation in all cases? How can we be sure, for example, that the case we are being asked to consider has been fully and accurately reported? How do we know that there might not be somewhere a fragment of evidence that, if it were available, would cast a different light on the case as a whole? Perhaps there are telltale clues buried in the data that, if we could but interpret them, would invalidate the claim. It took, after all, some thirty years and recourse to computers before definite evidence of data manipulation was finally discovered in the famous Soal-Shackleton series. (See the chapter by Betty Markwick in this volume.) Certainly, if the demand for a counter-explanation meant putting one's finger on exactly what was amiss in a given case, we could well be accused of trying to force the issue. But it is not unreasonable to expect a critic to indicate the weak points in the evidence and state where we should look for the most promising counter-explanation.

This much, at least, is presumably now common ground between parapsychologists and their critics. Where they still cannot agree is whether a given counter-explanation is more or less credible than the alleged facts that it purports to dispose of. Understandably, most critics concentrate on the latest experiments to attract attention, where information about methods and conditions are still open to inspection. But, although the task of finding a counter-explanation in this area is becoming increasingly more difficult because, with the advent of computers and automation, so many of the pitfalls that were relevant in the days of J. B. Rhine now no longer apply, for the reasons I have discussed, I do not think this is the ground where we can yet expect a showdown. If asked what it is that makes me side with the believers rather than with the skeptics, I would have to say, I suppose, that it is less this or that particular case than the global impression I derive from my survey of the literature that something real is going on that defies conventional explanations. However, one cannot argue about global impressions, so it is necessary for me to pick out a concrete example that can serve as the basis of discussion. What should that example be? People differ with regard to what they find persuasive so I can only say that, for my part, the most convincing evidence I know in the literature of psychical research is to be found in the careers of those exceptional individuals who (a) appeared to possess psi ability to a very high degree and (b) were willing to allow themselves to be used in the interests of research. This combination has, unfortunately, become increasingly rare over the years, but there still remains a galaxy of such star subjects from whose well-documented case-studies one can choose. The one I have chosen to illustrate my theme is Eusapia Palladino.

The Case of Eusapia Palladino (1854-1918)

The case of Palladino will no doubt strike some of my readers as little short of perverse. Was she not long ago discredited, I can hear them ask, when she was caught cheating and all her so-called phenomena were shown to be mere tricks? But, as so often in this treacherous field, a closer look shows how superficial such a judgment would be. There are undoubtedly a great many blemishes in her case but, equally, there are many valuable lessons we can learn from studying it. It was true enough that she preferred to operate under cover of darkness, as was the wont among mediums of that epoch, and reserved the right to veto any condition that she did not fancy. It is true enough that she cheated repeatedly, shamelessly, and outrageously. Nor can we take too seriously her own standard excuse that she could not be held responsible for anything she might do in her trances. Too many of her tricks were too contrived and rehearsed for that. And it is true, finally, that her phenomena were notoriously ludicrous, inconsequential, and repetitious even by the standards of the familiar mediumistic repertoire of the time. But, having said all that, one then has to add that all these facts were well known to her investigators from the very outset. And yet, in spite of this, they were undaunted, and their curiosity to observe ever more remained insatiable. Moreover, these same investigators were not obscure individuals or simple-minded spiritualists; they included some of the outstanding names in European science, who had everything to lose if it could be shown that they were being duped. For the fact is that Eusapia was investigated more frequently, more intensively, and by more different qualified investigators than any other individual in the annals of psychical research. Consequently, whatever construction we care to put on this fact, we cannot evade the question of how this uneducated peasant woman from Naples who could barely write her own name succeeded for nearly 20 years in enthralling the scientific elite of Europe. For, with very few exceptions, nearly all those who studied her at first hand, however incredulous they might be to start with, came to the conclusion that her phenomena were genuine—that is to say, whatever else they might portend, they were not due to trickery—and they adhered to this conclusion to the end.

So what were these strange phenomena that she purveyed?[4] They can be divided for convenience into the following main categories: (1) Acoustic phenomena, mainly loud raps. This was a very common accompaniment of sittings with physical mediums. (2) Kinetic phenomena, e.g., the movement of small objects, the playing of musical instruments, and—a prominent feature of her mediumship—the total levitation of the séance table; or very occasionally, of the medium herself. (3) A sudden loss of weight during a séance when the medium was seated on a weighing machine. (4) Cool breezes of sufficient force to cause the window curtains to billow out into the room or the medium's skirts to billow outwards. (5) Luminous phenomena, e.g., transient light effects, luminous apparitions, etc. And, perhaps the queerest item of the whole repertoire, (6) Materializations. These were much cruder than those associated with some of the famous materializing mediums and usually took the form of rudimentary heads or hands that would emerge from behind the curtains. Sometimes, however, it looked as if the medium herself had sprouted additional limbs, or "pseudopods," as they came to be known. Sitters would also sometimes feel themselves gripped or pinched as if by a living hand that they did not see. All the foregoing phenomena were familiar to psychical researchers of that era; indeed, Palladino's phenomena were much less spectacular than those of some other mediums. One phenomenon that does appear to be unique to her case was the jet of cool air that would sometimes be observed to emanate from a scar in her forehead, usually at the end of a séance.

Her phenomena always occurred within the vicinity of her body, although not necessarily within her reach. I know of no instance where she was able to exert an effect on a remote object or on one inside a sealed container. The arrangement at her séances, which eventually became standard, was to have at least two controllers, one on each side, to keep hold of her hands and feet, although sometimes another person would lie on the floor to hold her legs. She was seated in front of a curtained recess that diagonally cut off a corner of the room. This was known as the "cabinet" and was regarded by spiritualists as a sort of powerhouse for generating physical phenomena. Illumination varied a great deal even within a single séance, depending mainly on her whim. Sometimes the only illumination came from a bare window; but, as the sittings were always held in the late evening or at night, this was somewhat residual. Sometimes, however, artificial light was permitted, and toward the end of her career electric light was regularly used, but always shaded to give a red glow. In the more important investigations a stenographer would be employed, whose sole duty was to write down an account of every incident as it occurred, dictated by one or another of the sitters. In this way, nothing would be left to memory.

The list of those who sat with her is an imposing one. I do not think there is any doubt, however, that her most assiduous investigator, who could boast of having sat through more than a hundred of her séances, was Charles Richet of the University of Paris, a Nobel Laureate physiologist, a psychologist, and a psychical researcher. Richet has been portrayed as a rather credulous man,[5] so it is only fair to point out that, when he began his career in psychical research, he was just as skeptical as most of the other scientists of that time and even joined in the chorus of derision that greeted William Crookes, though he later had the good grace to retract his words.[6] His "credulity" seems to have consisted of an inability to doubt the evidence of his senses! But, in any case, he was by no means alone in his endorsement of Eusapia, and I must now try rapidly to cover the principal investigations of her that were undertaken between 1891 and 1907.[7]

The first person of international standing to be converted to a belief in Eusapia's abilities was the psychiatrist Cesare Lombroso of the University of Turin, now best remembered as the founder of criminology. He and a group of scientists held sittings with her in Naples in 1891 and duly issued a positive report. The following year a second investigation, in which Richet himself participated, was carried out in Milan, under the direction of G. Schiaparelli, the head of the Milan observatory. The report that issued from this investigation included photographs of complete table levitations obtained in good light. But it is of interest, in light of what I was saying about Richet's reputation for credulity, that he was not satisfied that every possibility of deception had yet been eliminated and refused to sign the report. Richet again participated in the series of sittings held in Rome from 1893 to 1894, but it was not until after he had held sittings under his own direction and at his own residence, in the summer of 1894, that he was ready to relinquish further doubts about the phenomena. "C'est absolument absurde mais c'est vrai," he used to say. These investigations took place partly at his château at Carqueiranne (near Toulon) and partly on the Ile Roubaud, a small Mediterranean island (near Hyères), where his cottage was the only dwelling and where, apart from the lighthouse-keeper and his wife, Richet, his family, and his servants were the only inhabitants, a fact that made him feel all the more confident that there could be no accomplices lurking in the vicinity.

The sittings with Eusapia on the Ile Roubaud were particularly productive of phenomena, including some of the most impressive that are attributed to her, although it must be admitted that artificial light was excluded so that the only illumination came from the windows and the night sky. The sitters, however, were all seasoned psychical researchers. Oliver Lodge and Frederic Myers of the Society for Psychical Research (SPR) were Richet's guests from England, and they were joined later by Henry and Eleanor Sidgwick. Julijan Ochorowicz, the Polish psychologist and psychical researcher, who completed the team, had already directed 40 sittings with Eusapia in Warsaw, which had impressed him. Otherwise there was just the professional stenographer to keep the minute-by-minute record of the proceedings. A very positive report on these sittings duly appeared in the *Journal of the SPR* in November 1894, written by Lodge but endorsed by Myers and by the Sidgwicks.[8] One detail is worth quoting. Lodge mentions that "raps on the table, which were frequent, were so strong as to feel dangerous: they sounded like blows delivered by a heavy mallet."

One outcome of the Ile Roubaud experience was that the SPR decided to investigate Eusapia for themselves. A series of sittings were held with her in the late summer of 1895 in Cambridge, at the house of Myers, where she stayed. They were a severe disappointment. The phenomena were sparse, and time and again she was caught cheating. Her ruse was to free one of her hands by first bringing her two hands together and then, after a certain amount of wriggling, contrive to make the controllers on either side think that each was still holding a different hand when in fact they were grasping different parts of the same hand. Why the Cambridge sittings were such a flop is still a matter for controversy and speculation. Eusapia's supporters protest that she was uncomfortable in the stuffy atmosphere of Cambridge academic society, although Eleanor Sidgwick denies that this was so and insists that they all did everything they could to make her stay a cheerful one.[9] Others lay the blame on Richard Hodgson.[10] Hodgson had come over from Boston especially for the occasion and soon took command of the situation. Ten years previously his report on Mme. Blavatsky had been issued by the SPR. He had openly accused her of fraud on an extensive scale. Probably he was now hoping to add Eusapia to his trophies. At all events, he had heard about her mode of cheating and decided that the best way to find out more about it was deliberately to let go of a hand at certain critical moments to see what she would then do. The result deeply shocked both Myers and the Sidgwicks, who felt that they had been betrayed and even doubted whether they could any longer assume that the events they had witnessed on the Ile Roubaud were all that they seemed to be. Lodge, on the other hand, took it more philosophically. But the upshot was that henceforth it became official SPR policy not to continue working with a medium who had once been caught cheating.

The policy was curiously illogical on the part of a philosopher of Sidgwick's caliber, since it was the medium's ability not her morals that were on trial. The question, after all, was never whether Eusapia *would* cheat if the opportunity arose but rather whether she *could* cheat in the circumstances and, if the answer is that she *could* cheat, then the test was invalid in the first place.[11] Fortunately, the Continental researchers were not so easily put off, so the Cambridge fiasco did not bring her career to an abrupt end. Thus, in 1898, in Paris, a large committee under the direction of Camille Flammarion, the astronomer, went into action in Flammarion's own house. One of the incidents described by Flammarion himself involved an accordion that apparently played of its own accord while he held the end opposite the keyboard and Eusapia's hands were tightly restrained. Richet participated in these sittings but then held some further sittings for her in the library of his own house in Paris. One of those invited was the distinguished Swiss psychologist Theodore Flournoy of the University of Geneva, who has given us his own account of these sittings, which fully convinced him of the authenticity of the phenomena.[12]

The next big investigation took place in Genoa under the direction of Enrico Morselli, head of a clinic for nervous and mental diseases, who held 20 sittings with Eusapia from 1901 to 1902 and then 6 further sittings there in the winter of 1906-1907. The latter attracted widespread publicity in the Italian press and Carrington describes them as "among the most remarkable and convincing that have ever been held," but Morselli himself thought that her powers already appeared to be waning when compared with her performance during the earlier sittings. One of the sitters at the Genoa investigation was Philippe Botazzi, head of the physiological institute of the University of Naples, who in 1907 had an opportunity to test Eusapia in his own laboratory and, as did so many others, underwent the process of having his initial incredulity converted into complete conviction.

In the same year, Lombroso came back into the picture. He organized a series of sittings in the department of psychiatry at the University of Turin that was attended by a number of medical men. It was followed by a fresh series of sittings in Turin under the direction of Pio Foà, professor of pathological anatomy and general secretary of the Academy of Sciences. His committee stated in their report: "Without the objective refutable documents which remained, we should have doubted our sense and intelligence." It is worth citing one incident that involved a strong white-wood table (2'9" high, 3' long, and 22" wide, weighing 17 lbs), which, instead of just receiving the loud raps like those Lodge had described, actually broke into pieces before their astonished gaze and in what is described as "very good red light" (Carrington 1909, 106). This incident followed an announcement by the medium herself that she intended to break the table for them. (It was characteristic of her to say in advance what was going to happen.) It must, one supposes, require an extra-strong dose of skepticism to doubt evidence of that magnitude!

There were still other investigations that need not detain us, but some mention should be made of the lengthy series of sittings with Eusapia in Paris, organized by the Institut Général Psychologique between 1905 and 1908. A report on these sittings was issued under the name of Jules Courtier, secretary of the Institute. The importance of this series is twofold: Photography and instrumentation, including electrical security devices for monitoring the medium's feet, were used more extensively than in any of the previous series. Secondly, the list of sitters included such luminaries as Pierre and Marie Curie and Henri Bergson. Eusapia was also subjected to a battery of psychophysiological tests, although nothing notable emerged from this. Many of the special tests devised for her failed, and on several occasions she was caught cheating, but the report is far from being dismissive of the phenomena in general.[13]

Yet, in spite of this load of testimony and the huge number of professional man-hours it represents, in 1908 it could still be said (quite unfairly in my opinion) that scientists are the last people who can be trusted to see through a wily impostor, that only a trained illusionist can appreciate the manifold possibilities of deception and sleight of hand.[14] This objection, however, does not apply to the investigation to which we must now turn, where all three investigators not only were themselves highly proficient in the art of conjuring but were, indeed, the acknowledged experts on the special techniques of fraudulent mediumship.

The Feilding Report

At the beginning of the year 1908, the American psychical researcher Hereward Carrington went to see Everard Feilding, then honorary secretary of the SPR. Some 22 official reports on Palladino had already appeared, but Carrington persuaded Feilding that, despite its earlier ban, it was time for the SPR to have another go before it was too late, and the consent of the Council was duly obtained. The two men took themselves off to Naples, where they were later joined by W. W. Baggally, a Council member and an expert on trickery, who had sat with Palladino but without becoming convinced that she was genuine. It was this trio who made up the "Naples Committee" and, as a testimonial to their competence for the task at hand, I cannot do better than quote the words of that distinguished scholar and erstwhile Fellow of the Committee for the Scientific Investigation of Claims of the Paranormal (CSICOP), Eric Dingwall (1950):

> I was intimately acquainted with all three investigators. Mr. Carrington was one of the keenest investigators in the United States. He had unrivalled opportunities to examine the host of frauds and fakers who flourished there, and his results led him to suppose that of the alleged physical phenomena the vast bulk was certainly produced by fraudulent means and devices, as he himself asserts in his book (*The Physical Phenomena of Spiritualism*. New York 1907, London 1908). Mr. Feilding was also a man of vast experience and one of the keenest and most acute critics that this country has ever produced. . . . Moreover his scepticism was extreme, although it was modified by an attitude of open-mindedness and an unwillingness to accept critical comments when these were not accompanied by properly adduced evidence. Mr. Baggally almost equalled Mr. Feilding in his scepticism and desire for investigation. He knew more about trick methods than his illustrious colleague and thus he was better able to concentrate on essentials. For over thirty years he had attended seances, but had come to the conclusion that rarely, if ever, had he encountered one genuine physical medium. This, then, was the committee which Eusapia consented to face.

The three men booked into the Hotel Victoria in Naples and there, in their rooms on the fifth floor, between November 21 and December 19, 1908, 11 sittings were held, the minutes of which go to make up what I am here calling "The Feilding Report" (though all three put their name to it). It was published the following year in the *Proceedings of the SPR* with a gracious foreword by

Eleanor Sidgwick (Feilding et al. 1909). It is a document that is still worth reading, not just as an account of certain extraordinary phenomena but also as a record of the moral struggle of each man with himself as he wrestled with his doubts and misgivings before finally succumbing to the only conclusion that honesty would allow. It was not until after the sixth séance, so Feilding informs us, that he himself was ready to commit himself. It is worth quoting at some length from the note he wrote on December 6, following this séance:

> My own frame of mind when starting on this investigation was that, in view of the concurrent opinion of practically all the eminent men of science who have investigated Eusapia's phenomena, it was inconceivable that they could, in turn, be deceived by the few petty tricks that have, from time to time, been detected, and that it was therefore probable that the phenomena were real. All my own experiments in physical mediumship had resulted in the discovery of the most childish frauds. Failure had followed upon failure. While, therefore, I tended to accept the general hypothesis that the facts of the so-called spiritualistic physical manifestations must, on the evidence, be regarded as probably existent, my mental habit had become so profoundly sceptical, when it came to considering any given alleged instance of them, that I had ceased to have any expectation of finding it able to bear examination. The first seance with Eusapia, accordingly, provoked chiefly a feeling of surprise; the second, of irritation—irritation at finding oneself confronted with a foolish but apparently insoluble problem. The third seance, at which a trumpery trick was detected, came as a sort of relief. At the fourth, where the control of the medium was withdrawn from ourselves, my baffled intelligence sought to evade the responsibility of meeting facts by har-bouring grotesque doubts as to the competency of the eminent professors who took our places, to observe things properly; while at the fifth, where this course was no longer possible, as I was constantly controlling the medium myself, the mental gymnastics involved in seriously facing the necessity of concluding in favour of what was manifestly absurd, produced a kind of intellectual fatigue.
>
> After the sixth, for the first time, I find that my mind, from which the stream of events has hitherto run off like rain from a macintosh, is at last begin-ning to be capable of absorbing them. For the first time I have the absolute conviction that our observation is not mistaken. I realize, as an appreciable fact in life, that, from an empty cabinet I have seen hands and heads come forth, that from behind the curtain of that empty cabinet I have been seized by living fingers, the existence and position of the very nails of which could be felt. I have seen this extraordinary woman sitting visible outside the curtain, held hand and foot by my colleagues, immobile except for the occasional straining of a limb, while some entity within the curtain has over and over again pressed my hand in a position clearly beyond her reach. I refuse to entertain the possibility of a doubt that we were the victims of a hallucination. I appreciate exactly the fact that ninety-nine people out of a hundred will refuse to entertain the possibility of a doubt that it was anything else. And, remembering my own belief of a very

short time ago, I shall not be able to complain, though I shall unquestionably be annoyed, when I find that to be the case [Feilding 1909, 461-462].

I sometimes think that the Feilding Report should be made mandatory reading for any would-be member of CSICOP. Only those whose skepticism survived this ordeal intact would then need to apply! Yet, as this passage shows, Feilding knew only too well what to expect from his critics, and it could have come as no surprise when Frank Podmore, always the implacable enemy of the physical phenomena, wrote to the *Journal of the SPR* to attack the report. In his letter, published in the December 1909 issue, he reverts to the possibility of Eusapia surreptitiously freeing a hand or foot and thereby accomplishing all the phenomena therein described (Podmore 1909). He was answered at length by Baggally (1910) in the following issue, February 1910, but alongside further letters supporting Podmore's criticisms. In his book *The Newer Spiritualism* Podmore (1910, Chap. 4) enlarges on this theme. He minutely dissects various séances in an effort to show where Eusapia might have been able to seize the advantage, but it is something of a tour de force and made no impact on the authors of the report. Podmore, we must remember, had never sat with Eusapia. In the end, he graciously admits that the job could not have been done more competently than it was by the Naples Committee, but he took his stand on his contention that no one, given the constraints within which they had to operate, could have got the better of Eusapia; and he urged that, unless she could produce effects inside sealed containers, the SPR would be well advised to leave her strictly alone.

Although many skeptics will sympathize with Podmore's attitude, Eusapia's reputation would have been safe after the publication of the Feilding Report had it not been for the subsequent debacle of her American tour. For, in the following year, 1909, Hereward Carrington, emboldened by the success of the Naples Committee, arranged for Eusapia to visit the United States. It was a decision he would live to regret. She arrived amid a blaze of publicity and was at once in demand from all quarters. According to Carrington (1913; 1954) some 31 sittings were held in all, including the 4 that took place at Columbia University in New York. She was, he alleges, tired, overworked, and ill at ease among investigators with no previous experience of dealing with mediums. Although her sittings were by no means unproductive, they were disappointing by previous standards and, as so often happened with her when things were not going well, she lapsed into her old bad habit of cheating in the usual fashion. This was all that was needed for the skeptics to raise the hue and cry. Eminent psychologists, like Hugo Münsterberg of Harvard and Joseph Jastrow of the University of Wisconsin, after just a few sittings, rushed into print in the popular magazines to denounce her and claim credit for exposing her, oblivious to the 20 years of patient work that had been done with her in Europe. Mark Hansel quotes at length from these outbursts as demonstrating the superior wisdom and discernment of the unbeliever and, today, if Palladino is still mentioned by psychologists, it was Münsterberg and Jastrow who said the last word on her, not Feilding, Baggally, or Carrington.

Conclusions

Are we then justified in dismissing the career of "this extraordinary woman," as Feilding called her, with the one simple word "trickery"? Trickery is, of course, another of those convenient open-ended and slippery concepts that, no less than the concept of the paranormal itself, can be invoked to explain anything whatsoever. All the same, it is not unreasonable to ask what conjurer would agree to perform under the conditions to which Eusapia regularly submitted? These included (1) performing in a private room that was first searched and then locked and sealed against intruders who might act as accomplices; (2) undergoing a thorough body search before the sitting began;[15] (3) allowing one's arms and legs to be held by sitters whose one duty was never to let go; (4) producing sometimes phenomena in light sufficient, it was said, to read the small print in one's Baedeker. At all events, one leading American magician who observed her during her American tour was so impressed by her performances that he offered to donate $1,000 to charity if any of his fellow magicians could do as much under comparable conditions. There were no takers. (See Rogo 1975, 27.)

Apart from sleight-of-hand trickery, the only other counter-explanation that was occasionally invoked in connection with Palladino was hallucination, especially with reference to her materializations and pseudopods.[16] It is a somewhat desperate explanation, especially as there was always more than one sitter; but, in the nature of the case, it is very difficult to deny. However, skeptics can always rely on one supreme ally: the poverty of the human imagination. Some things go so far beyond our familiar experience and are so inherently hard to credit that even to contemplate them imposes a severe strain on our intellectual equanimity. It is not, therefore, surprising that people are content to clutch at any straw as an excuse for not having to take these things seriously and are pathetically grateful to critics like Hansel whom they can cite in self-justification. To such people Eusapia's mismanaged American tour came as a godsend.

But, for those who are willing to make that leap of the imagination that is required if we are to put ourselves in the shoes of those who came face to face with her phenomena, who, so to speak, had their noses rubbed in them, there are a number of useful lessons we can learn from her career. In the first place, it reminds us that fraud can go hand in hand with genuine psychic ability, so that it is always risky to generalize from the discovery that cheating has occurred. There may be all kinds of psychological reasons why certain persons in certain situations indulge in trickery. We can also learn from her case that the more fantastic phenomena are not necessarily any less real than those of lesser magnitude. In particular, we can no longer justify dismissing materialization as too preposterous to warrant serious consideration.

This last point, in turn, reopens a host of other controversial historical cases that now demand to be looked at with a fresh eye and the received opinion if necessary challenged. What about the young Florence Cook, for example? Must we ignore her because in middle age she took to cheating? Must we continue to defame the memory of one of Britain's most illustrious (not to say bravest) scientists by insisting that he was either the dupe of this 16-year-old girl or else her lover, who for the sake of sexual favors betrayed his fellow scientists and the cause of truth?[17] And what of those cases that flourished in the decade after Palladino? What about poor "Eva C," with her ectoplasmic faces that looked to all the world so suspiciously two-dimensional? The SPR investigators could prove nothing against her, though they were reluctant to authenticate her phenomena; but Gustave Geley, of the Institut Métapsychique in Paris, insists that he watched the faces taking shape and was able to produce a certain amount of photographic evidence to support his contention.[18] And must we still ignore the mountain of evidence that exists on the Margery mediumship because of one compromising incident late in her career? After all, did not the great Houdini stake his reputation on exposing her and fail ignominiously?[19] To take one more example, the most fantastic of them all, what are we to make of the Brazilian medium Carlos Mirabelli? If the so-called Santos Report were to be credited, he would rank as by far the most powerful medium on record, surpassing D. D. Home.[20] Deceased individuals known to the sitters are said to have materialized in broad daylight while the medium was seated in full view strapped to a chair. These same entities conversed with the sitters, submitted to a medical examination on the basis of which they were pronounced anatomically perfect, allowed themselves to be photographed and later dissolved into nothingness while the sitters looked on incredulously. The witnesses, moreover, were mainly persons of professional standing, many of them physicians. The only objection one can raise in Mirabelli's case is that he was never tested outside Brazil. Plans to bring him to Europe fell through. It is, however, embarrassing to have to base one's counter-explanation on the assumption that what happens in Brazil need not be taken seriously and that Brazilians, even medically qualified ones, cannot be trusted to tell the truth. The point is, however, that, even in such an extreme case as this, where we have every reason to query the evidence and to express suspicion, we cannot escape the responsibility of putting forward *some* counter-explanation.

When cornered, there is always one last trump-card that the skeptic can brandish in the face of the believer: *Where are all these marvels now?* The harsh fact of the matter is that there are no more Palladini. For all I know to the contrary, the phenomenon of materialization may be extinct and may never recur. Except in connection with poltergeist cases, we cannot even be sure that there are any more strong phenomena. Hence, since historical cases can never compete in credibility with cases that are still open to further investigation, the skeptic cannot be faulted if, like Podmore, he prefers to suspend judgment pending the advent of more compelling evidence, always provided he does not invoke spurious reasons for rejecting what evidence there is. But, equally, if the negative option is still valid, so is the positive option. It is no less rational, and it is certainly more adventurous, to adopt an attitude of basic belief as one's working hypothesis. If we remain entrenched in a rigidly conservative stance, we are apt to neglect phenomena that may be both real and important. Moreover, the basic believer is spared those intellectual contortions to which a skeptic is now driven when confronted with evidence for which there is no plausible counter-explanation. Lastly, if in the future new cases of a spectacular nature should arise, the basic believer will be in a better position and better prepared to deal with them.

Acknowledgment

I am specially grateful to the late Piet Hein Hoebens for criticizing an earlier draft of this paper, as a result of which the paper has been completely rewritten.

Notes

1. David Hume, *An Enquiry Concerning Human Understanding*, 1748, Sect. 10, Of Miracles.

2. St. Augustine, *The City of God*, 21:8

3. Prompted by Scott, Piet Hein Hoebens of Amsterdam was able to obtain from Groningen an earlier version of the report, where, sure enough, this ambiguity was more apparent.

4. The most comprehensive account known to me is Carrington (1909), but see also entry under "Paladino" in Fodor (1966 [1934]) and Dingwall (1950, Chap. 5). Dingwall's essay is still the best general introduction that I know and has an invaluable bibliography.

5. Most recently by Ruth Brandon, who in her caustic book (Brandon 1983, 135) speaks of "his will to believe and his disinclination to accept any unpalatable contrary indications."

6. See Richet (1922, 35). His long treatise is dedicated to William Crookes and Frederic Myers. An account of Richet's involvement in psychical research is given in Fodor (1966 [1934]) under "Richet."

7. Much of this is taken from Carrington (1909, Part 3).

8. Lodge (1894) writes: "Any person without invincible prejudice who had the same experience would have come to the same conclusion, *viz*: that things hitherto held impossible do occur." Lodge never saw any reason to retract this conclusion and, in his autobiography (Lodge 1931), he amplifies his account of his experiences on the Ile Roubaud.

9. In a footnote to her review of Morselli's *Psicologia e Spiritismo* in the *Proceedings of the SPR*, 21 (1909): 522. She was even then not yet satisfied as to the authenticity of the phenomena.

10. This is certainly the view taken by Cassirer (1983a).

11. It is curious how often this point has been misunderstood. Thus Ruth Brandon (1983) writes: "In all other scientific fields to be caught out just once in fraud is to be instantly discredited." But this confuses the experimenter and the subject. An experimenter who cheats is instantly discredited in parapsychology as in all other sciences and all his results discounted as suspect. But, if a subject cheats, this shows only that the experimenter has been careless and should try harder.

12. See Flournoy (1911, Chap. 7). He mentions there that "Myers was this time—as were all the others—absolutely convinced of the reality of the phenomena" (p. 246).

13. A lengthy review of this report by Count Perovsky-Petrovo-Solovovo appeared as a supplement to the issue of SPR *Proceedings* that contains the Feilding Report (Feilding et al. 1909). Flournoy is rather more brusque with the Courtier Report, which he accused of prevarication. Since they appeared incapable of saying either *oui* or *non* when it came to the authenticity of the phenomena, Flournoy (1911, 272) suggested that they ought to reply in chorus: *Nouin!*

14. This view was first, I believe, put about by the celebrated illusionist, J. N. Maskelyne. He and his son had been invited to participate in the Cambridge sittings of 1895 and he soon formed a very poor opinion of Eusapia and perhaps an even poorer one of her investigators. "No class of men can be so readily deceived by trickery as scientists" he asserted. "Try as they may they cannot bring their minds down to the level of the subject and are as much at fault as if it were immeasurably above them" (cited in Brandon 1983, 138). Feilding, on the other hand insisted that scientists, as a class, are far more reluctant than conjurers to acknowledge any sort of supernormal force (see Feilding et al. 1909, Final Note). In fact, Maskelyne, himself, once admitted to a journalist who interviewed him that, as a result of personal experiences with friends, he had to admit that there was something we could not explain about "table-turning" phenomena, though he felt sure it was not the action of spirits (Brandon 1983, 166).

15. Hansel (1980, 61) suggests that Eusapia might have taken advantage of her female prerogative to refuse such a search. However, the task was usually given to female sitters, such as the two American ladies who were invited to attend the eighth séance of the Naples series, but Carrington mentions specifically that at the conclusion of the very successful sixth séance, Eusapia made no objections to letting the three men search her (Feilding 1950).

16. Alice Johnson, at one time honorary secretary of the SPR, would occasionally advance this hypothesis when all else failed; but for a recent discussion of the "pseudopods" phenomenon, see Cassirer (1983b).

17. This was the thesis of Trevor Hall's (1962) book and is the one favored by Ruth Brandon (1983, Chap. 4). Those who are not persuaded that Sir William Crookes, O.M., was either an imbecile or an unprincipled blackguard may wish to consult the analysis of the "Katie King" séances provided by Dr. G. Zorab (1980), a Dutch scholar, although his book has so far appeared only in Italian.

18. A re-evaluation of the case of Eva C. (Marthe Béraud) is given by Brian Inglis (1984, Chap. 4).

19. Margery (Mrs. Mina Crandon) was one of the most controversial mediums of the twentieth century. Inglis (1984, 167) reproduces a photograph of her encased in Houdini's fraud-proof box ("like an old-fashioned steam-bath with a hole for her neck and two for her arms"). Houdini is shown holding one of her hands. The séance had no sooner started when the lid burst open and the phenomena continued! Mrs. Marian Nester, of the American SPR, a daughter of Dr. Mark Richardson, Margery's chief investigator, is preparing a new book about this medium that should provide new grounds for reconsidering her case.

20. See Dingwall (1930). I am indebted to Brian Inglis for drawing attention to this document in his discussion of Mirabelli's mediumship. See Inglis (1984, 221-227). Further information on Mirabelli is provided in Playfair (1975, Chap. 3).

References

Baggally, W. W. 1910. Discussion of the Naples Report on Eusapia Palladino. *Journal of the SPR,* 14:213-228.

Beloff, John. 1980. Seven evidential experiments. *Zetetic Scholar,* 6:91-94, 116-120.

Brandon, Ruth. 1983. *The Spiritualists: The Passion for the Occult in the 19th and 20th Centuries.* Buffalo, N.Y.: Prometheus Books.

Carrington, Hereward. 1909. *Eusapia Palladino and her Phenomena.* London: Werner Laurie.

———. 1913. *Personal Experiences in Spiritualism.* London: Werner Laurie.

———. 1954. *The American Séances with Eusapia Palladino.* New York: Garrett.

Cassirer, Manfred. 1983a. Palladino at Cambridge. *Journal of the SPR,* 52:52-58.

———. 1983b. The fluid hands of Eusapia Palladino. *Journal of the SPR,* 52:105-112.

Dingwall, E. J. 1930. An amazing case: The mediumship of Carlos Mirabelli. *Journal of the American SPR,* 24:296-306.

———. 1947. *Some Human Oddities.* London: Home and Van Thal.

———. 1950. *Very Peculiar People.* London: Rider.

Feilding, E., W. W. Baggally, and H. Carrington. 1909. Report on a series of sittings with Eusapia Palladino, *Proceedings of the SPR* 23:306-569 (reprinted in E. Feilding, *Sittings with Eusapia Palladino and Other Studies* [with an introduction by E. J. Dingwall], University Books, New Hyde Park, N.Y., 1963.)

Flournoy, Theodore. 1911. *Mélanges de Métapsychique et de psychologie.* Geneva and Paris.

Fodor, Nandor. 1966 [1934]. *An Encyclopeadia of Psychic Science.* New Hyde Park, N.Y.: University Books.

Hall, Trevor H. 1963. *The Spiritualists: The Story of Florence Cook and William Crookes*. New York: Garrett 1963 (reprinted as *The Medium and the Scientist: The Story of Florence Cook and William Crookes*, Prometheus, Buffalo, N.Y., 1985).

Hansel, C. E. M. 1980. *ESP and Parapsychology*. Buffalo, N.Y.: Prometheus Books.

Inglis, Brian. 1984. *Science and Parascience: A History of the Paranormal, 1914-1939*. London: Hodder and Stoughton.

Lodge, Oliver. 1894. Experience of unusual physical phenomena occurring in the presence of an entranced person (Eusapia Palladino). *Journal of the SPR*, 6:306-360.

———. 1931. *Past Years*. London: Hodder and Stoughton.

Playfair, Guy. 1975. *The Flying Cow*. London: Souvenir Press.

Podmore, Frank 1909. The report on Eusapia Palladino. *Journal of the SPR*, 14:172-176.

———. 1910. *The Newer Spiritualism*. London: Fisher and Unwin.

Richet, Charles. 1922. *Traité de Métapsychique*. Paris: Alcan (English translation: *Thirty Years of Psychical Research*, London, 1923).

Rogo, D. Scott. 1975. Eusapia Palladino and the structure of scientific controversy. *Parapsychology Review*, 62:23-27.

Scott, Christopher. 1980. Comment on Beloff's "Seven Evidential Experiments." *Zetetic Scholar*, 6:110-112.

Zorab, George. 1980. *Katie King Donna o Fantasma?* Milano: Armenia Editore.

17

Parapsychology and Its Critics

DOUGLAS M. STOKES

This chapter will examine the irrational and "extrarational" factors underlying the acceptance and rejection of parapsychological phenomena. It will also examine the rational arguments in favor of belief and skepticism. The terms "paranormal phenomena" and "parapsychological phenomena" will be restricted to denote only ESP, psychokinesis (PK), and any phenomena suggestive of the survival of some portion of the human mind or personality beyond the death of the physical body.

"Irrational" and "Extrarational" Factors Underlying Belief and Skepticism

That belief in paranormal phenomena is occasionally generated by less than totally rational thought processes should come as a surprise to no one. Consider for instance the banner headline in the April 17, 1984, issue of *The Sun,* an American supermarket tabloid: "Priests and psychics confirm . . . GIRL AGE 4 MADE PREGNANT BY GHOST"; and the May 22, 1984, headline of the tabloid *Weekly World News,* also found in supermarkets: "Mental supermen locked in duel—then . . . FAMED PSYCHIC'S HEAD EXPLODES." The latter story was accompanied by a rather gruesome photo from the science-fiction movie *Scanners.* If anyone believes these stories (and I think we can safely exempt the writers of this material from this charge), that belief is probably not engendered by a hard-headed critical examination of the facts or a careful examination of alternative explanations.

Yet prejudice and closed-minded thought processes are not confined to believers in psychic phenomena. Consider for instance the following quotations of two eminent scientists, the psychologist Donald Hebb and the physicist Hermann von Helmholtz, both taken from Collins and Pinch (1979, 244). First Hebb:

> Why do we not accept E.S.P. as a psychological fact? Rhine has offered us enough evidence to have convinced us on any other issue . . . I cannot see what other basis my colleagues have for rejecting it . . . My own rejection of [Rhine's] views is in a literal sense prejudice.

Now Helmholtz:

> I cannot believe it. Neither the testimony of all the Fellows of the Royal Society, nor even the evidence of my own senses would lead me to believe in the transmission of thought from one person to another independently of the recognized channels of sensation. It is clearly impossible.

These quotations illustrate an unwillingness to consider the evidence on the part of certain skeptics that, if anything, exceeds that of the most ardent reincarnation enthusiast or UFO buff. In the remainder of this section, an attempt will be made to delineate the more or less nonrational bases that underlie such extreme positions.

Historical and Metaphysical Bases

The human mind, like nature, abhors a vacuum. People need to form a picture of the universe in which they live in order to arrive at an intuitive understanding of their own existence. Therefore they adopt a *Weltanschauung,* a religious or possibly a religious metaphysical world-view, in order to make sense of their own existence. Some people may pay lip service to suspending belief on metaphysical and untestable (and therefore unscientific) hypotheses; however, when pressed, all but a small minority will confess to having adopted some metaphysical outlook. Believers in psi have sometimes adopted unorthodox religious positions ranging from Theosophy to Scientology. Many disbelievers disclaim any religious proclivities. Yet, upon careful examination, they too may often be seen to have a profound belief in a particular metaphysical doctrine that goes by the name of "materialism." This doctrine denies the existence of such entities as minds, souls, and spirits and asserts that the physical universe constitutes the entirety of reality. As this doctrine cannot be said to be scientifically or philosophically proven (see below), this faith may be due in part to a reaction to certain events and trends in the history of science.

The rise of materialism. At one time, it was much more common to ascribe mental or spiritual properties to physical matter than it is today. Aristotle, for instance, taught that the crystalline spheres that carried the planets and stars on their celestial voyages were associated with incorporeal "movers" that provided the motive forces to keep them in motion. He taught that these "movers" were spiritual in nature and that the relation of a mover to its sphere was "akin to that of a soul to its body" (Mason 1962, 42). This view was somewhat distorted in the later interpretations of Aristotle by Christian thinkers, such as Dionysius in the fifth century and St. Thomas Aquinas in the thirteenth century, who equated the "unmoved movers" of Aristotle with the angelic beings described in the Scriptures.

Baser matter was likewise conceived to have psychological properties. Aristotle attributed the tendency for a terrestrial object to fall to the earth to its "aspiration" to reach its natural place. An extremely animistic or panpsychistic view of the universe is very much in evidence as late as the year 1600 in the work of William Gilbert, an English physician and the founder of the scientific study of magnetic phenomena. Gilbert (following the Greek philosopher Thales of Miletus) attributed magnetic attraction to the action of a "magnetic soul" in the lodestone, the attraction being mediated by the emission of a "magnetic effluvium" by the lodestone. Gilbert also attributed a magnetic soul to the earth as a whole, and the extreme animism of his view is exemplified in the following passage from Westfall (1977, 27):

> Placed near the sun, Gilbert asserted, the earth's soul perceives the sun's magnetic field, and reasoning that one side will burn up while the other freezes if it does not act, it chooses to revolve upon its axis. It even chooses to incline its axis at an angle in order to cause the variation of seasons.

Even as late as 1777, Joseph Priestley suggested that matter has no properties other than those of attraction and repulsion and hence is akin to "spiritual and immaterial beings."

Bit by bit, however, the animistic or panpsychistic views of matter described above crumbled under the onslaught of scientific advances. The Aristotelian doctrine of inertia asserted that the natural state of any body is one of rest, as opposed to the more modern view of inertia as elaborated by Galileo and Newton (which asserts that a body in uniform rectilinear motion tends to remain in that state of motion).

As early as the sixth century, the Alexandrian writer John Philoponos questioned the notion that Aristotle's unmoved movers or Dionysius' angelic beings were necessary to account for the perpetual motions of the heavenly spheres. He suggested that a force acted to supply an "impetus" to a body, which served to keep the body in motion. Thus motion did not require continual interaction with a mover. For his efforts, Philoponos was denounced as a heretic by the Church. The doctrine of impetus, however, was passed down through the generations and enjoyed a revived popularity during the fourteenth and fifteenth centuries, its most notable advocates at that time being Jean Buridan, Albert of

Saxony, and Nicolas Oresme. In the fourteenth century, William of Occam refuted the existence of the angelic "movers" of the heavenly spheres, and in doing so formulated his famous "razor" principle. There is, he stated, no need to postulate unnecessary entities like angels to explain phenomena that can be more economically treated by the concept of impetus. This principle, originally applied to deny the existence of a class of spiritual beings, is of course still the main justification used by modern scientists and philosophers to deny the existence of mental entities. Indeed, Herbert Butterfield (1957, 19) explicitly concludes that "the modern law of inertia, the modern theory of motion, is the great factor which in the seventeenth century helped to drive the spirits out of the world and opened the way to a universe that ran like a piece of clockwork."

Not only were hypotheses ascribing mental or spiritual properties to inanimate matter in retreat; "vital forces" were also eventually stripped from animate matter by means of analogies between processes involving living matter and processes involving inorganic matter (which had already been "devitalized" by such developments as the impetus theory). For instance, although Ernst Haeckel in the nineteenth century used an analogy between the growth of salt crystals and that of living cells to suggest that all matter has a vital aspect, saying that "no matter can be conceived without spirit, and no spirit without matter" (Mason 1962, 427), his contemporary, Carl Nageli, was able to turn the tables by using the same analogy to deny a vital force to organic cells, attributing their growth to mechanical forces. The synthesis of organic compounds, such as that of urea in 1828 by Friedrich Wohler, further undermined the vitalistic view of life, as did Lavoisier's demonstration that the ratio of emitted heat to carbon dioxide was the same for animals as it was for candle flames, which suggested that the energy of living organisms was derived from their food and not from a "vital force." Vitalism is by no means dead, although its modern versions are often in disguised form (e.g., Koestler's holons and Sheldrake's morphic resonance).

A strong factor in the final banishment of mind from its last stronghold in matter (the human brain) was, paradoxically enough, the dualistic model of mind-body interaction proposed by the French philosopher and mathematician René Descartes in the seventeenth century. Prior to Descartes, the physical universe had come more and more to be seen as governed by a clockwork mechanism. The Calvinist John Preston stated in 1628 that "God alters no law of Nature" (Mason 1962, 181). Divine intervention by deities or angels was no longer permitted; events were seen to be predictable from and governed by the laws of nature alone. Although it is true that vestiges of divine intervention persisted even later than the time of Descartes, such as in Newton's view that divine intervention was necessary to reestablish the regular order of the planets' orbits, which was constantly being deranged due to gravitational forces among the planets and comets and to a gradual reduction in orbital velocity due to "ether drag" (Mason 1962, 206; Christianson 1978, 407), in general the picture of the universe that was emerging during the seventeenth century was one of a huge impersonal machine governed by strictly mechanical principles.

Among the things that had previously suggested a mentalistic aspect to matter were those phenomena suggestive of action-at-a-distance, such as gravitation and magnetism. Descartes was able to propose theories of magnetism (the "vortex" theory) and gravitation (the "plenum" theory) that avoided the problem of action-at-a-distance by assuming that these two forms of attraction were transmitted through some substancelike medium. (Newton, also largely a mechanist, later proposed an explanation of gravitational attraction in terms of an all-pervading ether, which consisted of particles that mutually repelled one another.) Descartes extended his mechanical view of the universe to include all physical objects, even animate ones. He did not, however, deny the existence of mind but, rather, ruled that mind inhabited a different plane of existence from the physical world, although the human mind could interact with the physical body via the pineal gland. Descartes also saw the mind as a totally different kind of entity from matter; mind was indivisible and hence lacked a basic characteristic of matter—that of extension. In Descartes's view, only man possessed a soul, animals being mere mechanisms. Because Descartes's law of inertia held merely that the total quantity of motion in a system remains constant (but not necessarily its *direction*), he proposed that the soul acted upon the body by deflecting the direction of the motion of the "animal spirits," while not changing the intensity of the motion.

Leibniz, however, demonstrated that Descartes was incorrect and that directionality was conserved in the law of momentum. Leibniz thus closed the door on mind-action by showing that Descartes's universe was in fact a deterministic one (although mind retained a place in Leibniz's own cosmolgy based on the concept of the monad). As a deterministic clockwork physical universe allows no room for mind-action, it is not surprising that Descartes's dualism soon yielded to the materialism of Hobbes and La Mettrie (and more recently of Watson and Skinner). Indeed, Westfall (1977) sees the "rigid exclusion of the psychic from physical nature" as the "permanent legacy" of the seventeenth century (p. 41). We will now turn to a critical discussion of that legacy to see how viable modern versions of materialism are, both in terms of philosophical analysis and in light of scientific developments since the seventeenth century. This examination will be conducted in the context of a general discussion of what has become known as the "mind-body problem."

The mind-body problem. A logical place to start any discussion of the relationship between the mind and the body (the mind-body problem) is with a consideration of the traditional classification of solutions to that problem. Such solutions are usually divided into those that are monistic and those that are dualistic. Monistic solutions postulate only one type (i.e., either physical or mental) of entity in the universe, whereas dualistic solutions postulate the existence of both mind and matter as two radically different types of entities.

Monistic philosophies that postulate only the existence of mind are called idealistic philosophies. The prototype of the idealistic philosopher is often taken to be Bishop George Berkeley (who strangely enough lived in the eighteenth century, well after Westfall's "legacy" of materialism had been handed down). Idealistic philosophies postulate that the physical world is nonexistent but is erroneously postulated to exist in order to explain certain constancies and regularities in a person's sensory experience. (Indeed, in our century, the Swiss psychologist Jean Piaget has asserted that the basic properties of the physical world, including the concept of permanent physical objects, are not known a priori to a human infant but are constructed as hypotheses by the infant to account for certain regularities in his sensory experience and intercorrelations among his different sensory modalities.)

The doctrine that the physical world may be an illusion is in fact logically irrefutable. The reader, following the Taoist philosopher Chuang Tsu, may legitimately wonder whether he might be a butterfly temporarily dreaming that he is a human being reading a sentence about butterfly dreams. According to the doctrine of solipsism, all one can be certain of is one's own existence (in the words of Descartes, "I think, therefore I am") and that one is at the present time thinking certain thoughts, remembering certain memories, feeling certain feelings, and sensing certain sensations. One cannot know that the inferences one makes from these mental events about the nature of the physical world are valid, as the sensations could be hallucinatory, the memories false, the thoughts delusions, and the feelings baseless. The various agencies presumed by idealists to be responsible for producing the illusion of the physical world have included God, some sort of collective unconscious, and the illusion-producing state of craving and ignorance (according to certain schools of Buddhism).

The reply of modern (nonradical) philosophies of science to idealism in general and solipsism in particular is that theories that postulate the existence of the physical world with its associated entities and properties yield more testable scientific predictions than do idealistic theories and are therefore to be preferred over the latter as scientific hypotheses. (They are even covertly preferred by most solipsists, who prove strangely reluctant to step in front of illusory oncoming trucks.)

The second type of monistic philosophy is materialism. Radical materialism, as propounded by B. F. Skinner and others, asserts baldly that mental events do not exist. However, this contradicts the fact that I (and presumably the reader, if he or she is not a figment of my imagination) have directly experienced such mental events as sensations, thoughts, memories, and so forth. Skinner's position essentially contains its own refutation. Skinner cannot claim that he believes that mental events do not exist, as that belief would itself constitute a mental event. Therefore, by his own theory (and reportedly by his own contention), Skinner's expressions of belief in this doctrine are operantly conditioned responses (or generalizations thereof) which he has reinforced (through book sales, honoraria, etc.) for emitting in the past. However, if Skinner's arguments are in fact mere conditioned responses, it is difficult to see why one would need to take them seriously.

More interesting varieties of materialism are those that concede the existence of both mental and physical events but assert that mental events are in fact identical with neural events (neural identity theory and central state materialism) or that both are merely two aspects of a single underlying reality (double aspect theory).[1] These theories are reductionist in the sense that they assume that mental events are ultimately explicable in terms of physical events and that behavior is ultimately predictable solely by reference to physical events. A related dualist doctrine is that of epiphenomenalism, which, while conceding that mental events and physical events are "two separate things," denies any causal efficacy to mental events. Mental events are considered to be mere epiphenomena of physical events. They are themselves caused by physical events, but are themselves incapable of causing or influencing physical events.

From a scientific point of view, all these theories would seem to be operationally equivalent, as they all seem to make the same empirical predictions (mainly, that no violations of physical principles will occur in the brain and that no successful predictions regarding the behavior of the brain can be generated from theories involving "nonphysical" entities such as souls or "immaterial minds" that could not in principle at least be derived from theories referring solely to physical entities).[2] As it is difficult to see how one could devise a scientific experiment to test between these theories (as they all seem to make the same empirical predictions), they must be regarded from a scientific viewpoint as merely different verbal formulations of the same theory. Therefore, these doctrines will henceforth be referred to generically as "physicalistic theories."

It is commonly held, both by parapsychologists and skeptics, that psi phenomena (i.e., phenomena involving ESP or PK) are inexplicable in terms of physicalistic theories (as they seem to involve causation backward in time, not to weaken with increasing distance, etc.). Hence, it is usually taken that the existence of psi phenomena would falsify physicalism. As physicalistic solutions to the mind-body problem are subscribed to by the vast majority of scientists today, it is not surprising that they therefore reject the claims of parapsychology insofar as they perceive psi phenomena to contradict and threaten their world-view (and basic world-views of this type can be clung to with an almost religious tenacity). Parapsychologists have, on the other hand, exacerbated the problem by stressing the incompatibility of psi phenomena with a physicalistic picture of the universe. This may be due to the fact, as discussed below, that fear of death and the wish for an afterlife form an important motivation for the study of parapsychology. If psi phenomena exist and if psi phenomena cannot be explained in physical terms, then obviously the road is paved for the readmission of the spiritual (or at least mental) realm back into our pictures of the universe. On the other hand, however much parapsychological phenomena seem to contradict the physical determinism inherent in the Newtonian "clockwork" picture of the universe, it is not at all clear that they are in principle incompatible with post-Newtonian physics.

In fact, there has been a recent trend in parapsychology, beginning with Lawrence LeShan (1969; 1976) and Arthur Koestler (1972), to stress the compatibility of psi phenomena with modern physics. LeShan (1969) distinguishes between the "Sensory Individual Reality" (the commonsense view that things are separate from one another and that time can be absolutely partitioned into past, present, and future), which may be equated with the view of prerelativistic physics, and the "Clairvoyant Individual Reality" (in which all things are seen as interconnected and in which time is without unambiguous divisions into future, present, and past), which LeShan equates with the views of the universe contained in modern physical theories. LeShan proposes that the principle of "complementarity" be invoked to govern the use of these two ways of viewing the world, much as a physicist regards light as a wave in one context and as a particle in another. (If ever a solipsist needed proof of the nonexistence of the physical world, this behavior of light might do the trick!) Koestler (1972) has invoked Feynman's interpretations of antimatter as matter traveling backward in time as an example of the nonhostility of modern physics to backward causation (and hence to such parapsychological phenomena as precognition, in which a future event apparently sends a signal into its past).

After the rise of quantum mechanics, modern physics has relinquished the Laplacian idea of absolute determinism. Due to the Heisenberg uncertainty principle, it is no longer possible to predict the future state of the universe with total certainty; at best, physicists can assign probability values to various future states of the universe. This quantum indeterminacy has once again opened up the door to the possible influence of mind on the physical world. Several parapsychologists, among them Helmut Schmidt (1975), E. Walker (1975), and R. Mattuck 1982), have suggested in recent years that the mind may act on matter by determining which of the many possible future states of the universe will occur, thus explicitly or implicitly equating the mind with the "hidden variables" that determine the collapse of the quantum mechanical state vector. Some evidence that the mind may have this capability has been provided through a series of experiments by Schmidt and other investigators in which psychokinetic effect on quantum mechanical processes such as radioactive decay have been found. It has been suggested that the mind may interact with the brain in precisely this manner (see below). Many parapsychologists, among them Koestler (1978) and Zohar (1982) have made a great deal out of the fact that such "hidden variables," if they exist, cannot represent localized properties of physical particles but must be "nonlocal" in nature. The experimental demonstration that any "hidden variables" must be nonlocal involves the observation of the polarization of pairs of particles that have become widely separated after having been initially in contact. The act of measurement of the polarization of one particle seems somehow to determine "instantly" the polarization of the other, even though no causal (i.e., subliminal) signal could connect the particles. This apparent faster-than-light transmission of information is frequently called the "Einstein-Podolsky-Rosen," or EPR, paradox. If the correlation between the polarizations of the two particles is determined by local properties of the particles, then the numbers of pairs of particles observed with various types of polarization should obey an inequality called Bell's Theorem. Because this theorem is found to be violated by experimentally observed particles, the collapse of the wave function governing the two particles must be a "nonlocal" process (i.e., the particles are mysteriously "interconnected").

This "quantum interconnectedness" is taken by many parapsychologists as being compatible with, if not literally providing theoretical support for, the seeming mysterious interconnections between separated events implicit in such parapsychological phenomena as precognition, telepathy, clairvoyance, and psychokinesis. Some parapsychologists, most explicitly C. Nash (1984), have hypothesized that psi phenomena may indeed be literally mediated through such quantum interconnectedness. It is not clear, however, that such nonlocal quantum interactions could form the basis for the transmission of a telepathic message (for example) unless it is postulated that the mind or some other agency can force the state vectors to collapse in a highly coherent manner (otherwise both parties will observe a series of correlated but random and hence unintelligible signals).

If minds are to be granted the psychokinetic ability to collapse state vectors, it is difficult to see why this itself should be viewed as a localized process in view of the fact that the EPR paradox reveals that physics admits of nonlocal processes. It is also difficult to imagine how the sender's mind could keep track of which particles in its local vicinity are related in the appropriate manner to particles in the receiver's brain without assuming some sort of nonlocal monitoring (resulting in an infinite regress). Also the problem of decoding and encoding the signals would appear to be almost insurmountable. Rather than postulate that quantum interconnectedness directly mediates psi effects, parapsychologists should simply rest content in the knowledge that nonlocal processes are at least no longer unthinkable.

Interestingly enough, the argument that parapsychological effects may not be as incompatible with physics as they were once thought to be has not resulted in a sudden lessening of tension between parapsychology and its critics. Some critics, such as Martin Gardner and John Wheeler, have even accused parapsychologists of attempting to gain respectability for their field through the ploy of associating it with the more established and prestigious field of quantum mechanics. (See Gardner 1981 for a discussion.) While it is tempting to view this continued rejection as due to a persistence of cognitive set remaining from Newtonian physics, in view of John Wheeler's involvement it is more plausible to attribute it to continued concern about methodological errors, fraud, and replicability problems in parapsychological research (see discussion below).

If a physical or quasi-physical account of psi phenomena could be constructed, such an account might involve a radical reconceptualization of physics, to the extent that the new entities postulated might look more like the immaterial soul of the radical interactionalist than like any currently understood entity or process. Obviously, if mind and body interact, they form parts of one united system. Thus, any new entities introduced into physical theory to account for mental phenomena could be regarded as either nonmaterial (as they would not be a part of the physical world as previously understood) and thus a victory for the interactionists, or they could be regarded as new physical entities and thus as a victory for the physicalists. As the interactionists and the physicalists would at this point only be disagreeing on terminology, their disagreement would have no empirical content (i.e., their doctrines would be operationally equivalent) and hence they would both be advocating the same theory.

Two other forms of dualism (in addition to epiphenomenalism) are parallelism and interactionism. Parallelism asserts that mind and matter exist as two entirely separate types of entities that do not interact. Leibniz, the most prominent exponent of this position, asserted that God put the physical and mental realms in "preestablished harmony" so that they are forever in correspondence with one another, much as two synchronized clocks remain in harmony. Parallelism would seem, however, to be a most peculiar doctrine. After all, one postulates the existence of the physical world in order to explain certain regularities in one's sensory experience. If the physical world is assumed not to cause one's sensations, then there is no need to postulate its existence at all. To do so would violate Occam's Razor (the injunction not to multiply entities beyond necessity).

The remaining position is that of interactionism, the doctrine that the mind and brain are two "separate things" that nonetheless interact with one another (with causal efficacy in both directions, unlike epiphenomenalism). Some theorists (including J. B. Rhine) have difficulty understanding how such radically different types of entities as body and mind could interact with each other (especially when the mind is conceived in the Cartesian fashion as "unextended"). However, it is not clear that even all physical entities are of the same "type." Is the probability wave describing the motion of a particle in quantum theory (which is not even a wave in physical space) really the same type of entity as the particle itself after observation? Perhaps the terms *dualism* and *monism* denote outmoded concepts in light of recent developments in physical theory.

In discussing Descartes's theory of interactionism, it was noted that Newtonian determinism effectively closed the brain to any possible influence of mind. However, the Heisenberg uncertainty principle in quantum mechanics has reintroduced indeterminism into the physical world and has therefore opened the brain to possible influence from a "nonphysical" mind. The Nobel Laureate neurophysiologist Sir John Eccles once remarked that the brain is just "the sort of machine a 'ghost' could operate" (Koestler 1972, 78), functioning as it does by chemical neurotransmitters and minute electric potentials, and he has suggested that a change in the activity of even a single "critically poised" neuron could result in macroscopic changes in brain activity.

In the book *The Self and its Brain,* which Eccles coauthored with the distinguished philosopher of science Karl Popper (Popper and Eccles 1977), Eccles expresses doubt that influences at the level of quantum indeterminacy are sufficient to explain the influence of mind on brain, as he feels that quantum events are too random to account for the "precisely causal events" in the mind-brain interaction. In his contribution to the book, Popper initially agrees with Eccles but then apparently reverses himself by asserting that the mind could select the quantum state in the brain that it finds the most acceptable. At one point, Popper suggests that the mind may have its own source of (presumably physical) energy. In this latter view, the mind would be some sort of quasi-physical object that might be capable of greater influence on the brain than that allowed by Heisenberg's uncertainty principle. Thouless and Wiesner (1948) have proposed that extrasensory perception and psychokinesis are anomalous externalized forms of the usually internalized interactions between the mind and the brain (with the mind influencing the brain through psychokinesis and becoming aware of brain states through clairvoyance).

Eccles sees the integration of mental activity as the *raison d'être* of the mind, and he does not feel that the integration of mental activity in general and the visual field in particular can be explained on the basis of known neural processes. Wilder Penfield, another prominent neurophysiologist, has also found it necessary to postulate a mind external to the brain (although he balks at the use of the adjective "immaterial" to describe such an entity). As evidence for this dualistic position, Penfield (1975) cites the fact that movements or other activity produced by electrical stimulation of the brain are experienced as ego-alien and involuntary. Both Penfield and Eccles (1979) see conscious attention by the mind as necessary for memory formation.

The results of split-brain research are somewhat embarrassing to certain versions of interactionism. Under a naive interpretation of Thouless and Wiesner's "internal psi" theory, for instance, a commissurotomized patient should be able, through clairvoyant perception of the right hemisphere and psychokinetic influence of the left hemisphere, to describe verbally an object held in the left hand. That such an effect is not usually observed is therefore evidence against Thouless and Wiesner's theory. One way around this difficulty would be to limit the mind's influence to facilitation and inhibition of synaptic junctions. Under this interpretation, the mind would be unable to overcome disrupted neural pathways.

Another way out of the difficulty is to propose that the interaction between the mind and the brain is restricted to certain areas of the brain. Precisely this sort of restriction has been proposed by both Eccles and Penfield, although they disagree on the site of the interaction. To the extent that the nondominant hemisphere is to be granted a stream of consciousness of its own, it would be possible to account for this by postulating that more than one mind is associated with any given human brain, each mind having its own localized site or functional arena of interaction. Such a model of a "hierarchy of selves" was proposed by William McDougall (1926) and might account for certain types of dissociative phenomena, including multiple personality. It should be noted in passing that Eccles's and Penfield's theories by no means represent the mainstream of contemporary neurophysiological thought.

Emotional and Cognitive Bases

We will now turn from metaphysical and historical factors to a consideration of the psychological underpinnings of both belief and skepticism. This discussion will begin with religious motivations, a topic not unrelated to the discussion above.

Religious motives. There is no doubt that the same psychological needs that promote belief in various religions (including desires for control over the elements, knowledge of the future, protection from natural forces and the vagaries of chance, power over disease, and a life after death) are also responsible for the widespread belief in parapsychological phenomena. Modern science has discredited naive and literal interpretations of many religions, and for many people parapsychology fills the void thus created. Parapsychology not only has all the accoutrements of science itself but also promises to satisfy all the religious motives delineated above through its alleged demonstration of such paranormal phenomena as psychokinesis, precognition, psychic healing, and the survival of death.

Religious motivations and a desire to overthrow what they regarded as the depressing mechanistic cosmology proposed by nineteenth-century science formed an explicit and openly acknowledged part of the motivation of the founders of the Society for Psychical Research (SPR). Prominent among these concerns was unquestionably the fact of death with its promise of total annihilation of the human personality. This great concern of the early psychical researchers with the problem of the survival of death was undoubtedly in part attributable to the biological instinct for survival as well as to a desire to be reunited with departed loved ones (to use the mortician's term). It is well known, for example, that the incidence of and interest in mediumistic phenomena tend to increase markedly during and after times of great tragedy, such as world wars. As psi phenomena seemed to contradict physicalistic theories and to point to a mental realm over and above the physical world, they were readily embraced by persons seeking scientific support for the concept of a spiritual realm. Indeed, as recently as 1982, upon the occasion of the centenary of the founding of the SPR, the prominent British parapsychologist John Beloff asserted in his presidential address to the Parapsychological Association that the survival of death was contingent upon the existence of psi (Beloff 1983). This is probably an indefensible statement, as it is quite conceivable that the mind could survive death even if it did not possess the powers of ESP and PK, but it does show how closely related the issues of the existence of paranormal powers and the survival of death are in the minds of many parapsychologists.

The scientific community may in turn have feared (and may still fear) a trend toward irrationalism and a possible reemergence of religious persecution with an accompanying attempt to suppress scientific doctrines. Certainly the memory of the Christian resistance to the heliocentric model of the solar system and the theory of evolution has never been far from the consciousness of the scientific community. The history of parapsychology has done nothing to lessen these fears. Spiritualism, which formed the major impetus for the founding of the field of parapsychology, grew out of the mediumship of the Fox sisters, self-confessed frauds. Some members of the community of "professional" parapsychologists have shown an almost unbelievable lack of scientific caution, ranging from claiming to photograph the human aura through the technique of Kirlian photography to cataloging phone calls from the dead. The uncritical enthusiasm of the public, resulting in (among other things) the construction of a "levitation hall" at Maharishi International University, has not helped matters. It is thus clear that religious motives form part of the basis for belief in parapsychological phenomena and that fear of religious irrationalism forms part of the resistance of the scientific community to parapsychological "findings."

Attitudinal processes. Obviously, the subfield of social psychology known as "attitude theory" may have much to tell us about how attitudes toward parapsychology are formed. According to reinforcement theory (Hovland, Janis, and Kelly 1953), one tends to hold beliefs that one has been rewarded for expressing and to extinguish beliefs for which one has been punished. To the extent that the reward contingencies within the academic community would tend to favor anti-psi beliefs, one would expect them to engender skepticism. This would, however, neglect the propensity of the public to provide monetary support as well as adulation to authorities expressing belief in paranormal powers.

A more subtle view is provided by Leon Festinger (1957), whose theory of cognitive dissonance postulates a psychological pressure to achieve consistency between one's beliefs and actions. Thus, if a person succumbs to academic reinforcement contingencies and inhibits expression of his pro-parapsychology beliefs or makes public remarks in opposition to those beliefs, he will, according to dissonance theory, be in a state of tension due to the inconsistency between his overt behavior and his private belief. He can reduce this tension or "dissonance" by (a) changing his private belief from one of acceptance to one of skepticism, (b) reversing his decision and expressing his beliefs, or (c) magnifying the reward or punishment (e.g., "I only said it because I wouldn't get tenure if I didn't"). Strategy (c) would not succeed particularly well if the threatened punishment is communicated subtly and merely intimated and if the promised reward (salary, tenure, etc.) is small and/or unreliable (both conditions one would typically obtain in the case of the expression of parapsychological beliefs within the academic community); therefore, one might expect increasing recourse to strategy (a).

On the other side of the coin, any doubts about the existence of paranormal phenomena would create dissonance in anyone publicly expressing a belief in psi (as would any lost rewards, such as tenure, etc.). This dissonance could be reduced by eliminating whatever doubts about the existence of psi still remain. Thus, academic exile may have the boomerang effect of increasing rather than decreasing belief in psi (once that belief has been expressed).

One method of avoiding states of cognitive dissonance is to avoid exposure to high-quality communications and arguments that run counter to one's position. This might explain the tendency of some parapsychologists to ignore or repress legitimate and constructive criticisms of their methodology. Sometimes this can result in disaster, as has often happened in the case of research on paranormal metal-bending, most notably in the case of Project Alpha, in which researchers at Washington University in St. Louis were deceived by stooges of critic James Randi posing as psychics, primarily because the researchers failed to employ safeguards suggested by Randi (see Randi 1983 and Chapter 14 of this volume). On the other side, critics often fail to heed (or at least discuss) the better conducted studies in the field of parapsychology. Occasionally, critics write books and articles debunking the weakest claims in the field, such as Arthur Conan Doyle's alleged pictures of fairies (Randi 1980) and Kreskin's stage performances (Marks and Kammann 1980), while at the same time ignoring most of the best experimental studies, and subsequently claim to have debunked the entire field of parapsychology. This may be understandable in light of the fact that the scientific community's main concern may be directed toward a possible trend toward irrationalism (and the magicians' toward a dishonest and attention-stealing use of conjuring techniques). Both may be concerned not so much with so-called "legitimate" parapsychology but with clearly quack science and charlatanism. To the extent that this is the case, parapsychologists should applaud their efforts (but not their claim to have debunked the entire field).

Another dissonance-reducing technique is to reduce the psychological importance of an issue. The writer recalls the remarks of one prominent cognitive psychologist who told him that, although he did not know whether parapsychological phenomena existed or not, he did not see why they were of any importance or interest (perhaps reflecting his concerns as a psychological, rather than physical, theorist). A related technique for reducing the stress of cognitive inconsistency or "imbalance" described by R. Abelson and M. Rosenberg (1958) is to "stop thinking." To some extent, this has been the traditional response of academic psychology to the claims of parapsychology, which are almost never discussed in any detail in the academic curricula of psychology departments. Because of this "heads in the sand" approach, departments of psychology have in many instances failed in what should be their responsibility to provide a responsible (even if skeptical) discussion of alleged parapsychological phenomena, a topic that is of great interest to students and the public in general. (Perhaps if responsible discussions were more routinely provided, fewer adults would so credulously accept weak and ludicrous parapsychological claims.)

Lack of social support for one's beliefs is another source of cognitive dissonance, according to Festinger. Certainly, the tendency of people to conform to group opinion, the pressure placed upon the person by groups to conform, and the tendency of people to obey authority figures have been amply demonstrated in experiments by S. Asch (1958), S. Schachter (1951), and S. Milgram (1963; 1968). Within the academic community, one would expect such pressure to favor skepticism with regard to psi phenomena. One way to decrease the cognitive dissonance arising from lack of social support is, according to Festinger, to decrease the perceived attractiveness of the disagreeing parties (which might result in a skeptic classifying all parapsychologists as fairy-worshiping lunatics or a parapsychologist classifying all skeptics as unimaginative, narrow-minded bigots). A similar effect is postulated by "balance" theorists like Abelson and Rosenberg (1958). It would be expected that this strategy would be especially prevalent among persons scoring high on scales of dogmatism (see Rokeach 1960).

One adverse effect of the social isolation of parapsychologists from the mainstream academic community (which results from the rejection of even well-conducted parapsychological studies for publication in mainstream academic journals and the denial of academic posts to persons professing an interest in parapsychology) is that parapsychology is in danger of being methodologically isolated from the rest of science and is thus in peril of becoming a true pseudoscience rather than just a protoscience with no hard results, as it is at present. Part of this isolation is due to the fact that much of the dialogue between parapsychologists and their critics takes place in the popular press and other forms of mass media. This has resulted in an excess of rhetoric and a dearth of sophisticated and constructive methodological criticism. Some parapsychologists, perhaps employing the dissonance-reducing process of decreasing the attractiveness of one's opponents, have in recent years called for the abandonment of traditional scientific methodology. They have been aided and abetted in this movement by such radical sociologists of knowledge (and part-time parapsychologists) as H. M. Collins and T. J. Pinch (1982), who assert that there is no demonstrably correct form of reasoning and that it is essentially impossible to understand a theory unless one believes in it (theories or paradigms are said to be "incommensurable"). These views are similar to those of Paul Feyerabend, who asserts that all forms of reasoning are equally valid and who gives "three cheers to the fundamentalists in California who succeeded in having a dogmatic formulation of the theory of evolution removed from the textbooks and an account of Genesis included" and says "the more Lysenko affairs the better" (Feyerabend 1981, 163). Fortunately, only a small minority of parapsychologists adhere to such relativistic doctrines. However, should such radical ideas ever gain the ascendancy in parapsychology (with the resulting abandonment of traditional scientific methodology, such as the requirement that scientific results be repeatable before they are accepted as fact), a paradoxical effect of the social exile of parapsychology from the mainstream scientific community will have been the transformation of a potential science (even if one with null results) into a true pseudoscience. For this reason, it is important that communication between parapsychologists and their critics be improved. It would be helpful in this regard if critics would join professional organizations of parapsychologists and identify themselves as parapsychologists (albeit skeptical ones). Not only would this improve the quality of the dialogue, but it would decrease the tendency toward "black-and-white" thinking on both sides.

Cognitive factors. There is an implicit assumption on the part of a segment of the scientific community that existing scientific theories constitute a complete and final description of the universe. This has occasionally led to unreasonable resistance to new findings, as in the case of meteorites, and new ideas, as in the case of Wegener's theory of continental drift, which was proposed early in this century (1915) but was widely rejected until as late as the 1960s, when the overwhelming preponderance of geological evidence finally forced its acceptance. This attitude is exemplified in the following statement of Albert A. Michelson, which he made 20 years after his paradigm-shaking experiment on the velocity of the earth relative to the luminiferous ether, which led to the downfall of Newtonian mechanics and to the eventual acceptance of the special theory of relativity:

> The more important fundamental laws and facts of the physical universe have all been discovered and these are now so firmly established that the possibility of their ever being supplanted in consequence of new discoveries is exceedingly remote. [Quoted in Feuer 1974, 253]

Michelson added that, although there were apparent exceptions to most of these laws, these were due to the increasing accuracy of measurement made possible by modern apparatus and that the system of known physical laws would be adequate to deal with the "apparent exceptions." He went on to assert that "our future discoveries must be looked for in the sixth place of decimals" (Feuer 1974, 254). What is most amazing about these statements is that they preceded rather than followed the publication of Einstein's paper on special relativity. This tendency on the part of scientists to assume that the work of science is done and that all relevant laws are known is an example of what the Gestalt psychologists have called "the principle of closure"—the psychological pressure to achieve a solution to a given problem. This pressure may be reduced by entering a state of premature closure, in which problems are seen as having been solved when in fact they have not.

Not all rejected theories are correct of course, and the conservatism of science has proved useful in hindering the widespread acceptance of such nonexistent phenomena as the "N-rays" of René Blondlot, the "animal magnetism" of Franz Mesmer, and the "orgone energy" of Wilhelm Reich. (Just because they persecute you doesn't mean that you're a genius!) It should be noted, however, that present scientific theory is glaringly incomplete when it comes to explaining mental phenomena. There is no understanding at present of how or why certain patterns of neural activity give rise to conscious experience, nor is there any explanation for the psychological experience of the passage of time or the uniqueness of the present moment (neither of which has any place in physical theory).

At the other extreme, the need for novelty might underlie interest in psi phenomena. This might account for the grouping in bookstores of books on parapsychology with books on such topics as flying saucers, astrology, and the Loch Ness monster. Possibly it might also account for the fact that the headline "Reincarnation Shocker! Our son was reborn as a dog, say grieving parents" appeared atop the banner headline "TEEN DELIVERS BIGFOOT BABY" in the June 19, 1984, issue of the *Weekly World News*. Incidentally, even animals have been demonstrated to have a need for novelty in operant conditioning experiments using complex environments or novel stimuli for reinforcement (see Fowler 1965 for a discussion).

Psychodynamic factors. Paranoid mechanisms undoubtedly account for some portion of the belief in psychic powers, especially one's own psychic powers, and these mechanisms are particularly apparent in many persons who visit, write, or call parapsychological laboratories. Paranoid delusions of persecution, for instance, commonly include the belief that one's enemies are paranormally monitoring and manipulating one's thoughts. T. Lidz (1973) has attributed such paranoid mechanisms to the lack of properly defined ego boundaries in schizophrenics, and according to Piagetian as well as psychoanalytic theory fantasies of omnipotence (including the belief that one has psychic powers) have their roots in the infant's belief in the magical powers of his thoughts.

The idea of telepathy, with its implied intimate interconnections between human minds, may appeal to persons suffering from separation anxiety or what Karen Horney (1950) has called "basic anxiety"—the fear of being isolated and helpless in a hostile world. This may be a form of what McGuire (1960a; 1960b; 1968) has called "wishful thinking," the tendency to believe in what is pleasant and to disbelieve what is not pleasant. "Wishful thinking" undoubtedly underlies much of the belief in phenomena suggestive of survival after death as well.

Ardent disbelief could be construed as a defense against paranoid thoughts (and the causal efficacy of unconscious wishes) or as a fear of the uncanny and the unknown. Many people who reject the evidence for an afterlife also express a distaste for the idea that they themselves will survive death. Charles Tart (1982) has attributed skepticism toward psi phenomena to a "primal repression" of threatening telepathic interactions between mother and child. This argument of Tart's will, however, no more convince skeptics to believe in psi than the threat of eternal damnation will convince an atheist to attend church.

"Rational" Bases for Skepticism and Belief

This section will, very briefly, examine the evidence for various types of paranormal phenomena as well as the attacks upon that evidence by various skeptics. The evidence will be divided into three areas: spontaneous cases, experimental studies, and the evidence for a life after death.

Spontaneous Cases

The phrase "spontaneous cases" denotes incidents suggestive of psi phenomena that occur in everyday life. Consider, for instance, the following case of apparent precognition taken from Louisa Rhine's collection (1961, 198-199):

> In Washington State a young woman was so upset by a terrifying dream one night that she had to wake her husband and tell him about it. She had dreamed that a large ornamental chandelier which hung over their baby's bed in the next room had fallen into the crib and crushed the baby to death. In the dream she could see herself and her husband standing amid the wreckage. The clock on the baby's dresser said 4:35. In the distance she could hear the rain on the windowpane and the wind blowing outside.
>
> But her husband just laughed at her. He said it was a silly dream, to forget it and go back to sleep; and in a matter of moments he did just that himself. But she could not sleep.
>
> Finally, still frightened, she got out of bed and went to the baby's room, got her and brought her back. On the way she stopped to look out the window, and saw a full moon, the weather calm and quite unlike the dream. Then, feeling a little foolish, she got back into bed with the baby.
>
> About two hours later they were wakened by a resounding crash. She jumped up, followed by her husband, and ran to the nursery. There, where the baby would have been lying, was the chandelier in the crib. They looked at each other and then at the clock. It stood at 4:35. Still a little skeptical they listened— to the sound of the rain on the windowpane and wind howling outside.

Skeptics wishing to debunk such a case might attribute the apparent precognition to sensory cues, possibly asserting that the mother may have noticed falling plaster indicating that the chandelier was coming loose and may have incorporated the evening's televised weather prediction into the dream. The time of the chandelier's fall (4:35 A.M.) could have been added later as an additional detail in order to improve the account of the dream (confabulation). The woman may in fact believe that she dreamed the time when in fact she did not (memory distortion or "secondary elaboration").

Spontaneous cases are sometimes attributed by skeptics to coincidence, delusion, and inference as well. For instance, consider a case in which a man breaks out in a cold sweat before boarding an airplane, decides not to go on the flight, and then the airplane subsequently crashes. This case might be attributable to chance, as it might be expected to be a fairly common occurrence that people back out of airplane flights due to anxiety and that some of these planes will crash. As an example of an explanation in terms of inference, consider the case of a woman who dreams her husband is in a car crash the night before he is in fact killed in an automobile accident. She may have noticed that her husband has been driving more and more recklessly, has shown an inordinate amount of interest in car accidents on the television news, and looked particularly depressed (i.e., suicidal) the day before the crash. Explanations in terms of memory distortion, fraud, and delusion are not so easy with cases in which the ESP experience has been related to another person before the confirming event (as in many of the cases collected by the early SPR) or in which a psychokinetic occurrence (clock-stopping, etc.) is witnessed by several people. Explanations in terms of inference, sensory cues, and coincidence are, however, no less viable in these types of cases.

It is sometimes argued that, while each individual spontaneous case is like a twig that may be broken by counter-explanation in terms of normal processes (although sometimes at the expense of considerable mental gymnastics), when taken together the spontaneous cases constitute an unbreakable bundle. G. N. M. Tyrrell (1957) called this the "fagot theory" (not to be confused with Arthur Conan Doyle's fairy theory). It is true that these cases follow certain patterns (a great many involve death, severe physical injury, etc.) and that these patterns suggest a recurrent natural process. It is also true that spontaneous cases do not resemble invented ghost stories like those found in fictional literature. It could still be maintained, however, that the similarities among the stories reflect modal human thought processes (archetypal patterns?) rather than being characteristics of a naturally occurring phenomenon.

Two other forms of spontaneous psi occurrences that will be mentioned briefly because of their prominence are poltergeist phenomena and paranormal healing. Poltergeist phenomena involve inexplicable physical events, which may include object movements, sounds, misbehavior of electrical apparatus, and the sudden appearance of fire and water, to name only a few. In the majority of cases, these phenomena have centered around a focal person, who is presumed to cause the phenomena psychokinetically (hence the use of the term "RSPK"— standing for "recurrent spontaneous psychokinesis"—to describe these phenomena has come into vogue). Poltergeist occurrences are relatively rare, and several purported poltergeist agents (who are often maladjusted adolescents) have been detected producing the alleged phenomena through the use of fraud. In one of William Roll's cases (the "housing project" poltergeist in Newark), Ernie, the presumed agent, was observed through a one-way mirror to secrete measuring tapes under his shirt and then to throw the tapes. A subsequent polygraph test revealed Ernie to be "telling the truth" when he claimed that he did not know how the movement of the tapes was produced (Roll 1972). Ostensibly paranormal phenomena, and particularly the beginnings of object movements, are hardly ever observed directly by the investigators of poltergeist cases. This "shyness effect" makes it easy to ascribe at least the vast majority of such cases to fraud.

Another type of spontaneous effect of wide popular interest is paranormal healing. In cases of faith healing, as practiced by Kathryn Kuhlman and others, it is usually possible to attribute most cures to suggestion, as many of the illnesses involved, such as blindness and paralysis, may be due to conversion hysteria or may have a strong psychosomatic component. Hence these are probably primarily psychological rather than organic illnesses in the first place. In the few cases of documented organic illnesses that have undergone cure, the healing may be attributable to naturally occurring processes (such as the spontaneous regression of cancer). A related technique, psychic surgery, is almost invariably accomplished through the use of "sleight of hand" and other fraudulent techniques, as has been shown in an impressive exposé by William Nolen (1974). There are a handful of laboratory studies pointing to the existence of some genuine effects produced by healers employing the technique of laying-on-of-hands (e.g., Grad 1965; Smith 1968); but questions have been raised about the methodological adequacy of many of these studies, and it is not certain how replicable these effects will prove to be.

There is a consensus within the parapsychological community that the evidence from spontaneous cases is insufficient to prove the existence of psi and that experimental evidence is required in order to rule out the existence of sensory cues, confabulation, coincidence, inference, delusion, and memory distortion. This position was even shared by one of the most prominent investigators of spontaneous cases, Louisa Rhine (although it was not shared by some of the investigators in the early days of the Society for Psychical Research, many of whom felt that spontaneous case material was sufficient in and of itself to prove the existence of psi). This dismissal of spontaneous case material, while appropriately conservative from a strict scientific point of view, is perhaps made a bit too facilely by most parapsychologists. Anyone who has interviewed many people directly about their experiences cannot help but feel a great sense of unwarranted mental gymnastics when attempting to ascribe all these experiences to normal causes. Even if the experimental evidence for psi must in the final analysis be dismissed, the large body of spontaneous case material must raise at least a suspicion that something truly strange is occurring.

Experimental Evidence

Because of the above-mentioned doubts about spontaneous case material, parapsychologists have undertaken experimental studies in order to prove the existence of psi. To rule out the hypothesis of chance coincidence, they employ target materials for which the probability of guessing a target correctly by chance is well defined (such as a deck of cards). To rule out sensory cues, the targets are shielded from the subject's view (with varying degrees of efficacy in the early experiments). Under these conditions, many experiments have been reported that yield statistically significant evidence for psi. This experimental work has, however, been criticized by skeptics on the basis of residual sensory cues, motor artifacts, nonblindness of judging, improper randomization of targets, inappropriate statistical analysis, fraud, and the poor replicability of the effects. We will consider each of these criticisms in turn.

Sensory cues. The early days of experimental parapsychology were not characterized by the stringent safeguards against sensory cues that are (usually) employed today. For instance, an "agent" might sit at one end of a table, pick up an "ESP card," and attempt to project its identity into the mind of a "percipient" seated at the other end of the table. Under these circumstances, the percipient might learn the card's identity by seeing the card reflected in the agent's eyes or by picking up on cues unconsciously provided by the agent (such as tilting the head when viewing a "star," etc.). The behaviorist B. F. Skinner pointed out that the Zener cards employed by Rhine could be read from the back under certain lighting conditions, invalidating any experiment in which the percipient could see the backs of the cards. Parapsychologists were quick to respond to such critiques by totally isolating the subject from the targets (such as by having them in separate buildings, for instance). Most, but by no means all, forced-choice experiments in parapsychology today are characterized by adequate sensory shielding of the target from the percipient. (A forced-choice experiment is one in which the subject's guess must correspond to one of a finite number of targets on each trial.) Exceptions still occur. For instance, Martin Gardner (1981) has noted that a light system used by the agent to signal the next trial to the percipient in a recent experiment by Charles Tart allows the agent to provide cues as to the identity of the next target through the use of a "time-delay" code.

Persi Diaconis (Chapter 24 of this volume) points out the danger of giving trial-by-trial feedback to a subject guessing a target pool that is being sampled without replacement (as the feedback will enable the subject to improve his chances by avoiding guesses corresponding to already sampled targets). This criticism to a large extent misrepresents the actual practice of experimental parapsychology, as the practice of giving trial-by-trial feedback when sampling without replacement rarely occurs in forced-choice experiments and is regarded as a sign of incompetence when it does (and usually results in the rejection of the study concerned for publication).

This criticism does however apply to some free-response experiments. (Free-response experiments are those in which the subjects give their subjective impressions of the target rather than guessing it directly. Subjects in this type of experiment usually have no prior knowledge of the actual targets in the target pool, save for general information, such as the targets being geographical sites, pictures, objects, etc.) For instance, Harold Puthoff, Russell Targ, and Charles

Tart (1980) report a remote-viewing experiment in which a subject was required over ten trials to describe objects sampled without replacement from a set of ten target objects. Because the subject was told the identity of the target after each trial, she could, on subsequent trials, avoid giving descriptions corresponding to previously seen targets, thus artifactually inflating the probability that her descriptions would be correctly matched to the targets by the judges. Marks and Kammann (1978; 1980) have argued that in Targ and Puthoff's main remote-viewing research, the subjects' remarks contained clues as to trial order (by referring to "two previous targets," for instance) and target identity (by explicitly referring to previously seen targets, which the judges would then know not to match with the present transcript). Tart, Puthoff, and Targ (1980) have argued that the results are still statistically significant ($p < 10^{-4}$) when these cues have been edited out of the transcripts. One can of course argue about the efficacy of the editing process, and, in any event, the basic problem (namely, avoiding giving responses descriptive of previously seen targets) arising from the use of trial-by-trial feedback when sampling without replacement remains.

A related problem in free-response experiments involves the sensory cuing of judges. For instance, in remote-viewing experiments reported by J. Bisaha and B. Dunne (1979), judges were provided with pictures of the target location taken on the day of the trial. Thus cues as to weather conditions, seasonal variations (e.g., foliage conditions), time of day, and so forth, could have been present in both the subject's transcripts and the pictures, which the judges could then use to match the transcripts to the targets. Bisaha and Dunne deny that such cues exist; but, in the only two picture sets they reproduce from their first experiment, the leaves are still on the trees in one, whereas the trees are bare in the other. A similar problem exists in two dream telepathy experiments reported by I. Child, H. Kanthamani, and V. Sweeney (1977). In each study, the agent attempted to send a different target picture into the dreams of a percipient on each of eight different nights. The eight sets of dreams and impressions were then ranked by the agent against the eight targets. However, as the agent knew which target was used on which night and as the percipient's dreams would be expected to incorporate certain "day residues" reflecting the events of the prior day, the agent could have used this knowledge to match the dreams against the targets. Thus, while sensory cues do not pose much of a problem for forced-choiced experiments in parapsychology, the sensory cuing of subjects and judges is a problem that has yet to be worked out for free-response experiments that involve sampling without replacement. (The majority of free-response experiments, which have the responses judged against a different target pool for each trial, as opposed to the actual set of targets used in the experiment, do not suffer from this problem to the same extent.)

Motor artifacts. In certain types of psychokinesis experiments, it is very important to ensure that the subject cannot use his or her motor skills to influence the target apparatus. For instance, in a "placement PK" experiment in which a subject is attempting to use psychokinesis to influence a series of balls rolling down a chute to go into the left or right side of a collection bin, it is important to ensure that the subject cannot influence the balls by the use of his or her motor apparatus, such as by breathing on them, rocking the table, altering the air currents by changing his or her body position, and so forth. Also, it is important to ensure that the balls be placed in the apparatus in exactly the same way at the beginning of each trial, so that no initial placement artifacts occur. Experiments that involve an attempted psychokinetic influence of living targets should also involve precautions against normal sensory-motor influence. For instance, in an experiment reported by J. Barry (1971), subjects sat for 15 minutes at a distance of 1.5 meters from a set of ten petri dishes, attempting to inhibit the growth of the fungus in five experimental dishes while "ignoring" the control dishes. Under these conditions, it might be possible for a subject to influence the growth by, for instance, breathing on the dishes. N. Richmond (1952) reported an experiment in which he was successful in influencing paramecia to swim to a specified target quadrant as he viewed them through a microscope. As Richmond was obviously close to the microscope, he could have influenced the paramecia through his breath or by jiggling the slide. Another problem in this experiment is that, while the target quandrant was randomly selected, Richmond did not use a random process to select the paramecium to be influenced; thus he may have selected paramecia already predisposed to move to the desired quadrant, as has been pointed out by Martin Johnson (1982). It is obviously sometimes very difficult to exclude motor artifacts from these types of experiments. Fortunately, most modern PK research uses such targets as quantum-mechanically based random-number generators, which are not so easily influenced through motor artifacts.

Violations of blindness. It is important in parapsychology, as in other disciplines, that measurement of certain variables be done by a person who is blind as to the values of other variables. For instance, if an experimenter who is rating a person's extroversion based on clinical observation during an interview already knows that person's score on an ESP test, the experimenter may consciously or unconsciously tend to give higher extroversion ratings to persons with high ESP scores, thus artifactually producing another "confirmation" of the positive relation between ESP and extroversion. This sort of blindness violation is now widely recognized as improper procedure by parapsychologists, and studies containing this sort of error rarely find their way into the professional literature. Other types of blindness violation continue to exist in parapsychology, however, as they do in all sciences. (What science can claim that none of its practitioners makes methodological errors?) For instance, J. Palmer and R. Lieberman (1976) report an "out-of-the-body experience" study in which an experimenter who knew the identity of the target was in the room with the subject, allowing the possibility of sensory cuing. Persons who interact with subjects before they make their response should always be blind as to target identity. Persons physically interacting with PK target materials should also be kept blind as to the target. For instance, in an experiment reported by C. Nash (1982), the experimenter placing fungus samples in an incubator was not blind as to which funguses were to be psychokinetically inhibited and accelerated and which were controls. Thus the experimenter might have been able to influence the outcome in the desired direction by selective placement of the funguses in the incubator. Obviously, in such experiments it is important that the person measuring the fungus growth also be blind as to the experimental condition. While such violations of blindness do occasionally occur in parapsychology, it is probably safe to say that parapsychologists are more, not less, conscientious about blindness of measurement than are most researchers in the social sciences.

Nonrandomness of targets. In order to eliminate the hypothesis of chance coincidence, it is important that targets in parapsychological experiments be selected randomly. It will not do, for instance, to have a person select a target by thinking of a number between 1 and 10, as certain numbers are more likely to pop into his mind (and the guesser's) than are others, raising the probability of a correct guess (a "hit") above the chance level of 10 percent. For instance, in an experiment by G. Tyrrell (1936), a subject had to guess which of five target lamps would be lit on each trial. In the initial stages of the research, Tyrrell himself selected the targets, attempting to be "random" but not employing any formal randomization procedure. Thus the subject could quickly learn Tyrrell's favorite targets and guess these more frequently than the others. She could also increase her score by not calling lamps that had just been lit (as people attempting to produce a random sequence of targets avoid repetitions, thus creating sequential dependencies in the target sequence). Therefore, the subject could expect to do much better than the 20 percent hit rate expected by chance. The sequential dependency problem was pointed out to Tyrrell by G. W. Fisk, and the experiment was continued using random numbers to select the targets. Under these conditions, the subject was still able to achieve a highly significant score (although the significance level may be questioned on the basis of data selection in this study).

Randomness of target selection has also been a problem in some free-response experiments involving the drawing of pictures, including such classic experiments as those by René Warcollier (1963) and Upton Sinclair (1962). The problem continues to the present day, as exemplified in the Stanford Research Institute picture-drawing experiments with Uri Geller reported by Targ and Puthoff (1977). In these experiments, the target was generated by opening a dictionary "at random" and drawing the first "drawable" word on the page. (What is "drawable" is an arbitrary decision that may itself disqualify the target selection process as a random procedure.) The investigators allowed considerable latitude in the interpretation of the word in the target drawing. For instance, the one target selection that Targ and Puthoff describe in detail involved the word *farmer*. In the target drawing, the farmer is equipped not only with a pitchfork, but also with horns and an elaborate tail; in addition, the label *"Devil"* appears above the figure. If Geller and the target preparer had just been viewing *The Exorcist*, for instance, that common experience could account for both the target drawing and Geller's religiously oriented response. This amount of latitude in target selection is unacceptable in a parapsychological experiment.

The overwhelming majority of experiments in parapsychology use appropriate randomization procedures, sometimes involving tables of random numbers and sometimes mechanical random-number generators. There is of course always the possibility that a random-number generator may malfunction through mechanical or human error. For instance, the target sequence in Tart's famous "learning-to-use-ESP" experiment (Tart 1976) was nonrandom, as was pointed out by mathematicians Aaron Goldman, Sherman Stein, and Howard Weiner (see Gardner 1981 for a discussion). The departure from randomness consisted of a shortage of target doublets (the same target appearing twice in a row). Tart hypothesizes that this effect was due to the agent's thinking he had failed to push the button when the same target remained in the display. This sequential dependency not only invalidates Tart's study, but also can account for his claimed evidence for "trans-temporal inhibition" (see Stokes 1978 for a discussion).

Most parapsychological experiments cannot be faulted on the basis of target randomization. It is a common practice to run extensive randomness tests on any random-number generator before and after it is used in an ESP or PK experiment. James Alcock (1984) has recently criticized parapsychologists for failing to use control groups in their research and for comparing their data against theoretical statistical distributions rather than empirically observed distributions.

First, the randomness tests that are usually run on random number generators before and/or after they are used as targets in psychokinesis experiments serve essentially as control groups (although it is true that the scores are typically compared to a theoretical distribution rather than to the scores obtained in the randomness test). Also, to counteract biases in target apparatuses in PK research (such as a die loaded such that the "six" face comes up more than one-sixth of the time), parapsychologists routinely use each target alternative an equal number of times (by aiming for each face of the die on one-sixth of the trials, for instance). Thus, in a coin-toss experiment, aiming for "heads" would serve as a control group for aiming for "tails." Alcock suggests that the use of control groups "makes artifact only a minor problem" in "normal" science (Alcock 1984, 317). However, in the above-mentioned coin-toss experiment, if the coins were tossed by hand (which incidentally would be unacceptable in a parapsychological experiment), motor skills could be used to increase the number of heads in the "heads" condition and the number of tails in the "tails" condition. Thus, the use of a control group would hardly eliminate all artifacts in this case, as it would not in the case of a psychology experiment in which violations of blindness could lead to differential treatment of experimental and control groups, producing an artifactual result. Use of a control group does not automatically eliminate all sources of experimental error, as Alcock seems to assume.

Some critics have even chastised parapsychologists for their use of control groups. C. E. M. Hansel (1980) has criticized Schmidt for using a high-aim condition (in which subjects try to guess which of four lamps will be lit) and a low-aim condition (in which subjects try to guess a lamp that will not light) in the second experiment in his well-known investigation into the precognition of a quantum process (Schmidt 1969). In Schmidt's experiment, the subject indicated his or her response by pushing a button on the machine, and the machine recorded on tape the guess and target for each trial as well as the type of condition (high- or low-aim). Thus Schmidt's low-aim condition served as an excellent control for his high-aim condition (and would guard against some types of possible machine artifacts). Hansel makes the point that the overall results were not significantly different from chance. However, when the results are scored in the *intended* direction (i.e., high- or low-aim), the results are highly significant. Hansel also recommends that different machines be used for the high- and low-aim conditions. However, as the machines could be artifactually biased in the desired direction, this negates the advantage of using the same machine as a control group for itself.

Thus parapsychologists are caught in a double bind, as critics will castigate them both for their employment of a control condition and for their failure to employ one. They use theoretical distributions to attack parapsychological work (as Hansel does in attacking Schmidt) but disapprove of parapsychologists' use of the same distribution (Alcock). Hansel (1980) also uses a theoretical distribution to attack results showing differential effects between groups of subjects (extroverts and introverts, for example) when he notes that, although the groups differ from one another (one scoring above chance and one below), the overall score does not differ significantly from chance.

It should be noted that any statistical test of differences between experimental and control data must itself eventually rest on a theoretical distribution (such as the *t* distribution). Alcock (1981) seems to follow some critics, such as George Spencer Brown (whom he cites enthusiastically), who would rather call into question statistical theory than accept the results of parapsychology. This would seem to be a pretty heavy price to pay in order to continue to reject psi phenomena and would seem to be a case of throwing the baby out with the bath water. (After all, the statistical theory of chance distributions has received considerable empirical support from parapsychological experiments!)

Despite Alcock's remonstrations, parapsychologists frequently employ control groups (although not as frequently as they ought to in certain areas, such as psi optimization studies). One reason that parapsychologists often fail to employ control groups is that they consider it to be virtually impossible to eliminate psi from an experimental condition. For instance, Hansel (1980) has noted that in an early telepathy experiment conducted by John E. Coover in 1915 there was no significant difference between the telepathy condition and the control condition (in which the cards were guessed when no "agent" was looking at them). Coover considered this to represent a negative result. Hansel notes that, if the scores in the telepathy and control conditions are combined, the results are significantly above chance but says this "proves nothing and is a completely illegitimate procedure, since all control over the experimental conditions brought about by using a control series is then lost" (Hansel 1980, 40). However, clairvoyance, an ability not recognized as a possibility by Coover, could have operated in both conditions. Thus Hansel's argument is invalid. Because psi powers are assumed to operate in strange ways (such as the "linger effect," in which a PK influence is postulated to continue for a time even after the subject has terminated his conscious effort), parapsychologists have preferred to compare their data to the chance distribution expected under the hypothesis of no psi rather than to some control condition in which a psi influence of unknown magnitude and direction may be present.

Statistical errors. Parapsychological research has also been criticized on the basis of possible errors in statistical analysis. At one time, it was commonly asserted that the significant results in parapsychology might be due to errors in recording and transcribing data as well as errors in statistical computations. Parapsychologists have done much to reduce the probability of such errors by keeping duplicate records and having all statistical analyses double-checked. More recently, many parapsychological experiments have employed computers and other mechanical devices to record the data and perform the statistical analyses. Many of these experiments have yielded significant results. Of course, as receivers of strange phone bills know, machine errors and programming mistakes do occur, so it is still vital that such significant results be replicated by independent investigators (see below).

In the early days of experimental parapsychology, the basic statistical tests used by parapsychologists came under attack. Some of these criticisms were valid, such as Chester Kellogg's observation that, because the deck of ESP cards was sampled without replacement in the typical ESP experiments of that time, the normal approximation to the binomial distribution was an inappropriate statistical technique to use because of the increased variance produced by the sampling-without-replacement procedure. Joseph Greenwood, a defender of parapsychology, was able to produce a correction formula to account for this slightly increased variance. When this formula was applied to the experimental data, the significant ESP effects remained. Mauskopf and McVaugh (1979) have noted that, due to the attacks on the parapsychologists' use of abstract theoretical distributions and the fact that statistics was at that time in the process of establishing itself as an academic discipline, many statisticians perceived the attack on parapsychology as an attack on their own field. As Mauskopf and McVaugh note, this may be in part responsible for the issuance of a statement upholding the parapsychologists' use of statistics by Burton Camp, the president of the Institute of Mathematical Statistics, in 1937.

In general, the statistical methods employed by parapsychologists are as good or better than those of most other fields. Certainly parapsychologists occasionally use inappropriate statistical tests, such as when Puthoff and Targ (1979) used a binomial test to evaluate rankings of remote-viewing data that could not be considered to be independent of one another (and thus could not represent a Bernoulli process). Of course no field can claim to be free of statistical errors, and those errors that do occur in parapsychology are in no way responsible for the more striking effects reported in the field.

One statistical problem that does pose a threat to parapsychology is the tendency to accept as real effects those whose significance may be due to multiple analysis, post hoc analysis, or data selection. Suppose, for example, that in a parapsychological study analyses are performed for differences in scoring patterns between extroverts and introverts, for increased score variances within each group and for both groups combined, and for overall decline effects within each group and when the groups are combined. If one of these effects is significant at the .05 level, it cannot be concluded that psi occurred in the experiment, as one in twenty analyses should be significant by chance and ten analyses were performed in the study. Similarly, if the results of a free-response study are judged in several different ways, as is all too frequently the case, the overall results cannot be considered to be significant if only one of the judgings yields a moderately significant score. A related problem occurs when the results of a parapsychological experiment are inspected and an unexpected effect is seen in the data. As unexpected patterns frequently appear in random data, a significant post hoc statistical test for the effect should be considered only as suggestive evidence that a real effect occurred. The effect must be replicated before it can be concluded that the evidence for it is statistically significant. Of the papers reporting empirical results subjected to statistical evaluation in *Research in Parapsychology, 1982*, the most recently published proceedings of an annual convention of the Parapsychological Association, slightly more than half reported results whose significance is questionable because the analyses upon which they were based were either post hoc or embedded in a sufficiently large number of analyses as to render it debatable whether the results were truly significant or merely an artifact of data overanalysis. Of the remaining papers, roughly half reported results that were clearly significant based on the primary analysis and half reported nonsignificant results.

A related problem is that of data selection. If there is a tendency for authors not to publish nonsignificant studies, it might be assumed that many of the published studies that are marginally significant (at the .05 or .01 level) may represent Type I errors (rejecting the chance hypothesis when it is true), as it would be expected that one out of every twenty parapsychological experiments would yield significant evidence of psi at the .05 level. (It should be noted that data selection cannot account for results in parapsychology that reach high levels of significance, unless it is assumed that literally quadrillions of un-published studies exist.) Another way in which data selection can produce a bogus significant effect is when a parapsychologist only analyzes that portion of his data that seems to contain positive results, disregarding the rest as "pre-liminary trials" or "the inevitable decline effect," or when he stops his study as soon as the results become significant (optional stopping). A way around these difficulties is to require authors to register their experimental designs before the study is conducted, a publication policy currently in use by the *European Journal of Parapsychology.*

When a parapsychologist enthusiastically accepts as genuine effects that may be due to multiple analysis, post hoc analysis, or data selection, he may be deluding himself. In order to avoid this sort of promulgation of bogus findings, J. B. Rhine recommended that parapsychologists adhere to a pilot-confirmation paradigm in which all significant effects found in a pilot study would have to be replicated in a confirmation study before they would be accepted as real. If more parapsychologists would adhere to this recommendation of Rhine's, the false positive rate in parapsychology would drop markedly.

A final problem concerns the method of presentation of published studies. Many parapsychologists at present are content to publish their findings in abstract form in the annual *Research in Parapsychology* (*RIP*) series. By doing so, not only do they elude the formal refereeing system of the academic journals, but they render it almost impossible for outside observers to assess their re-search, as the *RIP* abstracts do not contain the kind of detail that would allow a skeptic (or anyone) to evaluate the correctness of their procedures. This publica-tion practice has been lamented by many prominent parapsychologists in recent years, and it is a further cause of the proliferation of bogus findings in para-psychology. Clearly, if the parapsychologists wish their results to be taken seriously by scientists, they must return to the practice of publishing their experimental procedures and statistical analyses in full.

Fraud. Another reason for the reluctance of skeptics to accept the results of parapsychological research is the possibility of fraud by subjects and experimenters. Subject fraud is an ever present possibility in experiments involving special subjects (professional psychics or others claiming unusual psychic abilities) and has been documented in the cases of the Smith-Blackburn telepathy team and the Jones boys mind-reading act, as discussed by Hansel (1980; and in Chapter 2 of this volume). In the latter case, sensory cues, such as coughing and leg movements, were undoubtedly employed by the boys as a means of cheating in telepathy experiments. It has been hypothesized that special subjects have employed various devices to cheat in experiments on "macro-PK" (i.e., PK experiments using macroscopic objects rather than quantum processes as targets). These postulated devices have included concealed magnets to move compass needles (Uri Geller and Nina Kulagina) and concealed transparencies to produce "psychic photographs" (Ted Serios). Occasionally, special subjects have been caught red-handed, such as the "mini-Geller" cutlery benders observed cheating through a one-way mirror, as reported by B. Pamplin and H. Collins (1975). Some parapsychologists, desperate to observe a psi effect, have employed experimental conditions with special subjects that are far more lax than any they would ever think of using with unselected subjects. They justify the looseness of their conditions by saying that they are needed to facilitate psi, as tight conditions result in a hostile, psi-inhibiting atmosphere. (Special subjects are notoriously reluctant to be tested by skeptics or by the more rigorous parapsychologists, often using precisely this reason as an excuse.) However, if the conditions are made so lax as to permit cheating, nothing can be learned from any effects obtained, since there is no assurance that they represent genuine psi effects rather than fraud. It should go without saying that parapsychologists should employ the same stringent precautions to eliminate normal sensory-motor channels that they use with unselected subjects (who presumably do not cheat) when testing selected subjects (who presumably will cheat, given the opportunity). As Randi's Project Alpha has amply demonstrated, this is far from being the case at the present time in parapsychology. It should be noted that most parapsychological research does not employ special subjects but rather volunteers unselected for psi ability or, in some cases, animals. Here, fraud by subjects is not of such great concern. Fraud by experimenters is.

That some of the more central and striking results in parapsychology have been produced through the use of fraud on the part of the experimenters is now an established fact. Experimental studies of telepathy by S. G. Soal, long regarded as among the most impressive evidence for ESP, have been demonstrated through statistical analyses by Scott and Haskell (1974) and a computer analysis of Soal's target series by Markwick (1978; Chapter 11 of in this volume) to be due to data manipulation on the part of Soal. A most impressive series of investigations of the psi powers of animals was called into question when the principal investigator, Walter J. Levy (who was at that time the director of the Institute for Parapsychology and J. B. Rhine's heir apparent), was discovered by his co-workers to be producing the significant results in a pyschokinesis experiment with rats through the manipulation of the data-recording equipment (see Chapter 12 of this volume). Some critics, including Hansel (1980), have alleged fraud in a great many other investigations. Hansel provides lengthy analyses of experiments showing how significant results could have been produced by fraud on the part of one or more members of the investigating team. His postulation of honesty on the part of some participants in the experiment is generous and increases the fun of his analyses, but of course any significant results could simply be the result of collusion on the part of everyone concerned. Occasionally, Hansel goes somewhat overboard, as when he fishes through the data of the famous Pratt-Woodruff experiment until he finds an anomalous pattern in the data and then proceeds to use that pattern as evidence for a fraud hypothesis—a hypothesis that was itself undoubtedly constructed on the basis of the pattern in the first place (although Hansel does not present it that way). Such flagrantly circular reasoning and unwarranted inferences from post hoc analyses are no more appropriate tactics when they are employed by a skeptic like Hansel than when they are employed by the parapsychologists he criticizes.

One long-term critic of parapsychology, Martin Gardner, has said that "cheating and self-deception are greater in parapsychology than in most sciences, especially the physical sciences, but not by much" (Gardner 1981, 130). Gardner's remarks may in fact be a bit overgenerous. Only a very small minority of parapsychological workers regularly report highly significant results. The proportion of these experimenters who have been exposed as fraudulent certainly exceeds the normal rate of exposure of fraudulent researchers in science (although that may be due to the greater attention paid to them and the more microscopic examination of their data by critics). The question remains, however, whether all the research that cannot be ascribed to the methodological errors discussed in the previous sections can be ascribed to fraud. Surely it is conceivable that, out of the billions of members of the human race, a handful will emerge who will be willing to seek the fame and adulation of being a "psi-conducive experimenter," a being with first-hand knowledge of the mysteries of the universe. Most fraudulent research is not exposed, remember, and only a few experimenters in the world are able to obtain significant results on any regular basis.

As a solution to the problem of experimenter fraud, J. B. Rhine recommended that experimenters work in teams so that each member could monitor the activities of the others. This system is not foolproof. Walter J. Levy produced significant results over a fairly long period of time as a member of several research teams, sometimes under conditions in which experiments were run and the data recorded by computer. Thus any policing system can be defeated, at least for a time. Also, collusion among the entire experimental team can never be ruled out, although this is much less likely than fraud by a single experimenter.

Replication failures. One scientific safeguard against the promulgation of bogus findings due to methodological errors or fraud is the replication of experimental results by independent researchers. Even the parapsychologists themselves have used failure of replication as an argument against the acceptance of Cleve Backster's claim to have demonstrated a "primary perception" in philodendrons (Backster 1968), even though some successful replications of Backster's work have been reported. This rejection is probably based in part on the claimed strength of Backster's effects, as well as the outrageousness of his claims and his flamboyant style in presenting them (both of which promoted ridicule of the field of parapsychology).

Although, in general, most investigators both inside and outside the parapsychological community have been unable to replicate reported parapsychological effects in their own laboratories, it is claimed that some lines of research are highly replicable. Charles Honorton (1977) has argued that the percentage of published studies reporting significant results is 50 percent or higher in many lines of research investigating "internal attention states," such as meditation, hypnosis, relaxation, and the ganzfeld (homogeneous visual field) state. (Similar high rates of replication have been claimed for studies demonstrating relationships between ESP scores and extroversion, belief in psi, and defensiveness.) Ray Hyman (1983; and Chapter 1 of this volume) has questioned Honorton's claim that 55 percent of all ganzfeld experiments are statistically significant on the basis of (*a*) unreported studies, (*b*) multiple analyses, (*c*) the classification of studies showing a missing effect as "successful," and (*d*) a positive correlation between the level of success and the number of methodological flaws in the study. In his reply to Hyman, Honorton (1983) concedes the validity and importance of Hyman's criticisms regarding multiple analysis, but he presents his own analysis opposing Hyman's claim of a positive relationship between methodological flaws and success level in ganzfeld studies, although he apparently does concede that the estimate of the success rate of published ganzfeld experiments should be revised downward and probably should lie somewhere between 33 and 40 percent. In a presidential address to the Parapsychological Association, Honorton has argued that, even if five nonsignificant unpublished studies existed for every published study of extrasensory perception, "the rate of replication of the ESP hypothesis would still be highly significant" (Honorton 1976, 204). Here Honorton appears to be confusing replicability with statistical significance. It is possible for a small group of "psi-conducive" experimenters to produce a large number of successful replications of one another's work, the results of which would still significantly exceed chance levels even if it is assumed that large numbers of unsuccessful studies are going unreported. If, however, the rate of successful replication by investigators outside of this group were sufficiently low, it might be assumed that the successful studies were due to methodological error and/or fraud (rather than chance or data selection). Perhaps if 50 percent of all *investigators* (rather than all published studies) obtained significant results, then it could be argued that ESP effects should be considered to have at least some degree of replicability. (Even a hard-nosed skeptic might balk at attributing fraud or incompetence to 50 percent of all investigators.)

Parapsychologists have postulated several reasons for the lack of replicability of psi effects. Most prominent among these is the experimenter effect. J. B. Rhine contended that it takes a great deal of skill, personal warmth, and enthusiasm on the part of an experimenter to elicit psi from his subjects. The rarity of these traits would explain the scarcity of "psi-conducive" experimenters. Many parapsychologists today talk of a "psi-mediated experimenter effect," in which the experimenter produces successful results in a parapsychological experiment through the use of his or her own psi powers, such as by "PKing" the extroverts to score above chance and the introverts to score below chance in an ESP test. Some studies (e.g., Sargent 1980) have shown that psi-conducive experimenters outperform psi-inhibitory experimenters in tests of their own psi ability. Other evidence in favor of a psi-mediated experimenter effect includes studies suggesting that the person who tabulates the data of an experiment can influence the outcome of the experiment (the "checker effect"), possibly by using "retroactive psychokinesis" to influence the subjects. Some authors, such as B. Millar (1978), have suggested that psi ability is comparatively rare in the population and that successful experimenters in fact represent some of the few available "psi sources." Of course, if the successful experimenters are causing their results through the exercise of their own psi powers, their so-called "findings" about psi (such as extroverts scoring higher than introverts on ESP tests) cannot be taken seriously, as the experimenter might merely be "PKing" the results to conform to his own hypothesis.

It is certainly true that a great number of apparently methodologically sound experiments reporting highly significant results exist in the parapsychological literature. In order to claim that the existence of psi phenomena has been experimentally proven, however, it is necessary that at least some effect be repeatable by a majority of investigators in order to rule out the hypothesis of fraud and/or undetected error. Even if one obtains significant results oneself, it is impossible to be certain that one has not made some undetected error. (This suggests an analogy with Gödel's theorem that no proof of the consistency of a sufficiently powerful formal system can be given within the system itself. In a similar manner, no competent scientist can ever prove his absolute competence to himself; only incompetent scientists can do this.)

The fact that psi effects have not proved strongly replicable as yet does not prove the nonexistence of psi. Many types of natural phenomena (e.g., meteorites, ball lightning, gravity waves, and fractional charge on niobium balls) cannot be observed on demand. On the other hand, a hypothesis that cannot be disproved does not qualify as a scientific hypothesis under Popper's falsifiability criterion. Certainly some assumptions about when and where psi effects may be observed will be necessary in order to render the hypothesis of psi falsifiable and hence worthy of scientific attention.

The Survival Problem

An ever-shrinking subfield of parapsychology is that concerned with the evidence for the survival of the human personality (or some portion thereof) of bodily death. This evidence consists of several different types of phenomena, including dreams, apparitions and hauntings, out-of-body and near-death experiences, mediumship, and cases suggestive of reincarnation.

Certain types of dreams suggest the existence of a discarnate agency. For instance, in the "Dordrecht Case" discussed by Zorab (1962), the son of a deceased bookkeeper who had been accused of embezzling approximately 1,800 guilders had a dream in which a white figure appeared to him, saying, "Look in the ledger at the dates." Upon checking, it was found that his father had included the date at the top of a column in one of his additions. A skeptic might explain this case by hypothesizing that the son might have unconsciously noted the identity between the disputed sum and the date and presented the solution to himself in the form of a dream. Such unconscious problem-solving activity in dreams has long been recognized by psychologists, a notable example being Kekulé's discovery of the ringlike structure of the benzene molecule, which was presented to him in the form of a dream in which the molecules became a group of dancing snakes that suddenly took their own tails in their mouths.

Other cases involve apparitions. One famous case, called the "Red Scratch" case, involved a traveling salesman whose deceased sister appeared to him with a red scratch on the right side of her face. When he related this incident to his mother, she nearly fainted, later explaining that she had unintentionally scratched the dead sister's face before the funeral and had repaired the damage with makeup without mentioning it to anyone. The skeptic could hypothesize that the man had subconsciously perceived the damage to his sister's face at the time of the funeral or had heard his mother talking to herself about it later.

The parapsychologist could assert that he learned of the scratch through ESP, although this explanation is not available to the skeptic. Somewhat more impressive are cases of collectively perceived apparitions (i.e., apparitions seen by more than one person) and hauntings (in which an apparition is seen repeatedly in a given location by a number of persons). However, haunting cases are quite rare, and the skeptic can readily attribute such cases as do exist to suggestion (ambiguous sounds and visual stimuli being quickly perceived as ghostly footsteps and apparitions in houses with a reputation for being "haunted"). Certainly, it could be argued that if hauntings did represent a real phenomenon, good haunting cases should not be so rare as they apparently are.

Out-of-body experiences (in which a person experiences himself or herself to undergo separation from the physical body and to travel to remote locations) and near-death experiences (in which people who are close to death experience visions of deceased friends, experience enhanced sensations of colors, travel down a corridor or tunnel, encounter a "being of light," and often undergo out-of-body experiences and a "life-review" as well) are frequently taken as evidence of a "nonphysical" existence and of an afterlife. Of course both out-of-body experiences (OBEs) and near-death experiences (NDEs) could simply be fantasies and hallucinations. Ronald Siegel (1980) pointed out the similarity between OBEs and NDEs and hallucinations induced by the consumption of psychedelic drugs, and Carl Sagan (1979) has argued that such experiences may be due to a reliving of the birth trauma. Experiments in which a person experiencing an out-of-body state is requested to describe target materials at the site to which he has "projected" have yielded results that are in general no more striking than when subjects are simply requested to use their ESP to gain knowledge of the target materials. Thus any veridical experiences occurring during the OBE can simply be ascribed to ESP by the parapsychologist (the skeptic can make up his own explanation). The fact that people are generally unable to describe target materials when they claim to be "astrally" located at a site is strong evidence in favor of a hallucination-fantasy explanation of OBEs and almost devastating evidence against the literal interpretation of the OBE as an "exteriorization" of an "astral body."

In general, the evidence from mediumship is no more compelling. Hyman (1977) has amply documented how a medium or psychic can give a "cold reading" by using vague statements and/or sensory cues to construct a seemingly accurate description of a client or deceased person. Mediums have frequently supplemented this technique with fraudulent practices. Many parapsychologists regard with skepticism virtually all physical mediumship (in which ostensibly paranormal physical effects occur during the séance), and fraud has been documented in the cases of many physical mediums, including Eusapia Palladino and Mina Crandon (whose "spirit fingerprint" proved to be that of her very much nondeceased dentist). The mental medium Arthur Ford is known to have kept files of information on likely clients, later claiming to have obtained the information paranormally during séances. Accurate details obtained from "drop-in" communicators (deceased personalities who manifest themselves unexpectedly during a séance) could be due to cryptomnesia on the part of the medium or Ouija board operators (the cryptomnesia possibly consisting of an unconscious memory of reading an obituary notice of the deceased personality— occasionally such accurate details have been demonstrated to have all been derived from such a single written source).

Parapsychologists are reluctant to consider accurate information given by a medium concerning a deceased personality as proof of a surviving spirit in any event, as the medium could have derived the information through the exercise of her ESP powers (the "super-ESP" hypothesis). Again, skeptics must come up with their own explanation. Many parapsychologists have considered that the exercise of special skills (such as solving partial differential equations) or the fluent speaking of a foreign language (xenoglossy) by the medium would constitute good evidence of the survival of a personality possessing these skills, so long as it could be demonstrated that the medium had not acquired these skills normally. However, such cases are rare to the point of nonexistence, and the handful that do exist are not very impressive in any event.

Reincarnation cases provide another source of evidence for survival. For many people, the concept of reincarnation is an appealing doctrine because of its similarity to many cyclical processes in nature. Also, as Voltaire once noted, it is no more surprising to be born twice than it is to be born once. The weaker evidence for reincarnation consists of cases in which a psychic reader, such as Edgar Cayce, exercises his clairvoyant powers to describe a person's past lives and cases in which a person is regressed to a past life through hypnosis. This evidence is weak primarily because there are very few cases on record in which accurate details about these past lives have been given that (a) have been verified and (b) were unlikely to have been obtained through normal means. Strangely enough, in cases of hypnotic regression, surprisingly few past-lives as Napoleon appear. Also Helen Wambach (1978) has shown that past lives recalled under regression have a fairly good statistical fit to what is known about past populations in terms of sex distribution, and so forth, which might not be expected under the hypothesis that recalled past lives are simply fantasies. The most impressive evidence is given by cases in which children spontaneously report memories of previous lives, as reported by Ian Stevenson (1966). A typical Stevenson case involves a child who at a very early age begins to speak of a previous life in a different village from the one in which he is now located. The family often takes him to the village of the previous personality, where many of his statements about the previous personality are verified and where the child frequently recognizes persons known in his previous life. Criticism of Stevenson's work has focused on the possibility that the child could have learned about the previous personality through normal means (such as by overhearing conversations, etc.), on the possibility of sensory cuing during the recognition process, and on the possibility of inaccurate recall of the order of events by the witnesss (as Stevenson usually arrives on the scene long after the families of the present and previous personalities have met and exchanged information). Also, the fact that the vast majority of Stevenson's cases come from cultures with a belief in reincarnation is evidence in favor of a normal explanation involving encouragement and perhaps "coaching" of such memories (although Stevenson interprets it as evidence of suppression of such memories in cultures hostile to the idea of reincarnation).

The evidence for survival includes many more strange phenomena. Unfortunately, space considerations and concern for the reader's mental health prohibit treatment of many lines of research, such as the seminal investigation of phone calls from the dead conducted by D. Scott Rogo and Raymond Bayless (1979).

Most survival research in parapsychology seems based on the assumption that the mind survives the death of the physical body with large portions of its memory, emotional make-up, and worldly concerns largely intact. However, the assertion that one's personality could remain unchanged in the face of the absence of the entire physical brain would seem ludicrous in view of the tremendous impact that brain states demonstrably have on emotions and cognitive activity. It is also difficult to believe that memories could persist after the destruction of the physical brain. Lesions of the hippocampal and thalamic areas of the brain, as well as such organic conditions as Korsakoff's psychosis in alcoholic patients, render a person apparently incapable of storing new long-term memories. Interference with (apparently physical) consolidation processes, through electrical shocks to the brain or chemical injections, also appears to inhibit the formation of long-term memory traces. On the other side, there are the celebrated failures of brain investigators, most notably Lashley, to find evidence for localized physical traces (engrams) corresponding to particular memories, although such traces have recently been found for simple classically conditioned reflexes (see Miller 1983). There have also been widespread failures to replicate much of the evidence suggestive of a chemical memory trace (such as R. A. McConnell's well-known studies of planaria). Theories asserting that memories are "holograms" are just metaphysical restatements of the general failure to find localized engrams, as no plausible physical storage mechanism corresponding to such "holograms" has been proposed. Interestingly, John Eccles (1979), who feels that there is strong evidence in favor of a synaptic modification theory of memory, has postulated the existence of a second, nonphysical memory system.

On the other side, it is difficult from an introspective point of view to accept the physicalists' equation of one's self with the collective of physical particles that constitutes one's physical body. Atoms are continually exiting from and entering into a person's brain and body, to the extent that a person's present body is an entirely different physical entity from his or her body of seven years ago. Yet most people feel that they are identical with the person who inhabited their body of seven years ago (of course this feeling could be illusory—just because one has access to a memory for an experience does not imply that one actually underwent that experience). If this belief in the continuity of the self (which, incidentally, some Buddhists do not share) is valid, then a person cannot be identified with a physical body. Also, if one's existence is contingent upon the existence of a particular assemblage of physical particles, the probability that one would exist and be conscious at the present time would be essentially zero. Thus, one could argue from the introspective fact of one's own existence that the hypothesis of physicalism must face statistical rejection as a null hypothesis.

If a person assumes himself to have a continual and ongoing existence in this present life, then that person cannot consistently maintain that he is identical with a particular set of emotions, memories, thoughts, or physical particles, as these things are ephemeral. More consistently, the person should equate himself with what Hornell Hart (1958) has called the "I-thinker," that entity that thinks one's thoughts, remembers one's memories, and senses one's sensations, rather than with the thoughts, memories, and sensations themselves. As it would be hard to imagine what identifying characteristics this "I-thinker" would have, it would seem impossible to obtain an empirical demonstration of its survival after death, given the current state of development of science. As the science of the mind becomes unimaginably more sophisticated, however, such a demonstration might one day be possible.

Miscellaneous Objections

Some skeptics have dismissed parapsychology on the basis of the fact that it has no agreed-upon theory to explain psi phenomena and does not conduct systematic research in order to construct and test theories. The lack of an agreed-upon theory is primarily due to the fact that there are no stable, replicable paranormal effects upon which a theory can be tested. Theories cannot be built and refined on an unstable and capricious data-base. There have been some attempts to do systematic theoretically oriented research, but these have typically become short-circuited due to the unrepeatability of the effects. The most progress has probably been made in the area of psychodynamic theories, where the overwhelming majority of significant studies have shown certain personality variables, such as extroversion, nondefensiveness, and belief in psi, to be positively correlated with scores on ESP tests. Again, these effects are not generally replicable by skeptical investigators.

Another objection is that, if psi powers exist, they should be strongly selected for in the course of evolution. Thus, one would expect a much greater level of psi ability than now exists in the general population. On the other hand, the noted philosopher Henri Bergson argued that the brain acts as a filter, restricting the mind's attention to events in the physical brain. After all, it will not do from an evolutionary perspective for a person to be clairvoyantly enjoying an orgy down the street while his apartment is burning down around him. In a similar vein, N. Dehn and R. Schank (1982) have pointed out that effective cognitive functioning in computers often requires a limited information-processing capacity, quickly terminating (rather than infinite) search procedures, and a forgetting mechanism. The parapsychologist and psychoanalyst Jan Ehrenwald has proposed on several occasions that the reason for the weakness of most psi effects in the laboratory is that they are dependent on "flaws" in Bergson's filter, whereas psi phenomena in real life tend to be "need-relevant" and evolutionarily adaptive.

Summary and Recommendations

A fair and objective examination of spontaneous case material raises at least a reasonable suspicion that psi phenomena exist. There are hints from the experimental literature that it may be possible to bring such phenomena under experimental control. Because the reported effects are not as yet repeatable by the majority of investigators, it cannot be claimed that psi phenomena have been scientifically demonstrated to exist. It would however be premature to close the book on the issue; psi phenomena are worthy of further study.

Notes

1. I have classified double-aspect theory as materialistic because the "single reality" underlying both mental and physical events is usually taken to be the physical world by most double-aspect theorists, who assert that mental events are simply physical events "experienced from the inside." It should be noted that some double-aspect theorists assert that the common "substance" underlying mental and physical events is neither mental nor material but is instead some neutral substance. Such an interpretation of double-aspect theory has recently led F. Dommeyer (1982) to classify such a seemingly radical dualist as J. B. Rhine as a double-aspect theorist.

2. The fact that some forms of human behavior are at present better predicted by

theories that employ mentalistic concepts, such as attitudes and memories, than by theories that refer only to physical events does not falsify the doctrine of physicalism, as it has not been shown that any physical principles are in fact violated or that physical theories are *in principle* incapable of making the same predictions (although practical difficulties make such an actual reduction impossible at the present time).

References

Abelson, R., and M. Rosenberg. 1958. Symbolic psycho-logic: A model of attitudinal cognition. *Behavioral Science*, 3:1-13.

Alcock, J. 1981. *Parapsychology: Science or Magic?* New York: Pergamon Press.

———.1984. Parapsychology's past eight years. A lack of progress report. *Skeptical Inquirer*, 8:312-320.

Asch, S. E. 1958. Effects of group pressure upon the modification and distortion of judgments. In *Readings in Social Psychology*, edited by E. Maccoby, T. Newcomb, and E. Hartley, 174-183. New York: Holt, Rinehart and Winston.

Backster, Cleve. 1968. Evidence of primary perception in plant life. *International Journal of Parapsychology*, 10:329-348.

Barry, J. 1971. Retarding fungus growth by PK. In *Progress in Parapsychology*, edited by J. Rhine, 118-121. Durham, N.C.: Seeman Printing.

Beloff, John. 1983. Three open questions. In *Research in Parapsychology, 1982*, edited by W. Roll, J. Beloff, and R. White, 317-327. Metuchen, N.J.: Scarecrow Press.

Bisaha, J., and B. Dunne. 1979. Multiple subject and long-distance precognitive remote-viewing of geographical locations. In *Mind at Large*, edited by C. Tart, H. Puthoff, and R. Targ, 107-124. New York: Praeger.

Butterfield, H. 1957. *The Origins of Modern Science*. New York: Macmillan.

Child, I., H. Kanthamani, and V. Sweeney. 1977. A simplified experiment in dream telepathy. In *Research in Parapsychology, 1976*, edited by J. Morris, W. Roll, and R. Morris, 91-93. Metuchen, N.J.: Scarecrow Press.

Christianson, G. 1978. *This Wild Abyss*. New York: Macmillan.

Collins, H. M., and T. J. Pinch. 1979. The construction of the paranormal. In *On the Margins of Science*, edited by R. Wallace. Sociological Review Monograph 27, University of Keele.

———.1982. *Frames of Meaning: The Social Construction of Extraordinary Science*. London: Routledge and Kegan Paul.

Dehn, N., and R. Schank. 1982. Artificial and human intelligence. In *Handbook of Human Intelligence*, edited by R. Sternberg. 352-391. New York: Cambridge University Press.

Dommeyer, F. 1982. J. B. Rhine and philosophy. In *J. B. Rhine: On the Frontiers of Science*, edited by K. Rao, 117-133. Jefferson, N.C.: McFarland.

Eccles, John. 1979. *The Human Mystery: The Gifford Lectures, 1977-1978*. New York: Springer International.

Festinger, L. 1957. *A Theory of Cognitive Dissonance*. Evanston: Row Press.

Feuer, Lewis. 1974. *Einstein and the Generations of Science.* New York: Basic Books.

Feyerabend, Paul. 1981. How to defend society against science. In *Scientific Revolutions,* edited by I. Hacking, 156-167. New York: Oxford University Press.

Fowler, H., ed. 1965. *Curiosity and Exploratory Behavior.* New York: Macmillan.

Gardner, Martin. 1981. *Science: Good, Bad and Bogus.* Buffalo, N.Y.: Prometheus Books.

Grad, B. 1965. Some biological effects of the "laying on of hands": A review of experiments with animals and plants. *Journal of the American SPR,* 59:95-129.

Hansel, C. E. M. 1980. *ESP and Parapsychology: A Critical Re-Evaluation.* Buffalo, N.Y.: Prometheus Books.

Hart, H. 1958. To what extent can the issues with regard to survival be reconciled? *Journal of the SPR,* 39:314-323.

Honorton, Charles. 1976. Has science developed the competence to confront the claims of the paranormal? In *Research in Parapsychology, 1975, edited by J. Morris, W. Roll, and R. Morris, 199-223.* Metuchen, N.J.: Scarecrow Press.

———. 1977. *Psi and internal attention states. In Handbook of Parapsychology,* edited by B. B. Wolman, 435-472. New York: Van Nostrand Reinhold.

———. 1983. Response to Hyman's critique of psi ganzfeld studies. In *Research in Parapsychology, 1982,* edited by W. Roll, J. Beloff, and R. White, 23-26. Metuchen, N.J.: Scarecrow Press.

Horney, Karen. 1950. *Neurosis and Human Growth.* New York: Norton.

Hovland, Carl, Irving L. Janis, and H. Kelly. 1953. *Communication and Persuasion.* New Haven: Yale University Press.

Hyman, Ray. 1977. "Cold reading": How to convince strangers that you know all about them. *Zetetic (Skeptical Inquirer),* 1 (2):18-37.

———. 1983. Does the ganzfeld experiment answer the critics' objections? In *Research in Parapsychology, 1982,* edited by W. Roll, J. Beloff, and R. White, 21-23. Metuchen, N.J.: Scarecrow Press.

Johnson, Martin. 1982. An attempt to select for psi ability in paramecium aurelia. *Journal of the SPR,* 51:272-282.

Koestler, Athur. 1972. *The Roots of Coincidence.* New York: Random House.

———. 1978. *Janus.* New York: Random House.

LeShan, Lawrence. 1969. *Toward a General Theory of the Paranormal.* Parapsychological Monograph No. 9. New York: Parapsychology Foundation.

———. 1976. *Alternate Realities.* New York: Ballantine.

Lidz, T. 1973. *The Origin and Treatment of Schizophrenic Disorders.* New York: Basic Books.

Marks, David, and Richard Kammann, 1978. Information transmission in remote viewing experiments. *Nature,* 274:680-681.

———. 1980. *The Psychology of the Psychic.* Buffalo, N.Y.: Prometheus Books.

Markwick, Betty. 1978. The Soal-Goldney experiments with Basil Shackleton: New evidence of data manipulation. *Proceedings of the SPR,* 56:250-277.

Mason, S. 1962. *A History of the Sciences.* New York: Macmillan.

Mattuck, R. 1982. A model of the interaction between consciousness and matter using Bohm-Bub hidden variables. In *Research in Parapsychology, 1981,* edited by W. Roll, R. Morris, and R. White, 146-147. Metuchen, N.J.: Scarecrow Press.

Mauskopf, S., and M. McVaugh, 1979. The controversy over statistics in parapsychology, 1934-1938. In *The Reception of Unconventional Science*, edited by S. Mauskopf, 105-123. Boulder, Colo.: Westview Press.

McDougall, W. 1926. *An Outline of Abnormal Psychology*. London: Methuen.

McGuire, W. 1960a. Cognitive consistency and attitude change. *Journal of Abnormal and Social Psychology*, 60:345-353.

———. 1960b. A syllogistic analysis of cognitive relationships. In *Attitude Organization and Change*, edited by M. Rosenberg and C. Hovland, 65-111. New Haven: Yale University Press.

———. 1968. Theory of the structure of human thought. In *Theories of Cognitive Consistency: A Sourcebook*, edited by R. Abelson, E. Aronson, W. McGuire, T. Newcomb, M. Rosenberg, and P. Tannenbaum. Chicago: Rand-McNally.

Milgram, Stanley. 1963. Behavioral study of obedience. *Journal of Abnormal and Social Psychology*, 67:371-378.

———. 1968. Some conditions of obedience and disobedience to authority. *International Journal of Psychiatry*, 6:259-276.

Millar, B. 1978. The observational theories: A primer. *European Journal of Parapsychology*, 2:304-332.

Miller, J. 1983. One archive of memory, *Science News*, 124:380.

Nash, C. 1982. Psychokinetic control of bacterial growth. In *Research in Parapsychology, 1981*, edited by W. Roll, R. Morris, and R. White, 61-64. Metuchen, N.J.: Scarecrow Press.

———. 1984. Quantum physics and parapsychology. *Parapsychology Review*, 15, (3):4-6.

Nolen, William. 1974. *Healing: A Doctor in Search of a Miracle*. Greenwich, Conn.: Fawcett.

Palmer, John, and R. Lieberman. 1976. ESP and out-of-body experiences: A further study. In *Research in Parapsychology, 1975*, edited by J. Morris, W. Roll, and R. Morris, 102-106. Metuchen, N.J.: Scarecrow Press.

Pamplin, B., and H. Collins. 1975. Spoon bending: An experimental approach. *Nature*, 257:8.

Penfield, Wilder. 1975. *The Mystery of the Mind*. Princeton, N.J.: Princeton University Press.

Popper, Karl, and John Eccles. 1977. *The Self and Its Brain*. New York: Springer International.

Puthoff, Harold, and Russell Targ. 1979. A perceptual channel for information transfer over kilometer distances: Historical perspective and recent research. In *Mind at Large*, edited by C. Tart, H. Puthoff, and R. Targ, 11-76. New York: Praeger.

Puthoff, Harold, Russell Targ, and Charles Tart. 1980. Resolution in remote-viewing studies: Mini-targets. In *Research in Parapsychology, 1979*, edited by W. Roll, 120-122. Metuchen, N.J.: Scarecrow Press.

Randi, James. 1982 [1980]. *Flim-Flam*, rev ed. Buffalo, N.Y.: Prometheus Books (originally published by Lippincott & Crowell, New York, 1980).

———.1983. The Project Alpha experiment. Part I. The first two years. *Skeptical Inquirer*, 7(4):24-33.

Rhine, Louisa. 1961. *Hidden Channels of the Mind.* New York: Sloane.

Richmond, N. 1952. Two series of PK tests on paramecia. *Journal of the SPR,* 36:577-588.

Rogo, D. Scott, and Raymond Bayless. 1979. *Phone Calls from the Dead.* Englewood Cliffs, N.J.: Prentice-Hall.

Rokeach, M. 1960. *The Open and Closed Mind.* New York: Basic Books.

Roll, William. 1972. *The Poltergeist.* New York: Signet.

Sagan, Carl. 1979. *Broca's Brain.* New York: Random House.

Sargent, C. 1980. A covert test of psi abilities of psi-conducive and psi-inhibitory experimenters. In *Research in Parapsychology, 1979,* edited by W. Roll, 115-116. Metuchen, N.J.: Scarecrow Press.

Schachter, S. 1951. Deviation, rejection and communication. *Journal of Abnormal and Social Psychology.* 46:190-208.

Schmidt, Helmut. 1969. Precognition of a quantum process. *Journal of Parapsychology,* 33:99-108.

———. 1975. Toward a mathematical theory of psi. *Journal of the American SPR,* 69:301-319.

Scott, Christopher, and P. Haskell. 1974. Fresh light on the Shackleton experiments. *Proceedings of the SPR,* 56:43-72.

Siegel, R. 1980. The psychology of life after death. *American Psychologist,* 35:911-931.

Sinclair, Upton. 1962. *Mental Radio.* Springfield, Ill.: Thomas.

Smith, J. 1968. Paranormal effects on enzyme activity. *Proceedings of the Para- psychological Association,* 5:15-16.

Stevenson, Ian. 1966. *Twenty Cases Suggestive of Reincarnation.* Charlottesville, Va.: University of Virginia Press.

Stokes, Douglas. 1978. Review of *Research in Parapsychology. 1977,* edited by W. Roll. *Journal of Parapsychology,* 42:313-319.

Targ, Russell, and Harold Puthoff. 1977. *Mind Reach.* New York: Delacorte Press.

Tart, Charles. 1976. *Learning to Use Extrasensory Perception.* Chicago: Univerity of Chicago Press.

———. 1982. The controversy about psi: Two psychological theories. *Journal of Para- psychology,* 46:313-320.

Tart, C., H. Puthoff, and R. Targ. 1980. Information transmission in remote viewing experiments. *Nature,* 204:191.

Thouless, R. H., and B. Wiesner. 1948. The psi process in normal and "paranormal" psychology. *Journal of Parapsychology,* 12:192-212.

Tyrrell, G. 1936. Further research in extra-sensory perception. *Proceedings of the SPR* 44:99-168.

———. 1953. *Apparitions.* New York: Collier.

Walker, E. 1975. Foundations of paraphysical and parapsychological phenomena. In *Quantum Physics and Parapsychology,* edited by L. Oteri, 1-53. New York: Para- psychology Foundation.

Wambach, Helen. 1978. *Reliving Past Lives.* New York: Harper and Row.

Warcollier, R. 1963. *Mind to Mind.* New York: Collier.

Westfall, R. 1977. *The Construction of Modern Science*. New York: Cambridge University Press.

Zohar, D. 1982. *Through the Time Barrier*. London: Heinemann.

Zorab, G. 1962. Cases of the Chaffin will type and the problem of survival. *Journal of the SPR*, 41:407-416.

18

The Adventures of a Psi-Inhibitory Experimenter

SUSAN BLACKMORE

I get negative results. Indeed, I have been doing so for ten years. The dilemma I now confront is how to weigh the results of my own failures against the published successes of others. This is just the last and most difficult in a long series of dilemmas forced on me by my failure to observe psi.

This is a personal account—and I apologize for being so egocentric, but I want to use my own experiences to illustrate some of the fundamental problems faced by parapsychology: in particular by a parapsychology bedeviled by unrepeatability.

My interest in parapsychology first developed when I ran the Oxford University Society for Psychical Research and came into contact with parapsychologists, psychical researchers, and occultists. I was challenged by the contradiction between what I learned from them and what I was learning in physiology and psychology—especially in the area of memory. I then conceived a "memory theory of ESP" (Blackmore 1979), which was to mold the first few years of my research. Roughly, this involved the (not original) notion that memory was not stored in individual brains but was in some way common to all. Memory would then be seen as a special case of ESP. This seemed to explain so much—which at the time I mistakenly took for an advantage. And it fit with the fact that then, as now, psychology did not understand the physiological basis of memory.

I set out to test these ideas by asking a fairly simple question: Does ESP behave more like perception or memory? This question formed the basis of the research for my Ph.D. at Surrey University. It was deliberately "process-oriented" research; that is, assuming (rather than seeking evidence for) the existence of psi and trying to understand the processes involved. To answer the question, I carried out about 20 experiments using large groups of unselected subjects. I looked at the kinds of errors and confusions that were made in ESP tasks (Blackmore 1981a); errors and confusions I found, but ESP I did not. I looked at the types of targets that were most effective (Blackmore 1981b), but I found that none was. I explored the kinds of memory skills that correlated with ESP (Blackmore 1980a)—except that none did. The results of all these experiments were close to chance expectation. In other words, I failed to find any ESP and was therefore unable to get any answer to my question.

So what could be concluded from these results? This is really the first step in the creation of the dilemma: knowing what to do with negative results. The problem is twofold. First, what do negative results tell us; and, second, what should the "failed" experimenter do next?

It has long been argued that, since ESP is negatively defined, negative results tell us nothing. I shall return to this point later but for the moment simply dispute it. Negative results at least tell us that something is not the case. This is not very helpful if no one thought it was the case anyway, as so often happens with ESP. But it is important to realize that the value of negative or positive results can only be judged in relation to current theory and expectations. In the case of my experiments, we are certainly justified in saying that my predictions were invalid as applied to those specific situations at that specific time. The difficult question is how far one can reasonably generalize from this failure. Should we throw out just those particular experimental tests—or the whole of parapsychology?

The problem is an inverse of the usual one in experimental science—that is, to know how far one can generalize the positive findings of specific experiments. In this case, we must ask how many of the original ideas have to be rejected. On the one hand, it is surely possible that there is ESP, and even that my memory theory was correct but that the way I tested it was wrong. On the other hand, it is possible that there is no psi and the whole idea was totally misconceived. There are numerous possible conclusions one might draw from one end of this spectrum to the other—and each of these leads to a different course of action. Some possible responses to negative results may be categorized as follows.

1. Psi does exist and my theory and predictions might be correct but I had bad luck with the experiments. I should try again.

2. Psi might exist but I was using the wrong experimental designs. I should change procedures, subjects, etc., and try again.

3. Psi might exist but my negative results are due to an experimenter effect. I should keep doing psi experiments but change experimenter.

4. The laboratory is the wrong place to look for psi. I should turn to spontaneous cases.

5. Psi may not exist. I should try to find out whether it does or not by looking for ways of testing this skeptical hypothesis.

6. Psi does not exist. People who believe in it are wrong and should be enlightened. I should seek to debunk the positive findings and persuade people of the "correct" view.

7. The whole subject is a waste of time. I should leave the field altogether.

8. We need a "New Parapsychology."

I have arranged these possible conclusions more or less in the order I have followed during ten years of research. During that time I have explored the extreme believer's position and the extreme disbeliever's position and concluded that neither is satisfactory. Instead, I shall propose that what we need is a different kind of parapsychology. I shall discuss each of these paths in turn, the particular problems and questions each raises, and the places each took me.

1. My first response to my negative results was that they might have been just bad luck. This enormously optimistic approach is fine—if one does end up with success. Success in this case means statistical success, and it is of course possible that bad luck produced a false negative when the hypothesis was true. However, this becomes increasingly unlikely the longer the experiments continue.

At one point I calculated that I had performed 34 independent significance tests in almost as many experiments and obtained two values significant at the 0.05 level. In other words, I had results as close to chance expectation as one could reasonably expect. Skeptics suggested that this simply confirmed that I had done the experiments correctly—assuming that of course there is no psi. At the time, I was not convinced; but I did soon abandon this line of reasoning, and I think that was the right thing to do. Sooner or later you have to admit that nature might be telling you something—in this case that this experiment does not work. So it is reasonable to move on.

2. The second possibility I considered was that I had got the techniques wrong. This hypothesis is even more attractive but of course means more work. To explore it fully one must try out all sorts of new designs. Indeed, there may be an infinite variety of possible experiments, and it is always possible to argue that the perfect one is just around the corner. With increasing numbers of experiments two things happen: The motivation to find something and the chances of spurious results both increase.

These are important problems. If 20 experiments are carried out and in each of them a dozen analyses are performed, of which half were planned and many are interdependent, then the chances of spurious "significance" are high—and incalculable. (Hyman [1985] has recently discussed these issues in an extensive study of the ganzfeld literature.) So, regardless of whether any psi is involved, one is likely to obtain quite a few "significant" findings along the way. Positive findings are a great stimulus to further work and increased belief. And it is hard to admit that a significant finding that fits in with your own theory may nevertheless be an artifact of overanalysis or of minor misuse of statistics. It is easy to be persuaded that there must be "something there." If you have spent years looking for the "something," the temptation is even greater.

I should add that I am assuming that there are no other artifacts and that the experiments are otherwise well done. However, if there are other causes of error, the same argument applies. It is hard to conclude that those positive findings that fit one's theory really were only artifact or chance. If they don't fit one's theory, it is much easier. All this means that the believer is likely to go on hunting while the disbeliever stops at the first hurdle.

As for myself, I pursued this approach for many years, convinced that there was psi to be found in laboratory experiments if I only could get the techniques right. I admitted that most of my early experiments had used boring tasks in boring classroom environments, and so I tried as many other methods as I could.

Thinking that the subjects might be wrong, I began testing people who came to me claiming to have psychic powers. As far as possible I tested them in accordance with their own claims and preferred tasks but found no confirmation of their abilities.

At that time, Spinelli (who was also doing a Ph.D. at Surrey University) was obtaining staggeringly impressive results in GESP experiments with young children. I therefore redesigned some of my memory experiments to use children aged between three and five years (Blackmore 1980b). These studies were not replications of Spinelli's work but drew heavily on his findings, using similar tasks and children of the age he had found best. They too gave only chance results.

I also wanted to try using subjects to whom I was personally much closer. An especially promising technique at that time seemed to be the ganzfeld, so I carried out a ganzfeld study using friends and family as subjects (Blackmore 1980c). Several of us, including students from my parapsychology class, formed a small training group and practiced imagery, relaxation, and other relevant techniques before carrying out further experiments. But the results of all of these studies were the same—chance expectation.

There came a point at which I simply stopped believing that I would ever find any psi however I varied my experimental techniques. I began to become just a little skeptical.

3. At this point, I was forced to consider another problem—the experimenter effect (see Kennedy and Taddonio 1976 for a review). Many parapsychologists suggested that the reason I didn't get results was quite simple—*me*. Perhaps I did not sufficiently believe in the possibility of psi.

Now this is an invidious argument, as I hope to show. On the one hand, it seems reasonable. It is certainly possible that psi is a funny kind of thing and only appears for certain people or when there are believers around. Understanding this might hold the key to unlocking psi. So the idea deserves serious consideration.

The experimenter effect might be either a normally mediated or a psi-mediated one. For example, it could be that a disbelieving experimenter conveys this doubt to the subjects in quite normal ways and that the subjects are then inhibited from producing psi. Even more simply, the experimenter may have inadequate personal skills for encouraging psi, whether or not he believes in it. Potentially this is a perfectly testable idea. One could carry out comparative studies of the results obtained by different experimenters using the same experimental design. Indeed, this has been done, for example, by manipulating experimenter expectancy (Taddonio 1976), but the argument is complicated by the second possibility.

The idea of a psi-mediated experimenter effect is more complex. There are several ways in which it could work. For example, the experimenter might impress his beliefs on his subjects by psi and they then conform to his wishes by producing no psi. Or the expectations of the experimenter could directly affect the results (whether by acting on subjects or random-number generators or by any mixture of effects). The disbelieving experimenter would then get no psi. And in various other ways the psi-inhibitory power of the experimenter could be imagined to work. Now this could also be tested by comparative studies, except for the problem of knowing who is to count as the experimenter.

Where one person designs, carries out, and analyzes the results of an experiment it is obvious who is the "experimenter," but in many cases several people are involved and any one of them could be blamed for being "psi-inhibitory." This can lead to interesting work. For example, there have been studies showing that, when different people check two halves of the data from one experiment, the results may be different—implying a psi-mediated-checker effect (Feather and Brier 1968; Bierman 1978). However, it can also become a nasty game of blaming, and of course there is really no end to the people who might be affecting the results. The observational theories suggest that anyone who observes the results of a given experiment may influence them by retroactive psychokinesis (PK). This interesting idea has led to important work on the "divergence problem" (see, e.g., Bierman and Houtkooper 1981); and, if the observational theories have any validity, it could be precisely the effect of so many observers that makes psi so elusive.

However, this is extremely hard to test, and these ideas extend the problem of the experimenter effect still further. In fact, there seems to be a slippery slope from using perfectly reasonable arguments about possible experimenter effects to making the whole notion vacuous and untestable.

I tried to take the argument seriously and wondered whether I was actually inhibiting psi from occurring in my experiments. How could I find out? Obviously I could not manipulate my beliefs as an independent variable. One cannot easily change beliefs at will. But I also found that it is surprisingly hard even to know what your own beliefs are. I concluded that you have to judge them just like anyone else does, by your actions and responses.

When accused of inhibiting psi because of my disbelief I recalled the vehemence of my early arguments against narrow-minded psychology. I recalled the disappointment I faced again and again as I did the final calculations. But can I honestly be sure that it wasn't what I expected all along? I remember the tingles of apprehension and even fear later on when people told me about exciting positive results; and finally, even now, I know the excitement I feel when someone tells me that high profits are being made by psi in California. So what did I and do I believe? I think I did believe in psi at the start and, if belief is crucial to getting results, then I should have been getting them then, but I didn't. However, I can never be sure about these beliefs or convince anyone else about them. This is no ground for rejecting the possibility of an experimenter effect. So I tried two different approaches.

First, I decided to try experiments with something I did believe in. I had been reading the Tarot cards for about eight years, and they seemed to be uncannily accurate. They appeared to reveal information that I could not have gained normally. So I set about designing an experiment to test this. I had ten subjects each rate and rank ten readings, of which one was their own. I tried to keep the experimental Tarot reading as close to the "real thing" as I could while making sensory communication impossible. And my first experiment was successful! Subjects ranked the readings intended for them significantly higher than those intended for others (Blackmore 1983a).

I can honestly say that I was thrilled. Here at last it seemed that I had found something. Perhaps I could begin building theories again instead of destroying them. But Carl Sargent (private communication) pointed out a potential flaw. The analysis I had used (Solfvin, Kelly, and Burdick 1978) assumed independence of the rankings, but, he pointed out, the subjects all knew each other, so their rankings would not be independent even though they did them in isolation. I could not believe that this could really make a difference. It seemed so subtle a problem. However, I repeated the experiment twice more without this flaw, just in case.

What happened? I got negative results. It is impossible to say whether there was psi in the first experiment. I only know that when I eliminated the flaw the effect disappeared. I am not justified in drawing any conclusion other than that the flaw was responsible; that is, unless I could demonstrate it in further experiments. After just two I chose to stop and conclude that there was no psi. Others might have carried on the search longer. But I was becoming skeptical— and the skeptic is likely to give up far sooner!

A second, more direct test of the experimenter effect would obviously be to compare myself with a psi-facilitatory experimenter at the same experiment. I had recently completed a ganzfeld study and, of course, obtained only chance scores. However, at the same time Carl Sargent was getting highly significant results with ganzfeld experiments in Cambridge (see Sargent 1980). Julian Isaacs (private communication) suggested that I go to Cambridge and try some experiments with Sargent—perhaps I could learn from his techniques how to find psi, or at least we might be able to find out if it was an experimenter effect.

Sargent agreed to the idea enthusiastically, and so in November 1979 I went to Cambridge for a preliminary week of observing his experiments and methods. The intention was for me to return after Christmas for a further few weeks so that we could do a comparative experiment together.

During that first week I observed numerous successful trials. The subjects in the ganzfeld, and that included myself on one occasion, really seemed to be describing the target picture. Out of 13 sessions observed, 6 were first-rank hits—in other words, the subject chose the right picture out of four. I was impressed.

However, I began to have some doubts about the complex and cumbersome radomization procedure being used. I observed very carefully the way this operated, and I predicted effects that would be observed if the randomization procedure were not being used correctly. When I looked for these effects, I found them. It was clear that errors had been made in the randomization. Neither Sargent nor I were ever entirely sure how the errors came about (Blackmore 1980d), nor how important they were to the final results. However, they were enough to dent my confidence in those results.

I never was able to test the experimenter effect directly in the way planned, which I much regretted, but then it appeared that I might not need to exploit the experimenter effect to explain the difference between my own results and those of Sargent. It began to seem that the more deeply I looked into claims for psi, the less convincing they appeared.

What then should we conclude about the experimenter effect? Someday there might be sufficient evidence to show whether it occurs and, if so, where its limitations lie. It is certainly possible that it was responsible for my negative results. But in the light of my findings I remain dubious. I did not and do not believe that it was.

4. The fourth possibility I considered was that psi may exist, but looking for it in the laboratory is futile. After all, it was the spontaneous experiences that motivated the founders of the Society for Psychical Research in the eighteenth century (Gauld 1968; Haynes 1982) and still motivate many parapsychologists today. Psi is not in any sense a laboratory discovery. The very notion arose

from people's experiences of telepathy and precognition in everyday life. Perhaps that is the place to look for it now.

Assessing spontaneous case material is quite a different task from assessing results obtained in the laboratory. Statistical rules make for a consensus on what is to count as psi in a laboratory experiment, but in the field there is more room for dispute over the interpretation of any claim or event. The determined believer can read psi into every strange occurrence. The determined disbeliever can more easily demand extra conditions and refuse to be satisfied by the evidence. As we move through the different approaches, we get deeper and deeper into the problem of what is to count as evidence. Similarly, I had to face the personal problem of what would convince me that I had found psi.

I had tended to assume that the spontaneous case material was stronger than the laboratory evidence, and since I knew less about it I was prepared to give it the benefit of the doubt. However, as soon as I began to explore it in more depth, I began to change my mind.

My interest in spontaneous cases centered around out-of-body experiences (OBEs) because of my own experience (Blackmore 1982). In my first OBE (nearly three hours long) I learned a lot about the experience but nothing that provided evidence of psi. However, I assumed that that was my problem and that other people's OBEs were more "psychic." Certainly there were plenty of books on the subject to convince me that this was so (see Rogo 1978; Mitchell 1981), but my own research soon convinced me otherwise.

The laboratory work on OBEs seemed largely unconvincing. There were a few outstanding successes, including Charles Tart's (1968) experiment with Miss Z, in which she appeared to read a 5-digit number on a shelf above the bed she was lying on, and an experiment in which Blue Harary apparently succeeded in calming down one of his two kittens while having an OBE in the laboratory (Morris et al. 1978). However, most of the results were much like those of any other ESP experiments. That is, the effects were always small and often inconsistent. This may seem an unfair assessment of the evidence and many disagree with me, but I have reviewed it in more detail elsewhere (Blackmore 1982, 1983b). The more important question at this stage is whether ESP occurs during spontaneous OBEs if not in the laboratory.

Among the many claims that it does, there are famous cases that are repeated in book after book. These include the Wilmot case (Myers 1903) and the Landau case (Landau 1963), to mention just two. While I began to study this material in more depth I was amazed to find that even these two were extraordinarily badly documented and really provided nothing like acceptable evidence for psi (see Blackmore 1983b).

It is not just that they are old cases. Reasonable ground-rules for accepting cases were laid down very early on in the subject. For example, Myers (1903) had a clear idea of what would constitute evidence for him. If someone claimed to have made a prediction or visited someone while out of the body, he required signed or witnessed statements of both the experience and the confirming event, made independently. This is much the same as we would expect today, and if he had obtained it I think we should take the evidence seriously. However, he did not. A clear example is the Danvers case, awarded the highest "evidentiality rating" in H. Hart's (1954) assessment of 99 convincing psychic experiences. Miss Danvers regularly "visited" a friend and claimed to be able to see what she was doing. Myers (1903, 695) sensibly asked her to record her attempts before checking and send the (postmarked) letter to him. The friend was to record her experiences independently. In the event, Myers's reasonable precautions were not observed, and he received notes of the attempt and the confirmation posted together—hardly a convincing outcome and a sad reflection of the standard of spontaneous case material!

My own investigations of spontaneous OBEs have only fueled my growing conviction that nothing psychic is usually involved. In fact, the association of psi with OBEs seems to have been blown up by the psychic literature and sensational books. Very few of the many cases sent to me or obtained from my surveys (e.g., Blackmore 1984a) include any mention of the paranormal—even when the experiences themselves are dramatic and life-changing.

Also, some of the few claims of paranormal OBEs have been proved to be false, like the case sent to me by Karlis Osis in which a Canadian architect had had an impressive-sounding OBE in which he seemed to travel across the Atlantic to a very specific area of London. He claimed that what he saw had been verified as accurate, but my enthusiastic checking of the area proved otherwise (Blackmore 1983b).

All this made me wonder whether there was any point in going on searching for psi. It seemed that wherever I looked it evaded me. Indeed, I began to think that the deeper I looked into any evidence, the less convincing it appeared. I began to think that whatever I did I wasn't going to find any psi. Suddenly I had to consider quite seriously the possibility that psi did not exist at all anywhere. The explanation of my negative results might be very simple—there is no psi.

So, I had taken the step of seriously questioning the existence of psi. What did this step entail and what then are the routes open to the novice skeptic?

5. As soon as I began to face the idea that psi might not exist, I found myself up against all sorts of new and serious problems.

It is obviously desirable, when considering a new hypothesis, to try to think of ways of testing it. In this case my new hypothesis was that there was no psi. I therefore tried to think of ways of directly testing this hypothesis. Obviously looking for psi and failing to find it is not enough. But why is it not enough? And could it ever be enough? Why aren't negative results good evidence for the skeptical hypothesis?

First, there is the difficulty of proving a negative, in this case that psi does not exist. It has often been assumed that it is impossible to prove a negative, but this could be, in the words of Tony Pasquarello (1984, 260), "one of the universally accepted platitudes that unfortunately just happens to be false!" In practice, we "prove negatives" all the time by looking for things and failing to find them. But these things are usually well defined, like my looking for my toothbrush in the bathroom cabinet. If I can't find it, I can be fairly confident that it is not there. I can specify the shape, size, color, and so on, of both toothbrush and cabinet and can search it all. To be confident of my negative I need only make some generally acceptable assumptions about things not disappearing when I look and reappearing a moment later and not fitting into spaces much smaller than they are. If I cannot see the toothbrush and, better still, if others cannot see it either, then we can all agree that it is not there. This is the kind of agreement we could wish for on the issue of psi.

But psi is not like this. It is not easily specifiable. There is the old, often discussed, and apparently insuperable problem of its negative definition. Psi is always defined by reference to what it is not. It is "extrasensorimotor communication with the environment" and includes ESP, which is ". . . without sensory contact," and PK, which is "extramotor" and "nonmuscular" (*Journal of Parapsychology* Glossary). So, in order to prove that psi is not there, we have to prove that something that is not normal (muscular, motor, sensory, or whatever) does not occur. In other words, we must prove a rather difficult proposition—that everything is "normal"!

In addition, the search area is infinite. In a sense, my progression through arguments 1 to 5 can be seen as a process of ever widening the search area for psi. In the beginning, it was supposed to appear in my specific experiments but, when it did not, it could have been hiding in the different conditions, the experimenter, the "real world," and so on. In other words it is an open-ended search. If you find psi all is well, but if you fail to find it you have to keep on looking. The negative definition of psi need not be a problem if psi does exist, but it certainly is if it doesn't.

Finally, no one can agree on the probability of finding psi. Some people are convinced that it is there somewhere and will keep looking for it, if necessary forever, while others only have to take a cursory glance to be convinced that it is not there. By contrast, in many areas of science, theory provides some kind of expectation about whether the thing will be found or not. If everyone thinks it unlikely and it is found, then a great discovery has been made. If everyone expects to find something and it does not appear, then that is a discovery too. A fair balance can then be struck between how much will be learned from positive or negative results, and experiments can be planned so that either way you will learn something. This is just not possible in parapsychology. There is little in the way of commonly accepted theory and everyone's expectations are different. Negative results provide some information to some people but none to others.

So we can now answer the question: Why aren't negative results good evidence for the skeptical hypothesis? Any given negative result tells us the most when (1) the thing or event being searched for is well defined and easily measured, (2) the search area is finite and searchable (and preferably small!), and (3) the prior probability of a positive finding is high. Psi is negatively defined and practically impossible to measure; the search area is infinite; and the expected probability of finding it depends on whether you are a believer or a disbeliever.

So it is not surprising that negative results tell us so little. Indeed, in the light of these three points, it becomes clearer why the argument between believers and disbelievers is so fierce and so unproductive.

To resolve the problem we might redefine psi so that we know exactly what we are looking for. That is, we could give it positive as well as negative characteristics. The demand for process-oriented research is obviously an attempt toward finding such characteristics, but so far it has not been very successful. Alternatively, we could specify more precisely the search area so that we would stop looking once we had searched far enough. Or we could develop theories sufficiently to come to some agreement about expected results. However, none of these seem likely to happen and achieve any kind of consensus. Unless we can build a radically new parapsychology we must accept that negative results provide little or no support for the skeptical hypothesis.

To return to my own research, it was obviously no use my doing more ESP experiments. I no longer believed that I would get significant results, and more negative results would teach me little or nothing. I therefore tried to find other ways of testing the skeptical hypothesis by asking what other testable predictions could be drawn from it.

One prediction concerns the reasons for people's belief in psi. The believer thinks that people believe in psi because it is there. The disbeliever thinks that belief is based on error and would therefore predict that there must be powerful reasons for belief in psi other than the existence of psi itself. I became interested in this as an alternative way of testing the skeptical hypothesis.

If you ask people why they believe in psi, you find that it is usually because of their own experiences, often very simple things like apparently precognitive dreams, communication with close relatives and friends by telepathy, and so on. Experiences of this kind usually have as their basis a judgment of probability. For example, when a person dreams that their Aunt Matilda is dead and the next day hears that she did die, the psi "explanation" is offered as an alternative to chance. It seems too unlikely to have been "just a coincidence." But our judgments of probability are notoriously inaccurate, even in simple situations (Tversky and Kahneman 1974; and others). Troscianko and I (1983) suggested that if poor judgment of probability were the reason for much belief in psi, then "sheep" should show much worse judgment than "goats."

We set about testing this with computer games and questionnaire studies. We found some evidence suggesting that sheep systematically underestimated the probability of chance events. Therefore, when they got chance scores in an experiment in which they thought they had done very well, they sought an explanation. We called this the chance baseline shift. However, this effect was fairly limited and did not appear in all the experiments. We are still exploring it.

I originally thought that this work might provide powerful evidence for the skeptical hypothesis. In the enthusiasm of my new-found skepticism I thought that other people would be equally convinced by it. But I now see why they were not. If it were regularly found that sheep did worse than goats we could conclude that some belief in psi came about in this way. Indeed we would have learned something interesting about the mechanisms of belief. But we would not be justified in arguing that all belief arises in this way and even less that psi does not exist. This was pointed out to me by numerous parapsychologists after I presented this work, and I am grateful for their discussions (Blackmore 1984-85). However, this kind of work is not entirely irrelevant as I shall discuss below.

6. I have not yet mentioned an obvious prediction of the skeptical hypothesis, which is that if you look more closely into published "successes" they too will be explicable in normal terms. In other words, the skeptical hypothesis predicts successful debunking. This is something done by many skeptics and I can see why. It is one of the few ways of testing their position. But it too is fraught with problems.

First, there is almost always disagreement about the relative merits of the "normal" and "paranormal" explanations offered (e.g., Price 1955; Rhine 1955; Hansel 1980). There have been some remarkable exceptions. Markwick's (1978) investigation of Soal's experiments with Basil Shackleton must gain first prize. This work has been almost universally accepted as showing that Soal manipulated some of his data. This alone has convinced many former believers that they might have been wrong. However it is a rare investigation that convinces everyone. More often there is still room for the believers to keep believing. Moreover, an unconvincing "normal" explanation only polarizes the two sides still further, with the believers laughing at those who will consider multiple fraudulent collusion rather than admit to the possibility of psi. All this is just another result of the fact that we cannot agree on any a priori probabilities.

The second problem is that even if you are prepared to consider very far-fetched possibilities you may not always be successful. You may find cases for which you can find no suitable alternative. What does this mean? It might mean that you just haven't looked hard enough although the explanation is there to be found. Or it might mean that the hypothesis was wrong, that there was psi after all. So how can you tell?

You cannot, because debunking is necessarily specific. You may be successful at showing that some claimed results were not paranormal, but is a great leap from there to the conclusion that there are none that are. If you personally have a good go at several experiments and succeed in finding really convincing alternative explanations, then you personally will probably be convinced that the leap is justified. But others may not be and can always produce another experiment. Debunking—like looking for psi—is an open-ended process, and so we are back again to some of the problems I have already discussed. They are just the same problems approached from the other side. I began to see that the believer's and disbeliever's positions very much mirror each other.

The skeptical position was now beginning to look distinctly less attractive. I decided that a career in debunking was not for me, but the whole issue is only one aspect of a very real problem—the positive results. There are positive results; there is evidence for psi. And necessarily entailed in the disbeliever's position is a rejection of it all.

This is no mean obstacle, and it is not good simply to dismiss it all en masse as bad experiments, bad reporting, bad statistics, and so on. One may do that in total ignorance or conceivably after very thorough investigation, but I was not totally ignorant and I had not done any such investigation. I knew of plenty of experiments that sounded convincing, and I knew several experimenters who were getting significant results. I had to ask myself how this could be.

It was here, finally, that I reached the most difficult of dilemmas. No longer was I confronting just the evidence from my own experiments, but I felt compelled to make some assessment of all the evidence from everyone else's experiments too. And the two were in conflict. The problem is this: How do you fairly weigh your own experience against what other people tell you of theirs?

My experience seemed to tell me the following. First, I could not find any psi. Second, lots of other people said they had found it. Third, every time I looked into other people's evidence I found that the deeper I looked the less psi there seemed to be. The inexorable direction I was taking was toward the conclusion that all evidence, if I looked into it thoroughly enough, would prove to be equally empty. But this is an indefensible position. Science cannot operate unless scientists generally believe the results of other people's work as well as of their own. And other people's work apparently provided evidence for psi.

This created a vast gulf between what I actually believed on the basis of my own experience and what I could reasonably argue I should believe. At that time I honestly did not any more believe in psi. So being honest meant stating beliefs that I could not reasonably defend.

What I could defend as reasonable belief depended on objectivity, logical argument, and impartial assessment of published work. Impartiality forced me to admit that there is evidence for psi. It cannot all be successfully debunked, and there will always be more "successes" coming along. But I could not be impartial. The positive findings were other people's and the negative ones were my own. So what could I do?

I admire honesty and I admire "scientific" impartiality, but in this case they seemed to be in conflict. I wondered whether this conflict is peculiar to parapsychology or whether it applies to all science. I think the answer is that it is always there but normally is a very minor problem and can be overlooked. This is so because repeatability, in its many varied forms, leads to agreement among scientists about their findings. But where there is no repeatability there can be no agreement. And where there is no agreement, as in parapsychology, impartiality and honesty part company.

Some people may be happy either to reject one of these ideals or to live with the conflict. I could do neither. Instead I concluded that there was only one solution. I had to bring the two together. I could only do this in one way: by giving up my new-found conviction and cultivating an open mind. I now understand why, in spite of good intentions to the contrary, people tend to polarize into belief or disbelief. The cognitive dissonance involved in not making up one's mind is quite painful! Nevertheless, I concluded that the evidence could only justify uncertainty. I had to refuse to make up my mind. This was, by a long way, the hardest thing I had tried to do.

7. It now appeared to me that both the extreme believer's and extreme disbeliever's positions were equally uncomfortable, and I began to see that many of my arguments had been futile. More than ever I wanted an answer to the question "Does psi exist?" but that answer seemed ever more remote and the question ever more nonsensical. So is the situation hopeless? Should I just leave the field altogether and forget about it?

I think not for one reason, that is, that science does not generally progress by seeking for proofs or disproofs all along the way and ruthlessly rejecting any refuted hypothesis. Rather, there are usually rival approaches, paradigms, research programs, or whatever. Each does a better or worse job of accounting for the data and convincing people. In the end, some approaches get abandoned and others progress.

So, I imagine, it will be with psi. The rivals at the moment are not so much the believers versus the disbelievers as the proponents versus the debunkers (or the parapsychologists versus the skeptics), each building their separate research programs based on their own convictions. I do not believe we shall see some crucial experiment that proves or disproves one viewpoint or the other. Rather, the two research programs will struggle along until one or the other, or some completely different one, will come to seem obviously better. In the end, the question "Does psi exist?" will no longer be asked because, within the prevailing program, the answer will seem obvious.

So how do we get to this position, and which viewpoint will win? Do we have the basis for a viable approach already or must we start again with a "New Parapsychology"?

Imre Lakatos provides a helpful philosophical framework here. In his terms, an approach that provides a progressive problemshift will win over a degenerating one. He explains: "A research programme is said to be *progressing* as long as its theoretical growth anticipates its empirical growth, that is, as long as it keeps predicting novel facts with some success (*'progressive problemshift'*); it is stagnating if its theoretical growth lags behind its empirical growth, that is, as long as it gives only *post hoc* explanations either of chance discoveries or of facts anticipated by, and discovered in, a rival programme (*'degenerating problemshift'*). If a research program progressively explains more than a rival, it 'supersedes' it, and the rival can be eliminated (or, if you wish, 'shelved')" (Lakatos 1978, 112 [his italics]).

So we may ask whether our two rival programs are degenerating or progressing. I have little doubt that judged against Lakatos's criteria both are fairly stagnant. I would argue that parapsychology has long been based on a degenerating program. Indeed, the steps I have followed are an example of that degeneration. In the face of the facts I was forced into ever weaker and weaker theoretical positions.

In parapsychology theoretical growth has not anticipated empirical growth. Rather, the accumulation of data goes on more or less unguided by theory—or guided by isolated theoretical attempts. Even the classic findings, such as the sheep-goat effect or position effects, remain isolated in weak theoretical structures incapable of providing further progress. There have been some notable examples of theory predicting novel facts, such as the prediction of retroactive PK within the observational theories. It is effects like this that hold out the hope of turning parapsychology into a progressive research program. But so far it has not come about. Indeed, historically, it is fascinating to see the lack of progress. As I showed in the case of OBE research, some of today's experiments are essentially asking the same questions as those asked 50 or even 100 years ago. There has been no problemshift.

But the problem is more serious even than this. Parapsychology has chosen definitions that force it into failure. It is defined as the study of psi, or paranormal phenomena. This immediately means that the field is committed to a particular hypothesis, that paranormal phenomena do occur. In other words it is hypothesis-driven. This is not how most other sciences operate. Biology, chemistry, and physics define themselves as studying a range of topics regardless of how they are to be explained and, roughly speaking, the theories change as time goes by but the topic area stays the same. Exceptions, such as quantum mechanics and thermodynamics, are based on hypotheses that are of quite a different order of sophistication to the psi hypothesis. By defining itself this way, parapsychology is restricted to studying phenomena whose explanation is deemed to be paranormal. Parapsychology has not claimed a range of topics for its own but a hypothesis that may prove to be empty.

This means that parapsychology is an ever-shrinking field. Hypnosis was an important part of early psychical research but has long since been taken over by medicine, psychology, and other "normal" sciences. Deathbed phenomena and near-death experiences were traditionally part of psychical research but are now being rapidly taken over by other fields, with notable success and with little or no reference to the psi hypothesis. There is progressive research on lucid dreams and OBEs that more or less ignores the paranormal aspects, and there are now whole societies and journals devoted to just these topics. How long will it be before such things as poltergeists, apparitions, and hauntings are tackled without any need for the psi hypothesis?

And what will parapsychology's response be? Judging by past performance it will simply shrink yet further and try to defend itself yet harder against the flood. In the end it may be left only with psi—and psi is a hypothetical process. Like any other hypothesis it may prove not to be very useful. If this is the case, parapsychology will finally have nothing left to work on. The believer runs the risk not only of being on the losing side but also of being left with no subjects to study.

What then of the rival program—the "skeptic's" approach? I don't think it is much better. Skeptics often point out the weaknesses in the believers' untestable positions but, as we have seen, there is not much to choose between them in this respect. Much of the skeptic's effort consists simply in destroying paranormal claims rather than replacing them with anything better. But then, just as the field of parapsychology shrinks, so must its parasite, the skeptical hypothesis. Remember it is not the "skeptics" who are taking topics away from parapsychology.

So we have two inadequate programs both doomed to failure. They are still rivals because they are totally interdependent and neither is in a strong enough position to supersede the other. People are divided by definition into those within parapsychology who work on psi and those opposing it who must be outside the field though dependent upon it. This produces unnecessary antagonism and is wasteful of knowledge, expertise, and research. Meanwhile the real progress goes on elsewhere while our two inadequate rivals battle over the vanishing remains.

There must be a better prospect for our subject.

8. The solution seems simple, but it is apparently not at all acceptable to many people. If the definition of parapsychology is at fault, then let us redefine it. I suggest that we go back to the roots of parapsychology—that is, to the phenomena that began it all. That includes spontaneous experiences interpreted as ESP or PK, out-of-body experiences, apparitions and hauntings, near-death and deathbed visions, poltergeists, and so on. There is little doubt that these experiences happen. All the doubt surrounds their interpretation. Let us define parapsychology as the study of these phenomena rather than as the study of psi. Let us have a new parapsychology.

This has numerous advantages. First, there would no longer need to be separate camps. Anyone working in the area could be considered within parapsychology. Our resources and knowledge could be shared more easily and the great gulf between the two factions done away with. Believers and disbelievers in psi could all work on the same topics from different points of view but with pooled resources and expertise.

Second, as I have explained elsewhere (Blackmore 1983c), this removes at a stroke one of parapsychology's major problems— unrepeatability. For it is only psi that is unrepeatable. Many experiences, beliefs, and other phenomena show all kinds of repeatable patterns. A parapsychology free from the bonds of psi could explore them freely and, who knows, perhaps in the end it might need something like psi. But at least it would not be committed from the start.

Third, I think we should be nearer to studying what the founders of psychical research and parapsychology intended and what motivates many people who get interested in the subject today. I don't think those early psychical researchers would be at all impressed with our progress so far. They urged us to study the phenomena "without prejudice or prepossession and in a scientific spirit" (from the aims of the Society for Psychical Research). I fear we have not lived up to that aim. And consider the motivation of J. B. Rhine. He spent most of his life working on psi, but his real desire appears to have been to study the mysteries of the mind (Brian 1982), and his laboratory was called the "Foundation for Research on the Nature of Man." Although he would certainly disagree, I submit that we shall be closer to understanding the nature of man if we abandon the psi hypothesis.

Why then has this not already happened? The answer became clear to me when parapsychologists began responding to my previous suggestions (Blackmore 1983c, 1983d, 1984-85). The general opinion seemed to be that either I was just playing with words or I was suggesting something unacceptable. Adrian Parker (1984-85) put it most clearly when he said: ". . . Should she prove to be correct and parapsychology be redefined as the psychology of psychic beliefs and experiences, then the subject would lose all interest to me."

So I am apparently alone in finding the experiences themselves fascinating, whether or not they prove to be paranormal. For many parapsychologists, pursuing my current line of research is more or less equivalent to taking that final path and leaving the field. Perhaps I should simply agree that it is a matter of words and definitions only and not bother to ask. In the end, what counts is the research. So I shall conclude by explaining the research to which all these paths finally led me.

My own first OBE, already mentioned, was the impetus for much of my recent research. I expect I shall continue until I feel I have explained that experience to my own satisfaction, but at the moment this is a remote prospect.

I began my search for an explanation with occult and paranormal theories of the OBE, most of which suggest that something actually leaves the body and travels around, taking consciousness with it. I rapidly found these unsatisfactory because they neither seemed to make sense nor fit with the evidence (Blackmore 1982). Nor have they led to any progress. The same questions are being asked today as in 1903 when Myers tried to get Miss Danvers to provide evidence of her nocturnal travels. The "something leaves" theories have provided no progressive problemshift.

The alternative theories are also unsatisfactory. Suggestions that it is imagination or a traveling fantasy plus ESP (e.g., Tart 1978; Osis 1975) are simply putting together two catch-all phrases and explaining nothing. The OBE may or may not be psi-conducive, but this cannot account for the nature of the experience. There have also been several psychological theories, most important of which is John Palmer's (1978). But, as D. Scott Rogo (1982) has pointed out, none of these is capable of satisfactorily accounting for the phenomenology of the OBE.

Finally, skeptics tend to dismiss the experiences as "just imagination." Obviously we must do better than that. One of the outstanding features of the OBE is that people always report it as seeming so real and not at all like imagination or dreaming. What we need is a theory that will explain how and why OBEs come about and why they take the form they do. I determined to go back to the actual experiences, to the phenomenology of the OBE, and try again.

There are certain features of the OBE that demand explanation. The conditions under which OBEs occur seem to be oddly variable, from near-death or drug states to relaxation and ordinary activity. The "exit" may be a gradual floating process or a sudden rushing. Sometimes the person seems to be hurtling along a tunnel at the start of the experience. Then usually the person's point of view is no longer in the head but above it and sometimes slightly behind, and he or she can look around and see what is going on. Most interesting is the nature of the perceived world. It is very odd, distorted, colorful, and stylized. It is almost like a dream world but yet seems more stable and realistic. Then there is the role of thought. Everything seems to proceed by thinking it to happen. Thought rules in the astral world! Movement seems to occur by thought alone. The experience usually ends fairly abruptly with a sudden return to normal perspective. One is not more or less out of body; rather, the experience seems to be discrete, both in the way it begins and ends and in the fact that most people clearly distinguish it from dreaming or imagination. Finally, and perhaps most important, is its "special" quality. Everything seems more real and more impressive than in normal life. Some people claim that they seem to be really awake for the first time in their lives. This is something that no theory has even begun to account for.

For me these are the kinds of things that need explaining, not the rare and disputed occasions on which ESP seems to be involved. So I set about trying to account for them.

Several pointers seemed important. One is that a reduction of sensory input seems to be the only common feature implicated in the induction of OBEs (see Blackmore 1982; Palmer 1978; Rogo 1983). It is as though one needs to be cut off from the normal world of the senses. Another is that the OB world is very much like the cognitive map—that is, it resembles the way we recall and imagine the world, rather than the world as it appears to our senses. Telltale signs are the distortions, additions and omissions of details, and the effects of thought (Blackmore 1978). But it is not sufficient just to conclude that it is imagination. Why does this imagined world seem real?

This seemed to me the most important single question, and I set about answering it in the following way. Suppose that we have been asking the wrong questions about altered states of consciousness. Instead of measuring physiological variables or looking at perceptual skills, let us ask what "model of reality" a person has in a given state of consciousness. I suggest that this higher level of explanation is more appropriate for understanding what the states are like and can actually lead to a new model of the OBE.

Most of the time we are busy building models of the world. For example, I now have a model of the room around me and the fields outside the window, another of the paper I am trying to write and other bits and pieces about what I'm going to do at the weekend and where the children are. These models are more or less distinct; they don't get muddled up with each other. Three of them might be called imagination or fantasy and one represents the external world of reality. But how does the cognitive system know which one is the "reality" model?

You may think this is obvious, but why? After all, perception is a process of model building just as thinking is. I suggest that this is actually an important choice that the brain makes and that "reality" is as much a constructed feature as anything else. I suggest that all the time it chooses one and only one model to represent external reality. Now in most cases you would be right—it is obvious which is which, because one model is extremely stable and complex while the others are fleeting and ephemeral things. So let us suppose that the stable one is called "reality."

This is fine under most circumstances, but what happens when sensory input is reduced (as in sleep, meditation, deep relaxation, and so on) or when it is greatly distorted (as in certain drug states, under severe stress, or close to death)? The model based on sensory input may degenerate or become distorted. If this process goes far enough it may cease to be an effective model of the input, and new (possibly noisy) input will not make sense anymore. The input model may now no longer be the most stable. Since I have assumed that the most stable model is always considered as representing reality, whichever model is now most stable will take over. It will seem real. In other words, one is hallucinating.

Of course this is a dangerous state for the organism to get into, and it will seek to get back to normal. But how can this be achieved? One possibility is to try to start again and build a new model of the external world. In most cases we need not assume that memory has been affected as well as perception. So the person will remember that he is lying in bed or sitting at his desk. He may then try to build up a new model of the world around him, but he must use predominantly information from memory and imagination. And what is that model like? Of course it is like the cognitive map; the internal representation of the world that we all hold in memory. And what about the viewpoint? Recent studies (e.g., Nigro and Neisser 1983) have shown that, for some people at least, scenes are often remembered as in a bird's-eye view—from above.

So a new model is built, from memory and imagination, and it may well be that this is more stable than any other and so it takes over as reality. Everything in that model seems real because it is real in exactly the same way as anything is ever real. If that model is from a bird's-eye viewpoint, then an OBE has occurred.

This way of looking at the OBE immediately leads to many predictions about when the OBE should occur, which people should have it more often, and so on. It accounts for the viewpoint and for many crucial features of the experience, such as the nature of the OB world, the effects of thought, and the "realness" of the experience. It can also explain why the experience is relatively discrete, since only one model can assume reality status at once (Blackmore 1984b). There are many outstanding problems, such as why people sometimes see a "silver cord," and how the OB viewpoint is related to imagined viewpoints, but I am hopeful that these are at least amenable to research. It does not directly account for the tunnel, but there is great progress being made on physiological theories of the tunnel, and it rather seems that it has its origin in the organization of the visual cortex (Cowan 1982).

I believe that this approach can help us to understand the OBE, but its implications go much wider. The OBE now appears as the closest to normality of a whole range of possible states. It arises out of the attempt to get back to normal. If you stop worrying about normality and allow other models to take over, then almost anything is possible—and whatever you can imagine can be experienced as real.

This raises the possibility of explaining certain occult and magical teachings in terms of the cognitive processes involved in model building. The astral worlds and other "planes" are seen as products of such models. Their common features and boundaries are imposed by the limits of the cognitive system. People who have explored these "places" can suddenly contribute to our understanding. Ideas that had seemed very far-fetched might now seem to make more sense.

More generally, this approach suggests that what is altered in altered states of consciousness is a person's model of reality. And it places our normal model of reality firmly within the context of all those other possible ones. Indeed, it might even throw light on the nature and pervasiveness of the illusion that there is one reality and a persistent self who perceives it. For the self is a part of the model of reality too. In this way cognitive psychology could come closer to mysticism.

It is odd that many parapsychologists are very interested in and know-ledgeable about magic, occultism, and mysticism. Many meditate or follow other disciplines, and many have wide experience of altered states and even mystical experience. But these topics are only rarely mentioned in conferences and even less in journals. It is as though they are avoided for fear of making parapsychology seem "unscientific." But I would say forget about trying to *seem* scientific. What is important is not using the external trappings of scientific methodology but actually making progress in understanding and theory. If we want to understand these things, then let us put science to work in whatever way we can. I think the most exciting prospect for the "New Parapsychology" is that it could begin to learn about these things.

I don't put these ideas forward as the solution to all our problems. I want only to point out that there are alternatives to the slavish adherence to the hypothesis of psi. If we stopped defining parapsychology as the study of psi, the schism between the proponents and the skeptics might be healed, the repeat-ability problem could be shelved, and we might find ourselves studying all the same phenomena we have always studied but also able to tackle those human experiences and occult and mystical teachings that we could never approach through the study of psi.

If this is not parapsychology, then so be it—I have left the field. If it all proves to be nonsense, then so be it—I shall at least have tried. In any case, it is a lot more fun than the never-ending search for ESP.

References

Bierman, D. J. 1978. Observer or experimenter effect? A fake replication. *European Journal of Parapsychology*, 2:115-125.

Bierman, D. J., and J. M. Houtkooper. 1981. The potential observer effect or the mystery of irreproduceability. *European Journal of Parapsychology*, 3:345-372.

Blackmore, S. J. 1978. *Parapsychology and Out-of-the-Body Experiences*. London: Transpersonal Books and Society for Psychical Research.

———. 1979. Is ESP perceiving or remembering? *Parapsychology Review*, 10(4):23-27.

———. 1980a. Correlations between ESP and memory. *European Journal of Parapsychology*, 3:127-147.

———. 1980b. A study of memory and ESP in young children. *Journal of the SPR*, 50:501-520.

———. 1980c. *Extrasensory Perception as a Cognitive Process*. Unpublished Ph.D. thesis, University of Surrey.

———. 1980d. *Report of a Visit to Carl Sargent's Laboratory in Cambridge*. Unpublished, Archives of the Society for Psychical Research.

———. 1981a. Errors and confusions in ESP. *European Journal of Parapsychology*, 4:49-70.

———. 1981b. The effect of variations in target material on ESP and memory. *Research Letter*, Parapsychology Laboratory, Utrecht, 11:1-26.

———. 1982. *Beyond the Body*. London: Heinemann.

———. 1983a. Divination with Tarot cards: An empirical study. *Journal of the SPR*, 52:97-101.

———. 1983b. Parapsychology—with or without the OBE? *Parapsychology Review*, 13, (6):1-7.

———. 1983c. Unrepeatability: Parapsychology's only finding? Paper presented at the Parapsychology Foundation Conference, San Antonio, October.

———. 1983d. Prospects for a psi inhibitory experimenter. In *Research in Parapsychology, 1982*, edited by W. G. Roll, J. Beloff, and R. A. White, 17-20. Metuchen, N.J.: Scarecrow Press.

———. 1984a. A postal survey of OBEs and other experiences. *Journal of the SPR*, 52:225-244.

———. 1984b. A psychological theory of the OBE. *Journal of Parapsychology*, 48:201-218.

———. 1984-85. Prospects for a psi inhibitory experimenter (with commentaries). *Zetetic Scholar*, No. 12-13.

Brian, D. 1982. *The Enchanted Voyager: The Life of J. B. Rhine*. Englewood Cliffs,

N.J.: Prentice Hall.

Carington, W. 1945. *Telepathy: An Outline of Its Facts, Theory and Implications*. London: Methuen.

Cowan, J. D. 1982. Spontaneous symmetry breaking in large scale nervous activity. *International Journal of Quantum Chemistry*, 22:1059-1082.

Feather, S. R., and R. Brier. 1968. The possible effect of the checker in precognition tests. *Journal of Parapsychology*, 32:167-175.

Gauld, A. 1968. *The Founders of Psychical Research*. London: Routledge and Kegan Paul.

Hansel, C. E. M. 1980. *ESP and Parapsychology: A Critical Re-Evaluation*. Buffalo, N.Y.: Prometheus Books.

Hart, H. 1954. ESP projection: Spontaneous cases and the experimental method. *Journal of the American SPR*, 48:121-146.

Haynes, R. 1982. *The Society for Psychical Research: A History, 1882-1982*. London: Macdonald.

Hyman, R. 1985. The ganzfeld/psi experiment: A critical appraisal. *Journal of Parapsychology*, 49(1):3-50.

Kennedy, J. E., and J. L. Taddonio. 1976. Experimenter effects in parapsychological research. *Journal of Parapsychology*, 40:1-33.

Lakatos, I. 1978. *The Methodology of Scientific Research Programmes. Philosophical Papers*, vol. 1, edited by J. Worrall and G. Currie. Cambridge: Cambridge University Press.

Landau, L. 1963. An unusual out-of-the-body experience. *Journal of the SPR*, 42:126-128.

Markwick, B. 1978. The Soal-Goldney experiments with Basil Shackleton: New evidence of data manipulation. *Proceedings of the SPR*, 56:250-281.

Marshall, N. 1960. ESP and memory: A physical theory. *British Journal for the Philosophy of Science*, 10:265-286.

Mitchell, J. L. 1981. *Out-of-Body Experiences: A Handbook*. Jefferson, N.C. and London: McFarland.

Morris, R. L., S. B. Harary, J. Janis, J. Hartwell, and W. G. Roll. 1978. Studies of communication during out-of-body experiences. *Journal of the American SPR*, 72:1-22.

Myers, F. W. H. 1903. *Human Personality and Its Survival of Bodily Death*. London: Longmans Green.

Nigro, G., and U. Neisser. 1983. Point of view in personal memories. *Cognitive Psychology*, 15:467-482.

Osis, K. 1975. Perceptual experiments on out-of-body experiences. In *Research in Parapsychology, 1974*, edited by J. D. Morris, W. G. Roll, and R. L. Morris, 53-55. Metuchen, N.J.: Scarecrow Press.

Palmer, J. 1978. The out-of-body experience: A psychological theory. *Parapsychology Review*, 9:19-22.

Parker, A. 1984-85. Comments on Blackmore's "Prospects for a psi-inhibitory experimenter." *Zetetic Scholar*, No. 12-13.

Pasquarello, T. 1984. Proving negatives and the paranormal. *Skeptical Inquirer*, 8:259-270.

Price, G. R. 1955. Science and the supernatural. *Science,* 122:359-367.

Price, H. H. 1939. Haunting and the "psychic ether" hypothesis. *Proceedings of the SPR,* 45:307-343.

Rhine, J. B. 1955. The controversy in *Science* over ESP. *Journal of Parapsychology,* 19:236-271.

Rogo, D. S., ed. 1978. *Mind Beyond the Body.* New York: Penguin.

———. 1982. Psychological models of the out-of-body experience. *Journal of Parapsychology,* 46:29-45.

———. 1983. *Leaving the Body: A Practical Guide to Astral Projection.* Englewood Cliffs, N.J.: Prentice-Hall.

Roll, W. G. 1966. ESP and memory. *International Journal of Neuropsychiatry,* 2:505-512.

Sargent, C. L. 1980. Exploring psi in the ganzfeld. Parapsychological Monograph, No. 17.

Sheldrake, R. 1981. *A New Science of Life.* London: Blond and Briggs.

Solfvin, G. F., E. F. Kelly, and D. S. Burdick. 1978. Some new methods of analysis for preferential-ranking data. *Journal of the American SPR,* 72:93-109.

Taddonio, J. L. 1976. The relationship of experimenter expectancy to performance on ESP tasks. *Journal of Parapsychology,* 40:107-114.

Tart, C. T. 1968. A psychophysiological study of out-of-the-body experiences in a selected subject. *Journal of the American SPR,* 62:3-27.

———. 1978. Paranormal theories about the out-of-body experience. In *Mind Beyond the Body,* edited by D. S. Rogo, 338-345. New York: Penguin.

Troscianko, T., and S. J. Blackmore. 1983. Sheep-goat effect and the illusion of control. In *Research in Parapsychology, 1982,* edited by W. G. Roll, J. Beloff, and R. A. White. Metuchen, N.J.: Scarecrow Press.

Tversky, A., and D. Kahneman. 1974. Judgment under uncertainty: Heuristics and biases. *Science,* 185:1124-1131.

19

Skeptical Literature on Parapsychology: An Annotated Bibliography

GERD H. HÖVELMANN
with Marcello Truzzi and Piet Hein Hoebens

The following annotated bibliography was prepared by three authors sympathetic to parapsychological research and is highly critical of what they consider to be "hard-line" skepticism. The first draft was begun by Piet Hein Hoebens, a "soft-line" skeptic. It was completed by Gerd Hövelmann, a skeptical parapsychologist, with the assistance of Marcello Truzzi, who is in both camps.

It should be pointed out that this bibliography does not necessarily represent the point of view of the editor of this volume or of other skeptics. Nevertheless, it does provide a helpful guide.—ED.

I. Introduction

Skeptical reactions to parapsychological research are as old as this research itself. More than one hundred years of skeptical inquiry have produced an unwieldy mass of skeptical literature from both outside and inside the parapsychological community, in which almost every aspect of parapsychological experimentation and theory-building has been subjected to skeptical scrutiny. The quality, meticulousness, and reliability of publications, however, cannot generally be claimed to be superior in the skeptical literature to that of the

Inclusion of an annotated bibliography of the skeptical literature in this *Skeptic's Handbook of Parapsychology* was suggested by the late P.H.H., and the plan for its format and scope was drawn up jointly by G.H.H. and P.H.H. However, the final selection of the works to be included, as well as the writing of both the introduction and annotations, was done by G.H.H. and M.T. only after P.H.H.'s untimely death in October 1984. P.H.H. should not be held responsible for any shortcomings or inadequacies the introductory section and annotations may contain.

proponents. Also, while inside criticisms have mostly appeared in parapsychological journals and anthologies, the vast majority of outside skeptics have chosen to publish their critiques in journals of the established sciences, in book form, or in their own specialized periodicals, such as the *Skeptical Inquirer*. Although understandable in terms of the skeptics' and the parapsychologists' affiliations with different professional organizations and their respective publication channels, these publication policies certainly form a major obstacle to rational communication between the two groups. While many skeptics seem to overlook the fact that most parapsychological periodicals insist that they remain open to skeptical outsiders' contributions, parapsychologists still meet with considerable difficulties when they try to publish articles—even skeptical or self-critical ones—in journals of the established disciplines. This apparent asymmetry adds to the communication problems. Also, while a number of parapsychologists, like Prince (1930), Pratt et al. (1940), Ransom (1971), Honorton (1975), Rao (1982), Bauer (1984), and, most recently, Palmer (1984), have published more or less comprehensive reviews of the skeptics' arguments, there has been hardly any effort on the part of the skeptics to do comparable surveys of their own literature. This is regrettable, because a systematization of skeptical objections to parapsychology, which itself is written from a skeptical point of view, may prove useful to both skeptics and parapsychologists and facilitate future communication between the two groups.

The term *skeptic* technically means one who doubts rather than one who denies, thus it properly refers to nonbelief rather than disbelief. However, in recent years the term has been used to designate all critics of psi whether they be agnostic or hold actively negative views. This blurs an important distinction, but because critics of parapsychology typically call themselves "skeptics" rather than "deniers," and it is their writings we review here, we will adopt the term *skeptic* in its currently broad (though somewhat corrupt) usage.

The apparent lack of systematic surveys of the skeptical literature in the skeptics' own publications may justify the present attempt to provide, as a first step, an overview of skeptical books and major articles in the form of a brief introduction and an (inevitably incomplete) annotated bibliography. We hope that, in addition, this bibliography will serve as a guide to the skeptical literature not only for those who, in one way or the other, are actively involved in the continuing debates around the paranormal but also for those readers of this book who have not themselves been engaged in any of these controversies and may wish to read further on the subject matters with which the present volume is concerned.

Anyone who has taken the trouble to become acquainted with the debates around parapsychology and its legitimacy as a scientific endeavor and to carefully read the relevant literature is likely to agree that it is glaringly inadequate to simply and summarily refer to *the* parapsychologists and *the* skeptics as if there were sociologically well-defined groups of people who either believe in or doubt the claims of the paranormal. The reality of the psi debate is far more complex than is apparent from this manner of speaking, which does not take into consideration that, on closer inspection, we find many different types of skepticism as well as a great variety of activities that are commonly subsumed under the term *parapsychology*. It also ignores the fact that in recent years a small but significant informal group has established itself that consists of moderates from both sides who are more interested in rational discourse than in propagandistic overselling of their respective convictions or in thinking in terms of black and white, winners and losers. Despite this recent development, widely varying degrees of scientific competence, seriousness, intellectual self-discipline, and methodological sophistication are to be found on either side of the debates around parapsychological research. Just as in the 1950s anyone could throw up a sign in most states and call oneself a psychologist, today anyone is free to present oneself as a parapsychologist or a critic of parapsychology. Consequently, the fact that the field is replete with self-appointed parapsychologists and self-appointed skeptics considerably adds to the difficult and at times obviously strained relations between the parapsychological and the skeptical communities that lead all too frequently to acrimonious disputes.

There have been a number of attempts (usually by parapsychologists or sociologists of science) to divide the skeptical literature into different categories according to a variety of more or less plausible criteria. Thus skeptical publications have been classified according to the respective professional backgrounds of those who advance objections to parapsychology's practices or theories (e.g., philosophers, natural scientists, psychologists, members of the medical profession, magicians), to the focus of their criticisms (e.g., folk or paranormal beliefs, psychic sleuths, experimental work), to what parapsychologists perceive as the skeptics' relative degrees of fairness/unfairness, knowledge of the relevant experimental literature or lack thereof, or to a skeptic's membership/nonmembership in skeptical organizations like the Committee for the Scientific Investigation of Claims of the Paranormal; quite a few further distinctive criteria are to be found in the literature. A distinction that, to us, seems to hold some promise for future systematic analyses of skeptical publications is the one recently suggested by one of us, M. Truzzi (1982), who distinguishes between "empirical," "conceptual," and "methodological" critics, which he defines as follows:

> *Empirical critics* take issue with the basic facts being alleged. They are commonly concerned with matters of possible fraud, both by subjects and experimenters, incomplete or incompetent observation, and purported contradiction between the events claimed and empirical generalizations (such as the laws of physics) accepted by most scientists.

Conceptual critics take issue with the basic units of analysis (the variables) posited by parapsychologists; this attack is mainly on a priori grounds and seeks to call into question definitional congruence between ideas like psi, precognition, and clairvoyance, and the normal prerequisites of scientific analysis.

Methodological critics take issue with the operational and procedural aspects of research, including such matters as the use of theoretical rather than empirical statistical distributions, problems of falsifiability, and related matters.

For the purpose of the present basic bibliography, however, we have chosen the following, more narrowly defined subject categories in which we will list and briefly discuss contributions to the skeptical literature:

1. General Criticisms
2. ESP Research
3. PK Research
4. Mediumism
5. Psychic Healing
6. Dowsing
7. Survival Research and Reincarnation
8. Statistics
9. Conceptual Criticisms

In addition to dividing the outside skeptical literature into these nine subject categories (which are relatively arbitrary), we list some important *inside* criticisms of parapsychology (category 10) that deserve the careful attention of skeptical outside commentators on the paranormal, as well as those works that we think make the best case not for the reality of psi or any other paranormal phenomenon but for the scientific legitimacy and respectability of parapsychology (category 11) and which therefore are required reading for every serious skeptic. We include a brief list (category 12) of old and new skeptical periodicals and end with a list of unannotated but relevant literature (category 13). In addition to books, major articles are included in several of the subject categories, and references are given to important reviews of many of the books listed, to possible rejoinders, and to major controversies around skeptical books. Given the very large number of skeptical books and essays, it is evident that the present compilation cannot be anything close to a complete bibliography.

Works that contain skeptical commentaries on a number of different areas of parapsychological research and that are therefore difficult to subsume under one of the other subject headings are gathered under the first heading "General Criticisms." The main entries in the bibliography are arranged alphabetically by the first author's last name under the major subject headings. The main entries are numbered consecutively, starting with the first skeptical publication listed and continuing through the last. The numerous "Additional References" to book reviews, rejoinders, or major controversies are not numbered.

It is always difficult to decide which works should be included in a basic bibliography like this and which can be omitted; inevitably, selection criteria remain arbitrary to a certain extent. As noted above, books and major articles were selected from a huge mass of skeptical publications. They are included because, in our opinion, they are reasonably representative of certain *types of skeptical inquiry* and/or of certain *areas of skeptical activity.* Our third and most important criterion was that the works selected should have a lasting *influence* on or *relevance* for contemporary discussions of parapsychological research.

Finally, we wish to emphasize the need for close and rational cooperation between skeptics and parapsychologists. Only cooperation, not competition or partisanship, of all those who are sincerely interested in scientific truth, as well as continued and collaborative empirical research by both parapsychologists and skeptics, can hold out any promise for an eventual solution to the problems of the paranormal—whatever this solution may turn out to be. We hope that the present annotated bibliography will be used in this spirit and serve this end.

References

Bauer, Eberhard. 1984. Criticism and controversies in parapsychology—an overview. *European Journal of Parapsychology,* 5:141-165.

Honorton, Charles. 1975. "*Error Some Place!*"*Journal of Communication,* 25:103-116.

Palmer, John. 1984. Criticism of parapsychology: Some common elements. Paper presented at the 33rd Annual International Conference of the Parapsychology Foundation, New Orleans, August.

Pratt, J. Gaither, Joseph B. Rhine, Burke M. Smith, Charles E. Stuart, and Joseph A. Greenwood. 1940. *Extra-Sensory Perception After Sixty Years: A Critical Appraisal of the Research in Extra-Sensory Perception.* New York: Henry Holt, (reprinted in 1966 by Bruce Humphries, New York).

Prince, Walter Franklin. 1930. *The Enchanted Boundary: Being a Survey of Negative Reactions to Claims of Psychic Phenomena 1820-1930.* Boston: Boston Society for Psychic Research (reprinted in 1975 by Arno Press, New York).

Rao, K. Ramakrishna. 1982. J. B. Rhine and his critics. In: *J. B. Rhine: On the Frontiers of Science,* edited by K. R. Rao, 192-212. Jefferson, N.C., and London: McFarland.

Ransom, Champe. 1971. Recent criticisms of parapsychology: A review. *Journal of the American SPR,* 65:289-307.

Truzzi, Marcello. 1982. J. B. Rhine and pseudoscience: Some zetetic reflections on parapsychology. In *J. B. Rhine: On the Frontiers of Science,* edited by K. R. Rao, 177-191. Jefferson, N.C., and London: McFarland.

II. Annotated Bibliography

1. General Criticisms

(1) Abell, George O., and Barry Singer (Eds.), *Science and the Paranormal: Probing the Existence of the Supernatural.* New York: Scribner's, 1981, xi + 414 pp.

An important but highly uneven anthology that contains 22 contributions (both original papers and reprinted articles) dealing with many different areas of anomaly research. Those of immediate relevance to parapsychology include, among others, "Parapsychology and Quantum Mechanics" by Martin Gardner (see Chapter 25 in this volume), "Scientists and Psychics" by Ray Hyman, "On Double Standards" by Barry Singer, "Life after Death" by Ronald K. Siegel, "Psychic Healing" by William A. Nolen, and "Science and the Chimera" by James Randi. The book is intended as an exposition for the lay public of the evaluation of claims of paranormal and related phenomena by informed mainstream scientists. However, the book does not always live up to this advertised goal, although its editors try to be constructive in their criticism. In particular, papers on anomaly areas other than parapsychology seem to be more thoroughly researched and more carefully written than some of those dealing with parapsychology proper. The book's main weakness probably is that it largely neglects the voluminous literature on experimental parapsychological research. Readers may thus be misled into believing that a certain topic (including the relevant literature) is fully and adequately covered when this actually is not the case. The book's title (as well as a few of its authors) confuse interest in parapsychology as a naturalistic endeavor with interest in the "supernatural." Nevertheless, this is probably the best anthology by critics of the paranormal and related anomaly areas published in the past few decades.

Additional References: An extensive and well-balanced book review was published by Robert L. Morris: "Mainstream Science, Experts, and Anomaly: A Review of *Science and the Paranormal: Probing the Existence of the Supernatural,* edited by George O. Abell and Barry Singer," *Journal of the American Society for Psychical Research,* 76 (1982):257-281.

(2) Alcock, James E. *Parapsychology: Science or Magic?* Elmsford, N.Y., and Oxford: Pergamon Press, 1981, 224 pp.

This certainly is one of the most important skeptical books on parapsychology. Although most of his criticisms are not new, the author makes many good points that should set parapsychologists rethinking and changing some of the ways they carry out their research. The book contains a number of thought-provoking chapters, especially "Magic, Religion and Science," "The Psychology of Belief," "The Psychology of Experience," and "The Fallibility of Human Judgment." In our opinion, a major weakness of this book seems to be that its author presents a one-sided picture of the role of belief systems in distorting people's perceptions of events; that is, he fails to fully recognize that many of the cognitive errors he charges parapsychologists with may be made by skeptics as well. A further, and probably the most important, weakness of this book is that its author, even more so than most of his fellow skeptics, fails to confront the actual empirical data of parapsychology. Both of these points should be kept in mind when reading this book, which otherwise has much of value to offer to both skeptics and parapsychologists.

Additional References: John Palmer's extensive review of this book ("In Defense of Parapsychology: A Reply to James E. Alcock," *Zetetic Scholar,* #11 [1983]:39-70) launched a major and exceedingly polemical controversy between Palmer and Alcock in the pages of the *Zetetic Scholar* (James E. Alcock, "Science, Psychology, and Parapsychology: A Reply to Dr. Palmer," *Zetetic Scholar,* #11 [1983]:71-90; John Palmer, "A Reply to Dr. Alcock," *Zetetic Scholar* #11, [1983]:91-103; James E. Alcock, "A Final Note," *Zetetic Scholar* #11 [1983]:104). Despite the polemical nature of the exchange (provoked by ad hominems in both Alcock's book and Palmer's review), it is most instructive reading insofar as it makes obvious many of the mutual misunderstandings and prejudices as well as many of the reasons for insufficient communication between skeptics and parapsychologists in general, and insofar as it serves to clarify a number of underlying assumptions about parapsychology made (but not unambiguously stated) in Alcock's book. Other important and more or less extensive reviews of this book were written by skeptics Ray Hyman (*Parapsychology Review,* 13 [1983]:2, 24-27), Andrew Neher (*Skeptical Inquirer,* 6, no. 4 [1982]: 54-56), and Barry Singer (*Contemporary Psychology* 27 [1982]:688-689), as well as by parapsychologists Robert L. Morris (*Journal of the American Society for Psychical Research,* 76 [1982]:177-186), and Rex G. Stanford ("Is Scientific Parapsychology Possible? Some Thoughts on James E. Alcock's *Parapsychology: Science or Magic?" Journal of Parapsychology,* 46 [1982]:231-271).

(3) Christopher, Milbourne. *Mediums, Mystics and the Occult.* New York: Crowell, 1975, 275 pp.

This book is intended "to give those not familiar with deceptive techniques a better understanding of what too often are called 'unexplained phenomena.'" The author complains that researchers who are "convinced" that human beings have extrasensory and other paranormal powers frequently fail to take proper precautions to rule out fraudulent manipulation. He argues that only magicians can be relied upon to guard against fraud. Therefore, he insists that investigators in parapsychology either be "experts in the subtle techniques used by magicians

and mentalists or have someone who is to assist them during their experiments."
The book contains many instructive examples of the public's will to believe in
paranormal phenomena. The performances of "psychic" stars Geller, Hurkos,
Ford, Slade, "Margery," the Fox sisters, and several others are discussed in
some detail, as is "psychic surgery" and "eyeless vision." In each case, the author
tries to show how the investigators were (or could have been) hoodwinked by
the "psychics" being studied. The historical segments of the book have fascinating illustrations.

(4) Frazier, Kendrick (Ed.). *Paranormal Borderlands of Science.* Buffalo, N.Y.:
Prometheus Books, 1981, xiii + 469 pp.

This is a collection of 47 articles reprinted from the *Skeptical Inquirer.* Of
the 11 subject headings, 4 (comprising 19 articles) are more or less directly
related to parapsychology ("Psi Phenomena and Belief," "Tricks of the Psychic
Trade," "Geller-type Phenomena," and "Stories of Life and Death"). The book
is intended "to help the reader to separate sense from nonsense when evaluating
claims of the paranormal" and to "attempt to distinguish real science from
pseudoscience." The book fails, however, to seriously address philosophical,
procedural, methodological, and evidential issues in parapsychology, and all too
frequently open hostility replaces proper argumentation against "paranormal"
practices or theories. Readers are easily misled to believe that all parapsychologists must be wishful thinkers, charlatans, or gullible fools. Nevertheless, careful
reading of a number of the articles in this book (such as Paul Kurtz's assessment
of the scientific status of parapsychology, the three contributions on "cold
reading" by, respectively, Ray Hyman, Ronald A. Schwartz, and James Randi,
several of the papers on Geller-type phenomena, and the debunking of the
"Amityville Horror" by parapsychologist Robert L. Morris) is highly recommended to both skeptics and parapsychologists. However, this book falls short
of its stated goal to distinguish science from pseudoscience. It does little to
clarify this important matter.

Additional References: Reasonably critical reviews appeared in both the
Journal of the Society for Psychical Research, 51 (1981):173-174 (by Denys
Parsons), and the *Journal of Parapsychology,* 46 (1982):280-283 (by Kerry S.
Walters).

(5) Gardner, Martin. *Fads and Fallacies in the Name of Science.* New York:
Dover, 1957, x + 363 pp. (This is a revised and expanded edition of the work
originally published by Putnam's in 1952 under the title *In the Name of Science*).

The book is a critical examination of various cults, fads, and quack theories
(such as dianetics, orgonomy, flat and hollow earth, and approximately 20 other

"theories"). It is included here because it also contains, as chapter 25 ("ESP and PK"), "a serious appraisal of the reputable work of Dr. Rhine . . . who has done more than any one man in history to give scientific respectability to the investigation of psychic forces." Gardner starts out emphasizing that "it should be stated immediately that Rhine is clearly not a pseudoscientist to a degree even remotely comparable to that of most of the men discussed in this book. He is an intensely sincere man, whose work has been undertaken with a care and competence that cannot be dismissed easily." He then goes on to review some important criticisms that have been leveled against Rhine's early work at Duke University's parapsychology laboratory. He discusses the possibility of data-selection and recording errors, and he charges Rhine and his collaborators with using optional stopping techniques and a number of other practices, most of which, however, had already been out of use for quite some time when this book was published. The chapter closes with brief discussions of other parapsychological investigations and opinions (e.g., those of Upton Sinclair and Nandor Fodor).

(6) Gardner, Martin. *Science: Good, Bad, and Bogus*. Buffalo, N.Y.: Prometheus Books, 1981, xvii + 408 pp.

This is a collection of (updated) articles and book reviews written over the past 30 years. Chapters of immediate relevance to parapsychology include, among others, a skeptical examination of Charles Tart's research on "learning to use ESP," a critique (two chapters) of the research of Russell Targ and Harold Puthoff at the Stanford Research Institute, two chapters on Einstein's beliefs regarding ESP, a critical general overview of the field of parapsychology (entitled "A Skeptic's View of Parapsychology"), a chapter on Conan Doyle's beliefs in fairies (its relevance to contemporary parapsychological research remains more than doubtful, however) as well as criticisms (some of them devastating) of metal-bending research, including chapters entitled "Magic and Parapsychology," "Geller, Gulls, and Nitinol," and "Quantum Theory and Quack Theory." While Gardner is far from gentle with those who he feels are disregarding the rules of science, many of his more substantive criticisms of parapsychological research are thoughtful and accurate. He makes quite a few important points on several of the studies he examines from a skeptical point of view, and parapsychologists are well advised to take these criticisms seriously. On the other hand, Gardner does not refrain from making a number of poorly founded overgeneralizations, and when he has a choice between a good argument and a less-than-good joke, he all too frequently decides in favor of the latter. Thus, despite the many good points made in this volume, it should be read with the same concern for sound argument that Gardner frequently finds absent in the works he attacks.

Additional References: Several members of the Parapsychological Association expressly welcomed publication of this book and emphasized its many sound criticisms but pointed out that it could have been much more useful had its author resisted the tendency to overgeneralize and to employ ad hominem and guilt-by-association arguments: for instance, cf. Douglas M. Stokes, "Book Review," *Journal of the American Society for Psychical Research*, 78 (1984):87-95; Gerd H. Hövelmann, "Verkannte Genies and Spinner für immer" (Unappreciated geniuses and incorrigible crackpots [review of the abridged German edition]), *Psychologie heute*, 10, no. 10 (1983):74-75. Other important reviews, written from differing perspectives, are those by George Adelman (*Parapsychology Review*, 13, no. 3 [1982]:24-26), Michael R. Dennett (*Skeptical Inquirer*, 7, no. 3 [1983]:68-70), and Hartmut von Voigt (*Bild der Wissenschaft* #4, [April 1984]:186-187 [review of the abridged German edition]). Gardner commented on one of the critical remarks in Stokes's review in "Notes of a Psi-Watcher: The Relevance of Belief Systems," *Skeptical Inquirer*, 9 (1985):213-216.

(7) Goran, Morris: *Fact, Fraud, and Fantasy: The Occult and Pseudosciences.* South Brunswick, N.J.: Barnes, 1979, 189 pp.

This book fails to live up to its stated goal to present "analyses of the pseudo- and occult sciences so that an intelligent person can view them objectively." Although the book occasionally raises valid objections to a number of parapsychological practices (these parts deserve to be read carefully and taken seriously), its analyses generally remain superficial, and the author shows little familiarity with the actual parapsychological research literature.

Additional Reference: For a critical review, see that by W. Teed Rockwell (*Journal of Parapsychology*, 45 [1981]:352-354).

(8) Marks, David, and Richard Kammann. *The Psychology of the Psychic.* Buffalo, N.Y.: Prometheus Books, 1980, 232 pp.

This certainly is one of the most important skeptical books on parapsychology. It contains an instructive skeptical discussion of the performances of Kreskin, an "internationally known mentalist" (full descriptions and conjectured explanations of the tricks he uses are given), extensive (though not always reliable) critiques of the experiments with Uri Geller at the Stanford Research Institute and of Targ and Puthoff's remote-viewing experiments (including detailed criticisms of the research methods of the SRI parapsychologists). The authors also describe their own personal investigations of alleged paranormal phenomena. The final chapters and appendices are of particular importance because they contain very useful discussions of cognitive biases leading to self-fulfilling prophecies, self-perpetuating beliefs, and what the authors call the fallacy of "subjective validation." There is much good advice on how to avoid being deceived by false psychic claims. Even if one does not agree with all of the authors' assessments of the quality of parapsychological research and with their claim that the powerful psychological mechanisms they describe are sufficient to explain away all cases of alleged ESP and other psychic performances, this book has much of value to offer to parapsychologists and skeptics alike. Its main shortcoming probably is the exaggerated assessments the authors make of its scope. While they claim that they have covered the whole field of parapsychology, that the cases they investigated typify parapsychological research, and that they have successfully demolished the evidence for psi, their scope is in fact much narrower.

Additional References: Robert L. Morris's critical and detailed review of this book ("Some Comments on the Assessment of Parapsychological Studies: A Review of *The Psychology of the Psychic,* by David Marks and Richard Kammann," *Journal of the American Society for Psychical Research,* 74 [1980]:425-443) led to a constructive dialogue between the reviewer and the book's first author that clarified a number of the points at issue: David Marks, "On the Review of *The Psychology of the Psychic:* A Reply to Dr. Morris," *Journal of the American Society for Psychical Research,* 75 (1981):197-203; Robert L. Morris, "Reply to Dr. Marks," *Journal of the American Society for Psychical Research,* 75 (1981):203-207. Another review of the book in the parapsychological literature by Eric Farge (*Journal of the Society for Psychical Research,* 51 [1981]:174-176) concluded by "strongly recommend[ing] *The Psychology of the Psychic.* It is revealing and thought-provoking, at no point is it dull, and the research was worth while." Another important review was contributed by skeptic Ray Hyman in the *Skeptical Inquirer,* 5, no. 2 (1980-81):60-63.

(9) Murchison, Carl A. (Ed.). *The Case For and Against Psychical Belief.* Worcester Mass.: Clark University Press, 1927. Reprinted by Arno Press, New York, 1975, 365 pp.

This book contains papers presented at a public symposium at Clark University in 1926 (some of them had originally been published elsewhere). The contributions represent widely varying opinions on and attitudes toward parapsychological research. There are three parts, one for each of the three major attitudes held by the symposiasts: those convinced of the reality of paranormal phenomena, those "convinced of the rarity of genuine phenomena," and those claiming that such phenomena do not exist. Skeptical contributors include John E. Coover, Joseph Jastrow, and magician Harry Houdini.

(10) Neher, Andrew. *The Psychology of Transcendence.* Englewood Cliffs, N.J.: Prentice Hall, 1980, xx + 361 pp.

This book, which begins with forewords by parapsychologist Robert L. Morris and skeptic Ray Hyman, attempts to show that many apparently inexplicable experiences—"transcendental experiences" as the author terms them—may not be that inexplicable after all. Psychological, psychic, and occult experiences, automatisms, hypnosis, creative imagery, hyperesthesia, and a variety of other transcendental experiences are discussed. A long chapter covering all kinds of psychic experiences is particularly useful. Considerable attention is given to a variety of alternative, nonparapsychological explanations, such as mechanisms of suggestion, subliminal and selective perception, motivation or learning, physiological processes, memory distortions, and so on. Although, at places, the author's counterexplanations are a bit simplistic, although his discussions tend to be somewhat superficial and imbalanced, and although the book lacks an adequate methodological framework, it is a useful and welcome reminder of possible pitfalls in parapsychological and related research. Although the author prefers a skeptical position, he encourages further systematic parapsychological experimentation.

Additional References: Parapsychologist George P. Hansen's favorable review of this book in the *Journal of Parapsychology,* 46 (1981):69-71, led to a minor controversy in the same journal (46 [1981]:288-289) between the reviewer and Brian Inglis, who had previously published an unfavorable (and superficial) review of the book in the *Journal of the Society for Psychical Research,* 51 (1981):108-109. This exchange is instructive insofar as it makes obvious different attitudes toward rational skepticism in the parapsychological community. Other reviews worth noting are those by parapsychologists William G. Braud (*Theta,* 10 [1982]:41-44) and Ralph G. Locke (*Journal of the American Society for Psychical Research,* 76 [1982]:189-191), as well as by skeptic James E. Alcock (*Skeptical Inquirer,* 6, no. 4 [1982]:57-58).

(11) Price, George R. "Science and the Supernatural," *Science,* 122 (1955): 359-367.

This has been one of the most influential and controversial critical works in the history of skepticism, and it contains the most explicit statement of the "Humean argument." The author starts out crediting parapsychologists with winning a "decisive victory" and silencing the opposition as a "result of an impressive amount of careful experimentation and intelligent argumentation." As Price nevertheless accepts the premise that "parapsychology and modern science are incompatible," his only way out of this dilemma seems to him to adopt the famous notion of philosopher David Hume "that the knavery and folly of men are such common phenomena, that I should rather believe the most extraordinary events to arise from their concurrence, than admit of so signal a violation of the laws of nature." Price goes on quoting rhetorically from Thomas Paine, who asked, "Is it more probable that nature should go out of her course, or that a man should tell a lie?" Consequently, Price's opinion concerning the findings of parapsychologists (and, in particular, concerning the experimental work of Rhine and Soal) "is that many of them are dependent on clerical and statistical errors and unintentional use of sensory cues, and that all extrachance results not so explicable are dependent on deliberate fraud or mildly abnormal mental conditions." "Let us remember," Price continues, "that those who seek to deceive us possibly are smarter than we are and probably have had more practice in simulating honesty than we have had in detecting dishonesty." Price's verdict, then, is that it is more probable that the best of psi results are due to "a few people with the desire and the ability artfully to produce false evidence for the supernatural" than that they demonstrate the existence of impossible phenomena like ESP. He suggests, therefore, that the most reasonable explanation of the results of Rhine's and Soal's experiments is that these researchers have cheated (which in fact, as was shown many years later [see No. 19], Soal most probably did).

Additional References: Price's article stirred up a hornet's nest of controversy. *Science,* 123 (1956):9-19, published a number of rejoinders and comments by Samuel G. Soal ("On 'Science and the Supernatural,'" pp. 9-11), Joseph B. Rhine ("Comments on 'Science and the Supernatural,'" pp. 11-14), Paul E. Meehl and Michael Scriven ("Compatibility of Science and ESP," pp. 14-15), and Percy W. Bridgman ("Probability, Logic, and ESP," pp. 15-17), as well as a reply by Price ("Where Is the Definitive Experiment?" pp. 17-18) and another rejoinder by Rhine ("The Experiment Should Fit the Hypothesis," p. 19). This controversy has been reprinted in its entirety in Jan K. Ludwig (Ed.), *Philosophy and Parapsychology,* Prometheus Books, Buffalo, N.Y., 1978, pp. 145-204. Eight additional "Communications on the Price Article in *Science*" (by James C. Crumbaugh, Ralph W. Erickson, Waldron R. Gardiner, Edmond P. Gibson, Jack Kapchan, Robert A. McConnell, Charles E. Ozanne, and Kendon Smith) were printed in the *Journal of Parapsychology,* 19 (1955):247-266. They were followed by Rhine's "Editorial Comment: The Balance of the View," *Journal of Parapsychology,* 19 (1955):267-271. Seventeen years after his original article was published in *Science,* Price apologized for what he had said about Rhine and Soal in his 1955 article: George R. Price, "Apology to Rhine and Soal" (letter), *Science,* 175 (1972):359.

(12) Randi, James. *Flim-Flam! Psychics, ESP, Unicorns and Other Delusions,* Buffalo, N.Y.: Prometheus Books, 1983 xii + 342 pp. (A revised edition of the book published in 1980 by Lippincott and Crowell.)

Parapsychologists will be disappointed to find their research treated, along with astrology, the Bermuda Triangle, and the Cottingley fairy photographs, as "delusive" and "pseudoscientific." They have frequently complained about Randi's lack of fairness, and this book suggests that their complaints are not entirely unfounded. In fact, this book is far from being the last word on the question of whether parapsychology is a "delusion." It contains many gross overgeneralizations, guilt-by-association arguments, and dogmatic verdicts on the quality of parapsychological research. This may provide parapsychologists with a welcome pretext to ignore or dismiss the many valid and important criticisms of a variety of aspects of individual parapsychological investigations that this volume also contains. Without doubt, this is an important skeptical book, and it has considerable merit.

Additional References: An important critical review of this book was written by Randi's fellow skeptic Piet Hein Hoebens in German in the *Zeitschrift für Parapsychologie und Grenzgebiete der Psychologie,* 23 (1981):246-251. Some of Randi's criticisms of the parapsychological work at the Stanford Research Institute led to a heated controversy in the pages of *Fate* magazine: D. Scott Rogo, "James Randi, the 'Flim-Flam' Man," 34, no. 6 (1981):74-83; James Randi, "Flutters Over Flim-Flam," 34, no. 11 (1981):111-113; D. Scott Rogo, "The Author Replies," 34, no. 11 (1981):113-118, 128-129.

(13) Rawcliffe, D. H. *Illusions and Delusions of the Supernatural and the Occult.* New York: Dover Publications, 1962, 551 pp. (Originally published under the title *The Psychology of the Occult,* Derricke Ridgway, London, 1952.)

Rawcliffe's book is an important but idiosyncratic and frequently flawed attack against psychical research. The author seems to have been an isolated scholar, a nonacademic quietly living and writing in Pelynt, Cornwall, who maintained very little if any communication with either fellow critics or proponents of the paranormal. His book presents all psychical research as occultism and supernaturalism hiding beneath a scientific facade rather than as a legitimate scientific research program seeking to explain anomalous phenomena. Thus he sharply concludes: "The resurgence of supernatural beliefs within the precincts of modern universities cannot be regarded otherwise than as a retrograde step of the first magnitude. It is virtually a reversion to the irrational beliefs of the Middle Ages" (p. 490). This outlook is the source of both the strength and weakness of his book. Rawcliffe displays an exceptional breadth of scholarship, including reference to much usually neglected background literature in areas like folklore. Certainly anyone concerned with topics like firewalking, the Indian rope trick, lycanthropy, stigmata, dowsing, scrying, automatic writing, hallucinations, physical mediumship, and hypnosis will learn much from this book. The sections dealing with parapsychology are far weaker and depend upon some rather extreme arguments (e.g., extraordinary auditory cues to explain away Soal's experiments). Despite its limitations and occasional factual errors (e.g., Richet is misdescribed as a believer in spirits), Rawcliffe's book has much to recommend it and has not been given the consideration it deserves among both critics and proponents.

Additional References: R. H. Thouless gave this book a sharply critical review in the *Journal of the Society for Psychical Research,* 33 (1952):624-627, See also S. G. Soal's reply to Rawcliffe's proposed explanation of "double whispering" for Soal's results with Basil Shackleton in the *Journal of the Society for Psychical Research,* 33 (1952):633-634.

(14) Zusne, Leonard, and Warren H. Jones. *Anomalistic Psychology: A Study of Extraordinary Phenomena of Behavior and Experience.* Hillside, N.J.: Lawrence Erlbaum, 1982. xiii + 498 pp.

One of the most important skeptical books of recent years. It is a comprehensive, skeptical, and fair-minded attempt to account for what appear to be paranormal or unusual psychological phenomena (ESP, PK, psychic healing, spiritualism, poltergeists, automatic writing, dermo-optical perception, and very many others) through the judicious application of standard psychological principles. This book is a must for both skeptics and parapsychologists.

A major limitation of this book is its inadequate consideration of the social-psychological, including experimental, work dealing with subjects' reactions to legitimately anomalous phenomena (e.g., experiments in which subjects are shown a deck of cards with black diamonds and hearts and red spades and clubs yet fail to notice anything anomalous). A fully balanced approach should examine errors by both those who misperceive the normal as anomalous and those who misperceive the truly anomalous as normal.

Additional References: Important reviews were written, for instance, by skeptic Victor A. Benassi (*Skeptical Inquirer,* 7, no. 3 [1983]:63-64) and parapsychologist Joseph H. Rush (*Journal of the American Society for Psychical Research,* 77 [1983]:171-180). See also review by K. R. Rao in the *Journal of Parapsychology,* 47 (1983):251-254. A relevant work that might well have been cited by the authors is: Helen Ross, *Behavior and Perception in Strange Environments,* Basic Books, New York, 1974.

2. ESP Research

(15) Gubisch, Wilhelm. *Hellseher, Scharlatane, Demagogen—Kritik an der Parapsychologie* [Clairvoyants, Charlatans, Demagogues—*A Critique of Parapsychology*]. Munich and Basel: Ernst Reinhardt, 1961, 213 pp.

This is a masterful study of the psychology of preconceived (paranormal) beliefs. In a long series of more than 5,000 lectures with demonstrations, the author observed that the public, guided by its will to believe, uncritically approves pseudo-psychic assertions. In his lectures, he always introduced himself as an authentic psychic, and he gave psychic readings for people in the audience.

Gubisch found that 78 percent of his arbitrary "psychic" statements were cheerfully accepted as "correct and exact" by the subjects. At the end of each lecture and demonstration, he always explained his procedure to the puzzled audience but did not always succeed in convincing those who had consulted him: Many preferred to continue to believe in his outstanding psychic gifts. According to Gubisch, the people's credulity and their will to believe in paranormal phenomena are the cause of all the successes attributed to psychics. He further maintains that the solution to the problem of ESP is not to be sought in the paranormal capacities of gifted psychics but in the psychological structure of those who believe in the paranormal. From the observations he made in his numerous informal lectures, however, the author draws the questionable conclusion that all alleged paranormal phenomena, including those recorded in controlled and standardized laboratory experiments, are nothing but delusions based on preconceived beliefs. The manner in which Gubisch presents his conclusions leaves the reader wondering whether the author himself has become the victim of a preconceived belief: the preconception that ESP is impossible.

Additional References: A good English summary and discussion of Gubisch's book is to be found in Bonaventura Kloppenburg's review in the *Journal of Parapsychology,* 26 (1962):226-229. Almost an entire issue (vol. 7, no. 2/3, 1964, pp. 85-173) of the German *Zeitschrift für Parapsychologie und Grenzgebiete der Psychologie* is devoted to critical discussions of Gubisch's book. While the authors of the different contributions (esp. Anton Neuhäusler, John Mischo, and Hans-Volker Werthmann) emphasize the relevance and importance of Gubisch's findings on the public's suggestibility and its will to believe in the paranormal, they try to demonstrate that, methodologically, Gubisch was a naive researcher, that he was almost completely unaware of the more technical parapsychological research literature, that he distorts the literature he mentions, that the book contains many factual inaccuracies, and that his treatment of statistics displays his ignorance of the basic principles of probability theory and of applied statistics. Nevertheless, Gubisch's book, which has been almost completely ignored in the English literature by both skeptics and parapsychologists, remains one of the best and most useful treatments of the public's credulity with regard to ESP phenomena. Of special importance in connection with Gubisch's book is a discussion between Bender and Gubisch: Hans Bender, "Parapsychologie" (Parapsychology), *Zeitschrift für praktische Psychologie,* 1 (1961):173-184; Wilhelm Gubisch, "Parapsychologie—Wissenschaft oder Glaube?" (Parapsychology—Science or Belief?), *Zeitschrift für praktische Psychologie,* 1 (1961):185-202.

(16) Hansel, C. E. M.: *ESP: A Scientific Evaluation.* New York: Scribner's, 1966, 263 pp. (An updated edition of this book appears in the following listing, No. 17.)

This is certainly the most influential (and maybe the most controversial) single book in the history of skeptical evaluations of parapsychology. It contains the classical statement of the fraud hypothesis as well as a restatement of the hypothesis of the a priori improbability of ESP, which George Price, among others, had advanced previously [No. 11]. According to Hansel, the processes being investigated by parapsychologists are "both hypothetical and a priori extremely unlikely. Any possible known cause of the results is far more likely to be responsible for it than the hypothetical process [ESP] under consideration." As "cheating in one form or another is one of the commonest of human activities," Hansel concludes that the most reasonable solution to the problem of ESP is to suspect that all positive experimental results are due to fraudulent manipulations by experimenters or subjects, or both. Starting from this premise, Hansel sets out to present a penetrating examination of four parapsychological experiments, three of which belong to the "classical" and allegedly conclusive ESP experiments: the Pearce-Pratt (1933-1934) and the Pratt-Woodruff (1939) series, both from the early Duke period; Soal's experiments with Gloria Stewart and Basil Shackleton (1954); and the Soal-Bowden experiments with three "gifted" Welsh school boys (1958). With remarkable ingenuity, Hansel tries to demonstrate how fraud could have been committed in these experimental series. According to Hansel, this is already quite sufficient to question any claim of convincing evidence for ESP: "It cannot be stated categorically that trickery was responsible for the results of these experiments, but so long as the possibility is present, the experiments cannot be regarded as satisfying the aims of their originators or as supplying conclusive evidence for ESP." Despite its numerous shortcomings, which were pointed out in many critical reviews (see below), this book is required reading for anyone interested in (or opposed to) parapsychology.

Additional References: An earlier version of Hansel's critique of Soal's experiments with Shackleton and Stewart is to be found in his "A Critical Review of Experiments with Mr. B. Shackleton and Mrs. G. Stewart as Sensitives," *Proceedings of the Society for Psychical Research,* 53 (1960):1-42. Earlier versions of Hansel's critical examinations of the Pearce-Pratt and Pratt-Woodruff experimental series as well as discussions around them were published in the *Journal of Parapsychology* in 1961: C. E. M. Hansel, "A Critical Analysis of the Pearce-Pratt Experiment," *Journal of Parapsychology,* 25 (1961):87-91; rejoinder by Joseph B. Rhine and J. Gaither Pratt, "A Reply to the Hansel Critique of the Pearce-Pratt Series," *Journal of Parapsychology,* 25 (1961):92-98; C. E. M. Hansel, "A Critical Analysis of the Pratt-Woodruff Experiment," *Journal of Parapsychology,* 25 (1961):99-113; rejoinders by J. Gaither Pratt and J. L. Woodruff, "Refutation of Hansel's Allegations Concerning the Pratt-Woodruff Series," *Journal of Parapsychology,* 25 (1961):114-129, and by J. Gaither Pratt, "Run Salience in the Pratt-Woodruff Series," *Journal of Parapsychology,* 25

(1961):130-135.

While the nonparapsychological world considered it the definitive work on parapsychology and the final word to be wasted on ESP research (see E. Slater's review in the *British Journal of Psychiatry,* 14 [1968]:653-658), Hansel's book was heavily attacked by parapsychologists who pointed out the apparent bias underlying Hansel's arguments and justly criticized numerous factual errors and inaccuracies in the book; they also emphasized what they considered the unfalsifiability of the fraud hypothesis. The most important criticisms of Hansel's book include: Ian Stevenson, "An Antagonist's View of Parapsychology: A Review of Professor Hansel's *ESP: A Scientific Evaluation,"* *Journal of the American Society for Psychical Research,* 61 (1967):254-267; R. G. Medhurst, "The Fraudulent Experimenter: Professor Hansel's Case Against Psychical Research," *Journal of the Society for Psychical Research,* 44 (1968):217-232 (cf. Christopher Scott, "Correspondence: The Fraudulent Experimenter," *Journal of the Society for Psychical Research,* 44 [1968]:299-302); Charles Honorton, "Book Review," *Journal of Parapsychology,* 31 (1967):76-82; Hans-Joachim Grünzig, "Rezension" (Book review), *Zeitschrift für Parapsychologie und Grenzgebiete der Psychologie,* 10 (1967):137-139; Hans-Joachim Grünzig, "Das Pierce-Pratt Experiment im Brennpunkt der Kritik" (The Pearce-Pratt experiment in the focus of criticism), *Neue Wissenschaft,* 15 (1967):83-92; Robert A. McConnell, "The ESP Scholar" (a letter), *Contemporary Psychology,* 13 (1968):41; Hans Jügen Eysenck et al., "Correspondence: ESP: A Scientific Evaluation," *British Journal of Psychiatry,* 114 (1968):1471-1483. Also of special interest is the discussion between Hansel and E. Slater in the *British Journal of Psychiatry,* 114 (1968):1471-1480, and 115 (1968):743-745.

Up to this day, Hansel's book continues to be the subject of many controversies and discussions. Among the more important contributions of recent years are: R. G. Medhurst and Christopher Scott, "A Re-examination of C. E. M. Hansel's Criticism of the Pratt-Woodruff Experiment," *Journal of Parapsychology,* 38 (1974):163-184; J. Gaither Pratt, "Comments on the Medhurst-Scott Criticism of the Pratt-Woodruff Experiment," *Journal of Parapsychology,* 38 (1974):185-201; Christopher Scott, "The Pratt-Woodruff Experiment: Reply to Dr. Pratt's Comments," *Journal of Parapsychology,* 38 (1974):202-206; J. Gaither Pratt, "Reply to Dr. Scott," *Journal of Parapsychology,* 38 (1974):207-214; Lila A. Gatlin, "The Pratt-Woodruff Experiment and Viable Explanatory Hypotheses," *Journal of Parapsychology,* 39 (1975):228-235; J. Gaither Pratt, "New Evidence Supporting the ESP interpretation of the Pratt-Woodruff Experiment," *Journal of Parapsychology,* 40 (1976):217-227; Michael Martin, "The Problem of Experimenter Fraud: A Re-evaluation of Hansel's Critique of ESP Experiments," *Journal of Parapsychology,* 43 (1979):129-139. While a number of parapsychologists and other commentators declared Hansel's fraud hypothesis unfalsifiable (e.g., Harry M. Collins and Trevor J. Pinch, "The Construction of the Paranormal: Nothing Unscientific Is Happening," in R. Wallis [Ed.], *On the Margins of Science: The Social Construction of Rejected Knowledge*, 237-270, University of Keele, Staffordshire, 1979, pp. 237-270), the late skeptic Piet Hein Hoebens ("Die Legitimität des Unglaubens" [The legitimacy of unbelief], *Zeitschrift für Parapsychologie und Grenzgebiete der Psychologie*, 24 [1982]:61-73) defended the fraud hypothesis and tried to show that, in principle, it can be falsified.

(17) Hansel, C. E. M. *ESP and Parapsychology: A Critical Re-Evaluation.* Buffalo, N.Y.: Prometheus Books, 1980, v + 325 pp.

This is essentially an updated edition of Hansel's earlier book with some new material, including critical chapters on Uri Geller, remote viewing, dream telepathy, and the experiments of Helmut Schmidt. Regrettably, this new edition suffers from the same shortcomings as the old one, because Hansel has chosen to ignore almost completely the many criticisms mentioned in the "Additional References" section under No. 16, above. In view of these criticisms, many of which seem valid, readers will be surprised to find Hansel state in the preface to the updated edition that "no reason could be found to change what has already been written." While the book still has the merits of the 1966 edition, many readers (parapsychologists and responsible skeptics alike) will be disappointed that Hansel made no effort whatsoever to consider these many criticisms and to correct the numerous demonstrable factual inaccuracies of the old edition. On the other hand, a number of Hansel's own criticisms of parapsychological research remain valid and cannot be dismissed easily.

Additional References: Although Hansel failed to consider their previous counterarguments, prominent parapsychologists have welcomed the publication of this new edition as a useful reminder of experimental standards and of the possibility of experimental flaws. On the other hand, they have tirelessly pointed out what they take to be the book's many shortcomings. Thus, Donald J. West concluded his sensible book review in the *Journal of the Society for Psychical Research,* 51 (1981):27-28: "Provided his wilder pronouncements and sweeping denunciations can be ignored, Professor Hansel can be credited with giving us good cause to reflect on our standards for evaluating evidence." In a like manner, Irvin Child concludes his book review in the *Journal of Parapsychology,* 44 (1980):358-361. West's review provoked a critical correspondence by K. Ramakrishna Rao (mainly dealing with Hansel's evaluation of the Pratt-Woodruff experiments) in the *Journal of the Society for Psychical Research,* 51 (1981):191-194.

Other parapsychologists (such as Theodore Rockwell in his book review in

Parapsychology Review, 11 no. 3 [1980]: 12-14) commented less charitably on the new edition of Hansel's book. Rockwell's review led to a controversy over Hansel's book and Rockwell's specific criticisms between the reviewer and skeptic Ray Hyman: Ray Hyman: "Correspondence: Dr. Hyman Protests. . . ," *Parapsychology Review*, 12 no. 2 (1981):25-26; Theodore Rockwell: "Correspondence: Theodore Rockwell Replies. . . ," *Parapsychology Review*, 12, no. 2 (1981):26.

Another minor but highly relevant controversy between Hansel and skeptic Marcello Truzzi was published in the *Zetetic Scholar*, #7 (1980):4-5. Other important book reviews were published in the *Journal of the American Society for Psychical Research*, 75 (1981):155-166 ("Beyond the Reach of Sense: Some Comments on C. E. M. Hansel's *ESP and Parapsychology: A Critical Re-Evaluation*," by Charles Honorton), in *Alpha*, no. 8 (May-June 1980):12 (by Carl Sargent), in *Fate*, 33 (June 1980):108-111 (by D. Scott Rogo), in *Contemporary Psychology* (by John Palmer), and in the *Skeptical Inquirer*, 4, no. 3 (1980):60-62 (by Martin Gardner).

(18) Ray Hyman: "The Ganzfeld Psi Experiment: A Critical Appraisal," *Journal of Parapsychology*, 49 (1985):3-49.

This paper describes an important critical evaluation of 42 ganzfeld psi experiments reported from 1974 through 1981. The author challenges the claimed rate of 55 percent of successful replication of this type of parapsychological experiment. He criticizes the applied significance level in this research, points out a variety of procedural flaws, and tries to show that some of these flaws (including inadequate randomizaton and insufficient documentation) correlate with the significance and effect size reported in the studies in the author's data-base. He concludes that this data-base is too weak to support any assertions about the existence of psi. Perhaps the most important aspects of this study are the facts that a leading skeptic attempts a critical but fair-minded examination of the actual technical research literature of experimental parapsychology and that, at least to a certain extent, this skeptic consulted and collaborated with some of the investigators who were involved in the research that is subjected to skeptical scrutiny. For these reasons alone, Hyman's study can serve as a model for future responsible skeptical examinations of parapsychological research.

Additional References: In his detailed reply to Hyman's study ("Meta-analysis of Psi Ganzfeld Research: A Response to Hyman," *Journal of Parapsychology*, 49 [1985]:51-91), Charles Honorton reports an evaluation—confined to the 28 out of the 42 studies in Hyman's data-base that reported the number of direct hits—that eliminates multiple-analysis problems. He tries to show that the significance of the psi ganzfeld effect does not depend on any one or two experimenters and that for various reasons selective reporting cannot account for the reported findings. He further criticizes Hyman's procedural-flaws analysis and concludes that no significant relationship is found between study outcomes and measures of study quality. Honorton's paper contains, as Appendix B, a critique by David R. Saunders of Hyman's factor analysis and its interpretation. Saunders concludes that both are faulty. We consider this recent exchange between skeptic Ray Hyman and parapsychologist Charles Honorton a promising sign that may encourage future improved and reasonable communication between parapsychologists and skeptics.

(19) Markwick, Betty: "The Soal-Goldney Experiments with Basil Shackleton: New Evidence of Data Manipulation," *Proceedings of the Society for Psychical Research,* 56 (1978):250-277.

This paper by statistician-parapsychologist Betty Markwick may be adequately described as an inside criticism of parapsychology. It is included in this section of the bibliography (rather than in section 10) because it is much indebted to previous attempts by skeptics (especially C. E. M. Hansel, Christopher Scott, and P. Haskell) to debunk S. G. Soal's experiments with Shackleton. Soal's experimental project was long believed to have provided the strongest evidence for the reality of psi in the history of the field and hailed as the *non plus ultra* of fraudproof experimental design, although suspicions as to the accuracy of the reports had already begun to arise in the 1950s. In an ingenious critical examination, the author provides evidence that extra digits were inserted into the "prepared random number" sequences used by Soal to determine the targets (cards bearing animal symbols) in the Shackleton tests. The insertions closely coincided with Shackleton's guesses and apparently account for the high level of scoring in the record sheets (the results drop to chance level when these suspicious hits are removed). Markwick's astute analysis makes the conclusion almost inescapable that Soal manipulated the target sequences in this experiment.

Additional References: Earlier suspicions as to the accuracy of Soal's reports and his integrity as an experimenter are presented, reviewed, and discussed by Christopher Scott, P. Haskell, Kathleen M. Goldney, Clement W. K. Mundle, Robert H. Thouless, John Beloff, J. Gaither Pratt, Mary Rose Barrington, Ian Stevenson, and J. R. Smythies: "The Soal-Goldney Experiments with Basil Shackleton: A Discussion," *Proceedings of the Society for Psychical Research,* 56 (1974):41-131. A pertinent discussion of some of the implications of the Soal scandal for parapsychological research practice is provided by Donald J. West: "Correspondence: Checks on ESP Experimenters," *Journal of the Society for Psychical Research,* 49 (1978):897-899.

3. PK Research

(20) Girden, Edward: "A Review of Psychokinesis (PK)," *Psychological Bulletin*, 59 (1962):353-388.

The author presents what is perhaps the most important skeptical evaluation of the evidence for psychokinesis. In his examination of 200 PK experiments, Girden distinguishes between the early PK tests at Duke University and the more sophisticated work done afterward. He finds numerous flaws in the first group, including the possibility of recording errors, statistical pooling of nonhomogeneous data, lack of empirical control tests, inadequate control for dice bias, badly defined experimental procedures, and others. He recognizes that the experiments of the latter group generally were better both in design and execution, but still finds a number of important flaws. This leads him to conclude that "evidence of PK as a psychological phenomenon is totally lacking. And this deficiency will persist until the effect is produced in the presence of a specified psychological variable, and the effect does not appear in its absence." Parapsychological commentators conceded the adequacy of many of Girden's criticisms of early PK research but criticized him for exaggerating the flaws of the experiments under consideration and for ignoring experiments to which his objections are not applicable.

Additional References: Girden's paper launched a major controversy about the quality of evidence for PK. It provoked a rebuttal by Gardner Murphy: "Report on a Paper by Edward Girden on Psychokinesis," *Psychological Bulletin*, 59 (1962):520-528, to which Girden wrote a brief rejoinder, "A Postscript to 'A Review of Psychokinesis (PK),'" in *Psychological Bulletin*, 59 (1962):529-531. This controversy is summarized and commented upon by J. Gaither Pratt, in "The Girden-Murphy Papers on PK," *Journal of Parapsychology*, 27 (1963):199-209. The papers by Girden and Murphy are reprinted (along with additional contributions to the controversy by John Beloff, Jule Eisenbud, Antony Flew, Joseph H. Rush, Gertrude R. Schmeidler, and Robert H. Thouless), under the title, "A Discussion of Psychokinesis," *International Journal of Parapsychology*, 6 (1964):26-137.

In 1978, Girden updated (and considerably radicalized) his 1962 review of psychokinesis research to cover parapsychology as a whole: Edward Girden, "Parapsychology," in E. C. Carterette, and M. P. Friedman (Eds.), *Handbook of Perception*, vol. 10: *Perceptual Ecology*, Academic Press, New York, 1978, Chapter 14. While Girden's new polemical examination still contains legitimate criticisms, it largely and grossly misrepresents not only the field of parapsychology but also the writings of some of his fellow skeptics (Hansel, Medhurst, Scott, Haskell). A counter-critique refuting some of these misrepresentations and exaggerations was published by Charles Akers: "A Reply to Edward Girden," in W. G. Roll (Ed.), *Research in Parapsychology 1979*, Scarecrow Press, Metuchen, N.J., and London, 1980, pp. 180-181.

(21) Dingwall, Eric J., Kathleen M. Goldney, and Trevor H. Hall. "The Haunting of Borley Rectory: A Critical Survey of the Evidence," *Proceedings of the Society for Psychical Research*, 51 (1956):1-181 (published in book form by Duckworth, London, 1956).

A survey and devastating critique of the evidence of the alleged haunting of Borley Rectory (according to Harry Price, the chief investigator and popularizer of the case, "the most haunted house in England" and "the most extraordinary and best-documented case" in the annals of psychical research). In a painstaking examination of the published literature and unpublished materials, the authors demonstrate that the case of the Borley haunting is one of story fabrication (and possibly fraudulent manipulation) by both the chief investigator and one or more major witnesses rather than one of genuine paranormal phenomena. An important aspect of this study is that it not only provides a report on a badly investigated and fraudulent case. As the authors point out, "It is . . . much more than that, for here we have tried to show how this kind of evidence is to be appraised, how important it is to understand the psychology of testimony, and how fatally easy it is to be led astray in this field, when those who should exhibit the most absolute integrity in their work are themselves in the plot to deceive their followers and the public who believe in their good faith. Finally, the report illustrates the influence of suggestion in this work and shows how, once the mind has been affected, belief can be strengthened and simple events misinterpreted in order to fit them into the desired pattern."

Additional References: Critical comments on the study by Dingwall, Goldney, and Hall were made by Michael Coleman: "The Borley Report: Some Criticisms," *Journal of the Society for Psychical Research*, 38 (1956):249-258, with their reply on pp. 259-264. Thirteen years later, a major (and, in our opinion, unsuccessful) attempt to refute the critique of the Borley case and to restore the reputation of Harry Price was undertaken by Robert J. Hastings: "An examination of the 'Borley Report,'" *Proceedings of the Society for Psychical Research*, 55 (1969):65-175. The author succeeds only in pointing out some minor inaccuracies in the Borley Report. See the rebuttal by Eric J. Dingwall, Kathleen M. Goldney, and Trevor H. Hall, "Mr. Hastings and the Borley Report," *Journal of the Society for Psychical Research* 45 (1969):115-124, and the rejoinder by Robert J. Hastings, "Reply to the authors of the 'Borley Report,'" *Journal of the Society for Psychical Research*, 45 (1970): The report by Iris M. Owen, and Paulene Mitchell, "The Alleged Haunting of Borley Rectory," in the *Journal of the Society for Psychical Research*, 50 (1979):149-162, presents interview and correspondence material of one of the main suspects of fraudulent manipulation. The account of this witness clearly supports Dingwall, Goldney, and Hall's appraisal of the evidence in the case of the alleged Borley haunting.

(22) Randi, James. *The Truth About Uri Geller*. Buffalo, N.Y.: Prometheus Books, 1982 (substantially revised and expanded edition of *The Magic of Uri Geller*. New York: Ballantine, 1975). 234 pp.

This is an exceptional debunking analysis of the internationally famous "psychic" from Israel whose "powers" were attested to by many scientists, most notably by experimental physicists at SRI International. Magician James ("The Amazing") Randi's book is highly recommended as an impressive and generally convincing analysis and case study. The Randi–Geller debate continues, and Geller remains professionally active. Randi's book makes an excellent case against scientific acceptance of Geller's claims, but it does not produce any "smoking gun" definitely proving fraud by Geller. Randi's analysis convinced most scientists, including many parapsychologists, that Geller was merely a clever but rogue conjurer. This revised edition updates events and is noteworthy for its inclusion of Randi's replies to objections raised by Russell Targ and Harold Puthoff about Randi's alleged misrepresentations in this book's first edition.

Additional References: Good discussions of the controversy around Geller can be found in: Martin Ebon (Ed.), *The Amazing Uri Geller*, New American Library, New York, 1975. For a fine conjurer's parody of Geller, revealing many methods that produce effects similar to those claimed for Geller see: Uriah Fuller [Martin Gardner], *Confessions of a Psychic* and *Further Confessions of a Psychic*, Karl Fulves, Teaneck, N.J., 1975 and 1980. For further references to these debates see: Marcello Truzzi and Ray Hyman (compilers), "Uri Geller and the Scientists: A Basic Bibliography," *Zetetic Scholar*, no. 1 (1978):39-46.

4. Mediumism

(23) Abbott, David Phelps. *Behind the Scenes With the Medium*. Chicago: Open Court, 1970, vi + 340pp.

This book is viewed by many as *the* great exposé by a conjurer of the methods of false mediums. Abbott, a successful businessman in Omaha, Nebraska, had briefly traveled as a professional magician in his youth, but he was best known among magicians as the inventor of several outstanding tricks. He had a special interest in fraudulent mediumship and became an authority in the field. In addition to books, Abbott wrote numerous articles on the fraudulent methods of mediums, including five on slate writing and billet readings in the 1907 and 1908 issues of the *Journal of the American Society for Psychical Research.*

Additional References: Abbott's book is one in a long line of other books by magicians exposing the methods of mediums. An excellent group of such studies can be found in: James Webb (Ed.), *The Mediums and the Conjurors,* Arno, New York, 1976, including three of the classic ones: John Nevil Maskelyne, *Modern Spiritualism: A Short Account of Its Rise and Progress, With Some Exposures of So-Called Spirit Media,* London, 1876; Herr Dobler [George Smith Buck], *Exposé of the Davenport Brothers,* Belfast, 1869; and George Sexton, *Spirit-Mediums and Conjurors: An Oration Delivered in the Cavendish Rooms, London, on Sunday Evening, June 15th, 1873,* London, 1873. Another reissue of a classic work of this kind is: Harry Price and Eric J. Dingwall, *Revelations of a Spirit Medium,* Arno, 1975, New York (reprint of the 1922 London edition). Other such early works include: Lionel A. Weatherly and J. N. Maskelyne, *The Supernatural?* J. W. Arrowsmith, Bristol and London, 1891; and William E. Robinson, *Spirit Slate Writing and Kindred Phenomena,* Munn, New York, 1899. More recent important volumes in this genre include: Julien J. Proskauer's *Spook Crooks! Exposing the Secrets of the Prophet-eers Who Conduct Our Wickedest Industry,* A. L. Burt, New York, 1932, and *The Dead Do Not Talk,* Harper and Row, New York, 1946; and John Mulholland's *Beware Familiar Spirits,* Scribner's, New York, 1938.

Abbott's book makes an interesting contrast with another book that came out the same year that also detailed the methods of false mediumship: Hereward Carrington, *The Physical Phenomena of Spiritualism: Fraudulent and Genuine,* Herbert B. Turner, Boston, 1907. Carrington was a psychical researcher and amateur magician who wrote several conjuring books and endorsed several mediums as genuine.

(24) Dessoir, Max. *Vom Jenseits der Seele: Die Geheimwissenschaften in kritischer Betrachtung* (The "beyond" of the soul: Occult sciences critically examined). Ferdinand Enke Verlag, Stuttgart, 1967 (reprint of the 6th edition, 1930 [1st ed., 1917; 5th ed., 1920]), xi + 562 pp.

In the first part of this book (pp. 1-367), Dessoir, who in 1889 coined the term *Parapsychologie,* provides an excellent skeptical discussion of mental and physical mediumship. He presents both critical examinations of the published research reports and accounts of his personal investigations of, especially, physical mediums. The performances of many well-known mediums are carefully discussed, such as those of Leonore Piper, Gladis Osborne Leonard, Henry Slade, Anna Rothe, Maria Silbert, Willi and Rudi Schneider, Jean Guzik, Franek

Kluski, Eleonora Zugun, Carlos Mirabelli, "Margery," and several others. Dessoir's own investigation of Eusapia Palladino leads him to suspend final judgment on this medium. Dessoir's criticisms frequently are devastating, though always thoughtful and fair-minded. He is adequately familiar with the parapsychological literature of his time, and despite his skeptical attitude he is uniformly appreciative, and very respectful, toward the early work of the British Society for Psychical Research. Dessoir's account of "Professor Bert Reese" is a valuable contribution to the history of trickery in parapsychology. The second part of this book is devoted to a critical examination of occult and mystical philosophies and belief systems.

Additional Reference: A highly informative essay review of the 1967 edition of Dessoir's book was written by Eberhard Bauer: "Max Dessoir und die Parapsychologie als Wissenschaft" (Max Dessoir and parapsychology as a science), in *Zeitschrift für Parapsychologie und Grenzgebiete der Psychologie,* 10 (1967): 106-114. Dessoir's book is discussed in the context of his other publications on psychical research, psychology, and philosophy, and his influence on the development of German parapsychology over a period of about sixty years is described.

(25) Dingwall, Eric J., and Trevor H. Hall. *Four Modern Ghosts.* London: Duckworth, 1958, 111 pp.

The authors discuss four cases of modern alleged "ghosts." Three are concerned with reputedly haunted houses (the Yorkshire Museum Ghost, the Runcorn Poltergeist, and the Ousedale Haunt) and one, the Rosalie case, related by Harry Price, with an alleged materialization of a child. They discuss and suggest "normal" explanations of each of these cases, including hallucination, trickery, Lambert's theory of underground water, as well as—in the case of Price's account of the Rosalie materialization—deliberate story fabrication.

(26) Dunninger, Joseph. *Inside the Medium's Cabinet.* New York: Davis Kemp, 1935, vii + 228 pp.

A general survey of the investigations by magician-mentalist Joseph Dunninger into fraudulent mediumship, the book includes many anecdotes about various mediums tested by Dunninger over the years and contains an excellent section on the alleged spirit message from Harry Houdini to Arthur Ford. Although some of the mediums encountered by Dunninger had reputations among spiritualists (e.g., Nino Pecoraro), he casts little light on the great physical mediums (e.g., Palladino and Home) who impressed early psychical researchers. Although Dunninger, like Houdini before him, was an antagonist of spiritualism, he was not opposed to parapsychology. Dunninger was best known for his stage simulations of extrasensory perception, and he even published two books purporting to teach telepathy: *What's On Your Mind?* World Publishing, New York, 1944, and *The Art of Thought Reading,* Clark Publishing, Highland Park, Ill., 1962. However, it is well known among those magicians who knew him privately that Dunninger genuinely believed in telepathy.

Additional References: Dunninger wrote numerous other works dealing with fraudulent spiritualism, most importantly: *How To Make a Ghost Walk,* David Kemp, New York, 1936, and *Houdini's Spirit World and Dunninger's Psychic Revelations,* Tower Books, New York, 1968 (a reprinting of pieces that first appeared in *Liberty Weekly* in 1925).

(27) Gulat-Wellenburg, W. von, Carl von Klinckowstroem, and Hans Rosenbusch. *Der Okkultismus in Urkunden. 1. Der physikalische Mediumismus* (Occultism documented. Vol. 1, Physical mediumism) (ed. by Max Dessoir), Ullstein Verlag, Berlin, 1925, xiii + 494 pp.

This book, which soon acquired the sobriquet "Drei-Männer-Buch" (Three men's book), is certainly the most important critical survey of physical mediumship to appear in the first three decades of this century. Although later commentators have correctly pointed out a considerable number of misrepresentations and factual errors, the book's skeptical examination of evidence for physical mediumship and its many thoughtful and valid criticisms remain among the best in the history of skeptical inquiry and make it a lasting contribution to the skeptical literature. Of special importance, aside from the investigation of individual physical mediums, such as Eva C., Eusapia Palladino, Kathleen Goligher, Stanislawa Tomczyk, Lucia Sordi, Linda Gazerra, Ladislaus Laszlo, Willi Schneider, Franek Kluski, Jean Guzik, Einer Nielsen, Maria Silbert, and others, is the chapter (and a great number of pertinent observations scattered throughout the book) on methods of investigation, in which the weaknesses and flaws in mediumistic inquiries are ruthlessly examined. The authors conclude that no scientifically valid proof of physical mediumship has been brought forward.

Additional References: A detailed and enthusiastic book review, which nevertheless points out a number of weaknesses of the book, was published by the then-psychical researcher Eric J. Dingwall in the *Proceedings of the Society for Psychical Research,* 36 (1926):333-340. Dingwall concluded that "whatever we may think of the conclusions of the authors of this volume, it must, we think, be agreed that they have contributed a permanent addition to the scanty material on physical mediumship. The book is one for the student and not for the propagandist. . . . [It is] the most important critical survey of physical mediumship since that made by Mr. Podmore." In 1926, Albert von Schrenck-Notzing, one of the psychical researchers under attack, edited a detailed, though mostly low-quality, rejoinder that appropriately became known as "Sieben-Männer-Buch" (Seven men's book): *Die physikalischen Phänomene der grossen Medien. Eine Abwehr* (The physical phenomena of the great mediums: A defense), Union Deutsche Verlagsanstalt, Stuttgart, Berlin & Leipzig, 1926.

(28) Hall, Trevor H. *The Spiritualists: The Story of Florence Cook and William Crookes.* London: Duckworth, no date [1962]; New York: Garrett/Helix, 1963. Reprinted as *The Medium and the Scientist* by Prometheus Books, Buffalo, N.Y., 1984.

In this much-debated book, the author tries to prove that William Crookes was not only the chief investigator but also the lover of the materialization medium Florence Cook and that Crookes protected and assisted her in her fraudulent production of the "phantom," Katie King.

Additional References: The book caused more or less heated controversies between its author and several commentators: George Zorab, "Side Lights on Mr. Trevor Hall's *The Spiritualists,*" *Journal of the American Society for Psychical Research* 58 (1964):204-209; R. G. Medhurst and Kathleen M. Goldney, "William Crookes and the Physical Phenomena of Mediumship," *Proceedings of the Society for Psychical Research,* 54 (1964):25-157; Ian Stevenson, "Reflections on Mr. Trevor Hall's 'The Spiritualists,'" *Journal of the American Society for Psychical Research,* 57 (1963):215-226; Trevor H. Hall, "Reply to Dr. Ian Stevenson's Review of 'The Spiritualists,'" *Journal of the American Society for Psychical Research,* 58 (1964):57-65; Ian Stevenson, "Rejoinder to Mr. Trevor Hall's Reply," *Journal of the American Society for Psychical Research,* 58 (1964):128-133. Hall's bold theory is also discussed in detail in George Zorab's Italian book *"Katie King: Donna o fantasma?* (Katie King: Woman or phantom?) (Milano: Armenia Editore, 1980). There were, however, also favorable reviews of Hall's book on Cook and Crookes in the parapsychological literature, such as that by Hans Bender in the *Zeitschrift für Parapsychologie und Grenzgebiete der Psychologie,* 6 (1963):195-196.

(29) Hall, Trevor H. *The Strange Case of Edmund Gurney.* London: Duckworth, 1964, xi + 219 pp.

In this book, Hall advances the controversial claim that Edmund Gurney, one of the founders and most active members of the Society for Psychical Research, withheld indications of fraud and that this may have been one of the reasons Gurney later committed suicide.

Additional References: Again, Hall's book provoked a heated controversy: Alan Gauld, "Mr. Hall and the SPR," *Journal of the Society for Psychical Research,* 43 (1965):53-62; J. Fraser Nicol, "The Silences of Mr. Trevor Hall,"

International Journal of Parapsychology, 8 (1966):5-59; Trevor H. Hall, "Some Comments on Mr. Fraser Nicol's Review," *International Journal of Parapsychology,* 10 (1968):149-164. See also: Simeon Edmunds, "Cooking the Evidence?" *Tomorrow,* 10 (Autumn 1962):35-44, Hall's "*The Spiritualists* in Retrospect," *Tomorrow,* 11 (Winter 1963):54-56, and Hall's "Florence Cook and William Crookes: A Footnote to an Inquiry," *Tomorrow,* 11 (Autumn 1963):342-359.

(30) Hall, Trevor H. *New Light on Old Ghosts.* London: Duckworth, 1965, xvi + 142 pp.

A series of essays dealing with diverse topics, including the Wesley Poltergeist (alleged to create disturbances in the Epworth Rectory in 1716-1717), the purportedly paranormal bell-ringing at Bealings House in 1834, an alleged ghost in the Leeds Library in 1884, the famous Cock Lane Ghost of 1762, the possible collusion between psychical researcher William Crookes and the medium Florence Cook, the alleged levitation by D. D. Home at Ashley House, and opening and closing pieces on the supposed hauntings at Borley Rectory. Though Hall's historical detective work is often impressive, his conclusions sometimes go beyond his data. Despite the flaws in some of Hall's efforts, his writings should be required reading for everyone interested in early psychical research.

Additional References: A highly critical review of this book, by R. G. Medhurst, was published in the *Journal of the Society for Psychical Research,* 44 (1967):94-100. The reviewer points out a great number of inaccuracies, misrepresentations, and factual errors in Hall's book. Many of the topics and themes in this book are elaborated upon in Hall's other books. In addition to his books listed above, see Hall's *Search for Harry Price,* Duckworth, London, 1978, and *The Strange Story of Ada Goodrich Freer,* Duckworth, London, 1980 (reprinted from 1968).

(31) Hall, Trevor H.: *The Enigma of Daniel Home: Medium or Fraud?* Buffalo, N.Y.: Prometheus Books, 1984, 148 pp.

This provoking but rather imperfect book purports to answer the question of whether D. D. Home was a medium or a fraud. While Hall presents a number of valid criticisms, this book is far from reaching its advertised goal. Parapsychological and skeptical reviewers agreed that the author's presentation is highly selective and that he has chosen the easy way out by largely confining his critical examination to cases carefully selected for their debunkability and ignoring the more striking examples of Home's mediumship. The best chapter of the book, and that which deserves to be seriously considered by those who come to Home's defense, is that dealing with Home's famous window levitation at Ashley House. Though some of the points Hall makes here were already made long ago, he has done a creditable job suggesting a reasonable nonparanormal explanation.

Additional References: Important critical reviews of Hall's book were written by Stephen E. Braude (*Journal of the Society for Psychical Research,* 53 [1985]:40-46); Eric J. Dingwall (*Zetetic Scholar* #12/13 [in press]), and George Zorab (*Journal of Parapsychology,* 49 [1985]:103-105).

(32) Houdini, Harry. *Miracle Mongers and Their Methods: A Complete Exposé.* New York: E. P. Dutton, 1920. Reprinted, with a foreword by James Randi, Buffalo, N.Y.: Prometheus Books, 1981, xv + 240 pp.

This is a fascinating debunking volume but unfortunately replete with pseudo-explanations for many of the incredible phenomena described. For example, a woman identified as "Thardo" (almost certainly a misidentification of the performer Evatima Tardo) is correctly described as regularly demonstrating how she could be clearly and openly bitten by a rattlesnake; immediately afterwards physicians extracted venom from the serpent and injected it into a rabbit who promptly died, while "Thardo" showed no discomfort. Houdini states the preposterous conclusion that her "immunity was the result of an absolutely empty stomach, into which a large quantity of milk was taken shortly after the wound was inflicted, the theory being that the virus acts directly on the contents of the stomach, changing it to a deadly poison" (p. 177). The book is generally accurate in its descriptions of the phenomenal effects produced for audiences (at least as these effects were *perceived* by the audiences), but the frequent false explanations given by Houdini constitute an excellent example of a critic discrediting rather than disproving an extraordinary claim. In some cases, Houdini may have done this intentionally since he may have wished not to reveal the real secret method of a fellow conjurer.

Additional References: In general, the real methods of the fakers and professional miracle mongers are available only through conjuring literature not generally available to the public but sold through dealers within the conjuring fraternity. Two relevant works available to the general public are: Ormond McGill, *How to Produce Miracles,* New American Library, Signet Books, New York, 1977, and Ottley R. Coulter, *How to Perform Strong-Man Stunts,* Johnson Smith, Detroit, no date indicated.

(33) Houdini, Harry. *A Magician Among the Spirits.* New York: Harper, 1924, xxi + 294 pp.

When this book first appeared, George H. Johnson, reviewing it in the *Journal of the American Society for Psychical Research,* 18 (1924):681-682, opened with the statement: "Houdini has produced a very excellent book, both entertaining and instructive, which should be read by the public generally and in particular by every Spiritualist, magician and researcher." Despite some flaws in the book's details, that recommendation still holds. Houdini's cool debunking of physical mediumship is among the very best of such studies and should be required reading for anyone interested in such exponents as the Davenport Brothers, D. D. Home, Eusapia Palladino, Dr. Slade, and many others. It is important to recognize that, although Houdini was very much the enemy of spiritualism, this work does not directly deal with his view on nonspiritualist psychical research. Houdini's opposition to the supernatural did not necessarily extend to the merely paranormal (in which he seems to have been more a doubter than a denier). Thus, when criticizing the magician Robert Houdin's letters endorsing the abilities of Alexis Didier, Houdini dismisses them by writing that they have "no bearings whatsoever on Spiritualism, but refer only to sittings with a clairvoyant . . ." (p. 253).

Additional Reference: A critical discussion of Houdini's book is included as Chapter 4 of Part I (pp. 144-162) of Walter Franklin Prince, *The Enchanted Boundary: Being a Survey of Negative Reactions to Claims of Psychic Phenomena 1820-1930,* Boston Society for Psychic Reserarch, Boston, Mass., 1930 (reprinted by Arno Press, New York, 1975).

(34) McComas, Henry Clay. *Ghosts I Have Talked With.* Baltimore, Md.: Williams, 1935, 192 pp.

The majority of case studies presented by the author are expositions of fraudulent mediums, based on his own investigations on behalf of the American Society for Psychical Research. Dr. McComas was a psychologist who worked with the ASPR during a leave of absence he took from Johns Hopkins University, and this memoir of his case investigations, including two chapters on the "Margery" mediumship, is very fair-minded and instructive. It is a good example of a constructively skeptical work.

(35) Rinn, Joseph F., *Sixty Years of Psychical Research: Houdini and I Among the Spiritualists.* New York: Truth Seekers Co., 1950, xx + 618 pp.

This is a flawed but nonetheless very important critical work by a man prominent in conjuring circles (Rinn was a successful businessman and part-time magician and exposer/investigator of spirit mediums) who has given us material in this memoir that today appears nowhere else. Because Rinn deals with his own direct experiences and, especially, because he quotes at length from now obscure and forgotten newspaper records, the book is invaluable. It is a book full of opinions, gossip, and anecdotes, and it needs to be read that way—not as a work of objective scholarship. Aside from its wealth of detail, the book is also an important document showing the outlook of a strong skeptic who has had direct encounters with many—if not most—of the "greats" of early psychical research and here gives his own, often stinging, evaluations. It is easy to understand why some of the excesses in this book so infuriated defenders of psychical research, but it remains a major document dealing with the pitfalls (and pratfalls) that have been present in psychical research.

Additional References: Readers should consult the highly critical reviews that call attention to many of the factual inaccuracies in Rinn's book: W. H. Salter's in the *Journal of the Society for Psychical Research,* 36 (1952):431-438; and Laura A. Dale's in the *Journal of the American Society for Psychical Research,* 45 (1951):77-83.

5. Psychic Healing

(36) Nolen, William A. *Healing: A Doctor in Search of a Miracle.* New York: Random House, 1975, 275 pp.

Dr. Nolen, a prominent surgeon, describes his personal investigation into the healing claims of the late evangelist Kathryn Kuhlman, Houston's spiritual healer Norbu Chen, and several "psychic surgeons" in the Philippines. In addition to his visits to these healers, he follows up many of the cases for which cures were claimed. Nolen presents a highly readable and very disenchanting picture of these alleged "miracle" healers, and the study is an excellent example of the medical perspective on these cases. Faults with the book include Nolen's seeming lack of familiarity with the substantial literature on this subject, possible overgeneralization from the relatively small number of cases he examined, and too little consideration given to some of the same psychosomatic effects as they operate within conventional (orthodox) medicine. Despite such limitations, the book is an excellent first-hand account, and the freshness of Nolen's approach makes this an important introduction to the subject.

Additional References: For a strongly critical reaction to Nolen's book—one which asks if it is not really "A Doctor in Search of a Best Seller?"—is: Stanley Krippner and Alberto Villoldo, *The Realms of Healing,* Celestial Arts, Millbrae, Cal., 1976. Nolen's views on the Philippine healers should be contrasted with the sympathetic but also critical section on them in: George W. Meek (Ed.), *Healers and the Healing Process,* Theosophical Publishing House, Quest Books, Wheaton, Ill., 1977. Important critical works relevant to the issues in psychic healing include: Louis Rose, *Faith Healing,* Penguin Books, Baltimore, 1971; George Bishop, *Faith Healing: God or Fraud?* Sherbourne Press, Los Angeles, 1967; Eve Simson, *The Faith Healer,* Pyramind Books, New York, 1977; Ralph H. Major, *Faiths That Healed,* Appleton-Century, New York, 1940; C. J. S.

Thompson, *Magic and Healing*, Rider, New York, 1947; and Jerome D. Frank, *Persuasion and Healing*, Johns Hopkins University Press, Baltimore, 1973. Two works of special relevance for describing psychological and social processes involved are: Theodore X. Barber, "Changing the 'Unchangeable' Bodily Processes by (Hyponotic) Suggestions: A New Look at Hypnosis, Cognitions, Imagining, and the Mind-Body Problem," in Anees A. Sheikh (Ed.), *Imagination and Healing*, Baywood Publishing, Farmingdale, N.Y., 1984, pp. 69-127; and L. Kay Gillespie, *Cancer Quackery: The Label of Quack and Its Relationship to Deviant Behavior*, R & E Research Associates, Palo Alto, 1979. There is also a vast relevant anthropological literature on healing. For typical surveys see: Ari Kiev (Ed.), *Magic, Faith and Healing*, Free Press of Glencoe, New York, 1964; and Peter Morley and Roy Wallis (Eds.), *Culture and Curing: Anthropological Perspectives on Traditional Medical Beliefs and Practices*, Peter Owen, London, 1978.

6. Dowsing

(37) Vogt, Evon Z., and Ray Hyman: *Water Witching USA*. 2nd ed. Chicago and London: University of Chicago Press, 1979 (originally published in 1959). 260 pp.

This volume, which includes a special preface and a "Postscript 1979," is the outstanding scientific evaluation of dowsing claims. In most cases, the skeptical arguments are powerful though fair-minded, and the authors do not fail to provide adequate accounts of the believers' arguments. Their treatment of the fallibility of human observation is of importance far beyond the subject matter that is dealt with in this book. On the other hand, their discussion of other claimed paranormal phenomena remains somewhat superficial.

Additional References: Two detailed reviews of the 1959 edition of this book appeared in the parapsychological literature: *Journal of the American Society for Psychical Research*, 53 (1959):147-155 (by J. L. Woodruff); *Journal of Parapsychology*, 23 (1959):274-277 (by Horace C. Levinson). Interestingly, the 1979 edition seems to have been more favorably received by parapsychologists than was the earlier one, as can be seen when one compares the reviews by Woodruff and Levinson (which already contained rather positive comments on the book) with David Christie-Murray's review of the second edition in the *Journal of the Society for Psychical Research*, 51 (1981):28-29. Vogt and Hyman's survey should be compared for scope and conclusions with: George P. Hansen, "Dowsing: A Review of Experimental Research," *Journal of the Society for Psychical Research*, 51 (1982):343-367.

7. Survival Research and Reincarnation

(38) Christopher, Milbourne. *Search for the Soul: An Insider's Report on the Continuing Quest by Psychics and Scientists for Evidence of Life After Death.* New York: Thomas Y. Crowell, 1979, 206 pp.

An excellent and lively review of about 100 years of attempts to discover the "soul," to weigh or photograph it, or to encounter it in out-of-the-body and near-death experiences or in cases of the reincarnation type. Christopher's book is both informative and entertaining, and the author's healthy skepticism is most useful in setting the record straight for the general reader who may have been confused by all sorts of publications purporting to present evidence for the soul or survival. Much of this alleged evidence for the soul evaporates in the course of Christopher's study. Without doubt, the book contains a number of factual errors and other inadequacies, but it well deserves to be read by both skeptics and parapsychologists.

Additonal References: This book was favorably received by both parapsychologists and skeptics, as will be seen from more or less detailed reviews by parapsychologist George Adelman (*Parapsychology Review,* 11, no. 3 [1980]:14-16) and skeptic Piet Hein Hoebens (*Zeitschrift für Parapsychologie und Grenzgebiete der Psychologie,* 23 [1981]:252-253). On the other hand, parapsychologist Michael Grosso published a rather sharp review in the *Journal of Parapsychology,* 44 (1980):375-378, which ends with the exaggerated conclusion that "the close student of the subject will find [Christopher's book] a waste of time."

(39) Kline, Milton V. (Ed.). *A Scientific Report on "The Search for Bridey Murphy."* New York: Julian, 1956, xxxi + 224 pp.

Contrary to its claim to provide a critical examination of the methodological and logical shortcomings of Morey Bernstein's report on the case of Bridey Murphy (alleged recollections of a former life), this book, which contains contributions by the editor and by Bowers, Marcuse, Raginsky, and Shapiro, as well as an introduction by Rosen, does not live up to this goal. There certainly is ample reason to be skeptical of the claims made in Bernstein's report. But, while there are a number of valid criticisms in this book (which may justify its inclusion in the present bibliography), large parts of the authors' analyses are marred by open prejudgments, ad hominem attacks, and apparent ignorance of important details of the case.

Additional References: A critical review, written by Ian Stevenson, was published in the *Journal of the American Society for Psychical Research,* 51 (1957):36-37. Curt J. Ducasse's "How the Case of *The Search for Bridey Murphy* Stands Today," *Journal of the American Society for Psychical Research,* 54 (1960):3-22, also contains a critical appraisal of the book Kline edited.

8. Statistics

(40) Brown, George Spencer. *Probability and Scientific Inference*. New York: Longmans, Green, 1957, 163 pp.

In this highly controversial monograph, the author gives a new twist to the statistical controversy in parapsychology and the debates around it by directing his criticisms not against technical details of the application of statistical procedures, as earlier and later critics of parapsychology have done (not included in this bibliography), but against the basic assumptions of probability theory itself.

Additional References: Brown had presented an earlier version of his assessment of the role of statistics in parapsychology in an article entitled "Statistical Significance in Psychical Research," *Nature,* 172 (1953):154-156. In a detailed critical review of Brown's book in the *Journal of the American Society for Psychical Research,* 55 (1961):112-117, Malcolm E. Turner points out numerous problems with Brown's unorthodox treatment of probability theory, but warns: "Any psychical researcher who does not study this book with care is doing himself and his field a great disservice." Another critical commentary on Brown's book was contributed by parapsychologist-turned-skeptic Christopher Scott: "G. Spencer Brown and Probablility: A Critique," *Journal of the Society for Psychical Research,* 39 (1958):217-234.

9. Conceptual Criticisms

(41) Flew, Antony G. N. *A New Approach to Psychical Research*. London: C. A. Watts, 1953, 161 pp.

Flew provides a critical linguistic analysis of the claims of psychical research, especially of survival. The "new approach to psychical research" that the book claims to represent is to consist of "the combination of a resolute, yet not invincible, skepticism . . . with a constant awareness of language." Consequently, extensive attention is paid to language as the tool with which paranormal phenomena are described and explained. Given the limited size of the book, Flew's discussion of selected instances of spontaneous, mediumistic, and experimental phenomena necessarily remains somewhat superficial, and a number of his conclusions are open to criticism. On the other hand, his language-philosophical examination of many parapsychological and other concepts (such as "survival" and "mind") make this book a lasting contribution to the skeptical literature that should be read and discussed by both parapsychologists and critics much more thoroughly than has hitherto been the case.

Additional References: Flew's book met with favorable reception in the parapsychological literature as is evident from book reviews in the *Journal of the*

American Society for Psychical Research, 48 (1954):78-80 (by J. L. Woodruff), and in the *Journal of Parapsychology,* 18 (1954):130-132 (by R. L. Patterson).

10. A List of Important Inside Criticisms of Parapsychology

Contrary to what a number of skeptics have alleged, the parapsychological literature is replete with high-quality inside criticism. Whether or not parapsychology can be considered a full-blown science, it is evident that there are more or less well-functioning self-correcting mechanisms and a scientific security system operating in the field. The literature clearly shows that many of the most rigorous criticisms of parapsychological practice and theory have been made by the parapsychologists themselves. Therefore, no responsible critic can afford to ignore this mass of skeptical inside publications, examples of which can be found in almost every volume of the *Proceedings of the Society for Psychical Research,* the oldest parapsychological periodical, and any other of the leading parapsychological journals. For obvious reasons, it cannot be the purpose of this bibliography to provide anything close to an adequate survey of these inside criticisms. All we can do here is to compile a very brief list of what we take to be *representative* examples of old as well as more recent inside criticisms and to encourage skeptical readers to carefully inspect the parapsychological literature.

(42) Akers, Charles. "Methodological Criticisms of Parapsychology." In Krippner, Stanley (Ed.), *Advances in Parapsychological Research,* vol. 4. Jefferson, N.C., and London: McFarland, 1984, pp. 112-164.

(43) Blackmore, Susan J. *Beyond the Body: An Investigation of Out-of-the-Body Experiences.* London: William Heinemann, 1982 (cf. the very favorable review by skeptic James E. Alcock in *Skeptical Inquirer,* 8, no. 1 [1983]:74-77).

(44) Davey, S. John. "The Possibilities of Mal-observation from a Practical Point of View." *Journal of the Society for Psychical Research,* 3 (1887):8-44.

(45) Ellis, David J. *The Mediumship of the Tape Recorder.* Harlow, Essex: D. J. Ellis, 1978.

(46) (Hodgson, Richard et al.:) "Report of the Committee Appointed to Investigate Phenomena Connected with the Theosophical Society." *Proceedings of the Society for Psychical Research,* 3 (1885):201-400.

(47) Hodgson, Richard. "Mr. Davey's Imitations by Conjuring of Phenomena Sometimes Attributed to Spirit Agency." *Proceedings of the Society for Psychical Research,* 8 (1892):253-310.

(48) Hodgson, Richard, and John Davey. "The Possibilities of Mal-observation and Lapse of Memory from a Practical Point of View." *Proceedings of the Society for Psychical Research,* 4 (1886-1887):381-495.

(49) Podmore, Frank. *Modern Spiritualism: A History and a Criticism,* 2 vols., London: Methuen, 1902 (reprinted as *Mediums of the 19th Century,* 2 vols., University Books, Secaucus, N.J., 1963).

(50) Podmore, Frank. *The Naturalisation of the Supernatural.* New York and London: Putnam's, 1908.

(51) Podmore, Frank. *The Newer Spiritualism.* London: Fisher Unwin, 1910 (reprinted by Arno Press, New York, 1975).

11. A List of Pro-Parapsychology Books

As we emphasized in the introduction, the books listed here are included because we think they are among those that make the best case not for the reality of psi or any other claimed paranormal phenomenon but for the scientific legitimacy and respectability of parapsychology. Again, the books listed here are selected from a much larger number of other works that make a reasonably good case for parapsychological research as a legitimate scientific endeavor.

(52) Bauer, Eberhard, and Walter von Lucadou (Eds.). *Spektrum der Parapsychologie. Festschrift für Hans Bender* (Spectrum of Parapsychology. Festschrift for Hans Bender). Freiburg i.Br., FRG: Aurum Verlag, 1983, 253 pp.

(53) Beloff, John (Ed.). *New Directions in Parapsychology.* London: Elek Science, 1974, 174 pp.

(54) Beloff, John. *Psychological Sciences: A Review of Modern Psychology.* London: Crosby Lockwood Staples, 1975 (Chapter 8, pp. 282-320: "Parapsychology").

(55) Houtkooper, Joop M. *Observational Theory: A Research Programme for Paranormal Phenomena.* Lisse, Holland: Swetz & Zeitlinger B. V., 1983, viii + 123 pp.

(56) Johnson, Martin: *Parapsychologie: Onderzoek in de grensgebieden van ervaring en wetenschap* (Parapsychology: Investigation of border areas of experience and science). Baarn, Holland: De Kern, no date [1982], 191 pp. [cf. the most favorable comments on this book were made by skeptic Piet Hein Hoebens in

his "Sense and Nonsense in Parapsychology," *Skeptical Inquirer*, 8 (1983-1984):
121-132]

(57) Krippner, Stanley (Ed.). *Advances in Parapsychological Research*. Vol. 1,
Psychokinesis (New York and London: Plenum Press, 1977), xi + 235 pp.; Vol.
2, *Extrasensory Perception* (New York and London: Plenum Press, 1978), ix +
308 pp. Vol. 3 (New York and London: Plenum Press, 1983 xiv + 338 pp. Vol.
4), (Jefferson, N.C., and London: McFarland, 1984), ix + 254 pp.

(58) Rao, K. Ramakrishna (Ed. and Compiler), *The Basic Experiments in Parapsychology*. Jefferson, N.C., and London: McFarland, 1984, viii + 264 pp.

(59) West, Donald J. *Psychical Research Today*. New York: Hillary House,
1956, 144 pp.

(60) Wolman, Benjamin B. (Ed.), *Handbook of Parapsychology*. New York:
Van Nostrand Reinhold, 1977, xxi + 967 pp.

12. Important Skeptical Periodicals

(61) *Skeptical Inquirer* (formerly *The Zetetic*), 1976–present; quarterly. Editor,
vol. 1, Marcello Truzzi; vols. 2–present, Kendrick Frazier. The *Skeptical Inquirer* is the journal of the Committee for the Scientific Investigation of Claims
of the Paranormal (order from: CSICOP, Box 229, Central Park Station, Buffalo, NY 14215).

This journal is today's leading voice of anti-paranormal advocacy. As such it
represents an important and much needed balancing force against advocates for
the paranormal. The journal is *must* reading for anyone seeking to construct an
objective appraisal of the evidence and arguments in these debates. The journal
is particularly concerned with misrepresentations by the mass media and regularly criticizes journalistic reports it considers pseudoscientific. Its frequent attention to popular reports on the paranormal like those in such publications as the
National Enquirer, which few legitimate parapsychologists would endorse, sometimes blurs the line between pseudoscience and legitimate protoscientific research
programs. The *Skeptical Inquirer* is an unabashedly hard-line skeptical journal,
and it has sometimes been accused of being more interested in discrediting than
impartially examining claims of the paranormal. And, as might be expected,
some proponents of the paranormal have characterized the journal as the arm of
a kind of "Rationalist's Inquisition" rather than as an objective scientific forum.
A by-product of the resulting polarization between critics and proponents this
has produced is that few parapsychologists have sought publication in the

journal, and this makes its articles appear to them to be one-sided. Nonetheless, there have been occasional sharp exchanges between the critics of parapsychology in its pages, and there is a growing spectrum of skeptical opinion to be found in the journal.

Additional References: An excellent discussion and defense of the journal can be found in "World Views in Collision: The *Skeptical Inquirer* versus the *National Enquirer*," by Douglas R. Hofstadter in his book *Metamagical Themas: Questing for the Essence of Mind and Pattern,* Basic Books, New York, 1985, pp. 91-114. A key paper on parapsychology in the journal, written by the chairman of its sponsoring committee is: Paul Kurtz, "Is Parapsychology a Science?" *Skeptical Inquirer,* 3 (1978):14-32 (see Chapter 21 of this volume). For a reply by a softer-line skeptic, see: Marcello Truzzi, "A Skeptical Look at Paul Kurtz's Analysis of the Scientific Status of Parapsychology," *Journal of Parapsychology,* 44 (1980):35-55. Critical reactions to the *Skeptical Inquirer* by scientists not party to its internal controversies can be found in: T. J. Pinch and H. M. Collins, "Private Science and Public Knowledge: The Committee for the Scientific Investigation of Claims of the Paranormal and its Use of the Literature," *Social Studies of Science,* 14 (1984):521-546; Leonard Lewin, *Science and the Paranormal,* Tinbridge Wells, Institute for Cultural Research, Kent, 1979; and Louis Lasagna "Let Magic Cast Its Spell," *The Sciences* (May–June 1984):10-12.

(62) *Zeitschrift für Kritischen Okkultismus* (Journal for Critical Occultism), 1926-1928; quarterly. Editor, Richard Baerwald.

Although this journal, which was supported by both outside skeptics and critical insiders like Dessoir, Dingwall, Hellwig, von Klinckowstroem, Rosenbusch, Tischner, et al. was published over a period of only three years, it contained some of the most important skeptical investigations of claims of the paranormal (especially of mental and physical mediumship) in the annals of skepticism. Today, the three volumes of this journal still deserve to be read and considered. The journal's (not always successful) policy of providing a forum for rational communication between critics and proponents of parapsychology was similar to what, in our day, is attempted by the *Zetetic Scholar* (No. 63).

(63) *Zetetic Scholar,* 1978–present; published irregularly but approximately twice per year. Editor, Marcello Truzzi. The *Zetetic Scholar* is the journal of the Center for Scientific Anomalies Research (order from Marcello Truzzi, Department of Sociology, Eastern Michigan University, Ypsilanti, MI 48197).

This journal seeks to promote dialogues rather than debates between proponents and critics of the protosciences. It features extensive bibliographies, book reviews, and peer commentaries and exchanges. As such, it seeks to act as a kind of *amicus curiae* or "friend of the court" to the scientific community. It seeks to represent a highly tolerant and constructive form of skepticism, placing great faith in science's self-correcting method. Some hard-line critics have criticized it for lending legitimacy to some "obviously pseudoscientific" and even "occult" efforts, and for making a fetish out of "due process over common sense." At the other extreme, some proponents of the paranormal have criticized it for masking an underlying even harsher skepticism under a cloak of public reasonableness. *Zetetic Scholar* also seeks to promote an interdisciplinary new science of *anomalistics*, which looks for methodological common denominators among the protosciences and welcomes valid scientific anomalies as opportunities to advance theory.

Additonal Reference: For a discussion of the philosophical differences in the forms of skepticism found in the *Zetetic Scholar* and the *Skeptical Inquirer*, see: Nicholas Wade, "Schism Among Psychic Watchers," *Science* (Sept. 30, 1977): 1344; Nicholas Wade, "Washington Shuttle: Paranormal Claims Adjustments," *The Sciences* (Nov. 1978):30-31; Boyce Rensberger, "Skeptics Criticized on Paranormal Issue," *New York Times* (June 26, 1978); and "The Crusade Against the Paranormal" (an interview with M. Truzzi), *Fate*, (Sept. 1979):70-75, and (Oct. 1979):87-94. An important feature of *Zetetic Scholar* is its attempt to give optimum consideration to the best version of any opposing position. On the advantages to this strategy, see: Charles G. Lord, Mark R. Lepper and Elizabeth Preston, "Considering the Opposite: A Corrective Strategy for Social Judgment," *Journal of Personality and Social Psychology,* 47 (1984):1231-1234.

13. A Note on Some Exclusions

In light of our selection criteria, some of the skeptical books we chose not to annotate but that readers might find relevant include (listed here alphabetically and not in terms of importance): Barber, Theodore X., *Pitfalls in Human Research* (New York: Pergamon, 1976). Brandon, Ruth, *The Spiritualists: The Passion for the Occult in the Nineteenth and Twentieth Centuries* (New York: Alfred A. Knopf, 1983). Carpenter, William B., *Mesmerism, Spiritualism, etc., Historically and Scientifically Considered* (New York: Appleton, 1877). Culpin, Millais, *Spiritualism and the New Psychology: An Explanation of Spiritualist Phenomena and Beliefs in Terms of Modern Knowledge* (London: Edward Arnold, 1920). Dingwall, Eric J., *How to Go to a Medium: A Manual of Instruction* (London: Kegan Paul, Trench, Trubner, 1927); *Ghosts and Spirits in the Ancient World* (London: Kegan Paul, Trench, Trubner, 1930); *Some Human Oddities: Studies in the Queer, the Uncanny and the Fanatical* and *Very Peculiar People: Portrait Studies in the Queer, the Abnormal and the Uncanny* (New Hyde Park, N.Y.: University Books, both 1962); *The Critics' Dilemma* (Sussex, privately published, 1966). Dingwall, Eric J., and John Langdon-Davies, *The*

Unknown—Is It Nearer? (New York: New American Library, Signet, 1968). Edmunds, Simeon, *Spiritualism: A Critical Survey* (Letchworth, Hertfordshire: Aquarian Press, 1966). Evans, Bergen, *The Spoor of Spooks and Other Nonsense* (New York: Alfred A. Knopf, 1954). Evans, Christopher, *Cults of Unreason* (New York: Farrar, Strauss and Giroux, 1973). Fair, Charles, *The New Nonsense: The End of the Rational Consensus* (New York: Simon and Schuster, 1974). Goldenson, Robert M., *Mysteries of the Mind* (Garden City, N.Y.: Doubleday, 1973). Jahoda, Gustav, *The Psychology of Superstition* (London: Penguin Press, 1969). Jastrow, Joseph, *Wish and Wisdom: Episodes in the Vagaries of Belief* (New York: Appleton-Century, 1935). Leahy, Thomas Hardy, and Grace Evans, *Psychology's Occult Doubles: Psychology and the Problem of Pseudoscience* (Chicago: Nelson Hall, 1983). Mann, Walter, *The Follies and Frauds of Spiritualism* (London: Watts, 1919). McCabe, Joseph, *Spiritualism: A Popular History from 1847* (New York: Dodd, Mead, 1920). Mertens, Gerald C., editor, *Behavioral Science Behaviorally Taught* (Lexington, Mass.: Ginn Custom Publishing, 1980). Planer, Felix E., *Superstition* (London: Cassell, 1980). Rachleff, Owen S., *The Occult Conceit* (Chicago: Cowles, 1971). Radner, Daisie and Michael, *Science and Unreason* (Belmont, Calif.: Wadsworth, 1982). Shadowitz, Albert, and Peter Walsh, *The Dark Side of Knowledge: Exploring the Occult* (Reading, Mass.: Addison-Wesley, 1976). Sladek, John, *The New Apocrypha: A Guide to Strange Sciences and Occult Beliefs* (New York: Stein and Day, 1973). Tanner, Amy E., *Studies in Spiritism* (New York: Appleton, 1910). Taylor, John, *Science and the Supernatural* (New York: E. P. Dutton, 1980). and Wilson, Ian, *All in the Mind* (Garden City, N.Y.: Doubleday, 1983).

Additonal skeptical articles similarly unannotated but which should be listed for the reader include: Boring, Edwin G., "Statistical Frequencies as Dynamic Equilibria," *Psychological Review,* 48 (1941):279-301; and "The Present Status of Parapsychology," *American Scientist,* 43 (1955):108-117. Crumbaugh, James C., "A Scientific Critique of Parapsychology," *International Journal of Neuropsychiatry,* 2 (1966):523-531; and "The Spirits Against Bosh," *Contemporary Psychology,* 6 (1961):149-151. Gridgeman, N. T., "Parapsychology and All That," *Queen's Quarterly,* Winter (1964):491-507. Heinlein, Christian Paul, and Julia Heil, "Critique of the Premises and Statistical Methodology of Parapsychology," *Journal of Psychology,* 5 (1938):135-148. Hutchinson, G. Evelyn, "Marginalia," *American Scientist,* 36 (1948):291ff. Hyman, Ray, "Psi: A Challenge to Critics and Believers," *Contemporary Psychology,* 23 (1978):644-646. Kennedy, John L., "A Methodological Review of Extra-Sensory Perception," *Psychological Bulletin,* 36 (1939):59-103; Moss, Samuel, and Donald C. Butler, "The Scientific Credibility of ESP," *Perceptual and Motor Skills,* 46 (1978):1063-1079 (for replies see: McConnell, R. A., "ESP and the Credibility of Critics," *Perceptual and Motor Skills,* 47 (1978):875-878; and Rao, K. Ramakrishna, "On the Scientific Credibility of ESP," *Perceptual and Motor Skills*, 49 (1979):415-429]; and "Comments on Rao's Article on the Scientific Credibility of ESP," *Perceptual and Motor Skills*, 50 [1980]:502). Skinner, B. F., "Card Guessing Experiments," *American Scientist*, 36 (1948):456-462. Stevens, S. S., "The Market for Miracles," *Contemporary Psychology*, 12 (1967):1-3. Szasz, Thomas S., "A Critical Analysis of the Fundamental Concepts of Psychical Research," *Psychiatric Quarterly*, 31 (1957):96-108. See also the synopses of papers presented by Antony Flew, John Taylor, C. E. M. Hansel, Trevor Hall, and E. J. Dingwall at the Rationalist Press Association's Annual Conference, 1975, with a critical report on the conference by Carl Sargent and a reply by Nicolas Walter, all in *New Humanist*, 91 (1975):175-185.

Finally, we would call readers' attention to a growing number of papers relevant to the psi debate by sociologists of science: Collins, H. M., and T. J. Pinch, *Frames of Meaning: The Social Construction of Extraordinary Science* (London: Routledge and Kegan Paul, 1982). "The Construction of the Paranormal: Nothing Unscientific Is Happening," in Roy Wallis, editor, *On the Margins of Science: The Social Construction of Rejected Knowledge* (University of Keele: Sociological Review Monograph 27, March 1979). Pinch, T. J., and H. M. Collins, "Is Anti-Science Not Science? The Case of Parapsychology," in Helga Nowothy and Hilary Rose, eds., *Counter-Movements in the Sciences* (Boston: R. Reidel, 1979), pp. 221-250. Koefed, Peter A., and Willem A. Verloren van Themaat, "The Rejection of Parapsychology Research Results," paper presented at the annual meeting of the Society for Social Studies of Science, Atlanta, Georgia, Nov. 5-7, 1981.

Annotation to the Annotated Bibliography

RAY HYMAN

The Hövelmann-Truzzi-Hoebens Annotated Bibliography is a welcome contribution. (Although Truzzi had some input and Hoebens would have probably agreed to the final version, I will assume that the annotations reflect mainly Hövelmann's views.)

Hövelmann finds good things to say about almost all of the 41 items he has felt were worth annotating. Some are considered to be "important," "influential," and even "fair-minded." In those he describes as "flawed," "dogmatic," and "superficial," he finds much to recommend, even suggesting, in some cases, that these so-called inadequate critiques should be "required reading."

The most frequent shortcomings of the skeptical items Hövelmann notes are: the author falls short of his stated goals; the author fails to show sufficient acquaintance with the relative literature and claims; the author is unfair; the discussions are superficial and selective; the arguments are overgeneralized from a few, possibly atypical, cases; and the author seems more intent on discrediting than disproving the claims being attacked.

Although I tend to agree with much of what Hövelmann has to say, I find myself uncomfortable with some of the evaluations. Obviously any set of annotations is highly subjective and represents the annotater's standards. But the application of a set of standards to a collection of critical contributions implies that the contributors were all attempting to achieve the same goals and thus can be judged on the same criteria.

But it is far from obvious that these various contributions make such a coherent set or that it makes sense to judge them all by one set of standards. The authors vary greatly in backgrounds and credentials. More important, they differ greatly among themselves in their objectives. Some restrict themselves to evaluating the extent to which parapsychological arguments are based on accepted scientific principles. Others try to suggest plausible nonparanormal alternative accounts of the phenomena. Still others try to supply psychological and social reasons for the belief and/or disbelief in such phenomena.

In addition, the readership has to be taken into account. Although Hövelmann writes that my critique of the ganzfeld literature "can serve as a model for future responsible skeptical examinations of parapsychological research," the technical nature of the critique and Honorton's rebuttal require, for adequate comprehension, a reader who has a reasonable background and training in statistical theory and methods, scientific procedure and the conduct of controlled experiments with humans, and specific problems related to parapsychological investigations. For example, as part of his rebuttal, Honorton included an appendix by David R. Saunders that argued that my particular application of factor analysis was wrong and yielded meaningless conclusions. To be able to evaluate this charge, as well as my future response to it, the reader would have to be familiar with such esoteric concepts as eigenvalues, the multivariate general linear model, and the various legitimate and illegitimate uses of linear combinations of variables. If all critics were required to write at this level of technical sophistication, the entire debate over parapsychological claims would be restricted to a very small number of highly trained specialists.

My own judgment of the skeptical literature is colored by my interest in its pedagogical implications. When I began teaching a course in pseudopsychologies in 1970, I found it difficult to find skeptical books to use as texts. The available skeptical works seemed to be dogmatic, ill-informed, and irrelevant. The students were sharp enough to detect the overgeneralizations and the misrepresentations. As a result, many of these books were counterproductive. They tended to make the students more sympathetic to the claims that were being attacked.

The situation has improved markedly in the past ten years. I now find it much easier to find suitable textbooks. I look for books that both my critical and my pro-paranormal students will find credible and from which they can extract general principles and tools that will help them cope with and understand future paranormal claims. In this regard I have found Andrew Neher's *The Psychology of Transcendence*, Marks and Kammann's *The Psychology of the Psychic*, and Susan Blackmore's *Beyond the Body* superb, because they go beyond mere debunking and provide explanations of how normal and intelligent individuals can be led astray. They also provide the students with models of how such difficult topics can be successfully investigated.

Hövelmann faults Andrew Neher's book because his "counterexplanations are a bit simplistic" and "his discussions tend to be somewhat superficial and imbalanced." In a sense this might be true, but in an even more important sense it is irrelevant and somewhat misleading. Neher's book is not aimed at debunking the many psychic, occult, and mystical beliefs he surveys. He does attempt to provide rather brief critiques of the evidence for each. But to discuss the evidence for each in any detail would have entailed a volume many times the size of its 350 pages. In place of detailed discussion of each belief, he documents his brief critiques with an impressive total of 747 references. Not only did he consult all these references; he devoted a considerable amount of time to personally interviewing a number of parapsychologists and critics in preparing his book.

Neher's book serves as just one example of how the annotation might be affected by the context in which the book is judged. If we attempt to judge it by how well it confronts the parapsychological literature and analyzes it on a number of highly technical and methodological grounds, then one is tempted to fault it as being superficial and simplistic. But this is like finding fault with Shakespeare's *Richard the Third* because it deviates from historical accuracy. Judged in terms of Neher's objectives, as well as in terms of pedagogical achievements, the book is faultless. My students not only find Neher's message to be positive and interesting but are encouraged to use his comprehensive bibliography to consult the original literature.

As you can tell from my chapter in this volume, I have long been dismayed by what I consider to be the inadequacies of the critical literature in parapsychology. My dismay, in this latter context, arises from considering the impact of external criticism upon the conduct of parapsychological research. I agree with Hövelmann that better-informed, less strident, and more relevant critiques would be more constructive and could influence parapsychological research for the better. My own exchanges with Honorton, for example, have already had visible changes on the design of new ganzfeld experiments.

Fortunately, there are signs that criticism is becoming more constructive. Most of this constructive criticism, it is true, is being done by internal critics. But I think this is as it should be. If the internal constructive criticism has an impact, it will result in parapsychological research that, when it is presented to the outside critics, will have fewer obvious flaws and will be taken more seriously.

But again I want to emphasize that the type of constructive criticism that will be useful to the parapsychologists will probably be quite different from the critical literature that can reach the lay public. And both these will have to be evaluated according to quite different standards.

Given that any annotated bibliography is a personal matter, Hövelmann has provided us with a valuable and useful guide. I especially appreciate the fact that he has been able to include important German contributions along with those in English. I also find it helpful that his annotations include references and accounts of the responses to the entries.

It is to be expected that bibliographies by different compilers would differ somewhat. There are some entries on his list that I would not have included. And I cannot resist this opportunity to list a few references omitted from Hövelmann's annotated and unannotated listings that I strongly feel are very important critical contributions:

(1) Davenport, Reuben B. *The Death-blow to Spiritualism.* New York: Arno Press, 1976, 247 pp. (reprint of the 1888 edition).

(2) Flournoy, T. *From India to the Planet Mars.* New Hyde Park, N.Y.: University Books, 1963 (reprint of 1900 edition).

(3) Jackson, H. C., Jr. *The Spirit Rappers: The Strange Story of Kate and Maggie Fox.* Garden City, N.Y.: Doubleday, 1972.

(4) Keene, M. L. *The Psychic Mafia.* New York: St. Martin's Press, 1976.

(5) McKay, C. *Extraordinary Popular Delusions and the Madness of Crowds.* New York: Noonday, 1970 (originally published in 1841).

(6) Sargent, W. *The Mind Possessed.* New York: Penguin, 1974.

(7) Seybert Commission. *Preliminary Report of the Commission Appointed by the University of Pennsylvania to Investigate Modern Spiritualism in Accordance with the Request of the Late Henry Seybert.* Philadelphia: J. B. Lippincott, 1920 (reprint of the 1887 edition).

(8) Wilhelm, J. *The Search for Superman.* New York: Pocket Books, 1976.

Part 4

Parapsychology: Science or Pseudoscience

20

Why Parapsychology Demands
a Skeptical Response

CHRISTOPHER SCOTT

The evidence presented by parapsychologists has several features that are rare or unique in the scientific domain and that together account for the persistence, and perhaps the character, of the conflict that has always surrounded the subject. The best known of these features is *nonrepeatability*.

Though the exact sense in which psi is nonrepeatable can be disputed, there is no doubt about the following negative formulation: *Failure* to replicate is never regarded by parapsychologists as evidence *against* psi. This position, while not in itself unscientific, rules out at one stroke the normal avenue of scientific falsifiability—namely, experimentation—and allows falsification to be attempted only by attacking the individual experiments done by parapsychologists. Thus there is no evidence against psi, only criticism of the evidence for psi. This accounts for the confrontational character of the controversy. Moreover, it gives the evidence a historical rather than an experimental character: Evidence for psi consists not of experiments but of reports of experiments. The distinction is important, because reports may be inaccurate or incomplete, and the critic must raise this as an issue, along with the almost inevitable implications of motivated incompetence or even fraud.

A second unusual feature of parapsychology is its essentially negative definition. The parapsychologist aims to get a result that is, in normal terms, inexplicable. He then argues: I cannot think of a normal explanation, so this must be a psi effect. If the critic *can* think of an explanation, the ensuing dialogue takes the form of an argument about the feasibility, or plausibility, of this alternative. To define a concept purely by eliminating alternatives, with no positive content whatever in the concept, seems to be unknown outside parapsychology. In other sciences, when a hypothetical substance or structure is invoked to explain observed phenomena, the "dialogue" proceeds by a consideration of the properties of the hypothesized entity and experiments are devised to test these. But in parapsychology this never happens, because psi has no properties. Indeed, I suspect that the failure of parapsychologists to come up with something that psi can *not* do is the main reason, rather than nonrepeatability, for the continuing skepticism of mainstream science in regard to psi. This merits further discussion.

Parapsychologists can reasonably blame nature for the nonrepeatability of psi. It is not their fault if results refuse to come at the will of the investigator. On the other hand, they have only themselves to blame for not investigating the *properties of psi*. I pointed out long ago one direction in which such an investigation might be pursued (*Proceedings of the Society for Psychical Research*, 1961, 195). There are many others. For example, by using unsymmetrical shapes on transparent cards, it would be easy to determine, given a source of psi, whether the target is being viewed from one side or the other. One could proceed from this to more or less exact localization in space of the ESP point of view. Parapsychologists have systematically shunned any experiment of this type. There seems to be a hidden agreement that you do not investigate the modus operandi of psi. This strange attitude has received surprisingly little comment. Yet what makes psi remarkable is that it seems to do things that should be impossible; surely the priority questions ought to be: What can it do? and How does it do it? But, for many years now, virtually the only feature of psi that has interested parapsychologists has been its psychological correlates. Why? It is as if they do not *want* to find out how it works.

A third unusual feature of the evidence for psi is the fact that only some people seem able to produce it. This so-called "experimenter effect" not only aggravates the problem of conducting parapsychological research, it threatens by implication practically the whole of science, which is based on the assumption that objective observation is possible. What becomes of the concept of the controlled experiment, fundamental to medicine and the behavioral sciences, if the observer determines the data?

Besides being obstacles to research, the three features I have mentioned—nonrepeatability, the absence of any properties for psi, and the correlation between results and the experimenter—are a potent source of suspicion among skeptics, for each feature is exactly what would be expected if psi were an artifact of selection of evidence, incompetence, and fraud. And at the same time the deliberate avoidance of experiments on the properties, or limitations, of psi encourages a further suspicion: that parapsychologists are, by motivation, not problem-solvers but mystery-mongers.

But to these suspicious features we must add an even more obvious reason for doubt: the fact that psi conflicts with the corpus of existing scientific knowledge. This conflict, though sometimes denied, is in fact inherent in the definition of the paranormal as well as in the explicit objectives of bodies like the Society for Psychical Research and the Parapsychological Association. But it is also, in my view, obvious enough at the nuts-and-bolts level: To believe that there is no basic conflict between current scientific knowledge and, for example, the ability to read "down-through" a deck of cards thousands of miles away in a place whose location is not even exactly known is to deceive oneself—I would say grossly and absurdly.

If psi does involve a fundamental conflict with existing science, then this is an extremely strong argument for caution; for this scientific understanding is founded on a body of experimentation and scholarly thought far more extensive than the whole corpus of parapsychology. The evidence needed to overturn such a huge volume of work would have to be extremely powerful.

Finally, a fifth reason for doubt: the constant crumbling of the evidence in the face of skeptical criticism. The history of parapsychology is full of experiments, initially proclaimed as exceptionally convincing or crucial, that are ultimately shown to contain basic flaws. When this happens, they retire into obscurity but are soon replaced by more recent experiments that skeptics have not yet had time to investigate. Often the process takes a long time. Exposure of the Soal-Shackleton experiments as fraudulent involved six researchers over a period of 35 years, and even then was made possible only because Soal, like President Nixon, kept copies of the ultimately fatal evidence (though, again like Nixon, he tried his best to prevent their use by his critics). Perhaps the only important psi research that has more or less stood the test of time is the work of Helmut Schmidt, but it is also striking that Schmidt's experiments are much less fully documented than most of the famous series in parapsychology. Schmidt has systematically avoided the detailed reporting of results that other parapsychologists have accepted as obligatory. All of this provides another injection of fuel to keep the fires of skepticism burning. Where so much of the "best" work has proved faulty or fraudulent, and so much of what remains is inaccessible to the critics, it is natural to suspect that if the critics had sufficient time and full enough access to original materials there might be nothing of the evidence to survive.

It is the role—the duty, perhaps—of the skeptic to keep this pot boiling by constant critical examination of the new crucial experiments as they arise. Let me therefore report briefly on two attempts at this kind of assessment with which I have been involved.

In the July 1980 issue of *Zetetic Scholar*, John Beloff listed seven "evidential experiments," presumably representing the best available evidence for psi phenomena. The first of these was the Brugmans (or Heymans) experiment, carried out in 1920, and I selected this for careful re-examination. For detailed results see *Zetetic Scholar*, Nos. 6 and 7.

To indicate his response, the subject pointed to the appropriate square on a kind of chessboard, and this was observed from the room above through a glass window in the ceiling. We do not know who recorded the response, and we do not know whether this person was ignorant of the target. To rely on recording of the response by a person who knows the target would be inadmissible in any modern study. We know that the response was frequently ambiguous (27 percent of the unsuccessful calls were explicitly recorded as ambiguous). With the subject's finger wandering over the board, two crucial elements are the method of signaling the start of a trial and the method of signaling the moment of response. On the first point, all contemporary reports are silent; the only report is second-hand, 18 years after the event, and not fully explicit. On the second point the first report suggests an inadequate signal ("pressing down with the finger"); the second report is silent; and the third report, dated three years after the experiment, is reassuring ("subject tapped twice").

Subsequent publications, including an important rehabilitation of the experiment by Schouten and Kelly in 1978, have always accepted the third, reassuring report and the second-hand, 18-years-after report. In other words, on these issues we see a progressive after-the-event tidying up of the experiment to make it look better. There is, in fact, statistical evidence of biased recording of responses, in that the percentage of calls recorded as ambiguous falls to 7 percent among the hits from the 27 percent mentioned above. The experiment could be explained in nonparanormal terms by supposing that the response recorder knew the target and frequently misrecorded the response so as to agree with the target, taking advantage of the uncertainties I have mentioned.

Turning to my second example, in 1978–79 Francis Hitching surveyed 200 parapsychologists and found that, as evidence for psi, their most favored research was the "remote viewing" studies of Harold Puthoff and Russell Targ. I therefore decided to examine the Price and Hammid experiments that constitute the principal experiments concerned. As it turned out, there is little for me to contribute. A long drawn out controversy is still in course in *Nature* with David Marks as critic. The issue now turns on the exact content of the experimental transcripts and can only be settled by looking at those transcripts. However, Puthoff and Targ have not made them available. I wrote requesting copies but got no reply. Since crucial evidence is not accessible to other investigators, these experiments cannot be considered as falling within the scientific domain. In the present forum, this rules them out from further serious consideration.

Let me summarize. At least three features of the evidence for psi differentiate it from ordinary scientific evidence. Moreover each of these can be seen as supporting the hypothesis that psi is an artifact. Further, I have cited two additional strong reasons for caution in accepting the evidence for psi, and I have given two recent examples in support of the second of these.

Parapsychologists should recognize that, by simple objective criteria, their science is *not* a normal one and that there are good and honest reasons for doubting their conclusions and for requiring from them more rigorous evidence than is often demanded in other sciences. Parapsychology is in a unique position and will need to make unique efforts if it is to convince mainstream science to accept its results.

Comment on the Soal-Goldney Experiments

Betty Markwick's scholarly account of the collapse of the Soal-Goldney experiments as evidence for ESP (Chapter 11 of this volume) serves to emphasize once again the necessity for caution in the interpretation of claims of the paranormal. But it also teaches a more subtle lesson, which deserves comment.

Although everyone now accepts that Soal's experiments were fraudulent, this was not so until Markwick's crucial dénouement. Up to that time virtually the whole parapsychological community was still defending Soal, despite the overwhelming evidence of fraud that skeptics had already assembled. It will be recalled that, before Markwick's findings, we had a report of a witness who claimed to have seen Soal cheating and described exactly what he did. The score sheets for the sitting concerned had been analyzed by Scott and Haskell and showed conclusively the presence of statistical anomalies closely reflecting the reported manipulation. Supporting analyses ruled out the counter-argument that this evidence was "fitted" after the fact. All this was dismissed by parapsychologists as inadequate to justify an accusation of fraud, and confidence in Soal was reaffirmed.

The evidence against Soal was remarkably strong, but it was not strong enough to convince parapsychologists. This is the first disturbing fact.

The second is that the final downfall of the Soal experiments, repeatedly cited earlier as among the most compelling in the whole field of parapsychology, has in no way led to the collapse of belief in the paranormal among parapsychologists. Believers now simply cite other experiments.

Put these two facts together and ask a simple question: If it should be true that the paranormal does not exist, how is this ever to be established? Clearly we would need *very strong* positive evidence of fraud or error for *every experiment* that has reported significant findings.

There seems to be no conceivable hope of achieving this, if only because many fraudulent experimenters will cover their tracks better than Soal, and many of those who make errors will not preserve the records that could prove it. In short, it is highly improbable that the evidence of the strength needed exists for more than a handful of the defective experiments, much less that it can be found. Thus there will always remain a core of positive findings that are, essentially, unassailable even if the reality is that the paranormal does not exist.

This is one good reason why sensible people should always maintain an attitude of skepticism toward the paranormal, at least unless and until a paranormal phenomenon is found that can be demonstrated at will.

21

Is Parapsychology a Science?

PAUL KURTZ

The "Paranormal"

An observer of the current scene cannot help but be struck by the emergence of a bizarre new "paranormal world-view." How widely held this view is, whether it has penetrated science proper or is simply part of the popular passing fancy, is difficult to ascertain.

Many of those who are attracted to a paranormal universe express an anti-scientific, even occult, approach. Others insist that their hypotheses have been "confirmed in the scientific laboratory." All seem to agree that existing scientific systems of thought do not allow for the paranormal and that these systems must be supplemented or overturned. The chief obstacle to the acceptance of paranormal truths is usually said to be skeptical scientists who dogmatically resist unconventional explanations. The "scientific establishment," we are told, is afraid to allow free inquiry because it would threaten its own position and bias. New Galileos are waiting in the wings, but again they are suppressed by the establishment and labeled "pseudoscientific." Yet it is said that by rejecting the paranormal we are resisting a new paradigm of the universe (à la Thomas Kuhn) that will prevail in the future.

Unfortunately, the meaning of the term *paranormal* is often unclear. Literally, it refers to that which is "beside" or "beyond" the normal range of data or experience. Sometimes "the paranormal" is used as an equivalent of "the bizarre," "the mysterious," or "the unexpected." Some use it to refer to phenomena that have no known natural causes and that transcend normal experience and logic. The term here has been used synonymously with "the supernormal," "the supernatural," or "the miraculous." These definitions, of course, leave little room for science. They mark a limit to our knowing. Granted there

---

This chapter is based on a talk delivered at the Smithsonian Institution on April 19, 1978, in a debate with J. B. Rhine. An earlier version was published in the *Skeptical Inquirer*, Winter 1978.

are many areas of knowledge that at the present time are unknown; yet one cannot on a priori grounds, antecedent to inquiry, seek to define the parameters of investigation by maintaining that something is irreducibly unknowable or inexplicable in any conceivable scientific terms.

Some use the term *paranormal* to refer to that which is "abnormal" or "anomalous," that is, that which happens infrequently or rarely. But there are many accidental or rare events that we wouldn't ordinarily call "paranormal"— e.g., a freak trainwreck, a lightning strike, or a meteor shower.

Some use the term *paranormal* simply to refer to the fact that some phenomena cannot be given a physical or materialistic explanation. In some scientific inquiries, physicalist or reductionist explanations are, indeed, not helpful or directly relevant—as, for example, in many social-science studies, where we are concerned with the function of institutions, or in historical studies, where we may analyze the influence of ideas or values on human affairs. But this surely does not mean that they are "nonnatural," "unnatural," or "paranormal"; for ideas and values have a place in the executive order of nature, as do flowers, stones, and electrons. Although human institutions and cultural systems of beliefs and values may be physical at root, they are not necessarily explainable in function as such. There seem to be levels of organization; at least it is convenient to treat various subject matters in terms of concepts and hypotheses relative to the data at hand. To say this in no way contravenes the physical laws of nature as uncovered in the natural sciences.

The term *paranormal*, however, has also been used in parapsychology, where something seems to contradict some of the most basic assumptions and principles of the physical, biological, or social sciences and a body of expectations based on ordinary life and common sense. C. D. Broad (1949) has pointed out a number of principles that parapsychologists would apparently wish to overthrow: (*a*) that future events cannot affect the present *before* they happen (backward causation); (*b*) that a person's mind cannot effect a change in the material world without the intervention of some physical energy or force; (*c*) that a person cannot know the content of another person's mind except by the use of inferences based on experience and drawn from observations of his speech or behavior; (*d*) that we cannot directly know what happens at distant points in space without some sensory perception of it, or energy, transmitted to us; (*e*) that discarnate beings do not exist as persons separable from physical bodies. These general principles have been built up from a mass of observations and should not be abandoned unless and until there is an overabundant degree of evidence that would make their rejection less likely than their acceptance—if I may paraphrase David Hume (1739; 1748; 1779). Nevertheless, those who refer to the "paranormal" believe that they have uncovered a body of empirical facts that call into question precisely those principles. Whether or not they do remains to be seen by the course of future inquiry. These scientific principles are not sacred and may one day need to be modified—but only if the empirical evidence makes it necessary.

Some who use the term *paranormal* refer to a range of anomalous events that are inexplicable in terms of our existing scientific concepts and theories. Of course there are many events not now understood. For example, we do not know fully the cause of cancer, yet we would hardly call it paranormal. There have been many reports of loud explosions off the Atlantic coast that remain unexplained and that some have hinted are "paranormal." (These may be due to methane gas, test flights, or distant sonic booms.) If we were to use the term *paranormal* to refer to that which is inexplicable in terms of current scientific theory, with the addition that it cannot be explained without major revisions of our scientific theory, this would mean that any major advance in science, prior to its acceptance, might be considered to be "paranormal." But then new developments in quantum theory or relativity theory, the DNA breakthrough, or the germ theory of disease would have been paranormally related. But this is absurd. There are many puzzles in science and there is a constant need to revise our theories; each new stage in science waiting to be verified surely cannot be called "paranormal."

In actuality, the term *paranormal* is without clear or precise meaning; its use continues to suggest to many the operation of "hidden," "mysterious," or "occult" forces in the universe. But this, in the last analysis, may only be a substitute for our ignorance of the causes at work. Although I have used the term because others have done so, I think that it ought to be dispensed with as a meaningless concept.

Pseudoscience

It is clear that science is continually changing and growing. As new facts are discovered, existing concepts and theories must be either extended to account for them or abandoned in favor of new and more comprehensive explanations.

In the current context, any number of new fields have recently appeared alongside the established sciences. These begin with a number of alleged anomalous events that proponents say cannot be readily explained in terms of the existing sciences. One may ask, Do these subjects qualify as sciences? One must always be open to the birth of new fields of inquiry. At first a new or proto science may be rejected by the existing body of scientific opinion; but in time, if it can make its case, it may become accepted as genuine. This has been a familiar phenomenon as new branches of inquiry emerge in the natural, social, and behavioral sciences. Unfortunately, not all of the claimants to scientific knowledge are able to withstand critical scrutiny, and many turn out to be psuedo or false sciences.

A classical illustration of this is phrenology, which swept Europe and America in the nineteenth century. It was formulated by F. J. Gall, and developed by his followers J. K. Spurzheim and G. Combe. According to the phrenologist: (1) the brain is the organ of the mind; (2) mental powers can be distinguished and assigned to separate innate faculties; (3) these faculties each have their seat in a definite region of the brain surface; (4) the size of each region is the measure to which the faculty forms a constituent element in the character of the individual; (5) the correspondence between the outer surface of the skull and the brain surface beneath it is sufficiently close to permit the scientific observer to ascertain the relative sizes of these organs by an examination of the head; and (6) such an examination provides a method by which the disposition and character of the subject can easily be ascertained. The theory was allegedly based on empirical observations from which generalizations were formulated. Gall and his associates examined the heads of their friends, men of genius, and inmates of jails and asylums in order to map the organs of intelligence, murder, sexual passions, theft, and so on. The theory seems quite mistaken to us today—not that behavioral functions may not be correlated in some sense with regions of the brain, but that they could be mapped by examining the exterior skull cap and that the permanent disposition of the persons could be so determined. Yet so great a degree of popularity did phrenology enjoy that in 1832 there were 29 phrenology societies in Great Britain alone, and several phrenology journals in America and Britain—all of which have virtually disappeared (*Encyclopaedia Britannica*, 11th ed., 534 ff.). Indeed, I know of only one practicing phrenologist in North America. He tells me he is the leading phrenologist in the world, and that he predicts a revival of the field!

The term *pseudoscience* has been used in many ways. One must be careful not to indiscriminately apply it to budding fields of inquiry that may have some merit. Perhaps it should be used for those subjects that clearly: (*a*) do not utilize rigorous experimental methods in their inquiries, (*b*) lack a coherent testable conceptual framework, and/or (*c*) assert that they have achieved positive results, though their tests are highly questionable and their generalizations have not been corroborated by impartial observers.

There are a great number of candidates for "pseudoscience" today, many of them ancient specialties that still persist: numerology, palmistry, oneiromancy, moleosophy, aleuromancy, apantomancy, psychometry. And there are new ones constantly appearing. Perhaps some may in time develop testable and tested theories.

Astrology—which had all but died out by 1900 and is now very strong—is a good illustration of a pseudoscience. The principles of astrology remain largely unchanged from the days of Ptolemy (first century C.E.), who codified the ancient craft. And astrologers still cast their horoscopes and do their analyses very much as Ptolemy did, in spite of the fact that its original premises have been contradicted by modern post-Newtonian physics and astronomy. Most astrologers have considered astrology to be an occult field of paranormal study; others have attempted to develop it as a science. Yet astrology does not use rigorous experimental standards of inquiry by which it can reach conclusions, it lacks a coherent theory of what is happening and why, and it draws inferences and makes predictions that are highly dubious. Michel Gauquelin is a critic of traditional astrology on these grounds, though he has attempted to develop his own field of astrobiology. Based on careful statistical analysis, he has attempted to correlate personality characteristics with planetary configurations. Thus, for example, he maintains that there is a relationship between the position of Mars and the time and place of birth of sports champions. Thus far, the results of his study, in my judgment, are inconclusive, though his procedure is far different from the usual approach of astrologers.

Biorhythm appears to be another false science. It also claims to have its foundations in empirical data; yet when independent examination is made to see whether its predictions are accurate, the results appear to be negative.

The Need for Replication

What are we to say about parapsychology? Is it a science or a pseudoscience?

Interest in psychic phenomena appears throughout human history, with reports abounding from ancient times to the present. There is a fund of anecdotal material—premonitions that seem to come true, apparent telepathic communication between friends or relatives, reports of encounters with discarnate persons, and so on—that leads many people to believe that there is some basis in fact for psi phenomena. It has been more than a century since the Society for Psychical Research was founded in 1882. In October 1909, William James, a president of the Society, wrote "The Last Report: Final Impressions of a Psychical Researcher," summarizing his experiences (Murphy and Ballou 1960, 310). The Society, he said, was founded with the expectation that if the material of "psychic" research were treated rigorously and experimentally then objective truths would be elicited. James reported: ". . . Like all founders, Henry Sidgwick hoped for a certain promptitude of results; and I heard him say, the year before his death, that if anyone had told him at the outset that after twenty years he would be in the same identical state of doubt and balance that he started with, he would have deemed the prophecy incredible." Yet James relates that his experiences had been similar to Sidgwick's.

More than three-quarters of a century have elapsed since James's comments. Has any more progress been made? Since that time psychic research has given way to parapsychology, especially under the leadership of J. B. Rhine and the establishment of his experimental laboratory. Where there were before only a handful of researchers, now there are hundreds. We may ask, Where does parapsychology stand today? I must confess that for many researchers, both within and outside the field, not much further along than before.

One thing is clear: many researchers today at least attempt to apply experimental methods of investigation. This was not always the case; and the field today, as then, has been full of deception, conscious or unconscious—perhaps more than most fields of inquiry. Even some of the most sophisticated scientists had been taken in by illusionists posing as pyschics. In spite of this there are many parapsychologists today who are committed to careful scientific inquiry and the use of rigorous laboratory methods. Whether they achieve it is not always clear; critics are constantly finding loopholes in their methodology.

What about the results? Are the hypotheses proposed by parapsychology testable? Have they been tested? Here there are also wide areas of dispute. Skeptics are especially unimpressed by the findings and believe that parapsychology has not adequately verified its claims—even though some parapsychologists believe that ESP, precognition, and PK have been demonstrated and need no further proof. I reiterate that, since the chief claims of parapsychology in these areas contravene the basic principles of both science and ordinary experience, it is not enough to point to a body of inconclusive data that has been assembled over the years; the data must be *substantial.* This is not to deny that there seems to be some evidence that certain individuals in some experiments are able to make correct guesses at above-chance expectations. The basic problem, however, is the *lack of replicability* by other experimenters. Apparently, some experimenters—relatively few—are able to get similar results, but most are unable to do so. The subject matter is elusive. It is rare for a skeptic to be able to replicate results, but it is even relatively rare for a *believer* in psi to get positive results. The problem of replicability has been dismissed by some parapsychologists who maintain that their findings *have* been replicated. But have they? For the point is that we cannot predict *when* or *under what conditions* above-chance calls will be made (with Zener cards, in precognitive dream labs, with random-number generators, in remote-viewing testing situations); one is much more likely to get negative results.

One explanation offered by parapsychologists for the difficulty in replication refers to the well-known "sheep/goat" distinction of Gertrude Schmeidler— that is, that subjects with a positive attitude toward psi (sheep) will get better results than those with a negative attitude (goats). Similar considerations are said to apply to the attitude of the experimenter. Is the explanation for this that when the experimenter is a believer he is often so committed to the reality of psi that he tends to weaken experimental controls? If so, perhaps we should distinguish between the donkey and the fox. The skeptic is accused of being so stringent that he dampens the enthusiasm of the subject. Yet parapsychologists Adrian Parker and John Beloff report on experiments at the University of Edinburgh by pro-psi experimenters that consistently score negative results. The same is true of the work of Susan Blackmore (see Chapter 18 of this volume) and others. Most parapsychologists want positive results, but few receive them. Many or most people don't display ESP; or if they do, they do so infrequently. And those few that allegedly have the ability eventually seem to lose it.

According to John Beloff (1977): "There is still no repeatable experiment on the basis of which any competent investigator can verify a given phenomenon for himself." And Beloff (1973) wrote: "The Rhine revolution . . . proved abortive. Rhine succeeded in giving parapsychology everything it needed to become an accredited science except the essential: the know-how to produce results where required."

Adrian Parker (1978) writes: "The present crisis in parapsychology is that there appear to be few if any findings which are independent of the experimenter. . . . It still remains to be explained why, if the experiment can be determined by experimenter psi, only a few experiments are blessed with success. Most experimenters want positive results, but few obtain them."

Charles Tart (1977, 500) says: "One of the major problems in attempting to study and understand paranormal (psi) phenomena is simply that the phenomena don't work strongly or reliably. The average subject seldom shows any individually significant evidence of psi in laboratory experiments, and even gifted subjects, while occasionally able to demonstrate important amounts of psi in the laboratory, are still very erratic and unpredictable in their performance."

And Rhine (1947) himself says: "Psi is an incredibly elusive function! This is not merely to say that ESP and PK have been hard phenomena to demonstrate, the hardest perhaps that science has ever encountered. . . . Psi has maintained an unknown quantity so long . . . because of a definite characteristic of elusiveness inherent in its psychological nature. . . . A number of those who have conducted ESP or PK experiments have reported that they found no evidence of psi capacity. . . . Then, too, experimenters who were once successful may even then lose their gift. . . . All of the highscoring subjects who have kept on very long have declined. . . ."

All of this means not only that parapsychology deals with anomalous events but that it may indeed be a uniquely anomalous science, for findings depend upon who the experimenter is. But even that is not reliable and cannot be depended upon. If any other science had the same contingent results, we would rule it out of court. For example, a chemist or biologist could not very well claim that he could get results in the laboratory because he believed in his findings whereas his skeptical colleagues could not because they lacked this belief. We say in science that we search for conditional lawlike statements: namely, that if *a*, then *b*; whenever *a* is present, *b* will most likely occur. Yet in viewing the findings of parapsychology the situation seems to be that we are not even certain that *b* occurs (there is a dispute about the reliability of the experiments). Moreover, we don't know what *a* is, or if it is present that *b* would occur; *b* may occur sometimes, but only infrequently. A high degree of replicability is essential to the further development of parapsychology. Some sciences may be exempt from the replicability criterion, but this is the case only if their findings do not contradict the general conceptual framework of scientific knowledge, as parapsychology seems to do. According to the parapsychologist, for example, ESP seems to be independent of space and does not weaken with distance; precognition presupposes backward causation; psychokinesis violates the conservation-of-energy law.

It is not enough for parapsychologists to tell the skeptic that *he*, the parapsychologist, on occasion has replicated the results. This would be like the American Tobacco Institute insisting that, based on its experiments, cigarette-smoking does not cause cancer. The neutral scientist needs to be able to replicate results in his own laboratory. Esoteric, private road-to-truth claims need to be rejected in science, and there needs to be an intersubjective basis for validation. Until any scientist under similar conditions can get the same results, then we must indeed be skeptical. Viewing what some parapsychologists have considered to be replication often raises all sorts of doubts.

In the 1930s S. G. Soal attempted to replicate in Britain the findings of Dr. Rhine in regard to clairvoyance and telepathy. He tested 160 subjects, always with negative results, indeed with results far below mean chance expectations. After the tests were completed, he reviewed the data and thought he had found a displacement effect in two cases, which he considered evidence for precognition (that is, above-chance runs in regard to one or two cards before and after the target). Soal then went on to test these two subjects, Basil Shackleton and Gloria Stewart, with what seemed to be amazing results. These results have often been cited in the parapsychological literature as providing strong proof for the existence of ESP. In 1941, in collaboration with the Society for Psychical Research, Soal designed an experiment with Shackleton that included 40 sittings over a two-year period. Among the people who participated were C. D. Broad, professor of philosophy at Cambridge, H. H. Price, of Oxford, C. A. Mace, C. E. M. Joad, and others.

Broad described the experiment as follows: ". . . Dr. Soal's results are outstanding. The precautions taken to prevent deliberate fraud or the unwitting conveyance of information by normal means . . . [are] seen to be absolutely water-tight" (1944, 261). And "... There can be no doubt that the events described happened and were correctly reported; that the odds against chance-coincidence piled up to billions to one (1978, 44).

On the basis of his work in precognitive research, Soal was awarded a doctorate of science degree from the University of London. Even Rhine (1947, 168) described the Soal-Goldney experiment as "one of the most outstanding researches yet made in the field. ... Soal's work was a milestone in ESP research."

C. E. M. Hansel (1966), in his work, found, on the contrary, that the Soal-Goldney experiments were full of holes, and he suggested the highly positive results might be due to collusion between the experimenters and/or the participants, especially in the scoring procedures. Broad responded to "Hansel and Gretel," denying the possibility of fraud. It now seems clear that Hansel was correct. And even parapsychologists now doubt the authenticity of these famous experiments. In 1978 Betty Markwick (1978a; 1978b) reported that there was substantial evidence that extra digits were inserted into the "random number" sequences prepared by Soal to determine the targets in the Shackleton tests. These insertions coincided with Shackleton's guesses and apparently accounted for the high scores on the record sheets. (See Chapter 11 of this volume.) Interestingly, Soal was present at every session in which the subject recorded high scores. When he was absent, the results were null.

Thus the classical tests usually cited as "proof" of ESP often employed improper shuffling and scoring techniques or had other flaws in the protocol. More recent developments in parapsychology have been more hopeful in this regard. Parapsychologists have attempted to tighten up test conditions, to automate the selection of targets, to use random-number generators and ganzfeld procedures, and to design ingenious dream research and remote-viewing experiments.

One might consider the use of random generators in testing situations to be an advance over previous methods, except for the fact that it is still the experimenter who designs and interprets the experiment. Walter J. Levy, who fudged his results, it may be noted, used machines in his testing work. No wonder the critic is still skeptical of some recent claims made in this area. Great results have been heralded in ESP dream research. Yet here, too, there are many examples of failed replication. For example, David Foulkes, R. E. L. Masters, and Jean Houston attempted to repeat the results obtained at the Maimonides laboratory with Robert van Castle, a high-scoring subject, but they met with no success at all. Charles Honorton has reported what he considers to be impressive results using ganzfeld techniques (in which subjects are deprived of sensory stimulation). To date there have been upward of 42 published studies. Some parapsychologists claim they are significant. Ray Hyman has carefully evaluated those studies and found them inconclusive. (See Chapter 1 of this volume.) Given the sad experience in the past with other alleged breakthroughs, we should be cautious until we can replicate results ourselves. Moreover, we do not know how many negative results go unreported. (I should say that I have never had positive results in any testing of my students over the years.) Parker, Miller, and Beloff in 1976 used the ganzfeld method to test the relation of altered states of consciousness and ESP and reported nonsignificant results: "A total of over 30 independent tests were conducted on the data without a single significance emerging. Whatever way we look at the results, they not only detract from the reliability of the ganzfeld, but also argue against the view that psychological conditions are the sole mediating variable of the experimenter effect" (Parker 1978).

Similarly, Targ and Puthoff at the Stanford Research Institute, in widely reported remote-viewing experiments, have allegedly achieved results that have been replicated. But the critic has many unanswered questions about the method of target selection and the procedures for grading "hits." Given their shockingly sloppy work with Uri Geller, Ingo Swann, and other "super-psychics" in the laboratory, the skeptic cannot help but be unconvinced by their claimed results.

The Need to Convince Skeptics

The accounts above have been introduced as a general comment on the field of parapsychological research: If parapsychology is to progress, then it will need to answer the concerns of its critics about the reliability of the evidence and the replicability of the results.

But difficulties become even more pronounced when we examine other kinds of inquiries that go on in this field; for the parapsychological literature contains the most incredibly naive research reports along with the most sophisticated. A perusal of the parapsychological literature reveals the following topics: clairvoyance, telepathy, precognition, psychokinesis, levitation, poltergeists, materialization, dematerialization, psychic healing, psychometry, psychic surgery, psychic photography, aura readings, out-of-body experiences, reincarnation, retrocognition, tape recordings of the voices of the dead, hauntings, apparitions, life after life, regression to an earlier age, and so on.

We now face a puzzling situation. There has been a marked proliferation of claims of the paranormal in recent years, many of them highly fanciful. Presumably, scientific researchers should not be held responsible for the dramatization of results by fiction writers. Yet some parapsychologists have aided, whether consciously or unconsciously, the breakdown in critical judgment about the paranormal. Few parapsychologists have attempted to discourage hasty generalizations based on their work. There are often extraordinary claims made about psychic phenomena, yet there are no easily determinable objective standards for testing them. Because parapsychologists are interested in a topic and do some research, it is said by some that, ipso facto, it is validated by science. (Lest one think that I am exaggerating, one should consult the *Handbook of Parapsychology,* the most recent comprehensive compilation in the field, which includes discussions of psychic photography, psychic healing, reincarnation, discarnate survival, and poltergeists, among other topics.) Professor Ian Stevenson, for example, of the University of Virginia, is well known for his work in reincarnation, which is of growing interest to many parapsychologists. After discussing the case of a young child who his parents think is a reincarnation of someone who had recently died, Stevenson (1977, 657) says: "Before 1960, few parapsychologists would have been willing to consider reincarnation as a serious interpretation of cases of this type [recall] . . . Today probably most parapsychologists would agree that reincarnation is at least entitled to inclusion in any list of possible interpretations of the cases, but [he added] not many would believe it the most probable interpretation."

Rhine was himself more cautious in his judgment and implied that only clairvoyance, precognition, and psychokinesis had been established and that adequate test designs had not been worked out for other areas. If one asks if parapsychology is a genuine science of a pseudoscience, it is important that we know if one is referring to the overall field or to particular areas. Surely the critic is disturbed at the ready willingness to leap to "occult" explanations in the name of science in some kinds of inquiry.

Although Rhine was committed to an objective experimental methodology, I have substantive doubts about his views on clairvoyance, precognition, and PK. The problem here is that one may question not simply the reliability and significance of the data but the conceptual framework itself. Rhine and other parapsychologists have performed tests in which they maintain that they have achieved above-chance runs. What are we to conclude at this point in history? Simply *that* and no more. ESP is not a proven fact, only a theory used to explain above-chance runs encountered in the laboratory. Here I submit that the most we can do is simply fall back on an operational definition: ESP is itself an elusive entity; it has no identifiable meaning beyond an operational interpretation. Some researchers prefer the more neutral term *psi,* but this still suggests a psychic reality. Of special concern here is the concept that is often referred to in trying to explain the fact that some subjects have significant below-chance runs—"negative ESP," or "psi-missing"—as if in some way there is a mysterious entity or faculty responsible for both above-chance and below-chance guessing. All this seems to me to beg the question. If ESP is some special function of the mind, then we need *independent* verification that it exists, that is, replicable predictions.

One of the problems with ESP is that parapsychologists have noted a "decline" effect; namely, that even gifted subjects in time lose their alleged "ESP" ability. At this point, I must confess that I am unable to explain why there are significant above-chance or below-chance runs: to maintain that these are due to psi, present or absent, is precisely what is at issue. How many validated cases do we actually have of significant below-chance runs in the laboratory. Are they as numerous as above-chance runs? If so, perhaps the overall statistical frequencies begin to reduce, particularly if parapsychologists stop testing those who have shown psychic ability once they lose their alleged powers. We still need to come up with possible alternative explanations. Some that have been suggested are bias, poor experimental design, fraud, and chance. There may be others.

Rhine's reluctance to accept telepathy because of the difficulty in establishing test conditions is surprising to some. Of all the alleged psi abilities, this seems prima facie to be the most likely. Ordinary experience seems to suggest spontaneous telepathy, especially between persons who know each other very well or live together. If telepathy is ever established, I would want to find the mechanism for it—perhaps some form of energy transmission, though most parapsychologists reject this suggestion, possibly because they are already committed to a mentalistic interpretation of the phenomenon.

There are very serious scientific objections to precognition—the notion that the future can be known beforehand (without reference to normal experience, inference, or imagination). The skeptical scientist believes that, where premonitions come true, coincidence is most likely the explanation. If one examines the number of times that premonitions do not come true, the statistics would flatten out. The conceptual difficulty with precognition is that, although we allegedly can know the future by precognition, we can also intervene so that it may not occur.

Louisa Rhine (1954) cites the following case to illustrate this: "It concerns a mother who dreamed that two hours later a violent storm would loosen a heavy chandelier to fall directly on her baby's head lying in a crib below it; in the dream she saw her baby killed. She awoke her husband who said it was a silly dream and that she should go back to sleep as he then did. The weather was so calm the dream did appear ridiculous and she could have gone back to sleep. But she did not. She went and brought the baby back to her own bed. Two hours later just at the time she specified, a storm caused the heavy light fixture to fall right where the baby's head had been—but the baby was not there to be killed by it."

If the future is veridically precognized, how could one act to change it? There are profound logical difficulties with this concept. Some parapsychologists discuss a possible alternative explanation for the event: one suggests (without himself accepting it) that the dream itself might have contained enormous energy that forced the calm weather to change into a storm, which cracked the ceiling holding the light fixture. "This alternative, then, is not precognitive but of the mind-over-matter, or PK variety" (Dean 1974, 55).

This illustrates a basic problem endemic to parapsychology: the lack of a clearly worked out conceptual framework. Without such a causal theory, the parapsychologists can slip from one ad hoc explanation to another. In some cases we cannot say that telepathy is operating—it may be clairvoyance; and in others, if it is not precognition, then psychokinesis may be the culprit. (Even an ESP shuffle may be at work!) I fear that the central hypothesis of parapsychology, that mind is separable from body and that the "ghost in the machine" can act in uncanny ways, often makes it difficult to determine precisely what, if anything, is happening.

A number of familiar conceptual problems also concern psychokinesis. What would happen to the conservation-of-energy principle if PK were a fact? How can a mental entity cause a physical change in the state of matter? Comparing the alleged evidence for PK with the need to overthrow a basic, well-documented principle of physics is questionable.

J. B. Rhine (1947, 209 and 214) at times expressed an underlying religious motive: "What parapsychology has found out about man most directly affects religion. By supporting on the basis of experiment the psychocentric concept of personality which the religions have taken for granted, parapsychology has already demonstrated its importance for the field of religion. . . . If there were no ESP and PK capacities in human beings it would be hard to conceive of the possibility of survival and certainly its discovery would be impossible. . . . The only kind of perception that would be possible in a discarnate state would be extrasensory, and psychokinesis would be the only method of influencing any part of the physical universe. . . . Telepathy would seem to be the only means of intercommunication discarnate personalities would have."

Unfortunately, many parapsychologists appear to be committed to belief in psi on the basis of a metaphysical or spiritualist world-view that they wish to vindicate. Charles Tart (1977b, vii-viii), a former president of the American Parapsychological Association, admits this motive. Giving an autobiographical account of why he became interested in parapsychology, he says: "I found it hard to believe that science could have *totally* ignored the spiritual dimensions of human existence. . . . Parapsychology validated the existence of basic phenomena that could partially account for, and fit in with, some of the spiritual views of the universe."

Of course, parapsychologists will accuse the skeptic of being biased in favor of a materialist or physicalist viewpoint and claim that this inhibits him from looking at the evidence for psi or accepting its revolutionary implications. Unfortunately, this has all too often been the case; for some skeptics have been unwilling to look at the evidence. This is indefensible. A priori negativism is as open to criticism as a priori wish-fulfillment. On the other hand, some constructive criticism is essential in science. All that a constructive skeptic asks of the parapsychologist is genuine confirmation of his findings and theories, no more and no less.

I should like to make it clear that I am not denying the possible existence of psi phenomena, remote viewing, precognition, or PK. I am merely saying that, since these claims contravene a substantial body of existing scientific knowledge, in order for us to modify our basic principles—and we must be prepared to do so—the evidence must be *extremely* strong. But that it *is*, remains highly questionable.

In the last analysis, the only resolution of the impasse between parapsychologists and their critics will come from the *evidence* itself. I submit that parapsychologists urgently need at this juncture to bring their claims to the most hard-headed group of skeptics they can find. In a recent review, C. P. Snow (1978) forcefully argues for this strategy. He admits that there are a good many natural phenomena that we don't begin to understand and ought to investigate. Moreover, phenomena exist that are not explained by natural science but which do not contradict it. It is when such phenomena allegedly do so that we should take a hard look. Snow says:

> An abnormal number of all reported paranormal phenomena appear to have happened to holy idiots, fools, or crooks. I say this brutally, for a precise reason. We ought to consider how a sensible and intelligent man would actually behave if he believed that he possessed genuine paranormal powers. He would realize that the matter was one of transcendental significance. He would want to establish his powers before persons whose opinions would be trusted by the intellectual world. If he was certain, for example, that his mind could, without any physical agency, lift a heavy table several feet, or his own body even more feet, or could twist a bar of metal, then he would want to prove this beyond, as they say in court, any reasonable doubt.
>
> What he would not do is set up as a magician or illusionist, and do conjuring tricks. He would desire to prove his case before the most severe enquiry achievable. It might take a long time before he was believed. But men with great powers often take a long time for those powers to be believed. If this man had the powers which I am stipulating, it probably wouldn't take him any longer to be accepted than it did Henry Moore to make his name as sculptor.
>
> Any intelligent man would realize that it was worth all the serious effort in the world. The rewards would be enormous—money would accrue, if he was interested in money, but in fact he would realize that that was trivial beside having the chance to change the thinking of mankind.
>
> It would now be entirely possible for such a man to have his claims

considered with the utmost urgency and rigor. For a number of eminent Americans of the highest reputation for integrity and intellectual achievemen have set themselves to examine any part of the paranormal campaigns. The group includes first-class philosophers, astronomers, other kinds of scientists and professional illusionists. They are skeptical as they should be. This is too important a matter to leave to people who want to believe. So there they are, the challenge is down. It will be interesting to see if any sensible and intelligent man picks it up.

This, then, is an invitation and a challenge to parapsychologists to bring their findings to the most thoroughgoing skeptics they can locate and have them examine their claims of the paranormal under the most stringent test conditions. If parapsychologists can convince the skeptics, then they will have satisfied an essential criterion of a genuine science: the ability to replicate hypotheses in any and all laboratories and under standard experimental conditions. Until they can do that, their claims will continue to be held suspect by a large body of scientists.

References

Beloff, John. 1973. *Psychological Sciences: A Review of Modern Psychology.* New York: Barnes and Noble.

———. 1977. Parapsychology and Philosophy. In *Handbook of Parapsychology,* edited by B. B. Wolman, 757-768. New York: Van Nostrand Reinhold.

Broad, C. D. 1949. The experimental establishment of telepathic precognition. *Philosophy,* 19:261.

———. 1978. The relevance of psychical research to philosophy. In *Philosophy and Parapsychology,* edited by Jan Ludwig, 43-63. Buffalo, N.Y.: Prometheus Books. (Originally published in 1949 in *Philosophy,* 24:291-309.)

Dean, Douglas. 1974. Precognition and retrocognition. In *Edgar D. Mitchell. Psychic Explorations: A Challenge for Science,* edited by John White. New York: Putnam.

Encyclopaedia Britannica, 11th edition.

Hansel, C. E. M. 1966. *ESP: A Scientific Evaluation.* New York: Scribner's. (Revised edition published as *ESP and Parapsychology: A Scientific Re-Evaluation,* Prometheus Books, Buffalo, N.Y., 1980.)

Hume, David. 1739. *Treatise on Human Nature.*

———. 1748. *Essay Concerning Human Understanding.*

———. 1779. *The Dialogues Concerning Natural Religion.*

Markwick, Betty. 1978a. Checks on ESP experimenters. *Journal of the SPR,* 49:897-899.

———. 1978b. The Soal-Goldney experiments with Basil Shackleton: New evidence of data manipulation. *Proceedings of the SPR,* 56:250-278.

Murphy, Gardner, and Robert O. Ballou, eds. 1960. *William James on Psychical Research.* New York: Viking.

Parker, Adrian. 1978. A holistic methodology in psi research. *Parapsychology Review,* 9:4-5.

Rhine, J. B. 1947. *The Reach of Mind.* New York: William Sloane.

Rhine, L. E. 1954. Frequency of types of experience in spontaneous precognition. *Journal of Parapsychology,* 18 (2):99.

Snow, C. P. 1978. Passing beyond belief (a review of *Natural and Supernatural: A History of the Paranormal,* by Brian Inglis). *Financial Times,* London. January 28.

Stevenson, Ian. 1977. Reincarnation: Field studies and theoretical issues. In *Handbook of Parapsychology,* edited by B. B. Wolman, 631-665. New York: Van Nostrand Reinhold.

Tart, Charles. 1977a. Drug-induced states of consciousness. In *Handbook of Parapsychology,* edited by B. B. Wolman, 500-527. New York, Van Nostrand Reinhold.

———. 1977b. *Psi: Scientific Studies of the Psychic Realm.* New York: E. P. Dutton.

22

Parapsychology: Science or Pseudoscience?

ANTONY FLEW

1

One thing has to be said with emphasis at the start: The case of parapsychology is quite different from most of the other paranormal claims falling within the scope of the Committee for the Scientific Investigation of the Claims of the Paranormal.[1] It is quite different, that is to say, from the factitious, but richly profitable mysteries of the Bermuda Triangle and the Chariots of the Gods, from astrological prediction, from the extraterrestrial identification of Unidentified Flying Objects, and from most of the other affairs dealt with so faithfully in that committee's useful and entertaining journal, the *Skeptical Inquirer*.[2] The crucial difference from these other cases mentioned is that there either we know from the beginning that it is all bunkum, or else we can come to know this very soon after serious and honest investigation has begun.

Thus the moment someone concerned to discover what's what, rather than to produce a best-selling real-life mystery, began to probe the Bermuda Triangle story it became apparent that there was no sufficient reason to believe that more ships and aircraft vanish without trace in that area than anywhere else with comparable traffic densities and comparable natural hazards. Again, there just is no good reason to believe that there have been any close encounters of the third kind; nor indeed of the first or second either. The truth here is that the content of visions, dreams, and misperceptions is always in part a function of the wishes, beliefs, and expectations of the subject. So the Chinese, under the old emperors, used to dream dreams of dragons and Confucian officials; but not of Red Guards, chanting doubleplus good Chairman Mao-think. So too Bernadette Soubirous in her nineteenth-century French village had a vision of the Blessed Virgin, as represented in pictures and images in her local church; but not of

First published in *Science, Pseudoscience, and Society*, edited by Marsha Hanen, Margaret J. Osler, and Robert G. Weyan (Waterloo, Ontario: Calgary Institute of Humanities and Wilfred Laurier University, 1980). © 1980 by University of Southern California. Reprinted with permission.

Shiva the Destroyer, as represented in Indian temple sculptures. So, again and likewise, when contemporary North American readers of science fiction misperceive celestial phenomena, what they believe they have seen are neither gods nor dragons but spaceships. Such false identifications are, in one of the finest phrases of Karl Marx, "the illusion of the epoch."

Parapsychology, however, is a horse of quite another color. One of the properly uncelebrated silver jubilees of 1978 was that of the publication of my own first book, entitled, with all the brash arrogance of youth, *A New Approach to Psychical Research.*[3] Yet it is just worth saying that, after reviewing the literature as it then was, I concluded that, although there was no repeatable experiment to demonstrate the reality of any of the putative psi phenomena, and although the entire field was buried under ever-mounting piles of rubbish produced by charlatans and suckers, nevertheless one could not with a good academic conscience dismiss the case as closed. Too much seemingly sound work pointing to the genuineness of at least some of these phenomena had been done. Too many honest, tough-minded, methodologically sophisticated, and often formidably distinguished persons had been involved in this work. Not even the youngest and most wholehearted of Humeans could recommend that we commit it all to the flames as "containing nothing but sophistry and illusion."[4] The research had to go on.[5]

With, it must be confessed, precious little participation by the author of "that juvenile work," the research has indeed gone on. In all probability its sum in the years between is as great or greater than the total for all the years before. Yet is is hard to point to any respect in which the general situation is better now than it was then. Certainly there is still no repeatable experiment to demonstrate the reality of any putative psi phenomenon. Now as then the experts are inclined to construe the night on night regularity of the performance of any stage or screen psychic as proof that the performance is nothing but conjuring. Even worse or—according to taste—even better S. G. Soal's work on Gloria Stewart and Basil Schackleton has been progressively discredited. This work had won Soal a D.Sc. from the University of London, and was hailed by so tough a nut as C. D. Broad as involving, among other things, "The Experimental Establishment of Telepathic Precognition."[6] Nevertheless, not to put too fine a point on it, Soal, who was in his later years to present the crudely fraudulent Jones brothers as *The Mind Readers,*[7] seems to have been faking the scores.[8]

Having so far in the present section labored in the main to distance parapsychology from some wholly disreputable exercises in deception and self-deception, I intend in the remaining three sections to consider three respects in which it appears to differ from all the established high-status sciences. First, its field has to be defined negatively. Second, there is no repeatable demonstration that it does in truth have its own peculiar and genuine data to investigate. And, third, there is no even halfway plausible theory with which to account for the materials it is supposed to have to explain.

II

In his Gifford lectures, Sir Charles Sherrington remarked that the names given to the vitamins were at first "non-committal in order that scientific ignorance should not be cloaked. Under fuller knowledge they are already being christened properly and chemically. Vitamin C is ascorbic acid. . . ."[9] It is now usual for parapsychologists to begin by following this excellent example; although here, regrettably, there is no sign of progress toward legitimate re-christenings. "Parapsychology" is thus defined as "the study of the psi phenomena," "psi" being the name of the initial letter of the Greek word from which our "psychic" is derived. Psi phenomena are divided into two fundamental categories: psi-gamma and psi-kappa. "Gamma" and "Kappa" are again names for Greek letters; the initial letters, respectively, for the Greek words for knowledge and movement. The word "psi-gamma" covers both of what are elsewhere more tendentiously described as "clairvoyance" (clear seeing) and "telepathy" (distant feeling). The word "psi-kappa" substitutes for the equally tendentious "psychokinesis" (movement by the mind).

(i) We speak, or would speak, of psi-gamma when some subject comes up with information; and when that subject's acquisition of this information cannot be put down either to chance, or to perception, or to inference from materials ultimately obtained through sensory channels. These phenomena, or alleged phenomena, are then subdivided in two ways. One distinction is between clairvoyant and telepathic conditions. The idea is to distinguish two kinds of psi-gamma information: that already available to some person other than the subject, and presumably being somehow acquired from that other person; and that not available to any other person but immanent in the nonpersonal world, and presumably being somehow acquired directly from that nonpersonal world. The tradition, strongly challenged yet dominant still, takes a Platonic-Cartesian view of the nature of man for granted. So it describes the former as mind to mind, the latter as matter to mind.

The other distinction refers to temporal order. If the information produced in or by the subject is only going to become normally available in the future, then it is usual to speak of paranormal precognition or of precognitive psi-gamma. With appropriate alternations the same formula will give the meanings of "paranormal retrocognition" and "retrocognitive psi-gamma." When there is no such qualifying adjective we may take it that the psi-gamma is neither precognitive nor retrocognitive but simultaneous.

522 Parapsychology: Science or Pseudoscience?

Once these several definitions are given and understood, it must become immediately obvious that it is inept—not to say perverse—to characterize psi-gamma as a new form of either perception or knowledge.

(*a*) If the word "extra" in the expression "Extrasensory Perception" (ESP) is construed as meaning outside of—like the "extra" of "extramarital sex"— then that expression becomes self-contradictory. It becomes equivalent to "extra-perceptual perception"; and hence, as Thomas Hobbes would have had us add, parallel to "incorporeal substance." If, on the other hand, "extrasensory" is interpreted as referring to a hypothetical additional sense, then that hypothesis is at once falsified by two decisive deficiencies. First, there is no bodily organ or area whose masking or local anesthetization suppresses psi-gamma. Second, there is no accompanying sixth mode of sensory experience as different from visual, tactual, gustatory, auditory, and olfactory as each of these is different from all the others. For good measure we may conclude the paragraph by mentioning a further deficiency. It seems that the subjects who come up with the information are unable at the time to recognize the deliverances of this supposed new sense and to distinguish them from plain ordinary guesses or hunches or imaginings.

(*b*) Since psi-gamma information is defined as precisely not being acquired through the senses, it really is, as has just been urged, perverse to insist upon thinking of psi-gamma in terms of a perceptual model. It is almost equally perverse to think of such information as constituting a kind of knowledge. For the definition stipulates that the subject must not be in a position to know, either on the basis of perception or on the basis of inference from antecedently available material. If, but only if, subjects were at the time of coming up with the information able to pick out some of the items as coming from a fresh, special, and reliably veridical source, then indeed we might quite properly begin to speak of belief in the truth of these items as knowledge, knowledge duly grounded in that source or faculty. But that ability is no part of the accepted definition of "psi-gamma." Nor would it be sensible to require it by adding a further clause. For it appears that such ability is rather seldom claimed, and never in fact found, among those responsible for what are, on the established weaker definition, ostensible cases of psi-gamma.[10]

Since the suggestion that we have here a fresh form of knowledge is, for the reasons given, wrong, I regret that no one took up my proposal to make the temporal distinctions by applying to the Greek noun "psi-gamma" the appropriate member of a trio of more familiar Latin letters: M (for minus, replacing retrocognitive); S (for simultaneous); or P (for plus, replacing precognitive).

(ii) For present purposes the most important feature of the definitions presented in subsection (i) is that they stipulate what psi-gamma is not, rather than what it is, or would be. In the opening words of one especially thoughtful presidential address to the Society for Psychical Research (London): "The field . . . must be unique in one respect at least: no other discipline, so far as I know, has its subject matter demarcated by exclusively negative criteria. A phenomenon is, by definition, paranormal if and only if it contravenes some fundamental and well-founded assumption of science."[11]

(*a*) There is, I imagine, no disputing but that this must make it harder to establish that there really is psi-gamma: the difficulty of proving negatives is notorious and trite. But some other consequences are less obvious and more disputatious. Take first the points of subsection (i) (*b*), above, and especially the last two; that subjects are not able to pick out items as coming from a fresh, special, and reliably[12] veridical source; and that it neither is nor ought to be part of the meaning of "psi-gamma," that they should be so able.

From all this it surely follows, as indeed is the case, that psi-gamma can only be identified by subsequent checkups; and hence that it is not an independent source of knowledge. Thus, in the experimental work, the only way of telling whether or not we have any psi-gamma effect is by scoring up the subjects' guesses against the targets, and then calculating whether the proportion of hits to misses is too great to be dismissed as no better than what could have been expected by the "law of averages."

The case is substantially the same with what Broad would have us describe as sporadic rather than spontaneous psi-phenomena. There is again no way of identifying information coming telepathically or clairvoyantly save by comparing the hunches, dreams, visions, thoughts, or what have you of the subject with whatever it is to which they may or may not correspond; and then estimating as best we can whether or not the degree of correspondence is greater than might reasonably be put down to chance, perception, or conscious or unconscious inference from materials ordinarily available to the subject.

The conclusions that psi-gamma as at present defined can only be identified by subsequent sensory checkups, and that it is therefore not an independent source of knowledge, carry an interesting corollary. This corollary seems to have been noticed only once or twice, and never discussed.[13] It is that, even supposing that we were able to construct a coherent concept of an incorporeal soul surviving the dissolution of its body, we could not consistently suggest that such souls might first learn of one another's existence and then proceed to communicate through psi-gamma.

For suppose first that there were such incorporeal Cartesian subjects of experience. And suppose further that there is from time to time a close correspondence between the mental contents of two of these beings; although such a fact could not, surely, be known by any normal means to anyone in either our world or the next. Now, how could either of these two souls have, indeed how could there be, any good reason for hypothesizing the existence of the other; or of any others? How could such beings have, indeed how could there be, any good reason for picking out some of their own mental contents as—so to speak—messages received; for taking these but not those to be, not expressions of a spontaneous and undirected exercise of the imagination, but externally provoked communication input? Suppose these two challenging questions could be answered, still the third would be "the killing blow." For how could such beings identify any particular items as true or false, or even give sense to this distinction?

The upshot seems to be that the concept of psi-gamma is essentially parasitical upon everyday, this-worldly notions; that, where there could not be perception, there could not be "extrasensory perception" either. It is assumed too often and too easily that psi-capacities not only can be, but have to be, the attributes of something immaterial and incorporeal; mainly for no better reason than that they would be nonphysical in the quite different sense of being out of touch with the scope of today's physical theories. Yet the truth is that the very concepts of psi are just as much involved with the human body as are those of other human capacities and activities. In the gnomic words of Wittgenstein: "The human body is the best picture of the human soul."[14]

(b) A second important, but too rarely remarked, consequence of the fact that the definition of "psi-gamma" is negative is that the concept itself (not just the best available evidence that psi-gamma does in fact have some application) is essentially statistical. Consider first a standard experiment in which a subject guesses through a well-shuffled pack of Zener cards—five sets of five identical cards—while an agent, suitably concealed from the subject, exposes to himself, and briefly contemplates, each card in turn. We are, that is, supposing telepathic as opposed to clairvoyant conditions. And suppose that, after this procedure has been many times repeated, it emerges that the subject has scored significantly better, or worse, than the expected chance average rate of one in five. Then on the face of it we have a case of psi-gamma.

But now notice that we have absolutely no way of picking out from the series any single hit, or any collection of particular hits, and identifying this, or these, as due to the subject's psi-capacity rather than to chance. Or, rather, that is misleading; it is not that we as a matter of fact at this time cannot thus divide the singly paranormal from the singly normal. The crux is that no meaning has been given to this distinction: psi-gamma just is understood as a factor that manifests itself, if at all, only in the occurrence of significant deviations from mean chance expectation over a series of guesses—or over a series of whatever else it may be.

This is also one of the reasons why it is misleading to speak of a subject who puts up a score significantly better, or worse, than mean chance expectation as doing this *by* or *by means of* telepathy, clairvoyance, or other paranormal power. For while it remains possible, at least as far as the present consideration goes, for theorists to hypothesize some so far unrecognized kind of radiation through which information is conveyed to subjects; still psi-gamma is at this time defined as precisely not the product of any means we can think of.[15] If the subject used the methods of the conjurer, or cheated by stealing a peek at the target cards, or had some hand in the determination of their values, then the results are on these grounds disqualified as not genuine psi-gamma.

Some have thought to dismiss the contention of this subsection on the ground that it does not apply to sporadic psi-gamma. But it does. Consider, for instance, the person who—"on the night when that great ship went down"—had had a dream that both the dreamer and the parapsychologists are inclined to rate as telepathic. Their case will rest, not upon any particular correspondence between the dream images and the reality, but upon the total amount of that correspondence. A perfect fit of the whole would be the sum of fits at every particular point. Once again, there is no way of determining, and no sense in asking, which of these particular fits should be scored to chance and which to psi-gamma.

(iii) In this paper I am concentrating on psi-gamma, without asking systematically how much of what I say applies to psi-kappa. But I cannot leave the point about the essentially statistical character of the former without—not for the first time—drawing attention to a most remarkable fact. The fact is that all the evidence for the latter, and almost all the work on it, is similarly statistical. Yet the concept of psi-kappa is not. In the Glossary printed in every issue of the *Journal of Parapsychology* "psi-kappa (PK)" is defined as "the direct influence exerted on a physical system by a subject without any known intermediate physical energy or instrumentation." More popularly, it is the putative power to move something, or at least to impress a force upon it, by just willing, and without touching it or employing any electrical or mechanical device to bring this result about.

Now, it should be immediately obvious that there is no analogue here for those mere chance correspondences that investigators of psi-gamma through their statistical calculations labor to discount. There seems to be no a priori reason why psi-kappa should have to be detected and studied as the production, by a subject just "willing," of a significant surplus of sixes among the falls of dice mechanically rolled ten or more at a time; rather than as the production, by the same subject just "willing," of particular single movements in some highly sensitive and scrupulously shielded physical instrument. On the contrary: it would seem a priori far more likely that subjects would be able to direct their— shall we say?—willpower at a single stationary target than at (presumably at most one or two of the) several dice moving rapidly yet raggedly in midair. For would not such direction require a find-fix-and-strike mechanism comparable with what is needed in an antiballistic missile (ABM) defence system?[16]?

Of course nature neither has to be nor is slave to our notions of the a priori probable or improbable. So it may be that in fact it is easier or only possible to deploy the force—May the force be with you, investigators!—against either a confusion of dice spinning in midair or a jostling mob of paramecia. But the observation of the present subsection must still raise questions about experimenters who seem never in the first decade or so, and rarely later, either to have effected tests of the most obvious kind, or to have provided any rationale for their long-sustained refusal to do so. Rhine, I believe, spoke truer than he either knew or would have cared to know when, in 1947, he insisted: "The most revealing fact about PK is its close tie up with ESP. . . ."[17] For the uncanny resemblances between, on the one hand, the methods and findings of the experimental investigation of psi-gamma and, on the other hand, those of psi-kappa, do in truth constitute strong, though much less than decisive, reason for concluding that what we have in both cases is evidence, not so much of some previously unrecognized personal power, but rather of a lot of fraud, self-deception or incompetence—and maybe of some real statistical oddities not significant of causal connections. There certainly is "Something Very Unsatisfactory" about what is supposed to be evidence of putative personal power, yet in which there seem to be no close concomitant variations between the effects alleged and any psychological variables in the supposed effectors.[18]

III

One of the most important similarities between the two main subareas of the field of parapsychological experimentation is that, typically, the work of one investigator cannot be repeated by another, not even when the second is able to use the same subjects as the first.[19] This fact is one of several that give purchase for the representation here of Hume's once notorious arguments about the difficulty, amounting usually to the impossibility, of establishing upon historical evidence that miracles have occurred.[20] These arguments were thus a few years ago redeployed in the present context by G. R. Price.[21] This Price, it has to be said, must not be confused with two others better known in this field: the late disreputable Harry Price, who surely faked some of the Borley Rectory phenomena that he was pretending to investigate, and H. H. Price, the most excellent sometime Oxford professor, well known for an almost Kantian integrity.

Hume, it will be remembered, contended "that no testimony for any kind of miracle has ever amounted to a probability, much less to a proof; and that even supposing it amounted to a proof, it would be opposed by another proof derived from the very nature of the fact, which it would endeavor to establish." Confronted by such a conflict of evidence, and—the interpreter must interject—remembering Hume's unfortunate ambition to develop a psychological mechanics, "we have nothing to do but substract the one from the other, and embrace an opinion, either on one side or the other, with that assurance which arises from the remainder." However, for reasons that are not made altogether clear, "this substraction, with regard to all popular religions, amounts to an entire annihilation; and therefore we may establish it as a maxim, that no human testimony can have such force as to prove a miracle, and make it a just foundation for any such system of religion."[22]

(i) A miracle for Hume would be much more than a fact "which . . . partakes of the extraordinary and the marvellous." For, by the force of the term, "A miracle is a violation of the laws of nature . . . ." (A footnote adds a supplementary clause: "A miracle may be accurately defined, *a transgression of a law of nature by a particular volition of the Deity, or by the interposition of some invisible agent.*"[23]) Waiving on this occasion the scholarly question whether Hume himself was in any position to provide an account of laws of nature strong enough to permit this contrast between a miracle and a fact that merely "partakes of the extraordinary and the marvellous," we need first to show that reports of psi phenomena would lie within the range of Hume's argument.

(*a*) There is no doubt but that they would, or do. Certainly it is not easy to think of any particular named law of nature—such as Boyle's Law or Snell's Law or what have you—that would be, or is, as Hume would have it, "violated" by the occurrence of psi-gamma or psi-kappa. What that threatens is more fundamental. For the psi phenomena are in effect defined in terms of the violation of certain "basic limiting principles," principles that constitute a framework for all our thinking about and investigation of human affairs, and principles that are continually being verified by our discoveries. If, for instance, official secret information gets out from a government office, then the security people try to think of every possible channel of leakage; and what never appears on the checklists of such practical persons is psi-gamma. When similarly there has been an explosion in a power station or other industrial plant, then the investigators move in. At no stage will they entertain any suggestion that no one and nothing touched anything, that the explosion was triggered by some conscious or unconscious exercise of psi-kappa. Nor shall we expect them to turn up any reason for thinking that their, and our, framework assumptions were here mistaken.

It is some of these usually unformulated "basic limiting principles" that both psi-gamma and psi-kappa would, or do, violate, and that C. D. Broad formulated in his much reprinted *Philosophy* article titled "The Relevance of

Psychical Research to Philosophy."[24] Broad's formulations here are pervasively Cartesian. They thus provide for "the interposition of some invisible agent," if not for "a particular violation of the Deity." What, for instance, psi-kappa would violate is the principle: "It is impossible for an event in a person's mind to produce directly any change in the material world except certain changes in his own brain. . . . [I]t is these brain-changes which are the immediate consequences of his volitions: and the willed movements of his fingers follow, if they do so, only as rather remote causal descendants."[25]

A Rylean, of course, would attribute any psi feats to the flesh and blood person rather than to his putative incorporeal mind or soul. But Broad, taking absolutely for granted a fundamentally Cartesian view of the nature of man, is instead so misguided as to conclude that it is the supposed establishment of the reality of the psi phenomena, rather than this unnoticed and unargued preconception, which "has undermined that epiphenomenalist view of the human mind and all its activities, which all other known facts seem so strongly to support. . . ."[26]

(b) In their first response to G. R. Price's paper "Science and the Supernatural," Paul Meehle and Michael Scriven wrote: "Price is in exactly the position of a man who might have insisted that Michelson and Morley were liars because the evidence for the physical theory of that time was stronger than that for the veracity of these experimenters."[27] It is important to appreciate why this is not so. Two of the reasons I shall consider here and now; the third is the subject of section IV, below.

First, the Michelson–Morley experiment was not one in a long series including many impressively disillusioning instances of fraud and self-deception. Second, there was in that case no reason at the time—nor has any reason emerged since—for suspecting that the experiment would not be repeatable, and repeated, as well as confirmed indirectly by other experiments similarly repeatable, and repeated. It is these two weaknesses together which lay parapsychology wide open to the Humean challenge, each weakness reinforcing the other. The black record of fraud would not carry nearly so much weight against what might seem to be strong new cases of psi if we only possessed some repeatable demonstration of the reality of such phenomena. We should not be in such desperate need of that repeatable demonstration if there had only not been so much fraud and self-deception.

This is perhaps the moment to perform the nowadays mandatory genuflexion toward Thomas Kuhn's *The Structure of Scientific Revolutions*. Normal science—here to be construed as contrasting with pseudoscience rather than science in revolution—involves "research firmly based upon one or more past scientific achievements . . . that some particular community acknowledges for a time as supplying the foundation for its further practice."[28] Such an acknowledged achievement, if the acknowledgment and diploma title "science" are to be deserved, must surely embrace some measure of demonstrable repeatability. For—becoming now a brazen and reactionary non-Kuhnian—remember that the aim of science is, after discovering what sorts of things happen, to explain why the qualification "sorts of" has to go in to cover the point that, unlike history, science is concerned with the type rather than the token. The formula for the repetitive production of a type is at the same time an initial, no doubt inadequate, explanation of the occurrence of any and every particular token of that general type; while in these two aspects together the achievement of that formula constitutes a pledge of more and better yet to come.

So, until and unless the parapsychologists are able to set up a repeatable demonstration, they will at best be making preparations for the future development of a future science—with no guarantees that these aspirations ever will in fact be realized. One moral to draw from this point, and indeed from the whole paper in which it is made, is that, if affiliation to the American Association for the Advancement of Science (AAAS) is thought of as a recognition of actual achievement rather than of good intentions, then the Parapsychological Association is not yet qualified for admission, and ought now to be politely disaffiliated.

(c) It is sometimes suggested either that repeatability does not matter or that there already is as much of it in parapsychology as there was in say the study of magnetism before electricians learned how to construct artificial magnets, or as there is now in abnormal psychology.[29] But these analogies break down. Certainly alleged star-performers in psi-gamma or psi-kappa are, like natural lodestones or calculating boys, rare. But, when the latter are found, different investigators regularly repeat the same results. The same, unfortunately, is not true with psi.

Nor will it do to dismiss the demand for repeatability as arbitrary or unreasonable. For, if only it could be satisfied, then parapsychology would escape the Humean challenge. But, as it is, any piece of work claiming to show that psi-phenomena have occurred is in effect a miracle story. So, in order to form the best estimate we can of what actually happened, we have to resort to the methods of critical history. This means that we have to interpret and assess the available evidence in light of all we know, or think we know, about what is probable or improbable, possible or impossible. But now, as we saw earlier in the present subsection, psi phenomena are implicitly defined in terms of the violation of some of our most fundamental and best evidenced notions of contingent impossibility. So, even before any Humean allowance is made for the special corruptions afflicting this particular field, it would seem that our historical verdict will have to be, at best, an appropriately Scottish, and dampening: "Not proven."

(ii) Hume started with a general argument about the difficulty of establishing upon historical evidence the occurrence of a miracle. He then proceeded to contend that this difficulty is compounded when the miracle stories in question have "regard to . . . popular religions." So much so that he felt entitled to conclude "that no human testimony can have such force as to prove a miracle, and make it a just foundation for any such system of religion."

Whatever force Hume's worldly contentions here may have must bear equally against the miracle stories of parapsychology. For the Founding Fathers unanimously believed that to establish the reality of what we now call the psi phenomena would be to refute philosophical materialism, thus opening the way to an empirically grounded doctrine of personal survival, even personal immortality. Frederic Myers, for instance, in his 1900 presidential address to the original Society for Psychical Research (London) said, in as many words, that their goal was to provide "the preamble of all religions," and to become able to proclaim: "Thus we demonstrate that a spiritual world exists, a world of independent and abiding realities, not a mere 'epiphenomenon' or transitory effect of the material world."[30]

Again, Henry Sidgwick in his own second presidential address, speaking of the motives of the whole founding group, explained how "it appeared to us that there was an important body of evidence—tending *prima facie* to establish the independence of soul or spirit . . . evidence tending to throw light on the question of the action of mind either apart from the body or otherwise than through known bodily organs."[31] In his third presidential address he added: "There is not one of us who would not feel ten times more interest in proving the action of intelligence other than those of living men, than in proving communication of human minds in an abnormal way."[32]

In our own day J. B. Rhine's best-selling accounts of the research at Duke University present it all as proving some sort of Cartesian view of the nature of man, and refuting philosophical materialism. "The thread of continuity," he writes, "is the bold attempt to trace as much as we can see of the outer bounds of the human mind in the universe."[33] Descriptions of familiar flesh and blood creatures guessing cards, or "willing" dice to fall their way, are spiced with references to minds—their powers, frontiers, and manifestations; their unknown, delicate, and subtle capacities—and the experimental findings are all construed as striking hammer blows for "spiritual values" in the global battle against "materialism." Always Rhine deplores "the traditional disinclination to bring science to the aid of our value system."[34]

It is, by the way, a noteworthy indication of the enormous power and fascination of the Cartesian picture that, as we have seen, even so acute and so unspiritually minded a professor as C. D. Broad took it as obvious that to establish the reality of paranormal human powers is to establish the reality of incorporeal thinking substances as the bearers of these powers, and to undermine the plausibility of the epiphenomenalist account of the relation between consciousness and the conscious organism. Yet what reason did Broad have for attributing these putative powers to such unidentified and unidentifiable metaphysical entities,[35] rather than to those familiar flesh and blood creatures who to the philosophically uncontaminated eye are the ostensible performers?

IV

In Section I, I distinguished, as the third peculiarity prejudicing the scientific pretensions of parapsychology, the fact that "there is no even halfway plausible theory with which to account for the materials it is supposed to have to explain." This deficiency bears on the question of scientific status in two ways. For a theory that related the putative psi-phenomena to something else less contentious would tend both to probabilify their actual occurrence and to explain why they do thus indeed occur. Here we have the third reason that refusing to accept the reality of such phenomena is not on all fours with dismissing the result of the Michelson–Morley experiment. For, even if no one then was ready immediately with an alternative theory, still in that case there was no good reason to fear that such a theory could not be produced. But, in the case of parapsychology now, our investigators have had a hundred years for theoretical cogitation, while there is also reason to believe that at least some of the phenomena alleged are so defined as to be necessarily impervious to causal explanation.

(i) The situation is confused by the fact that most investigators have been, and are, attached to a conceptual scheme whose actual explanatory power they tend vastly to exaggerate. For, as we have seen, most of them, taking the Cartesian concept of soul to be quite unproblematic, are ready to construe any proof of the reality of psi phenomena as at the same time proof of the existence and activities of Cartesian souls. So, as they come to believe in this reality, they forthwith attribute all such performances to those putative agents. When they leap to this congenial conclusion, not only do they overlook the by now surely notorious difficulties of offering any serviceable description to enable those incorporeal somewhats to be identified, individuated, and reidentified through time; they also fail to provide their proposed hypothetical entities with any characteristics warranting the expectation that these could, and naturally would, achieve what for mere creatures of flesh and blood must be simply impossible. If, as C. W. K. Mundle put it in his 1972 presidential address to the Society for Psychical Research (London), "Materialism is to be rejected in favor of dualism on the ground that materialism cannot explain all kinds of ESP, it needs to be shown that, and how, all kinds of ESP can be explained in terms of immaterial minds."[36]

Where detail is vouchsafed sufficient to yield a piece of discussable and even testable theory, the result is almost if not quite always a fragment, a fragment that could at best serve only to explain one kind of psi phenomenon—simultaneous psi-gamma under telepathic conditions. This applies, for instance, both to Whately Carington's proposals about the association of ideas[37] and to Ninian Marshall's physicalistic postulation of the assimilative force by which all physical things tend to make others more like themselves.[38] But the evidence for straight simultaneous psi-gamma under telepathic conditions now appears to be neither substantially stronger than, nor of a significantly different kind from, the evidence for "precognitive" psi-gamma, simultaneous psi-gamma under clair-voyance conditions, or psi-kappa. So it looks as if our choice is either to think up a comprehensive theory covering all kinds of psi-phenomena, and presumably a lot else besides, or else to go back in the end to the position that we could not in good academic conscience adopt at the beginning—that of committing the whole pseudo-subject to the flames, in high Humean style, "as containing nothing but sophistry and illusion."

(ii) Already in section II (iii) I hinted at the great obstacle in the way of an explanation of psi-kappa: This is the problem of describing some believable "find-fix-and-strike" mechanism for directing the force "at (presumably at most one or two of the) several dice moving rapidly yet raggedly in mid-air," and when those dice or larger objects may not be within the sensory range of the "willer." We have now to notice in passing a similar massive obstacle standing in the way of any attempt to explain psi-gamma under clairvoyance conditions. Suppose that someone does spectacularly better than mean chance expectation in guessing the values of the cards in a well-shuffled pack, guessing these "down through" with no one touching that pack until the complete guess-run is later scored. What conceivable mechanism could that subject have employed—unconsciously, of course—to acquire the information needed to achieve such scores? (An appreciation of the force of this question has held many psychical researchers back from accepting clairvoyance even when they have no remaining doubts about telepathy.)

(iii) These are both formidable difficulties for the spectator. But the obstacle barring the way to any explanations that accept the genuineness of P psi-gamma (precognition) is an altogether different kind, and totally decisive. For if the various conditions usually specified as essential to a genuine case of P psi-gamma are in truth all satisfied simultaneously, then what is going on just is not susceptible to explanation in terms of causes or of causally interpretable natural laws. It is significant that when Broad offered a theory "to explain precognition" he added this warning: ". . . notice that, on the theory of 'precognition,' no event is ever 'precognized' in the strict and literal sense."[39]

The crux is that inexplicability is built into what is here rather oddly called "the strict and literal sense" of (paranormal) precognition. For consider, to start with we must have highly significant correlations between what someone says, or does, or experiences and what later is said, or done, or happens. But, though necessary, this is by no means sufficient. If the subject played any part in bringing about those later ongoings, then that would be enough to disqualify that subject's anticipations as a case of P psi-gamma. Suppose next that the correlation between these anticipations and their later fulfillment could be explained in terms of some common causal ancestry; maybe the guesser is an identical twin of the person choosing the targets, and they share genetically determined patterns of guessing and choosing dispositions. Here too the correlations would be disqualified: It is indeed mainly in order to avoid disqualification by reference to a common causal ancestry that experimenters insist that the targets must be randomly selected.

But now, what possibility of causal explanation is left? If anticipations and fulfillments are causally connected, then either the anticipations must cause the fulfillments, or the anticipations and the fulfillments must both be partly or wholly caused by something else, or the fulfillments must cause the anticipations. The first two disjuncts are, as we have just seen, ruled out by the force of the (expression) term (paranormal) "precognition." The third is radically incoherent. Because causes necessarily and always bring about their effects, it must be irredeemably self-contradictory to suggest that the (later) fulfillments might cause the (earlier) anticipations. By the time the fulfillments are occurring the anticipations already have occurred. It would, therefore, be futile to labor either to bring about or to undo what is already unalterably past and done.[40]

I indicated in the first paragraph of this final section how a well-supported theory may probabilify the occurrence of whatever it predicts. So I trust that it will not look like a lapse into anti-empirical dogmatism to conclude with a maxim from Sir Arthur Eddington, a leading British physicist of the period between the wars: "It is also a good rule not to put overmuch confidence in the observational results until they are confirmed by theory."

Notes

1. This committee was set up on the initiative of Professor Paul Kurtz of the State University of New York at Buffalo, in hopes of doing something to stem the rising tide of popular credulity.

2. Formerly the *Zetetic,* now edited by Kendrick Frazier from 3025 Palo Alto Drive NE, Albuquerque, NM 87111.

3. London: C. A. Watts, 1953. This book was long ago remaindered, and its publishers were later absorbed into the fresh-founded firm Pemberton Books. But two chapters, revised, are still current in philosophical anthologies: see, for one, Note 34.

4. Hume, *An Inquiry Concerning Human Understanding,* 12 (iii), *ed. fin.*

5. See the "Advertisement," referring to the *Treatise,* added by Hume to what in the event became the first posthumous edition of that *Inquiry.*

6. Compare this article under this title in *Philosophy* (London), 19 (1966): 261–275. Broad was only perhaps the most distinguished of the many who accepted this work at its face value. That throng—or should I say rout?—included the author of *A New Approach to Psychical Research.*

7. London: Faber and Faber, 1959.

8. See, most recently, Betty Markwick, Chapter 11 in this volume and "The Soal-Goldney Experiments with Basil Shackleton: New Evidence of Data Manipulation" in *Proceedings of the SPR* (London), 56 (1978): 250–278. Compare D. J. West, "Checks on ESP Experimenters" in the *Journal* of the same society, 59 (1978): 897–899, also further references given in these articles and in Edward Girden, "Parapsychology," Chapter 14 of E. C. Carterette and M. P. Friedman, eds., *Handbook of Perception,* vol. 10 (New York: Academic Press, 1970), pp. 385–412, especially pp. 366 ff. All this sheds a very bright light upon Soal's "calm, but perfectly devastating reply" to B. F. Skinner's contention that mechanical scoring devices should have been employed to reduce the possibilities of cheating. (See G. R. Price: "Where is the Definitive Experiment?" reprinted in J. Ludwig, ed., *Philosophy and Parapsychology* (Buffalo, N.Y.: Prometheus, 1978), pp. 197–198.

9. *Man on His Nature* (Cambridge: Cambridge University Press, 1946), p. 96.

10. Almost everyone embarking on a discussion of "the philosophical implications of (paranormal) precognition" has in fact got off on the wrong foot by first thinking of P psi-gamma on the model of either cognition or perception or both. See, for instance, my article "Precognition" in Paul Edwards, ed., *The Encyclopedia of Philosophy* (New York: Macmillan and Free Press, 1967), vol. 1, pp. 139–150; or, more fully, my "Broad and Supernormal Precognition" in P. A. Schilpp, ed., *The Philosophy of C. D. Broad* (New York: Tudor, 1959), pp. 411–435.

11. John Beloff, reprinted in J. Ludwig, ed., loc. cit., p. 356; the first printing was in the Society's journal, 42 (1963): 101–116.

12. See, for instance, C. J. Ducasse in J. Ludwig, ed., loc. cit., p. 131.

13. See my "Is There a Case for Disembodied Survival?" in the *Journal of the American SPR,:* 46 (1972): 129–144; perhaps more easily found in J. M. O. Wheatley and H. L. Edge, eds., *Philosophical Dimensions of Parapsychology* (Springfield, Ill.: C. C. Thomas, 1976) or—in a revised and retitled version—in my own *The Presumption of Atheism* (New York: Barnes and Noble, 1976).

14. *Philosophical Investigations,* tr. G. E. M. Anscombe (Oxford: Blackwell, 1953), p. 278.

15. So far as I know the first person to make much of this point that psi-gamma is essentially meansless was Richard Robinson. See his contribution to the Symposium "Is Psychical Research Relevant to Philosophy?" originally published in the *Proceedings of the Aristotelian Society,* Supp., vol. 24 (1950), but reprinted in J. Ludwig, ed., loc. cit. The relevant passage is at pp. 80–83 in that reprinting.

16. Compare my "Something Very Unsatisfactory," in the *International Journal of Parapsychology,* 6 (1964): 101–105.

17. See E. Girden, "A Review of Psychokinesis (PK)" in the *Psychological Bulletin* 54 (1962): 353 ff.

18. Compare Note 16, above. The only apparent exception to the generalization in the text is the sheep/goat work initiated by Dr. Gertrude Schmeidler: The "sheep," who believe in the reality of psi phenomena, usually put up better scores than the "goats," who do not. But, even if the findings here were unequivocal, they would not provide the sort of dramatic concomitant variation reported in—and, apparently, reported only in—the since discredited work of Soal: Then when the conditions were suddenly and secretly changed from telepathy to clairvoyance one subject's scores at once dropped to a chance level, recovering equally immediately when the original experimental conditions were restored.

19. Compare, again, Girden loc. cit.

20. I develop and defend an interpretation of these arguments in Chapter 8 of my *Hume's Philosophy of Belief* (New York: Humanities Press, 1961). So here I follow without defending that same interpretation.

21. This Humean challenge was first published in *Science*, 122 (1955): 359-367; but it is now more easily found, along with one or two counter-blasts, in Ludwig loc. cit.

22. *An Inquiry Concerning Human Understanding*, 10 (ii), p. 127 in the standard Selby-Bigge edition. I suppose that "the principle here explained"—a principle that so remarkably ensures that "substraction" of the lesser quantity from the greater neither leaves the greater undiminished, nor diminishes it by the amount "substracted," but instead always yields a zero remainder—is the sum of all the considerations, which Hume has been deploring in Part II of this Section 10, for thinking that the evidence for the occurrence of miracles, which, if they occurred, would support "popular religions," is peculiarly rubbishy and corrupt. The upshot should be that it is all this superstitious evidence that is thus annihilated, and hence that there is here nothing to "substract" from the strong contrary evidence that whatever laws are in question do in fact obtain universally. But this is not what Hume actually wrote; which is, it has to be admitted, just muddled.

23. Ibid., pp. 113, 114, and 115n: italics in original.

24. *Philosophy* for 1949, 24: 291-309; reprinted in J. Ludwig, loc. cit., pp. 43-63.

25. Ibid., p. 46: italics in original. This principle is Broad's "(2) Limitations of the Action of Mind on Matter."

26. Ibid., p. 63; and perhaps compare my *A Rational Animal* (Oxford: Clarendon, 1978).

27. J. Ludwig, loc. cit., pp. 187-188.

28. (Chicago: University of Chicago Press, 1962), p. 10.

29. For the second of these see M. Scriven, "The Frontiers of Psychology" in R. G. Colodny, ed., *Frontiers of Science and Philosophy* (Pittsburgh: University of Pittsburgh Press, 1962), reprinted in Wheatley and Edge, eds., loc. cit., pp. 46-75. The relevant paragraphs are in this reprint at pp. 64-65.

30. *Proceedings of the SPR*, 15: 117.

31. Ibid., 5: 272-273.

32. Ibid., 5: 401.

34. *Telepathy and the Human Personality* (London: Society for Psychical Research,

1950), p. 36. For critiques of such Cartesian misconstructions compare: first, my "Minds and Mystifications," in *The Listener,* 46 (1951): 501–502, reprinted in P. A. French, ed., *Philosophers in Wonderland* (St. Paul, Minn.: Llewellyn, 1975), pp. 163–167; and, second, "Describing and Explaining," in the book mentioned in Note 3, revised and reprinted in J. Ludwig, ed., loc. cit., pp. 207–227.

35. Compare Terence Penelhum "Survival and Disembodied Existence," a potpourri from his book under the same title, cooked up specially for inclusion in Wheatley and Edge, loc cit., pp. 308–329.

36. "Strange Facts in Search of a Theory," in Wheatley and Edge, loc. cit., pp. 76–97; the sentence quoted is at p. 88.

37. *Matter, Mind and Meaning* (London: Methuen, 1949), pp. 203 ff.

38. "ESP and Memory: A Physical Theory," in the *British Journal for the Philosophy of Science,* 10 (1960): 265–286.

39. *Religion, Philosophy and Psychical Research* (London: Routledge and Kegan Paul, 1953), p. 80.

40. Compare the unusually hard-hitting symposium "Can an Effect Precede Its Cause?" in *Proceedings of the Aristotelian Society,* Supp., vol. 28 (1954): 27–62. By altogether ignoring the second contribution A. J. Ayer contrives to repeat in his *The Problem of Knowledge* (Harmondsworth: Penguin, 1956), pp. 170–175, the main mistakes of the first.

Nowadays someone is likely to object that modern physics gives hospitability to the notion of backward causation. Here I can and will do no more about this than quote yet again from Broad, this time pillaging his contribution to J. R. Smythies, ed., *Science and ESP* (London: Routledge and Kegan Paul, 1967), p. 195: "May I add that it would not be enough to cite eminent physicists who talk as if they believed this. What is nonsense if interpreted literally, is no less nonsense, if so interpreted, when talked by eminent physicists in their professional capacity. But when a way of talking, which is nonsensical if interpreted literally, is found to be useful by distinguished scientists in their own sphere, it is reasonable for the layman to assume that it is convenient shorthand for something which is intelligible but would be very complicated to state in accurate literal terms."

23

Parapsychology As a "Spiritual" Science

JAMES E. ALCOCK

Parapsychology, once the despised outcast of a materialistically-oriented ortho-doxy, may now claim pride of place among the spiritual sciences, for it was parapsychology which pioneered the exploration of the world beyond the senses.

J. L. Randall, *Parapsychology and the Nature of Life*

Whether in séance parlors, in "haunted" houses, in simple laboratories using decks of cards and rolling dice, or in sophisticated research centers employing equipment of the atomic age, the search for psychic ("psi") forces has been under way, in the name of science, for more than a century. The quest to demonstrate the reality of these putative forces which are said to lie beyond the realm of ordinary nature, at least insofar as it is known by modern science, has not been an easy one. Yet, despite the slings and arrows of sometimes outrageous criticism, many men and women have dedicated themselves over the years to the pursuit of psi and to the task of attempting to convince skeptical scientists of the necessity of taking the psi hypothesis seriously.

Many, too, are the people who have come and gone who have claimed to possess psychic powers. From those who can allegedly predict the future or influence delicate processes at the subatomic level to those who are supposedly able to project their thoughts onto photographic film or to bend forks and spoons by sheer will-power, from "healers" who can apparently demonstrate their psychic powers by retarding the growth of laboratory fungi to people whose minds can ostensibly leave and subsequently return to their bodies, the psychic claimants have offered a vision of an extraordinary world where the power of the mind can overcome the material limitations imposed by flesh and blood, atoms and mole-cules, space and time. Many such claims are sensational and unworthy of any serious attention, being more at home in the pages of the *National Enquirer* than in the journals of science. Yet there exists a substantial corpus of experimental work that has been executed with considerable care and with dedication to the traditions and canons of scientific methodology and that is claimed by para-

537

psychologists to substantiate the hypothesis that psi does exist.

Wherever one stands in the debate about parapsychological claims, it is important to recognize that experimental parapsychology, at its best, should never be confused with the tea-readers and professional psychics who earn their livelihoods from performing miracles upon demand. Professional parapsychologists are for the most part dedicated to the principles and methods of science, and in many ways professional parapsychology operates in much the same manner as any other discipline that wears or aspires to wear the mantle of Science. There are research laboratories dedicated to parapsychological research. There are annual research meetings and symposia at which empirical findings and theoretical ideas are discussed. There are peer-reviewed technical journals in which the best of parapsychological research is published. There are research grants, including some from government, albeit much too few in number from the point of view of parapsychologists. Parapsychological courses are taught at a number of universities around the world, and in some universities, undergraduate and advanced degrees are awarded for parapsychological study and research. The Parapsychological Association, an organization of professional researchers founded in 1957 by J. B. Rhine, has been affiliated with the prestigious American Association for the Advancement of Science (AAAS) since 1969. Parapsychologists can also point with pride to a number of prominent scientists who, over the years, have come out in support of paranormal claims.

On the basis of the summary above, one would expect that parapsychology would enjoy the same status as any other research discipline. Yet, despite all this, the scientific establishment continues today, as it did a century ago, to refuse to recognize the existence of psychic ("psi") phenomena, claiming that parapsychological studies have been riddled by experimental artifacts resulting from poor methodology, by overinterpretation of weak and nonreplicable effects, and even by fraud. The Parapsychological Association's affiliation with the AAAS notwithstanding, most scientists do not take psychic forces seriously. As J. McClenon (1982) found in his survey of "elite scientists" (all of them Council members or selected section committee members of the AAAS), only 29 percent were favorably disposed toward extrasensory perception (ESP), while 50 percent considered it to be a remote possibility or an impossibility. That this is frustrating for parapsychologists, there is no doubt; however, this chilly reception in the halls of science seems only to strengthen their resolve to establish the reality of psi.

I have elsewhere evaluated paranormal claims (Alcock 1981) and my own conclusion is straightforward: There has been no evidence adduced for the paranormal that cannot be explained more parsimoniously, and, for me at least, more compellingly, in terms of "normal" science and psychology. Moreover, an understanding of the psychology of human perception, cognition, and behavior suggests that, even if psi phenomena were not to exist, the kinds of *experiences* that people report under the rubric of "psychic" should be *expected* to occur from time to time. The evidence presented to support the psi-hypothesis is, I contend, the result of the fact that parapsychologists for the most part begin with the implicit assumption that psi exists and then use this hypothesis to "explain" extra-chance success rates in guessing experiments or in experiments in which supposedly random events accumulate in a manner not predicted by probabilistic models.

The invocation of psychic explanations in order to explain phenomena that, besides usually being small in size of effect, are not amenable to replication before neutral observers puts parapsychology into an adversarial position with the natural sciences. This conflict between parapsychology and natural science did not occur by happenstance, since the very definition of paranormal phenomena is based on their incompatibility with the scientific world-view (Alcock 1981; Boring 1966; Flew 1980; MacKenzie and MacKenzie 1980); in order to be considered "paranormal," a phenomenon must be inexplicable in terms of normal science. For example, at one time parapsychologists suspected that a psychic ability might be involved in bats' extraordinary skill at navigating in the dark. Once bat sonar was discovered, the phenomenon was no longer of interest to psychic researchers.

The parapsychologists' interest in and study of strange, anomalistic, or seemingly "inexplicable" phenomena is, in itself, both proper and commendable, and psychologists and others have long been remiss in their tendency to ignore such phenomena. However, research into these phenomena certainly need not, and should not, begin with the idea that a psychic process is at work. Indeed, apparent inexplicability can be due to a number of things, including unfamiliarity with what *is* known in science and errors in human perception and information-processing. Because one cannot immediately provide a natural explanation does not mean that such explanation does not exist. Indeed, Susan Blackmore (1983), a parapsychologist as well as a psychologist, recently discussed the inability of parapsychologists to produce a repeatable demonstration of psi and urged them to abandon the psi-hypothesis even while they continue to study anomalistic phenomena. (See Blackmore's Chapter 18 in this volume.) This advice is sound; only if phenomena were to be found that could not be fit into an existing model of nature would it be necessary to speculate about changes in that model. Unfortunately, there are likely to be few in parapsychology who will submit to Blackmore's radical, and rather apostatical, advice.

Some parapsychologists, of course, believe that psi has already been adequately demonstrated and that the use of psi as an explanation is therefore quite acceptable; however, this viewpoint is unlikely to win any sympathy among scientists, the large majority of whom do not share that view. The evidence offered for psi has been in the form of experiments that to date have never been repeatable by neutral investigators. This lack of "strong" repeatability, in the sense that any competent researcher following the prescribed procedure can obtain the reported effect (as compared with "weak" repeatability, which refers to a situation in which "a given experiment or hypothesis or phenomenon in question has been independently confirmed by at least one other experimenter" [Beloff 1984]) puts the very existence of psi in doubt.

It is important to recognize that within parapsychology there is a wide spectrum of belief about what has been demonstrated with regard to the paranormal. On the one hand are those who believe that the reality of psi has been long since proven and that the time has come to begin working on practical applications of psi. On the other hand, there are those who readily admit that the evidence for psychic forces is hardly indisputable, although they believe that enough has been discovered to justify continued research. Such people are frustrated by the continued disinterest shown by the scientific community. For example, John Palmer is a leading parapsychologist who comes from the more conservative end of the belief spectrum, and he regrets the fact that more scientists don't take seriously what he believes has been accomplished by parapsychological research. He commented (1984, 72): "All this raises the question of whether there is anything we can do short of producing undeniable evidence for psi that would provide parapsychology with scientific legitimacy." The cautious and skeptical scientist may well respond that of course undeniable evidence must be presented before a hypothetical construct that involves drastic violations of the currently accepted laws of nature will be taken seriously. This demonstrates part of the reason for the gap between parapsychologists and most scientists: The former are prepared to accept, at least tentatively, the reality of psi even without undeniable evidence, while the latter, for the most part, are not.

This difference in outlook can perhaps best be expressed through Robert Jahn's (1982) likening of parapsychological research to the search for bizarre, rarely seen, and scientifically unrecognized forms of fauna in a vast, fog-shrouded swamp: Some researchers claim that they have searched and found nothing but shadows and sunken stumps that mislead the gullible, while others report with equal conviction and in minute detail their observations of "a variety of extraordinary beings of awesome dimensions and capability" (p. 136). Jahn concluded: "When fully sifted, only a very few legitimate specimens seem to have been captured, by tediously deliberate trolling of the brackish domain, or by more incisive invasion of its turbid interior, and even these have proven so incomprehensible and so delicate to exposure, and the imposed criteria for their credibility have been so severe, that they have not been fully persuasive. Yet the goal remains alluring, and the search continues."

The goal remains alluring and the search continues. That statement expresses the theme of this chapter, which is to attempt to understand why, after a century or more of formal empirical inquiry, and in the absence of undeniable evidence, the search for the paranormal not only goes on but continues to attract intelligent and capable people who, despite the skepticism and even the derision of some of their more conventional colleagues in "normal" science, press the search with great conviction and great dedication.

The Persistence of Belief

If one is to dedicate one's life to the pursuit of something, one must surely believe that it is likely that that "something" exists. If researchers did not believe it is possible to cure diseases, they would hardly be motivated to try to find the cure. If Columbus did not believe it possible to arrive in the East by sailing west, he surely would have not undertaken his famous voyage. While curiosity can explain why researchers initially turn their attention to the study of particular phenomena, the researcher's belief structure is very important in maintaining enthusiasm for continued research when no convincing evidence is forthcoming. Otherwise, he or she might well decide that the trail being followed was a false one.

There are some very deeply held beliefs that are all but unshakable for the vast majority of people. That the earth is spherical is an example of such a belief; it is extremely resistant to change despite the fact that it flies in the face of our own *personal* experience, which suggests that the earth is indeed flat. The belief in extrasensory perception and other paranormal phenomena, too, is not only widely held but also very difficult to change (e.g., Gray 1984). However, it is not only the general public that is somewhat unshakable in such belief. Researchers into the subject often show unrelenting tenacity in the maintenance of their belief that paranormal forces are real: Despite their professional frustration with the paucity of evidence, and despite the difficulties they face in the effort to win legitimacy in university communities and in the halls of science, they continue to persevere, confident, it would seem, in the view that, just as the great Lavoisier had to come to admit that he was wrong when he denied the extraterrestrial source of meteorites, the day will come when science will be forced to recognize the reality of psi and all their efforts will be vindicated.

It is important, if we are to understand the persistence of parapsychology, to acknowledge that it is an underlying belief in the reality of the paranormal and the desire to substantiate that belief that serve as the driving force behind empirical inquiry. Parapsychological research has never been motivated by anomalous observations occurring in normal scientific research. It is not from physicists' using extremely sensitive equipment in their study of delicate subatomic processes that the claim comes that one must posit the existence of some mental influence on matter in order to explain certain empirical anomalies. If Dr. X hypothesizes that a certain particle should tend to veer toward the left in a linear accelerator experiment, while Dr. Y argues that it should veer to the right, there are no reports that when Dr. X is near the accelerator his prediction tends to be confirmed whereas when Dr. Y is in the vicinity the particles tend to move in the direction predicted by her theory. Parapsychology is not the search to understand the anomalies that puzzle normal science; it is much more the quest to demonstrate that certain anomalies can be found that demand for their explanation the existence of forces or concepts as yet not accepted as possible by science.

The Assay Table of Science

Science thrives on informed speculation, and such speculation has produced a vast number of hypotheses about the workings of nature. Some of these hypotheses have been exciting, some pedestrian; some have been revolutionary and still others simply preposterous. Like a prospector's ore samples dumped with great hope onto the assayer's table, they are subjected to scrutiny in the attempt to find the gold and to separate it from the pyrites and the dross. It is empirical testing and replication that serves as the assayer's principal tool in this case. Of the many fantastic ideas put onto the assay table of science, some have proven golden; many others have not. N-rays, polywater (cf. Franks 1981), the transfer of knowledge from one worm to another via ingestion of parts of the trained worm's brain (McConnell 1962), and the use of milk transfusions as a preferred substitute for blood transfusions (Oberman 1969) are among the many ideas that initially seemed worthy of scientific attention but are now considered to have been false diversions on the path to knowledge. No one today espouses alchemy, despite the fact that in Newton's day the pursuit of alchemy was not seen as irrational, and Newton himself engaged in such research. Phrenology at one time was seen to merit serious attention. Phlogiston theory was, during the seventeenth and a large part of the eighteenth centuries, part of the dominant scientific paradigm, until it was refuted by Lavoisier's research, which established the true nature of combustion. Before the classic experiment of Albert Michelson and E. W. Morley in 1887, it was accepted by most scientists that light is transmitted via the medium of ether, a colorless, odorless, and all but indetectable substance believed to permeate all space.

While belief in the ether and in phlogiston are long gone, belief in paranormal phenomena in the form of divination, prophecy, scrying, and so forth, albeit dressed up with new terminology, continues to flourish on the edges of science. Why should these phenomena continue to tantalize while alchemy and phrenology do not? Why should spoon-bending excite parapsychologists while

N-rays do not?

There may be many reasons for this, including, of course, the possibility that the persistence of such interest reflects an underlying reality of the phenomena. However, one important reason is this: Because the putative phenomena of parapsychology are so delicate, so ephemeral, and so unpredictable, it is all but impossible to show that paranormal phenomena are absent when claimed to be present; this makes the psi hypothesis unfalsifiable. As for N-rays, specific and testable claims were made that could be and were falsified: When Professor Blondlot, the discoverer of N-rays, continued to "see" them even after a skeptical researcher had surreptitiously removed the essential aluminum prism from his N-ray spectrograph, it seemed obvious that N-ray theory was in error. Similarly, it was relatively straightforward for almost anyone with the requisite training to put phrenological claims or the efficacy of milk transfusions to the test. Alchemical notions lost their appeal following the development of the periodic table of elements. However, psi cannot be so readily examined, for it is claimed that even the *psychic* abilities of the researcher may be of critical importance, thus perhaps making it impossible for some researchers to ever detect the phenomena. That being so, it is difficult to imagine any way by which the case for the existence of the phenomena could be weakened. Nonobservance can be readily explained away.

Yet unfalsifiability alone cannot explain the persistence of parapsychological research and belief. Freudian theory is almost unfalsifiable for the most part, yet its hold over psychology and psychiatry has largely withered away. There must be some important *motivation* to continue to believe in the reality of psi and to continue to pursue its study. In the pages that follow, it will be argued that this motivation is, for most parapsychologists at least, a quasi-religious one. Such a viewpoint is bound to anger many in parapsychology who see themselves simply as dedicated researchers on the trail of important phenomena that normal science has refused to study. However, were that the case, one would expect to see much more disillusionment and abandonment, given the paucity of results, than actually occurs. There are several, perhaps many, instances in parapsychology of researchers who admit not only to never having produced a single indication of psi in their laboratories but to not even having had personal experiences of a seemingly psychic sort; yet they continue to be active within parapsychology and to express a conviction that psi is real. Such behavior is hard to understand until one examines the history of parapsychology, until one sees the reasons that distinguished scholars were in the past drawn to the study of the paranormal. In order to understand the rise of parapsychology, it is necessary to begin with the development of science itself.

The Rise of Science

Human beings everywhere have always tried to come to grips with the mysteries of existence through the erection of powerful belief-systems by which to explain them. Both through natural magic, based on the notion that nature operates in a lawful way that can be discovered and then used to control natural processes, and through religion, which is based in a belief in supernatural beings who hold in their power the destiny of the world and all that is in it, humankind has tried to forge a link with nature and with forces that may lie beyond it.

In the sixteenth and seventeenth centuries, when modern science began to form out of a swill of superstitious ignorance mixed with practical knowledge, belief in spirits, witchcraft, and divination was still taken very seriously, not just by the untutored masses but by the educated elite as well. The scientific revolution, beginning with Copernicus's challenge to the geocentric model of the universe, reflected in part a growing sense of dissatisfaction with the dogmatic theological philosophy that had been predominant in Europe for centuries, a dissatisfaction that had already given rise to the Protestant Reformation. As scientific thought developed and spread, the belief in magic began to decline, although the reason that this is so is not as obvious as it might seem and indeed is not fully understood even today (Thomas 1971).

The keystone to the development of science, as K. E. Boulding (1980) pointed out, was the high value placed on the combination of informed speculation and empirical testing, with the latter being used as a check on the former. It was the attempt to fit theory to observation, rather than the use of sophisticated logic by itself, that led to the Copernican challenge to the geocentric model of the solar system, a challenge that began the scientific revolution. Copernicus's ideas, especially as later promoted by Galileo, ran headlong into opposition with Catholic dogma, and this led to considerable friction between the emerging scientific world-view and theology. Yet the degree of conflict between science and religion has usually been greatly overstated (Rudwick 1981). The giant figures at the roots of modern science, people like Isaac Newton, Robert Boyle, and others, in no way doubted the existence of a divine creator, nor were they hindered by organized religion in their attempts to explain the workings of nature. Indeed, it may be in no small part due to religious ideas that modern science arose, for it can be argued that it was principally the evolution of religious thought that gave rise to the quest to discover immutable natural laws of nature. The rise of Protestantism, whether reflecting or generating the shift away from magical thought, brought with it a dramatic change with regard to belief about divine intervention in human affairs and promoted an attitude that was far less oriented toward the miraculous and the supernatural than was that of the Roman Catholic faith.

While the Catholic God regularly manifested himself through miracles and the sacraments, Protestantism, especially the Lutheran and Calvinistic strains of it, downplayed or denied the immanence of God. The Protestant belief in a transcendent God led to the view that the universe is a legal-mechanical creation that operates according to divine law. Thus Newton, Boyle, and others carried out their research secure in the belief that immutable laws of nature, imposed by God, were there to be discovered (Klaaren 1977). Protestantism no doubt further influenced the development of the scientific method through its belief that one could *personally* question theological dogma, for it was necessary to have both the will and the freedom to challenge the Aristotelian pronouncements that had for so long dominated the world-view of the Roman Catholic church.

Yet, in many specific instances, organized religion did do battle with science and technology. This was especially true of the Roman Catholic church in the early days of science. This was partly because the church, under the guidance of St. Thomas Aquinas, had linked theology *and* morality to Aristotelian science, and thus any significant departure from the latter threatened the former. Consequently, as Andrew D. White (1955 [1895]) described, the Catholic church attempted to suppress not only the heliocentric theory of the solar system but many other ideas and products of science as well, from inoculation to lightning rods. This is not to suggest that Protestant leaders were always foursquare on the side of science, for nothing could be further from the truth, although some Protestant sects do appear to have been more tolerant and inspiring with regard to scientific thought than were others (Kemsley 1973). Despite the individual freedom to question dogma, and despite a new view of the role of the divinity, some Protestant leaders exceeded their Catholic counterparts in their zeal to halt the rise of science and technology. However, even when Protestant clerics were outraged by scientific claims, Protestantism as a whole could not mount as effective an opposition as the Catholic church for several reasons: there was a diversity of competing sects; there was no body like the Inquisition to enforce orthodox belief in Protestant countries; and, perhaps most important, Protestantism did not possess the concept of infallibility, so that scriptural interpretation was left to individual judgment, and thus it was possible for individuals to accommodate scientific ideas through modification of their interpretation of the Bible (Russell 1961 [1935]). Yet is is clear that, where Protestant clerics have been able to mount effective protests, they have often done so; the Scopes "monkey trials" and the recent attempts to promote "scientific creationism" as an alternative to evolutionary theory through insistence that science textbooks give equal time to creationism bear witness to the fact that at least some Protestant sects continue to view science as a threat.

It is important to note that during the same epoch that gave rise to science, the late sixteenth and early seventeenth centuries, there was also a sharp recrudescence in magical thinking and practice. As John Beloff (1976, 193) commented: ". . . The challenge to orthodoxy in religion and philosophy, especially to Aristotelian scholasticism, had left something of an intellectual vacuum which science had not yet been able to fill. The result was a great upsurge of interest, not only in the two traditional occult sciences of astrology and alchemy, but also in all manner of old and new systems of magic."

Two centuries later, beginning in the second half of the nineteenth century, there was another explosion of scientific and technological achievement and, just as in the sixteenth century, interest in magic and the occult flourished; this was the very time that modern psychical research was born.

The Birth of Psychical Research

In the second half of the nineteenth century, a number of influences combined to set the stage for the development of "scientific" parapsychology:

1. The growing interest within medical circles with regard to hypnotism and dissociation stimulated speculation about the hidden potentialities of the human mind. Hypnotized subjects occasionally seemed to demonstrate clairvoyant or other psychic qualities, and this aroused curiosity about the possibility of true psychic powers. Although the concept of hypnosis itself was not quite respectable in scientific circles because of a pedigree that tied it back to mesmerism, respectable medical researchers were beginning to assess its properties.

2. Because of the religious opposition that had met some aspects of scientific and technological advancement, there was great suspicion in science about anything that was redolent of the religious beliefs that had so dominated thought throughout the Middle Ages and beyond. Christianity became a target for those who found scientific thought more compelling than religious dogma. For example, Sir Francis Galton initiated an experimental attack on the manifestation of religion with his famous "Statistical Inquiries into the Efficacy of Prayer," first published in the *Fortnightly Review* in 1883 (Hearnshaw 1973). The latter 1800s also saw a number of critical analyses of biblical material, such as Ernest Renan's *Life of Jesus*, which made it difficult for those of a logical, rational bent to continue to accept the Bible as being literally correct.

Ironically, just as Protestantism seems to have been responsible, at least in part, for the changes in thinking that led to the scientific revolution and to the consequences of that revolution that challenged all religion, so too can Protestantism be linked to the birth of psychical research, an endeavor that in its turn ultimately stands as a challenge to traditional religion. J. J. Cerullo (1982) suggests that it is no accident that psychical research emerged in Great Britain and the United States rather than elsewhere; this is because, he says, the Protestant versions of Christianity make some particular demands on the individual: The believer is led to understand his own selfhood in terms of an ineffable, unique, and immortal soul. Yet he argues, as did Georg Weber before him, that Protestant belief systems were also particularly vulnerable to secularizing forces, as a result of the denial of supernatural interventions into the day-to-day world: "During the nineteenth and early twentieth centuries, scientists attempted to move into the cultural territory vacated by religion. But science's alternative view of selfhood (or, perhaps, its failure to provide any singular or cogent view of self-hood) was disquieting. First in Spiritualism and then in psychical research, what we see is an attempt to come to terms with scientific thought while retaining the understanding of the self that religious tradition had transmitted" (1982, xi-xii).

The attempt to save the concept of the soul, while at the same time casting it into a form more acceptable within the framework of science, led to the formulation of what Cerullo calls the "secular soul": "It was a vision of selfhood that whittled down the Western religious sensibility to its barest essence and, in doing so, magnified its most intoxicating assertion. It was a vision of the self that incorporated what had been the supernatural qualities of the soul into the worldly persona itself, with the vitalism religion would truly unleash only after death operational in the here and now. It was a vision of protean man" (p. xii).

3. The Darwinian theory of evolution and the challenge it posed to religious beliefs made many people, scientists among them, uneasy about the future of their beliefs and pushed them to attempt to find evidence of an empirical nature to buttress them. It was Darwin's *Origin of Species* that most threatened the Christian concept of the soul. It was as serious a challenge to theology as had been Copernicus's heliocentric model of the solar system; for, if evolutionary theory were true, it would be necessary to abandon the idea of the fixity of species, to accept that humankind descended from the lower animals rather than having been the special creation of a divine being, and to accept that the world was created much, much earlier than calculations based on biblical descriptions would suggest. As one clergyman in Darwin's day expressed it: "If the Darwinian theory is true, Genesis is a lie, the whole framework of the book of life falls to pieces, and the revelation of God to man, as we Christians know it, is a delusion and a snare" (cited by A. D. White, 1955 [1895], 71).

Catholics and Protestants alike condemned Darwin's ideas. Some theologians argued that "Christ died to save men, not monkeys" (Russell 1961 [1935]), while Pope Pius IX wrote of Darwinism: "A system which is repugnant at once to history, to the tradition of all peoples, to exact science, to observed facts, and even to Reason herself, would seem to need no refutation, did not alienation from God and the leaning toward materialism, due to depravity, eagerly seek a support in all this tissue of fables. . . . And, in fact, pride, after rejecting the Creator of all things and proclaiming man independent, wishing him to be his own king, his own priest, and his own God—pride goes so far as to degrade man himself to the level of the unreasoning brutes, perhaps even of lifeless matter. . . ." (cited by A. D. White, 1955 [1895], 75).

Darwin himself was uncomfortable with the implications his work had for religious beliefs, and Alfred Russel Wallace, who independently discovered natural selection, never accepted that this process was responsible for moral and mental abilities. Some process other than natural selection must account for these, Wallace believed, and ultimately he turned to spiritualism since it seemed to offer to him a "scientific explanation for the development of human moral character" (Turner 1974).

4. The spiritualist movement, with its claims of empirical demonstrations of mediumistic communication with the dead, called out for scientific appraisal, especially since spiritualists presented themselves not as religous worshipers but as empirically oriented investigators.

Spiritualism was a direct ancestor of modern parapsychology. The roots of the spiritualist craze that swept North America and western Europe during the late nineteenth and twentieth centuries can be traced to the Shaking Quakers, a Protestant sect (Dingwall 1929). Ann Lee, a young Englishwoman, joined the Shaking Quakers in the latter part of the eighteenth century and began to show a mediumistic capability. She emigrated to the United States in 1774 and was well known for her mediumistic abilities when the religious revival broke out in 1779. She died in 1784 and was succeeded by others of similar talent. The belief in mediumistic communication with the dead continued to he held by that sect, and in 1837 a series of disturbances occurred at various Quaker settlements: Small girls began to sing in a strange fashion and to describe visions of angels. This was followed by adults being attacked by convulsions that sometimes took them into trancelike states in which they ostensibly carried on conversations with the dead. Their bodies were said to have been taken over and controlled by these spirits, who spoke and acted through them. Indeed, just as occurred later in the séance parlors of Europe, the spirits of the recently dead presented evidence of their identities through mediums. In Eric Dingwall's words, "The Shakers had sown the seed: the harvest had merely to be gathered in" (1929, 329). This harvesting began in Hydesville, New York, in 1848, when the now famous Fox sisters produced their mysterious spirit-rappings. Out of this, the spiritualist mania was born, and a system of belief began to grow up around it.

No doubt because of the high value given to scientific thought in those days, and because of the fact that spiritualism was in part a reaction to materialistic science and appealed to those whose religious beliefs had given way to scientific thought, the spiritualists wanted and claimed to be on the side of science; they saw themselves as empiricists investigating observable phenomena, and they rejected supernaturalism, claiming that natural laws were immutable

(Moore 1977). An opportunity to explore the afterworld without having to give up life or science and without the need to obey biblical injunctions or to believe religious mythology was a welcome refuge for many for whom the struggle between science and theology was too uncomfortable. As Dingwall (1929, 329) said: "The claim to be able to furnish evidence of human survival after death naturally compelled the attention of those over whom the influence of orthodox religion was beginning to weaken."

These four factors, and possibly others as well, provided a *Zeitgeist* conducive to psychical research. It was in this time of previously unparalleled scientific advancement that threatened deeply held convictions about the nature and meaning of life that the first organization dedicated to the scientific study of psychic phenomena was born.

The Society for Psychical Research

The Society for Psychical Research (SPR) was organized in England in 1882. Its objectives included the study of the extent to which one mind can affect another beyond the limits of normal sensory communication; the study of hypnotism and clairvoyance; the investigation of reports concerning apparitions and hauntings; and an inquiry into physical phenomena associated with spiritualism (Shepard 1980). While its working goal was to investigate the mediumistic claims, the SPR's leaders also hoped that they would one day be able to put the existence of the soul on a sound scientific footing (Mauskopf and McVaugh 1980) or, at the very least, show that there is a nonmaterial aspect to the human mind (Cerullo 1982).

It is commonly believed that the SPR was organized by Cambridge scholars who were upset by the challenges made by science to their religious beliefs. While it was just such scholars who formally led the Society and who served as its principal investigators, the organization and control of the Society were actually in the hands of spiritualists (Nicol 1972). Indeed, the very idea for the Society grew out of a conference held in the offices of the British National Association of Spiritualists in January 1882 (Shepard 1980). When the Society was being set up, Dawson Rogers, who was vice-president of the Central Association of Spiritualists, and William Barrett, a professor of physics at the Royal College of Science in Dublin and a spiritualist, decided that they must have someone of intellectual strength and respectability to be the head of the new society; their choice fell upon Henry Sidgwick, a Cambridge philosopher of considerable repute.

Sidgwick and the other major figures who contributed to the founding of the SPR had previously undergone religious crises. Although raised by parents who put heavy emphasis on the central importance of religion in one's life, their education put their religious belief into doubt (Gauld 1968; Moore 1977; Turner 1974). Henry Sidgwick's belief in Christianity had been shaken both by Darwin's theory of evolution, which denied to humankind its special place in the world described by the account in Genesis, and by the criticisms of the accuracy of the Bible made by Ernest Renan. This was very upsetting, since without the Bible there would be no moral code, and consequently Sidgwick sought to find some other basis upon which to anchor morality. According to Cerullo (1982, 41): "Without a solution in the form of a system of ethics on a firmly rationalistic foundation, Sidgwick could foresee little but social chaos and an uninhabitable world. For his ethical system to achieve coherence, Sidgwick found himself required to postulate that the human personality survives bodily death, so that the sacrifice of personal gratification necessitated by social duty could eventually be compensated. Demonstration of survival, for Sidgwick, became something of an obsession."

In order to demonstrate the existence of postmortem survival, it would be necessary to demonstrate a nonphysical aspect of the human personality while the person was still alive, an aspect not tied to the material world and therefore not subject to disintegration upon the death of the physical body. Sidgwick saw in telepathy the possibility of demonstrating the existence of spirit, and he saw in the SPR the opportunity, in Cerullo's words, to "secularize the soul," to demonstrate, in a scientific way, the existence of a soul, without all the attendant beliefs that surround the concept of soul in the religious context.

After Sidgwick became president of the SPR, several of his friends and colleagues at Cambridge joined the Society, including F. W. H. Myers and Edmund Gurney, who became the principal researchers. Myers had a particular horror of the idea of death and the dissolution of the human personality into nothingness. He, too, surrendered his belief in Christianity to the rationality of science. During a life-threatening bout of pneumonia in 1869, he realized that he was no longer a Christian, and for the next year he vacillated between agnosticism and semi-belief; he *needed* religion in order to make life meaningful (Gauld 1968). He then began the search for evidence that the soul lives on beyond bodily death, using as his tool the very science that had robbed him of his religious beliefs. Indeed, Myers wanted nothing less than to build a new religion, a religion whose basic spiritual tenets would be scientifically demonstrable. It was his belief in telepathy that convinced Myers that the mind existed separately from the physical body, and he felt that the spiritual sphere of existence may exist side by side with the material sphere (Turner 1974).

Edmund Gurney also became estranged from orthodox religion; in his case, the suffering in his own life, including the deaths of three sisters in a boating accident on the Nile, led him to reject the possibility of the existence of a kindly God. Yet he felt that there had to be more to human existence than materialism allows; in psychical research, he saw the opportunity to demonstrate the ineffable aspects of the inner person.

There was nothing inherently irrational, or course, in the desire to investigate the claims of mediums. Even Michael Faraday, the great physicist, turned his attention to the examination of table-tilting during séances; he reported that nothing unusual was occurring and that the movements of the table were unconsciously made by the hands of the participants. However, the difference between the approach of Faraday and the approach of the SPR was that, despite their dedication to scientific empiricism, the SPR investigators hoped to find evidence for the existence of paranormal phenomena in order to shore up their faith in postmortem survival and in morality. This is not to suggest that they did not take a rigorous stance in their evaluation of evidence, for they certainly tried to do so, to the dismay of the spiritualists, who left the SPR in large numbers once the SPR investigators' hard-nosed attitude toward mediums became evident.

The Birth of American Parapsychology

No sooner had psychical research formally begun in Britain than an organization was set up in the United States to pursue similar research. The American Society for Psychical Research (ASPR) was founded in Boston in 1885. The officers of this group included four prominent psychologists: William James, G. Morton Prince, Stanley Hall, and Joseph Jastrow, the latter two later becoming outspoken critics of parapsychology. Unlike their British counterparts, these men, with the notable exception of James, had no interest in trying to demonstrate the reality of postmortem survival, but they shared with the SPR an interest in investigating the claims of spiritualists. On the whole, these people were critical of the SPR, viewing it as being in large part a spiritualist organization (Mauskopf and McVaugh 1980). When they were unable to come up with any solid evidence, most of the group lost interest, and the ASPR was disbanded in 1889 and its remnants absorbed by the British SPR. James continued to support psychical research and went on to become president of the SPR. In 1905, James Hyslop of Columbia University set up the new American Society for Psychical Research. However, Hyslop died in 1920, and in 1923 the spiritualists managed to legally assume control of the organization. Walter Prince, who had been Hyslop's assistant and protégé, then founded, under the sponsorship of psychologists William McDougall and Gardner Murphy, the Boston Society for Psychical Research in an effort to keep experimental parapsychology alive in the United States. It was only in 1941 that Gardner Murphy and George Hyslop (James Hyslop's son) managed to wrestle the ASPR away from the spiritualists and again turn it into an organization dedicated to scientific investigation of parapsychological phenomena.

Just as in Britain, disaffection with conventional religion played an important role in bringing people into psychical research. For one notable example, Gardner Murphy, a giant in the history of modern parapsychology, just as he was a giant in the history of psychology, gave up his religious faith because of its conflict with his education. He was the son of an Episcopal minister and, perhaps because of this, the loss of religion was not easy for him to accept. As had Sidgwick, Myers, and others, he found comfort in psychical research, which he viewed as "a potential hostage in the scientific camp and through which he might eventually find his way back to religious belief" (Mauskopf and McVaugh 1980, 60). Murphy saw psi as a means for human beings to reach out to one another: ". . . Because man cannot bear to be sealed up within the little cell of his own individuality he uses to the limit of his powers the senses and the outreaching arms which immerse him in the world of his fellows; that when his senses fail him or his arms cannot reach to those whom he seeks, he contrives other modes of seeking, of which two are through the mystical and through the paranormal" (Murphy 1952, 141).

Throughout his life, Murphy was a driving force in parapsychology, and perhaps more than anyone else in the modern era he brought respectability to the study of the paranormal by virtue of his stalwart reputation within mainstream psychology. However, it fell to Joseph Banks Rhine, who devoted his entire professional career to the subject, to lead American parapsychology into world predominance.

Joseph Banks Rhine

The history of parapsychology would no doubt have been very different indeed were it not for Joseph Banks Rhine and his wife Louisa, for it was the Rhines, especially J. B., who put the study of parapsychology on an empirical footing that was based on laboratory studies.

J. B. Rhine had planned a career as a minister but, as was the case with Sidgwick, Myers, and others we have already discussed, his university studies led him to doubt the validity of his religious beliefs. He grew to see scientific materalism as a substitute for his religious outlook and pursued an education in science that led to a Ph.D. in plant physiology from the University of Chicago in 1925; Louisa Rhine also obtained a Ph.D. in the same domain. However, the Rhines were never totally at ease with scientific materalism. Despite their dedication to the scientific method, they harbored many doubts about strict materialism, and they wondered about the place of human beings in the natural order of things and about the existence of a soul (MacKenzie 1981).

Even before the Rhines obtained their Ph.D.'s, they had become interested in psychical research. When they attended a lecture given by Sir Arthur Conan Doyle, who toured the United States in 1922 speaking on spiritualism and describing the wondrous feat of mediumistic communication with the dead, they were impressed by Doyle's belief that psychical phenomena could be subjected to scientific evaluation. It seemed to them that psychical research might be able to serve as a bridge between science and religion, a view that was to persist throughout their lifetimes (Mauskopf and McVaugh 1980).

The Rhines sought out William McDougall, an eminent psychologist and a committed opponent of the wave of behaviorism that was sweeping through North American psychology. McDougall shared with the Rhines a vitalistic view of life, believing that there is more to human existence than materialism can account for. In 1927, McDougall was appointed to the chair of the psychology department in the newly created Duke University. Shortly after, it was arranged that J. B. Rhine would spend a semester at Duke during which time he would examine, under McDougall's supervision, a body of evidence relating to mediumistic communications. He was to be supported by a private donor, indeed the same individual who had furnished the mediumistic evidence. Thus Rhine's parapsychological career was born out of the study of the survival problem (Rhine et al. 1965). Rhine was soon appointed to the position of assistant professor of philosophy and psychology (in 1929), and he subsequently founded the parapsychology laboratory at Duke. He and his wife spent the rest of their careers, indeed the rest of their lives, pursuing parapsychological research.

To Rhine, it was essential to demonstrate the reality of extrasensory perception and psychokinesis (PK) if one were to have any hope of putting the existence of a soul, or at least the principle of mind-body dualism, on a solid scientific footing. In 1943, in an editiorial in the *Journal of Parapsychology*, which had been founded by Rhine and his colleagues, Rhine (1943, 227) wrote that it was essential to demonstrate "that man possesses ESP and PK capacities in order to make any tentative conception of an existence beyond the transitions of bodily death a reasonable one. Without them, such survival could not occur and be discovered."

As time went on, Rhine became convinced of the reality of paranormal phenomena, ESP and PK in particular, and he began to write about their implications for philosophy and for living. In his book *New World of the Mind* (1953, 227), he said, "But the work in parapsychology does more than refute materialism. It is more, too, than a new method of solving problems. There are, at least, still other definite implications and possibilities. Since this new science has penetrated the physical barrier that has hidden man's true nature from the scientists of the past, it has become literally the science of the spiritual aspect of nature."

In the same work (p. 229), he speculated on the relationship between religious communication and paranormal communication: "If prayer *is* effective and if the thoughts of men *do* reach out to other personalities in the universe beyond the range of the senses, it must be through the medium of extrasensory perception. If, originating in any personal agency anywhere, celestial or mundane, there is an effect produced upon the physical world in answer to prayer, it would have to be a psychokinetic effect, a psi phenomenon. Psi, then, would be the scientific concept of the operations underlying any demonstrable spiritual manifestation involving either cognitive or kinetic effects."

Rhine, it seemed, had done something of which Myers, Sidgwick, and Gurney had only dreamed. He had scientifically demonstrated the reality of extra-materialistic processes, which indeed must put the lie to the monistic, materialistic view of humankind. Toward the end of this life, Rhine reiterated his belief that parapsychological research deals with the same phenomena that gave rise to religious belief: "On the whole, the types of psi that have been quite independently outlined by laboratory research closely resemble the kinds of exchange that religious men have assumed in the theologies that arose out of human experience long before the laboratories of parapsychology began their work" (cited by Hall 1981).

Other eminent parapsychologists shared the view that the existence of psi ruled out materialism. One such individual, Henry Habberley Price, a professor of logic at Oxford University, commented in 1949: "We must conclude, I think, that there is no room for telepathy in a Materialistic universe. Telepathy is something which ought not to happen at all, if the Materialistic theory were true. But it does happen. So there must be something seriously wrong with the Materialistic theory, however numerous and imposing the *normal* facts which support it may be" (cited by Randall 1977, 186).

Likewise, it could be argued, as John Beloff (1976, 19) has done: "If ever scientific materialism should win the day it [is] hard to see how religion, in any meaningful sense, could survive. . . ."

The triumph of materialism would be, for many, the death of existential meaning. It is the fear of this that seems to have motivated so many of the leaders in parapsychology. R. L. Moore (1977) concluded, in his study of the history of parapsychology in the United States, that not only were the leaders of parapsychology motivated by the quest to find meaning in life after having lost their religious convictions, and not only were the people who showed the greatest interest in Rhine's results people who also happened to disbelieve in the existence of God, but "most parapsychologists, from the very time they lapsed into agnosticism, began searching for evidence to sustain the view that individual life held meaning" (p. 239).

In a similar vein, Ruth Brandon (1983; 1984), who has studied the history of parapsychology in Britain, reported that in her examination of scientists who have become involved in the study of the paranormal: "In almost every case I have looked into, the facts turn out to be singularly revealing. Time and again they present a curious dichotomy between the publicly proclaimed spirit of pure scientific inquiry in which the investigations in question were undertaken, and the underlying emotional motivation which prompted those investigations in the first place" (1983, 785).

That the founders of modern parapsychology were motivated by the need to find a bridge between science and religion, by a desire to demonstrate through the methods of science that human personality and thought is more than an epiphenomenon, there can be little doubt. This by itself does not of course necessarily weaken the evidential value of the products of their labors. After all, as mentioned earlier, the founders of modern science were steeped in religious beliefs. One difference, however, is the fact that psychical research was not carried out *despite* religious needs and beliefs but, it seems, *because* of such needs. The quest was not simply to understand nature but, rather, to demonstrate that nature is more than what is dreamt of in the materialists' philosophy, and it has, historically at least, been associated with a dissatisfaction not just with scientific materialism but also with the mythological aspects of conventional religion.

It is important to stress that it would be quite unfair to automatically attribute such motivation to any and all who work within parapsychology. Nonetheless, it would be equally imprudent to ignore the major role that antimaterialistic sentiment has historically played and continues to play in parapsychology. It may well be that modern parapsychologists are not all motivated by the needs that pushed Sidgwick, Myers, Rhine, and the others. Nonetheless, there are prominent parapsychologists even today who explicitly see parapsychology as a bridge between science and religion. Some contemporary parapsychologists talk openly along these lines: Charles Tart, one of today's most prominent parapsychologists, has had this to say:

> Because I was so impressed with the power and accomplishments of the scientific enterprise, I found it hard to believe that science could have *totally* ignored the spiritual dimensions of human existence. I began reading intensively in the fringe areas of science and discovered the greatly neglected field of psychical research. . . .
>
> I had happened upon a partial resolution of my personal (and my culture's) conflict between science and religion. Parapsychology validated the existence of basic phenomena that could partially account for, and fit in with, some of the spiritual views of the universe. . . .
>
> I now understand that the personal conflict I experienced between my religious upbringing and the scientific world view was and *is* shared by many of us. [1977, xii-xiii]

Indeed, in recent years, the parallelism between parapsychological and religious thought has been made more apparent by parapsychologists themselves. This is not to suggest that parapsychologists are surrendering themselves to the charge that they are motivated by other than pure scientific curiosity but only that the similarities between parapsychological phenomena and religion are so obvious that some researchers are beginning to reinterpret religious concepts, and particularly miraculous ones, including prayer, in terms of parapsychological constructs. It is to this subject that we shall now turn.

The Convergence of Parapsychology and Religion

Not only have some parapsychologists seen in parapsychology vindication of their belief in the wrongness of the philosophy of materialism, but there have been many calls to examine the accounts of miraculous religious phenomena from a parapsychological point of view. Indeed, miraculous events that occur in a religious context seem to be drawing increasing interest among parapsychologists in recent years (Grosso 1983). Some take the position that psi and religious forces are one and the same, while others, such as W. H. Clark (1977), contend that it is perfectly possible to separate religious and paranormal occurrences, although there does seem to be a "deep-lying kinship."

R. H. Thouless (1977) argued that reports of miracles in the religious literature take on a new credibility in the light of parapsychological findings and that parapsychology can bring a belief in God back into respectability: "Belief in God or in any spiritual reality has seemed to many people to have become impossible, because these beliefs contradict the expectations raised by the scientific views which have come down to us from the last century. These views regard reality as being bounded by the physical world and necessarily exclude any spiritual world. Parapsychological investigations tend to undermine this 'physicalistic' view of the world and, thus, to remove one of the obstacles to religious belief. . . . Parapsychological research seems to reveal a world in which it is more reasonable to suppose that God and the supernatural play a part" (pp. 175-176).

J. L. Randall (1977, 242-243) made a similar point: "Despite the contempt with which religion is regarded in some intellectual circles, the vast majority of mankind still seeks relief from the misery of the existential vacuum through ritual, sacrament and prayer. Now at last we are witnessing the extension of scientific procedures into these spiritual areas of human experience: is it too much to hope that the result will be a deepening of understanding which will lead to yet another advance in the liberation of the human spirit?"

It is true that, if the Bible or the literature from other religions is examined from a paranormal viewpoint, there is an abundance of seemingly parapsychological phenomena: telepathy, clairvoyance, precognition, mediumship, psychokinesis and out-of-body experiences (Clark 1977; Perry 1979, 1982; R. A. White 1982). Indeed, D. Scott Rogo (1982) devoted an entire book to the examination and discussion of miraculous religious phenomena and offers explanations based on parapsychological principles. Perry (1982, 370) argued: "The paranormal and the miraculous are not identical phenomena, though they overlap; to remove either from the pages of the Bible would be to emasculate it intolerably."

Rhine (1972, 117), too, commented on the parallels between scriptural reports of miracles and the discoveries made by parapsychology: ". . . What parapsychology had discovered and labeled *psi* communication in all its types, forms, and conditions has turned out to have a remarkable parallel to the whole communication system of religion. . . . Had the founders of the religions been working with the 34-volume set of the *Journal of Parapsychology*, or had the workers in parapsychology been guided by the scriptures of the great religions, the parallelism of the two systems of communication could hardly have been more nearly perfect."

M. Grosso (1983, 344) advocates even more interest by parapsychologists in religious phenomena and miracles: ". . . Psychical research branched out in two directions: scientific parapsychology and, through William James, the psychology of religion. . . . The parapsychology of religion would reunite these distinctive strands into one discipline and begin to forge a powerful new science of the human spirit."

There are many other examples of a growing interest in the similarities between paranormal constructs and certain religious ones. R. A. McConnell (1982) suggested, in effect, that religion arose out of ignorance of the true nature of paranormal processes: "What does it mean that throughout history the phenomena of parapsychology have been in the province of religion? Perhaps organized religion is nothing more than the cultural expression of psi phenomena and the truth behind religion may be waiting for discovery by science" (p. 140).

Even paraphysicists Russell Targ and Harold Puthoff (1977) have linked parapsychology and religion: "When man first began modeling the universe around him, paranormal functioning was gracefully accepted as one of the phenomena to be accounted for, and therefore occupied an important place in religion and philosophy" (p. 212).

These several excerpts are intended to help convey the seriousness with which some modern parapsychologists view the correspondence between religion and parapsychology. Of course the former is typically seen as a somewhat mistaken interpretation of the latter. However, it is fascinating, given what has been said about the historical motivation underlying parapsychology that, in a sense, parapsychology not only supplants religion's role of supplying meaning to life and hope about postmortem existence but is now taking over its miracles as well.

On the other hand, there are also parapsychologists who show a decided disinterest in anything touching on religion and yet accept the basic dualistic philosophy that underlies virtually all religion. It is the the the axiom of mind-body dualism, with its obvious anti-materialistic ramifications, that not only links parapsychology and religion but keeps parapsychology outside of science.

Mind-Body Dualism

There is still much in contemporary parapsychology that directly reflects the tradition of mind-body dualism, of a soul that can survive bodily death. William Roll's studies of poltergeists, Karl Osis' pursuit of near-death out-of-the-body experiences, and Ian Stevenson's studies of reincarnation are obvious examples. Yet it is hard to say whether or not these form part of the mainstream in modern parapsychology, for it is difficult to say just what the mainstream is. Certainly some eminent parapsychologists will deny any interest in proving mind-body dualism. They would claim to be simply good scientists, in hot pursuit of anomalous phenomena that do not fit the contemporary world-view. However, others openly embrace dualism; consider the words of M. A. Thalbourne (1984, 13): "Whether we like it or not, and despite the best efforts of an Eccles or a Popper . . . the dominant mode of thinking among present-day scientists is that of Central-State Materialism. Parapsychologists alone constitute a professional group where Dualism is still the most popular assumption."

As John Beloff (1977) pointed out, these two different guiding philosophies exist side by side in modern parapsychology. For those in the first camp, there is the view that ultimately the phenomena of parapsychology will be understood within the context of an expanded scientific world-view. The concept of "paranormal" will no longer be needed. For those in the other camp, there is the viewpoint that has historically dominated parapsychology, the one we have been describing, which argues that paranormal phenomena mark the boundary limits of the scientific world-view: "Beyond that boundary lies the domain of mind liberated from its dependence on the brain. On this view, parapsychology, using the methods of science, becomes a vindication of the essentially spiritual nature of man which must forever defy strict scientific analysis" (Beloff 1977, 21).

However, even the first view must surely lead one to a dualistic position, for as Gardner Murphy (1961, 276) commented, the nature of psi seems to require "the assumption of some kind of fundamental dualism, some basic difference, between normal and paranormal processes. One way of stating the situation is that paranormal processes do not represent a part of the time-space-event system which the physical sciences describe. . . . There is a certain timeless, spaceless, or we might say transtemporal and transpatial character at the very heart of the paranormal. This is indeed one of the major reasons why the phenomena do not belong to and are rejected by official science."

Yet, there may be many present-day parapsychologists who conduct their studies without even considering the dualistic implications of the phenomena they hope to demonstrate. As Louisa Rhine (1967, 241) wrote: "It is not only outside the field but also within it that sometimes an appreciation of the objective behind present-day parapsychological research is lacking. It is entirely possible to do work in parapsychology today and never once consider the antithesis between the parapsychological and the physical."

B. MacKenzie and S. L. MacKenzie (1980), in their analysis of the development of parapsychological thought, found the earlier philosophical approach to the paranormal more in keeping with the essence of parapsychological inquiry: "Even if modern researchers are not driven by the motive of disproving mechanism, materialism, etc., the objects of their study are still phenomena barred from the universe by the assumptions and implications of the natural sciences. . . . Parapsychology remains tied to its historically conditioned adversary relationship with the natural sciences. Without that, it has no continuing basis for identity. Achievements in the field, therefore, are important just to the extent that they are incompatible with, and as a result have revolutionary implications for, the modern scientific world picture. For these reasons, we feel that the old-fashioned ideologues in the field, such as J. B. Rhine and J. G. Pratt, had a more accurate conception of parapsychology's significance than some of the less philosophical newcomers" (p. 163).

If the philosophy of materialism is incorrect, once that misunderstanding is put right the implications for humankind could be overwhelming, at least in the view of some parapsychologists whose writings suggest that the harnessing of our psychic potentials will herald a new chapter in human history. Theirs is the dream of a better age to come, the dream of a psychic millennium.

Parapsychology and the New Millennialism

Humankind has often dreamed of the future transformation of society into one in which personal problems and social evils have been vanquished through the coming of a "new age" (Wilson 1973). These dreams have taken many forms, from those of the Cargo Cults awaiting salvation from the air to those of the Judeo-Christian tradition awaiting the Messiah, or to the more secular and perhaps less seriously held wish of the 1960's youth for the dawning of the "age of Aquarius."

There is a certain strain of such millennialism to be found in the writings of some contemporary parapsychologists. Although the idea that the human condition will be greatly improved once psychic forces are understood has been held throughout the history of parapsychology, it seems that in recent years, perhaps because of growing disillusionment with the ability of science and technology to alleviate human social problems and suffering, there has been a growing tendency in some parapsychological quarters to look to the flowering of psychic abilities to save the world.

Even though most parapsychologists would likely be hesitant to make predictions about the future in a world in which psi is understood and harnessed, that has not stopped some prominent parapsychologists from rhapsodizing about just how great the future is going to be. Some write about the supposedly soon-to-come "paradigm shift" that will force science to accommodate psi and, consequently, open the door to a multitude of new discoveries about the place of humankind in nature. Of course, if it were true that parapsychological research will ultimately be able to answer the question "What is man as a person in a physical universe?" (L. Rhine 1967), and if the answer is that humanness transcends material existence, then, obviously, the meaning of human existence would take on quite an exciting new flavor. However, some speculation has gone far beyond that, to dreams of the psychic *control* of the material world. For example, Targ and Puthoff (1977) have speculated about the "peaceful use of psychic energy" in terms of "executive ESP," medical diagnosis, psychic exploration of space, and forecasting future social and political trends. R. O. Becker (1977, ix-x) was even more obviously millennialistic:

> The scientific revolution and scientific medicine have both failed humanity, and a new appraisal of our situation and a new scientific revolution are in order. The opposition of the scientific establishment to such a new revolution is obvious and determined, and its power is not to be underestimated. . . .
>
> The discipline of parapsychology is uniquely suited to lead the new revolution. It deals directly with the core of the living process. . . . It can lead to a new vision of the human being and his place in the universe. Indeed, it may be the last and best hope we have. . . .

R. A. McConnell (1982, 140) too has referred to parapsychology as our last hope, calling it "the wild card in a stacked deck." He argued that the ethical and philosophical implications of psi "offer the only hope I know—and slim it is—for a continuation of the human experiment."

There are many other examples of millennialistic thought to be gleaned from the pages of parapsychological writing. Although such thinking may not reflect the viewpoint of the majority of parapsychologists, and indeed would be challenged by many, it does represent yet another motivation behind the search for the paranormal—again a motivation held in common with most religions.

Concluding Comments

It remains for us to consider just what role this quasi-religious/dualistic motivation plays in parapsychology apart from giving many parapsychologists a reason to continue their quest. Has it colored their research? Does it taint their findings? One could properly point out that we don't question Newton's motives when we examine his classical laws of motion; we don't inquire about Einstein's philosophical or religious beliefs when we evaluate his theory of relativity; we don't accept or reject the usefulness of pasteurization on the basis of Pastuer's motives for his research.

Should we not equally ignore the motivational orientation of parapsychologists when we examine their data? Before answering this question, it is important to note that it is not because of Newton's testimony or Newton's beliefs that his classical laws are accepted as principles underlying certain aspects of nature on a macrolevel. It is not even because of his data, some of which was fudged (Westfall 1973). Nor is it because of Einstein's philosophy that most scientists now believe that his theory of relativity is substantially correct. It is not because of Pasteur's beliefs or motivations or even his data that we believe that pasteurization of milk is efficacious and essential. Clearly, personal motivations are irrelevant here; in all these cases, we believe because subsequent empirical testing of these ideas has repeatedly supported them. On the other hand, we would be wise to refuse to accept any of them if only people who were already persuaded of their reality could find empirical support.

In parapsychology, as in these cases just cited, the motivations of the researchers are also irrelevant to the evaluation of their claims. They become important only in our understanding of the *persistence* of the quest. Some, perhaps many, parapsychologists carry out their empirical researches in a scientific manner from a methodological point of view (although there is sometimes considerable sloppiness in experimental design and procedures, a problem far from peculiar to parapsychology). However, the *major* problem with parapsychology is at the level of *interpretation* rather than that of data-collection. It is precisely here that the motivational system exerts its greatest influence: ESP is taken to be a more likely explanation than subtle cuing or some other unrecognized but normal influence when guessing is successful at a level above chance; psychokinesis is seen to be more probable than experimental artifact when subatomic events apparently violate probabilistic views. It is in the preference for paranormal explanations over any other, and the attempt to explain away failures to replicate, and the insistence by some parapsychologists that science should accept the reality of the paranormal even though the normal criterion of strong replicability has not been met, that parapsychologists often stray from the pathways of science.

Our reluctance to accept the reality of the paranormal should never be on the basis of the parapsychologists' motivations. Rather, our hesitation must properly be on the grounds that demonstrable phenomena have yet to be produced. Should one day such demonstrations be forthcoming, our history books may well indicate that the quasi-religious orientation of parapsychologists pushed them to pursue their quest despite the skepticism and even occasional derision of mainstream scientists, just as we now attribute some advances in basic chemistry to the attempts of early researchers to turn base metals into gold.

In the final analysis we are left with one question: Is the goal of parapsychology to explain anomalous experiences, be they labeled telepathic, precognitive, out-of-body, or phantasmagoric, or is the goal to vindicate the core beliefs of the founders of parapsychology—the beliefs that telepathy, clairvoyance, precognition, and psychokinesis, and ultimately postmortem survival of the human personality, are real? If the answer to the first question were yes, then parapsychology would have no particular raison-d'être except to inquire into those phenomena that mainstream psychology has for so long ignored. In this case, a rapprochement between psychology and parapsychology would not be long in coming, for such phenomena, in my view at least, do not require the introduction of the concept of psi for their explanation. However, parapsychology began not because of any anomalies encountered in scientific research but, rather, because parapsychologists believed that emerging scientific laws threatened the concepts of the soul (Cerullo 1982) and morality (R. A. White 1982). Although modern-day parapsychology may not directly concern itself with the soul or with morality, the search to find evidence for paranormal processes continues to be, by its very nature, an attempt to challenge the current scientific-mechanistic world-view rather than simply the study of anomalistic experiences and phenomena.

To call parapsychology a "spiritual science," as a few parapsychologists have done, would appear to be a contradiction in terms: How can a science of the spirit exist, given that science is by its very nature materialistic? If one believes in the reality of the paranormal, then one must either ultimately change the basic foundations of science or accept that paranormal phenomena lie beyond science, in either case overthrowing materialism. While both approaches coexist within modern parapsychology, perhaps it is this contradiction inherent in the phrase "spiritual science" that best reflects both the persistence of parapsychology and its estrangement from science: Parapsychology is quasi-religious in nature while attempting to follow the path of science, a path laid down upon the foundation of materialism.

Parapsychologists are not, for the most part at least, just fishers of facts on the prowl for scientific anomalies, for if that were so they would surely have long ago migrated to the much richer fishing grounds of normal science. Nor, it seems to me, are they merely practical-minded investigators tramping through the foggy night in Robert Jahn's swampland, looking for rarely seen specimens. Rather, the specimens, the anomalies, are for most parapsychologists only the means to an end; ultimately, they hope, these specimens will demonstrate once and for all that science as we know it is badly mistaken in its materialistic orientation and that human existence involves an ineffable, nonmaterial aspect that may very well survive the death and decay of the physical body. As long as the need exists to find meaning in life beyond that which is forthcoming from a materialistic philosophy, the search for the paranormal will go on. That being said, in all likelihood it will go on, in one form or another, until the end of the human story.

Acknowledgment

I wish to express my gratitude to Professors Ronald Cohen and Ray Hyman for reviewing an earlier version of this manuscript, and for their thoughtful suggestions, most of which have been incorporated herein.

References

Alcock, J. E. 1981. *Parapsychology: Science or Magic?* Oxford: Pergamon.
Becker. R. O. 1977. Preface to *Advances in Parapsychological Research,* vol. 1: *Psychokinesis,* edited by S. Krippner. New York: Plenum.
Beloff, John. 1976. On trying to make sense of the paranormal. *Proceedings of the SPR,* 56:173-195.
———. 1977. Historical overview. In *Handbook of Parapsychology,* edited by B. B. Wolman, 3-24. New York: Van Nostrand Reinhold.
———. 1984. Research strategies for dealing with unstable phenomena. *Parapsychology Review,* 1:1-7.
Bird, J. M. 1929. The crisis in psychical research (as seen by Eric J. Dingwall). *Journal of the American SPR,* 23:323-336.
Blackmore, Susan. 1983. Unrepeatability: Parapsychology's only finding. Paper presented to the Parapsychology Foundation Conference, San Antonio, Texas. October.
Boring, E. G. 1966. Paranormal phenomena: Evidence, specification and chance. Introduction to *ESP: A Scientific Evaluation,* edited by C. E. M. Hansel, xiii-xxi. New York: Scribner's.
Boulding, K. E. 1980. Science: Our common heritage. *Science,* 207:831-836.
Brandon, Ruth. 1983. Scientists and the supernormal. *New Scientist,* 20:783-786.
———. 1984. *The Spiritualists.* Buffalo: Prometheus Books.
Cerullo, J. J. 1982. *The Secularization of the Soul.* Philadelphia: Institute for the Study of Human Issues.

Clark, W. H. 1977. Parapsychology and religion. In *Handbook of Parapsychology*, edited by B. B. Wolman, 769-780. New York: Van Nostrand Reinhold.

Dingwall, E. J. 1929. The crisis in psychical research. *Journal of the American SPR*, 23:323-336.

Flew, Antony. 1980. Parapsychology: Science or pseudoscience? *Pacific Philosophical Quarterly*, 61:100-114. (See Chapter 22 of this volume.)

Franks, F. 1981. *Polywater*. Cambridge, Mass.: MIT Press.

Gauld, A. 1968. *The Founders of Psychical Research*. London: Routledge & Kegan Paul.

Gray, T. 1984. University course reduces belief in paranormal. *Skeptical Inquirer*, 8:247-251.

Grosso, M. 1983. The parapsychology of religion: Remarks on D. Scott Rogo's "Miracles: A parascientific inquiry into wondrous phenomena." *Journal of the American SPR*, 77:327-345.

Hall, James A. 1981. The work of J. B. Rhine: Implications for religion. *Journal of Parapsychology*, 45:55-63.

Haynes, R. 1982. *The Society for Psychical Research: A History*. London: MacDonald and Co.

Hearnshaw, L. S. 1973. The psychology of religion. In *The Psychology of Religion*, edited by L. B. Brown. Harmondsworth, England: Penguin.

Jahn, R. G. 1982. The persistent paradox of psychic phenomena: An engineering perspective. *Proceedings of the IEEE*, 70:136-170.

Kemsley, D. S. 1973. Religious influence in the rise of modern science. In *Science and Religious Belief*, edited by C. A. Russell, 74-102. London: University of London Press.

Klaaren, E. M. 1977. *Religious Origins of Modern Science*. Grand Rapids, Mich.: W. B. Eerdmans.

MacKenzie, B. 1981. The place of J. B. Rhine in the history of parapsychology. *Journal of Parapsychology*, 45:65-84.

MacKenzie, B., and S. L. MacKenzie. 1980. Whence the enchanted boundary? Sources and significance of the parapsychological tradition. *Journal of Parapsychology*, 44:125-166.

Mauskopf, S. H., and M. R. McVaugh. 1980. *The Elusive Science*. Baltimore: Johns Hopkins University Press.

McClenon, J. 1982. A survey of elite scientists: Their attitudes toward ESP and parapsychology. *Journal of Parapsychology*, 46:127-152.

McConnell, J. V. 1962. Memory transfer through cannibalism in plenarians. *Journal of Neuropsychiatry*, 3:42-48.

McConnell, R. A. 1982. *Parapsychology and Self-deception in Science*. Pittsburgh: R. A. McConnell.

Moore, R. L. 1977. *In Search of White Crows*. New York: Oxford.

Murphy, Gardner. 1952. The natural, the mystical and the paranormal. *Journal of the American SPR*, 46:125-142.

———. 1961. *Challenge of Psychical Research*. New York: Harper and Row.

Nicol, F. 1972. The founders of the Society for Psychical Research. *Proceedings of the*

SPR, 55:341-367.

Oberman, H. A. 1969. Early history of blood substitutes: Transfusion of milk. *Transfusion,* 9:74-77.

Palmer. J. 1984. Review of R. A. McConnell's "Parapsychology and self-deception in science." *Journal of the American SPR,* 78:70-74.

Perry, M. 1979. Psi in the Bible. *Parapsychology Review,* 10:9-14.

———. 1982. Psychical research and religion. In *Psychical Research,* edited by I. Grattan-Guinness. Wellingborough, England: Aquarian Press.

Randall, J. L. 1977. *Parapsychology and the Nature of Life.* London: Sphere Books.

Rhine, J. B. 1943. Editorial: ESP, PK and the survival hypothesis. *Journal of Parapsychology,* 7:223-227.

———. 1953. *New World of the Mind.* New York: William Sloane.

———. 1972. Parapsychology and man. *Journal of Parapsychology,* 36:101-121.

Rhine, J. B., and associates. 1965. *Parapsychology: From Duke to FRNM.* Durham, N.C.: Parapsychology Press.

Rhine, L. E. 1967. Parapsychology, then and now. *Journal of Parapsychology,* 31:231-248.

Rogo, D. S. 1982. *Miracles.* New York: Dial Press.

Rudwick, M. 1981. Senses of the natural world and senses of God: Another look at the historical relation of science and religion. In *The Sciences and Theology in the Twentieth Century,* edited by A. R. Peacocke, 241-262. Notre Dame, Ind.: University of Notre Dame Press.

Russell, B. 1961 [1935]. *Religion and Science.* Oxford: Oxford University Press.

Shepard, L. A., ed. 1980. *Encyclopedia of Occultism and Parapsychology.* New York: Avon.

Targ, R., and H. E. Puthoff. 1977. *Mind-Reach.* Delacorte Press.

Tart, C. T. 1977. *Psi: Scientific Studies of the Psychic Realm.* New York: E. P. Dutton.

Thalbourne, M. A. 1984. The conceptual framework of parapsychology: Time for a reformation. Paper presented at the 27th Annual Meeting of the Parapsychological Association. Dallas, August.

Thomas, K. 1971. *Religion and the Decline of Magic.* Harmondsworth, England: Penguin.

Thouless, R. H. 1977. Implications for religious studies. In *Advances in Parapsychological Research,* vol. 1: *Psychokinesis,* edited by S. Krippner, 175-190. New York: Plenum.

Turner, F. M. 1974. *Between Science and Religion.* New Haven: Yale University Press.

Westfall, R. S. 1973. Newton and the fudge factor. *Science,* 179:751-758.

White, Andrew D. 1955 [1895]. *A History of the Warfare of Science with Theology in Christendom.* New York: George Braziller.

White, R. A. 1982. An analysis of ESP phenomena in the saints. *Parapsychology Review,* 13:15-18.

Wilson, B. R. 1973. *Magic and the Millennium.* New York: Harper and Row.

Part 5

Some Methodological and Theoretical Issues

24

Statistical Problems in ESP Research

PERSI DIACONIS

Is modern parapsychological research worthy of serious consideration? The volume of literature by reputable scientists, the persistent interest of students, and the government funding of ESP projects make it difficult to evade this question. Over the past ten years, in the capacity of statistician and professional magician, I have had personal contact with more than a dozen paranormal experiments. My background encourages a thorough skepticism, but I also find it useful to recall that skeptics make mistakes. For example, the scientific community did not believe in meteorites before about 1800. Indeed, in 1807 when a meteorite fell in Weston, Connecticut, an extended investigation was made by Professors Silliman and Kingsley of Yale. When Thomas Jefferson—then President of the United States and scientist of no small repute—was informed of the findings, he reportedly responded, "Gentlemen, I would rather believe that those two Yankee Professors would lie than to believe that stones fell from heaven" (quoted in Nininger 1933).

Critics of ESP must acknowledge the possibility of missing a real phenomenon because of the difficulty of designing a suitable experiment. However, the characteristics that lead many to be dubious about claims for ESP—its sporadic appearance, its need for a friendly environment, and its common association with fraud—require of the most sympathetic analyst not only skill in the analysis of nonstandard types of experimental design but appreciation of the differences between a sympathetic environment with flexible study design and experimentation that is simply careless or so structured as to be impossible to evaluate.

In this article I use examples to indicate the problems associated with the generally informal methods of design and evaluation of ESP experiments—in particular, the problems of multiple endpoints and subject cheating. I then review some of the commentaries of outstanding statisticians on the problems of

Reprinted with permission from *Science*, July 14, 1978, copyright 1978 by the American Association for the Advancement of Science.

evaluation. Finally, as an instance of using new analytic methods for non-standard experiments, I give examples of some new statistical techniques that permit appropriate evaluation of studies that allow instant feedback of information to the subject after each trial, an entirely legitimate device used to facilitate whatever learning process may be involved.

Informal Design and Evaluation

A common problem in the evaluation of ESP experiments is the uncertainty about what outcomes are to be judged as indicative of ESP. Sometimes the problem can be dealt with by setting up a second experiment to verify the unanticipated but interesting outcome of a first experiment.

In a much discussed card-guessing experiment reported by Soal and Bateman (1954), a receiving subject tried to guess the name of a card that was being thought about by a sending subject. When the data were first analyzed, no significant deviations from chance were observed. Several years later the experimenters noticed that the guessing subject seemed to name not the card the sender was thinking about but rather the card two cards down in the deck (an example of precognition). Once this hypothesis was clearly formulated, the data were reanalyzed and new data were collected. The results stood up. The publication of Soal and Bateman's book touched off a series of lively articles (Soal and Bateman 1954; Price 1955; Soal 1956; J. B. Rhine 1956; Meehl and Scriven 1956; Bridgman 1956; Price 1956; Price 1972). The validity of Soal's experiment is still being debated (there are claims that the records are unreliable [Scott and Haskell 1975; Hansel 1966; see also Chapter 11 of this volume]), but that he subjected the data to reanalysis after finding an unusual pattern seems acceptable to almost everyone. Whatever the view about reanalysis, the design and evaluation of the later experiments fall squarely within the domain of familiar scientific practice. The problems are more acute in the next example.

Three papers from the *Journal of Parapsychology* describe experiments with a young man called B. D. (Kelly and Kanthanani 1972; Kanthanani and Kelly 1974). These experiments took place at J. B. Rhine's Foundation for Resesarch on the Nature of Man in Durham, North Carolina. The effects described, if performed under controlled conditions, seem like an exciting scientific breakthrough. In May 1972, I witnessed a presentation by B.D., arranged by the Psychology Department of Harvard University. I was asked to observe as a magician and made careful notes of what went on. Although the experiments were not controlled, I believe they highlight many problems inherent in drawing inferences from apparently well controlled experiments.

Most of the demonstrations I witnessed B.D. perform involved playing cards. In one experiment, two onlookers were invited to shuffle two decks of cards, a red deck and a blue deck. Two other onlookers were asked to name two different cards aloud: they named the ace of spades and the three of hearts. Both decks were placed face down on a table. We were instructed to turn over the top cards of each deck simultaneously and to continue turning up pairs in this manner until we came to either of the named cards. The red-backed three of hearts appeared first. At this point, B.D. shouted, "Fourteen," and we were instructed to count down 14 more cards in the blue pack. We were amazed to find that the fourteenth card was the blue-backed three of hearts. Many other tests of this kind were performed. Sometimes the performer guessed correctly, sometimes he did not.

Close observation suggested that B.D. was a skilled opportunist. Consider the effect just described. Suppose that, as the cards were turned face upwards, both threes of hearts appeared simultaneously. This would be considered a striking coincidence and the experiment could have been terminated. The experiment would also have been judged successful if the two aces of spades appeared simultaneously or if the ace of spades was turned up in one deck at the same time the three of hearts was turned up in the other. There are other possibilities: suppose that, after 14 cards had been counted off, the next (fifteenth) card had been the matching three of hearts. Certainly this would have been considered quite unusual. Similarly, if the fourteenth or fifteenth card had been the ace of spades, B.D. would have been thought successful. What if the fourteenth card had been the three of diamonds? B.D. would have been "close." In one instance, after he had been "close," B.D. rubbed his eyes and said, "I'm certainly having trouble seeing the suits today."

A major key to B.D.'s success was that he did not specify in advance the result to be considered surprising. The odds against a coincidence *of some sort* are dramatically less than those against any prespecified *particular one* of them. For the experiment just described, including as successful outcomes all possibilities mentioned, the probability of success is greater than one chance in eight. This is an example of exploiting multiple endpoints. To further complicate any analysis, several such ill-defined experiments were often conducted simultaneously, interacting with one another. The young performer electrified his audience. His frequently completely missed guesses were generally regarded with sympathy rather than doubt, and for most observers they seemed only to confirm the reality of B.D.'s unusual powers.

Subject Cheating

In the experiments at Harvard, B.D. occasionally helped chance along by a bit of sleight of hand. During several trials, I saw him glance at the bottom card of the deck he was shuffling. He then cut the cards, leaving a quarter of an inch step in the pack. This fixed the location of the card he had seen. The cards were then spread out, and a card was selected by one of the onlookers. When the selected card was replaced in the deck, B.D. secretly counted the number of cards between the card he had seen and the selected card. B.D. named a "random" card (presumably the card he had glanced at) and asked someone to name a small number. He disregarded the first number named and asked someone else to name another small number—this time the difference in location between the card B.D. had seen and the selected card. One of the observers counted down in the pack until he came to the "randomly" named card. Addressing the observer who originally selected a card, B.D. asked, "What card are you thinking of?" Sure enough, when the second small number was counted off, the selected card appeared. When presented in the confusing circumstances I have described, the trick seemed impossible. About ten of the observers were psychology faculty, the remaining five were graduate students. When they tried to reconstruct the details of this presentation, they could not remember exactly who had thought of the number and who had selected the card. They muddled the circumstances of this particular test with those of previous tests. I call this blending of details the "bundle of sticks" phenomenon. It is a familiar element in standard magic tricks: An effect is produced several times under different circumstances with the use of a different technique each time. When an observer tries to reconstruct the modus operandi, the weak points of one performance are ruled out because they were clearly not present during other performances. The bundle of sticks is stronger than any single stick.

B.D.'s performance went on for several hours. Later, some of the observers realized that B.D. often took advantage of the inevitable lucky breaks. However, his performance must have made quite an impression on some of the observers because the July 13, 1973, issue of *Science* reported that B.D. had been given a grant from Harvard "to explore the nature of his own psychic ability." My personal curiosity about the possibility of B.D. having powers that upset the known physical laws is fully satisfied—in the negative. This position is further discussed below.

Another exposé of which I have first-hand knowledge concerns Ted Serios. Serios claimed that he could create psychic photographs on Polaroid film in cameras he had never seen before. A group of scientists in Chicago and Denver had become convinced that there was no trickery involved; indeed, they believed that Serios had extraordinary psychic abilities. I became involved when Eisenbud's (1967) book, *The World of Ted Serios*, was being considered for review by *Scientific American*. A team of experienced magicians went to Denver to take a close look at Serios's performance. When we arrived, Serios was attempting to produce psychic images on TV film at a Denver TV station. Conditions were chaotic. Several news teams were present, each team having brought its own Polaroid film. After a short time, I managed secretly to switch about 20 boxes of their film with marked film we had brought along. We wanted to determine whether their film had been previously exposed. It had not been. The fact, however, that it had been so easy for me to switch the film by sleight of hand clearly indicated that the investigators did not have adequate control over the essential materials. Conditions remained like this during our several days stay, and our observation revealed irreparable methodological flaws in all phases of the experiments. Serios openly used a small paper tube that he placed on his forehead pointing toward the camera "to help focus the thought waves." I observed that he occasionally placed this tube in front of the camera lens. On one trial, I thought I saw him secretly load something into the tube. When I asked to examine the tube, pandemonium broke loose. Several of the Denver scientists present jumped up, shouting things like, "You can't do that!" Serios hastily put the tube in his pocket. He was not searched. We were later able to duplicate Serios's pictures in several ways. After our exposé of how we believe Serios obtained his results (Eisendrath and Reynolds 1967; Eisenbud 1967), *Life* magazine published an article about Serios's psychic powers, with no mention of our findings. Paranormal claims tend to receive far more media coverage than their exposés.

There are many other reports of subject cheating in ESP experiments. For example, Gardner (1966) figured out how Russian women "saw" with their fingertips and, in a later paper (1977a) exposes Uri Geller's supposedly "foolproof" alteration of the internal memory of several pieces of Nitinol wire. Nitinol is an alloy of nickel and titanium that has a memory. Under intense heat, a piece of Nitinol wire can be given a shape. When cold, it can easily be reshaped between the fingers. After being heated, it snaps back to the original shape. One of the most persistently quoted proofs of Geller's paranormal powers is Eldon Byrd's claim that "Geller altered the lattice structure of a metal alloy in a way that cannot be duplicated" (Byrd 1976). As usual, there is a story of amazing feats performed under test conditions. Gardner's competent detective work reveals the usual tale of chaotic conditions and bad reporting. There is an interesting twist here. Supporters of Geller argue that the event is amazing, even in light of chaotic conditions, since Geller could not have had access to a heat source of about $500°C$, "the only known way to get this result" (Byrd 1976). Gardner found he could easily alter the memory of a piece of Nitinol wire with a pair of pliers or even by using his teeth.

Unfortunately, a nonmagician's memory of a magic feat is unreliable. For example, Hyman (1977a), a psychologist and magician, has described his visit to the Stanford Research Institute, during which Geller demonstrated many of his psychic feats. Hyman reports observing sleight of hand performed under uncontrolled conditions, much at variance with the published report of the SRI scientists involved (Puthoff and Targ 1977). Geller probably ranks as the most thoroughly exposed psychic of all times (Hyman 1977a; Randi 1976; Marks and Kammann 1977), yet the parascience community continues to defend him as a psychic who is often genuine even though he occasionally cheats.

Some Conclusions

Rejecting the claims of a psychic who has been caught cheating raises thorny scientific problems. I am sure that B.D. used sleight of hand several times during the performance I witnessed. Yet, as one of the other observers remarked, "The people who introduced B.D. never said he didn't do card tricks; they just claimed he had extraordinary powers on occasion." During my encounter with Serios, a psychologist present put it differently: "Suppose he was only genuine 10 percent of the time; wouldn't that be enough for you?" My position is conservative: The similarity of the descriptions of the controlled experiments with B.D. and Serios to the sessions I witnessed convinces me that all paranormal claims involving these two performers should be completely discounted.

The fact that a trained observer finds reason to discredit two psychics is not, of course, sufficient evidence to discredit the existence of ESP or the integrity of other potential psychics. However, the pervasiveness of fraud in so many claims for ESP makes it extremely difficult for the disinterested observer to identify evidence worthy of credit. Whether Houdini was a disinterested witness, as he claimed, is hard to judge. But his tireless investigation and exposure of spiritualists in England and America (Houdini 1924) give powerful evidence of the extent of fraud in this domain and of the difficulties of detecting it. Randi, also a professional magician, has undertaken a detailed exposé of Uri Geller. Randi (1976) repeatedly documents the discrepancy between actual circumstances and those reported in newspapers and scientific journals.

Even if there had not been subject cheating, the experiments described above would be useless because they were out of control. The confusing and erratic experimental conditions I have described are typical of *every* test of paranormal phenomena I have witnessed. Indeed, ESP investigators often insist on nonnegative observers and surroundings. Because of this, skeptics have a difficult time gaining direct access to experimental evidence and must rely on published reports. Such reports are often wholly inadequate. According to Davey (1887), Hansel (1966), and others, it is not easy to notice crucial details during ESP experiments. For example, each of the studies referred to above describes experimental conditions beyond reproach. My own observation suggests that the conditions were not in control. Some of these problems can be overcome by insisting that expert magicians and psychologists, skilled at running experiments with human subjects, be included in study protocols.

Statisticians and ESP

The only widely respected evidence for paranormal phenomena is statistical. Classical statistical tests are reported in each of the published studies described above. Most often these tests are "highly statistically significant." This only implies that the results are improbable under simple chance models. In complex, badly controlled experiments, simple chance models cannot be seriously considered as tenable explanations; hence rejection of such models is not of particular interest. For example, the high significance claimed for the famous Zenith Radio experiment is largely a statistical artifact (Goodfellow 1938). Listeners were invited to mail in their guesses on a random selection of playing cards. The proportion of correct guesses was highly significant when calculations were based on the assumption of random guessing on the part of each listener. It is well known that the distribution of sequences produced by human subjects is far from random (Slovic, Fischoff, Lichenstein 1977; Tversky and Kahneman 1974), and hence the crucial hypothesis of independence fails in this situation. More sophisticated analysis of the Zenith results gives no cause for surprise.

In well-run experiments, statistics can aid in the design and final analysis. The idea of deliberately introducing external, well-controlled randomization in investigation of paranormal phenomena seems due to Richet (1884) and Edgeworth (1885a; 1885b). (See also McVaugh and Mauskopf 1976.) Later, Wilks (1965a, 1965b) wrote a survey article on reasonable statistical procedures for analyzing paranormal experiments popular at the time. Fisher (1924; 1928; 1929) developed new statistical methods that allow credit for "close" guesses in card-guessing experiments. Good (1974) suggests new experiments and explanations for ESP. The parascience community, well aware of the importance of statistical tools, has solved numerous statistical riddles in its own literature. Any of the three best known parascience journals is a source of a number of good surveys and discussions of inferential problems. (For a useful survey of this literature see Burdick and Kelly 1977.)

The actual circumstances of even well-run ESP tests are sufficiently different from the most familiar types of experiments as to lead even able and well-regarded analysts into difficulty, and the statistical community has a mixed record, with errors in both directions. On one hand, the celebrated statement by the Institute of Mathematical Statistics (Camp 1937, Notes) was widely regarded as an endorsement of ESP analysis methods, a position that seems hard to justify. As an example of unjust criticism of ESP, consider Feller's review (1940) of the methodology of ESP research (Greenwood and Stuart 1940).

Feller was an outstanding mathematician who made major contributions to the modern theory of probability. He attacked some of the statistical arguments used by J. B. Rhine and his co-workers (see Feller 1940). It appears now that several of Feller's criticisms were wrong. To give one instance: a standard ESP deck consists of five symbols repeated five times each to make up a 25-card deck. Feller found published records of the order of ESP decks before and after shuffling. He noticed that one could match up long runs of consecutive symbols in the two orders and took this as evidence of "unbelievably poor results of shuffling" (Feller 1968, 56 and 407). In a follow-up article, Greenwood and Stuart (1940) pointed out that such runs of matching symbols did not prove poor mixing. Since each symbol is repeated five times, long runs of matching symbols are inevitable. Feller had no respect for their remarks: "Both their arithmetic and their experiments have a distinct twinge of the supernatural," he wrote years later (Feller 1968).

I believe Feller was confused. As proof of this, consider one of the experiments that Greenwood and Stuart (1940) carried out to prove their point: they simulated two arrangements of ESP decks from a table of random numbers, and they showed that random arrangements exhibited long runs of matching symbols. Feller completely misunderstood this experiment; he thought that Greenwood and Stuart chose a sample of 25 from a set of five symbols *with* replacement. If the simulation were done by sampling with replacement, only those outcomes that had exactly five of each symbol would be useful. Since these are rare, the time required to complete the situation reported by Greenwood and Stuart would have been lifetimes long. Thus, Feller found the report of the resulting samples "miraculously obliging." The comments of Feller that I have quoted, suggesting that the investigators were at best incompetent, persisted through three editions of his famous text. I have asked students and colleagues of Feller about this, and all have said that Feller's mistakes were widely known; he seemed to have decided the opposition was wrong and that was that.

Feedback Experiments

If ESP phenomena are real, we still do not know a reliable method for eliciting them; and any serious exploration of the subject requires that as much leeway as possible be provided for experimental designs that seem likely to produce an effect. In their search for replicable experiments, psychic investigators have modified the classical tests of ESP. Important changes include the use of targets of increasing complexity, such as drawings or natural settings, and greater use of feedback, either telling the subject whether the guess was right or wrong or, in a card-matching experiment, what the last target card actually was. Unfortunately, the statistical tools for evaluating the outcome of more complex experiments are not available, and the ad hoc tests created by researchers are often not well understood. An article on remote viewing (Puthoff and Targ 1976) provides an example. Apparently, in a typical phase of the experiment, nine locations (a local swimming pool, tennis court, and others) were selected from a list of 100 locations chosen to be as distinct as possible. A team of sending subjects went to each of the nine locations in a random order. A guessing subject tried to describe where they were. After each guess the guessing subject was given feedback by being taken to the true location. This is clearly a complex experiment to evaluate, and there are several reasons to discount the findings presented by Harold Puthoff and Russell Targ (1976). I give some of these reasons at the end of the next section. I first focus on the analysis of simpler feedback experiments.

Feedback of some sort is a much-used technique in modern ESP research (Tart 1976, Chaps. 1 and 2). The appropriate analysis of a feedback experiment is easy in some simple cases but not at all clear in other cases. The assessment of such experiments requires new methods. R. L. Graham and I have explored some of the problems in a situation simple enough to allow mathematical analysis (Diaconis and Graham 1978), and the following examples are drawn from that research.

Let us consider an experiment that involves a sending subject, a receiving subject, and a well-shuffled deck of 52 cards. The sending subject concentrates on each card in turn, and the receiving subject attempts to guess the suit and number of the card correctly.

No information case. If no additional information is available to the receiving subject, the chance of a correct guess at any point in the experiment is 1 in 52; thus the expected number of correct guesses in a single run through the 52-card deck is 1. If we do not accept ESP as possible, it can easily be shown that any system of guessing leads to one correct guess on the average. However, the distribution of the number of correct guesses can vary widely as a function of the guessing strategy: if the same card is guessed 52 times in succession, then exactly one guess will be correct. It has been shown that the variance of the number of correct guesses is largest when each card is called only once (Greenwood 1938).

Complete feedback case. Next, let us consider an experiment that includes giving information to the guesser. After each trial he is shown the card he has attempted to identify. The most efficient way the guesser can use this information is always to name a card he knows to be still in the deck. This strategy leads to an expected number of correct guesses of

$$\frac{1}{52} + \frac{1}{51} + \frac{1}{50} + \cdots + 1 = 4.5$$

in a single run through the deck, much larger than the one correct guess we expect with no information.

Partial information case. A third situation is created by giving only partial information. The guesser is told only if each guess is correct or not. In this situation, it can be shown that the guesser's optimal strategy is to name repeatedly any card—for example, the ace of spades—until he is told his guess is correct. After he is told that he has guessed correctly, he repeatedly calls any card known to be in the deck until that card is guessed correctly or the run through the deck is completed. The expected number of correct guesses, if this optimal strategy is used, is

$$\frac{1}{52!} + \frac{1}{51!} + \frac{1}{50!} + \cdots + 1 = e - 1 = 1.72$$

where e is the base of the natural logarithms. A subject given partial information can minimize the expected number of correct guesses by naming cards without repeating the same card until a correct guess is made. The guesser then repeatedly calls the card known not to be in the deck for the remaining calls. The expected number of correct guesses in this situation is well approximated by

$$1 - \frac{1}{e} = .632$$

Similar analysis can be carried out with the standard 25-card ESP deck, consisting of five different symbols repeated five times. If no feedback information is given to the guessing subject, then, under the hypothesis of chance guessing, each guess has probability $1/5$ of being correct. In a run through the 25-card deck, five correct guesses are expected. In the case of complete feedback, the best strategy is to guess the most probable card at each stage. This leads to 8.65 as the expected number of correct guesses, as shown by Read (1962). In the case of partial information—telling the guesser only if each guess is right or wrong—things are more complicated. For example, the optimal strategy no longer is to choose the most probable card for each guess. It is easy to give a simple strategy that gets six cards correct on the average: guess a fixed symbol until told that five correct guesses have been achieved, and then guess a second symbol for the remaining cards. There seems to be no simple closed-form expression for the optimal strategy, but the expected number of correct guesses, if the optimal strategy is used, satisfies a multivariable recurrence that makes dynamic programming techniques available. M. A. Gatto at Bell Laboratories succeeded in putting this problem on the computer and, by solving the recurrence, showed that the expected number of correct guesses is 6.63, if the optimal strategy is used (personal communication). The result took about 15 hours of CPU (central processing units) time on a large computer.

These examples show that feedback can drastically change the expected number of correct guesses.

Simple Guessing Experiments with Feedback: Scoring Rules

Available evidence (Slovic, Fischoff, and Lichenstein 1977; Tversky and Kahneman 1974) suggests that subjects do not use their best possible strategies in simple probabilistic experiments. In more complicated situations—for example, if the experimenter uses a deck of cards with values repeated several times and gives the subject feedback as to whether his guess is "close" or not—the most difficult strategy may be very difficult to compute. Tart (1976, Chaps. 1 and 2) gives references to the use of scoring rules that range from not taking into consideration the amount of information available to including the assumption that the subject is using the optimal strategy. Both of these approaches seem unnecessarily crude. The former might give an untalented subject a high score, while the latter might penalize a skillful subject who does not make efficient use of the information available to him.

For problems of this type, there exists a class of scoring rules that depend on the amount of information available to the subject and on the way the subject uses the information given. The idea is to subtract at the ith stage the probability of the ith guess being correct, given the history up to guess i. For example, if a guesser names a card he knows not to be in the deck, no penalty is subtracted. More formally, if G_i is the subject's guess on the ith trial and Z_i is one or zero as the ith guess is correct or not, then the skill-scoring statistics for n trials is defined by

$$S = \sum_{i=1}^{n} \{Z_i - E(Z_i|G_1, G_2, \cdots, G_i,$$

$$Z_1, Z_2, \cdots, Z_{i-1})\} \tag{1}$$

The conditional expected values that appear in Eq. 1 can be calculated for any past history with the use of new combinatorial formulas related to problems of permutations with restricted positions (Diaconis and Graham 1978). The statistic S is related to the skill-scoring rules used to evaluate weather forecasters (Glahn and Jorgensen 1970). S has the property that, in the absence of skill (that is, ESP or talent), the expected score is zero for any guessing strategy, optimal or not.

TABLE 1

Card Guessing With Ten Cards and Partial Feedback

Column 1 is trial number; column 2 is subject's guess; column 3 is feedback to subject; column 4 is the probability of the ith guess being correct, given the history up to time i; for example, subject guessed card 9 on trial 2 after being told that the guess on trial 1 was wrong, penalty = probability (9 on trial 2 given that the guess was wrong on trial 1) = 8/81; column 5 is the actual card in i^{th} position.

$$S = 3 - 1.0874 = 1.9126$$

Trial	Guess	Feedback	Penalty	Card
1	1	Wrong	0.1000	3
2	9	Wrong	0.0988	4
3	6	Wrong	0.0976	8
4	3	Wrong	0.0965	6
5	2	Right	0.0955	2
6	1	Wrong	0.1189	10
7	4	Wrong	0.1031	9
8	7	Right	0.1019	7
9	6	Wrong	0.1282	5
10	1	Right	0.1470	1
Total			1.0874	

Let us consider an example made explicit in Table 1. A deck of 10 cards numbered from 1 to 10 was well mixed. A sender looked at the cards in sequence from the top down, and a guesser guessed at each card as the sender looked at it. After each trial the guesser was told whether she was correct or not. There were three correct guesses. If one ignores the availability of partial information, one comes to the conclusion that this response was two more than could be expected by chance. If one assumes that the guesser used the optimal strategy outlined in the partial information example in the previous section, then one would compare the number of correct guesses with 1.72, the expected number of correct guesses under the optimal strategy. Thus, one would conclude that the score of 3 was 1.28 higher than "chance." The guesses that were actually made are far from the optimal strategy. For example, on the second trial the optimal guess was 1, not 9; on the third trial the optimal guess was 1 or 9, not 6. In this case, the skill-scoring statistic scores this experiment as 1.91 higher than chance. Skill-scoring statistics can be tested by using an appropriate normal approximation available via Martingale central limit theorems (Diaconis and Graham 1978).

Skill-scoring provides an example of how mathematical statistics can be used to evaluate experiments under nonstandard conditions. Clearly, experiments designed to include both feedback and sampling with replacement will be far easier to evaluate. The problems dealt with above—dependent trials coupled with feedback—arise in practice. For example, the analysis can be applied for reassessing experiments where subjects were seated within sight or hearing of one another, and an investigator suspects that unconscious sensory cuing has taken place. To be specific, a sender might, by his behavior, unconsciously indicate to the receiver whether his last guess was correct or not. This assumes, of course, that right and wrong were the only information cues transmitted. If the investigator thinks that the sender cued the guesser with information about each card as he looked at it, no statistical analysis can salvage that data.

One problem with feedback experiments is that they seem highly sensitive to clean experimental conditions. If the conditions break down, it will be hard to make sense of the data. For example, if a random number generated in an experiment with feedback is faulty, it may be that subjects can learn something of the pattern from the feedback (Gardner 1977a). In the remote-viewing experiment (Puthoff and Targ 1976) referred to above, subjects included reports of where they had been taken during a "feedback trip" in the description of a current target. When a judge is given the subjects' nine transcripts, the judge is told which nine targets were visited but not the order of the visits. Information within a transcript allows a judge to rule out some of the potential targets and renders analysis of the results impossible. This is only one of many objections to the findings by Puthoff and Targ (1976). Because of inadequate specification of crucial details (Hyman 1977b; Stokes 1977), I find it impossible to interpret what went on during this experiment.

Conclusions

To answer the question I started out with, modern parapsychological research *is* important. If any of its claims are substantiated, it will radically change the way we look at the world. Even if none of the claims is correct, an understanding of what went wrong provides lessons for less exotic experiments. Poorly designed, badly run, and inappropriately analyzed experiments seem to be an even greater obstacle to progress in this field than subject cheating. This is not due to a lack of creative investigators who work hard but rather to the difficulty of finding an appropriate balance between study designs that permit both analysis and experimental results. There always seem to be many loopholes and loose ends. The same mistakes are made again and again. The critiques and comments of S. J. Davey (1887) and G. S. Hall (1887) seem as relevant for modern studies as they did at the turn of the century. Regrettably, the problems are hard to recognize from published records of the experiments in which they occur; rather, these problems are often uncovered by reports of independent skilled observers who were present during the experiment.

There have been many hundreds of serious studies of ESP, and I have certainly read and been told about events that I cannot explain. I have been able to have direct experience with more than a dozen experiments and detailed second-hand knowledge about perhaps 20 more. In every case, the details of what actually transpired prevent the experiment from being considered seriously as evidence for paranormal phenomena.

Acknowledgment

I thank Tom Cover, Bradley Efron, David Freedman, Maryin Gardner, Mary Ann Gatto, Seymour Geisser, Judith Hess, Ray Hyman, William Kruskal, Paul Meier, Lincoln Moses, Frederick Mosteller, David Siegmund, Charles Stein, Stephen Stigler, Charles Tart, and Sandy Zabell for comments on earlier versions. Partially supported by NSF grant MPS74-21416.

References

Bridgman, W. 1956. *Science*, 123, no. 9:15.

Burdick, D. S., and E. F. Kelly. 1977. Statistical methods in parapsychological research. In *Handbook of Parapsychology*, edited by B. B. Wolman. New York: Van Nostrand Reinhold.

Byrd, E. 1976. In *The Geller Papers*, edited by C. Panati. Boston: Houghton Mifflin.

Camp, B. H. 1937. *Journal of Parapsychology*, 1:305.

Davey, S. J. 1887. *Journal of the SPR*, 3:8.

Diaconis, P., and R. L. Graham. 1978. The analysis of experiments with feedback to subjects. *Annals of Statistics*.

Edgeworth, F. Y. 1885. *Proceedings of the SPR*, 3:190.

———. 1885. *Proceedings of the SPR*, 4:189.

Eisenbud, J. 1967. *The World of Ted Serios*. New York: Morrow.

———. 1967. *Popular Photography*. 61, no. 5:31.

Eisendrath, D., and C. Reynolds. 1967. *Popular Photography*. 61, no. 4:81.

Feller, W. 1940. *Journal of Parapsychology*, 4:271.

———. 1968. An *Introduction to Probability Theory and Its Applications*. New York: Wiley.

Fisher, R. A. 1924. *Proceedings of the SPR*, 34:181.

———. 1928. *Proceedings of the SPR*, 38:269.

———. 1929. *Proceedings of the SPR*, 39:189.

Gardner, Martin. 1966. *Science*, 151:645.

———. 1977a. *The Humanist*, 37:25. May/June.

———. 1977b. *New York Review of Books*, 24, no. 12:37. July 14.

Glahn, H. R., and D. L. Jorgensen. 1970. *Mon. Weather Review*, 98:136.

Good, I. J. 1974. *Parascience Proceedings*, 1(2):3.

Goodfellow, L. D. 1938. *Journal of Experimental Psychology*, 23:601.

Greenwood, J. A. 1938. *Journal of Parapsychology*, 2:60.

Greenwood, J. A., and C. E. Stuart. 1940. *Journal of Parapsychology*, 4:299.

Hall, G. S. 1887. *American Journal of Psychology*, 1:128.

Hansel, C. E. M. 1966. *ESP: A Scientific Evaluation*. New York: Scribner's.

Houdini, H. 1924. *A Magician Among the Spirits*. New York: Harper.

Hyman, R. 1977a. *The Humanist*, 37:16, May/June.

———. 1977b. *The Humanist*, 37:47, November/December.

Kanthanani, B., and E. F. Kelly. 1974. *Journal of Parapsychology*, 38:16, 355.

Kelly, E. F., and B. Kanthanani. 1972. *Journal of Parapsychology*, 36:185.

———. 1974. *Journal of Parapsychology*, 38:16, 355.

Marks, D., and R. Kammann. 1977. *Zetetic (Skeptical Inquirer)*, 1(2):3.

McVaugh, M., and S. H. Mauskopf. 1976. *Isis*, 67:161.

Meehl, P. E., and M. Scriven. 1956. *Science*, 123:14.

Nininger, H. H. 1933. *Our Stone-Pelted Planet*. Boston: Houghton Mifflin.

Price, G. R. 1955. *Science*, 122:359.

———. 1972. *Science*, 175:359.

Puthoff, H. E., and R. Targ. 1976. *Proceedings of the IEEE*, 64:329.

———. 1977. *Mind Reach*. New York: Delacorte.

Randi, J. 1976. *The Magic of Uri Geller*. New York: Ballantine [rev. ed., *The Truth About Uri Geller*, published by Prometheus Books, Buffalo, N.Y., 1983].

Read, R. C. 1962. *American Mathematics Monthly*, 69:506.

Rhine, J. B. 1956. *Science*, 123:11, 19.

Richet, C. 1884. *Review of Philosophy*, 18:41.

Scott, C., and P. Haskel. 1975. *Journal of the SPR*, 118:220.

Slovic, P., B. Fischoff, and S. Lichenstein. 1977. *Annual Review of Psychology,* 28:1.

Soal, S. G. 1956. *Science,* 123:9.

Soal, S. G., and F. Bateman. 1954. *Modern Experiments in Telepathy.* New Haven, Conn.: Yale University Press.

Stokes, D. M. 1977. *Journal of the American SPR,* 71:437.

Tart, C. 1976. *Learning to Use ESP.* Chicago: University of Chicago Press.

Tversky, A., and D. Kahneman. 1974. *Science,* 185:1124.

Wilks, S. S. 1965a. *New York Statistician,* 16(6).

———. 1965b. *New York Statistician,* 16(7).

25

Parapsychology and Quantum Mechanics

MARTIN GARDNER

Watson: "This is indeed a mystery. What do you imagine it means?"
Holmes: "I have no data yet. It is a capital mistake to theorize before one has data. Insensibly one begins to twist facts to suit theories, instead of theories to suit facts."

—Sir Arthur Conan Doyle,
A Scandal in Bohemia

Parapsychologists differ considerably about the "facts" of their trade, but there is a fairly solid core of beliefs on which most of them agree. They are convinced that psi powers (ESP and PK) are possessed in some degree by everybody, and to a high degree by a few. Almost all agree that psi forces are independent of time and distance. (ESP is defined here as the alleged ability to perceive or sense by means other than the known physical senses. PK is defined here as mind over matter—the alleged ability to move or alter objects by paranormal means.)

There is, of course, no way they can be sure that extrasensory perception (ESP) and psychokinesis (PK) are manifestations of a single power. Even ESP (which includes telepathy, clairvoyance, and precognition) may, from their point of view, be a name for several kinds of interactions. However, parapsychologists have always been partial to the notion that a single force is responsible for both ESP and PK. If so, what kind of force is it?

Modern physics recognizes four fundamental forces: gravity, electromagnetism, and the weak and strong nuclear forces. All are field phenomena with strengths that diminish with distance. As J. B. Rhine perceived early in the game, there is no reasonable way that any such force can explain the peculiar indifference of psi to distance and time. Moreover, electromagnetism, long a favorite among early researchers, seems ruled out by experiments that show that

Reprinted from *Science and the Paranormal*, edited by George O. Abell and Barry Singer (New York: Scribner's, 1983), with the permission of the Estate of George O. Abell.

electromagnetic shielding has no effect on psi. Because extremely low frequency (ELF) electromagnetic waves have strong penetrating power, some parapsychologists continue to think of photons as carriers of psi, but empirical evidence for this is nonexistent. (Electromagnetic waves of successively shorter wavelength are, respectively, radio waves, infrared radiation, light, ultraviolet radiation, X-rays, and gamma rays. All of these are essentially the same kind of energy and are transmitted in small, discrete packets of energy called photons.)

Nor is there evidence for theories that other particles, such as the "graviton" (conjectured carrier of gravity), or the neutrino (emitted in certain nuclear reactions), play a role in psi. There have been recent speculations that tachyons, alleged particles that can travel faster than light, may be psi carriers. Unfortunately, tachyons probably don't exist and, even if they did, if they were used for communication their faster-than-light speeds would create logical contradictions with the extremely well documented results of special relativity. Russian parapsychologists have proposed the "psychon," but this is just inventing a new particle to explain a force that nobody understands—and that may not exist in the first place.

Because psi phenomena seem to disobey all known physical laws, Rhine has always held the sensible view that psi is outside physics altogether. We simply don't know, he says, what psi is. Until more data are in, we had best confess our ignorance and patiently await new developments.

Today's paraphysicists are less patient. In recent years, mainly as the result of speculations by Evan Harris Walker, a paraphysicist now in the Department of Mechanics and Materials Science at Johns Hopkins University, the notion that quantum mechanics (QM) may explain psi has become fashionable in many psi circles. Walker's ideas, in modified form, have been loudly championed by Jack Sarfatti, a San Francisco paraphysicist and one-time admirer of Uri Geller.[1] They have received partial and less strident support from Nobel Prize winner Brian Josephson of England,[2] O. Costa de Beauregard of the Poincaré Institute in Paris,[3] Harold Puthoff and Russell Targ of Stanford Research Institute,[4] and other less well known physicists, such as Richard Mattuck at the Örsted Institute of the University of Copenhagen.

Before summarizing Walker's views it will be necessary to consider a few relevant aspects of QM. In QM the state of a particle or system of particles is given by the "wave function." The curious thing about this function is that it does not specify precise values for such properties as position, momentum, spin, polarization, and so on. It gives only the probabilities that each variable will have certain values when the particle is measured. The act of measurement, for reasons that QM does not explain, causes the particle to undergo what is usually called a reduction or collapse of its "wave packet." The particle "jumps" from a quantum state in which the value of the variable being measured is indefinite to a quantum state in which it has a definite value.

The situation seems to be similar to what happens when a rolling die comes to rest, but actually it is radically different. Our inability to predict which side of the die's face will be on top is no more than a reflection of our ignorance of all the physical forces influencing the die. In principle, if we could take into account all those forces, we could correctly predict the outcome of the roll. But an unmeasured particle does not behave like a die or a flipped penny or a roulette wheel or like anything else we are familiar with. In QM the value that a quantum property acquires when measured is the result of pure chance. For example, if the wave function says a particle can be spinning either clockwise or counterclockwise with equal probability, there is no way of specifying which spin it has; it's as if the particle actually has no definite spin until it is measured. Both spins are somehow latent in the particle. Nature does not "decide" which spin it will be until the act of measurement captures it.

Many QM experts are unhappy with this "pure chance" aspect of the theory. Einstein himself, one of the early contributors to what became QM, liked to say that he could not imagine God playing dice with the universe. He hoped that someday physicists would find deeper laws capable of restoring classical causality on the microlevel. To dramatize his belief that QM was incomplete, Einstein and two friends, Boris Podolsky and Nathan Rosen, devised a thought experiment that became known as the EPR (for Einstein, Podolsky, and Rosen) paradox.[5]

The paradox can be given in many forms. When an electron and a positron (positive electron) come into contact, they annihilate each other, turning into energy in the form of two photons. Suppose, for example, that an electron-positron annihilation sends off two photons in opposite directions. A photon can be plane polarized with the amplitude of its wave motion in either a horizontal or vertical orientation, or it can be circularly polarized, so that the plane of the wave displacement rotates as it moves through space. The circular polarization can rotate in a clockwise or counterclockwise direction. QM predicts that the two photons produced by the annihilation must have *opposite* polarization. Now each can be measured by a filtering device that allows the photon to pass through one of two channels. If a photon is measured for either polarization, then immediately allowed to pass through a second device of the same type, the type of polarization is unchanged. The first measurement has, in a sense, "forced" the photon into a definite state. According to QM theory, states are not "known"—even to the particle itself—until after the particle interacts with something else. The uncertainty is innate until the polarization is observed, or measured, at which point it is no longer possible for it to be one way or the other.

Two photons, produced by electron–positron annihilation, remain correlated in the sense that they must have (when measured) opposite plane polarizations or opposite circular polarizations. To dramatize the paradox, suppose they become separated by ten light-years. QM tells us that if one photon is measured for either variable, we know the value of that variable for the other photon *even though it has not been measured.*

As Robert Dicke and James Wittke put it in their *Introduction to Quantum Mechanics* (Addison Wesley, 1960), we cannot conceive how a photon can be plane and circularly polarized at the same time. Indeed, QM asserts that the photons have no definite values for either variable until one photon is measured and its wave packet collapses. Yet when measurement "forces" one photon into, say, a clockwise polarized state, the other instantly goes into a counterclockwise polarized state. They conclude, "The two photons constitute a *single* dynamic system. Any information obtained about the system is information about both photons. Any interaction on a single photon is an interaction on the system and affects the state of the whole system."

Now there would be nothing mysterious about this if we could think of the two photons as intricate little mechanisms that somehow possess opposite polarizations of both types before they are measured, but it is precisely this that QM forbids. It is not until the act of measurement that the photon's wave packet collapses and nature decides what to do. Dicke and Wittke, like the authors of almost all standard textbooks on QM, simply describe what happens and leave it at that. It may seem to be sheer magic, but QM works very well in that it is extremely successful in predicting how electromagnetic phenomena behave.

Einstein wanted to know how the trick works. It is unthinkable, he argued, that information can go instantly from one particle to another one that is ten light-years away—yet QM seems to demand this. Somehow, when one particle is measured, the other "knows" the outcome of the measurement. In the past few years, actual laboratory tests with correlated photons, together with a deep construct known as Bell's theorem, have confirmed the predictions of QM.[6] The new results based on Bell's theorem leave open two possibilities: One, conjectured by the London quantum physicist David Bohm and others, is that correlated particles may be connected on a subquantum level that is outside the space-time of relativity theory. The other possibility is that widely separated particles may be causally connected in space-time, but in a way that violates relativity theory.

An enormous ferment is now under way among quantum physicists over the implications of Bell's theorem and the new laboratory observations. More experiments are planned, so it is too early to guess how the EPR paradox will finally be resolved. Most working physicists probably belong to what has been called the pragmatic or "no-nonsense" school, which accepts the paradoxes of QM without worrying about what is "actually"going on. A no-nonsense physicist sees QM as essentially a mathematical tool that tells him, with astonishing accuracy, what he will see if he makes certain experiments. It tells him nothing about what goes on between experiments. The no-nonsense physicist is content with this tool and unconcerned about philosophical interpretations; he will continue to use QM unquestioningly until someone comes along with a new theory that has testable consequences and works better than classic QM.

Einstein was more philosophically minded. He was not content with being told no more than that, if you measure a particle here, another particle at a vast distance will abruptly alter its state. He ruled out as too "spooky" the notion that information could go from particle to particle at superluminal (greater than light) speed. That seemed to him as absurd as believing that a needle stuck in a voodoo doll could instantaneously cause pain in a victim many miles away. Now that Bell's theorem and new experimental results have ruled out local hidden variables, the possibility that Einstein considered unthinkable has become so thinkable that a number of quantum experts now favor it.[7] But note that only information of a curious, limited sort is transferred, not energy. No one has actually found a way that particle correlation can be used for transmitting any kind of message faster than light. But there is a possibility that widely separated particles may be connected in some as yet totally unknown way.

A useful metaphor—of course it is no more than that—is to think of our space-time as the "surface" of some vast hypersphere. (A hypersphere is the analogue of a three-dimensional sphere in four or more dimensions. It cannot be visualized, but is well defined mathematically.) Within space-time no information can go faster than light. But we do not know what laws govern the transfer of information through the hypersphere. On a subquantum level (a hypothetical unknown theory or principle that is more fundamental than that of quantum mechanics), perhaps information can travel at superluminal speeds—or even instantaneously.

It was necessary to sketch this background because Walker's theory of para-normal powers assumes the existence of a subquantum level. Walker regards the human mind, like all physical systems, as an ongoing QM process. We possess, he says, a "will" that is continually reducing wave packets in the brain to bring about new mental states. This process, he conjectures, involves "electron tunnel-ing across synaptic clefts." There is no experimental evidence of this, but he believes that such evidence may be forthcoming. Because, in Walker's view, all parts of the universe are connected on the subquantum level, he sees no reason why the human will cannot use this level to collapse wave packets of quantum systems outside the brain—regardless of how far away they are.

That the brain can do this is, of course, pure speculation. In QM it is not the human observer who collapses wave packets but the observing instruments. The human observer simply looks at certain macrostructures, such as photo-graphs and pointer readings, to learn the outcome of microlevel measurements.

When particles leave tracks inside bubble chambers, it is what goes on inside the chamber that reduces wave packets and gives to the tracks their precise positions and shapes. It is only after a long chain of macrointeractions (involving events that are irreversible) that a human mind "sees" the tracks in the same way it sees a star or a tree. No one supposes that this observation can alter the track any more than looking at a tree can alter the tree. In brief, there is no support for the notion that the brain can change the state of a quantum system outside itself.[8]

Walker's second assumption is even more staggering. Not only does he suppose that the mind can alter wave packets of distant objects, but he also assumes that it can alter a wave packet in such a way as to bring about a desired value for one of the variables. There is no reliable evidence of any sort for this fantastic claim; indeed, it runs counter to the very heart of QM's formalism, which asserts that the value acquired by a variable, after wave-packet reduction, is the outcome of absolute chance.

It is obvious that if both of Walker's assumptions are correct, a scaffolding exists on which to hang a theory of ESP and PK. In Walker's view, psi action is not a force that goes from brain to brain, or brain to object, or object to brain. There is not even a message that travels from here to there. A psi event occurs when one or more persons unite their quantum mechanical power to collapse wave packets in such a way as to select a mutually desired future state from among all the possible states permitted by the relevant wave functions.

Let us see how this works for telepathy. In classical psi theories, a mind sends out a wave of some sort that carries information to another mind. Walker's QM approach is strikingly different. Suppose a sender is turning ESP cards and a receiver is recording guesses. Eventually the receiver's list will be compared with the target list. If both sender and receiver want a successful outcome, their minds will collaborate to alter all the quantum systems involved so as to bring about the mutually desired state.

Clairvoyance may seem different but actually is not. An experimenter selects targets, the subject tries to "see" them, but the overall situation is the same as before. All persons participating in the test, including sideline observers, collaborate to influence the outcome. No information is transferred from target to subject. Rather, it is a case of all the participants using their wills to "select" a future state from among the myriad of possible states permitted by the relevant wave functions. Precognition is "explained" in exactly the same way. Thus telepathy, clairvoyance, and precognition are simply different names for essentially the same QM process.

Walker's theory clearly accounts for the seeming independence of psi from space and time constraints. Moreover, it accounts easily for the "sheep–goat" effect so often invoked by parapsychologists. The sheep (believers) are supposed to do better than the goats (skeptics) as both subjects and experimenters. Sheep naturally try to reduce wave packets to get successful results. Goats naturally want experiments to fail. This also explains, says Walker, why the mere presence of a skeptic as an observer may cause a psi test to fail. The skeptic keeps collapsing wave packets the wrong way.

Walker's conjectures become bolder when he speculates on how QM can explain ordinary psychokinesis. Historic PK tests, by Rhine and others, involved testing the mind's ability to influence rolling or falling dice. Although a die is made of billions of particles, it can be regarded as a single quantum system with its own overall wave function.

QM does not give the actual state of a particle (say, its position and velocity), but only the *probability* of various states. With extremely many particles, though, as in a die, the individual uncertainties nearly average out, and the state of the composite die is well determined. Similarly, the lot of an individual gambler in a casino is very uncertain; but, if there are thousands of gamblers present, the casino operator has a very good idea what the evening's take will be. Thus, statisically speaking, the die's quantum uncertainty is essentially zero—much smaller than the uncertainty arising from the actions of its individual molecules (called "thermal noise"); nevertheless, its uncertainty is not absolutely zero. Suppose the die does a good deal of bouncing as it rolls down a long runway and falls on a flat surface. If a mind can collapse the die's wave packet at the start of its roll, to throw it into one of its possible states, this inconceivably tiny microeffect will be magnified by the divergent process of bouncing. A minute alteration at the outset will, Walker reasons, have a slightly larger effect after the first bounce, a still larger one after the second, and so on. Such divergent effects are not uncommon in the macroworld; a stray spark from a cap pistol can start a forest fire, for example. As someone has said, the flutter of a butterfly's wings in Brazil could conceivably start a divergent chain of causes and effects that would end with a cyclone in Kansas.

If a die bounces enough as it rolls, Walker reasons, will not a tiny alteration of its position at the start be sufficiently magnified at the end of the roll to bring about a desired macrostate when the die comes to rest? He suggests ways in which this conjecture could be tested. For example, one would expect a stronger PK effect in tests with dice that do a lot of bouncing than in tests with little bouncing. Also, the more dice there are, the more they rattle (bounce) against one another; consequently, the more dice, the stronger the expected PK effect. The basic idea extends to such measuring devices as thermistors, magnetometers, radiation detectors, and so on. If the final readings are affected by any kind of natural noise that stems from a QM process, the noise provides a divergent sequence comparable to bouncing dice. This should improve the subject's chances to succeed in altering such readings by PK.

Walker's theory also accounts for the embarrassing fact that parapsychologists have been unable to detect a PK effect on a delicately balanced needle even when many minds are collaborating on the effort for a long period of time. Moving the needle requires a push proportional to the needle's mass. From Walker's point of view, quantum uncertainty is not strong enough to provide such a push (assuming the subject is not a superpsychic) unless it is magnified by a divergent process. Since no divergent phenomena are involved with the needle, the average subject is unable to work up enough PK power to move it.

To bolster his theory that a single wave-packet collapse can start a divergent process that ends with a desired macroresult, Walker relies almost entirely on the published results of experiments made over a period of some 20 years by a retired Swedish electrical engineer named Haakon Forwald. Most of Forwald's papers were published in the fifties in Rhine's *Journal of Parapsychology*. They dealt not with dice but with unmarked cubes of various sizes, weights, and surface textures, and made of different materials. Forwald allowed his cubes to roll down a long incline onto a walled surface divided into two identical parts. The idea was for the subject to influence the cubes so that more ended up in one region than in the other. Parapsychologists call it a "placement effect."

In his lengthy paper "Foundations of Paraphysical and Parapsychological Phenomena," Walker devotes many pages to a detailed analysis of Forwald's confusing results.[9] Walker is firmly persuaded that these results are unique in the literature on PK work with cubes, since they show a correlation between the magnitude of the effect and the nature of the cubes.

When I first learned that Walker relied so heavily on Forwald's work, I was astounded. Most parapsychologists today have a low opinion of this work. For one thing, almost all of it was solo—that is, Forwald acted as both experimenter and subject. No photographic records were made. Today, if a researcher submitted a paper to Rhine's journal reporting on placement effects with cubes in which the author was both subject and experimenter, the paper would be rejected. But at the time Forwald did his research, protocols were unbelievably lax.

After publishing many papers on the results of his solo work, Forwald went to Rhine's laboratory in 1957 to conduct rolling-cube experiments under the supervision of J. G. Pratt. Forwald's crusty temperament made it difficult for him to work with others. After a number of unsuccessful experiments, an assistant was finally found who was psychologically compatible with Forwald. The assistant was a 20-year-old married woman employed in the lab as a secretary. The positive results of this work prompted R. A. McConnell, at the University of Pittsburgh, to repeat the tests in 1959 at his laboratory. This time a motion-picture record was made and the cubes were individually numbered. "It was hoped in this way," McConnell wrote, "to tighten the evidence for the existence of the placement effect."[10]

Alas, with these simple controls the results were negative. McConnell's opinion is that this failure to replicate was entirely psychological. He noted that Forwald spent eight weeks in Durham in 1957 but only 19 days in Pittsburgh. And "even had he been able to remain longer, it would have been difficult to create in a biophysics department within an urban university the same air of southern relaxation and hospitality that was characteristic of the Duke University laboratory."

A disappointed Forwald returned to Sweden, where, working all by himself again, the placement effect returned. I know of no PK research, over so long a period, that was so consistently uncontrolled.[11]

Not only does Walker accept the validity of Forwald's sloppy solo work, he also accepts the reality of claims that some psychics can cause macroscopic objects to "translocate" (vanish here and appear there) as well as produce the "Geller Effect" (paranormal metal-bending). In neither case is there a divergent causal sequence, as with bouncing cubes, so Walker is forced to posit a different mechanism. He distinguishes normal or weak PK, such as we ordinary mortals have, from the "strong PK" of superpsychics.

How does strong PK work? As before, Walker offers nothing resembling a scientific theory. He simply makes another quantum jump from a mere possibility to a wild assumption. The superpsychic, by an "extraordinary" and "sustained" effort of will is able to alter *lots* of wave packets. By altering enough packets, he or she can bring about a "highly improbable state" that is nevertheless one permitted by the macro-object's overall wave function. For example, a Felicia Parise moves a plastic pill bottle form here to there, or a Uri Geller bends a spoon by "translocating" a portion of its metal.

What does all this add up to? It adds up to nothing more than a bare assertion that an intensive, sustained effort of will by a superpsychic can produce translocations and metal bending.

There is more. Walker believes that his "theory" will explain the great miracles of historical religions. At the close of his paper "Consciousness and Quantum Theory,"[12] he pulls out all the stops. Copernicus is taken as a symbol of the man of science, devoted to reason and empiricism, and skeptical of religious faith. Luther is taken as an opposite symbol: the man of faith who is skeptical of science. Today, proclaims Walker, religion is entering a new age. Thanks to QM we at last have a genuinely scientific explanation for the great miracles of Luther's faith, and presumably those of other religions as well. "We are at a point in time for which certain knowledge, factual knowledge, can provide a basis for the God concept," he asserts.

His QM theory of psi, Walker goes on, gives "only an inkling" of how the "collective will" of all the consciousnesses in the universe can be thought of as "God," and how this God can interact with history in ways that seem miraculous but that actually are nothing more than the collapsing of many wave packets to bring about desired future states. "It is to be through efforts of this nature that the present basis of acceptance of God, faith, will come to an end, and factual knowledge will become the basis for religion. This is to be the rock on which the new age is to be founded. This is the thesis I come to nail to your door."

The thesis he is nailing to our door! It seems clear that Walker sees himself as a new Martin Luther, nailing his QM theory of consciousness on the world's door to spark a new Reformation—a new age in which hitherto blind faith will be supplanted by certain scientific knowledge. For centuries, Christians have supposed, in their ignorance of QM, that when Jesus walked on the water it was a transcendent god suspending the laws of his creation. Now that Walker has nailed his thesis to the church door, Christians know better. It was Jesus, aided by the collective consciousnesses of the universe, who twiddled billions of wave packets to permit the highly improbable state of his levitation!

To readers unfamiliar with QM, Walker's papers seem enormously impressive because they swarm with equations and scientific jargon that only a physicist could understand. But, when it is all translated and you discover exactly what he is saying, his "theory" turns out to be only a collection of pious hopes. If our mind operates by quantum jumps, if all parts of the universe are connected on a subquantum level, if the human will can alter wave packets of distant objects, and if we can alter the packets to bring about desired states, then we have an "explanation" of how Uri Geller can bend a spoon. This is not a theory; it is a caricature of a theory. I am reminded of a letter that Wolfgang Pauli wrote to George Gamow. Pauli and Heisenberg had recently cooked up a hypothesis to explain some new results in particle theory. The hypothesis had been shot down. Pauli closed his letter with a "proof" that he could draw as well as Titian. The proof was an empty square with the note: "Only technical details are lacking."[13]

Walker has proposed ways in which his theory could be tested, but is it worthwhile to fund the testing of a theory of translocation, metal bending, and placement effects before it has been demonstrated that such psi effects actually take place? So far, the main support for Walker's theory is a series of questionable experiments with rolling cubes, conducted by an experimenter who liked to work alone and whose results are regarded with suspicion even by parapsychologists.

Although the general public remains unaware of it, the overwhelming majority of experimental psychologists around the world do not believe that the existence of ESP and PK has even been demonstrated. Yet for the past hundred years the true believers, in violation of Sherlock Holmes's advice, have been turning to the latest theories of physics in hopes of finding support for the shaky results they are convinced are genuine. It is a sad history. When Maxwell's theory of electromagnetic fields was new, it was fashionable to theorize about how magnetic forces could account for psi. When relativity theory was new, it was fashionable to explain psi by forces in hyperspace that move in and out of our world.[14] Today the big mysteries of physics are on the microlevel. It is not surprising that true believers, eager to underpin psi with science, would turn to QM.

For once I find myself agreeing with Rhine. Paraphysicists would do well to abandon theory and concentrate on devising experiments that can be replicated by unbelievers. At the end of the 23rd Annual International Conference of the Parapsychology Foundations in Geneva in 1974 on QM and psi, there was a roundtable discussion at which the writer Charles Panati, editor of *The Geller Papers,* made a good point. He had been enormously impressed, he said, by Puthoff and Targ's account of how their superpsychic Ingo Swann had altered a magnetometer. This, said Panati, is something "no magician would dare to claim he could duplicate." (Although Panati admits he is totally ignorant of conjuring methods, he is quick to tell magicians what they can't do.) Why not call an international conference of eminent physicists and let them witness Swann perform this miracle? Would it not hit them all like a "sledgehammer blow"?

Arthur Koestler thought the suggestion excellent. But immediately the paraphysicists began to toss cold water on the idea. If any of the observing scientists are skeptics, warned Costa de Beauregard, "the demonstration will come out zero." Walker allowed that Swann's magnetometer feat was closer to being *the* definitive demonstration than any other he knew, but he reminded everybody that he had once seen Uri Geller try to perform for skeptics at Berkeley; and, because their wills kept reducing wave packets the wrong way, Geller could do nothing. The final blow to Panati's innocent plan was struck by Targ in a memorable sentence. "Even if Geller walked on the water from Berkeley to San Francisco," said Targ, "skeptics would say, Oh, that's the old walking-on-the-water trick."

So the familiar deadlock remains. Believers keep getting sensational results, skeptics keep failing to replicate them, and the believers keep invoking their old Catch-22 to explain the failures. Work like Forwald's through which loopholes run like holes in swiss cheese, seems never to fade from the literature. There is no indication that paraphysicists have the slightest desire to train themselves in the subtle arts of deception, or seek the aid of knowledgeable magicians in any significant way. As a result, they continue to act like excited little children every time a new psychic charlatan shows them a trick they can't explain. In the report of the conference on QM and psi, there are numerous favorable references to Geller.[15] Not one person who spoke at the conference, least of all Walker, questioned Uri's psychic powers.

It looks as if Panati will have a long wait for that sledgehammer blow. In the meantime, paraphysicists would be well advised to stop rushing about pretending to be Martin Luther, nailing new paradigms on laboratory doors. They would do better to have Sherlock Holmes's advice that opened this chapter emblazoned on large shields and nailed above their own laboratory entrances.

Notes

1. See "The Physical Roots of Consciousness," by Jack Sarfatti, in *Roots of Consciousness: Psychic Liberation through History, Science and Experience*, by Jeffrey Mishlove (New York: Random House, 1975), pages 279–293; *Space-Time and Beyond*, by Bob Toben "in conversation with physicists Jack Sarfatti and Fred Wolf" (New York: Dutton, 1975).

2. See "Possible Connections Between Psychic Phenomena and Quantum Mechanics," by Brian Josephson (*New Horizons*, January 1975, pages 224–226).

3. See "Quantum Paradoxes and Aristotle's Two-fold Information Concept," by O. Costa de Beauregard in the Oteri book cited in Note 9, and his comments in the book's discussion sections.

4. See *Mind-Reach: Scientists Look at Psychic Ability*, by Russell Targ and Harold Puthoff (New York: Delacorte Press/Elinor Friede, 1977), page 170.

5. The EPR paradox was first set forth by Einstein, Podolsky, and Rosen in "Can Quantum-Mechanical Description of Physical Reality Be Considered Complete?" in *Physical Review*, vol. 47 (1935), pages 777–780. Niels Bohr's reply, which Einstein claimed he could never understand, appeared in the same journal, vol. 48 (1935), pages 696 ff. For a discussion between Bohr and Einstein about the paradox, see *Albert Einstein: Philosopher-Scientist*, edited by Paul Arthur Schilpp (Library of Living Philosophers, 1949), pages 231–241, 681–683. For discussions by Einstein and Max Born of the paradox, see *The Born-Einstein Letters*, edited by Born (New York: Walker, 1971), pages 164–165, 168–176, 178, 188–189, 214–215. A letter from Einstein to Karl Popper, in which he outlines his paradox, appears in Popper's *The Logic of Scientific Discovery* (New York: Basic Books, 1959), pages 457–464; see also pages 244–245, 444–448.

Einstein's objection is in no way met merely by restating the QM formalism that describes the paradox. This is the kind of "resolution" one finds in almost any standard textbook on QM theory. On this point see "Concerning Einstein's, Podolsky's, and Rosen's Objection to Quantum Theory," by Clifford A. Hooker (*American Journal of Physics*, vol. 38 [July 1970], pages 851–857) and Hooker's lengthy paper "The Nature of Quantum Mechanical Reality: Einstein Versus Bohr" in *Paradigms and Paradoxes*, edited by Robert G. Colodny (Pittsburgh: University of Pittsburgh Press, 1972).

6. In 1965, J. S. Bell showed that any theory of hidden variables designed to explain the correlation of two particles, that was both realistic and local, would lead to predictions that differ from those of QM and therefore can be tested. "Realistic" here means that the variables have a space-time structure independent of the observer, and "local" means that the particles, after becoming widely separated, are not in any kind of interaction with each other.

Stronger versions of Bell's proof were later found by others. All are known collectively as Bell's theorem. In 1969, J. F. Clauser, M. A. Horne, Abner Shimony, and R. A. Holt showed how actual tests could be made. Since 1972 there have been seven such tests, most of which clearly confirm QM. The experiments involved particles that remain correlated only for a distance of a few meters. No one can yet say whether the correlation will persist or grow weaker at greater distances.

For a detailed and excellent summary of these momentous results see "Bell's Theorem: Experimental Tests and Implications," by Clauser and Shimony, in *Reports on Progress in Physics*, vol. 41 (1978), pages 1881–1927. "Because of the evidence in favour of quantum mechanics from the experiments based upon Bell's theorem," they conclude, "we are forced either to abandon . . . a realistic view of the physical world (perhaps an unheard tree falling in the forest makes no sound after all)—or else to accept some kind of action-at-a-distance. Either option is radical, and a comprehensive study of their philosophical consequences remains to be made."

7. See H. P. Stapp, "Are Superluminal Connections Necessary?" in *Il Nuovo Cimento*, vol. 40B (July 11, 1977), pages 191–205. To avoid superluminal connection, Costa de Beauregard (in the book cited in Note 9) maintains that quantum information travels back in time from the measured particle to the event that produced the two particles, then forward in time to the other particle. The path is a "Feynman zigzag" that brings the information to the second particle at precisely the same moment it left the first one.

8. I am aware that some very eminent physicists, notably Eugene Wigner, contend that every "measurement" of a quantum system creates a new state that is in turn subject to measurement, and that this regress does not finally end until it reaches a mind. By this is a point of view held by an extreme minority of physicists. It rests partly on metaphysical suppositions and partly on desperation over the lack of any good theory of wave-packet reduction.

One objection to Wigner's view is that there seems to be no good reason to stop the process with the human observer—not to mention the difficulties that arise in asking whether the process can be said to terminate if the observer is, say, a cow. The observer, too, is an on-going quantum system with its own wave function that can acquire precise values for its variables only if someone observes the observer, and so into an infinite regress. This is sometimes called the "von Neumann catastrophe" (because it is suggested by John von Neumann's classic formalizaton of QM), and sometimes the "paradox of Wigner's friend." It is closely tied to the famous earlier paradox of "Schrodinger's cat." The issues are complex and technical, and loaded with semantic pitfalls, but they are largely irrelevant to our topic. Even if one believes that a falling tree has no "reality" until a "mind" observes it, it does not follow that a human mind can alter the way the tree falls.

In a paper on "Wave-Packet Reduction as a Medium of Communication," by Joseph Hall, Christopher Kim, Brien McElroy, and Abner Shimony (*Foundations of Physics*, vol. 7 [October 1977], pages 759–767), the authors report on an ingenious experiment designed to test the ability of observers to reduce wave packets. The results were negative. "Doubt is thereby thrown," the authors conclude with understatement, "upon the hypothesis that the reduction of the wave packet is due to the interaction of the physical apparatus with the psyche of an observer."

9. This paper, Walker's major statement of his theory, appears in *Quantum Mechanics and Parapsychology*, edited by Laura Oteri, published by the Parapsychology Foundation, New York, in 1975. The book contains eleven papers given at the 23rd Annual International Conference of the Parapsychology Foundation, held at Geneva in 1974. The topic had been proposed by Arthur Koestler, who attended as an observer.

10. "Psychokinetic Placement: II. A Factorial Study of Successful and Unsuccessful Series," by R. A. McConnell and Haakon Forwald, in *The Journal of Parapsychology*, vol. 31 (September 1967), pages 198–213.

11. For a listing of Forwald's principal papers and a critical survey, see "A Review of Psychokinesis (PK)" by Edward Girden, in the *Psychological Bulletin*, vol. 59 (September 1962), pages 374–377, 385. Forwald became convinced that the PK placement effect he thought he was getting is gravitational. In his monograph *Mind, Matter and Gravitation* (New York: Parapsychology Foundation, 1969) he argues that his "findings suggest that PK-forces are of a gravitational kind, and that they originate from a mental influence on atomic nuclei in the material which is used in the moveable bodies in the experiments." He believes this theory is tentatively confirmed by his late experiments with an oak ball rolling sideways on an inclined plane.

12. Published in *Psychic Explorations: A Challenge for Science*, edited by astronaut Edgar D. Mitchell and occult writer John White (New York: Putnam's, 1974).

13. Gamow reproduces Pauli's letters in facsimile in *Thirty Years That Shook Physics: The Story of Quantum Theory* (Garden City, N.Y.: Doubleday, 1966), page 162.

14. Hyperspace theories of the paranormal were popular during spiritualism's heyday. A classic crank work along such lines is *Transcendental Physics*, by Johann C. F. Zöllner, published in Germany in 1879 and later translated into English. Zöllner was typical of many of today's paraphysicists, learned in science but so gullible that he was easily bamboozled by a famous mountebank of the time, the slate-writing medium Henry Slade. Zöllner's book should be required reading for every executive of Stanford Research Institute.

Hyperspace theories of psi are still with us. See William A. Tiller, "The Positive and Negative Space/Time Frames as Conjugate Systems," and Charles Muses, "Paraphysics: A New View of Ourselves and the Cosmos." Both papers are in *Future Science*, edited by John White and Stanley Krippner (New York: Anchor Press, 1977). Muses, a panpsychist who believes that all basic particles are primitive life forms, explores hyperspaces with his "hypernumbers"—operators that describe how you can do such things as swing an object into hyperspace and back. They account for the Geller effect, the levitations of the British medium D. D. Home, and other wonders.

15. See *Quantum Mechanics and Parapsychology*, pp. 51–52, 124–126, 171, 230, 261, and 274.

26

Detective Work in Parapsychology

DENYS PARSONS

If I were invited to talk to a group of young people in the hope of interesting them in parapsychology, I would explain to them that research in parapsychology is very similar to research in any other subject, whether literary, historical, or scientific. I would assure them that much of its fascination lies in attention to detail—following up every trail, however unpromising—and that much of its satisfaction comes either when a long-shot pays off or when a painstaking assembly of fine detail leads to the resolution of a point at issue.

Indeed, research in parapsychology is akin to research in criminology and forensic medicine. Series on television, both fictional and documentary, have displayed ample evidence of the need for meticulously detailed investigation in those fields. There has been no comparable exposition of the back-room detective grind that goes into the exploration of parapsychology, so let me venture to portray something of the flavor of it through an account of some of my own research.

Fifty years ago, Mrs. Helen Duncan, the Scottish "materializing" medium, was at the height of her powers. Her specialty was the production of "ecto-plasm," allegedly emanating from her own body. In the darkened séance room the ectoplasm assumed the form of the spirits of departed relatives, friends, and even animal pets of the sitters. The late Harry Price (1931), a well-known British investigator, conducted a series of sittings with Mrs. Duncan in 1931 and took a number of photographs. Inspection of these photographs gives the overwhelming impression that the ectoplasm and the spirit forms were of mundane origin. What appear to be the warp, weft, and selvedge of butter muslin can be clearly identified, as can rents and folds in the material. In other photographs we can discern a rubber glove, a safety pin, and dolls' heads or masks.

At a séance in Edinburgh in 1933, the "spirit of a little girl" was seized by one of the "sitters" and proved to be a woman's undervest. Mrs. Duncan was arrested and convicted of fraud. Eleven years later, in 1944, the police intervened at a séance at Portsmouth. This resulted in Mrs. Duncan's being brought to trial at the Old Bailey, the famous criminal court in London. The prosecution was embarrassed to discover that there was no modern legislation to fit the case, and Helen Duncan had to be charged under the Witchcraft Act of 1735; this Act prescribes a year's imprisonment for anybody who may "pretend to exercise or use any kind of witchcraft, sorcery, inchantment or conjuration." She was again convicted.

Two years later, I heard a story about the Portsmouth séance from an ex-naval friend at third-hand. My friend said he knew a man who had met a sailor named Jacobs who had attended that séance. When the police shined their flashlights for the denouement, Jacobs, it was claimed, had grabbed hold of the "spirit" and secreted it in the pocket of his greatcoat. It turned out to be a substantial length of cheesecloth and, the story went on, Jacobs took it back to barracks and used it as a hammock.

If this is true, it is remarkable that the police did not witness the incident, and, if they did, it is incomprehensible that Jacobs had not been called as a witness at the trial. I considered it important to check out the story, and I set about tracking down the sailor, a task that I thought would present little difficulty. But first I wrote to the intermediary, James Robinson, who had told my friend that remarkable story.

Robinson replied as follows:

> At the time of the Duncan case I was, as you know, a Leading Seaman instructor in the Royal Naval Barracks at Portsmouth. Two of my friends, also instructors, had been to a séance by Mrs. Duncan and said they did not believe she was "on the level." The next evening [after a second visit] they returned to barracks and joyfully produced a piece of cheesecloth about eight feet square. When I questioned one of them, L/S J. Jacobs, this is the story he told me:
>
> Jacobs and his friend were sitting at the front of the audience and were becoming more and more convinced that the show was a lot of tripe, when suddenly there was a disturbance and Jacobs made a grab at the ghost and contacted a fist-full of cheesecloth which he immediately stuffed into his greatcoat. This, he is convinced, came off the figure purporting to be a ghost. They both made a hasty exit after this and returned to barracks.
>
> I do not think that either of my friends would make up a story like that as they were both very interested in psychical phenomena.

The story was now a little stronger in that it was second-hand instead of third-hand. Then, with the object of making it first-hand, I turned my attention to tracing J. Jacobs. I wrote to the Drafting Commander, R.N. Barracks, Portsmouth, asking for information and regretting that I could not give Jacobs's navy number. In reply I was told that "the details given are insufficient for the rating concerned to be traced in official records."

Later, I found out from Robinson that Jacobs had been on the staff of Lt.

Comdr. Crangham, and I wrote again to the barracks. I had a reply from the Chief of Regulating Staff: "Reports show that John Henry Jacobs, Leading Seaman—official number PJ/X 246351, was serving in the Royal Naval Barracks, Portsmouth, in 1944. He is at present serving in H.M.S. Diadem and any communication should be addressed c/o G.P.O. London." I wrote to this John Jacobs and sometime later received a reply in which he denied emphatically that he was the man concerned.

Robinson had also told me that he believed Jacobs had taken up poultry-farming after the war. An inquiry to the Poultry Association of Great Britain produced the reply that "an exhaustive search of our records has not produced any useful information."

Robinson could not remember the name of the other sailor who had accompanied Jacobs to the séance, but by lucky chance a full list of the sitters had been published in reports of the trial. When I fed Robinson the names White, Pickett, Williams, Coulcher, Green, and Bush, he immediately confirmed that Pickett was the name of the other sailor.

I then wrote to the naval authorities asking if they could trace the name Pickett; I described him as a friend of J. Jacobs. They replied: "Peter John Pickett, P/JX 515005, was drafted to H.M.S. Gosling on 9 March 1944. He is shown as 'Discharged Dead' on 17 August 1945." More remarkably, they came up with a second L/S J. P. Jacobs, with a different number, P/JX 607928, who, they said, was drafted to H.M.S. Loch Katrine on 19 January 1945. "This man, it is understood, was Rhodesian and the last trace held is that he was serving in H.M.S. Afrikander." I wrote a number of letters but failed to trace this man.

Next, I decided to enlist the help of the Portsmouth police. I wrote to them explaining the circumstances of my inquiry. This produced a stereotyped reply that information obtained during police inquiries could not be divulged.

Then, through a fellow member of the Society for Psychical Research, I was given an introduction to the barrister who had been prosecuting counsel at Mrs. Duncan's trial. He expressed interest in the story I told and offered to help. He wrote to the Portsmouth police on my behalf and later telephoned me to give the particulars of yet a third Jacobs—L/S Woolf Bentley Jacobs, P/JX 220123, with an address in north London. It now seemed clear that there were three Leading Seamen named Jacobs whose time at Portsmouth Barracks overlapped. It is perhaps not surprising that James Robinson transposed the first name, John, of two of them, to the third, who did not bear that name.

I lost no time in arranging to meet L/S W. B. Jacobs, and we had a long talk on the evening of May 3, 1948, four years after the trial. Jacobs admitted that he was the man concerned but described the story told by Robinson as "fantastic" and quite untrue—it had just grown in the telling. He and Pickett had in fact been seated at the back of the room and were in no position to seize the "ectoplasm." He had not brought back cheesecloth or any other material to the barracks and could not understand how the story arose.

Curiously enough my second detective venture in parapsychology involved the tracing of two airmen (Parsons 1962). The impetus came from an article on "telepathy" by Hunter Diack in the *New Statesman and Nation* of August 27, 1949. It was at the time of the triumphant rise to fame of the Piddingtons, a husband and wife team who performed an entertaining fake telepathy act that dominated the lighter side of British radio for many weeks. In reviewing the Piddingtons' act, Diack related an interesting experience he had had while he was an education officer in the Royal Air Force.

Two airmen, named Scathard and Stephenson, began in 1945 to entertain their mates during winter evenings in their billets with a telepathy performance. News of this soon spread to the officers of the station, who asked for a demonstration. Indeed, many such demonstrations were given to officers and men during that winter.

The performance was impressive. One of the partners (Scathard) would wander around the audience asking people to show coins from their pockets, select playing cards, or write down their birthday or favorite color.

Scathard did not speak a word, and apparently made no sign to his partner on the stage, who gave the correct replies almost simultaneously. All the time Scathard kept his back to the stage, where Stephenson paced casually to and fro, gazing into the air. Meanwhile, Scathard, endeavoring to transmit an impression of the object to him, concentrated till his face grew pale and beads of sweat stood on his brow.

Vaudeville telepathy acts are well known in the history of parapsychology, but Diack seemed so confident that these two were genuine telepathic subjects that I thought an investigation should be mounted to obtain full details. Accordingly I wrote to the Royal Air Force Records Office at Gloucester, asking for help in tracing Scathard—a name so unusual that I thought I would experience little difficulty. A printed form came back a week later: "From the information given, I regret that I have been unable to identify the above-named with my records."

Next I wrote to Hunter Diack. I asked whether he was sure of the name Scathard, or whether he had used a pseudonym to conceal the identity of the airman concerned. He replied: "I have no doubt at all about the name Scathard, nor little doubt that my memory is more dependable than the R.A.F. system of keeping records. Mr. D. G. Farrow, Education Officer, Great Yarmouth, ought to be able to confirm that this name Scathard is correct." In his letter he also put forward the view that the hypothesis of numerous accomplices was quite improbable, and he stated that the events described took place at RAF Station

Wing, Leighton Buzzard, during the autumn and winter of 1945.

I approached Mr. Farrow, who confirmed the name Scathard and gave the additional information that the pair had performed at Murray's Club in London in early 1946. A telephone inquiry and a letter to the club yielded no result.

A second inquiry was then addressed to the RAF Record Office, giving the additional information that Scathard had been stationed at Leighton Buzzard in autumn 1945. A second, identical negative reply was received.

Further reference to Diack's letter showed that Scathard was a Nottingham man in the building trade. A letter to the City Treasurer of Nottingham produced a negative reply, and an inquiry to the secretary of the local Trades Council was not answered.

Had I then had the experience of later years I would have conducted one more maneuver that I have since found profitable from time to time. I would have gone to a large reference library and looked through the 70-odd telephone books for the whole country seeking individuals named Scathard. This could well have been productive in tracing a relative of the man I sought. The search would have taken an hour at most.

But now it was April 1950, and clues were beginning to run short. It seemed to me inconceivable that the RAF Records Office should be unable to trace Scathard, Leighton Buzzard, autumn 1945. I wrote for the third time, and 11 days later received the familiar form: "From the information given I regret that I have been unable to identify the above-named with my records."

I now turned my attention to Stephenson. Diack told me that he believed Stephenson lived in Beckenham. A search of the London telephone directory revealed two Stephensons and four Stevensons in the Beckenham area. I wrote to all six. In the last reply received I read: "I have to admit to being the person you are looking for."

I hastened to get in touch with this Stephenson, and we met for a long talk over lunch. I was favorably impressed with his sincerity and straightforwardness. He readily admitted that his act with Scathard had been based on a code of the simplest kind. They had started the game in RAF billets for their own amusement and had been astonished at the enormous interest it had aroused. Within a week or two, quite unwittingly, they had got themselves into a position in which it became difficult to call off the hoax. It would have been highly embarrassing to reveal to the officers that they had been conned. (In *The Road to Endor*, the author E. H. Jones and his confederate, having started the "spirits" talking in a Turkish prison camp in 1918, found themselves in the same predicament.) Stephenson and Scathard felt most uncomfortable about keeping up the deception, but after long discussion between themselves they decided to keep silent. They kept up the highly popular act until they were demobilized and went their separate ways.

Hunter Diack was astounded at the results of my inquiries, but he was honest enough to publish a retraction in the *New Statesman*, about a year after his initial article.

How were Stephenson and Scathard able to maintain this deception when repeatedly tested by their superior officers, who, according to Diack, "were much more skeptical than even a scientific investigator"? The answer is that the art of the magician is to deceive. If he does not deceive then he is a poor magician.

In 1950 the Society for Psychical Research received a letter from Dr. Rolf Alexander, then living at Paignton, Devonshire, in which he offered to give a demonstration of the "ability of the human will to produce an effect upon a target at a distance." He claimed that, on a clear day with gentle or moderate wind, he could disintegrate a cumulus cloud by willpower, while control clouds on either side of it remained unchanged.

Psychic practitioners do not often make such precise, unambiguous claims, and it seemed to me that it should not be difficult to arrange suitable tests of his "cloudbusting" ability, as he called it. But first it was necessary to check on the claims made by Dr. Alexander of demonstrations he had given in the past.

Soon after the arrival of his letter, I arranged to meet Dr. Alexander in London. He claimed that various well-qualified people had witnessed successful demonstrations of his cloudbusting powers. Later, in a letter, he referred me to Mr. J. F. Strickler, Jr., assistant vice-president in charge of engineering at a well-known aircraft company in the United States, to the general manager of a chain of department stores in Canada, to a prominent real-estate operator in Illinois, and to a museum curator holding a doctorate. I wrote to all these gentlemen; the first three replied, the fourth did not.

The three respondents broadly supported Dr. Alexander's claims. The general manager referred me in turn to the production manager of Orillia Radio Station, who had witnessed a demonstration at Orillia, Canada, that had convinced him. In answer to a specific question I put, he replied that "no one was present who could be considered a qualified meteorologist."

Later I wrote again to Mr. Strickler to ask whether Dr. Alexander was correct in stating (1) that the aircraft company had made his book *Creative Realism* "required reading for certain of their executive and engineering groups," (2) that the company took an official interest in his claims, and (3) that many young scientists at that company had "transferred the Cloud Experiment indoors to the laboratory cloud chamber." Strickler replied: (1) *Creative Realism* has never been required reading for any of our people," (2) "the Corporation has never taken any *official* interest in this subject, and (3) "none of us have done any cloud chamber experiments."

Dr. Alexander also claimed that Fisher Body Corporation had made his book required reading for certain executive and engineering staff. There is no such company as Fisher Body Corporation, but an inquiry addressed to Fisher Body Division of General Motors Corporation in Detroit was answered by the general director of the public relations and advertising section as follows: "Neither our Industrial Relations Department nor this one has ever heard of Dr. Rolf Alexander's *Creative Realism*."

In February 1956, it came to my attention by chance that Dr. Alexander had written to a correspondent of his claiming that the Foreign Office, the National Research Foundation, and British Overseas Aircraft Corporation had "shown great interest."

There is no such body as the National Research Foundation—it turned out that Dr. Alexander meant the National Physical Laboratory; he told me he had been in touch with a Mr. L. H. McDermott there. I telephoned Mr. McDermott, who said that his contact with Dr. Alexander was limited to writing him one letter to the effect that the matter fell "quite outside the scope of the Laboratory's activity, and that therefore his proposals could not be entertained." Whereas Dr. Alexander had written to his other correspondent about "great interest" at NPL, he wrote to *me* that he had received "the usual 'brush-off' treatment" from the laboratory.

Similarly, the "great interest" of the Foreign Office turned out to be an exchange of letters privately with a member of the staff, who wrote in answer to my inquiry: "I have been in touch with Dr. Alexander and am aware of his cloud dissipation theories. My contact with him has been entirely unofficial, but it did seem to me that he had much information that could be of interest to the Government, but as a result of subsequently trying to pin him down to hard facts I have rather come to doubt this."

The Operations Department of British Overseas Airways Corporation wrote: "This Department has had no dealings whatsoever with Dr. Alexander and I have approached several other departments of the Corporation without success. It is possible, however, that Dr. Alexander has spoken to an individual member of the Corporation and, perhaps naturally, it is possible that he was told that the project was 'interesting.'"

It soon became evident to me, in my dealings with Dr. Alexander, that he was not interested in scientific tests but only in demonstrations in the presence of the press and television crews so that he could get publicity for the forthcoming British edition of his book.

I was instrumental in engineering the attendance at one of these press demonstrations of Dr. R. S. Scorer, then head of the Department of Meteorology of the Imperial College of Science and Technology. Dr. Scorer explained to the assembled company that clouds of this type "worked on" by Dr. Alexander disappeared in about 15 minutes anyhow, and he produced photographs illustrating the phenomenon for which Dr. Alexander had claimed to be responsible. The pictorial magazine concerned, *Illustrated*, dropped the proposed feature like a hot brick.

The cumulative effect of my routine inquiries had shown that statements made by Dr. Alexander were not to be taken at their face value. In modern parlance, I had shown his credibility to be low. On the occasion of the press demonstration referred to above, Dr. Alexander was heard by three witnesses to claim that he possessed a D.Sc. degree.

After taking legal advice I concluded my published report on the investigation (Parsons 1956) as follows: "I fancy that Dr. Alexander would find it difficult to prove that he has a D.Sc.; he does not appear to have that insistence on accuracy of statement which would become ingrained, if it was not inborn, in any man able to attain such a distinction."

There was no comeback.

In the classic *An Adventure* case, Miss Moberly and Miss Jourdain felt themselves transported at Versailles in 1901 back to the times of Marie Antoinette. Since that day there have been occasional reports of buildings and people seen with great clarity by normal individuals who on revisiting the scene have failed to find any trace of what they saw and have accordingly concluded that they had experienced a psychic transportation or hallucination. One such case was reported in the *Journal of the Society for Psychical Research* in December 1961. Mrs. Peggy Fraser (pseudonym) gave the following account:

> In November 1955 my husband and I decided to spend a week-end at a country hotel in Sussex, selected at random from a guidebook. We left London just after six on a Friday evening, but owing to torrential rain my husband drove slowly and it was nearly 7:30 when we approached the roundabout at Lower Dicker, where the road branches right to Eastbourne and goes straight ahead to Hastings.
>
> The rain was still beating down relentlessly and we had been travelling some ten minutes when, turning a gentle bend in the road, we saw on the left a lovely old country house, lying back from the roadway some twenty-five yards. My husband slowed down and we looked appreciatively at the hotel. It was covered with lichen and its windows were lighted with a diffused light that speaks of comfort and welcome. There was a gravel drive leading to the porticoed entrance, and on the left was a low sloping-roofed addition with the words "American Bar" in neon lighting. I can see as if it was only a moment ago the small red shaded lamps and the bar and bottles and small inviting tables.

Mrs. Fraser goes on to describe how, after dinner, they drove slowly back along the same road as far as the roundabout and then slowly forward again, but totally failed to find the hotel. They claimed to have since made many journeys along the same road without discovering the hotel, and said they had made many inquiries "but nothing was known of such a place."

When I read this account in the *Journal* I became convinced that the Frasers had indeed seen such a hotel. The description was so detailed and vivid. I embarked with some confidence on a search for the place they had described. I did not expect to find it in the place where they had located it—I thought it likely that in the "torrential" rain they had lost their way on the outward journey and had in fact approached Herstmonceux (where they stayed the night) on a parallel road. I went to the public library and spent an hour with the large-scale maps of the area. I studied the local road system and noted the names of all hotels within five miles of the road from Lower Dicker to Herstmonceux. I telephoned one or two of the hotels, but this line of inquiry led nowhere. Then I made a photocopy of the Frasers' account and sent it with a covering letter to the Inspector of Police, East Sussex Constabulary, Hailsham, the nearest town of any size. I received the following reply:

> I have to inform you with reference to your letter of the 16th instant that there is a 16th-Century Guest House named Walden Heath situated on the north side of the Lower Dicker to Herstmonceux road, A27, at Magham Down, Hailsham. As Mr. and Mrs. Fraser were travelling in a direction from west to east this would, of course, have been on their left-hand side when they were proceeding to their hotel. Walden Heath is situated about one and a half miles north-east of Hailsham.
>
> Walden Heath is similar in appearance to the premises described by Mrs. Fraser and is approximately 15 yards from the A27 road and easily visible when passing. Suppers in addition to other meals are supplied at Walden Heath and the interior would, therefore, undoubtedly have been illuminated at 7:30 P.M. when lights would have been visible through the windows to motorists using the road. . . .
>
> It is also possible that when they returned later that evening after dinner Walden Heath . . . had concluded business for that day and was in darkness. Although there are in fact unlighted signs at the edge of the road at Walden Heath premises, giving the name and indicating that it is a 16th-Century Guest House, if such signs were missed the premises would give the appearance of a good class country residence.

A few days after receiving this letter, I journeyed to Sussex with a friend, and we had a meal in the supposedly nonexistent building. It is Waldernheath Fifteenth Century Tea and Guest House (not Walden Heath and not "16th-Century" as stated in the police letter) and its address is Amberstone Corner, Hailsham. The best way to show that the building I found is identical with that seen by the Frasers is to analyze the Frasers' account, item by item, presenting the actual findings in a column alongside.

Ghost House	Guest House
1. On main road between Lower Dicker and Herstmonceux	Yes
2. About ten minutes travel eastwards from Lower Dicker roundabout	Depends on speed of car; distance is 2 miles.
3. After a gentle bend in the road	Yes
4. Hotel on left of road	Yes
5. Lovely old country house	Yes
6. Lying back 25 yards from roadway	Yes (not 15 yards as stated in police letter)
7. Covered with lichen	Yes
8. Windows lighted with diffused light	Yes
9. Gravel drive	Tarred drive with pebbles embedded
10. Drive leads to porticoed entrance	Yes
11. A low sloping-roofed addition	Yes
12. The addition is on left side	Yes
13. Neon sign "American Bar"	No
14. Small red-shaded lamps	Yes. Bright red shades on table lamps in east wing dining room visible from road
15. Small inviting tables	Yes
16. Bar and bottles	No. The guest house was not licensed
17. The building could not be located on the return journey after 9:00 P.M.	The lights in the two dining rooms would have been switched off at 8:00 P.M. according to the proprietor

The Frasers' "lovely old country house" hotel turns out to be exactly where they said it was, and there is spectacular agreement, except for the "American Bar," between the detailed features they described and the appearance of the actual hotel as seen from the road.

When I sent an account of my findings, together with a picture of the Guest House, to the Frasers, I was astonished to learn that they did not accept that I had found *their* building. This is in fact yet another example of a very interesting facet of human behavior. Once a percipient has convinced himself that he has had a psychic experience, he assumes jealous proprietorial rights over it. "This is *my* 'ghost story.'" he seems to be saying. "I'm very proud of it, and I'm not having anybody try to topple it. Keep your distance, you busybody."

The story of Waldernheath Guest House also conveys the lesson that the investigator should take with a large pinch of salt any such claim as: "We searched everywhere and made exhaustive inquiries." The layman does not know how to make a systematic search and often is not motivated to attempt such a task.

References

Parsons, Denys. 1956. Cloud busting: A claim investigated. *Journal of the American SPR*, 51:136-148. (Reprinted from *Journal of the SPR*, 1956, 38:352-364.)

———. 1962. A non-existent building located. *Journal of the SPR*, 41:292-295.

Price, Harry. 1931. *Regurgitation and the Duncan Mediumship.*

27

Can Meta-Analysis Resolve the ESP Controversy?

CHARLES AKERS

Meta-analysis is a quantitative, analytical approach to the review of scientific literature (Green and Hall 1984). The initial applications to psychology were in major areas of controversy, such as employment test validity (Schmidt and Hunter 1977), experimenter expectancy effects (Rosenthal and Rubin 1978), sex differences in conformity (Cooper 1979), and effects of psychotherapy (Smith and Glass 1977). Meta-analysis has become a popular technique for the exploration of many areas where experimental outcomes are in conflict, including parapsychology (Honorton 1985; Hyman 1985).

Meta-analytic methods do have some potential for resolving parapsychological controversies. However, I will argue that there are serious limitations to what such methods can accomplish with old data—data on which skeptics and believers disagree vehemently. It is apparent that skeptics and believers do not agree on the quality of parapsychological studies (and hence on how much weight each study should receive in the analysis). If this is true, then meta-analysis may be premature. It may be preferable to collect new data, under conditions prespecified by both parties to the debate. With research standards prespecified, the problem inherent to meta-analysis, of subjective bias in the coding of research quality, could be avoided.

Before exploring the issue of quality coding, and possible resolution of the issue, a brief account of meta-analytic methods is in order. The initial step in meta-analysis (after delineation of the problem area) is a definition of the data base. This involves setting explicit **criteria** for which studies should be included in the literature review and which should be excluded. The reviewer then defines the nature of the independent and dependent variables he wishes to consider. Methodological or design quality features can and should be included. All such study characteristics are then coded and assigned numerical values (if only for

Prepared with the support of the Hodgson Fund of Harvard University. I thank George Hansen, John Palmer, Robert Rosenthal, and E. H. Walker for their critical comments on earlier drafts.

the purpose of nominal classification). Once the quantification has been completed, the data can be statistically analyzed, either by conventional techniques or by methods specific to meta-analysis. The usual goal is to determine how (or whether) study outcomes are correlated with or influenced by certain independent variables (though conclusions about causality may not be warranted). "Study outcome" can be defined in terms of some quantitative measure of effect size, such as Cohen's (1977) d index.

The emphasis on quantification is one feature that distinguishes meta-analysis from a traditional, qualitative review. Another distinguishing feature of meta-analysis is the attempt to make every step in the inferential process explicit. In a qualitative review, the steps in the process are more likely to be implicit, requiring the reader to make inferences. An advantage of meta-analysis is that, with all steps in the inferential process made explicit, it should be easier than in a traditional review to identify sources of error or bias. If two meta-analysts disagree, it should be easier to identify the reasons for their disagreement.

Because all variables must be quantified and all inferences made explicit, meta-analysis involves difficult or even arbitrary judgments. In a review of the various pitfalls in the approach, M. J. Strube and D. P. Hartmann (1983) conclude that meta-analysis is best described as "a series of complex, subjective, and sometimes arbitrary-seeming decisions" (p. 25). They see meta-analysis as permitting all the sources of error that plague the traditional, qualitative review and as introducing its own unique statistical problems. Yet they are among the advocates of meta-analysis simply because the quantitative approach ought to yield more precise conclusions when properly applied.

Of course it is an open question whether meta-analysis will achieve these aims in any given instance. Quantitative methods can serve to clarify, but they can also serve to obscure. There is a danger that meta-analysts will assign pinpoint estimates to variables that cannot so readily be quantified. Their conclusions will then be based on false claims of precision. But, if this and other dangers can be avoided (see Strube and Hartmann 1983), the approach will represent a major advance in the review of social science research. This is so because meta-analysis, broadly defined, is simply an attempt to be objective and systematic (Fiske 1983).

What might meta-analysis contribute toward a resolution of the ESP controversy? The approach does not, of course, address the more philosophical issues of whether ESP is compatible with modern science. If G. R. Price (1955) was correct in arguing that ESP is incompatible with science, then meta-analysis becomes superfluous; the phenomena can be dismissed on an a priori basis. However, few critics have accepted Price's argument (which he recanted in Price 1972). Most critics are interested in knowing what the data have to show. They want to know whether the studies purporting to demonstrate ESP are methodologically sound and whether the outcomes are replicable. Skeptics and believers have different answers to these questions, and meta-analysis should help to clarify the reasons for their differences. The meta-analytic debate between Charles Honorton (1985) and Ray Hyman (1985), has already yielded such benefits.

It would be a mistake, however, to imagine that reanalysis of old data can resolve the empirical issue of whether ESP exists. The difficulty is that, in conducting such a meta-analysis, one must have some method of coding study quality, so that low-quality studies can be either excluded from the data base or included with a coding that reflects their low status. Yet there is disagreement on criteria for differentiating good from bad studies, both within parapsychology and between parapsychologists and their critics.

In part, this may simply reflect the existence of differing assessments of how likely or unlikely ESP is, from an a priori standpoint; critics believe the phenomena are highly unlikely and hence they set higher standards. However, the problem appears to be deeper than this; there is, as will become evident, considerable disagreement *among* believers, and *among* critics, on issues of quality.

Even in conventional areas, such as research on psychotherapeutic outcomes, disagreements on quality coding are common. Fiske (1983) sees such conflicting judgments as inevitable: Even where quality coders agree on the presence or absence of specific methodological flaws, they will probably disagree on the assignment of relative weights to these flaws in computing an overall measure of quality. The seriousnesss of the problem is evident from studies assessing the inter-judge reliability of quality codings. The reliability values, as measured by the intraclass correlation coefficient, rarely exceed .50 (Cooper 1984, 63-65).

Yet G. V. Glass, B. McGaw, and M. L. Smith (1981) have argued that there is an objective, empirical approach to quality coding. In their view, it is useful to compute a series of correlations between various design flaws, representing potential artifacts, and study outcomes. If a design flaw is found to be strongly correlated with the size of study outcomes, then it must be considered a possible source of artifact, and the results of the flawed studies discounted. If, however, the presence of the flaw is not correlated with effect size, then it has no immediate relevance, and its presence can be ignored for the purposes of meta-analysis; the "flawed" studies can be given the same weight as the "unflawed studies. The same logic can then be applied to overall ratings of study quality. If the overall ratings show no correlation with effect size, then "low-quality" studies can just as well be included in the data-base for whatever bearing they may have on the issues at hand. Glass, McGaw, and Smith were concerned with meta-analysis of psychotherapeutic outcomes, but Honorton (1979) has made a very similar argument in the area of parapsychology.

This argument for an "empirical" approach to quality coding has a certain appeal, but there is a circularity in such reasoning. The initial goal is to obtain an objective measure of study quality, so that the outcomes of poor-quality studies can be either ignored or heavily discounted in drawing conclusions from the meta-analysis. Can one at the same time reverse the direction of inference and attempt to judge quality on the basis of outcomes? The possible benefits of this approach have been questioned by J. Mintz (1983): "The recommendation appears to be that if poor-quality research agrees with good research, include it. But in that case, what information is being added? If poor research disagrees, disregard it. What, then, is the benefit from including research that is obviously flawed?" (p. 74).

One apparent benefit would be an increase in statistical power; conclusions would not be changed by the inclusion of poor research, but the statistical significance of the conclusions would be strengthened (as a result of increased N). Note, however, that the Glass, McGaw, and Smith procedure allows the increase in N only when the experimental results come out in a particular direction. Outcomes that conform with good-quality studies are allowed to increase N; outcomes that do not are excluded from the data base. Hence the unintended result of this decision rule is a type of data selection.

As Mintz argues, a poor-quality study should not be considered equal to one of high quality simply because the two yielded similar patterns of data. Neither should another study be ignored on the basis of its having yielded dissimilar data (though, admittedly, findings that are *wildly* discrepant with other research may provide grounds for caution). The weight that a study receives should depend very little on its outcome and very much on the quality of its experimental design, which is evaluated on an a priori basis.

However, Glass et al. (1981) and Cooper (1984) argue against any a priori judgments of design quality. Cooper (1984) concludes that so long as the overall effects are comparable, in good and bad studies, "it is sensible to retain the 'bad' studies because they contain other variations in methods (like different samples and locations) that, by their inclusion, will help solve many other questions surrounding the problem area" (p. 66). (See also Glass et al. 1981, 222). Cooper's implicit assumption is that if overall effect size is unaffected by quality, then relationships between effect size and other variables must also be unaffected by quality. But, as Mintz (1983) has observed, there is no real basis for such an argument. Flaws in a design could yield spurious correlations between effect size and the other variables while having no influence on overall estimates of effect size.

These debates are usually framed in terms of whether the low-quality studies should be included or excluded. The more appropriate question is, "What *weight* should a low-quality study receive?" Deciding to exclude a study is equivalent to assigning that study a weight of zero (Rosenthal 1984). If a study is very badly flawed, then it can safely be assigned a quality coding of zero (excluded from the meta-analysis). However, to assign all low-quality studies a weight of zero is to imply that there are no quality gradations among them (that they are all equally bad), and this may be inappropriate. While there are "obviously flawed" studies that deserve a "zero," many studies will have defects whose significance is less certain. These studies ought to be included in the meta-analysis, but with a quality coding that reflects their questionable status. Results from the studies can "add information" to the analysis, but only in proportion to their quality.

If it is not legitimate to decide quality by checking results, how can reliable judgments of quality be obtained? A priori judgments of quality may, after all, be highly subjective and reflect nothing more than outcome bias (e.g., Mahoney 1977). Rosenthal (1984) has suggested a method that ought to mitigate the effects of bias: He argues, first, that quality coding jobs be assigned to knowledgeable methodologists who have no emotional investment in the research area. Outcome bias may still occur, but this can be assessed by having these methodological experts make their ratings both before and after having read the results section of manuscripts. If intercoder correlations are low despite these precautions, then it is simply necessary to increase the number of such coders until the *average* ratings become highly reliable.

Rosenthal's approach seems a reasonable one for research areas where there is moderate initial agreement on what constitutes good research. Suppose, for example, that the initial interjudge correlation was .70. It would then seem appropriate to obtain the mean quality ratings across N coders and consider this as "representative" of all coders. Many coders would accept these mean values as fair, since the means would show a moderate or high correlation with their own individual ratings. Suppose, on the other hand, that the average initial intercoder correlation was .07. By increasing the number of such coders, one could, it is true, achieve a high reliability for the mean ratings. However, the correlation between these mean ratings and most individual ratings would still be quite low. Most coders would feel no compunction about rejecting the mean values, since these means bear little relation to their own evaluations.

Such low interjudge agreement (e.g., r = .07) might be taken as an indication that meta-analysis was premature. However, this is not necessarily the case. One must distinguish among several claims a meta-analyst might make: (*a*) that ESP results can be described and related to other variables by certain summary statistics, (*b*) that a *plausible* case has been made for a hypothesis about ESP effect sizes, or (*c*) that a *convincing* case has been made for a hypothesis about ESP effect sizes.

If the meta-analyst claims only that he has constructed a descriptive summary of ESP studies, agreement among quality coders may be desirable, but it is not at all necessary. The extent of disagreement on a given study, measured by the variance of its quality codings, could be entered into the meta-analysis as a study feature. Each study would then be associated with both a mean quality coding and a quality coding variance. By comparing studies with either high or low intercoder variance, it might be possible to identify those study characteristics that led to coder disagreement. Whether or not this is possible, the meta-analysis could serve another purpose: Hypotheses could be derived about the causes of ESP scoring that could be put to the test in future research.

What if the meta-analyst claims to have made a plausible case for ESP? Agreement among quality coders might still not be considered critical. It is doubtful, however, that a "plausible case," with low intercoder agreement, would contribute much toward a resolution of the ESP controversy. At best, it would succeed in converting some of those scientists who already considered ESP a likely possibility. It would have little effect on the large numbers of skeptics who consider ESP, on a priori grounds, as no better than a "remote possibility" (McClenon 1982). They are not interested in a "plausible case" scenario; they are interested solely in convincing evidence.

However, there is a legitimate use for the "plausible case" analysis if the meta-analyst claims, not that ESP has been proven, but that some particular area of ESP research (e.g., ganzfeld ESP) is a "good bet" and deserves continued allocation of parapsychology's limited resources. This appears to have been the rationale that Charles Honorton (1977) and John Palmer (1977) had in writing their *Handbook of Parapsychology* reviews. The reviews were not intended to "prove ESP" (though they have often been cited in that regard) but to encourage continued research. Even with this limited goal, the reviewers ought to have raised the issue of design quality, but that issue was not necessarily critical to their arguments.

On the other hand, a meta-analyst might claim to have made a convincing case for ESP. But could the case really be persuasive with low intercoder agreement? By averaging over large numbers of coders, high reliability could be achieved for the mean ratings. Yet the mean values would conceal strong differences of opinion among coders. Whatever the mean values indicated, believers in ESP would no doubt side with those coders whose quality ratings suggested support for ESP (as by findings of a near zero or positive correlation between quality and effect size). Skeptics would side with the other coders (whose ratings suggested an inverse correlation between quality and effect size).

The practical effects of coder differences could be assessed by plotting a distribution of statistics, representing individual coder tests of the meta-analytic hypothesis. Each statistic would reflect the way a single coder had weighted the contribution of different ESP studies. From this distribution, one could find the proportion of coders whose ratings, when entered as weights into the analysis, yielded support for the ESP hypothesis. Even if this proportion was unexpectedly high (e.g., 90 percent), a skeptical scientist might reasonably side with the minority coders. He could argue that their codings were more likely to be valid because they yielded the outcome that had a high a priori probability of occurrence (no ESP). Thus the outcome bias that was avoided at the level of individual studies (through Rosenthal's approach) could recur at this higher level of analysis. The only solution would be to obtain some consensus on quality from the start.

There is another way in which outcome bias could recur at the meta-analytic level. Suppose that coders had reached a high level of agreement on the weights that various design features should receive in assessing overall quality. This high level of agreement would provide evidence that the weighting system was reliable but not that it was valid. Its validity might still be in question, since the assignment of weights would often depend on an assessment of uncontrolled variables. The effects of uncontrolled variables are difficult to assess, especially when, as is often the case, they have not been measured in the experimental setting. Suppose that these effects are, nevertheless, assigned weights and that no correlation is found between quality and effect size. A skeptic might suspect that the subjectively derived weights were invalid. By employing multiple regression techniques, the skeptic could obtain a new set of weights that would yield the expected negative correlation between effect size and quality (e.g., Hyman 1985). Only through additional research could the skeptic be proved wrong.

The arguments above suggest that the ESP controversy may remain unresolved even if coders can initially agree on ratings on quality. However, such initial agreement is quite unlikely. Agreement on quality is much less likely in parapsychological research than in conventional areas of psychology (where agreement is none too high to begin with!). The quality of ESP research is often judged on the degree to which the procedures have excluded experimenter bias, subliminal perception, or fraud by the subjects and/or experimenters. Yet there is nearly as much controversy over these alternative explanations as there is over the parapsychological claims themselves. Thus the extent to which the experimenter expectancies can bias subject responses is still in dispute, and the mechanisms for such effects, when they do occur, are not yet well understood (see the commentaries following Rosenthal and Rubin's 1978 article). Hypotheses of "subliminal perception," or perception without awareness, are still more controversial (Dixon 1981; Glucksberg 1982; Merikle 1982). Fraud (by either subjects or experimenters) is a counterhypothesis that is frequently invoked by critics (e.g., Hansel 1980; Randi 1980a), but the actual incidence of fraud is unknown. Inevitably, the weights that quality coders assign to controls against such variables will vary, depending on the theoretical bias of the coder.

One might imagine that these disagreements on quality are primarily between skeptics and believers. However, this is not the case. Believers cannot agree among themselves on quality of evidence. J. F. Nicol (1956) discusses this situation, citing the fate of an early card-guessing experiment by B. F. Riess (1937; 1939): Pratt et al. (1966 [1940]), in a thorough review of psychical research, had cited the Riess study as one of the most convincing ESP experiments ever performed. In defending the Riess study, the authors considered 35 counter-hypotheses to ESP. These included every alternative explanation that critics of the field had proposed. Yet the Riess experiment survived this exhaustive analysis and remained "inexplicable except by the ESP hypothesis" (p. 180). Fourteen years later, Soal and Bateman published the English classic *Modern Experiments in Telepathy*. How did the Riess experiment fare? That venerable series was, by Soal and Bateman's standards, a "weak paper" that was "scarcely considered to be worthy of mention" (p. 180). Apparently, these authors saw possibilities for fraud that Pratt et al. discounted. Nicol cites further examples, indicating that this is not an isolated case of disagreement among parapsychologists.

For a more recent example, consider the critical response to two ganz-feld/ESP experiments by James Terry and Charles Honorton (1976): John Beloff (1980a) had cited these among his "seven evidential experiments," representing some of the best of ESP research (though he later [in Beloff 1980b, 118] conceded that the studies exhibited one "minor methodological flaw"). What happened when Ray Hyman (1985) examined the same studies? He found that their designs were flawed on six different bases. On a summary measure that Hyman labels "Controls," the Terry and Honorton experiments ended up among the worst of the forty-two studies reviewed. Even after considerable correspondence, Honorton (1985) and Hyman (1985) remained far apart on what should or should not be considered a "flaw."

In my own review (Akers 1984) I also had the task of evaluating the Terry and Honorton studies. It was difficult to decide when to assign a "flaw" and when to discount the possibilities for error and when not to do so. The decision was arbitrary in some instances. The one source of error I found especially difficult to assess arose because the experimenters had used a single target-set for both "sending" and judging. As the "senders" (or agents) briefly handled the targets (which were View-Master slides), they could have accidentally or deliberately left some imprint or smudge so that the subjects (who served as judges) would have had a sensory basis for discriminating the target from the control slides.

Honorton (1979) discussed this possibility at length but found it implausible from an a priori standpoint and deficient in empirical support. In a comparison of studies that had allowed handling cues and studies that had excluded them, Honorton found no difference in main effects for ESP. In his view, this meant that the handling cue "flaw" was really no flaw at all. Hyman (1985) disputed this conclusion. He observed that correlational data assembled on a post hoc basis cannot decide issues of cause and effect.

Another ESP ganzfeld researcher, John Palmer (1983), initially agreed with Honorton that such cues, if they existed, would probably be "very subtle." However, Palmer expressed doubts similar to those raised by Hyman about the value of post hoc analysis in deciding the relevance of design flaws. He argued that much more systematic investigation was needed before the status of the handling cue hypothesis could be decided. In two studies (not with the View-Master paradigm), Palmer (1983; in press) found a handling cue effect, but only when subjects were specifically instructed to look for such cues. Palmer (19??) concluded that "no experiment that fails to take reasonable precautions against such cueing should henceforth be admitted into the parapsychological literature."

A British ganzfeld researcher, Carl Sargent (1980a) has been especially concerned about the possibilities of handling cues, which he finds "most disturbing" (p. 265). However, Sargent (1980a; 1980b) has taken a position different from that of Palmer. He claims that such experiments can never be salvaged because they are conceptually invalid. ESP is negatively defined in terms of an exclusion of sensory cues. Therefore, to Sargent, an experiment that allows such cues is simply not a valid ESP experiment. Sargent's case is weakened by the fact that handling cues are not known to have been present in the experiments he criticizes. In that sense, his handling-cue hypothesis is speculative. On the other hand, it is certainly no more speculative than the ESP hypothesis itself.

Even if handling cues were present in some ganzfeld experiments, this does not mean that they were necessarily noticed or utilized by subjects (Honorton 1979). Hence I found myself in agreement with Palmer that further empirical study of the matter was warranted. Nonetheless, I took a conservative stance and assigned a "flaw" to studies like those of Terry and Honorton that had allowed such cues. In doing so, I took the position that ESP experiments should rule out alternative explanations that have at least some degree of plausibility. If handling cues were present, they were not necessarily "subtle" as presumed by Honorton. They may have been so blatant as to be easily recognized by subjects, and this is obviously the case if they were introduced deliberately.

If I were conducting a meta-analysis, my decision on the handling-cue issue would be still more difficult. I would need to assign a weight to this design weakness so that I could compute an overall measure of design quality. Depending on the weights that I assigned for this and other aspects of the Terry and Honorton studies, I could make their overall quality appear either high or low. Inevitably, my own subjective biases would determine the weights that I chose.

There is also a chance that I would be unconsciously biased in my assignments of weights by knowledge of the study outcomes. Research on the manuscript reviewing process has confirmed the existence of such biases, which depend on the reviewer's prior hypotheses (Lord, Ross, and Lepper 1979; Mahoney 1977). Hence, if I believed in ESP, I would tend to discount weaknesses in experiments like those of Terry and Honorton, which yielded evidence of ESP. If I were a skeptic, I would be inclined to discount weaknesses in those experiments that yielded no evidence of ESP.

E. H. Walker (1980) claims that skeptics did exhibit the latter type of bias in their response to a "remote viewing" study of E. W. Karnes et al. (1980). Skeptics J. L. Calkins (1980), David Marks and Richard Kammann (1980), and James Randi (1980b) accepted the Karnes study as a clear-cut failure to confirm the ESP findings of parapsychologists Harold Puthoff and Russell Targ (1976). In their view, Karnes and his colleagues had eliminated the artifactual sources of error that had plagued the work of the parapsychologists. E. H. Walker saw the matter differently. In his view, it was Karnes's design that was flawed, by the presence of seven "critical inadequacies." Walker (1980; 1981) argued that Karnes had departed from Puthoff and Targ's original design in ways that were not justified by a concern for elimination of error. In particular, Walker saw a possibility for experimenter bias if Karnes et al. had conveyed their skeptical outlook to the judges, whose rankings of subject protocols played a critical role in the experiment. When judges expect no ESP, perhaps they find none.

In a reply to Walker, Karnes (1981, 128) claimed that his judges were open-minded. He accused Walker of having gathered "ad hoc reasons" for the failure to replicate. Were Walker's objections ad hoc or had he found legitimate problems in the Karnes design? This is not an easy question to answer. If the remote-viewing effects were as robust as Puthoff and Targ had initially claimed, then small departures from their methodology should not have eliminated all ESP scoring. However, Walker's reading of the remote-viewing literature is different from that of Puthoff and Targ. In his view, the effects are generally only marginally significant with naive subjects (like those employed by Karnes), and they are sensitive to procedural changes. If Karnes's judges were somewhat biased, as Walker speculates, or lacked ability, then this could account for the failure to replicate. Karnes et al. did not assess judges' expectancies or abilities, so the effects of such variables are unknown. The experiment is thereby weakened, but it is difficult to say by how much it is weakened; there is no objective procedure for making an assessment of the uncontrolled variables. Yet, a properly done meta-analysis would require quantification of all such design weaknesses.

It should be noted that Puthoff and Targ also failed to assess judges' expectations and abilities. However, they did find evidence of ESP, so their results are not open to the same objections. In coding design quality, how should one weigh deficiencies like this that could hypothetically have flawed the experiment but that do not in fact appear to have? There is no easy resolution to the problem.

A similar problem arises in assessing the Karnes et al. experiment. In response to comments by Solomon Feldman (1980), Piet Hoebens (1980), Charles Tart (1980), and Walker (1980; 1981), Karnes (1980; 1981) acknowledged some deficiencies in his design: If he and his colleagues had obtained evidence for ESP, there would have been grounds for disputing it. One problem was that his experimenters knew the target sites, so they could conceivably have cued the subjects. There were also possibilities for subject cheating (Hoebens 1980). Yet, since there was no significant ESP scoring, these scenarios can be disregarded. The question remains, how should the study be coded for design quality? Should hypothetical flaws be counted or ignored? Proponents and opponents of ESP are likely to have very different answers to that question.

The general conclusion to which I have been leading is that, given the problems in quality coding, meta-analysis of the ESP literature is premature. A resolution of the controversy lies not in meta-analysis of old data but in the collection of new data. If conditions for the collection of the new data can be specified in advance, through collaboration between believers and skeptics, then there will be considerably less room for argument over the issue of quality coding. Meta-analysis will then become meaningful to those on both sides of the controversy.

Retrospective examination of old data has its uses. However, if the focus remains solely on past research, the larger issue of whether ESP exists will fall by the wayside. The old research has been defended by parapsychologists on the grounds that the methodological standards have approximated those of ordinary social science experiments and have yielded findings with some degree of repeatability (claims of 25 to 50 percent success). Yet, if the findings are truly repeatable (even if only at a 25 percent rate), there is no need to focus on the old research. New experiments can be designed that eliminate the methodological problems thus far identified.

Even though believers and skeptics differ in their evaluations of such problems, they can often agree on how the problems can be eliminated in future research. Consider, for example, the controversy over randomization. Both Hyman and I found that parapsychologists have often failed to specify their randomization procedures or have used some informal technique like shuffling (Akers 1984; Hyman 1985). As Hyman emphasizes, it is not simply a question of whether spuriously high scores arose as a result of poor randomization. Even if this did not occur, the presence of such design flaws, if frequent enough, may suggest that a study was carelessly planned. Hyman refers to this as the "symptomatic" aspect of flaw analysis; major design flaws are symptoms that a study may not have been a serious attempt to obtain evidence of ESP.

Informal randomization is surprisingly common in ESP research. In a review of 54 such studies (Akers 1984), I found that randomization was by informal means, or was poorly described, in nearly half my sample (26/45). The seriousness of this design weakness varies from study to study depending on the nature of the ESP rask, characteristics of the subject pool, the type of feedback that subjects received, and the size of the ESP effect that requires explanation. Given all the moderating variables, it is unreasonable to assume that any two meta-analysts would agree on an "objective" method for assessing whether a nonrandom artifact was likely or unlikely in a particular case.

Yet there is a good possibility that meta-analysis could agree on a future standard of randomization. Hyman (1985), in his review of ESP ganzfeld studies, implicitly endorses the familiar procedure of ordering targets on the basis of a well-tested source of random numbers, such as the Rand Corporation Tables (1955). Although some writers (e.g., Brown 1957) have questioned whether random number tables provide truly "random" numbers, most critics have accepted their use in ESP research, and no critic has suggested an acceptable alternative. As Wilson (1966) has observed, there are limitations on the degree to which any such table can approach ideal randomness. Yet the size of ESP effects that are typically reported are much larger than the small biases arising from a carefully designed source of random numbers (Davis and Akers 1974). Hence, there is a good chance of agreement on the use of this standard approach to randomization, which is already common in ESP research. (I am ignoring here the question of whether the results obtained with such tables are to be interpreted in terms of "extrasensory perception" or some other construct.)

It should also be possible to obtain an agreed-upon standard for randomization by ESP test machines. As Hyman (1981) has noted, there are a wide variety of such devices in use, and these are constantly being modified or replaced. The lack of standardization makes it difficult to assess what the possibilities for machine bias may be. Yet some of the "random-event generators" have been tested over sequences of a million trials and shown no evidence of either short-term or long-term bias (Davis and Akers 1974, 403-406). It should be possible to introduce a switching mechanism, as C. E. M. Hansel (1980, 321) has advocated, so that even if some bias arose, it could be automatically corrected. (Perhaps the Rand Tables could be incorporated into the switching system.) With random-event generators interfaced to computers, it becomes possible to generate control trials at the same time as experimental trials, so that the results can be systematically compared (Broughton 1982). Once controls like these become routine, the adequacy of ESP test machines should cease to be an issue. Those critics who have doubted the test machines can then work together with parapsychologists on the design of such procedures, which will guarantee adequate randomization.

It should also be possible for parapsychologists and their critics to agree on standards for the elimination of sensory leakage. Despite the heated controversy that has arisen over the handling-cue hypothesis, the elimination of this artifact through the use of duplicate target sets has been a simple matter. Of 54 ESP studies that I examined (Akers 1984), handling cues and feedback artifacts accounted for the more serious possibilities for sensory leakage. The feedback effects arose in attempts to discover personality correlates of ESP scoring: often, when subjects completed the personality inventory, they already knew their scores on the ESP test. This created the possibility that their knowledge of success or failure on the ESP test had somehow influenced their personality test scores. Simply by reversing the test order (with prior administration of the personality test), any feedback artifact is eliminated, so there is no reason to expect this artifact in any future research.

The statistical analysis of parapsychological experiments has raised other controversies. Hyman (1985) has found that parapsychologists often failed to prespecify their statistical analysis (as far as can be judged from the experimental reports) and thus left themselves open to a charge of multiple analysis. In my own review, I also found this to be the case, but I did not judge it a severe problem. I found that in many cases I could infer preplanning on the basis of an author's previous publications. In other cases, I could adjust the obtained probabilities for multiple analysis and still compute a significant result (as in Honorton 1985). Hyman (1985) however, sees no firm basis for making such adjustments. Whichever side of the question one adopts, the matter can be easily resolved in the future. All that is required is that investigators report which of their statistical tests were planned in advance of data collection. If several tests were planned, then the investigator must of course make corrections for multiple analysis.

In another statistical controversy, Alcock (1981), Calkins (1980), Girden (1978), and Moss and Butler (1978) have criticized parapsychologists for failing to use empirical baselines and relying instead on a priori conceptions of "chance expectation." In response to such criticism, parapsychologists Robert Morris (1982) and John Palmer (1981) have defended the use of theoretical baselines. Personally, I find the arguments of the parapsychologists convincing, since it is difficult to imagine any statistical analysis, whether or not it involves empirical control groups, that is not grounded in probability theory, and hence in a conception of "chance expectation." Yet, if future meta-analysts do insist on empirical control groups, there should be an ample supply of studies that meet this criterion. In the sample of 54 ESP studies I examined, the significance of the results depended on comparisons between empirically derived means in about two-thirds of the cases (Akers 1984, 147).

I do not mean to imply that all issues of design are so easily resolved. The problem of fraud, by either subject or experimenter, is particularly troublesome. In dealing with a self-proclaimed "psychic," stringent controls against fraud are obviously necessary. Are the same controls necessary in research with unselected subjects? Are the same controls necessary to prevent cheating by the experimenter? These questions are not easily answered, since the incidence of fraud is unknown and the possibilities for fraud vary with different experimental situations. In tests for precognition, cheating by either subject or experimenter may be quite easy to eliminate. In a test for telepathy, the elimination of fraud may be much more difficult.

Generalizations are hard to come by, since methods of cheating are so numerous. However, it is clear that possibilities for fraud could be substantially reduced if the issue was more often raised in the design stage of experimentation. At the 1983 meeting of the Parapsychological Association, the PA Council voted unanimously for a greater collaboration between parapsychologists and magicians. If this collaboration does occur, standards for controls against fraud should eventually emerge. Already, within parapsychology, Martin Johnson (1975) and Helmut Schmidt (1980) have proposed models for the control of fraud that should be applicable to some areas of research.

In summary, it is time for parapsychologists and their critics to shift attention away from past research and to focus on designs for future research. If experimental standards can be agreed upon before this research begins, much of the methodological controversy can be avoided. Once a body of data has been generated under conditions that satisfy those on both sides, the debate can shift to the meta-analytic level. Until that time, reanalysis of past ESP studies will only lead to endless debate as to which studies represented an adequate test of the ESP hypothesis.

References

Akers, C. 1984. Methodological criticisms of parapsychology. In *Advances in Parapsychological Research*, vol. 4, edited by S. Krippner. Jefferson, N.C.: McFarland.

Alcock, J. E. 1981. *Parapsychology: Science or Magic? A Psychological Perspective.* Elmsford, N.Y.: Pergamon Press.

Beloff, J. 1980a. Seven evidential experiments. *Zetetic Scholar*, 6:91-94.

———. 1980b. Seven evidential experiments: A rejoinder. *Zetetic Scholar*, No. 6:116-120.

Broughton, R. S. 1982. Computer methodology: Total control with a human face. *Parapsychology Review*, 13(2):1-6.

Brown, G. S. 1957. *Probability and Scientific Inference*. London: Longmans.

Calkins, J. L. 1980. Comments by James Calkins [commentary on the paper by Professor Karnes, et al.]. *Zetetic Scholar*, No. 6:77-81.

Cohen, J. 1977. *Statistical Power Analysis for the Behavioral Sciences*, rev. ed. New York: Academic Press.

Cooper, H. M. 1979. Statistically combining independent studies: Meta-analysis of sex differences in conformity research. *Journal of Personality and Social Psychology*, 37:131-146.

――――. 1984. *The Integrative Research Review: A Systematic Approach.* Beverly Hills, Calif.: Sage.

Davis, J. W., and Akers, C. 1974. Randomization and tests for randomness. *Journal of Parapsychology,* 38:393-407.

Dixon, N. F. 1981. *Preconscious Processing.* Chichester, England: Wiley.

Feldman, S. E. 1980. Solomon E. Feldman comments on Edward W. Karnes et al., re remote viewing. *Zetetic Scholar,* No. 7:131.

Fiske, D. W. 1983. The meta-analytic revolution in outcome research. *Journal of Consulting and Clinical Psychology,* 51:65-70.

Girden, E. 1978. Parapsychology. In *Handbook of Perception,* vol. 10, edited by E. C. Carterette and M. P. Friedman. New York: Academic Press.

Glass, G. V., B. McGaw, and M. L. Smith. 1981. *Meta-analysis in Social Research,* Beverly Hills, Calif.: Sage.

Glucksberg, S. 1982. Not seeing is believing [review of Norman F. Dixon's *Preconscious Processing*]. *Contemporary Psychology,* 27:856-858.

Green, B. F., and J. A. Hall. 1984. Quantitative methods for literature reviews. *Annual Review of Psychology,* 35:37-53.

Hansel, C. E. M. 1980. *ESP and Parapsychology. A Critical Re-Evaluation.* Buffalo: Prometheus Books.

Hoebens, P. H. 1980. Piet Hein Hoebens comments on Edward V. Karnes et al., re remote viewing. *Zetetic Scholar,* No. 7:131-132.

Honorton, C. 1977. Psi and internal attention states. In *Handbook of Parapsychology,* edited by B. B. Wolman, 435-472, New York: Van Nostrand Reinhold.

――――. 1979. Methodological issues in free-response psi experiments. *Journal of the American SPR,* 73:381-394.

――――. 1985. Meta-analysis of psi ganzfeld research. *Journal of Parapsychology,* 49:51-91.

Hyman, R. 1981. Further comments on Schmidt's PK experiments: Alternative explanations are abundant. *Skeptical Inquirer,* 5(3):34-40.

――――. 1985. The ganzfeld/psi experiment: A critical appraisal. *Journal of Parapsychology,* 49:3-49.

Johnson, M. 1975. Models of control and control of bias. *European Journal of Parapsychology,* 1, (1):36-44.

Karnes, E. W. 1980. Edward W. Karnes replies to Solomon E. Feldman, Piet Hein Hoebens, and Evan Harris Walker. *Zetetic Scholar,* No. 7:137-139.

――――. 1981. Edward W. Karnes replies to Evan Harris Walker's above comments. *Zetetic Scholar,* No. 8:128-130.

Karnes, E. W., E. Susman, P. Klusman, and L. Turcotter. 1980. Failures to replicate remote viewing using psychic subjects. *Zetetic Scholar,* No. 6:66-76.

Lord, C., L. Ross, and M. Lepper. 1979. Biased assimilation and attitude polarization: The effect of prior theories on subsequently considered evidence. *Journal of Personality and Social Psychology,* 37:2098-2109.

Mahoney, M. J. 1977. Publication prejudices: An experimental study of confirmatory bias in the peer review system. *Cognitive Therapy and Research,* 1:161-175.

Marks, D. and R. Kammann. 1980. Comments by David Marks and Richard Kammann [commentary on the paper by Professor Karnes et al.]. *Zetetic Scholar,* No. 6:83-84.

McClenon, J. 1982. A survey of elite scientists: Their attitudes toward ESP and parapsychology. *Journal of Parapsychology,* 46:127-152.

Merikle, P. M. 1982. Unconscious perception revisited. *Perception and Psychophysics,* 31:298-301.

Mintz, J. 1983. Integrating research evidence: A commentary on meta-analysis. *Journal of Consulting and Clinical Psychology.* 51:71-75.

Morris, R. L. 1982. Review of *Parapsychology: Science or Magic? A Psychological Perspective,* by J. E. Alcock. *Journal of the American SPR,* 76:177-186.

Moss, S., and D. C. Butler. 1978. The scientific credibility of ESP. *Perceptual and Motor Skills,* 46:1063-1074.

Nicol, J. F. 1956. Some difficulties in the way of scientific recognition of extrasensory perception. In *Extrasensory Perception,* edited by G. E. W. Wolstenholme and E. C. P. Millar. New York: Citadel Press.

Palmer, J. 1977. Attitudes and personality traits in experimental ESP research. In *Handbook of Parapsychology,* edited by B. B. Wolman, 175-201. New York: Van Nostrand Reinhold.

———. 1981. Methodological objections to the case for psi: Are formal control conditions necessary for the demonstration of psi? Paper presented at the convention of the American Psychological Association, Los Angeles, Calif., August.

———. 1983. Sensory contamination of free-response ESP targets: The greasy fingers hypothesis. *Journal of the American SPR,* 77:101-113.

——— (in press). Sensory identification of contaminated free-rsponse ESP targets: Return of the greasy finger. *Journal of the American SPR.*

Pratt, J. G., J. B. Rhine, B. Mott-Smith, C. E. Stuart, and J. A. Greenwood. 1966. *Extra-Sensory Perception after Sixty Years.* Boston: Bruce Humphries. (Originally published by Holt in 1940.)

Price, G. R. 1955. Science and the supernatural. *Science,* 122:359-367.

———. 1972. Apology to Rhine and Soal. Letter to *Science,* 175:359.

Puthoff, H. E., and R. Targ. 1976. A perceptual channel for information transfer over kilometer distances: Historical perspectives and recent research. *Proceedings of the IEEE,* 64:329-354.

Rand Corporation. 1955. *A Million Random Digits.* Glencoe, Ill.: Free Press.

Randi, J. 1980a. *Flim-Flam! The Truth about Unicorns, Parapsychology, and other Delusions.* New York: Lippincott & Crowell. [Revised edition published by Prometheus Books, Buffalo, N.Y. 1982.]

———. 1980b. Comments by James Randi. [commentary; on the paper by Professor Karnes et al]. *Zetetic Scholar,* No. 6:84.

Riess, B. F. 1937. A case of high scores in card-guessing at a distance. *Journal of Parapsychology,* 1:260-263.

———. 1939. Further data from a case of high scores in card-guessing. *Journal of Parapsychology,* 3:79-84.

Rosenthal, R. 1984. *Meta-Analytic Procedures for Social Research.* Beverly Hills, Calif.: Sage.

Rosenthal, R., and D. B. Rubin. 1978. Interpersonal expectancy effects: The first 345 studies. *Behavioral and Brain Sciences,* 3:377-386.

Sargent, C. L. 1980a. Comments on "Effects of associations and feedback on psi in the ganzfeld." Letter to the editor. *Journal of the American SPR,* 74:265-267.

———. 1980b. *Exploring Psi in the Ganzfeld.* Parapsychological Monographs, No. 17, New York: Parapsychology Foundation.

Schmidt, F. L., and J. E. Hunter. 1977. Development of a general solution to the problem of validity generalization. *Journal of Applied Psychology,* 62:529-540.

Schmidt, H. 1980. A program for channeling psi data into the laboratory and onto the critic's desk. In *Research in Parapsychology 1979,* edited by W. G. Roll. Metuchen, N.J.: Scarecrow Press.

Smith, M. L., and G. V. Glass. 1977. Meta-analysis of psychotherapy outcome studies. *American Psychologist,* 32:752-760.

Soal, S. G., and F. Bateman. 1954. *Modern Experiments in Telepathy.* London: Faber and Faber.

Strube, M. J., and D. P. Hartmann. 1983. Meta-analysis: Techniques, applications, and functions. *Journal of Consulting and Clinical Psychology,* 51:14-27.

Tart, C. T. 1980. Comments by Charles T. Tart [commentary on the paper by Professor Karnes et al]. *Zetetic Scholar,* No. 6:85-86.

Terry, J., and C. Honorton. 1976. Psi information retrieval in the ganzfeld: Two confirmatory studies. *Journal of the American SPR,* 70:207-217.

Walker, E. H. 1980. Evan Harris Walker comments on Edward W. Karnes et al., re remote viewing. *Zetetic Scholar,* No. 7:132-137.

———. 1981. Evan Harris Walker replies. *Zetetic Scholar,* 8:124-127.

Wilson, R. 1966. Deviations from randomness in ESP experiments. *International Journal of Parapsychology,* 8:387-395.

Part 6

Further Critiques

28

Reflections on Psychic Sleuths

PIET HEIN HOEBENS
with Marcello Truzzi

If the voluminous "psi" literature on the subject is to be believed, the Watsons in the world's police departments owe the solution of some of the most baffling mysteries they have ever confronted to the intervention of the psychic counterparts of Sherlock Holmes.

The blurb on the cover of Colin Wilson's *The Psychic Detectives* (1984) neatly summarizes the claimants' position: "No established psychological or criminological science can explain it . . . the astonishing and recurrent phenomenon of those who can simply touch a garment or some other item to trigger their extraordinary psychic powers to solve a crime, identify a murder, locate a corpse, even predict where a killer will strike again. . . ."

The employment of sensitives for police purposes has for many decades been a highly controversial topic. Professional opinion is sharply divided. Some police officers have championed the cause of their paranormally gifted colleagues, whereas others have acted as the spokesmen of implacable skepticism.

The controversy of course is intimately linked to that surrounding the existence of extrasensory perception in general. If such faculties as telepathy and clairvoyance indeed exist, it is only natural to expect that, at least in some cases, they might be of practical use. On the other hand, if the "paranormal" is a delusion, it would seem slightly foolish to believe that adding "third eyes" and "sixth senses" to the contents of the police officer's toolbox would serve any useful purpose.

It should be made clear from the outset that the author of this essay does not think that the question of the reality of psi can ever be settled by disputes over anecdotes pertaining to historical—and necessarily irreproducible—incidents. All accounts of psychic successes in police investigations are in this category. Psi can only be demonstrated to the satisfaction of the skeptical

---

This essay was edited by M. Truzzi from the notes left him by Piet Hein Hoebens, whose untimely death precluded its completion. © Copyright 1985 by the Center for Scientific Anomalies Research.

observer if the parapsychologists succeed in their attempts to distill from their vast collection of miraculous anecdotes at least one hypothesis that can be checked and rechecked by independent researchers, with results that consistently confirm what parapsychology predicts. The field's signal failure to meet this demand is at the bottom of what impatient proponents deplore as the persistence of skeptical obstinacy.

However, there is no denying that the claims surrounding psychic detectives (and the many other "spontaneous" or "real life" manifestations of psi) are of considerable interest to both the believing parapsychologist and his incredulous counterpart. Weak as the evidence may be, it does lend substance to the anemic experimental findings of parapsychology, and its heuristic value can hardly be overestimated.

A second reason such cases are of interest to the debate over the paranormal is that they can provide the sort of evidence (whether positive or negative) that would compel the Bayesian observer to modify his or her expectations as to the most probable outcome of the psi controversy. Although accounts of isolated incidents can never conclusively demonstrate the reality of ESP, I can conceive of a series of such incidents sufficiently striking and sufficiently resistant to debunking attempts that I personally would find it judicious to change my bets and provisionally join the moderate wing of the believer's party.

A third reason—which for the sake of argument assumes the nonreality of psi—is that a scientific examination of the claims of psychic detection may throw fresh light on the mechanisms of human error and human credulity—and perhaps also on some human abilities that, while not of a paranormal nature, are sufficiently unusual and unexpected to make it understandable that they have so often been taken for the miraculous.

Basic Questions

In discussing psychic detectives, it is essential to make a clear distinction between two very different questions: (1) Have persons claiming extrasensory abilities in fact been successful in solving police cases? and (2) Is ESP the most likely explanation for what we have reason to believe are the facts of psychic detection?

The distinction (rarely made in the popular or quasi-scholarly literature on this topic) is important, as it is quite conceivable that a psychic could score a remarkable success in paranormally obtaining accurate information that does not, however, lead to the actual solution of a police case. On the other hand, it is conceivable that a psychic could be successful in solving a crime or locating a missing person but not obtain the relevant information by nonparanormal methods.

In this essay, I will attempt to clearly differentiate between the reliability of the claims and the inexplicability of claims presumed to be factually accurate.

Sources, Theories, and Countertheories

A major problem confronting the critical investigator of psychic detectives is that the subject has been virtually ignored by the leading practitioners of parapsychology. The literature is vast, but very little of it can in fairness be said to be representative of parapsychological thinking at its best. In short, there is no accepted parapsychological theory of psychic detection that the skeptic could juxtapose with his own. This is regrettable, as the critic naturally prefers to focus his criticisms on the cases that are deemed "strong." To the extent that the relevant literature may claim to be scientific or scholarly, it is almost exclusively written by skeptics or by police officers who tend to approach the topic from the vantage point of the pragmatic law-enforcer rather than from that of the scientific researcher primarily interested in to what extent any factor unknown to conventional science might be involved.

The most authoritative source of information on psychic detectives remains the work of the prewar German Landesgerichts-direktor Albert Hellwig, notably his magnum opus *Okkultismus und Verbrechen* (1929). My own investigations into the claims surrounding the best-known Dutch "paragnosts" may be seen as a contemporary footnote to Hellwig, confirming his essentially negative conclusions. Experimental and semi-experimental findings supporting the skeptical position have been published by Martin Reiser (1979; 1982) and C. Brink (1960). At the moment of this writing, the long-term Psychic Sleuths Project, under the auspices of the Center for Scientific Anomalies Research (CSAR) and directed by the skeptic Marcello Truzzi, is under way.

On the psi side, the work of the Dutch parapsychologist Wilhelm Tenhaeff has long been hailed as exemplifying scholarly psychical research, but it has now been largely discredited. The literature in English is dominated by popular and sensationalist books like the monographs by Archer (1969), Tabori (1974), Pollack (1964), and Wilson (1984), and the autobiographies of noted psychics.

A renewed interest in practical applications of psi (exemplified by the California-based Mobius Society and the Canadian Psychic Systems Research group) may eventually lead to the emergence of a modern pro-literature of better quality.

The Skeptical Explanation

The standard skeptical explanation for the alleged successes of psychic detectives is that these sensitives offer their consultants the verbal equivalent of a Rorschach test. Their statements are typically vague, rambling, and verbose. The accuracy of the "readings" is evaluated post factum: "Good" sitters retroactively interpret their ambiguous and often contradictory statements in such a way that they fit the true facts and obligingly forget the many details that were too wide of the mark. Complete failures are ignored or suppressed. The possibility that some of the paranormal information could have been acquired by normal means is quietly discounted. Occasional lucky guesses (consistent with the chance hypothesis) are enhanced by selective reporting and editorial embellishment. Cautious parapsychologists usually concede that this explanation is adequate in the vast majority of cases. However, they point out that, in some instances, a sufficient number of "loose ends" remain even after a thoroughly skeptical examination of the relevant data to justify a suspension of judgment.

The CSAR Project. In 1980 the Michigan-based Center for Scientific Anomalies Research initiated a long-term research project into the gifts of psychic detectives. At the time of this writing [Fall 1984], the mass of documents carefully collected by the CSAR investigators does not yet justify an unambiguous verdict on all cases. While the findings generally support the case for skepticism, Truzzi and his collaborators (the author of this chapter included) prefer to suspend judgment in a few instances that, prima facie, seem to be exceptions to the negative rule.

The Reiser test. In 1978, Martin Reiser (Reiser et al. 1979), director of the Los Angeles Police Department's behavioral science section conducted a controlled test with 12 carefully selected sensitives who were asked to look at evidence from four crimes. According to the report, little if any useful information was elicited. A followup study showed that psychics are no better at making good guesses than are detectives and students. As the Reiser tests were rather limited in their scope, proponents of psychic detectives may be excused for declining to be entirely convinced until the results have been replicated in an in-depth series of similar experiments.

Reiser reports that the Behavioral Science Services staff of the LAPD "has received several first-hand accounts of reported success with psychics from several other departments." He has also suggested, however, that "perhaps the compelling manner in which self-identified 'psychics' tend to print the information may account for some of the positive beliefs about psychic abilities in law enforcement."

The Reliability of the Reports

One of the most damning arguments against psychic detection is that, of the reports of "prize cases" in the pro-literature, many upon critical examination turn out to be grossly misleading or even fraudulent. One may be forgiven for wondering why, if there are convincingly "genuine" cases, proponents delight in regaling us time and again with pseudo-miracles. Here follow a few brief examples (recently published in a more extensive form) of much publicized, apparently inexplicable successes subsequently shown to have been spurious. A somewhat more detailed section will be devoted to three classic cases from prewar Germany that feature in Paul Tabori's (1974) *Crime and the Occult*. To my knowledge, these cases of misreporting have not been exposed previously.

Claim: In 1951, the Dutch/American clairvoyant Peter Hurkos identified as the perpetrator of a series of arsons near Nijmegen the 17-year-old son of a respected local family whom the police believed to be beyond suspicion. To the utter amazement of the police chief, the boy confessed to the crime when confronted by Hurkos (Browning 1970; Hurkos 1961).

Facts: The 17-year-old arsonist, a mentally deranged farmer's son, had been the prime suspect almost from the beginning. He was arrested after the police at the site of one of the fires found candy wrappings of a brand the boy had recently bought in large quantity at the local confectioner's shop. Hurkos's attempts to solve the case began only on the day after the suspect had been arrested and the case had for all intents and purposes been solved (Hoebens 1981b).

Claim: Nutley, New Jersey, psychic Dorothy Allison told press reporters that she had given the name "Williams" to the Atlanta police long before a man of that name was arrested and convicted for the series of murders of black children. Moreover, she claimed, she had previously named "Williams" as the perpetrator of a series of homicides in Columbus, Georgia, and requested that the Columbus police forward this information to their Atlanta colleagues as soon as she heard of the slayings in that city. A spokesman for the Columbus police was cited in the press to the effect that Wayne Williams had indeed become a suspect in the Columbus murders before he was arrested by the Atlanta police.

Facts: It appears that, during her much publicized visit to terror-stricken Atlanta, Allison mentioned just about every name in the phone directory. James Randi quotes Atlanta's Sergeant Gundlach as saying that Allison had given 42 names for the murderer but (almost surprisingly) not the correct one.

Truzzi spoke to two police officers Allison had mentioned to him as witnesses. One could not confirm having heard the name "Williams." The other one recalled that, at one time, Allison had mentioned a number of names, one of which was "Williams." Wayne Williams was not a suspect in the Columbus case, and a spokesman for the police denied that his department had ever had any reason to forward Allison's information to the Atlanta task force (Randi 1982; Truzzi 1982).

Claim: In 1979, the Dutch clairvoyant Gerard Croiset was consulted by the police commander of Woudrichem about a mysterious outbreak of arson. Croiset's description of the perpetrator would only fit the most unlikely suspect: a quartermaster in the commander's own police department. The commander was dumfounded when he later discovered that the psychic had been right (Tenhaeff 1979).

Facts: A tape-recording of the actual consultation proved that Tenhaeff, professor of parapsychology at Utrecht University, had fabricated the psychic's amazing "hits." The "protocol checked and signed" by the Woudrichem commander who Tenhaeff claimed was the basis of his report simply never existed (Hoebens 1982a).

Claim: In 1958 the Dutch psychic Marinus B. Dykshoorn, now a United States resident, in a remarkable instance of long-distance clairvoyance, solved a theft case in Duisburg, Germany, while speaking on the telephone from his home in Breda, Holland. Dykshoorn identified the thief and gave very precise indications of where the booty had been hidden. The police confirmed to newspaper reporters that Dykshoorn had solved the case (Dykshoorn 1974; Tabori 1974).

Facts: The Duisburg police have repeatedly ..nd flatly denied the claim. They insist that the case was solved by normal investigating methods. The accounts by Dykshoorn and Tabori contradict each other at several points. Dykshoorn refused my request to be supplied with documentary evidence supporting the claim (Hoebens 1982c).

Tabori's German Prize Cases

In *Crime and the Occult—How ESP and Parapsychology Help Detection,* Tabori (1974) relates a number of classic instances in which crimes were supposedly solved by means of clairvoyance. Of particular interest is the case of the occult detective August Drost, whose trial in 1925 received wide publicity in Germany and abroad. According to Tabori, Drost, a teacher, had a considerable reputation as a clairvoyant. He had "succeeded in a number of cases where the police had given up or had been unable to produce quick results." A few of these cases will be critically examined presently.

The Ballenstedt incident. According to Tabori, Drost had attempted to shed light on a burglary that had been committed in the house of a distinguished physician in Ballenstedt. The clairvoyant went into a self-induced trance, but the séance produced nothing very helpful. "Yet," writes Tabori, "something strange *did* happen: Drost declared that the thief had taken from the sanitatsrat's desk a 'greenish book'—something 'with which one makes money.' When he was asked what he meant by this he said: 'Something with which one collects money.' Thereupon the victim went to his desk and found that his cheque book was missing—something he hadn't known himself. Two police officials who were present confirmed this incident under oath." According to Tabori, this is one of those cases where "coincidence can be excluded."

Although Tabori claims that all the material in the chapter "has been taken from police archives or the personal memc:rs of officials," his verison of the event actually appears to be a translation of a story published in the Berlin newspaper *Vossische Zeitung*.

In *Okkultismus and Verbrechen*, the classic work on psychic detectives, which is not even mentioned in Tabori's book, Hellwig (1929) has discussed this case and shown it to be a perfect instance not of clairvoyance but of pseudo-ESP, recalling the far better known case of Sir Edmund Hornby.

First it needs to be pointed out that Tabori is in error when he describes Drost as a clairvoyant. Drost was a hypnotist who worked with female mediums. It is true that the victim of the burglary (which took place in November 1922), Sanitatsrat Danziger, testified during the 1925 trial that Drost's medium, while unsuccessful in her attempt to solve the crime, during a séance in 1922 had spoken of the theft of a checkbook—a fact that at the time had not yet been discovered.

Hellwig, however, was able to prove beyond doubt that Danziger was mistaken. He had been able to consult the original police files and had discovered that Danziger had already reported the loss of this checkbook 19 days prior to the séance. Drost had been handed a list of all the items reported stolen.

When confronted with this evidence, Danziger admitted that he must have been the victim of an extraordinary lapse of memory. He then recalled that he had made his statement to the authorities as a result of a suggestive question posed to him by the hypnotist. Drost had asked him: "You remember, do you, that you went to your desk and said: 'Yes, it is true!'?" Danziger's recollection of the actual event was not good, as he had never attached much importance to the loss of his checkbook—an item that the thief would find of no use whatever. Hellwig points out that the case is more remarkable in that Danziger was very skeptical of the paranormal in general.

The Schade case. Drost had a quite undeniable success, Tabori claims, in his attempts to solve a burglary of which a watchmaker and jeweler named Schade had been the victim. One of Schade's assistants, Walter, was suspected at first but proved his innocence. Schade turned to Drost for help. This time Drost worked with the medium Louise Rennecke—who happened to be Walter's fiancée.

At the séance, Drost and Rennecke identified a man named Franz as the thief. Drost added that the stolen goods were hidden under a layer of straw in a house on the Grosse Wasserreihe in Bernburg. Soon after, the police arrested a man named Franz Muller. The stolen goods were found where Drost had said they had been hidden.

In discussing this case Hellwig (1929) quotes the testimony of the police commander Heilman, who had handled the case. Heilman had told him that Schade (not a jeweler, incidentally, but the manager of a chemical plant) had initially suspected not only Walter but also a second employee of his firm, a certain Franz Montag, who lived on the Grosse Wasserreihe. This was the Franz who was later convicted of the crime. Walter never "proved his innocence"; although legal proof against him was lacking, Heilman was sure he had been an accomplice. According to the police commander, the medium, since she was Walter's fiancée, knew exactly what had happened and where the goods were hidden. In order to protect her lover, she had pointed only to Montag. Drost later told Hellwig that the medium, while in trance, had implicated not only Franz but Walter as well. At the medium's request, the hypnotist had kept this secret.

The Rockmann case. According to Tabori (1974), "One of the most dramatic cases in which Drost had been involved concerned a murder and robbery in the house of a farmer named Rockmann in Calbe." In February 1923 intruders into the Rockmann farmhouse had been surprised by a certain Schlosser, who was brutally battered to death. There were no clues. Drost was called in, and he stated that the crime had been committed by two people, "Eddie" and Aefer." This was a hit; the culprits were soon arrested. Their names were "Ende" and "Schaeffer." The clairvoyant, according to Tabori, had "read" the names, "but phonetically rather than visually, which explained the discrepancy."

Hellwig's investigations revealed that two individuals, named Ende and Schaeffer, had already been suspected prior to the séance. Moreover, the case was hardly as dramatic as Tabori invites us to believe. Ende and Schaeffer had merely stolen some linen belonging to Rockmann. The brutal murder of Schlosser is a pure invention.

Inexplicable and Unexplained Cases

The examples above have in common that they are representative of the genre at its best and that they have been explained. Not only have skeptics found a plausible scenario to account for the data but the skeptical explanation has for all intents and purposes been shown to have been correct. The specific errors in the claims could be identified. Such debunkings are often the result of sheer luck.

Enthusiastic skeptics are fond of stating *ex cathedra* that there is not a shred of evidence to support the claim that psychics have been successful in assisting the police. In fact, this is an overstatement. Several such shreds exist and are available for critical examination. Contrary to what is often believed by insufficiently informed skeptics, police officers *have* testified that they have been very satisfied with the services of sensitives. Such testimonies cannot in all cases be dismissed as the products of a delusion and may legitimately be cited as evidence supporting the proponents' position.

One example: In response to an article in *Police Chief* magazine mentioning the Psychic Sleuths Project of the CSAR, a New Jersey chief of police [name here withheld but available to researchers from CSAR—M.T.] wrote to Marcello Truzzi to confirm that Peter Hurkos "had furnished us with a preponderance of leads that we could not have obtained using the standard investigative techniques." In this homicide case, he further wrote, "Mr. Hurkos, using his unbelievable psychic powers, named for us (by first and last name) the actual perpetrator. It was not until two years later that my officers were able to establish sufficient corroborative evidence to make the arrest of the person named."

While the police chief's statement certainly does not constitute conclusive proof, it *does* constitute evidence of the sort that many ultraskeptical publications have implicitly claimed does not exist.

In contrast to such "inexplicable" cases, I call cases "unexplained" when they continue to resist attempts at specific debunking even where the circumstances (the availability of documents and eyewitnesses, and so on) are such that a critical investigation might normally have been expected to yield information supportive of a specific naturalistic counterhypothesis.

It is tempting, especially if one is a psi proponent, to present such cases as prima facie evidence for the reality of the ESP phenomenon. However, in evaluating historical incidents, great caution is called for. Such cases may have a naturalistic explanation. Apparent success of psychic detection may in fact have been due to naturalistic causes whose traces have been irrevocably erased, removed, or can no longer be identified.

Perhaps the most amusing psychic failure on record involves the well-known Dutch paragnost Cor Heilijgers, who phoned me to reveal that he had "seen" where the body of a missing railway employee was buried. The next day, the newspaper reported that the buried man had been found alive and well and living in Antwerp, almost next door to where Mr. Heilijgers had recently lived.

The Value of Police Opinion

Police investigators and psychical researchers are interested in paranormal detective work for different reasons, and this may on occasion cause some confusion. The parapsychologist is primarily interested in deciding whether or not the psychic demonstrated genuine ESP, whereas the police officer wants to know whether or not the psychic actually helped in solving the case. The two groups use different criteria for measuring success. The law officer may have a low opinion of a sensitive who did not succeed in tracing a missing body but who may have nevertheless scored ESP hits that would enrapture the dedicated psi-researcher.

It is important, however, to note that in assessing the paranormality of a given psychic's feat the average police officer is a layman whose judgment has no more intrinsic value than that of the average citizen. Police officers do not need to be familiar with the numerous techniques of simulating telepathy or with the psychological principles underlying "cold reading" and other soothsayer's tricks. In fact, police officers may be at a disadvantage, as they are trained to quickly discover meaningful patterns in apparently chaotic data. They are conditioned to help the conveyor of information and to encourage the witness. They may be ideal victims for the talented psychic who relies on the cooperation of a sitter. This can be a serious problem as soon as a police officer momentarily steps outside his or her role as an expert in detection and starts playing the amateur parapsychologist. Quite a few police are personally interested in the paranormal and are every bit as desirous of witnessing the "inexplicable" as are other people. This may influence their testimony (and their recollections) if they are requested to comment on the genuineness of psychics—apart from the question of whether these sensitives are of actual practical use to the police.

Affidavits from police departments. Statements by police spokesmen to the effect that a psychic has been successfully consulted should be treated with some caution. Police officers as a rule take a purely pragmatic interest in paranormal detectives and rarely attempt (if they are competent to do so at all) to establish scientifically to what extent the sensitive's helpful perception has likely been of an extrasensory nature. Positive statements usually mean no more than that the police confirm that an individual provided accurate information in a given case. As a rule, they are not capable of deciding whether sensitives are correct in attributing their successes to paranormal gifts.

The trigger hypothesis. Psychic detectives typically confront the police with a great number of ambiguous, contradictory "impressions." Although perhaps containing actual information, these may on occasion act as a trigger. Police officers are forced to rack their brains to discover some signal in the noise and, presumably, will be in a state of intense concentration. A chance remark by a psychic may produce a chain of associations resulting in a lucky guess. The relevant piece of information is already stored inside the police officer's mind; the psychic merely helped to retrieve it by presenting the verbal equivalent of a Rorschach tableau. In cases where the investigation has become bogged down in a morass of false trails and vicious circles, such "brain-washing" applied by a loquacious sensitive may actually contribute to the solution of a case.

Psychics as allies. An individual policeman who has a theory of his own concerning an unsolved police case but who fails to convince his superiors of the plausibility of his conjectures may take a psychic into his confidence, on the assumption that a supposedly independent paranormal confirmation of his theory may persuade the authorities to change their minds.

Laundering of information. In certain circumstances, criminals may use psychics for "laundering" information on fellow-criminals. Here, the sensitive serves as a screen to protect the informant from retaliation. It is also conceivable that in rare cases the police, in order to protect actual sources, will pretend that the informative help vital to the identification of the criminal was obtained from a psychic.

Disinformation. Since a criminal is likely to be as superstitious as the next person, the police may deliberately leak the (false) information that a highly experienced psychic is involved in the investigation, in the hope that the unknown perpetrator of a crime may get nervous and make an injudicious move.

Bribes. In (it is hoped) atypical cases, a psychic in need of favorable publicity may obtain confidential information by bribing a member of the police force and relay this information (this time purportedly received by paranormal means) to other police—who will be duly amazed by the accuracy of the psychic's "vision."

Nonpsychic Alternatives

Ordinary methods. One of the most obvious (if rarely discussed) naturalistic explanations for apparent psychic successes is that many such psychics employ the same methods as do private detectives, police detectives, and Pinkerton employees: collecting evidence, reconnoitering, questioning witnesses, making informed guesses, and practicing the art of deductive thinking. In his autobiography, *Mihn Dubbele Leven* (My double life), the noted Dutch psychic Cor Heilijgers claims that he presented the police with highly accurate descriptions of the murderers of "Black John" at a time when the authorities had no clues whatsoever. However, Wim Jengsma, an Eindhoven police officer responsible for public relations, told me that everyone in the village where the crime had occurred had known exactly who had done it. "And they knew it before Heilijgers appeared on the scene. The psychic spent a few days in the village, heard all the gossip, and later claimed a reward for having helped trace the culprits." Heilijgers's unquestionable successes in locating the bodies of missing persons (confirmed by the police) do not seem necessarily psychic in nature. Clairvoyants may become experts in a limited area of (conventional) police work, to the extent that they can outperform professional police. For example, the late Gerard Croiset's enormous experience in searching for missing children presumed drowned had probably never been equaled by any professional police officer. Such experience makes it easier to see similarities between different events and to make an educated guess as to the most probable solution.

Unusual nonparanormal abilities. Recently, there was a lot of publicity surrounding an American physician who claimed to be able to identify a piece of music (and sometimes even the orchestra playing it) by merely looking at the grooves of a gramaphone record (the label of which had been covered). Initial suspicions of a hoax were dispelled when James Randi, the magician and debunker of spurious psychic claims, tested the claimant and found his ability to be perfectly genuine. "Record reading" is certainly not an example of extrasensory perception but no less baffling for that. The example is relevant to this discussion as it reminds us that laymen and scientists alike are prone to underestimate the range of *sensory* perception. Sensory abilities vary enormously in individuals, and some have developed the ability to perform apparent miracles by using their eyes, ears, or noses. Some successful psychic detectives may actually be able to detect traces too faint to be discerned by the average person and erroneously attribute this ability to ESP.

Stacking effects. If many psychics attempt to solve the same case, the "stacking effect" well known to statisticians may easily produce spurious "success." As a rule, the media will only report "hits" and keep silent about psychics who failed. In 1972, the Dutch paragnost R.G. was in close touch with the parents of 12-year-old A.P., who had disappeared on her way to school in Rotterdam. According to the report in the daily newspaper *De Telegraaf*, about 100 sensitives tried to be helpful. It seems almost a statistical oddity that none of the 100-plus "visions" (some psychics, such as the famous Gerard Croiset, tried twice) appreciably corresponded to what later turned out to be the tragic truth, that A.P. had been murdered and that her body had been left in a pool near the airport. (If the psychics involved had each agreed to select a different 100th part of the town, at least one of them would have been assured a "hit," with odds against chance of 100 to 1.)

References

Allison, Dorothy, and Scott Jacobson. 1980. *Dorothy Allison: A Psychic Story.* New York: Jove Books.

Archer, Fred. 1969. *Crime and the Psychic World.* New York: William Morrow.

Brink, F. 1960. Parapsychology and Criminal Investigation. *International Criminal Police Review,* 134. January.

Browning, Norma Lee. 1970. *The Psychic World of Peter Hurkos.* Garden City, N.Y.: Doubleday.

Dykshoorn, M. B. (as told to Russell H. Felton). 1974. *My Passport Says Clairvoyant.* New York: Hawthorn.

Heilijgers, Cor. 1976. *Mihn Dubbele Leven* (My double life). Bussum, Holland: Fidessa.

Hellwig, Albert. 1929. *Okkultismus und Verbrechen. Eine Einfürung in die kriminalistischen Probleme des Okkultismus für Polizeibeamte Richter Staatsanwälte, Psychiater und Sachverständige.* Berlin: Dr. P. Langenscheidt.

Hoebens, Piet Hein. 1981a. Gerard Croiset: Investigation of the Mozart of "Psychic Sleuths"—Part I. *Skeptical Inquirer,* 6(1):17-28.

———. 1981b. The mystery men of Holland, I: Peter Hurkos's Dutch cases. *Zetetic Scholar,* no. 8:11-17.

———. 1982a. Croiset and Professor Tenhaeff: Discrepancies in claims of clairvoyance. *Skeptical Inquirer,* 6(2):32-40.

———. 1982b. The mystery men of Holland, II: The strange case of Gerard Croiset. *Zetetic Scholar,* No. 9:20-32.

———. 1982c. The mystery men of Holland, III: The man whose passport says clairvoyant. *Zetetic Scholar,* No. 10:7-16.

———. 1983a. Croiset: Double Dutch? *The Unexplained: Mysteries of Mind, Space & Time,* No. 132:2630-2633.

———. 1983b. Less sensitive by half? *The Unexplained: Mysteries of Mind, Space & Time,* No. 138:2754-2757.

Hurkos, Peter. 1961. *Psychic.* New York: Popular Library.

Pollack, Jack Harrison. 1964. *Croiset the Clairvoyant: The Story of the Amazing Dutchman.* Garden City, N.Y.: Doubleday.

Randi, James. 1982. Private communication (letter, documents, and cassette tape) to Marcello Truzzi, available at the Center for Scientific Anomalies Research. March.

Reiser, Martin, and N. Klyver. 1982. A Comparison of psychics, detectives, and students in the investigation of major crimes. In *Police Psychology: Collected Papers,* edited by M. Reiser, 260-267. Los Angeles: LEHI Publishing Co.

Reiser, Martin, L. Ludwig, S. Saxe, and C. Wagner. 1979. An evaluation of the use of psychics in the investigation of major crimes. *Journal of Police Science and Administration,* 7(1):18-25.

Tabori, Paul. 1974. *Crime and the Occult—How ESP and Parapsychology Help Detection.* New York: Taplinger.

Tenhaeff, W. H. C. 1953. Aid to the police," *Tomorrow,* 10-18. Autumn.

———. 1960. The employment of paragnosts for police purposes. *Proceedings of the P.I.* (Parapsychological Institute of the State University of Utrecht), No. 1:33 f.

———. 1980. Der paragnost. *Esotera,* 31(9):816-827.

Truzzi, Marcello. 1982. Summary report on Dorothy Allison's claims re Atlanta murders perpetrator. Psi Sleuths Project Memorandum of March 21, 1982. Ann Arbor, Mich.: Center for Scientific Anomalies Research.

Wilson, Colin. 1984. *The Psychic Detectives.* London: Pan Books.

29

Evidence for Survival from Near-Death Experiences?
A Critical Appraisal

GERD H. HÖVELMANN

Introduction

Ever since 1848, when the Fox sisters produced those ill-famed and most probably fraudulent (Dessoir 1967, 339; Nicol 1979, 16) rapping sounds to use them as a means for purported communication with the spirit of a deceased man, the assumption that mind and personality survive the death of the body and brain has formed the basis for the quasi-religious spiritualistic movement. While the British Society for Psychical Research was not founded to pursue the problem of survival as such, at least one of the immediate reasons for its formation in 1882 was the hope that the assumption might be demonstrated to be correct by the meticulous application of scientifically sound empirical methods (Gauld 1968; 1982).

The early leaders of the SPR set afoot large-scale attempts to collect and critically assess ostensible evidence for survival. They conducted careful censuses and collected accounts of apparently veridical hallucinations of the dead and dying during the 1880s and 1890s; but their extensive reports, though sometimes suggestive, were far from conclusively resolving what these early psychical researchers had called "the problem of survival."[1] Thus scientific research into the problem of survival of human personality after death has been conducted for well over a century. More or less comprehensive accounts and evaluations of old as well as contemporary research and its results that may be usefully consulted include Myers (1903), Barrett (1918), Hyslop (1919), Murphy (1945), Salter (1961), Jacobson (1973), Palmer (1975), Gauld (1977, 1982), Stevenson (1977a; 1982a), Resch (1980), Anderson (1981), Roll (1982; 1984), Zorab (1982), and Thouless (1984).

There can be no doubt that the focal point of the parapsychologists' interest has shifted away from survival research to other areas of parapsychological investigation over the decades, and Zorab (1982, 128) even concludes that "the SPR's quest for survival practically came to an end at the beginning of World War II." In fact, between the late 1930s and the early 1960s, most parapsychologists considered it wiser to defer a direct attack on the problem of survival after death until after a more complete understanding had been achieved of the power and limitations of extrasensory perception on the part of living persons. So Zorab's opinion seems defensible at least as far as programmatic decisions of the SPR and other parapsychological organizations regarding the priority of certain areas of research over others are concerned. However, even during that period (c. 1930–1960) quite a few individual psychical researchers, including several leading figures of the field, continued to pursue various areas of survival-related research and theory-building, and there are reasons to suspect that, stimulated by an increasing public interest in questions related to death and dying since the late 1960s or early 1970s, survival research is gaining ground again. Gauld (1982, 7) provides a pertinent description of these developments:

> Investigations of mediumship, apparitions, and other survival-related phenomena have been to a considerable extent displaced by laboratory experiments on telepathy, clairvoyance and precognition. . . . Despite changes of emphasis the parapsychological enterprise today is recognizably continuous with the undertaking set afoot by those distinguished and earnest Victorians one hundred years ago. There has in fact been in the last decade or so something of a revival of interest in the problem of survival.

Beloff (1977, 14) concludes that "to this day parapsychologists are still divided between survivalists and nonsurvivalists," and in his 1982 presidential address to the Parapsychological Association (Beloff 1983), he called the perennial question of survival an "open question" as well as one of "the most important questions that concern us and that our founders bequeathed to us" (p. 317), and he argues that, "on current reckoning, a rational case can be made for either a positive or negative answer to the question of survival" (p. 323).

Since 1882, parapsychologists have tried to find evidence for the persistence of personality after bodily death in a variety of areas of survival-related research.[2] These include:[3]

—The study of physical and, in particular, mental *mediumship*: e.g., cf. Salter (1950), Roll (1960; 1982, 170-186), and Gauld (1982). These survival-related studies include the examination of cases of so-called "drop-in communicators," that is, "uninvited" communicators in mediumistic sessions who are ostensibly unknown to both medium and sitters (see, for instance, Stevenson [1970]; Gauld [1971; 1982, 58-73]), and cross-correspondences (Saltmarsh 1938).

—The collection and examination of reports of *apparitions:* cf. Gurney,

Myers, and Podmore (1886), Tyrrell (1953), Gauld (1982), 230–260), Stevenson (1982b), and Roll (1982, 150–170).

—The investigation of *hauntings* and *poltergeist* disturbances: see Stevenson (1972) and Roll (1982, 212–246). L. Stafford Betty's badly argued claim, which he supports with hardly any evidence at all and which is marred by a number of logical problems, that *all* poltergeist disturbances should be considered as being due to discarnate agency (Betty 1984), provoked a controversy betweeen Hövelmann and Zorab (1985a; 1985b), Betty (1985), and Stevenson (1985). For a decidedly nonsurvivalist approach to hauntings and poltergeists, see Zorab (1984).

—The study of alleged cases of *possession* and *obsession:* cf. Oesterreich (1930), Gauld (1982, 147–162); for a comprehensive criticism of a particularly well known case, see Mischo and Niemann (1983).

—The examination of evidence for *reincarnation* (which, according to most definitions, implies the survival at least of some personality characteristics) from claimed memories of former incarnations (especially, cf. Stevenson 1960a, 1960b, 1974a, 1977b, as well as Stevenson's continuing *Cases of the Reincarnation Type* series,[4] published by the University Press of Virginia; also, cf. Gauld 1982, 163–187) as well as from hypnotic regressions into what is alleged to be past lives (e.g., Bernstein 1956).

—Research into cases of *xenoglossy,* into cases, that is, in which persons speak a natural language of which they have ordinarily no knowledge: see Stevenson (1974b; 1984) as well as Hövelmann (1986).

—The construction of *combination lock* and *cipher tests* for survival: for instance, cf. Thouless (1948), Stevenson (1968; 1976), and Berger (1984).

—The collection and examination of reports of spontaneous *out-of-the-body experiences* (OBEs) as well as the experimental induction of OBEs in laboratory settings. Most survivalists within parapsychology consider the separability of mind and body, which many believe to be apparent in OBEs, a necessary precondition of the survival of personality after bodily death. Consequently, the occurrence of OBEs is viewed as an indirect proof of the possibility of survival. This interpretation of OBEs, as well as of other of the aforementioned ostensibly paranormal phenomena, rests on the assumption that the "mental-entity paradigm" is valid. (See Note 2.) A thoughtful nonsurvivalist, nonseparationist, "normal"-psychological theory of out-of-the-body experiences has been suggested recently by Blackmore (1982, and her Chapter 18 of this volume).

—One further area of survival-related research, which only came into prominence a few decades ago because it depends on the availability of relatively sophisticated technical recording apparatus, is the investigation of so-called *electronic voice phenomena* or *Raudive voices*. The earliest relevant publication I am aware of is a brief report by Bayless (1959). Later and more important and influential publications on such tape-recorded voices (more purportedly are produced by discarnate agencies) include those by Jürgenson (1967), Raudive (1971), and Köberle (1980). For critical discussions of these phenomena and their survivalist interpretation—which, fortunately, few parapsychologists have taken seriously—see Keil (1980b), Hövelmann (1982), and, especially, Ellis (1978).

There is one further area of research supposedly relevant to the problem of survival of bodily death that is not included in this inevitably incomplete list of parapsychologists' attempts to find a solution to that problem: the collection of and research into *near-death experiences* (NDEs) and *deathbed visions*.[5] It is on these experiences and their relevance to the question of survival that we will concentrate in the following pages, because this particular area of survival-related research seems to have been the most fashionable one during the past two decades. Quite obviously, this has been the area of survival-related research most appealing to the nonscientific general public after questions of death and dying ceased to be under taboo. This increasing public interest in these questions is no doubt largely responsible for what Gauld (1982), in the passage quoted above, referred to as "something of a revival of interest among parapsychologists in the problem of survival" (p. 7), and even as careful a parapsychological experimentalist as Keil (1980a) feels forced to admit that "recent research about near death experiences . . . has probably weakened" his otherwise nonsurvivalist position, although he still sees "no evidence which would compel me to accept the survival hypothesis" (p. 163). In addition, research into NDEs appears to answer Roll's call for "survival research with the living" (Roll 1973); and, at least at first sight, it seems particularly well suited to demonstrate the validity of the old assumption of the separability of mind and personality from body and brain, which we referred to at the outset of this paper. It must be stated immediately, however, that not all and, in fact, not even many of the researchers engaged in parapsychological investigations have ever considered near-death experiences evidence of survival. Nevertheless, quite a few parapsychologists as well as the vast majority of the general public decidedly believe that research into NDEs holds some promise for an eventual solution to the survival problem.

Since the early 1960s, an enormous (and still gradually increasing) number of books, both good and bad, on NDEs and deathbed visions have been published, including those by Osis (1961), Kübler-Ross (1975; 1978; 1980a; 1980b; 1982), Matson (1975), Moody (1977a; 1977b), Osis and Haraldsson (1978a), Kastenbaum (1979), Ring (1980a; 1982a), Sabom (1981), Gallup (with Proctor, 1982), Lundahl (1982), and others.[6] As can easily be seen from these and other publications, a considerable part of contemporary NDE research is conducted by investigators outside of the parapsychological community. A number of prominent figures in this field, such as Ring, Sabom, Kastenbaum, Lundahl,

Gallup, Moody, Kübler-Ross, et al., are not parapsychologists by any definition of the word. Nevertheless, parapsychologists have significantly contributed to (and initiated some of) this research, and it is they who are among the staunchest defenders of the relevance of NDE research to the survival hypothesis.

A review of the more strictly parapsychological literature on near-death experiences and deathbed visions befor 1977 was provided by Rogo (1978). Apart from the books just mentioned (most of which belong to the better ones on the topic), there also is an increasing number of popular writers trying to cash in on the public's interest in NDEs. This enormous number of recent books (some of which have proclaimed rhapsodically that NDEs already provide strong evidence of man's survival after death), as well as the recent upsurge of public and scientific interest in such experiences, may suggest that the investigation of near-death experiences and deathbed visions represents a relatively new line of research or that NDEs have only occurred in the past few years. Contrary to the general public's impression and contrary to what some less-than-well-informed skeptics have alleged, however, this is far from being the case. In actual fact, research on NDEs and deathbed visions (or "circumthanatology," as Lundahl [1982] would have us call it), has a long history in parapsychology, and occasionally it has also been conducted elsewhere: early studies include, for instance, those by Heim (1892), Bozzano (1906; 1923; 1947), Hyslop (1907; 1918), Flammarion (1922); Barrett (1926); and Pfister (1930).

There are at least two main reasons that these authors and their studies on NDEs had much less influence on their contemporaries than more recent works appear to have had. The first is that, as Johnson (1982, 19–37) has convincingly argued, there was an attitude of evasion of questions of death and dying, which were under taboo at least until the early 1960s. The second reason is explained by Blackmore (1982, 142):

> There is good reason for the recent upsurge of interest in NDEs, and that is that more people now survive close brushes with death. In the time of Myers, Barrett or Flammarion, deathbed accounts were more common as people lingered on with consumption and often died at home. But today they are rushed to hospital and resuscitated from states which, not so long ago, would have been called death. One can suffer a cardiac arrest and the cessation of breathing and even most brain activity, and still be "brought back to life." This has necessitated changes in the definition of death and the laws surrounding it,[7] but of most importance here, it has provided a large number of people who have been very close to death but have survived to tell the tale. [p. 142]

This also explains the (relative) shift away of interest from deathbed visions to NDEs. The developments described by Blackmore, I may add, have not only provided a large number of people who are in a position to relate the experiences they made in the face of death, but also a large number of people who wish to learn more about (and have explained) their own experiences, which not infrequently have changed their views of life.

The Phenomenology of Near-Death Experiences

A variety of important phenomenal aspects and experiential features of near-death experiences are easily distinguished. They have been described extensively by a number of NDE researchers, some of whom, in addition, have tried to formulate sets of experiential clusters or symptoms. Raymond Moody (1977a), an American doctor who interviewed a number of people who had had accidents or been resuscitated, has put together what he considers the most important aspects of the NDE cases he collected, and he has constructed an idealized version (or a "complete case") of a typical near-death experience. Moody emphasizes that no one person described the whole of this experience, that some of these elements are typically reported, but that no single element appears in every account and that the order in which these experiences occur may also vary. Since Moody's description contains virtually all of the different experiential features of NDEs that are also reported by other investigators, I can do no better than use his own words (as, at the time this paper is being written, only the German edition of Moody's book was available to me [again, see Note 6], I am quoting from Roll [1982]; numbers and italics were added by Roll):

A man is dying and, as he reaches the point of greatest physical distress, he hears himself pronounced dead by his doctor. He begins to hear an uncomfortable noise, a *loud ringing or buzzing* [1], and at the same time feels himself moving very rapidly through a *long dark tunnel* [2]. After this, he suddenly finds himself *outside of his own physical body* [3], but still in the immediate physical environment, and *he sees his own body from a distance* [4], as though he is a spectator. He watches the resuscitation attempt from this unusual vantage point and is *in a state of emotional upheaval* [5].

After a while, he collects himself and becomes more accustomed to his odd condition. He notes that he *still has a "body"* [3], but one of a very different nature and with very different powers from the physical body he has left behind. Soon other things begin to happen. Others come to meet and to help him. He glimpses the *spirits of relatives and friends* [6] who have already died, and a loving, warm spirit of a kind he has never encountered before—*a being of light* [7]—appears before him. This being asks him a question, nonverbally, to make him *evaluate his life* [8] and helps him along by showing him a panoramic, instantaneous *playback of the major events in his life* [9]. At some point he finds himself approaching some sort of *barrier or border* [10], apparently representing the limit between earthly life and the next life. Yet, he finds that he *must go back to the earth* [11], that the time of his death has not yet come. At this point he resists, for by now he is taken up with his experiences in the afterlife and *does not want to return* [12]. He is overwhelmed by intense *feelings of joy, love, and peace* [13]. Despite his attitude, though, he somehow *reunites with his physical body* [14] and lives.

Later, he tries to tell others, but he has trouble doing so. In the first place, he can find *no human words adequate to describe these unearthly episodes* [15]. He also finds that others scoff, so he stops telling other people. Still, the experience affects his life profoundly, especially his views about death and its relationship to life. [pp. 262–263]

Kenneth Ring (1979a), whose study was stimulated by Moody's informal sampling work, describes six types of experience constituting what he terms the "core NDE": (1) a profound sense of peace and contentment, (2) a sense of being detached from the physical body, (3) movement into a "space" between this world and another that seems to be without dimension, (4) the presence of another being who helps to assess one's life and offers a choice of remaining or not, (5) brilliant white or golden light that immerses one and brings contentment, and (6) unforgettable beauty of colors and/or heavenly music.

Later Ring (1979b; 1980a) reduced this six-type "core NDE," presenting a novel grouping of features of near-death experiences in five distinct, prototypical sequential stages of decreasing frequency and increasing depth: (1) peace, euphoric affect, and cessation of pain, (2) body separation (out-of-the-body experience), (3) entering a transitional region of darkness, (4) seeing an unearthly world of light, and (5) entering into that world of light. This final stage involves paradisiacal imagery and meeting religious figures and deceased relatives "out there." Various characteristics of the NDE are qualitatively described by Ring: the states of mind, detachment, calm, total relaxation, improved logic, increased sight, sensitive hearing, and, in general, a novel and thoroughly enhanced sense of awareness.[8] Still other, though related, classifications are applied by Sabom (1981) and Sabom and Kreutziger (1978; 1979). Finally, it may be noted that, in a study of the relationship between the phenomenology of the NDE and pre-existing conditions, Twemlow, Gabbard, and Coyne (1982) found that, apparently, "there are the 'haves' and the 'have nots'" (p. 138) with regard to near-death experiences.

In spite (or because) of these differing preliminary classifications of phenomenal aspects of near-death experiences, investigation into the mechanisms and effects of NDEs "has been impeded by the lack of quantitative measures of the NDE and its components" (Greyson 1983a, 369). Therefore, Greyson developed a useful 16-item NDE Scale as an easily administered instrument for the investigative and clinical "quantification of a near-death experience and its Cognitive, Affective, Paranormal, and Transcendental Components" (pp. 374–

375). Greyson's new NDE Scale certainly has major advantages over Ring's earlier Weighted Core Experience Index.

Surveys, Reviews, Case Studies

As already pointed out in the introduction, investigation into near-death experiences and deathbed visions by no means forms a new line of research. Quite the contrary, this type of research and case collection dates back at least as far as 1892, when Albert Heim, a Zürich professor of geology, published a report (in German) on the experiences of people, especially alpinists, who had survived falls (as Heim himself had), as well as on other NDE cases, such as those of wounded soldiers and persons who had fallen from roofs, been in railroad disasters, or in other near-fatal accidents (Heim 1892).[9] First systematic studies of NDEs, including what F. P. Cobbe (1877; 1882) had called "Peak-in-Darien" cases, that is, NDEs in which the experiencers are unaware that the people seen in their visions have died,[10] were conducted by Hyslop (1907; 1918), Bozzano (1906; 1923; 1947), Flammarion (1922), and Barrett (1926). Barrett's posthumously published study especially discussed collectively seen deathbed apparitions as well as OBEs by the dying.

Among the most popular (and, from a scientific point of view, the least useful) studies of near-death experiences and deathbed visions are those by Elisabeth Kübler-Ross (1975; 1978; 1980a; 1980b; 1982), which resulted from her work with dying patients. Another popular, though scientifically somewhat more interesting, collection of tales of NDEs is the one published by Moody (1977a; 1977b), from which I have quoted at some length already. It is quite obvious (which Moody himself frankly admits) that Moody's work has many shortcomings. Among the most serious of them is the fact that the author did not attempt any organized sampling or statistical analysis of his cases—he interviewed about 50 people who reported NDEs after resuscitation had brought them back from close brushes with death, and he mentions but does not describe or discuss in any detail some 100 additional NDEs from terminal patients. Nor did he determine whether the nature of the NDEs varied with the respective situations in which they occurred, the experiencers' personalities, or other factors.

After Osis (1961) had conducted, as early as 1959–1960, and published what he later referred to as his "pilot survey" under the auspices of the Parapsychological Foundation, Osis and Haraldsson (1974; 1977; 1978a) carried out large-scale surveys of physicians' and nurses' deathbed observations in both the United States and India (see also Osis 1966). They took the following steps:

In the U.S. the questionnaire, with a covering letter, was mailed to a stratified random sample of 2500 physicians and 2500 nurses. . . . A total of 1004 responses was received.

Our Indian consultants advised us not to use the mails to distribute the questionnaire. We therefore worked mainly in large university hospitals. Usually the professor of medicine or professor of surgery arranged meetings with the hospital staff during which we gave a short talk and distributed the questionnaire to be filled out. Practically all the physicians and nurses we approached returned the completed questionnaire (a total of 704). [Osis and Haraldsson 1977, 242]

Further explorations were made by means of telephone (in the U.S.) and personal interviews (in India) as well as follow-up questionnaires. Altogether 877 cases were obtained, about evenly distributed between the United States and India. Among a number of other interesting findings were the following:

The vast majority of patients involved were terminally ill (714). We also had 163 cases of patients who recovered from near-death conditions. Hallucinations of human figures, or seeing apparitions, was the type of phenomenon most frequently reported (by 591 patients). A total of 112 vision cases were primarily of heavenly abodes, landscapes, gardens, buildings. In 174 cases, patients did not report seeing anything unusual, but their moods became elevated to serenity, peace, elation, or religious emotions. [p. 243]

The vast majority of visions in this survey by parapsychologists Osis and Haraldsson were of dead people or religious figures (which reverses the trend for people in good health). Indian respondents reported more cases of religious visions, while in America there were more visions of the dead. Of all the dead people seen, 91 percent were relatives of the patients, and 65 percent (as compared with 50 percent in Osis's 1961 survey) seemed to have come with the purpose of taking the dying patient away. Here a remarkable difference emerged between the two cultures: The majority of Americans were willing to "go" with the apparitions while most Indians were not. In fact, of the 54 patients who refused to "go" 53 were Indians. Osis and Haraldsson (1977) suggest that "this difference in consent between the U.S. and Indian samples may be partly due to the patients' religion and partly to their nationality" (p. 247). The authors state that they considered psychological and quite a few other factors that may have caused hallucinations, but that no such effect could be found.

Major NDE studies that were stimulated by Moody's work include those by Ring (1979a; 1980a) and Sabom (1981) and Sabom and Kreutziger (1978; 1979). Ring studied and compared 102 NDE cases he had obtained in interviews of people who had come close to death or been resuscitated from clinical death as victims of illness (52 patients), accidents (26), or suicide attempts (24). He found that the near-death experience unfolds in the five distinct stages we already referred to in the preceding section. Among a number of other inter-esting results, he found, for instance, that the panoramic life-review was experi-enced by 55 percent of accident victims, but only by 16 percent of those in the two other groups. With attempted suicides, none reported the tunnel effect, saw the light, or encountered the presence. Sabom (1981) interviewed 106 persons who had been close to death (mostly cardiac-arrest patients). A surprising 43 percent of them reported actually having had a near-death experience. Even more so than in the cases reported in the other studies, the patients in Sabom's and Sabom and Kreutziger's studies seem to have experienced calm and peace during their NDEs.

Now all of the studies mentioned so far suffer from a number of more or less serious drawbacks with regard to both the sampling methods and the analyses. I am not going to discuss these shortcomings in this place, however, because, in this paper, I am mainly concerned with the claimed relevance of near-death experiences and deathbed visions, and their investigation, to the problem of survival.[11]

There can be no doubt that the studies mentioned so far are among the best known and, in a sense, the most popular ones available in the literature. How-ever, there are a large number of other surveys, reviews, and case studies of NDEs and deathbed visions—conducted for a variety of different purposes and with differing degrees of scientific rigor and sophistication—which deserve to be mentioned here. So, before I return to the question of whether studies of NDEs have contributed meaningfully to a solution of the survival problem, let me review some of these less well known investigations.[12]

Near-Death Experiences in Various Cultures or Populations

In a recent analysis of the data from a national poll of Americans' beliefs and experiences in relation to life after death (including NDEs), Gallup (with Proc-tor, 1982) concludes:

> There is a correlation between what the witnesses to deathbed scenes report and what those involved in near-death events claim to experience. Our findings suggest that as many as eight million Americans, or about one-third of those who have been involved in near-death occurrences, may have felt the presence of some being or otherwise have had a positive, otherworldly experience. Many of those reporting deathbed encounters are describing something quite simi-lar. [p. 14]

These findings seem less than reliable, however, as the question that attempted to solicit data on NDEs was very poorly formulated. Also, the analysis is marred by statistical inadequacies.

Green and Friedman (1983) present interviews with 41 Southern California residents who had experienced close brushes with death as the result of an accident, illness, or suicide attempt. A total of 50 NDEs is reported and are rated according to Ring's Weighted Core Experience Index. Results are presented in terms of the characteristics of Ring's five stages of the NDE, although "some of our respondents reported these components in reverse order" (p. 92). The authors favor a metaphysical interpretation of near-death experiences in terms of "altered dimensions of reality or existence" (p. 77) and emphasize what they believe may be "potentially . . . revolutionary" implications of NDEs.

Giovetti (1982) presents a survey of 120 Italian cases of near-death experiences and deathbed visions solicited from readers of several magazines. She finds that her cases are consistent with those collected at different times and in different cultures.

Counts (1983) reports three near-death experiences, one vision, and one dream by Melanesian villagers and analyzes them with regard to their cultural context. Comparison of these experiences with those reported by Moody (1977a) and Osis and Haraldsson (1978a) from the United States and India suggests that, while there are common features (visions of a paradise, apparitions), their interpretation is structured by and largely dependent on cultural expectations (such as the Melanesian cargo belief) on the part of the experiencers.

Bush (1983), on the other hand, in a review of 17 accounts of near-death experiences in children, found that NDEs that occur at early ages appear to "follow patterns simlar to those encountered with adults" (p. 192). With the exception of particular features like life-review and encounters with deceased persons, the children's experiences are comparable to those reported by adults. This leads Bush to the conclusion that "cultural conditioning is not a primary determinant of NDE contents" (p. 177). However, there is a possibly serious problem with both this conclusion and the entire study, because what is called "children's accounts" were made retrospectively after periods ranging from 11 to 65 years, when those who had had NDEs as children were teenagers or adults! So, contrary to Bush's conclusion, the fact that "children's accounts" and accounts made by adults are comparable may be due to the very fact that "cultural conditioning" is "a primary determinant of NDE contents."

Kohr (1982) conducted a questionnaire survey of a national sample of members of the Association for Research and Enlightenment (ARE). There were 547 respondents who filled in the 221-item questionnaire. Based on a series of questions regarding death, the respondents were divided into three groups, an Experiencing group (84 respondents), a Close to Death Only group (105), and a Non-Experiencing group (358). While analyses revealed little or no differences between the second and third group, there were a number of interesting differences between the Experiencing group and the two other groups. The Experiencing group showed a "significantly greater tendency to report psi or psi-related experiences such as general ESP in both the waking and the dream state, psychokinesis, auras, apparitions, and out-of-body experiences" (p. 51). As Kohr himself points out, however, "the respondents represent an atypical population of individuals who are attracted to an orgnaization like the ARE because of their own psi experiences and who are even willing to pay [a fee of $5.00—G.H.H.] to participate" (p. 50).

Particular Aspects, Characteristics, and Components of the Near-Death Experience

Ring (1982b) presents some "preliminary findings suggestive of the possibility that a small minority of near-death survivors may have had glimpses of the future disclosed to them during or after their NDEs" (p. 69). He distinguishes between two groups of such "glimpses of the future": so-called "Personal Flash-forwards," that is, those that concern one's personal future, which may "in some sense independently exist as part of a 'life design' that only gradually unfolds in manifestation," and so-called "Prophetic Visions," which "relate to the earth's future over the next twenty years" (pp. 69–70). Ring presents what he considers suggestive evidence from about a dozen cases of each type.

Locke and Shontz (1983) studied presumed personality and other differences between members of a group of nine persons who recalled at least moderate NDEs and those of a group of ten persons who had been near death but did not recall any such experience. "Contrary to expectation," however, "no patterns of personality were found that would distinguish persons who could recall an NDE from persons who had been exposed to similar physiological conditions but could not recall one; there were no differences between groups on any of the several tests of personality and intelligence. The data also failed to support the expectation that persons not experiencing NDEs would show Rorschach test signs implying the incapacity for psi. At least to the extent that this was measured in the present experiment, therefore, the difference between groups in occurrence or nonoccurrence of NDEs does not appear to be due to differences in personality traits normally associated with the ability or inability to process psi" (pp. 315–316).

In a study of 78 retrospective reports of near-death experiences using (self-selected) subjects' narratives, questionnaires, interviews, and medical records, Greyson and Stevenson (1980) report a number of interesting findings on predisposing and precipitating factors, as well as on a variety of features of NDEs, such as out-of-the-body experiences during NDEs; tunnel experiences; encounters with a "being of light," religious figures, deceased or living acquaintances, and unidentified strangers; unusual visual, somatic, auditory, olfactory, and gustatory phenomena; apparent extrasensory phenomena; panoramic memory; and the respondents' changes in attitudes. No single feature of the NDEs reported was significantly correlated with the respondents' prior knowledge about NDEs. Of particular interest is Greyson and Stevenson's finding that 52 percent of their subjects reported having believed during their NDEs that they were dying and that "this belief was inversely correlated with the subjective duration of the experience (X^2 = 7.38, df = 2, p < .05); that is, the longer the experience seemed to last, the less likely the subject was to believe that he or she was indeed dying" (p. 1195).

In a number of studies, Noyes and associates—Noyes (1972; 1981), Noyes, Hoenk, Kuperman, and Symen (1977), Noyes and Kletti (1976a; 1976b; 1977a; 1977b)—reported and analyzed accounts of near-death experiences in terms of psychological mechanisms. Among other things, the authors describe sequential phases of (1) resistance to death, (2) life review, and (3) transcendence of time and space. By factor analysis, they isolated independent symptom clusters of (1) hyperalertness, (2) depersonalization, and (3) mystical consciousness, including panoramic memory. They interpret the first two of these symptom clusters as adaptive psychological responses to the threat of death, but they conclude that no single or unified interpretation also can account for the reported experiences of mystical consciousness. (We will return to the studies by Noyes and associates in a later section.)

Gabbard, Twemlow, and Jones (1981) discussed the question of whether NDEs occur only near death, and they compared 34 OBEs occurring near death with 305 other OBEs. They found no features unique to the near-death state, although certain phenomena, including positive changes in attitude, were more frequently associated with near-death OBEs than with other OBEs. Twemlow, Gabbard, and Jones (1982) described the same 339 OBEs in terms of the conditions surrounding the experience, phenomenological features, and subsequent impact. OB experiencers did not differ from control subjects in terms of psychological health or background. Twemlow, Gabbard, and Coyne (1982) report the results of a multivariate analysis of data from 33 near-death experiences. They examined the relationship between the phenomenology of the experience and preexisting conditions. Five clusters of preexisting near-death conditions were isolated (low stress, emotional stress, intoxicant, cardiac arrest, and anesthetic); the authors propose that the statistical technique they used in their analyses is particularly suitable for near-death studies with few subjects and large numbers of variables.

A useful and informative review of the literature on an apparently paradoxical effect—suicide inhibiting effects of NDEs, even though these experiences near death are described as very pleasant by the vast majority of the experiencers—is provided by Greyson (1981a), who also presents several psychodynamic hypotheses to account for this puzzling finding.[13] Another study on alleged positive personality transformations following near-death experiences is presented by Flynn (1982). He reviews the previous literature on what he calls the "transformative effects of NDEs," and he presents preliminary data suggesting that NDEs greatly increase concern for others, religious interest, and belief in an afterlife, while they decrease fear of death, material desires, and need for approval of others. Greyson (1983c), on the other hand, in a questionnaire survey of 264 members of the International Association for Near-Death Studies "did not find that the study group [that is, those 89 respondents who had had NDEs—G.H.H.] valued self-actualization, altruism, and spirituality more highly than did the control group [those 175 respondents who did not claim NDEs—G.H.H.]" (p. 619).

The Survival Hypothesis

Quite a few NDE investigators, most of them parapsychologists, have claimed that near-death experiences are or may become relevant to the problem of survival, and some of them have maintained that research into NDEs has already provided evidence in support of the survival hypothesis. Among the staunchest defenders of the survival hypothesis with regard to near-death experiences and deathbed visions are parapsychologists Osis and Haraldsson (1977, 1978a). They constructed a bi-polar model contrasting the survival hypothesis and the destruction hypothesis, and the results of their American and Indian surveys led them to the conclusion that orthodox psychological factors are unlikely to have played any significant role in the production of the deathbed visions they had studied and that they had collected evidence favoring the survival rather than the destruction hypothesis: "The central tendencies of the data support the after-life hypothesis as it is formulated in the model we outlined briefly earlier in this paper" (Osis and Haraldsson 1977, 258).

While Osis and Haraldsson's stance has been roundly criticized by some of their fellow parapsychologists, such as Anderson (1981, 9), Blackmore (1982, 140-141), Palmer (1978, 1979), McHarg (1978), and Timm (1980a; 1980b), other psychical researchers, such as Stevenson (1977a), have defended the survival interpretation of NDEs. Giovetti's statement adaquately summarizes this position: "The occurrence of . . . common patterns, in spite of the great social, religious, and cultural differences of the subjects, offers—if not evidence, then an indication, at least, that life does not end with physical death" (Giovetti 1982, 13).

Grosso (1981a)—also see his note on "Questions and Prospects for Near-death Research" (Grosso 1981b)—likewise asserts that the universality, the paranormal components, and the beneficial effects of NDEs cannot be explained by currently available normal-scientific theories. He therefore proposes a nonreductionist approach that, he hopes, in terms of Jungian archetypes, can explain these aspects of NDEs, and he especially notes that, given the alleged fact that "the major tendency of parapsychological research is to upset the pretensions of physicalism" (Grosso 1981a, 57),[14] the survival hypothesis is "more intrinsically plausible" than nonsurvivalist interpretations of near-death experiences. And in his book review of Ring (1980a), Grosso (1981c) explains further:

[Ring] is at pains to stress that *proof* of survival doesn't follow from his findings. Certainly the word "proof" is too strong here; the most one could hope for would be the production of evidence that more or less bolsters or strengthens the survival hypothesis. With this more limited objective in mind, I think it is possible to construct models for the investigation of NDEs in such a way that the survival question is directly addressed. This has yet to be done with the near-death experience. (*It has, of course, been done* with deathbed visions.) . . . *Life At Death* . . . should be a forceful stimulus for further investigation of the ultimate enigma of survival. [p. 176; italics are partly mine—G.H.H.]

Greyson and Stevenson (1979) and Stevenson and Greyson (1979) also, though in less enthusiastic words, defend the legitimacy of the survival hypothesis when they write:

The evidence available is far from necessitating a conclusion in favor of . . . survival, but it is also far from deserving the neglect it has received from most scientists. One type of research that may contribute to this evidence is the investigation of near-death experiences. [Stevenson and Greyson 1979, 265]

Some of [the] universal features [of NDEs] may reflect widespread human adaptive responses to stress, but others may be more suggestive of the possibility of another realm of existence into which we pass after death. [p. 266]

Thus, with many parapsychologists the survival hypothesis seems to be a viable option with regard to near-death experiences.[15] And the late Robert Thouless (1978), one of the great old men of parapsychology, in his review of the book by Osis and Haraldsson (1978a), concluded: "These findings make a significant contribution to the evidence pointing toward a life after death . . . This is a book which takes a notable step forward in parapsychology" (p. 144).

For reasons that should become apparent in the following pages, I find myself unable to agree with Thouless's assessment of the relevance of NDE research to the survival question and of what past research has already achieved in this regard.

Nonsurvivalist Explanations of Near-Death Experiences

For several reasons, there should be no doubt that the near-death experiences and deathbed visions related by so many people from different cultures and with widely varying backgrounds are honestly reported and recorded. First of all, as Tetens (1983) has convincingly pointed out, there can be no conceivable and justifiable philosophical or epistemological a priori arguments against the *possibility* of *any* kind of private experience. Second, given the psychological conditions under which near-death states are experienced (and sometimes reported), hardly any doubt is justified with regard to the "subjektive Aufrichtigkeit dieser Berichte" (subjective sincerity of these reports) (Timm 1980a, 250). If someone reports an NDE, the person is to be believed, since the experience itself is private. This does not mean, however, that at the same time one accepts the contents of the reports as veridical. In fact, a great variety of alternative explanations have been proposed over the past decade that are much more mundane and prosaic than the survival hypothesis. And, in my opinion, some of them are much more likely to be true. Traditionally, responsible parapsychologists and responsible critics alike have insisted that only such findings should be considered evidence for paranormal effects that exclude all reasonable alternative explanations. I can see no reason that we should proceed more generously when it comes to the question of survival. Therefore, in the following pages a number of those alternative explanations of near-death experiences and deathbed visions will be discussed that have been proposed in recent years.

Dead or Alive?

> If we are to examine evidence for an after-life honestly and dispassionately we must free ourselves from the tyranny of common sense. [Spraggett 1974, 6]

This is Spraggett's advice to those who wish to assess the evidence for survival. Though the wisdom of this advice can be questioned on good grounds, it may well help some people to more or less cheerfully solve the survival problem, at least to their own satisfaction. Those among us, however, who, regrettably, have failed to get rid of tyrannical common sense and are inclined to make use of it once in a while will find that one of the most obvious and utterly devastating objections to the survival interpretation of near-death experiences lies in the fact that those who were still capable of telling the tale and having their experiences recorded, by definition, cannot have been dead and therefore cannot have had any experience of death. As Blackmore (1982) observed:

> It must be borne in mind that in every near-death experience the person did not die, and so he cannot be said to have been dead at the time of his conscious experience, even though physiologically he may have showed all the signs of death. The same applies to deathbed experiences. If the person was capable of recounting his vision or other experience then he cannot have been dead at the time. Therefore we shall not hear accounts from the dead, but only accounts from those who have stared death in the face. [p. 138]

Or, as Siegel (1981b) pointedly formulates, "a conscious physical body is always the one to make such reports!" (p. 162). In his discussion of related problems, Alcock (1981b), referring to survival claims based on NDEs reported by cardiac-arrest patients, wonders: "Why anyone would consider temporary cardiac inactivity to indicate a period of death is difficult to understand in this day and age" (p. 155). Stevenson summarizes the main argument:

> [Skeptics] point out that anyone who does not lie has not experienced death; therefore, no matter how close a person may have been to death, his experiences are still those of a living person and can tell us nothing about what may happen after we die. [Stevenson 1980, 271]

Certainly Stevenson's is a correct representation of this most fundamental objection to claims of survival evidence from near-death experiences. However, he then immediately adds the following argument, which seems of little relevance to both the survival interpretation of NDEs and the paper by Rodin (1980) that Stevenson is commenting upon:

> Yet most of these critics have not been near death themselves, and their incredulity has little influence on those who have. The two groups—recovered patients and healthy scientists—seem to talk across each other. [p. 271]

Stevenson here seems to miss the point of this particular objection to the survival interpretation of NDEs: that is, this objection is not a matter of the one group failing to convince or impress the other, but rather one of the logical semantics of our language that excludes sentences like, say, "Mr. X experienced death and told us afterwards what it is like," from the range of permissible, semantically well-formed (as opposed to grammatically well-formed) sentences.

Moreover, the presumed fact that most critics of the survival interpretation of NDEs and deathbed visions have not been close to death themselves does not detract in any way from the value and potential importance of their arguments and conclusions. And that is what really matters. (I can assure the unconvincible "recovered patients" Stevenson refers to that my own knowledge of near-death experiences is not derived only from the literature.) There is a similar disregard for the logic of language in a remark made by Grosso (1981a). He writes:

> The patient, having temporarily lost all vital functioning, would in the great majority of cases have soon joined the ranks of the permanently and irrevocably dead had it not been for the intervention of on-the-scene medical workers. In this sense, one is tempted to say that the *resuscitated* patient really *was dead.* [p. 39; italics are partly mine—G.H.H.]

Again, this last remark testifies to linguistic slovenliness, to say the least, because, by definition, "being resuscitated" and "being dead" are mutually exclusive; that is, a person (or animal) who has been resuscitated may not, at the same time, be said to have been dead before. So, if someone claims (and not, like Grosso, just feels "tempted to say") that a person has been "resuscitated" after he "really was dead," the claimant may be said to be ignorant of how the words "resuscitated" and "dead" are to be used.

Sources of Error

A number of commentators on near-death and deathbed investigations have emphasized that many reports of NDEs and almost all reports of deathbed visions are secondhand (e.g., Blackmore 1982; Timm 1980b; Alcock 1981b). There is only an almost negligibly small number of independently published first-hand accounts of NDEs (e.g., von Jankovich 1980) and still fewer first-hand reports of deathbed visions (e.g., Oxenham and Oxenham 1941). This predominance of second-hand reports may introduce a variety of bona fide errors and flaws into NDE and deathbed investigations, such as memory distortions and reporting errors on the part of the experiencers (who sometimes are not even available for further inquiries) as well as recording errors, data selection, and faulty data reduction on the part of the investigators. Alcock (1981b) illustrates one of these risks in a comment he makes on the survey of deathbed visions conducted by Osis and Haraldsson (1977, 1978a):

> The authors in this case didn't even interview the patients, but instead sent out large numbers of questionnaires to physicians and nurses (in the United States) or personally handed out the questionnaires to medical staff (in India). They

argue that these trained observers are likely to be more accurate in their ac-counts of what the patients reported than would be the patients themselves. This is difficult to accept, of course, since what they were really doing was asking for anecdotal reports about the observer's impressions of what a patient was experiencing in a situation that occurred in all likelihood years before. [p. 157]

The (presumably) long lapse of time between experience and report in Osis and Haraldsson's survey of deathbed visions, which Alcock points out, also can cause potentially serious problems in many NDE studies. Thus, the reports that formed the data-base for the study by Greyson and Stevenson (1980) were made between 1 and 67 years (with a median of 30 years) after the experiences. Likewise, the reports used by Bush (1983) in her study of children's NDEs, to mention just one more example, were made between 11 and 65 years after the fact. Even very important experiences, such as NDEs, that have made lasting impressions on (and in many cases have profoundly influenced the lives of) the experiencers hardly can be expected to be accurate, reliable, and unaffected by memory distortions when people try to recall them later, in some cases, periods of far more than half a century. Of course I am aware of the fact that many reports made after long periods of time usually contain the same elements as do those made relatively shortly after their experiences. However, (a) we cannot rule out the possibility that, say, the first type of reports (those made after long periods of time) are influenced by other reports of NDEs of which the experiencers may have learned in the interim (at least, the possibility of such distortions can be tested empirically by comparing reports the same person made at different times), and (b) the correspondences between different accounts may give us some confidence in the accuracy of these reports but do not solve the basic problem of the reliability of the experiencers' reports. An additional reason for concern about these long periods between experiences and reports has been pointed out by Schnaper (1980), who speculates that the time elapsed since the near-death experience may convert "the unpleasant to the pleasant" in the recollection of NDEs, thus inflating the number of pleasant features of the experiences. Rawlings (1978) made a similar point, suggesting that although patients may have unpleasurable experiences near death and recall them immediately afterwards, they tend to forget them with time, while more pleasurable aspects of the experiences are much more easily remembered. So, according to Rawlings, the reason that the vast majority of experiences reported are pleasant may be that the experiencers have been interviewed too long after they had their NDEs.

Another possible source of error—and a quite serious one—is mentioned by Stevenson and Greyson (1979):

> In one series, overenthusiastic interviewers may have unwittingly enticed patients to embellish their experiences; in another, skeptical interviewers may have subtly communicated to the patients the wisdom of keeping silent about any puzzling experiences they may remember. [p. 266]

It goes without saying that points about possible errors and distortions in NDE reports raised in this section concern questions of fact, not interpretation. They apply to all reports regardless of whether they are used to support survivalist or nonsurvivalist hypotheses.

Psychological and Related Approaches to the Near-Death Experience

Both parapsychologists involved in NDE research and other near-death investigators have made numerous—and some promising—attempts to provide psychological explanations for near-death experiences and their complex phenomenology. Also, both parapsychological and other observers of NDE research and conceptualizations have suggested alternative explanations.[16] Perhaps the most prominent among these alternatives are (1) the hallucination (Siegel and others) and (2) the depersonalization (Noyes and others) hypotheses. In addition, there have been (3) quite a few related or competing theories and conceptualizations.

(1) Siegel (1977; 1980; 1981a; 1981b; Siegel and Hirschman 1984) certainly is the most outspoken defender of the hypothesis that near-death experiences and deathbed visions are nothing but hallucinations triggered by the enormously stressful situation near death.[17] As already mentioned in earlier sections of this paper, Osis and Haraldsson and others who favor (or wish to keep open the possibility of) the survival interpretation of NDEs have contrasted the survival hypothesis and the destruction hypothesis in a bi-polar model and argued that the typical phenomenology of NDEs only *appears* similar to dreams and drug-induced or other hallucinations. However, they have failed to point out any significant differences between the two. So, if NDEs and deathbed visions are similar to and phenomenologically indistinguishable from other hallucinatory visions, one may be justified in wondering whether there actually *are* any important differences. Thus, the most reasonable conjecture seems to be that both near-death experiences and hallucinations have similar explanations that do not require recourse to the survival hypothesis and constructs of an afterlife. Therefore, Siegel (1981b) juxtaposes experiencers' descriptions of phenomenological features of near-death experiences and drug-induced and other hallucinatory

visions. This demonstrates the close similarity between the two types of phenomena and renders Osis and Haraldsson's claim that there are important differences between them utterly implausible.

Even worse, Osis and Haraldsson (1977), in their own juxtaposition of the survival and destruction hypotheses, claimed that "hallucinations will portray only memories already stored in the brain and express desires, expectations, and fears of the individual, as well as beliefs characteristic of his culture," while "after-life visions will be relatively coherent, and oriented to the situation of dying and the transition to another mode of existence, including 'otherworldly' messengers and environments" (p. 240). According to Siegel (1981b), this view of hallucinations is patently false: "Hallucinations (like dreams, images, thoughts, and fantasies) are often elaborate cognitive embellishments of memory images, not just mere pictorial replicas" (p. 178).

Siegel (1981b) further explains:

> The remarkable similarity of imagery in life-after-death experiences and in hallucinatory experiences invites inquiry about common mechanisms of action. The experiences can be considered as a combination of simple and complex imagery. . . . Recent electro-physiological research . . . has confirmed that hallucinations are directly related to states of excitation and arousal of the central nervous system, which are coupled with a functional disorganization of the parts of the brain that regulate incoming stimuli. Behaviorally, the result is an impairment of perceptions normally based on external stimuli and a preoccupation with internal imagery. . . . The specific context of complex hallucinatory imagery is greatly determined by set (expectations and attitudes) and setting (physical and psychological environments). For many dying and near-death experiences, the sets (fear of approaching death, changes in body and mental functioning, etc.) and settings (hospital wards, accident scenes, etc.) can influence specific eschatological thought and images. [pp. 180–182]

Rogo (1984) points out that the phenomenology that typically goes along with near-death experiences is also described as a by-product of ketamine, an anesthetic, and that NDE-type ketamine experiences are relatively common. "As food for thought" (p. 95), he discusses four conceptual models, all of which have "explanatory advantages and disadvantages" (p. 87). These include: (1) the NDE is a similar form of chemically induced hallucination; (2) ketamine induces objective OBEs; (3) ketamine-linked NDEs are artifacts produced by expectancy and the hospital setting, that is, ketamine does not produce NDE hallucinations at all; and (4) the NDE is an archetypal experience catalyzed under a variety of different situations.

Of the models discussed by Rogo, Siegel (1980), who has conducted clincal research into ketamine experiences, obviously would favor the first, reductionistic one, which, in effect, holds that NDEs are nothing but by-products of brain chemistry. Siegel has posited that both types of experience are hallucinations resulting from neurophysiological activity and have no metaphysical relevance. According to Siegel, the same holds for LSD and mescaline-induced hallucinations.[18] Incidentally, the "tunnel," a prominent feature in many NDEs, is one of eight "form constants" in Siegel's study of LSD images (Siegel 1977). Siegel and Hirschman (1984) discuss (and partly translate from French) early accounts of hashish-induced NDEs, which already show close similarities with nondrug NDEs. Siegel and Hirschman conclude that "the difference between the hashish NDEs and other nondrug NDEs appears to be more a function of dosage or intensity than the fact that a drug was or was not used to trigger the experience. . . . The hashish-induced NDE . . . is more strikingly similar to nondrug-induced experiences than was previously noted" (p. 84).

Aside from Siegel's work, there are a number of other studies favoring an explanation of near-death experiences and deathbed visions in terms of hallucination. Thus, Drab (1981) analyzed 71 descriptions of apparent movement through a tunnel-like space, and he concluded that these rather varied tunnel experiences are neither objectively real nor a metaphorical transition between states of consciousness or "realms of being," but are most likely hallucinatory events. Chari (1982) proposed a typology of six distinguishable tunnel experiences based on their apparent structural complexity and functions. He concluded that "the psi-induced pseudo-hallucinatory tunnel is an attempt to surmount the potential discontinuity between the pseudo-hallucinatory visual world and the ordinary perceptual world" (p. 123).

Some skeptics may be surprised to find that quite a few parapsychologists (and even some of the survival researchers among them) consider the hallucination theory of near-death experiences the most reasonable one and that which may be most likely true. Thus, Anderson (1981) observes:

There are a number of parapsychologists who have been impressed with the fact that these dreams of the near dead follow a broadly similar pattern. To suggest, however, that dreams of this kind support an otherworldly explanation seems clearly to go beyond what the facts themselves would warrant. . . . The experiences of the near dead . . . may well reveal a common reaction to the trauma of death without thereby implying anything at all about the true conditions prevailing in any supposed afterworld. On this view, such experiences are most naturally interpreted as simply hypnopompic hallucinations designed to alleviate the anxiety occasioned by imminent death. The broad similarity among such dreams may be regarded as either physiologically determined . . . or as simply reflecting the coping mechanism of the human mind when confronted with a uniquely distressing situation. Considering, furthermore, that such (usually) wish-fulfilling fantasies are culturally and emotionally appropriate

. . . there seems no reason to suppose them revelatory of any permanent reality.
[p. 9]

This interpretation is also favored by psychiatrist/parapsychologist Ehrenwald (1974) in his study of OBEs and the denial of death. It may be noted, however, that Ehrenwald's denial-of-death theory of OBEs seems relatively far-fetched and implausible when he applies it to out-of-the-body experiences that do not occur near death.

Palmer (1979), in his critical commentary on the survey of deathbed visions by Osis and Haraldsson (1977), wrote:

> In fact, much of the serenity often reported in some patients is likely to be an adaptive psychological reaction to stress that could provide an excellent background for hallucinatory visions. . . . We are dealing (according to the subjective hallucination hypothesis) with hallucinations, not daydreams. Given what we know about the complex processes and transformations that enter into the production of nocturnal dreams (a more common form of hallucination), it would be naive to assume any less complexity in the production of deathbed visions. [Palmer 1979, 95–96]

Finally, it is not without significance that even as prominent a survival researcher within parapsychology as Gauld (1982) feels forced to conclude that he "can at the moment find among the phenomena of OBEs and NDEs no strong grounds for disagreement with the hallucination theory" (p. 229).

(2) On the basis of Heim's falling experience (Heim 1892) and one additional account of a near-fatal event in World War I trench-warfare, Pfister (1930) ascribed the symptoms of near-death experiences to denial of death (again, cf. Ehrenwald [1974]) and profound regression under stress. He suggests that persons faced with death tend to exclude reality from their perceptions and to seek refuge from potentially inescapable danger in pleasurable fantasies.

In a number of studies, Noyes and Kletti and their collaborators (Noyes 1972; 1981; Noyes, Hoenk, Kuperman, and Symen 1977; Noyes and Kletti 1972; 1976a; 1976b; 1977a; 1977b), who conceive of near-death experiences as a type of depersonalization, have elaborated Pfister's interpretation. Noyes (1972) regards the near-death OBE as "an interesting negation of death. . . . The threat of death is reduced to a threat of bodily annihilation. By dissociating these aspects of the self the reality of death is excluded from consciousness" (p. 178). The depersonalization mechanism thus may serve as a kind of sacrifice of a part of the self in order to avoid actual death. According to Noyes and associates, there are three main phases distinguishable in the reaction to the threat of death: resistance, acceptance, and transcendence. The initial stage of terror, fear, and struggle is followed by acceptance of death, which in turn may lead to life-review and to the final phase of transcendence. Noyes (1972) describes the role of out-of-the-body experiences in this process as follows:

> Immediately, as fear is replaced by calm and as active mastery is replaced by passive surrender, a curious splitting of the self from its bodily representation may occur. . . . The subject may correctly view his body as near death but, being outside of it, he witnesses the scene with detached interest. [p. 178]

With regard to the panoramic life-review, also a frequently reported aspect of NDEs, Noyes (1972) suggests that such life-reviews, too, serve as a defense mechanism: "Loss of the future may necessitate regression . . . persons suddenly confronted with an end to their lives may experience an intense investment in their past lives" (p. 179). In a similar way, Noyes and Kletti (1977b) argue that, "In life-threatening circumstances, a person confronts the loss of himself and, consequently, becomes absorbed with images of his own past life . . . symbols of his own existence" (pp. 191–192).

Noyes and Kletti (1977a) gave a 17-item questionnaire to 85 victims of falls, drownings, automobile accidents, illnesses, and other near-fatal events. Of these, 75 percent experienced a slowing of clocktime, which for 68 percent was associated with increased speed and vividness of mentation. Others reported that features of NDEs were a sense of detachment (64%), feelings of unreality (63%), automatic movements in response to danger (60%), lack of or dampening of negative emotions (50%), detachment from the body (49%), sharper vision or hearing (46%), great understanding (37%), revival of memories (36%), impressive colors or visions (36%), a sense of harmony or unity (35%), perception of objects as small or far away (35%), experience of control by an external force (32%), vivid mental images (29%), and voices, music, or sounds (23%). In all instances, people who expected death to be imminent were more likely to respond affirmatively to the items than persons who had no such expectations.

Like the hallucination theory, the theory of depersonalization seems most useful to me in that it appears to adequately account for a large number of characteristic features of near-death experiences. On the other hand, it is quite obvious (as Noyes himself acknowledges) that there are other aspects of NDEs, such as what Noyes labeled the "hyperalertness" and "mystical consciousness" factors (mentioned earlier in the present paper), that the depersonalization theory cannot possibly explain.

(3) In addition to the hallucination and depersonalization theories, a variety of other or less plausible nonsurvivalist hypotheses have been advanced to account for the characteristics of near-death experiences and deathbed visions.

Some of them are directly related to or derived from one or the other of the theories we have just discussed; others have been developed independent of other conceptualizations. In what follows, some of the more important of these additional alternative explanations will be presented.

Similar to Roll (1982; and, again, see Note 10), Krishnan (1981) suggests that the "take-away" figures reported, for instance, in the Osis and Haraldsson survey, may be interpreted as constructions of the unconscious rather than deceased persons who try to take the patients with them. Osis and Haraldsson (1977) had reported that the majority of the dying persons who envisioned take-away apparitions might be real entities from a post-mortem world with a will of their own, since they appeared even to those patients who were recovering and could not, therefore, have been expecting to die. Krishnan (1981) comments:

> I think that this view needs to be reconsidered. For, the finding that most of those who saw take-away figures died, but not those who hallucinated living persons could mean that take-away apparitions are indicators or symbols of impending death, brought up to the conscious mind by the unconscious. Being products of the unconscious which, as Jung has shown, is autonomous, the take-away apparitions would appear to be independent of the percipient's expectations. This interpretation of the take-away figures receives support from the fact that the subjective experiences of survivors of clinical death contain symbols indicating that they will not die. [p. 10]

Like Noyes and his collaborators, Krishnan also holds that transcendental feelings and out-of-the-body experiences in near-death states may serve protective functions and not be regarded as evidence of post-mortem survival.

In his critical commentaries on the paper by Grosso (1981a), Greyson (1981b) proposed several psychological interpretations of near-death experiences that can accommodate the phenomena's universality, paranormal components, and allegedly beneficial effects, and he concluded that NDEs may serve a number of psychological functions, such as that of a defense mechanism in the face of impending death.

While Wilson and Barber (1983, esp. 361, 372-373) in their study of the fantasy-prone personality concluded that OBEs and NDEs "may be expected much more often among fantasy-prone individuals than among the remainder of the population" (p. 372), Alcock (1981a) reviewed arguments for the interpretation of near-death experiences as "glimpses of an afterlife" and as "reverie in a disturbed or dying brain," and he argued that the after-life hypothesis is based exclusively on faith and cannot be supported by empirical evidence from NDEs.

McHarg (1978), in his review of Osis and Haraldsson (1978a), criticized the authors for having failed to consider the possibility that many of the features of the cases they had collected may have been reducible to (*a*) "cerebral anoxia" and (*b*) "predisposition to paroxysmal temporal lobe disturbance":

Although they reasonably exclude four or five specific medical possibilities, they do not even mention the most important possibility of all—cerebral anoxia. Transitory cerebral anoxia is a well-known cause of visual hallucinations, often in a setting of clear consciousness, and, with or without hallucinations, must be even commonplace in the dying just prior to the lapse into terminal unconsciousness. Also, the authors do not take into account . . . predisposition to paroxysmal temporal lobe disturbance . . . I think immediately of no less than three currently attending patients, not approaching death, whose paroxysmal temporal lobe attacks are characterized by . . . apparitions of a deceased person. Also, the striking mood changes are simply *assumed* by the authors to have been *caused* by the apparitions and they show no awareness of the medical fact that such mood changes, in the direction of ecstasy, with a religious, "otherworldly" colouring, have been long recognized as being rather typical of temporal lobe paroxysms . . . Dr. Elisabeth Kübler-Ross, in the introduction, says this book is yet another confirmation of existence after death but I think it will be clear that at least one reader has not been so persuaded. [pp. 886-887; McHarg's italics]

An alternative explanation that, so far as can be ascertained on the basis of two brief presentations, seems consistent with that proposed by McHarg was suggested by Rodin (1980). He, too, explains NDEs in terms of physiological processes in the dying patient. "Unless death is instantaneous," he writes, "the final common pathway is anoxia" (p. 262). Anoxia (or hypoxia) is oxygen deprivation of organic tissue resulting in severe and permanent damage. Rodin further observes:

It is known that the earliest effect of hypoxia consists of an increased feeling of well being and a sense of power. This is accompanied by a decrease and subsequent loss of critical judgment. Just as in dream consciousness, the patently false is experienced as objectively true. As anoxia persists, delusions and hallucinations occur until, finally, complete unconsciousness supervenes. The loss of oxygen supply coupled with an increase of CO_2 and nitrogen induce a toxic psychosis during the process of dying." [p. 262]

Rodin's explanatory attempt has been roundly criticized by Stevenson (1980).

Another related theory of near-death experiences was suggested by Carr (1981), who proposed that certain frequently reported features of such experiences, such as euphoria, panoramic life-review, dissociation from the physical body, and hallucinations, are suggestive of a "limbic lobe syndrome" and may be precipitated in a near-death state by the release of beta-endorphin and related brain peptides. In a subsequent article, Carr (1982) elaborated his theory that endorphins and enkaphalins along with other peptide neuro-hormones released under stress provoke hippocampal neuronal activity and thereby trigger a limbic lobe syndrome.[19]

Conclusions

I think this critical survey of research into and conceptualizations of near-death experiences and deathbed visions has demonstrated that the defenders of the survival interpretation of these types of phenomena have failed to provide even a presumptive case for survival. Nor have they, in my opinion, been able to show that these phenomena at the very least are relevant to or hold some promise for an eventual solution to the problem of survival. Quite the contrary, there are a large number of psychological, physiological, and other alternative theories, many of which appear much more viable than the survival hypothesis and are free of the metaphysical ballast with which at least many versions of that hypothesis are fraught.

I cannot claim, of course, that there is no such thing as the survival of personality after bodily death, although I think there are very good reasons to suspect that the survival question is not even subject to a solution in terms of *empirical* science (Hövelmann 1985). Also, it should be clearly understood that I am far from convinced that proponents of alternative, nonsurvivalist approaches have all the answers already or have yet adequately accounted for all the complex features of NDEs and deathbed visions. A number of commentators on the alternative explanations have convincingly pointed out that no single one of these alternative explanations can account for all the reported characteristics of such experiences. However, this should provide little comfort to advocates of the survival hypothesis, because (a) despite my reservations with regard to some of the alternative explanations, I think that others are quite adequate to account for a number of features of NDEs, and (b) the burden of proof clearly falls on those who would claim (or be inclined to favor the notion) that the phenomena under investigation are indicative or suggestive of survival of (aspects of) human personality after death of body and brain. What the survivalists among NDE investigators need to demonstrate is that their research provides evidence that can be accounted for *more* readily by the survival hypothesis than by the hallucination, depersonalization, or any of the other hypotheses reviewed in the preceding pages. The conclusion seems inescapable that survivalists have yet to present data and conceptualizations that at least come close to meeting this requirement.

I have no argument with people's theology. As far as nonscientific ways of dealing with and talking about the problem of survival are concerned, everyone is free to hold the belief that pleases him. In scientific contexts, however, private beliefs and convictions are irrelevant and have to be replaced by rational arguments and sound evidence.

Finally, it should have become evident that I would prefer to see more (and more high-quality) rather than less work (both empirical and theoretical) on those puzzling experiences that have formed the subject matter of my paper. Greyson and Stevenson (1980) write:

> The investigation of near-death experiences may contribute not only to our understanding of the dying process but to our care of terminally ill patients, our ability to help grieving families, and our approach to suicidal patients. . . . Even if near-death experiences are the epiphenomena of adaptive defense-mechanisms or transient delirious states, their profound impact on subsequent attitudes justifies their further study. [pp. 1193, 1196]

I cannot but agree.

Notes

1. Some early critics of this research, who equated psychical research with spiritualism, conveniently overlooked that this manner of speaking chosen by the early leaders of the SPR is in marked contrast to the spiritualist doctrine that *presupposes* the reality of survival.

2. For a criticism of the search for evidence of the survival of *individual personality* after death (which is based on the presupposition of the validity of what may be called "mental-entity hypothesis" or "mental-entity paradigm") and the proposal of a competing theory of survival that questions basic assumptions of that hypothesis, see the extensive article by Roll (1982) as well as (1971).

3. As in the present paper I will concentrate on one particular area of survival-related research—near-death experiences. I will in the following paragraphs list only very briefly the most important of the other areas of research into survival after bodily death, and I will provide some references to representative publications by researchers engaged in these areas, as well as, occasionally, to critical evaluations of this resesarch, so that the reader unfamiliar with the relevant literature will know where to look for further information on related topics mentioned but not appropriately discussed in this paper. Also, skeptical readers are well advised to note (a) that quite a few of these publications are of a high quality even if they reach conclusions favorable to the survival hypothesis I find myself unable to agree with, and (b) that most of the more important criticisms of research in these areas have been made by fellow parapsychologists (and sometimes by fellow survival researchers) rather than by card-carrying outside skeptics (also cf. Zorab 1966, 1982).

It should be stated at this point that in this paper I am not going to discuss philosophical, semantic, etc., critiques of the survival hypothesis as they have been advanced, for instance, by Flew (1953; 1972) and Penelhum (1959; 1970), who try to show that the very notion of personal survival is based on a philosophical mistake and that therefore it is intrinsically meaningless. Suffice is to say here that I agree with considerable parts of these criticisms (cf. Hövelmann 1985).

4. Stevenson's extensive field investigations of cases of the reincarnation type have been substantially criticized by Nicol (1976) and, in particular, by Chari (1967; 1978; 1981). Chari always tried to back up his critique of some of Stevenson's Indian cases, which he prefers to interpret in terms of Indian social psychology rather than in those of reincarnation, with documents relating to these cases that he was able to obtain when he inquired into these cases in India but which have never been available for inspection by interested researchers. Through the courtesy of Professor Chari, I am in the possession of copies of a number of these documents, a detailed examination of which (which was begun with the collaboration of the late Piet Hein Hoebens) is currently under way. I will publish the results of this examination in due course; suffice it to say at this point that some of these documents support Chari's negative, social-psychological conclusions about a number of Stevenson's Indian reincarnation cases, while the case for the prosecution appears not as strong as Chari claims with a number of other cases that Stevenson studied in India. The documents available to me at this point are far from fatal to the whole of Stevenson's Indian case studies.

5. For the purposes of this paper, I will make no systematic distinction between near-death experiences (of people who were close to the threshold of death and may even have been clinically dead but survived) of the type reported, for instance, by Ring (1980a) and deathbed visions (of those who actually died shortly after they had these experiences) studied, for instance, by Osis (1961; 1966) and Osis and Haraldsson (1974; 1977; 1978a). I am going to deal with them together because both types of experience suffer from a number of common problems that, in my opinion, render them incapable of providing even a presumptive case for survival.

6. At the time this paper was written, I had no access to the original English editions of the works by Kübler-Ross (1980a; 1980b; 1982), Moody (1977a), Osis and Haraldsson (1978a), and Sabom (1981). Therefore, I used the German editions of these books for the purposes of the present paper. However, full references to the respective original English editions are added to the German references in the bibliography.

7. For a discussion of legal consequences, in particular with regard to the definition and identification of brain death, of what are taken to be advances in medical research, medical technology, and medical care over the past two or three decades, see Arnold (1976).

8. In his book, Ring (1980a) also advanced a far-fetched and utterly ill-conceived "parapsychological-holographic explanation of the near-death experience," which will not be discussed in this paper. For a scathing review of holographic models in general and of Ring's theory that near-death experiences involve a "holographic domain," see Braude (1981) who concludes that such models, particularly as applied to NDEs, are "fundamentally incoherent and confused."

9. Heim's 1892 report is now available in English in Noyes and Kletti (1972).

10. As Rogo (1978) argues, even Peak-in-Darien visions need not lend support to the survival interpretation of NDEs, because the patient might "unconsciously use ESP to learn who among his friends and relations had recently died" (p. 27), and on this basis create the hallucination. Thus "the 'inner dynamics' of a patient and the 'take-away' purpose of the apparition may be in agreement with the biological drama within the percipient, although its conclusion may be far from his or her conscious intention" (Roll 1982, 170). I may add that other, *nonparanormal* ways are easily conceivable by which a patient may learn, without being aware of it, of the death of another person. The same applies to patients' memories of conversations they cannot have perceived normally because they were anesthetized or otherwise ostensibly unconscious. Cherkin and Harroun (1971) report that such patients sometimes can assimilate, and afterward remember, conversations held in their presence although they were thought to be quite incapable of perceiving at the time.

11. Some critical commentaries are to be found, for instance, in Blackmore (1982, 133-152). Methodological and other aspects of Osis and Haraldsson's (1977; 1978a) study, in particular, have been subjected to a number of thorough criticisms by fellow parapsychologists: for instance, cf. Anderson (1981, 9), Blackmore (1982, 140-141), McHarg (1978), Timm (1980a; 1980b), Palmer (1978; 1979). Osis and Haraldsson (1978b) have replied to Palmer's critical commentaries.

12. A brief, though informative and useful, review of near-death studies conducted in 1981 and 1982 is provided by Greyson (1982).

13. For further studies of near-death experiences during attempted suicides and the survivors' subsequent attitudes toward life, death, and suicide, see, especially, Rosen (1975), Ring (1980b), and Ring and Franklin (1981-82).

14. There are quite a number of parapsychologists who would debate that contention.

15. In the literature on near-death experiences, there are also to be found a number of other, more outlandish claims that treat survival as fact and describe at length otherworldly landscapes and such. One of the numerous popular writers on NDEs, who notoriously and conspicuously fails to present any evidence at all for her survival and a number of other claims, is Elisabeth Kübler-Ross (1975; 1978; 1980a; 1980b; 1982). Grosso (1981b, 5) claims that NDEs may give rise to a new State Specific Epistemology, and elsewhere (Grosso 1981c) he argues that the occurrence of "core NDEs" as described by Ring (1980a) provides a "repeatable experimental situation" (Grosso 1981c, 172). Of course NDEs are not "experimental situations" at all (meaning empirical testing conditions under which certain effects are observed and recorded in dependence on one or more foregoing experimental manipulations), much less are they "repeatable" ones in any meaningful sense of that term (see Hövelmann 1984).

Davenport (1984a, 1984b), based on nuclear and relativity physics and a (not always pertinent) discussion of twentieth-century philosophy of science, postulates a "field theory conceptualization of reality" to account for NDEs, after, he believes, demonstrating the "inadequacy of Newtonian physics in illumining the content of NDE." (To the best of my knowledge, nobody has ever tried to "illumine the content of NDEs" with the help of the methodological and terminological means of Newtonian mechanics, anyway; nor can I see why anyone should have.) In addition to his grandiose "field theory conceptualization of reality," Davenport also provides an utterly unconvincing defense of Ring's holographic theory of NDEs.

16. For an overview, see Greyson (1983b).

17. Also, cf. what I think are important anthologies on hallucination by Siegel and West (1975) and West (1962), as well as the sections on hallucination in Bleuler's classical textbook of psychiatry (Bleuler 1969).

18. In 1981, Siegel's paper (Siegel 1980) provoked an interesting and lively discussion in the pages of the *American Psychologist*. Gibbs (1981) criticized Siegel's view that NDEs are only subjectively real, and he presented data from the literature that he—less than convincingly—claimed cannot be explained by Siegel's "naturalistic" explanation. Stevenson (1981) tried to point out logical fallacies in Siegel's argument and appealed to corroborative data that Siegel ignored. In his response to Stevenson, Siegel (1981a) defended his view of NDEs as only subjectively real as the most parsimonious one and dismissed the supportive data presented by Stevenson as indistinguishable from fiction.

19. In passing, I will mention another model of NDEs, now thoroughly discredited by Becker's careful study (Becker 1982), which was first described by Grof and Halifax (1977) and subsequently elaborated and popularized by Carl Sagan and other writers: the state-dependent reactivation of birth memories. According to this theory, at least some features of near-death experiences (especially the tunnel experience) may be related to stored memories of the birth experience, available to consciousness only in hyperaroused states like that induced by the threat of death. After Becker's thorough and persuasive criticism, at least a literal interpretation of this model seems no longer defensible.

References

Alcock, James E. 1981a. Pseudo-science and the soul. *Essence,* 5: 65–76.

Alcock, James E. 1981b. Psychology and near-death experiences. In *Paranormal Borderlands of Science,* edited by Kendrick Frazier, 153–169. Buffalo, N.Y.: Prometheus Books.

Anderson, Roger I. 1981. "Contemporary survival research: A critical review." In *Parapsychology Review,* 12 (5): 8–13.

Arnold, H. 1976. Hirntod. *Nervenarzt,* 47: 529–537.

Barrett, William Fletcher. 1918. *On the Threshold of the Unseen: An Examination of the Phenomena of Spritualism and the Evidence for Survival After Death.* New York: E. P. Dutton. (Original work published in 1917.)

———. 1926. *Death-bed Visions.* London: Methuen.

Bayless, Raymond. 1959. Correspondence. *Journal of the American Society for Psychical Research,* 53: 35–38.

Becker, Carl. 1982. Why birth models cannot explain near-death phenomena: The failure of Saganomics. *Anabiosis,* 2: 102–109.

Beloff, John. 1977. Historical overview. In *Handbook of Parapsychology,* edited by W. W. Wolman, 3–24. New York: Van Nostrand Reinhold.

Beloff, John. 1983. Three open questions. In *Research in Parapsychology 1982*, edited by W. G. Roll, J. Beloff, and R. A. White, 317–327. Metuchen, N.J., and London: Scarecrow Press.

Berger, Arthur S. 1984. Experiments with false keys. *Journal of the American Society for Psychical Research*, 78: 41–54.

Bernstein, Morey. 1956. *The Search for Bridey Murphy*. Garden City, N.Y.: Doubleday.

Betty, L. Stafford. 1984. The Kern City Poltergiest: A case severely straining the living agent hypothesis. *Journal of the Society for Psychical Research*, 52: 345–364.

———. 1985. The Kern City Poltergeist: A reply to Hövelmann and Zorab. *Journal of the Society for Psychical Research*, 53: 92–96.

Blackmore, Susan J. 1982. *Beyond the Body: An Investigation of Out-of-the-Body Experiences*. London: William Heinemann.

Bleuler, Eugen. 1969. *Lehrbuch der Psychiatrie*, 11th ed., revised by M. Bleuler. Berlin, Heidelberg, and New York: Springer Verlag.

Bozzano, Ernest. 1906. Apparitions of deceased persons at death-beds. *Annals of Psychical Science*, 5: 76–100.

———. 1923. *Phénomènes Psychiques au Moment de la Mort*. Paris: Editions de la B.P.S.

———. 1947. *Le Visioni dei Morenti*. Milano: Bocca Ed.

Braude, Stephen E. 1981. The holographic analysis of near-death experiences: The perpetuation of some deep mistakes. *Essence*, 5: 53–63.

Bush, Nancy Evans. 1983. The near-death experience in children: Shades of the prison-house reopening. *Anabiosis*, 3: 177–193.

Carr, Daniel B. 1981. Endorphins at the approach of death. *Lancet*, 1: 390.

———. Pathophysiology of stress-induced limbic lobe dysfunctions: A hypothesis for NDEs. *Anabiosis*, 2: 75–89.

Chari, C. T. K. 1967. Reincarnation: New light on an old doctrine. An essay review. *International Journal of Parapsychology*, 9: 217–222.

———. 1978. Reincarnation research: Method and interpretation. In *The Signet Handbook of Parapsychology*, edited by Martin Ebon, 313–324. New York: New American Library.

———. 1981. A new look at reincarnation. *Christian Parapsychologist*, 4: 121–129.

———. 1982. Parapsychological reflections on some tunnel experiences. *Anabiosis*, 2: 110–131.

Cherkin, A. and P. Harroun. 1971. Anesthesia and memory processes. *Anesthesiology*, 34: 469–474.

Cobbe, F. P. 1877. The Peak in Darien: The riddle of death. *Littell's Living Age and New Quarterly Review*, 134: 374–379.

———. 1882. *Peak in Darien*. London: Williams and Norgate.

Counts, Dorothy Ayers. 1983. Near-death and out-of-body experiences in a Melanesian society. *Anabiosis*, 3: 115–135.

Davenport, Arlice W. 1984a. Science and the near-death experience: Toward a new paradigm. Part I. *Journal of Religion and Psychical Research*, 7: 26–37.

———. 1984b. Science and the near-death experience. Toward a new paradigm. Part II. *Journal of Religion and Psychical Research*, 7: 98–108.

Dessoir, Max. 1967. *Vom Jenseits der Seele* (reprint of the 6th edition, 1930). Stuttgart: Ferdinand Enke Verlag. (Original work published in 1917).

Drab, Kevin. 1981. The tunnel experience: Reality or hallucination? *Anabiosis,* 1: 126–152.

Ehrenwald, Jan. 1974. Out-of-the-body experiences and the denial of death. *Journal of Nervous and Mental Disease,* 159: 227–233.

Ellis, David J. 1978. *The Mediumship of the Tape Recorder.* Harlow: Essex: D. J. Ellis.

Flammarion, Camille. 1922. *Death and Its Mystery: II. At the Moment of Death.* London: T. Fisher Unwin.

Flew, Antony G. N. 1953. *A New Approach to Psychical Research.* London: C. A. Watts.

———. 1972. Is there a case for disembodied survival? *Journal of the American Society for Psychical Research,* 66: 129–144.

Flynn, Charles P. 1982. Meanings and interpretations of NDE transformations: Some preliminary findings and implications. *Anabiosis,* 23: 3–14.

Gabbard, Glen O., Stuart W. Twemlow, and Fowler C. Jones. 1981. Do "near death experiences" occur only near death? *Journal of Nervous and Mental Disease,* 169:374–377.

Gallup, George, Jr. (with William Proctor). 1982. *Adventures in Immortality: A Look Beyond the Threshold of Death.* New York: McGraw-Hill.

Gauld, Alan. 1968. *The Founders of Psychical Research.* London: Routledge and Kegan Paul.

———. 1971. A series of "drop-in" commentators. *Proceedings of the Society for Psychical Research,* 55: 273–340.

———. 1977. Discarnate survival. In *Handbook of Parapsychology.* edited by B. B. Wolman, 577-630. New York: Van Nostrand Reinhold.

———. 1982. *Mediumship and Survival: A Century of Investigations.* London: William Heinemann.

Gibbs, John C. 1981. The near-death experience: Balancing Siegel's view. *American Psychologist,* 36: 1457–1458.

Giovetti, Paola. 1982. Near-death and deathbed experiences. An Italian survey. *Theta,* 10: 10–13.

Green, J. Timothy, and Penelope Friedman. 1983. Near-death experiences in a Southern California population. *Anabiosis,* 3: 77–95.

Greyson, Bruce. 1981a. Near-death experiences and attempted suicide. *Suicide and Life-Threatening Behavior,* 11: 10–16.

———. 1981b. Toward a psychological explanation of near-death experiences: A response to Dr. Grosso's paper. *Anabiosis,* 1: 88–103.

———. 1982. Near-death studies, 1981-82: A review. *Anabiosis,* 2: 150–158.

———. 1983a. The Near-Death Experience Scale: Construction, reliability, and validity. *Journal of Nervous and Mental Disease,* 171: 369–375.

———. 1983b. The psychodynamics of near-death experiences. *Journal of Nervous and Mental Disease,* 171: 376–381.

———. 1983c. Near-death experiences and personal values. *American Journal of Psychiatry,* 140: 618–620.

Greyson, Bruce, and Ian Stevenson. 1979. The contribution of near-death experiences to the evidence of survival after death. In *Research in Parapsychology 1978*, edited by W. G. Roll, 33. Metuchen, N.J., and London: Scarecrow Press.

———. 1980. The phenomenology of near-death experiences. *American Journal of Psychiatry*, 137: 1193–1196.

Grof, Stanislav, and Joan Halifax. 1977. *The Human Encounter With Death*. New York: Dutton.

Grosso, Michael. 1981a. Toward an explanation of near-death phenomena. *Journal of the American Society for Psychical Research*, 75: 37–60.

———. 1981b. Questions and prospects for near-death research. *ASPR Newsletter*, 7, 4–5.

———. 1981c. Book review (of *Life At Death*, by K. Ring). *Journal of the American Society for Psychical Research*, 75: 172–176.

Gurney, Edmund, Frederic W. H. Myers, and Frank Podmore. 1886. *Phantasms of the Living*, 2 vols. London: Trübner.

Heim, Albert. 1892. Notizen über den Tod durch Absturz. *Jahrbuch des Schweizer Alpenklubs*, 27: 327–337.

Hövelmann, Gerd H. 1982. Involuntary whispering, conversational analysis, and electronic voice phenomena. *Theta*, 10: 54–58.

———. 1984. Are psi experiments repeatable? A conceptual framework for the discussion of repeatability. *European Journal of Parapsychology*, 5: 285–306.

———. 1985–1986. A constructively rational approach to parapsychology and scientific methodology (responses to my commentators and some further attempts at clarification). *Zetetic Scholar*, No. 12–13.

———. 1986. Book review (of *Unlearned Language: New Studies in Xenoglossy*, by I. Stevenson). *Journal of the Society for Psychical Research* (in press).

Hövelmann, Gerd H., and George Zorab. 1985a. The Kern City Poltergeist: Some critical remarks on the quality of the evidence and the arguments. *Journal of the Society for Psychical Research*, 53: 87–92.

———. 1985b. Correspondence (reply to Dr. Betty and Professor Stevenson). *Journal of the Society for Psychical Research* (in press).

Hyslop, James H. 1907. Visions of the dying. *Journal of the American Society for Psychical Research*, 1: 45–55.

———. 1918. Visions of the dying. *Journal of the American Society for Psychical Research*, 12: 585–645.

———. 1919. *Contact With the Other World*. New York: Century.

Jacobson, Nils. 1973. *Life Without Death?* New York: Delacorte Press.

Jankovich, Stefan von. 1980. Erfahrungen während des klinisch-toten Zustandes. In *Fortleben nach dem Tode* (= IMAGO MUNDI, Band VII), edited by A. Resch, 409–424. Innsbruck: Resch Verlag.

Johnson, Martin. n.d. [1982.]. *Parapsychologie: Onderzoek in de grensgebieden van ervaring en wetenschap*. Baarn: de Kern.

Jürgenson, Friedrich. 1967. *Sprechfunk mit Verstorbenen*. Freiburg i.Br.: Hermann Bauer Verlag.

Kastenbaum, Robert, ed. 1979. *Between Life and Death.* New York: Springer.

Keil, H. H. Jürgen. 1980a. Parapsychology—Searching for substance beyond the shadows. *Australian Psychologist,* 15: 145–168.

———. 1980b. The voice on tape phenomena: Limitations and possibilities. *European Journal of Parapsychology,* 3: 287–296.

Köberle, Fidelio. 1980. Beweisen die Tonbandstimmen das Fortleben nach dem Tode? In *Fortleben nach dem Tode* (= IMAGO MUNDI, Band VII), edited by A. Resch, 395–401. Innsbruck: Resch Verlag.

Kohr, Richard L. 1982. Near-death experience and its relationship to psi and various altered states. *Theta,* 10: 50–53.

Krishnan, V. 1981. Near-death experiences: Reassessment urged. *Parapsychology Review,* 12: 4, 10–11.

Kübler-Ross, Elisabeth. 1975. *Death: The Final Stage of Growth.* Englewood Cliffs, N.J.: Prentice-Hall.

———. 1978. *To Live Until We Say Goodbye.* Englewood Cliffs, N.J.: Prentice-Hall.

———. 1980a. *Interviews mit Sterbenden,* 12th ed. Stuttgart: Kreuz Verlag. (Original English edition: *On Death and Dying,* Macmillan, New York, 1969.)

———. 1980b. *Was können wir noch tun? Antworten auf Fragen nach Sterben und Tod.* Gütersloh: Gütersloher Verlagshaus Mohn. (Original English edition: *Questions and Answers on Death and Dying,* Macmillan, New York, 1974.)

———. 1982. *Verstehen was Sterbende sagan wollen. Einführung in ihre symbolische Sprache.* Stuttgart: Kreuz Verlag. (Original English edition: *Living With Death and Dying,* Macmillan, New York, 1981.)

Locke, Thomas P., and Franklin C. Shontz. 1983. Personality correlates of the near-death experience: A preliminary study. *Journal of the American Society for Psychical Research,* 77: 311–318.

Lundahl, Craig R., ed. 1982. *Collection of Near-death Research Readings.* Chicago, Ill.: Nelson-Hall.

Matson, A. 1975. *Afterlife: Reports from the Threshold of Death.* New York: Harper and Row.

McHarg, James F. 1978. Book review (of *At the Hour of Death,* by K. Osis and E. Haraldsson). *Journal of the Society for Psychical Research,* 49: 885–887.

Mischo, Johannes, and Ulrich P. Niemann. 1983. Die Besessenheit der Anneliese Michel (Klingenberg) in interdisziplinärer Sicht. *Zeitschrift für Parapsychologie and Grenzgebiete der Psychologie,* 25: 129–194.

Moody, Raymond A., Jr. 1977a. *Leben nach dem Tod.* Reinbek bei Hamburg: Rowohlt Verlag. (Original English edition: *Life After Life: The Investigation of a Phenomenon—Survival of Bodily Death,* Mockingbird Books, Covington, Calif., 1975.)

———. 1977b. *Reflections on Life After Life.* New York: Bantam Books.

Murphy, Gardner. 1945. An outline of survival evidence. *Journal of the American Society for Psychical Research,* 39: 2–34.

Myers, Frederic W. H. 1903. *Human Personality and Its Survival of Bodily Death,* 2 vols. London: Longmans and Green.

Nicol, J. Fraser. 1976. Book review (of *Cases of the Reincarnation Type,* vol. 1: *Ten Cases in India,* by I. Stevenson). *Parapsychology Review,* 7: 5, 12–15.

————. 1979. Fraudulent children in psychical research. *Parapsychology Review,* 10: 1, 16–21. (See Chapter 10 of this volume.)

Noyes, Russell, Jr. 1972. The experience of dying. *Psychiatry,* 35: 174–184.

————. 1981. The encounter with life-threatening danger: Its nature and impact. *Essence,* 5: 21–32.

Noyes, Russell, Jr., P. R. Hoenk, S. Kuperman, and D. J. Symen. 1977. Depersonalization in accident victims and psychiatric patients. *Journal of Nervous and Mental Disease,* 164: 401–407.

Noyes, Russell, Jr., and Roy Kletti. 1972. The experience of dying from falls. *Omega,* 3: 45–52.

————. 1976a. Depersonalization in the face of life-threatening danger: A description. *Psychiatry,* 39: 19–27.

————. 1976b. Depersonalization in the face of life-threatening danger: An interpretation. *Omega,* 7: 103–114.

————. 1977a. Depersonalization in response to life-threatening danger. *Comparative Psychiatry,* 18: 375–384.

————. 1977b. Panoramic memory: A response to the threat of death. *Omega,* 8: 181–194.

Oesterreich, Traugott Konstantin. 1930. *Possession: Demoniacal and Other.* New York: R. R. Smith.

Osis, Karlis. 1961. *Deathbed Observations by Physicians and Nurses* (= Parapsychological Monograph, No. 3). New York: Parapsychology Foundation.

————. 1966. Second survey of deathbed observations by physicians and nurses (Abstract). *Journal of Parapsychology,* 30: 294–295.

Osis, Karlis, and Erlendur Haraldsson. 1974. Survey of deathbed visions in India. In *Research in Parapsychology 1973,* edited by W. G. Roll, R. L. Morris, and J. D. Morris, 20–22. Metuchen, N.J.: Scarecrow Press.

————. 1977. Deathbed observations by physicians and nurses: A cross-cultural survey. *Journal of the American Society for Psychical Research,* 71: 237–259.

————. 1978a. *Der Tod—Ein neuer Anfang: Visionen und Erfahrungen an der Schwelle des Seins.* Freiburg i.Br.: Hermann Bauer Verlag. (Original English edition: *At the Hour of Death,* Avon, New York.)

————. 1978b. Correspondence: Reply to Dr. Palmer. *Journal of the American Society for Psychical Research,* 72: 395–400.

Oxenham, John, and E. Oxenham. 1941. *Out of the Body.* London: Longmans, Green.

Palmer, John. 1975. Some recent trends in survival research. *Parapsychology Review,* 6: 3, 15–17.

————. 1978. Deathbed apparitions and the survival hypothesis. *Journal of the American Society for Psychical Research,* 72: 392–395.

————. 1979. Correspondence: More on deathbed apparitions and the survival hypothesis. *Journal of the American Society for Psychical Research,* 73: 94–96.

Penelhum, Terence. 1959. Personal identity, memory, and survival. *Journal of Philosophy,* 56: 882–903.

————. 1970. *Survival and Disembodied Existence.* London: Routledge and Kegan Paul.

Pfister, Oskar. 1930. Schockdenken und Schockphantasien bei höchster Todesgefahr. *Internationale Zeitschrift für Psychoanalyse*, 16: 430–455.

Raudive, Konstantin. 1971. *Breakthrough*. New York: Taplinger.

Rawlings, Maurice. 1978. *Beyond Death's Door*. Nashville, Tenn.: Thomas Nelson.

Resch, Andreas, ed. 1980. *Fortleben nach dem Tode*. (= IMAGO MUNDI, Band VII). Innsbruck: Resch Verlag.

Ring, Kenneth. 1979a. Further studies of the near-death experience. *Theta*, 7: 1–4.

———. 1979b. Some determinants of the core near-death experience. In *Research in Parapsychology 1978*, edited by W. G. Roll, 31–32. Metuchen, N.J., and London: Scarecrow Press.

———. 1980a. *Life At Death. A Scientific Investigation of the Near-death Experience*. New York: Coward, McCann, and Geoghegan.

———. 1980b. Do suicide survivors report near-death experiences? *Omega*, 11: 10–15.

Ring, Kenneth. 1982a. *Near-death Studies: A New Area of Consciousness Research*. Storrs, Conn.: International Association for Near-death Studies, Inc.

———. 1982b. Precognitive and prophetic visions in near-death experiences. *Anabiosis*, 2: 47–74.

Ring, Kenneth, and Stephen Franklin. 1981-82. Do suicide survivors report near-death experiences? *Omega*, 12: 191–208.

Rodin, Ernst A., 1980. The reality of death experiences: A personal perspective. *Journal of Nervous and Mental Disease*, 168: 259–263.

Rogo, D. Scott. 1978. Research on deathbed experiences: Some contemporary and historical perspectives. *Parapsychology Review*, 9: 1, 20–27.

———. 1984. Ketamine and the near-death experience. *Anabiosis*, 4: 87–96.

Roll, William G. 1960. The contribution of studies of "mediumship" to research on survival after death. *Journal of Parapsychology*, 24: 258–278.

———. 1971. A critical examination of the survival hypothesis. *A Century of Psychical Research. The Continuing Doubts and Affirmations*, edited by A. Angoff and B. Shapin, 123–130. New York: Parapsychology Foundation.

———. 1973. Survival research with the living. In *Research in Parapsychology 1972*, edited by W. G. Roll, R. L. Morris, and J. D. Morris, 183–185. Metuchen, N.J.: Scarecrow Press.

———. 1982. The changing perspective on life after death. *Advances in Parapsychological Research*, vol. 3, edited by S. Krippner, 147–291. New York and London: Plenum Press.

———. 1984. Survival after death: Alan Gauld's examination of the evidence. *Journal of Parapsychology*, 48: 127–148.

Rosen, D. H. 1975. Suicide survivors: A follow-up study of persons who survived jumping from the Golden Gate and San Francisco–Oakland Bay Bridges. *Western Journal of Medicine*, 122: 289–294.

Sabom, Michael B. 1982. *Erinnerung an den Tod. Eine medizinische Untersuchung*. München: Wilhelm Goldmann Verlag. (Original English edition: *Recollections of Death: A Medical Perspective*. Harper and Row, New York, 1982.)

Sabom, Michael B., and Sarah Kreutziger. 1978. Physicians evaluate the near-death experience. *Theta*, 6: 4, 1–6.

————. 1979. Recollections of patients while unconscious and near death. *Research in Parapsychology 1978*, edited by W. G. Roll, 32-33. Metuchen, N.J., and London: Scarecrow Press.

Salter, William Henry. 1950. *Trance Mediumship: An Introductory Study of Mrs. Piper and Mrs. Leonard.* London: Society for Psychical Research.

————. 1961. *Zoar, or the Evidence of Psychical Research Concerning Survival.* London: Sidgwick and Jackson.

Saltmarsh, Herbert Francis. 1938. *Evidence for Survival from Cross-Correspondences.* London: Bell.

Schnaper, Nathan. 1980. Comments germane to the paper entitled "The reality of death experiences" by Ernst Rodin. *Journal of Nervous and Mental Disease*, 268-270.

Siegel, Ronald K. 1977. Hallucinations. *Scientific American*, 23: 7, 132-140.

————. 1980. The psychology of life after death. *American Psychologist*, 35: 911-931.

————. 1981a. Reply to Stevenson. *American Psychologist*, 36: 1461-1462.

————. 1981b. Life after death. In *Science and the Paranormal: Probing the Existence of the Supernatural*, edited by G. O. Abell and B. Singer, 159-184. Scribner's.

Siegel, Ronald K., and Ada E. Hirschman. 1984. Hashish near-death experiences. *Anabiosis*, 4: 69-86.

Siegel, Ronald K., and L. J. West, eds. 1975. *Hallucinations: Behavior, Experience and Theory.* New York: John Wiley.

Spraggett, Allan. 1974. *The Case for Immortality.* New York: New American Library.

Stevenson, Ian. 1960a. The evidence for survival from claimed memories of former incarnations. Part 1: Review of the data. *Journal of the American Society for Psychical Research*, 54: 51-71.

————. 1960b. The evidence for survival from claimed memories of former incarnations. Part 2: Analysis of the data and suggestions for further investigations. *Journal of the American Society for Psychical Research*, 54: 95-117.

————. 1968. The combination lock test for survival. *Journal of the American Society for Psychical Research*, 62: 246-254.

————. 1970. A communicator unknown to medium and sitters. *Journal of the American Society for Psychical Research*, 64: 53-65.

————. 1972. Are poltergeists living or are they dead? *Journal of the American Society for Psychical Research*, 66: 233-252.

————. 1974a. *Twenty Cases Suggestive of Reincarnation*, 2nd rev. ed. Charlottesville, Va.: University Press of Virginia. (Original work published in 1966.)

————. 1974b. *Xenoglossy: A Review and Report of a Case.* Charlottesville, Va.: University Press of Virginia.

————. 1976. Further observations on the combination lock test for survival. *Journal of the American Society for Psychical Research*, 70: 219-229.

————. 1977a. Research into the evidence of man's survival after death: A historical and critical survey with a summary of recent developments. *Journal of Nervous and Mental Disease*, 165: 152-170.

————. 1977b. Reincarnation: Field studies and theoretical issues. In *Handbook of Parapsychology*, edited by B. B. Wolman, 631-663. New York: Van Nostrand Reinhold.

———. 1980. Comments on "The reality of death experiences: A personal perspective." *Journal of Nervous and Mental Disease,* 168: 271–272.

———. 1981. Comments on "The psychology of life after death." *American Psychologist,* 36: 1459–1461.

———. 1982a. Survival after death: Evidence and issues. In *Psychical Research: A Guide to Its History, Principles and Practices,* edited by I. Grattan-Guiness, 109–122. Wellingborough, Northamptsonshire: Aquarian Press.

———. 1982b. The contribution of apparitions to the evidence for survival. *Journal of the American Society for Psychical Research,* 76: 341–358.

———. 1984. *Unlearned Language: New Studies in Xenoglossy.* Charlottesville, Va.: University Press of Virginia.

———. 1985. The Kern City Poltergeist: Comments on the critique by Hövelmann and Zorab. *Journal of the Society for Psychical Research,* 53: 96–99.

Stevenson, Ian, and Bruce Greyson. 1979. Near-death experiences: Relevance to the question of survival after death. *Journal of the American Medical Association,* 242: 265–267.

Tetens, Holm. 1983. Erkenntnistheorie des kleinen Grenzverkehrs zwischen Wildnis und Zivilisation? Philosophische "Anmerkungen" zu Hans Peter Duerrs *Traumzeit.* In: *Der gläserne Zaun: Aufsätze zu Hans Peter Duerrs "Traumzeit,"* edited by R. Gehlen and B. Wolf, 278–283. Frankfurt/M.: Syndikat Verlag.

Thouless, Robert H. 1948. A test for survival. *Proceedings of the Society for Psychical Research,* 48: 253–263.

———. 1978. Book review (of *At the Hour of Death,* by K. Osis and E. Haraldsson). *Journal of Parapsychology,* 42: 143–144.

———. 1984. Do we survive death? *Proceedings of the Society for Psychical Research,* 57: 1–52.

Timm, Ulrich. 1980a. Thanatologie, Parapsychologie und das Survival-Problem. *Zeitschrift für Parapsychologie und Grenzgebiete der Psychologie,* 22: 249–258.

———. 1980b. Rezension (Book review) (of *Der Tod—Ein neuer Anfang,* by K. Osis and E. Haraldsson). *Zeitschrift für Parapschologie und Grenzgebiete der Psychologie,* 22: 259–260.

Twemlow, Stuart W., Glen O. Gabbard, and Lolafayne Coyne. 1982. A multivariate method for the classification of preexisting near-death conditions. *Anabiosis,* 2: 132–139.

Twemlow, Stuart W., Glen O. Gabbard, and Fowler C. Jones. 1982. The out-of-body experience: A phenomenological typology based on questionnaire responses. *American Journal of Psychiatry,* 139: 450–455.

Tyrrell, George N. M. 1953. *Apparitions.* New York: Pantheon Books. (Original work published in 1942.)

West, L. J., ed. 1962. *Hallucinations.* New York: Grune and Stratton.

Wilson, Sheryl C., and Theodore X. Barber. 1983. The fantasy-prone personality: Implications for understanding imagery, hypnosis, and parapsychological phenomena. In *Imagery: Current Theory, Research, and Application,* edited by A. A. Sheikh, 340–387. New York: John Wiley.

Zorab, George. 1966. The survival hypothesis: An unsupported speculation? *Journal of the American Society for Psychical Research,* 60: 248–253.

———. 1982. The forlorn quest. Paper presented at the 25th Annual Convention of the Parapsychological Association, Cambridge, U.K., August (abstracted in *Research in Parapsychology 1982,* edited by W. G. Roll, J. Beloff, and R. A. White, 125–128, Scarecrow Press, Metuchen, N.J., and London, 1982.)

———. 1984. *Spoken en spookverschijnselen: Feiten en hypothesen.* Den Haag: Leopold.

30

Magical Thinking and Parapsychology

LEONARD ZUSNE

Introduction

One characterization of parapsychological research points to the diametrically opposite views held by parapsychologists and their critics of the rate of success of the former group in demonstrating the reality of "psi." While parapsychologists assert that no further demonstrations are needed, their critics are still asking, "Where is the definitive experiment?" Arguments and counterarguments about the repeatability of experiments, fraud, the nature of the decline effect, the influence of the experimenter on the experimental results, and the need for a congenial atmosphere for psi demonstrations to succeed have been repeated many times but without leading to any resolution of these issues. There have been several well-known exchanges in scientific journals between prominent representatives of the sciences on the one side and parapsychologists on the other. The best-known exchange consists of an article by G. R. Price and a series of replies and comments that appeared in 1955 and 1956 in *Science* (Bridgman 1956; Meehl and Scriven 1956; Price 1955, 1956; Rhine 1956a, 1956b; Soal 1956). This exchange presents all the classic arguments for and against parapsychology, and it is as up to date today as it was in the 1950s. Similar, more recent exchanges that cover much of the same ground as well as new and additional points are those initiated in an article by Persi Diaconis on the statistical aspects of ESP (see Chapter 24 of this volume and Diaconis 1978a, 1978b; Puthoff and Targ 1978; Tart 1978) and in one on ESP and credibility in science by R. A. McConnell (McConnell 1969, 1978; Moss and Butler 1978a, 1978b). It is abundantly clear from these exchanges that, after all the logical, psychological, and scientific arguments have been traded, the parties to the argument part without their beliefs having been affected one iota. It appears that the problem lies not in a resolution of the objective issues but in an entirely different area.

The parapsychological experiment is in form and essence like any experiment in psychology. The crucial difference lies in the variables that, in a stimulus-organism-response system, are presumed to operate within the organism. Learning, perception, and thinking, like psi, are not directly observable processes, yet they are firmly anchored on both the stimulus and the response sides in terms of observable events. They are intervening variables (McCorquedale and Meehl 1948). The psi variable, on the other hand, cannot be completely anchored in observable reality. It is what McCorquedale and Meehl call a hypothetical construct, a variable with "surplus meaning," that is, dimensions that cannot be anchored in physical reality. This is where magical thinking comes in. The lower degree of operational validity of hypothetical constructs is of relatively little importance in theory building as long as the constructs remain fruitful, making predictions possible, explaining observed phenomena, and furthering advances in research. If hypothetical constructs are introduced in theorizing, they must be expected to produce supporting data within a reasonable time period or else be discarded. If, for whatever reason, empirically unconfirmed constructs remain in circulation too long, they may become accepted and treated like intervening variables. This has happened, for instance, in psychoanalysis as well as in parapsychology. In parapsychology, in addition, the hypothetical construct of psi has not only remained incompletely anchored in terms of stimulus and response variables but is described in terms that violate the laws of nature and cannot be logically, psychologically, or scientifically distinguished from constructs that are purely magical.

Laws of nature are statements of cause-effect relationships. It is in connection with the interpretation of cause-effect relationships that we come to grief over anomalistic natural phenomena, especially when living systems, such as the human being, are perceived as causal agents or the recipients of causal action. Physical or mechanical causation amounts to a transfer of energy between two systems. Although the human organism is certainly an energetic system and can transmit its energy to other systems, there exist in it other processes whose main function is not to transmit energy but information. Informational processes require some energy, but only as the means whereby information is transmitted. Their function is to inform, not to energize. Informational processes, although they are not energetic themselves, can trigger energetic events. Among the triggering processes are all those subjective processes of which one is aware "from the inside," such as thinking and other types of mentation, including sensations and perception, and others that one is ordinarily not aware of, such as the signals that trigger physiological processes within the organism and other instances of unconscious mentation. Both energetic and informational processes may revert to the organism itself, or their target may be another system, such as another person or an external object. In both cases either energy is transferred or information is transmitted. There are therefore eight types of interaction, all of which may be at least some of the time called causal, but of which only two are actually causal in the sense of energy transfer. What is more, every one of the eight instances of interaction may be conceptualized either scientifically or magically. This is illustrated in Table 1. Each instance of naturalistic interaction has a counterpart that is magical. The magical interactions embrace all of the topics studied by experimental parapsychologists as well as some that are considered only by their more tender-minded confreres. What this table underscores is that the crucial factor in distinguishing between magical and nonmagical thinking is how causation is interpreted and not so much the physical or psychological reality of the phenomenon in question.

The problem of parapsychologists and their critics being as far apart today as they have ever been can be restated in these terms: Given a natural phenomenon, especially one involving humans as either the source or the target of causal action, or both, what kind of person is more likely to describe the cause-effect relationship in non-natural (supernatural, paranormal, magical) terms than in scientific terms? An examination of the extant literature shows that, while there is a considerable body of research on the relationship between belief in the paranormal, including the acceptance of superstitions, and demographic, social, and personality characteristics of the believers, no direct investigation of the relationship between understanding of causation and personality characteristics has been made. However, one can assume that, since the belief in many of the items that typically appear on belief-in-the-paranormal inventories implies belief in causal action of the kind that is not scientifically acceptable, these studies have at least indirectly measured this relationship. They have been reviewed by Zusne and Jones (1982, 186-190), who conclude that the results of these studies have often been used to characterize the occult believer as "female, unintelligent, misinformed, poorly educated, authoritarian, and emotionally unstable." All is not well with these studies however: "There are several reasons for exercising caution when interpreting these data. For example, studies of intellectual, demographic, and personality correlates of believers often produce as many nonsignificant findings as significant findings, and in a few cases the findings are reversed. Also, many of the variables compared to belief in the paranormal are themselves correlated, so that it is difficult to determine which of several possibilities is responsible for the basic relationship. Finally, even the significant correlations tend to be of such a magnitude as to raise some doubt about the degree of contribution of these variables to the formation of belief in the paranormal." Zusne and Jones concluded:

> Despite the inconsistencies, there is an underlying theme to these results that may suggest that some configuration of personal factors contributes to the development of such beliefs. In particular, it would appear that variables related to feelings of uncertainty, the belief that one's fate is controlled externally, and social marginality may represent the composite dimension that often facilitates

TABLE 1

Conceptualizations of Informational and Energetic Processes and Causation in Persons

	Energetic Processes in Target		Informational Processes in Target	
	Scientific Conceptualizations	Magical Conceptualizations	Scientific Conceptualizations	Magical Conceptualizations
Energetic Processes in Source				
Source: Person Target: Person	Physiological processes	Magical transformations	Sensation and perception (interoception)	Clairvoyance (self)
Source: Person Target: Environment	Mechanical causation (energy transfer)	Alchemy, faith healing of others, possession	Sensation and perception (exteroception)	Clairvoyance (non-self)
Informational Processes in Source				
Source: Person Target: Person	Operants: self-healing, biofeedback; supplicatory prayer; therapeutic imaging	Magical self-transformations (into animals, objects)	Thinking, imagery, hallucinations, dreams	Precognition
Source: Person Target: Environment	Verbal control	PK, levitation, poltergeists; intercessory prayer; sympathetic magic; magical rituals	Communication	Telepathy

the development of paranormal beliefs. Directly, this would include such factors as authoritarianism, externality, life change, and emotional instability, and, indirectly, . . . such factors as education, social class, age, and status inconsistency. It may be that the experiences related to these variables predispose an individual to paranormal beliefs by alienation from conventional sources of truth and an increase in readiness to believe in mysterious external forces, thereby increasing the probability that extraordinary ideas will be accepted and internalized. It is also clear, however, that these are not sufficient causes in most instances and that paranormal beliefs may also occur for other reasons.

In the remainder of this chapter I shall consider what some of these other reasons might be. In a word, they are the different forms of magical thinking. Magical thinking is treated here as a predisposition to think along certain lines, one result of which may be the tendency to accept explanations of natural phenomena that are at variance with those of science. The phrase "magical thinking" is used here not because it is the best term available but because psychiatric and psychological usage has consecrated it. The term *thinking* is not quite the right term because commonly it suggests only symbolic activity, problem solving using symbols, and trains of ideas. The processes included under "magical thinking" include not only the internal manipulation of symbols in an orderly manner but also the manipulation of enactive representations (neural representations of actions) and iconic representations (images). A more comprehensive and therefore better phrase would be "magical ideation" or "magical cognition." It would be wrong to think of magical thinking as a single, homogeneous kind of process that has its origin in a single source. Rather, it is a syndrome of biological and psychological antecedents and a variety of corresponding behavioral and attitudinal consequents.

The Roots of Magical Thinking in Conflict and Uncertainty

Magical thinking is partly rooted in cognitive conflicts and their resolution and partly in the lack of cognitive closure (or uncertainty) concerning cause-effect relationships and the attempts to achieve such closure (to reduce the uncertainty). Because they have biological roots themselves, the sources of the conflict and of the uncertainty are never removed, but the temporary resolution of the conflict or the removal of the uncertainty act as cognitive reinforcers—it feels good not to experience conflict any more or to have knowledge where previously there was none—and thus the essential condition for maintaining magical thinking indefinitely is always present. The conflict arises over what might be called the "transcendence wish"; the uncertainty concerns the nature of causes and cause-effect relationships in instances where previous experience fails to supply an explanation. The transcendence wish describes the motivational state that arises from certain conflicting cognitions that are universal. One such cognition is that all humans are mortal. The conflicting cognition is that all human beings want to continue living, to transcend their mortality. How is the conflict between these two cognitions resolved? Cognitive dissonance may be resolved by ignoring or denying one of the cognitions, by changing one of them, or by adding other cognitions that serve to decrease or eliminate the conflict or dissonance. Here, the resolution of the conflict hinges on the fact that humans possess an ego, a self-awareness, an inner person, a subjectivity. We are aware that the subjective self is quite different from our physical bodies or anything else in the visible, tangible world. There is the I, the mind, the soul even, and then there is the body and all the rest of the physical world, and they are different. It is a simple and short step from here to resolve the mortality-survival conflict, and that is to add the cognition that, while the body is mortal, the inner person (psyche, soul, ka, etc.) is not and can transcend the body, perhaps not only in death but also in life. The consequence of such an added cognition is the postulation of a place or a world where immortal souls dwell after bodily death, the possibility of communication with the dead, "phantasms of the living," out-of-the-body experiences, and the like. Once the premise of immortality, immateriality, and transcendence is granted, every magic act on the part of the transcending self becomes possible: after all, it belongs to a different world, one that is not bound by the limitations of gravity, density, and time and space in general.

There is an intimate relationship between self-awareness, the transcendence wish, and the reification of the subjective. The illusion that the self-aware I is an entity separate and distinct from the physical body is an overwhelming and inescapable one. The ego and all its functions—perceptions, thoughts, dreams, images, memories, wishes, emotions—achieve such a degree of apparent autonomy that it may seem quite plausible to think that a wish or thought should be able to lead an independent existence outside the brain. Children quite literally think that dreams are a physical reality outside them, and the occultist may think of thoughts as "thought forms," roundish formations, perhaps with wings, that one may project outside oneself and propel toward other brains and minds. Thus, paradoxically, even though dualism is rooted in the separation of the objective and the subjective, it also leads to endowing the subjective with properties that are like those of the objective world. In other words, the subjective is reified. The process of reification does not apply only to one's own thoughts, dreams, wishes, or the inner person as a whole. It is also seen in the unconscious process of projection, an ego defense mechanism. Another person may not only be blamed for the things we do but that person may indeed be seen as possessing the undesirable characteristic that we ourselves display. It need not be even an actual person: demons and evil spirits are often seen as embodiments or personifications of the traits, tendencies, and thoughts that a person is most anxious not to be associated with.

That the physical body is irretrievably space- and time-bound is all too painfully obvious. This gives rise to another form of the transcendence wish. There are the dissonant cognitions that, while one can easily imagine the body unfettered by the laws of nature, the depressing fact is that our senses are limited; that we cannot see through walls or hear another person think; that the speed at which we propel our bodies through space or move our limbs is very slow; that neither our bodies nor the bodies of others can be changed at will; and that every act requires an effort to overcome gravitational pull and the solidity of matter. These compelling forces and circumstances make life monotonously predictable and wearisome. There is the wish to transcend the limitations of material bodies, the laws of nature. Why can't we be as free and unencumbered as our imagination allows us to be? Fantasy fiction and fairy tales, legends, myths, and magical traditions of the world are eloquent proof of the power and universality of this form of the wish to transcend. Those who have concerned themselves with the reasons why belief in the miraculous, the occult, and the paranormal persists have spoken of the will to believe, the need to believe, a yearning for the miraculous, and the like. All such phrases reflect in essence the transcendence wish, the wish that the world should not be as predictable, mundane, and constricting as it is, that fantasy should be allowed to soar within not only the subjective but the objective world as well. That the distinction between magic as imagination and magic as actuality becomes blurred as often as it does needs no special pointing out.

Lack of cognitive closure and uncertainty, which are forms of cognitive incompleteness, create the need to finish incomplete tasks and to obtain missing information. The need to obtain missing information about the causes of observed effects, the need to question why anything happens, is a need that is acutely felt. In many instances the information concerning cause-effect relationships is not available, but since the cognitive gap must be closed, uncertainty removed—leading to a satisfactory state of affairs or cognitive reinforcement—inadequate explanations may be resorted to.

There are several reasons that we may not have the correct or complete information concerning cause-effect relationships. The essence of physical causality is the transfer of energy between systems. Stated this way, causation is a relatively recent scientific concept and for that reason alone would be unavailable to persons not grounded in science. This is not to say that the ancients had no conception of causality. They did, but it took the form of observed regularities in natural phenomena, the concept of laws of nature. Because the underlying principle of transfer of energy was lacking, regularities that were not due to causation were also thought to be cause-effect linkages. Thus one condition leading to inadequate information concerning causation is inadequate understanding of the nature of the physical world. This can occur either because society as a whole has not yet reached the developmental stage where science becomes possible, or because the individual is as yet too young to have developed the necessary concepts for understanding causation the way the scientist understands it. Cognitive underdevelopment is therefore one major determiner of cognitive uncertainty concerning cause-effect relationships. But even an adult in an industrial society can succumb to magical thinking if that adult does not have a solid grounding in scientific thinking and lacks information concerning the true state of affairs in the phenomenon observed. This most often occurs when the energy transfer feature is not obvious, or under conditions that make its observation difficult or impossible, or when the phenomenon is rare or appears to be rare and therefore to lie outside the range of the more common phenomena governed by natural laws, or when the circumstances surrounding the phenomenon in question involve chance to such an extent that the phenomenon itself appears to be due to chance. Finally, psychopathological states may distort the thinking process to a degree where fantasy and therefore magical thinking replace causal thinking.

In spite of the ample opportunities to misperceive cause-effect relationships, even members of primal societies and developing children do not do too badly in following their daily routines. Stones and toys fall to the gound invariably, knives cut wood only when guided by hand, and water boils only if heated. The English philosopher David Hume made the point that this is precisely how we arrive at the notion of causality: We experience B following A so many times that a perfect correlation is established in our minds between A and B, meaning that we will fully expect A to lead to B every time A occurs and to perceive the relationship between A and B as a causal one. Perfect correlation can be established, however, without any sort of energy transfer between systems A and B, and the difference between those who think magically and those who do not is the awareness of a principle that allows one to distinguish between phenomena involving systems that are in fact in a causal relationship to each other and those in which the systems are merely statistically correlated.

It is clear that the transcendence wish and causal uncertainty will often interact. If I sit in a chair in my orchard wishing that an apple would fall down from the tree and it actually does fall down, then my tendency to think magically will be reinforced on two counts. First, the event has reinforced my assumption that wishing makes things happen because my wishing and the wished-for event occurred close together in time. In the absence of information about physical causes, such as wind, ripeness of the fruit, boring insects, and so on, I have substituted contiguity in time and space for true causality. Second, my hypothesis about the reality of thoughts acting as direct physical agents across space has also been confirmed, my transcendence wish has been satisfied.

Both philosophically and scientifically causation may be defined as a constant and unique production (Bunge 1979): If x happens, then (and only then) y is always produced by it. In the realm of physical events causation is the result of energy transfer between systems, such as from a rolling billiard ball to a stationary one, from a warm object to a colder one, from one chemical to another, and so on. The nature of causation is not the problem in the explanation of anomalous phenomena. The problem lies in how causality (causal connections in general) is perceived, how connected events, or seemingly connected events, are interpreted. When two events fail to become connected because one does not obviously produce the other, and a direct perceptual causal nexus fails to be established because the proper stimulus configuration is absent, a relation between these two events or objects may become established nevertheless, and this relation may be taken to represent a connection, that is, a production of a causal relationship. It is a case of simple associative learning, first formally taken cognizance of by Aristotle: If two ideas occur together in time and space, later each one of them may evoke the other. Aristotle cited spatial and temporal contiguity as well as contrast and similarity as factors that facilitate associative learning. Contiguity and similarity have been cited as the main factors in associative learning by everyone else who followed Aristotle in time and had something to say about the association of ideas, notably the members of the British school of associationism.

Resemblance and propinquity are all that is needed to establish an association between ideas. The point of the matter is that an association between two ideas may not correspond at all to any causal association of events. One significant aspect of magical thinking is that there is a confusion of semantic and physical relationships, a confusion between one's interpretive categories and the events they refer to. It is easy to fall into this confusion because similarity and contiguity are directly perceived from the earliest infancy, whereas contingency and other hierarchical relationships are not spontaneously available categories in human thought. To the child it may be the whiteness of the pebble that makes it sink in water or the yellowness of the moon that keeps it from falling down. To the voodoo sorcerer it is the similarity between the doll and the intended victim that will make the latter suffer when needles are stuck into the doll. Even the redness of blood and the redness of the planet Mars are linked, related to the war god Mars and brought to bear causally on human affairs on Earth in the magical thinking of the astrologer. Symbolic parallelism and analogies between words and events are operative even where the reality of events exists only in the magical thinker's imagination. For instance, if good and evil, God and Satan, are conceptualized as polar opposites or the reverse of each other, causation may be attributed to any physical act thought to be representative of one of them:

reciting the Lord's prayer backward is part of the Satan worshipers' black mass; children believe that such a recital will make the Devil appear and seldom dare try it (Opie and Opie 1959); and the "satanic message" flap of 1983, when some rock groups were alleged to have recorded pro-devil messages in their recordings that could be heard if the record was played backward clearly had a basis in the ancient principle of *demon est deus inversus.*

The Developmental Roots of Magical Thinking

The systematic study of children's thought begins with Jean Piaget's work, first published in the 1920s. The anthropologists' observations of "primitive" thought both preceded and influenced the work of developmental psychologists. Thus Piaget not only remarks on the similarities between the thinking in primal societies and children's reasoning but borrows from the anthropologists such terms as *animism* and *participation.*

The connection between the "primitive" mind and the mind of the child is that in both cases we are dealing with individuals whose conceptual development has not yet reached the stage of the educated adult in an industrial society. For this reason, both may show magical thinking under similar conditions, and the magical thinking of an adult who ought to know better is occasionally described as "primitive" or "childlike."

Piaget describes the development of reasoning, including causal reasoning, in terms of the development of concepts. Mental operations are operations performed on concepts, and the end result of a reasoning process in a child may differ from that of an adult if some of the necessary concepts are not there yet or are insufficiently developed. The bulk of Piaget's empirical and theoretical work on the development of the concepts involved in causation is to be found in three books (Piaget 1929; 1930; 1974).

Piaget distinguished two kinds of precausality in the infant and the very young child, efficacy and phenomenalism. Efficacy is the feeling that effort or wish are responsible for external happenings, and phenomenalism is the feeling that temporal contiguity between two events means that one has caused the other. According to Piaget, during the first year of life causality is an undifferentiated mixture of efficacy and phenomenalism. They then begin to separate, efficacy becoming psychological causality (volition as the cause of one's own actions), and phenomenalism becoming physical causality.

Between the ages of two and seven the thinking of the child (preoperational or prelogical thought) is characterized as transductive. The child reasons neither inductively (from the particular to the general) nor deductively (from the general to the particular) but from the particular to the particular. Although some of the conclusions arrived at in this way are correct, many are not, because in transductive reasoning the observation or statement that A causes B is no different from the statement that B causes A. A further characteristic of transductive reasoning is the inability to classify things hierarchically. Instead of arranging them in superordinate and subordinate categories, they are placed side by side because they may show some superficial resemblance. This in itself leads to magiclike conclusions.

The prelogical child fails to discriminate among causal, psychological, and logical explanations. Confusion of psychological and causal explanations leads to animistic explanations (attributing life and mind to inanimate objects and plants). While the confusion disappears by the time the child is seven or eight, there may still be difficulty with logical statements, and psychological explanations may be used instead ("Half of 6 is 3 because it's right"). Animism is only one of three tendencies that Piaget ascribes to the thought of the prelogical child. Because the child has only one viewpoint, his own, and hence does not differentiate between self and the world, there is no particular dividing line between the subjective and the objective. The child not only makes biological and psychological attributions to physical objects and events (animism) but also has the tendency to think of psychological events as physical realities external to the child (realism) and of physical phenomena as being created by humans for human purposes (artificialism).

Piaget borrows from the anthropologist Lucien Levy-Bruhl the term *participation,* which the latter uses to characterize thought in primal societies, to characterize the young child's thought, without suggesting that primal peoples' idea of participation and that of the child are necessarily identical. Participation is a mystical belief that everybody and everything form part of each other, with no strict boundaries drawn between one being and another, beings and things, the subjective and the objective.

It is easy to see the parallel between animism, realism, and participation in the child and the transcendence wish and reification of the subjective in the adult. Their psychological mechanisms may be the same if the underlying circumstances—incompletely developed concepts, lack of information—are the same. Piaget himself sees instances of participation in adults, especially under three conditons: involuntary imitation, anxiety, and monoideic desire. Involuntary imitation is exemplified in such phenomena as speaking louder to a person with laryngitis, as if in order to lend him strength, and in "body English," as when helping the bowling ball to reach its intended mark. Highly anxious people tend to perform ordinary routines in their minutest detail so as not to upset the balance of things, such as taking care not to omit any of the routine acts performed before any examination when about to take a particularly difficult or crucial one, or trying to sweep the floor, as usual in the morning, of one's house that has just burned down. Monoideic desires refer to all those cases where a desire is linked to the desired event, typically one that is difficult or impossible to control, such that experiencing the desire is felt to be connected to the occurrence of the event. This type of thinking is often accompanied by acts of countermagic: If you wish for good weather, do not wash your car (or do take the umbrella with you); if you have voiced a wish, knock on wood so the voicing does not interfere with the wishing, and so on.

The realist child who does not understand subjectivity and reifies internal events finds a counterpart in the adult whose main interest in life centers on observing, investigating, and understanding the workings of the physical world, such as the physicist. J. H. Leuba (1934) found that a greater proportion of scientists concerned with inanimate objects believed in God and immortality than did those who studied human behavior. The academic background that may be found among parapsychologists with much greater frequency than psychology, for instance, is physics, the psychologists' attitude toward parapsychology being the most skeptical among scientists. It is as if the physicist's excess of familiarity with the physical has lent, in his mind, the nonphysical a degree of objectivity that justified its treatment on a par with physical phenomena.

Magical Thinking and Individual Differences

The parallels between children and adults apply not only to contemporary adults but extend to those of earlier ages. In describing the progression from one type of causal explanation of cloud movement to the next, Piaget distinguishes five stages. "According to the children of the fourth stage, the wind pushes the clouds, but the wind itself has come out of the clouds" (Piaget 1930, 62). It is noteworthy that some of the ancient Greek philosophers held a notion concerning the movement of clouds that is very similar to that entertained by the child in the fourth stage: the wind moves the clouds, but the wind itself comes from the clouds. What are we to make of this parallel? Do children and philosophers think alike? Clearly not. The developmental factor is present in both, though, and incompletely developed concepts can lead to thinking that is magical, whether the thinker is a child or an adult in a prescientific society, be it an ancient one or a primal one in modern times. With the developmental factor held constant, does magical thinking show itself in the mentation of adults in contemporary industrial societies? Without any doubt. The child and the primitive may think magically because of uncertainty or lack of information concerning the natural order of things or because of incomplete differentiation between self and the world. In the adult, primitive or not, the transcendence wish may also be operating.

The question may be asked if, in addition to the motivational and developmental variables already discussed, variables that potentially affect everybody, there are additional modifying variables involved in magical thinking, such as individual differences. An observation easily made is that individuals with experiential backgrounds that should have steered them away from magical ways of thinking, such as training in the physical sciences, may show nevertheless unmistakable signs of such thinking. There are also well-known examples of individuals trained in the humanities or even theology who are now considered precursors of scientific thinking. They opted for the empirical method of ascertaining cause-effect relationships, even the experimental method, long before the advent of the seventeenth century and modern science.

The opposition between science and religion is assumed by many without question. The history of the development of science is adduced as evidence, the case of Galileo versus the Catholic church serving as the archetypal example. What remains unexplained is that Catholics, "good" Catholics, have been scientists from the very beginning of science, and that for some time now the Catholic church has not only not opposed science but has encouraged it. Unexplained also remains the fact that, while the mainstream religions see science as a way to find out about the glories of God, it is some of the Protestant sects that show opposition to such fundamental scientific notions as evolution. In examining the nineteenth-century controversy regarding the universal flood vs. glaciation theories of the origin of gravels, and so on, Stephen Jay Gould (1983) shows that the true relationship that exists between science and religion is not one of simple opposition but a more complex relationship involving a third element. Having written a treatise (in 1823) on how a universal flood of the biblical kind could account for the widespread existence of gravels and organic remains in caves, the geologist-clergyman William Ruckland was confronted with empirical evidence that gravels originate in periods of continental glaciation. he rethought his position, criticized his own earlier arguments and, along with other clergymen who were his supporters, accepted the glaciation theory. "Flood theory," writes Gould, "was disproved . . . largely by professional clergymen who were also geologists, exemplary scientists, and creationists. The enemy of knowledge is irrationalism, not religion."

Irrationalism indeed appears to be a key concept here. A few years ago Warren Jones and I had constructed a psychological instrument for measuring world-view (Zusne and Jones 1982). Had William James wanted to measure people on tough-mindedness and tender-mindedness, empiricism and rationality, and subjectivity and objectivity on a seven-point scale, he could have constructed a scale like ours. The scale has since gone through a series of refinements, but no version of it has shown very significant correlation with belief in the paranormal, as measured, for instance, by the Belief in the Paranormal Scale (Jones,

Russell and Nickel 1977). We had expected that those oriented toward the subjective side of life would be more likely to show belief in the paranormal, and they do, but we also found that there are individuals who believe in the paranormal regardless of where they fall on the subjective-objective continuum. At one point we were thinking of a third factor, a credulity or gullibility factor, that determined belief in the paranormal quite apart from world-view, but then decided that *magical ideation* would perhaps be a better term, and proceeded to study its relationship to world-view.

The continuum between the subjective and the objective extremes of the world-view scale may be thought of also in terms of rationality; both the "philosopher" and the "scientist" are rational, each in his or her own way, for there is dialectic rationality and there is demonstrative rationality. Irrationalism may be therefore a dimension that contrasts equally with both dialectic and demonstrative rationality. Is irrationalism the same as magical thinking? Perhaps, or, rather, these terms reflect different aspects of the same thing and therefore may be expected to be highly correlated. We are now using a Magical Ideation Scale, which consists of 14 magical ideation items proper interspersed with the World View Scale items to form a single instrument. Seven of the magical ideation items refer to superstitions and seven reflect reification of the subjective. The overall correlation between the total score on the World View items and the total score on the Magical Ideation items, while statistically significant, is very low. The scatterplot is an almost perfect triangle, the highest magical ideation scores corresponding to those who score in the middle of the World View Scale. The scatterplot is somewhat skewed, the subjectively oriented individuals showing a greater tendency to score high on the magical ideation items. This is because the two types of magical ideation items do not correlate the same with world-view scores: individuals who are high on the objective view reject both superstition and reification, those in the middle score high on both variables, while those who score high on the subjective world-view show a considerable degree of reification while rejecting superstition.

That magical ideation is indeed a third factor, orthogonal to the subjective-objective continuum, shows up in still another way. Although we tried to refine the World View Scale so that factor analysis would yield only two factors, the subjective and the objective, it actually yielded also a third one. At first it made no sense because only four items loaded significantly on it and because two of them belonged to the subjective subscale and two to the objective. The only thing common to all four items was that they contained the word "understanding." These items reflect the presence of a magical ideation factor in the World View Scale. The total Magical Ideation scores and the World View scores on these four items are highly correlated. The individual who scores in the middle of the World View Scale and is high on the Magical Ideation Scale is perhaps trying to solve the age-old problem of reconciling the subjective with the objective, solving the inside-outside problem, understanding the world and oneself in both their aspects. It is the same problem that William James faced all his life: Torn by the choice between two equally inacceptable alternatives of how to perceive the world, he sought a philosophical solution in pragmatism and a view that neither reduces the world to matter nor sees it in purely idealistic terms. It takes a James not to succumb to the lure of magical thinking in search of a solution to this problem, and although his explorations in psychical research show that he was certainly looking in that direction. many of us not only look but proceed in that direction, the direction that begins in the middle of the bipolar world-view continuum and is orthogonal to it.

Looking at the problem this way also throws some light on the way psychology has treated the paranormal. We respect William James, even though he did engage in psychical research, because he stayed within the bounds of both dialectic and demonstrative rationality. We think less of those who take off in the direction of irrationalism (or magical thinking), no matter how scientifically respectable may be the form in which their irrationalism is clothed.

Research like ours does not answer the question of whether there is or not a fundamental predisposition to see the world magically, a predisposition apart from the motivational and developmental determiners. In 1800, the German philosopher Johann Gottlieb Fichte wrote, "The kind of philosophy a man chooses depends upon the kind of person he is." That a person should choose parapsychology rather than psychology as his or her "philosophy" may well depend on whether he or she is the kind of person who thinks magically. The reason I think that the disposition toward magical thinking is more fundamental than the personality variables that it correlates with is, to repeat myself, that even under the worst of circumstances—where scientific education is not available or where the *Zeitgeist* militates against a naturalistic view of phenomena— some individuals do not succumb to magical thinking, and that even a background in modern scientific research in a physical science does not guarantee that magical thinking will not be engaged in. Obviously there is much room for fascinating research along these lines.

References

Bridgman, P. W. 1956. Probability, logic, and ESP. *Science,* 123:15-17.

Bunge, M. 1979. *Causality and Modern Science,* 3rd ed. New York: Dover.

Diaconis, P. 1978. Letter to editor. *Science,* 202:1146.

Fichte, J. G. 1838 [1800]. *Die Bestimmung des Menschen,* 2nd ed. Berlin: Voss. In vol. 2 of *Sämtliche Werke,* 8 vols., ed. by J. H. Fichte, 1845-46, reprinted 1965.

Gould, S. J. 1983. Unconnected truths. *Natural History,* March: 22-28.

Jones, W. H., D. W. Russell, and T. W. Nickel. 1977. Belief in the paranormal scale. *JSAS Catalog of Selected Documents in Psychology,* 7:100 (Ms. No. 1577).

Leuba, J. H. 1934. Religious beliefs of American scientists. *Harper's Magazine,* 169:297.

McConnell, R. A. 1969. ESP and credibility in science. *American Psychologist,* 24:531-538.

———. 1978. ESP and the credibility of critics. *Perceptual and Motor Skills,* 47:875-878.

McCorquedale, K., and P. E. Meehl. 1948. On a distinction between hypothetical constructs and intervening variables. *Psychological Review,* 55:95-107.

Meehl, P. E. and M. Scriven. 1956. Compatibility of science and ESP. *Science,* 123:14-15.

Moss, S., and D. C. Butler. 1978a. Comments on McConnell's paper. *Perceptual and Motor Skills,* 47:992.

———. 1978b. The scientific credibility of ESP. *Perceptual and Motor Skills,* 46:1063-1079.

Opie, J., and P. Opie. 1959. *The Lore and Language of School Children.* Oxford: Clarendon Press.

Piaget, J. 1929. *The Child's Conception of The World.* New York: Harcourt, Brace.

———. 1930. *The Child's Conception of Physical Causality.* London: Kegan Paul.

———. 1974. *Understanding Causality.* New York: W. W. Norton.

Puthoff, H. E., and R. Targ. 1978. Letter to editor. *Science,* 202:1145-1146.

Price, G. R. 1955. Science and the supernatural. *Science,* 122:359-367.

———. 1956. Where is the definitive experiment? *Science,* 123:17-18.

Rhine, J. B. 1956a. Comments on "Science and the supernatural." *Science,* 123:11-14.

———. 1956b. The experiment should fit the hypothesis. *Science,* 123:19.

Soal, S. G. 1956. On "Science and the supernatural." *Science,* 123:9-11.

Tart, C. T. 1978. Letter to editor. *Science,* 202:1145.

Zusne, L., and W. H. Jones. 1982. *Anomalistic Psychology.* Hillsdale, N.J.: Erlbaum.

Index

AAAS (American Association for the Advancement of Science): affiliation of Parapsychological Association, 301, 529, 538; criticizes Hare, 15; on quality of parapsychological research, 139-140; and *Science*, 51

Abbott, David, 254, 472-473

Abell, O., and Barry Singer, 454

Abelson, R., and M. Rosenberg: balance theorists, 393

Abraham, Saint: spiritual hygiene, 165

Achenbach, Joel, 221

Adams, E. T., 105

Adare, Lord: on Home's levitation, 189-190; relationship with Home, 190; séance with Home, 186-187

Adelman, George, 458, 482

Agassiz, Louis. *See* Boston Courier psi-testing committee

Aggazzotti, Dr., 260

Agrippa, 164

Air Force Laboratories: experiments with VERITAC, 139

Akers, Charles, 484, 611-627; book review, 471; on chance expectation, 623; on fraud, 623-624; on handling cues in meta-analysis, 619; on Markwick paper, 301; on multiple analysis, 623; on prematurity of meta-analysis for psychical research, 621, 624; on randomization problems, 621-622; on sensory leakage, 622-623; psi critic, 75, 87, 89; research on ESP, 75-76; and Rhine, 75; on Terry and Honorton's ganzfeld experiment, 618, 619

Albert of Saxony: doctrine of impetus, 381-382

Albert, Gretl: allegation, 58-62, 292-294. *See also* Soal/Goldney experiment

Alcock, James, 454-455, 537-565; after-life hypothesis and faith, 669; book review, 460; chance expectation, 623; on conflict between parapsychology and science, 539; on flaws in psychical experiments, 404-405; NDEs, 661-663; new millennialism, 559-560; normal explanations for psychical phenomena, 538-539; on religion and psi, 557-558; responds to critics, 445

Alexander, Rolf: cloud-busting, 604-606; false references, 604-605

Allison, Dorothy, 635-636

Allison, Lydia. *See* Schmeidler and Allison

Allsop, Kenneth, 329

altered states, 72, 307. *See also* ganzfeld

alternative explanation. *See* counter-explanation

American Association for the Advancement of Science. *See* AAAS

American Society for Psychical Research

(ASPR): use of complex targets, 112; criticisms of SPR, 551; founding, xiii, 147, 192, 551; Newcomb as first president of, 147; objectives, 551; taken over by Spiritualists, 551-552

Anderson, Roger: on NDEs as hallucinations, 666-667; on Osis and Haraldsson, 658, 674n; survival research, 645

Andre, E., 131

animal experiments, 111, 135-136; automated, 314, 316; Levy, 108-109, 135-136, 314; Levy scandal's implication for, 323-324; Rhine and McDougall, 108; Schmidt, 108, 135

animistic universe, 380-383

apparitions, 646-647

Aquinas, Saint Thomas: demonic influence on natural events, 163; interpretations of Aristotle, 381

Archer, Fred: on psychic detectives, 633

Aristotle: animistic universe, 380-381; associative learning, 693; doctrine of inertia, 381; science and Catholic church, 545

Arnold, H.: legal consequences of definition of death, 673n

Asch, S.: experiments on obedience to authority, 393

Asimov, Isaac: on D. D. Home, 12

Association for Research and Enlightenment, 655-656

astrology: as pseudoscience, 505-506

attitude theory: and psychical belief, 392-394

Augustine, Saint: on miracles, 361

Austin, Rev. John M., 180, 247

Backster, Cleve: experiments on plants, 135, 411

Baggally, W. W., 86. *See also* Feilding Committee

Balfour, Arthur James: mischievous youth, 275; president of SPR, 275

Balfour, Frederick H., 271; on Hornby's reporter-materialization, 270-271

Ballenstedt case, 636-637

Ballou, R. O. *See* Murphy and Ballou

Bancroft, George, 179

Barber, Theodore X., 481, 488

Barksdale, W. *See* Honorton and Barksdale

Barrett, Sir William, 649; and Creery sisters, 42, 280; Peak-in-Darien cases, 652; as psychical researcher, 30, 192; on psychical research and religion, 162; spiritual world as fact, 147-148; and SPR, 35, 549; supporters, 42; survival research, 645; thought-transference, 147-148

Barrett, Gurney, and Myers: Committee on